THE DREAMLAND CHRONICLES

BOOK THREE

THE DREAMLAND CHRONICLES: BOOK THREE
COPYRIGHT 2009 SCOTT CHRISTIAN SAVA

FOR MORE INFORMATION, PLEASE GO TO:
WWW.THEDREAMLANDCHRONICLES.COM

www.IDWpublishing.com

ISBN: 978-1-60010-309-4

12 11 10 09   1 2 3 4   Production by Chris Mowry • Edited by Justin Eisinger and Amy Betz

Operations: Moshe Berger, Chairman • Ted Adams, Chief Executive Officer • Greg Goldstein, Chief Operating Officer • Matthew Ruzicka, CPA, Chief Financial Officer • Alan Payne, VP of Sales • Lorelei Bunjes, Dir. of Digital Services • Marci Hubbard, Executive Assistant • Alonzo Simon, Shipping Manager • **Editorial:** Chris Ryall, Publisher/Editor-in-Chief • Scott Dunbier, Editor, Special Projects • Andy Schmidt, Senior Editor • Justin Eisinger, Editor • Kris Oprisko, Editor/Foreign Lic. • Denton J. Tipton, Editor • Tom Waltz, Editor • Mariah Huehner, Assistant Editor • **Design:** Robbie Robbins, EVP/Sr. Graphic Artist • Ben Templesmith, Artist/Designer • Neil Uyetake, Art Director • Chris Mowry, Graphic Artist • Amauri Osorio, Graphic Artist

FOR BRENDAN DANIEL AND LOGAN ALEXANDER...
MAY GOD BLESS YOUR ADVENTURES
AS YOU DISCOVER DREAMLAND
FOR YOURSELVES.

CHAPTER NINE

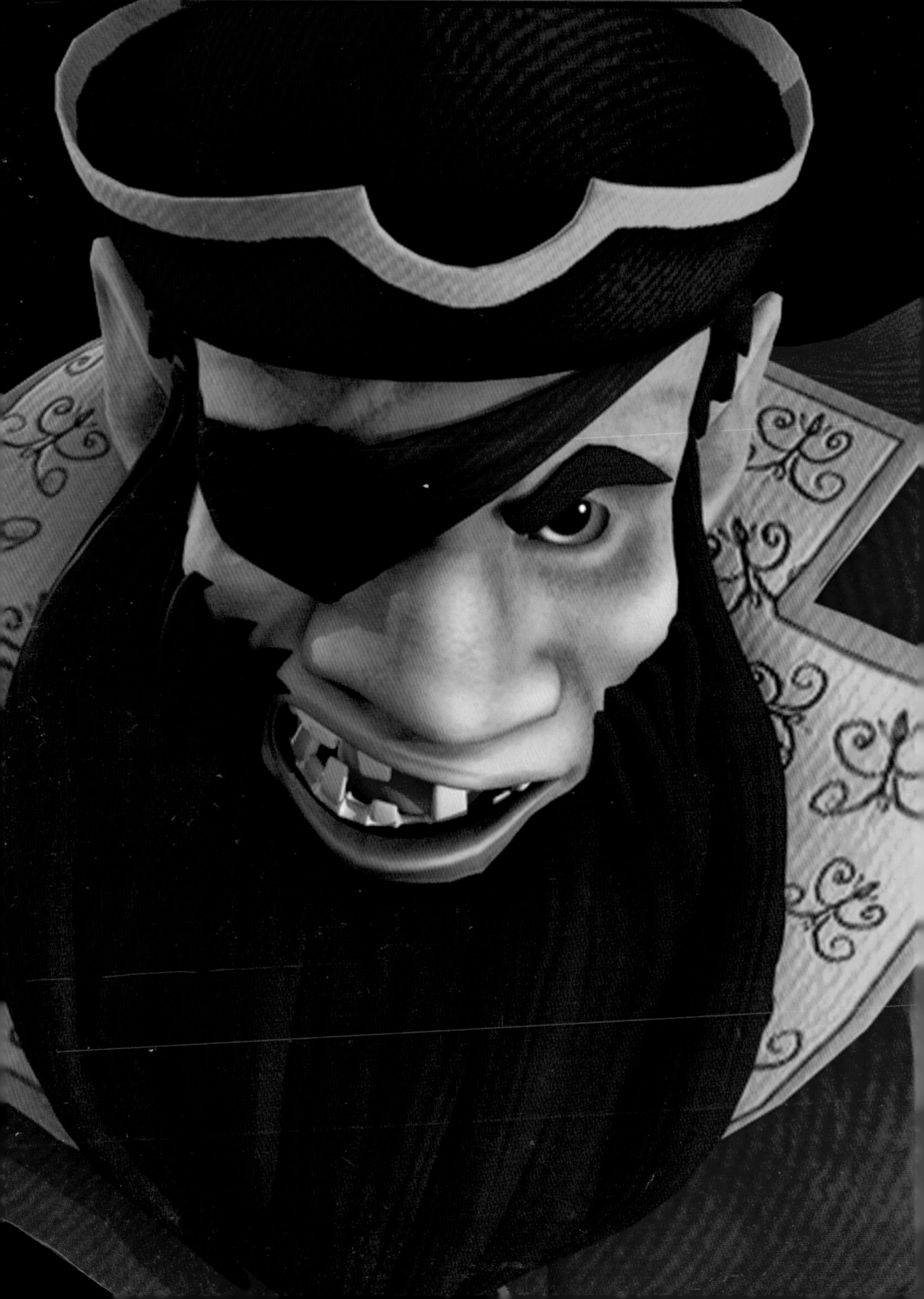

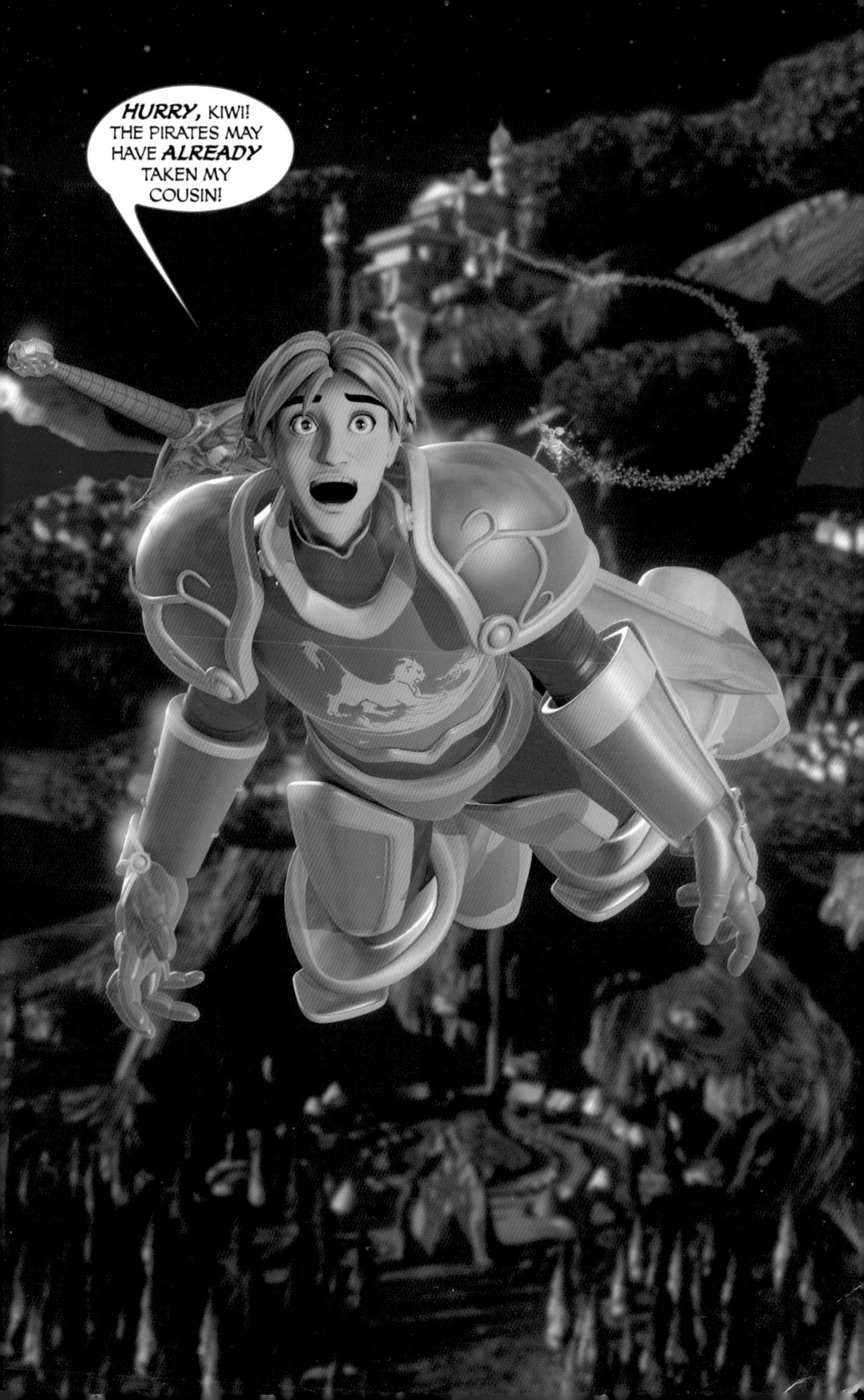
HURRY, KIWI! THE PIRATES MAY HAVE ALREADY TAKEN MY COUSIN!

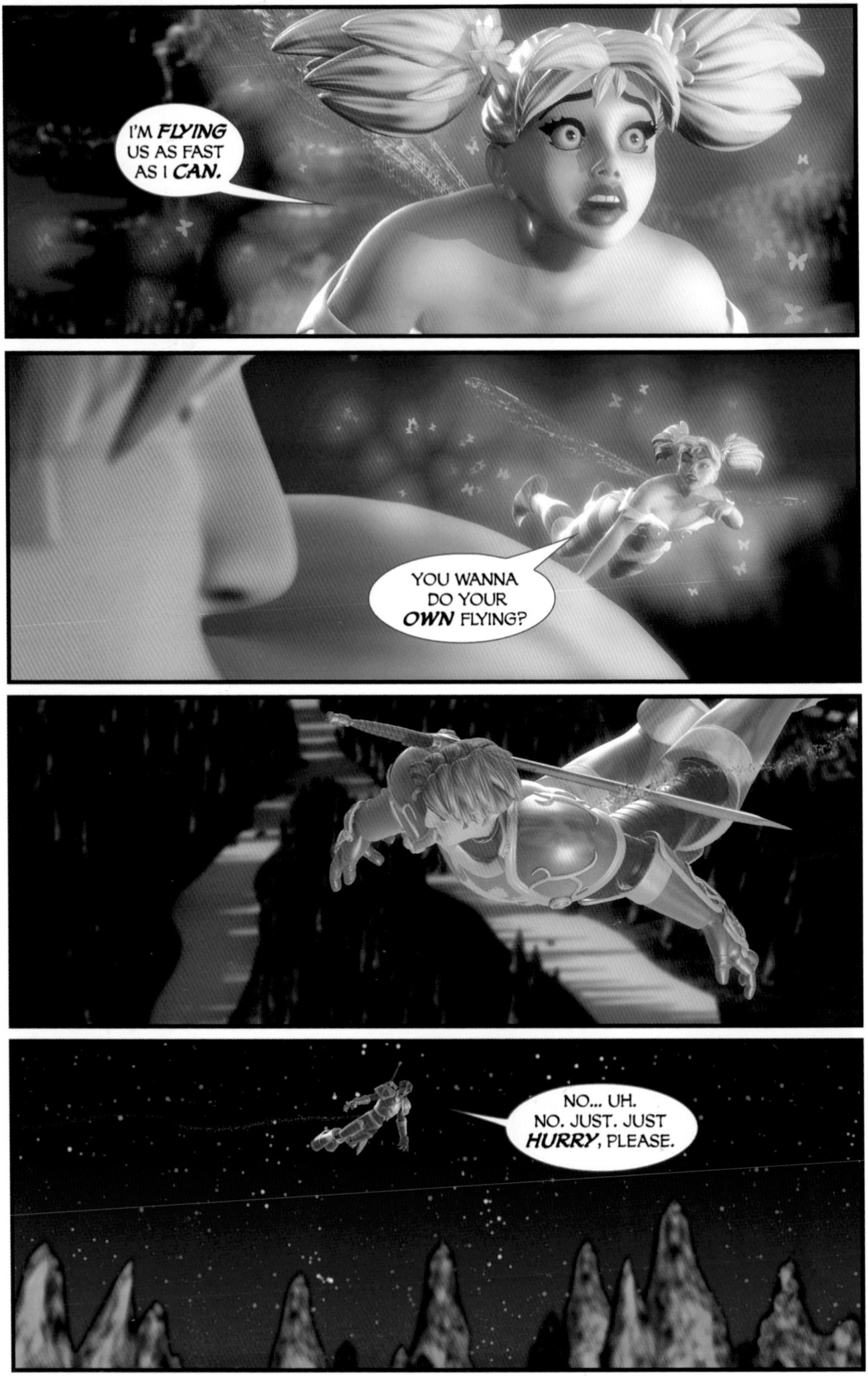
I'M FLYING US AS FAST AS I CAN.
YOU WANNA DO YOUR OWN FLYING?
NO... UH. NO. JUST. JUST HURRY, PLEASE.

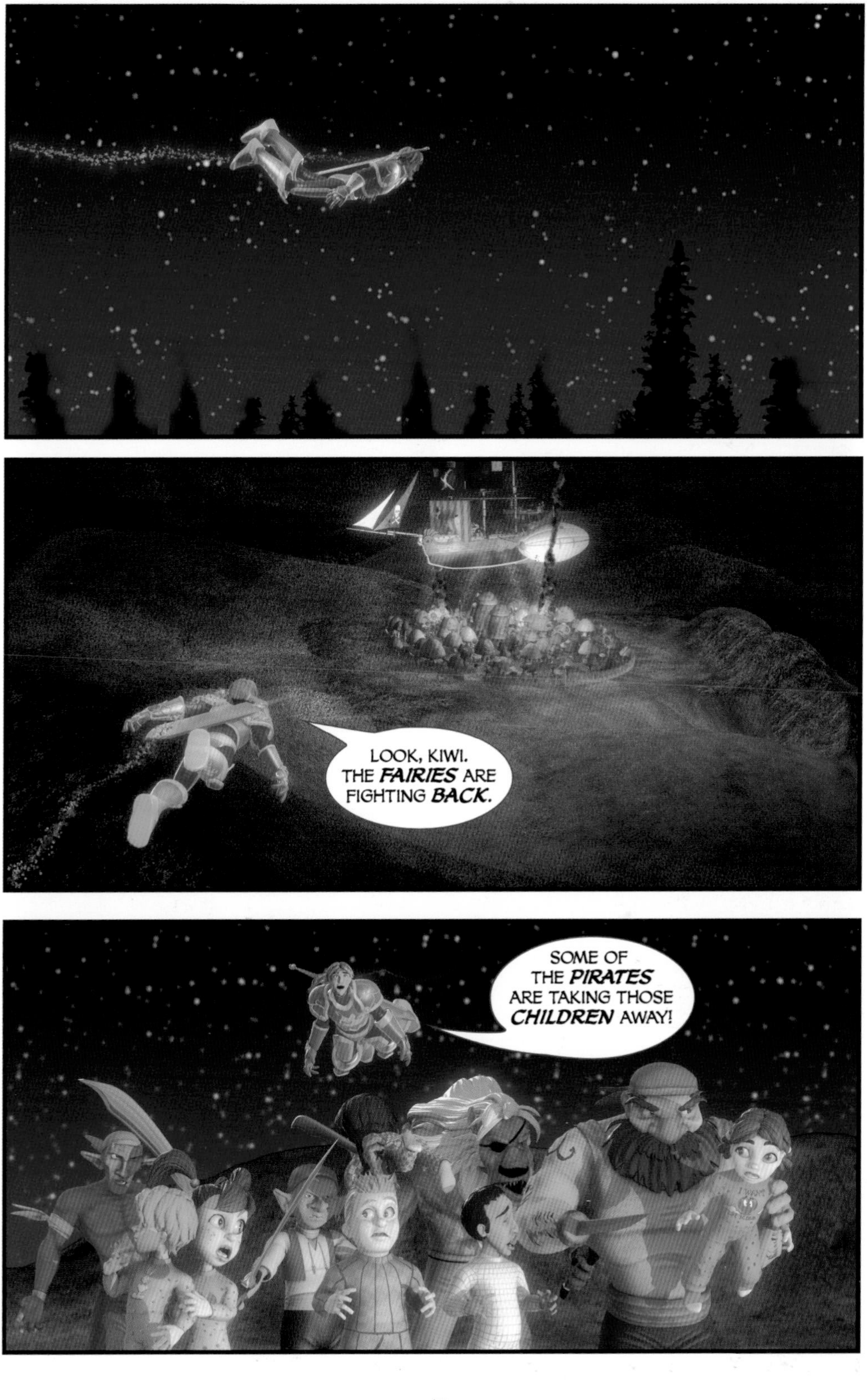
LOOK, KIWI. THE FAIRIES ARE FIGHTING BACK.
SOME OF THE PIRATES ARE TAKING THOSE CHILDREN AWAY!

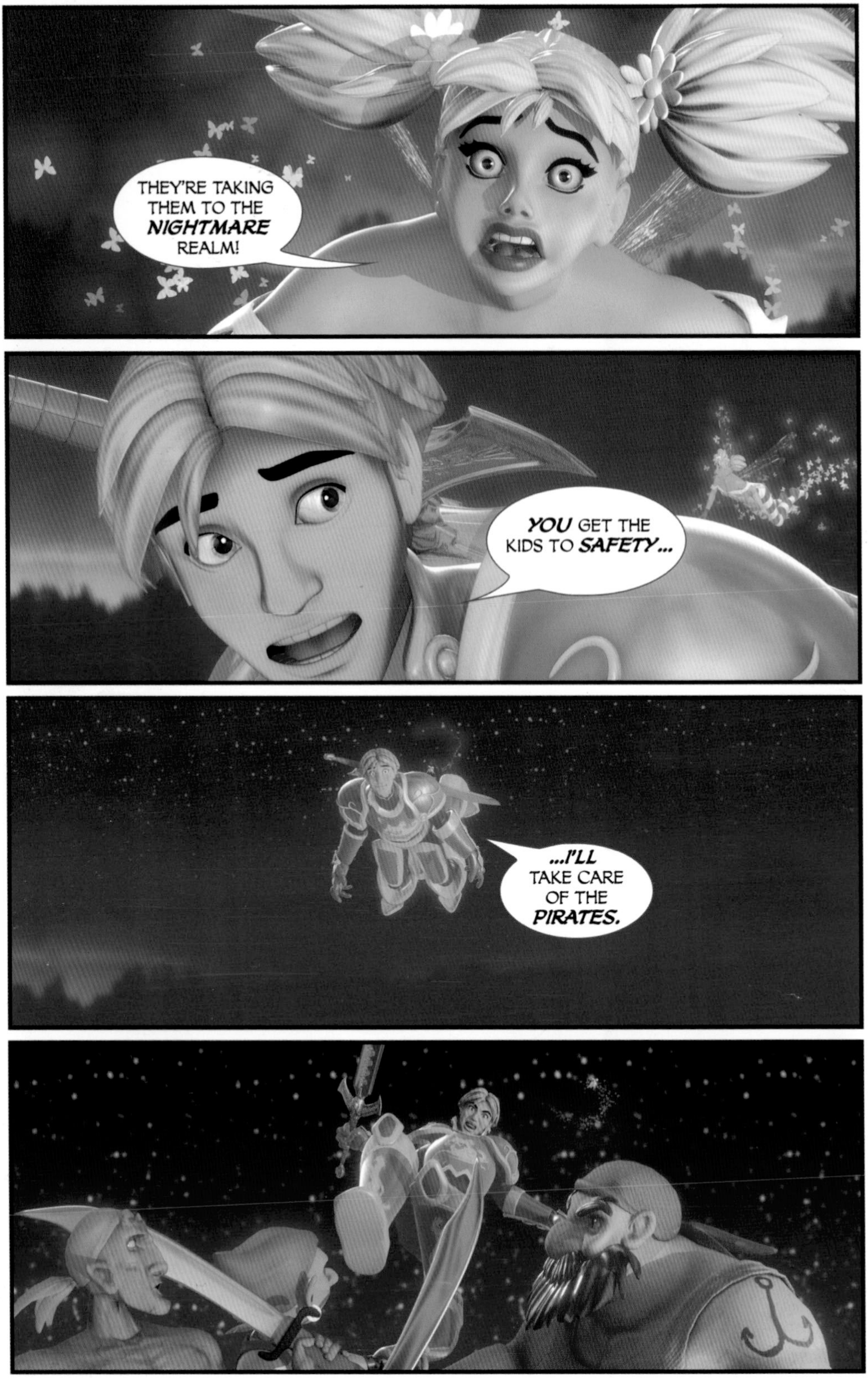
THEY'RE TAKING THEM TO THE NIGHTMARE REALM!
YOU GET THE KIDS TO SAFETY...
...I'LL TAKE CARE OF THE PIRATES.

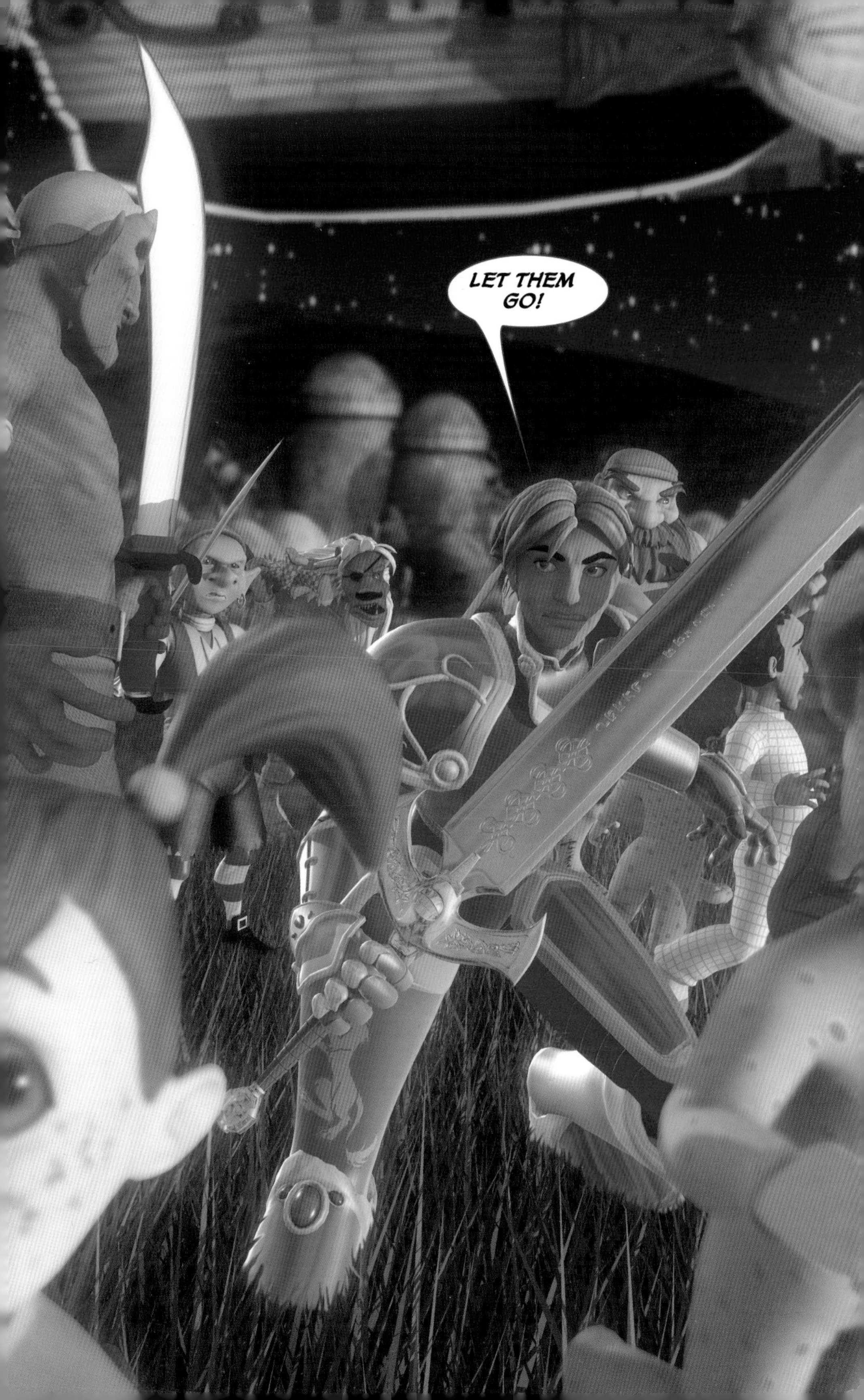
LET THEM GO!

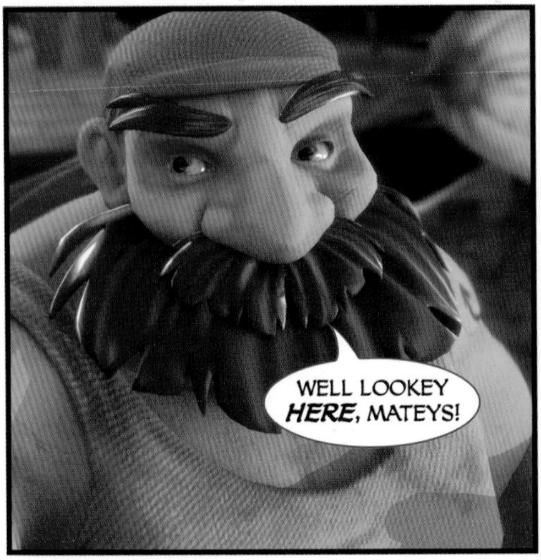
WELL LOOKEY **HERE**, MATEYS!

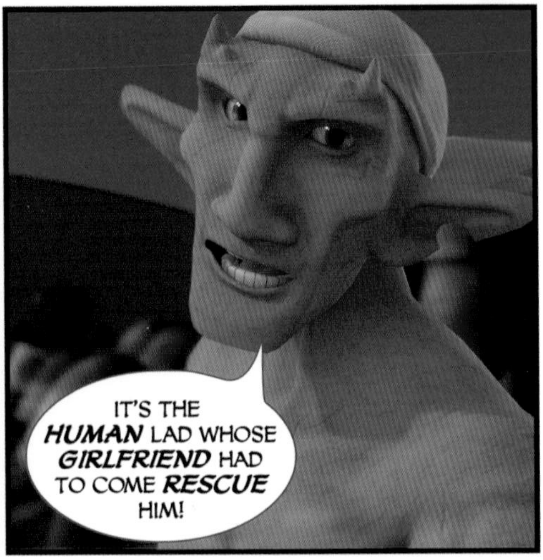
IT'S THE **HUMAN** LAD WHOSE **GIRLFRIEND** HAD TO COME **RESCUE** HIM!

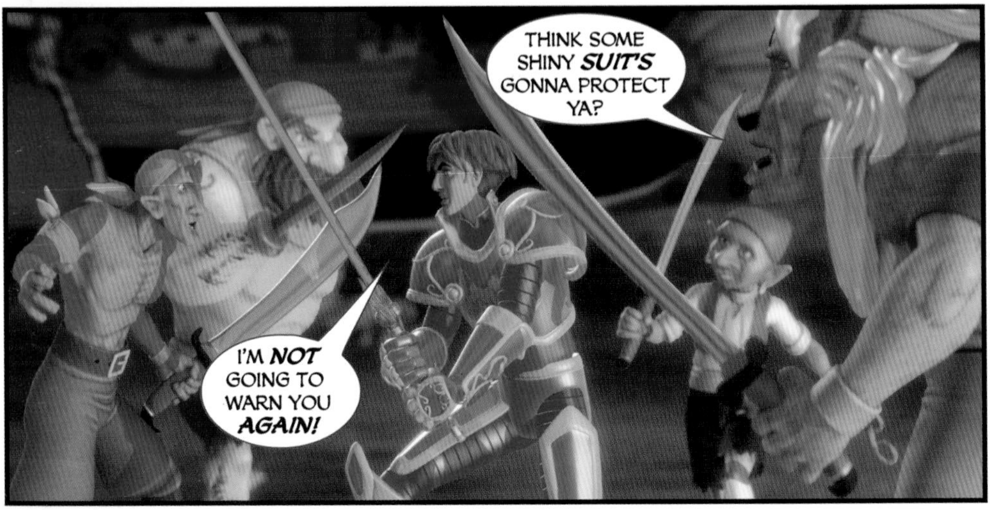
THINK SOME SHINY **SUIT'S** GONNA PROTECT YA?
I'M **NOT** GOING TO WARN YOU **AGAIN!**

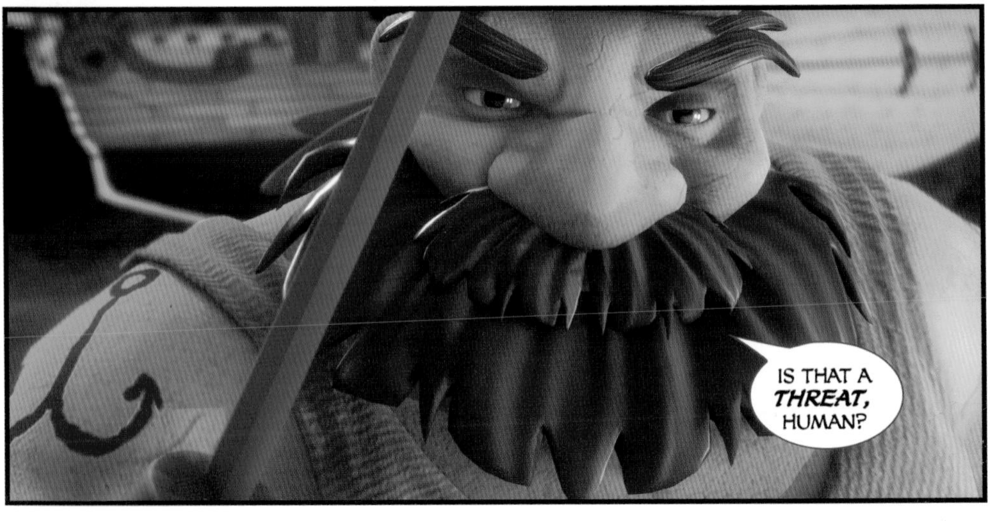
IS THAT A **THREAT,** HUMAN?

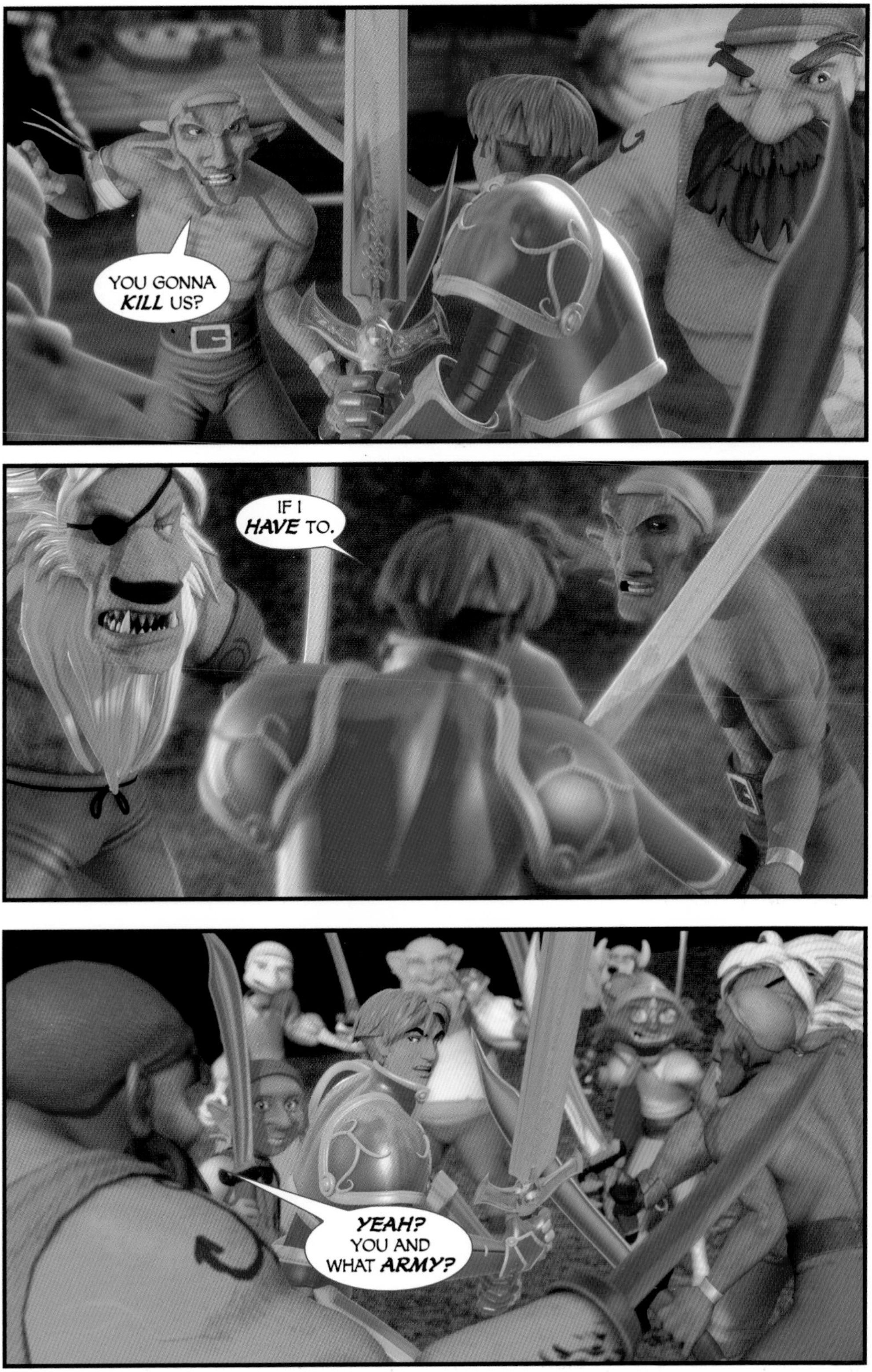
YOU GONNA *KILL* US?
IF I *HAVE* TO.
YEAH? YOU AND WHAT *ARMY?*

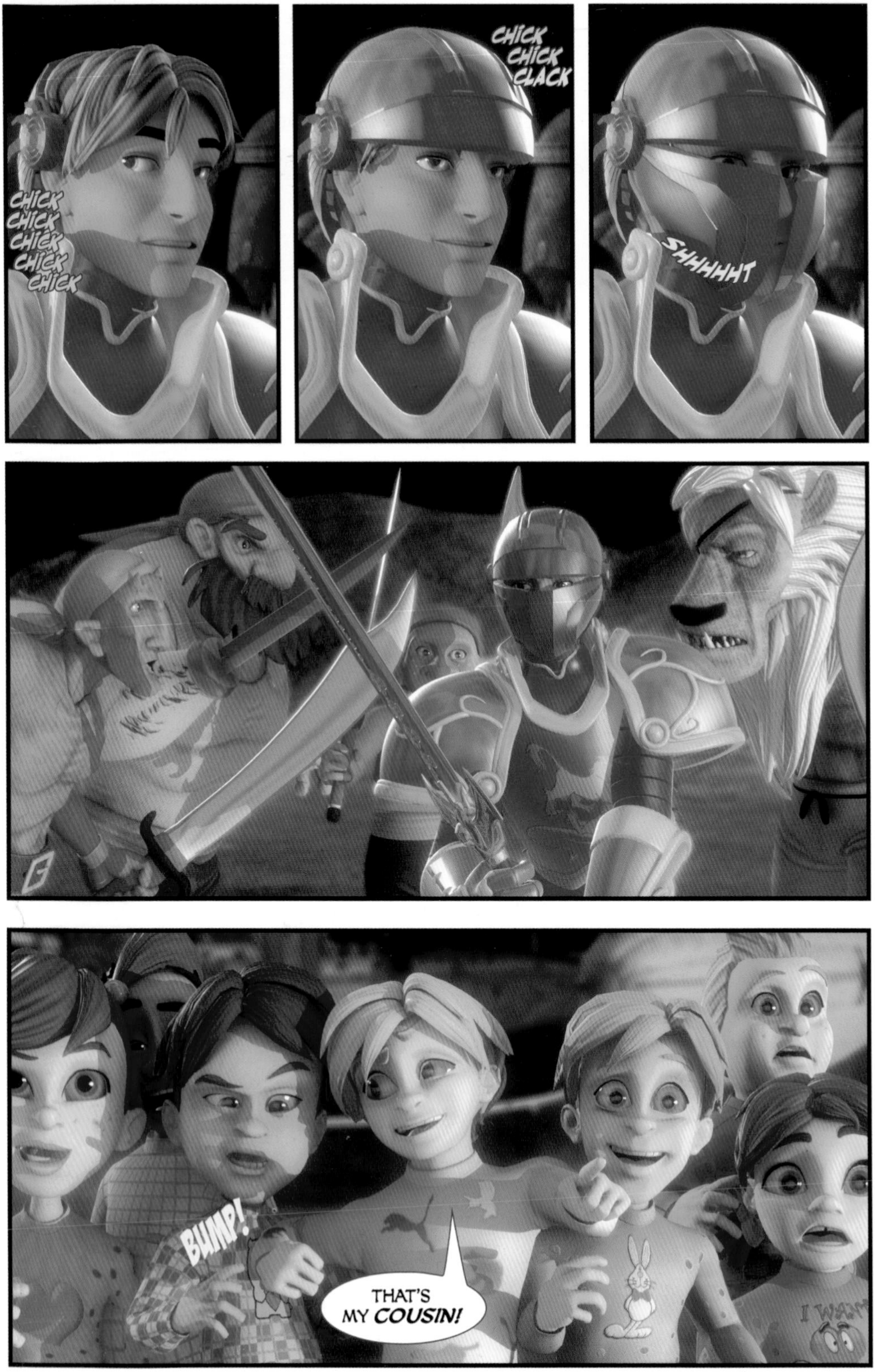
CHICK
CHICK
CHICK
CHICK
CHICK
CHICK
CHICK
CLACK
SHHHHHT
BUMP!
THAT'S MY *COUSIN!*

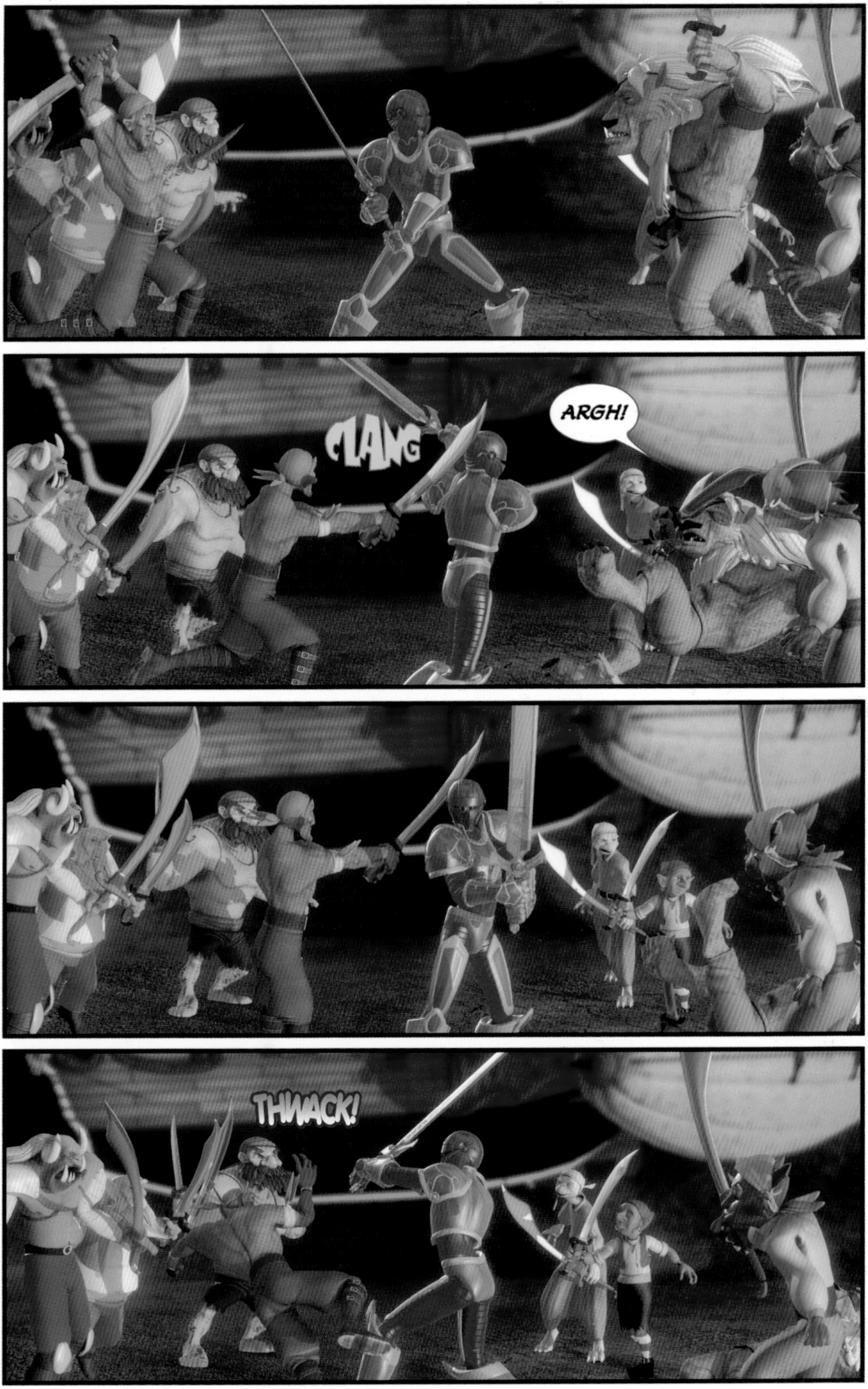
CLANG
ARGH!
THWACK!

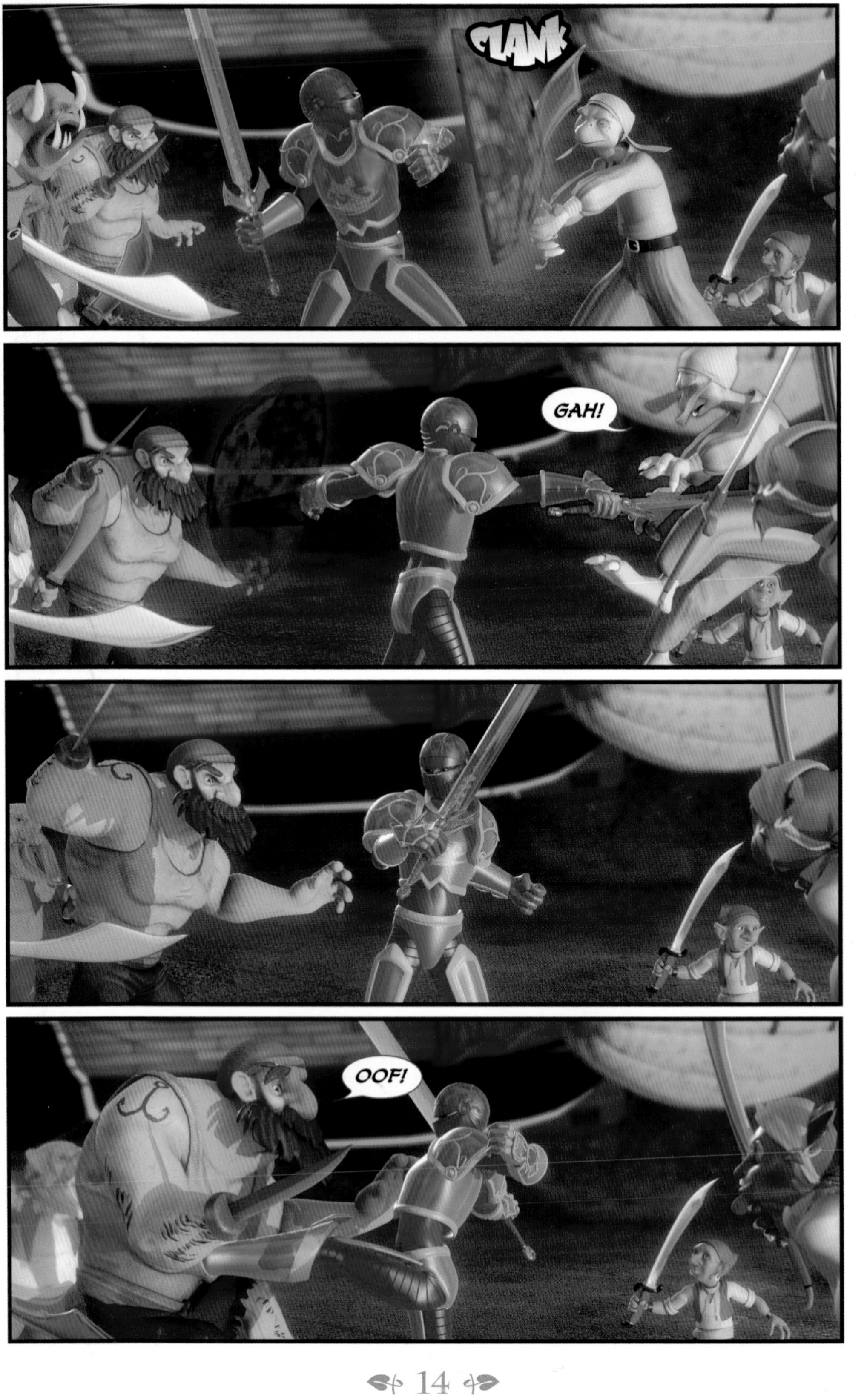
CLANK
GAH!
OOF!

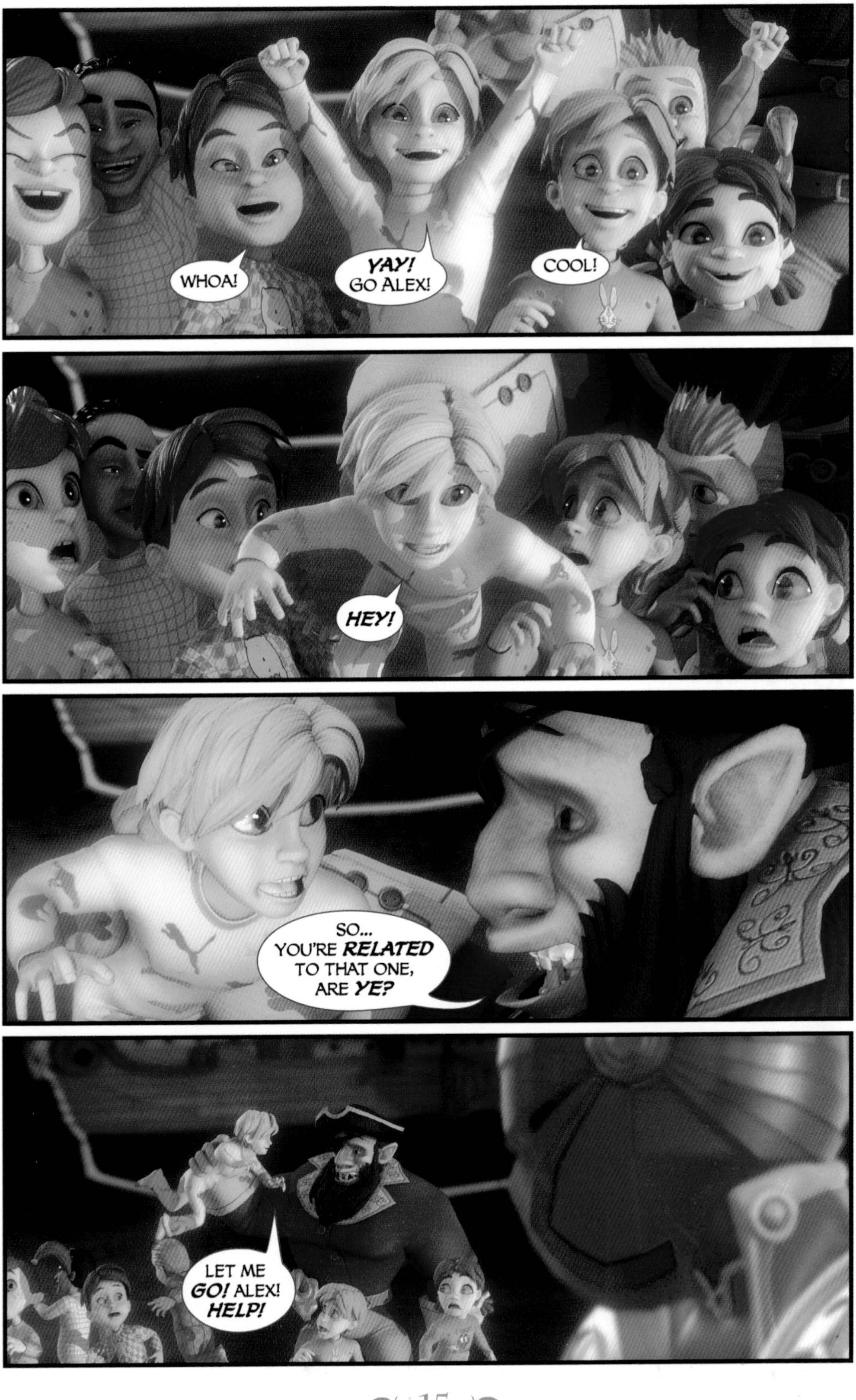
WHOA!
YAY! GO ALEX!
COOL!
HEY!
SO... YOU'RE RELATED TO THAT ONE, ARE YE?
LET ME GO! ALEX! HELP!

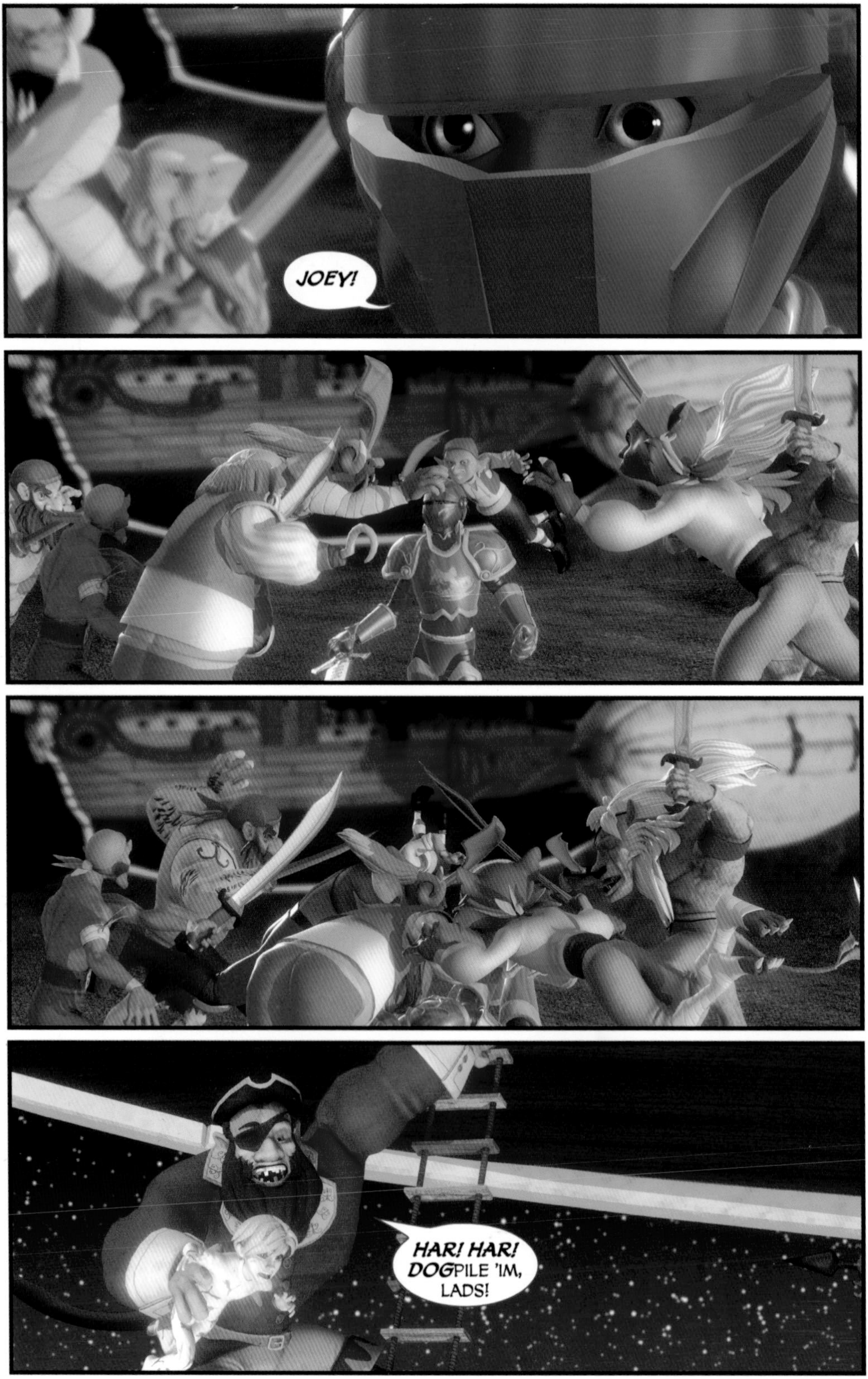
JOEY!
HAR! HAR! DOGPILE 'IM, LADS!

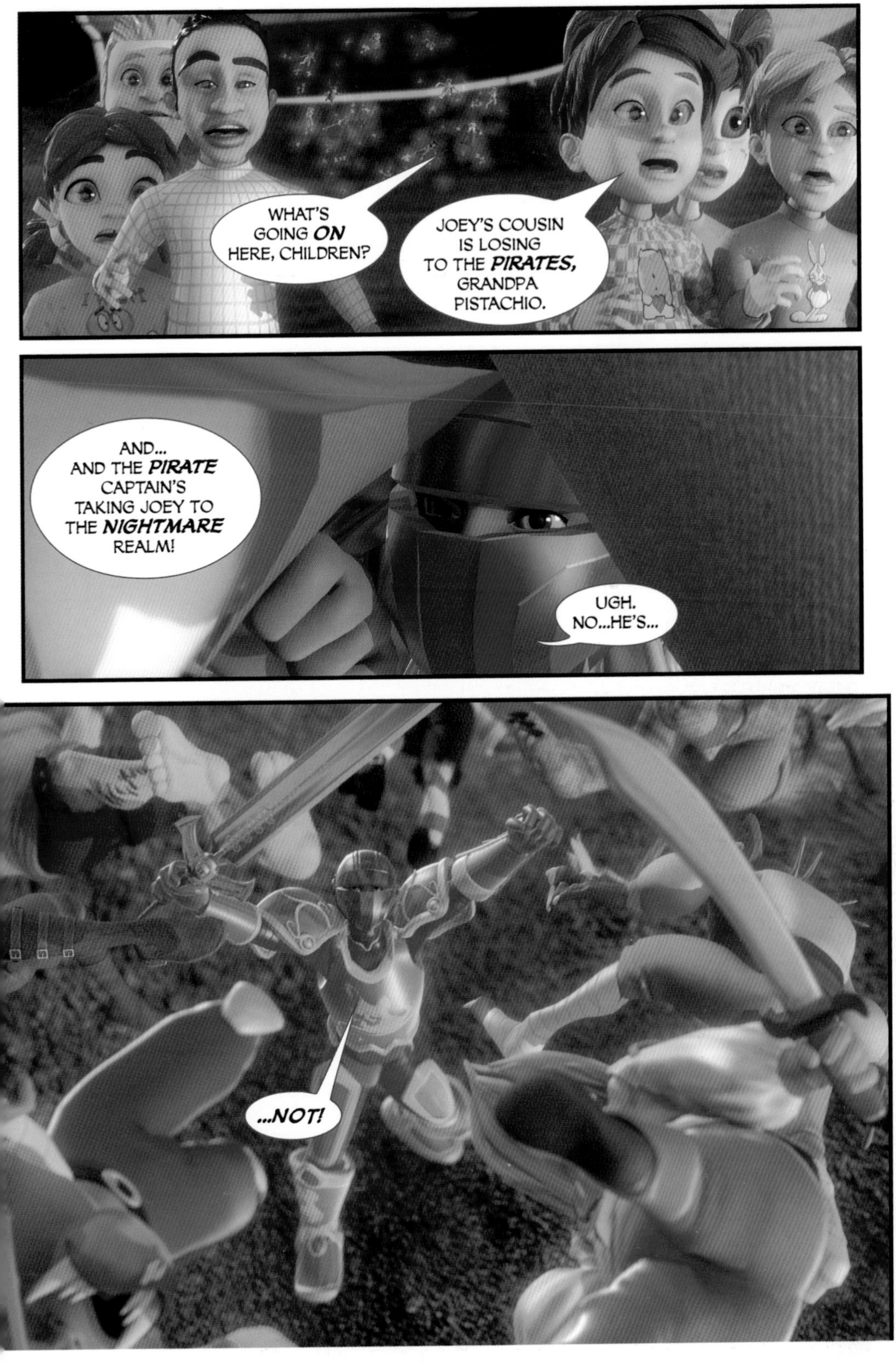
WHAT'S GOING ON HERE, CHILDREN?
JOEY'S COUSIN IS LOSING TO THE PIRATES, GRANDPA PISTACHIO.
AND... AND THE PIRATE CAPTAIN'S TAKING JOEY TO THE NIGHTMARE REALM!
UGH. NO...HE'S...
...NOT!

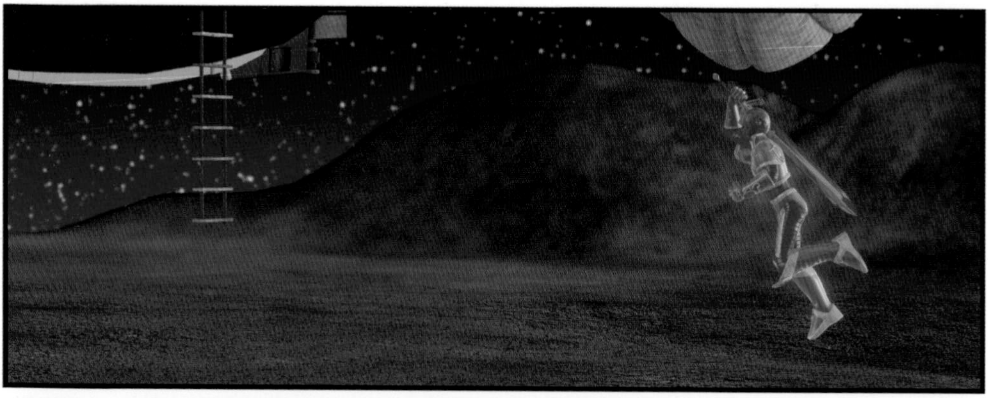

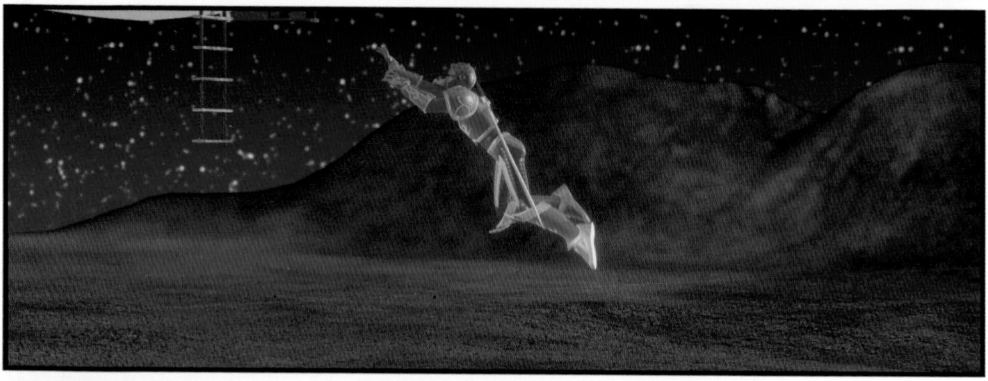

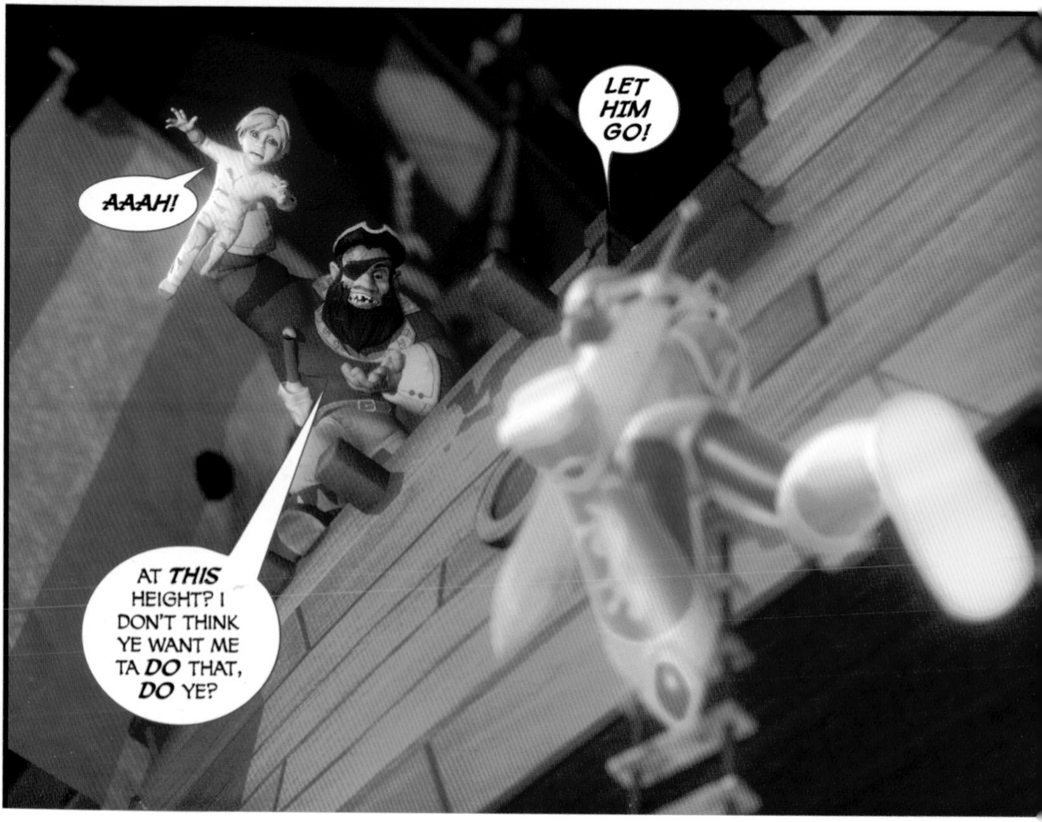
AAAH!
LET HIM GO!
AT THIS HEIGHT? I DON'T THINK YE WANT ME TA DO THAT, DO YE?

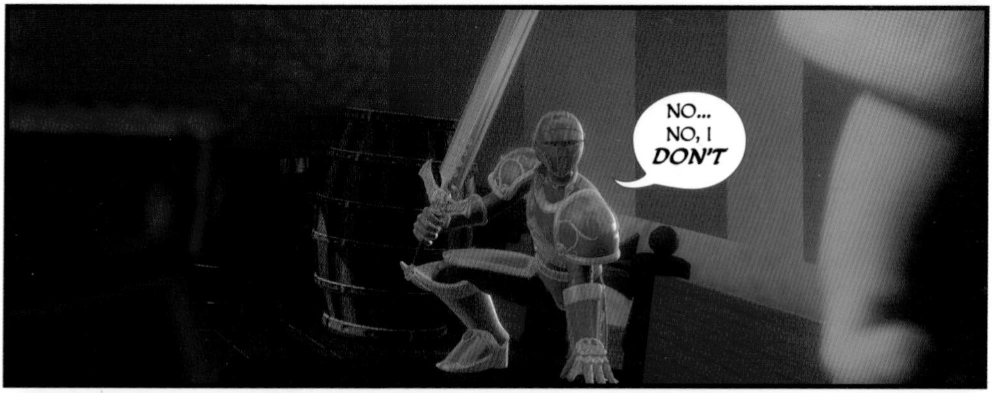
NO...
NO, I
DON'T

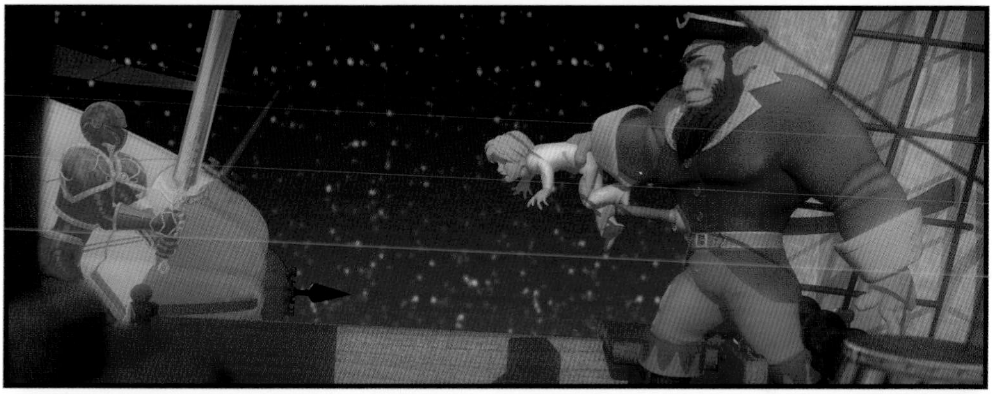

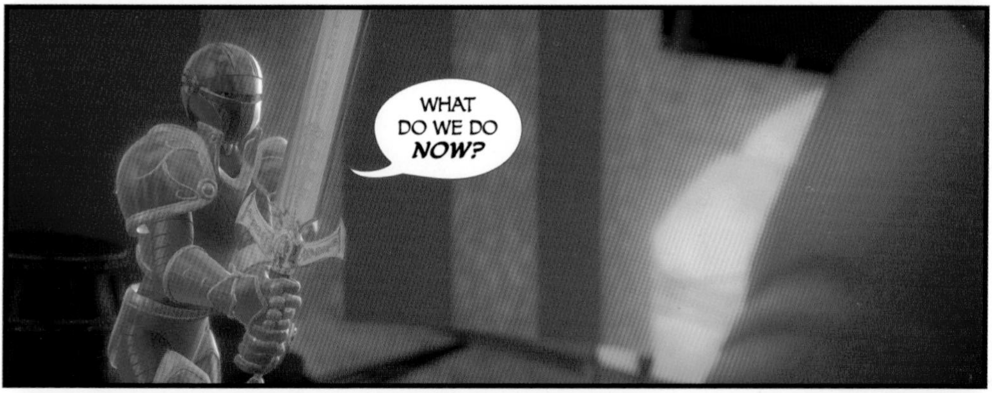
WHAT
DO WE DO
NOW?

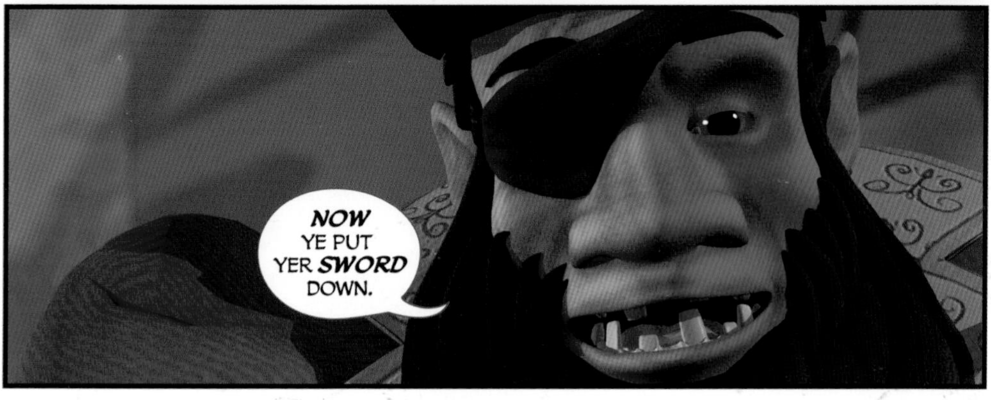
NOW
YE PUT
YER SWORD
DOWN.

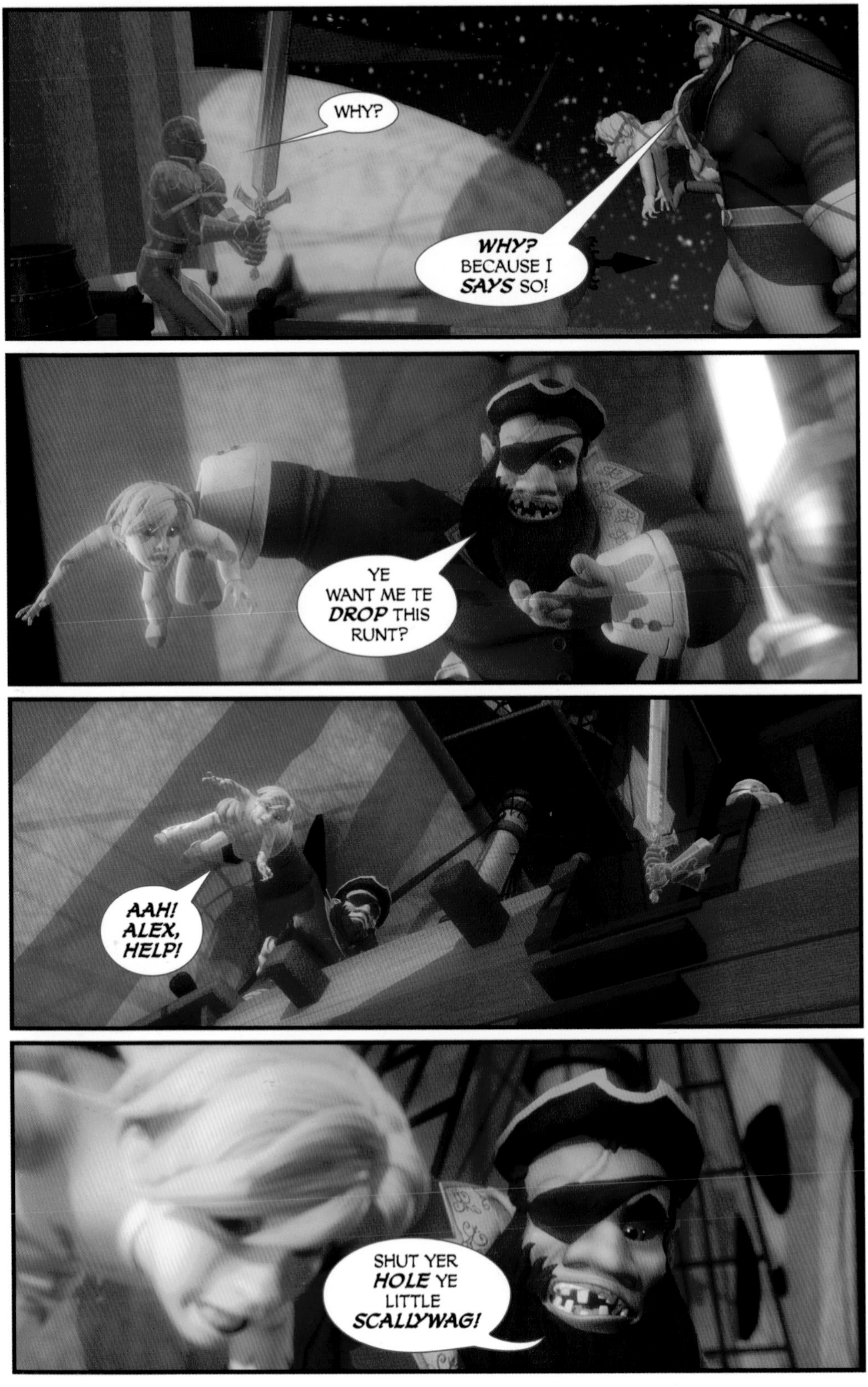
WHY?
WHY? BECAUSE I SAYS SO!
YE WANT ME TE DROP THIS RUNT?
AAH! ALEX, HELP!
SHUT YER HOLE YE LITTLE SCALLYWAG!

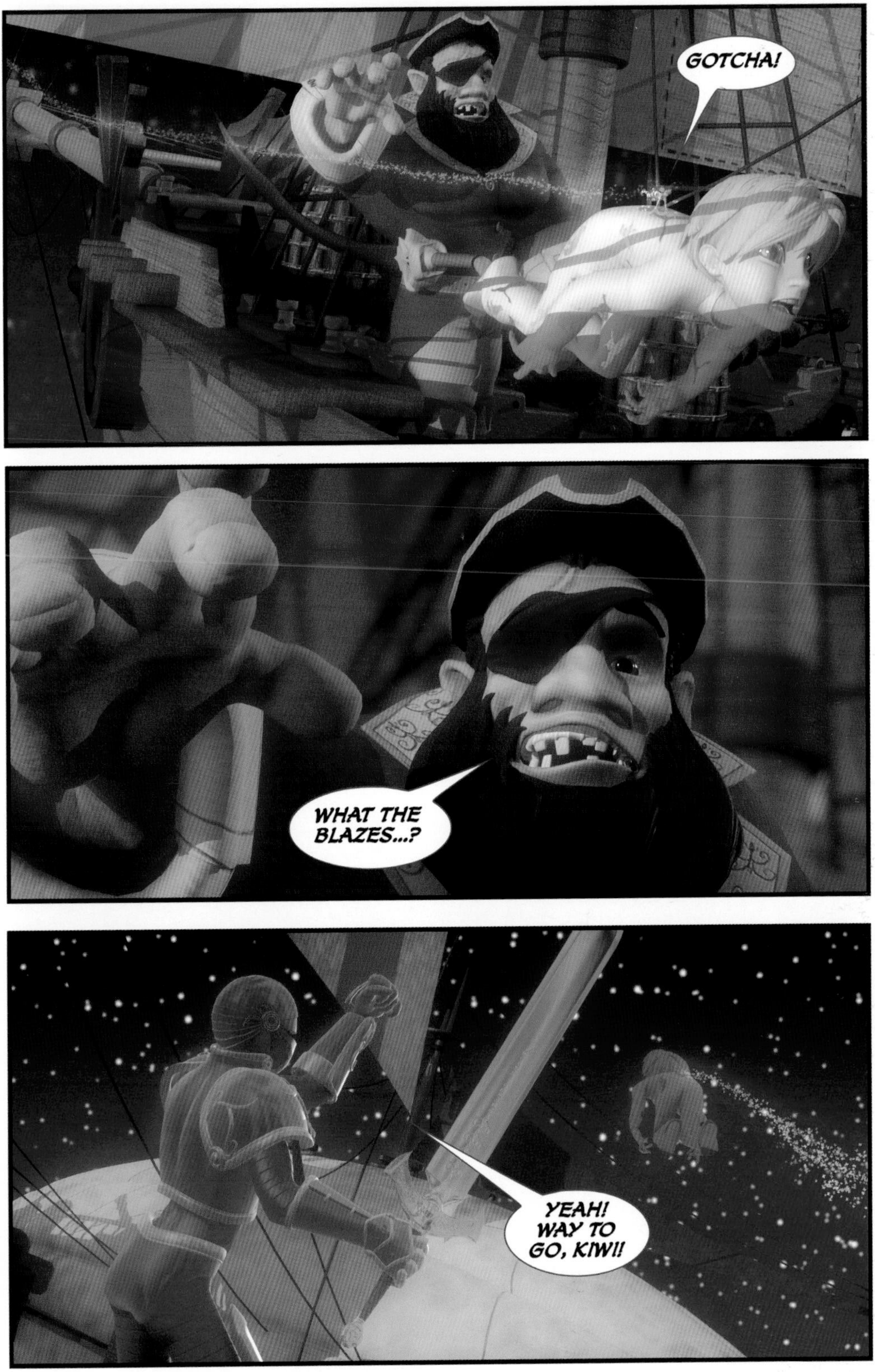
GOTCHA!
WHAT THE BLAZES...?
YEAH! WAY TO GO, KIWI!

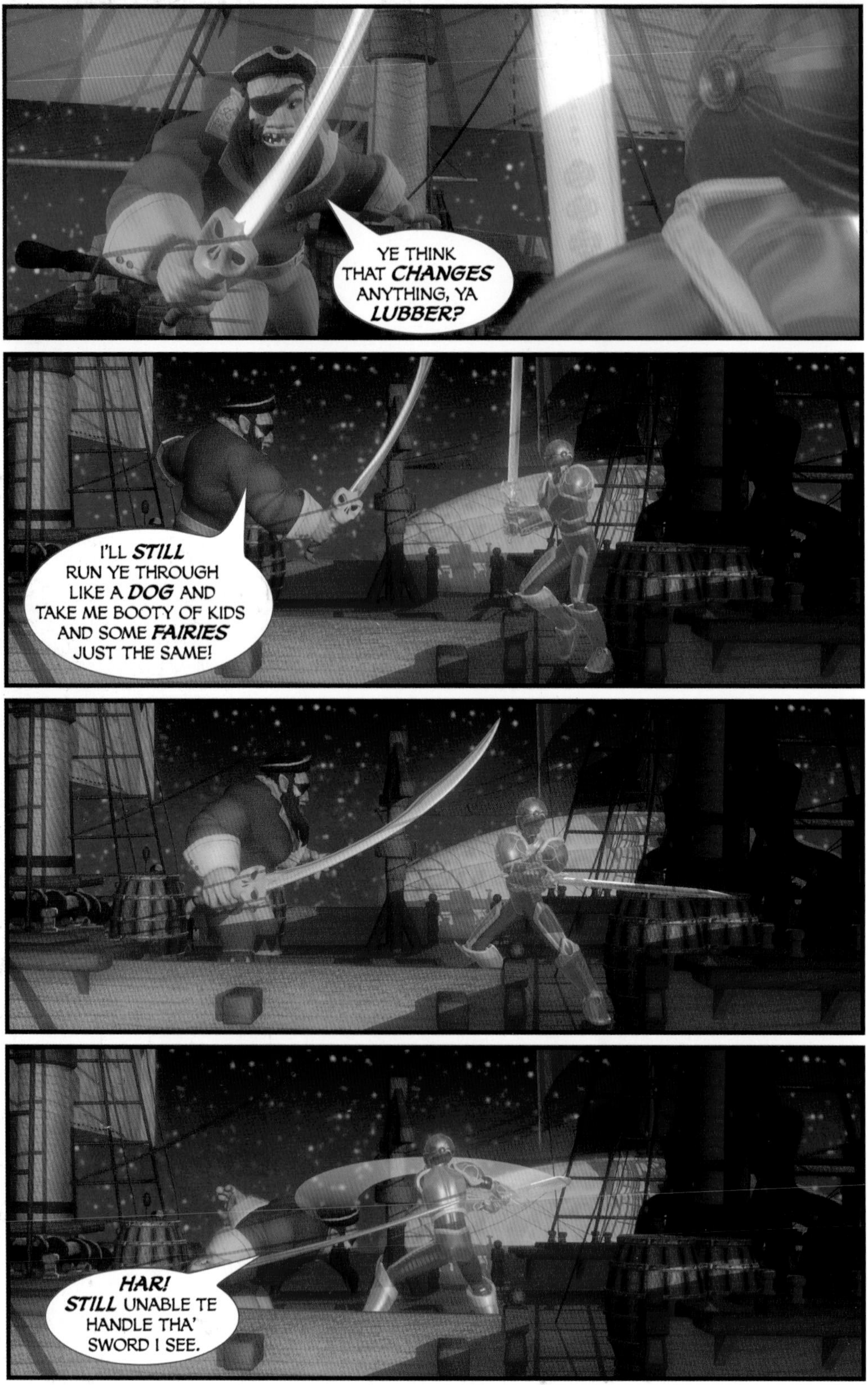
YE THINK THAT *CHANGES* ANYTHING, YA *LUBBER?*
I'LL *STILL* RUN YE THROUGH LIKE A *DOG* AND TAKE ME BOOTY OF KIDS AND SOME *FAIRIES* JUST THE SAME!
HAR! *STILL* UNABLE TE HANDLE THA' SWORD I SEE.

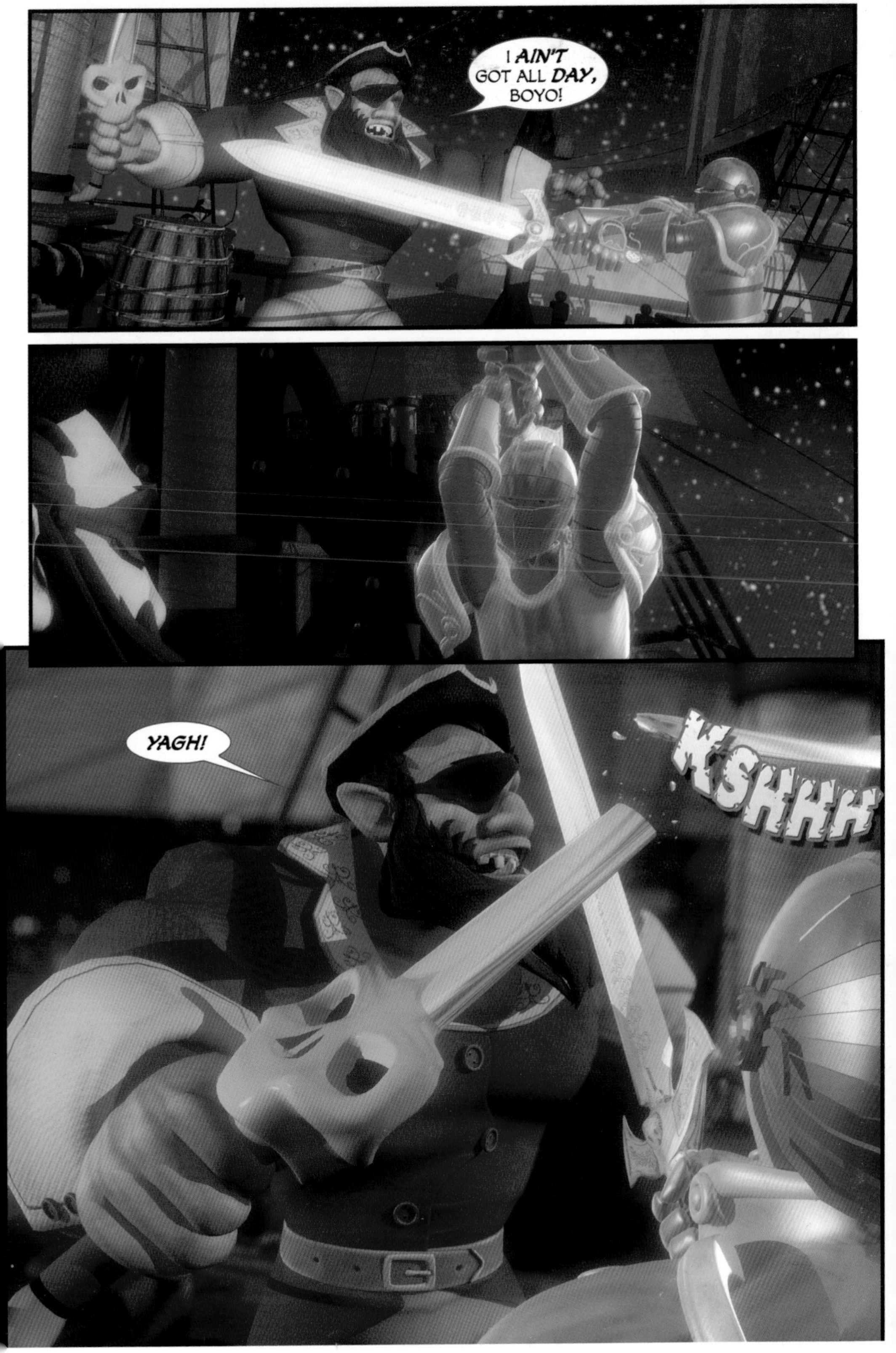
I AIN'T GOT ALL DAY, BOYO!
YAGH!
KSHHH

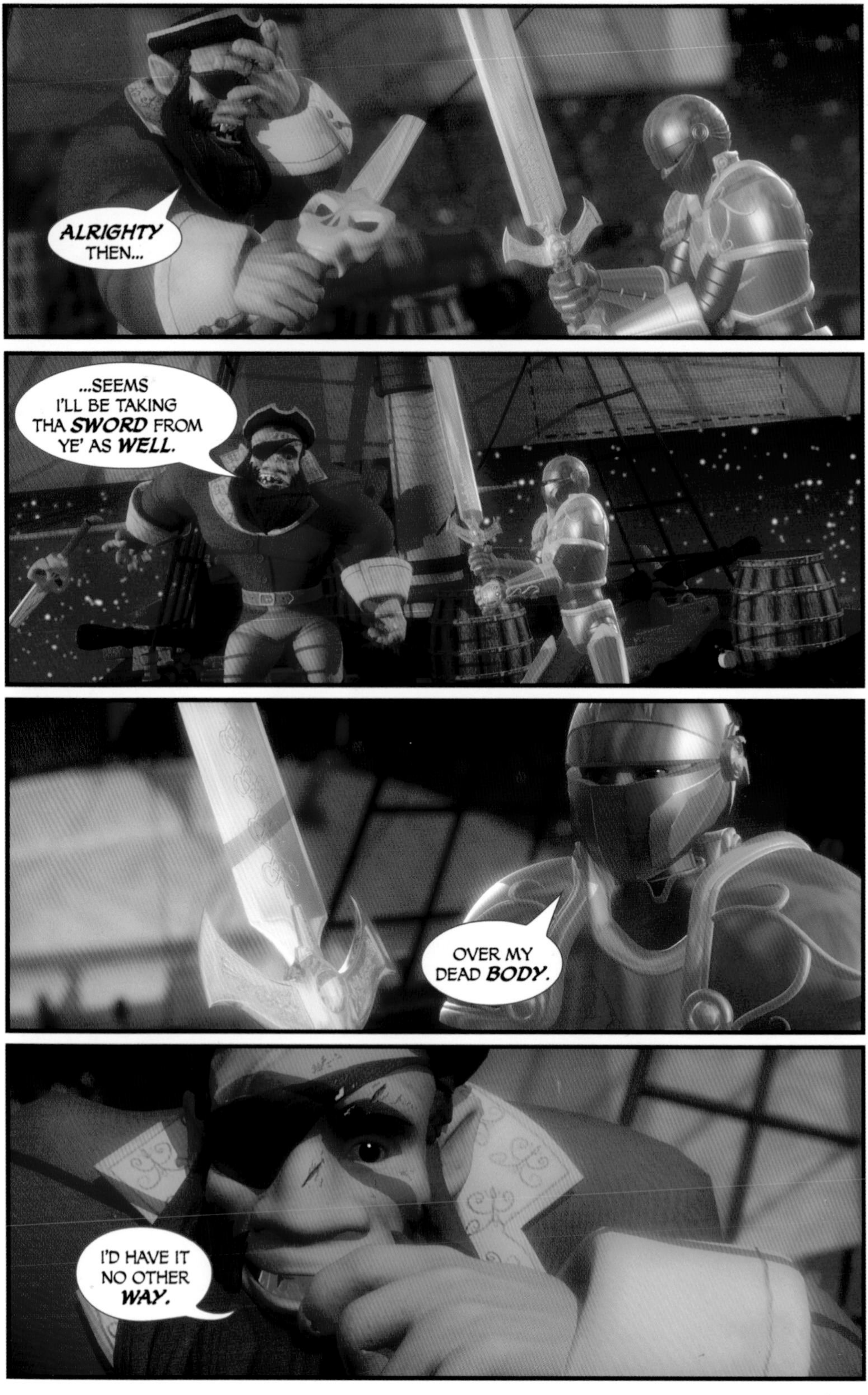
ALRIGHTY THEN...
...SEEMS I'LL BE TAKING THA SWORD FROM YE' AS WELL.
OVER MY DEAD BODY.
I'D HAVE IT NO OTHER WAY.

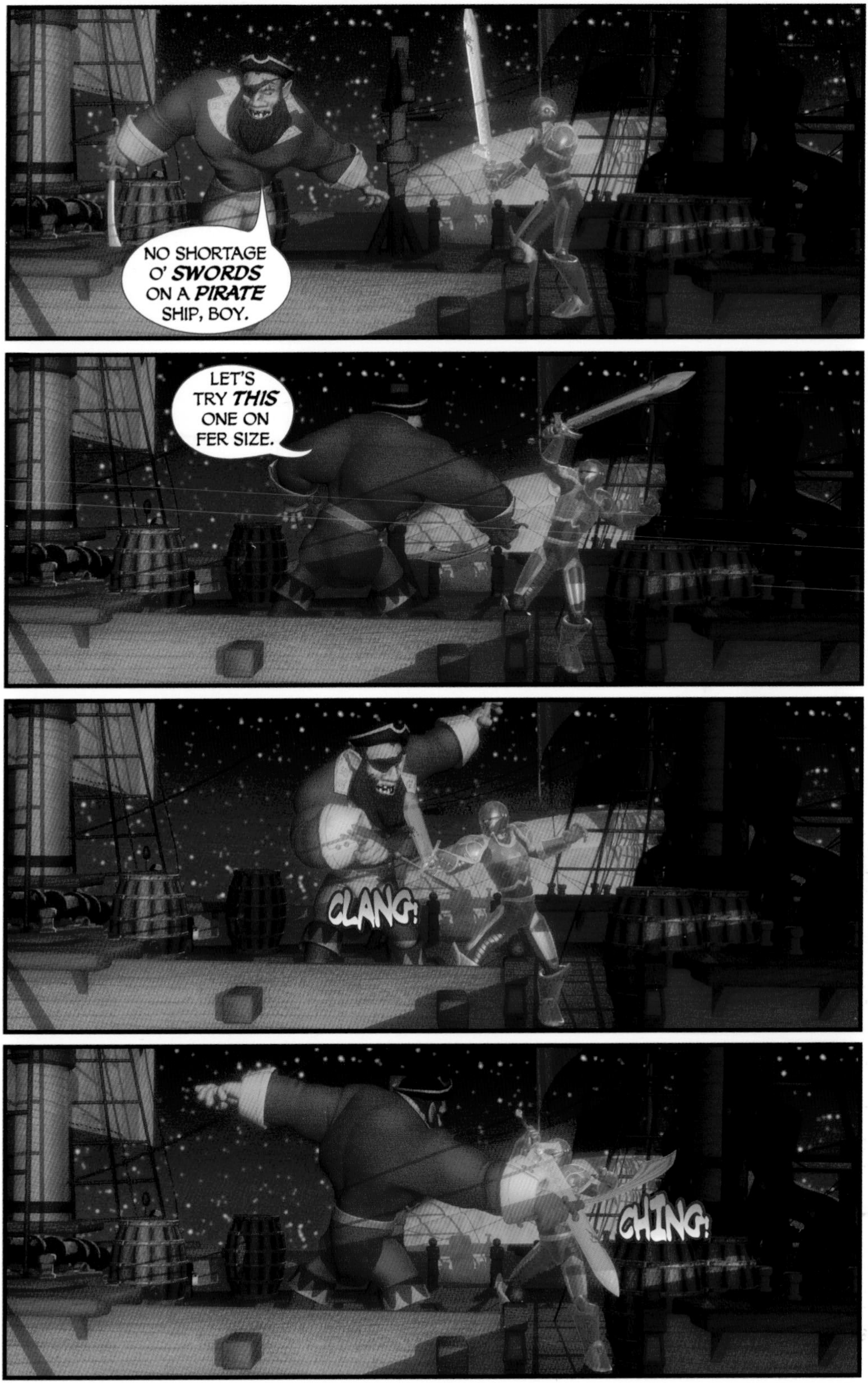
NO SHORTAGE O' SWORDS ON A PIRATE SHIP, BOY.
LET'S TRY THIS ONE ON FER SIZE.
CLANG!
CHING!

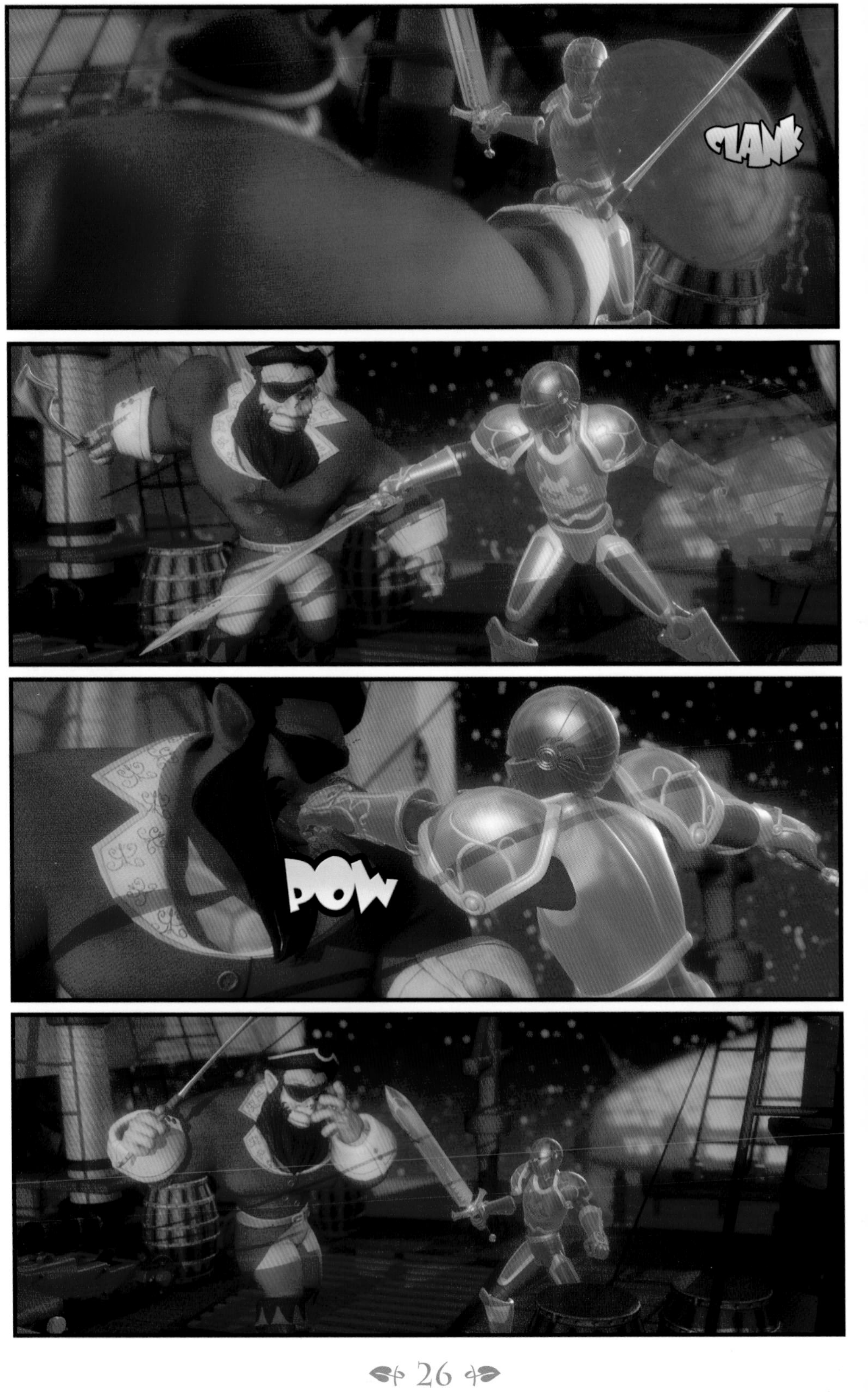
CLANK
POW

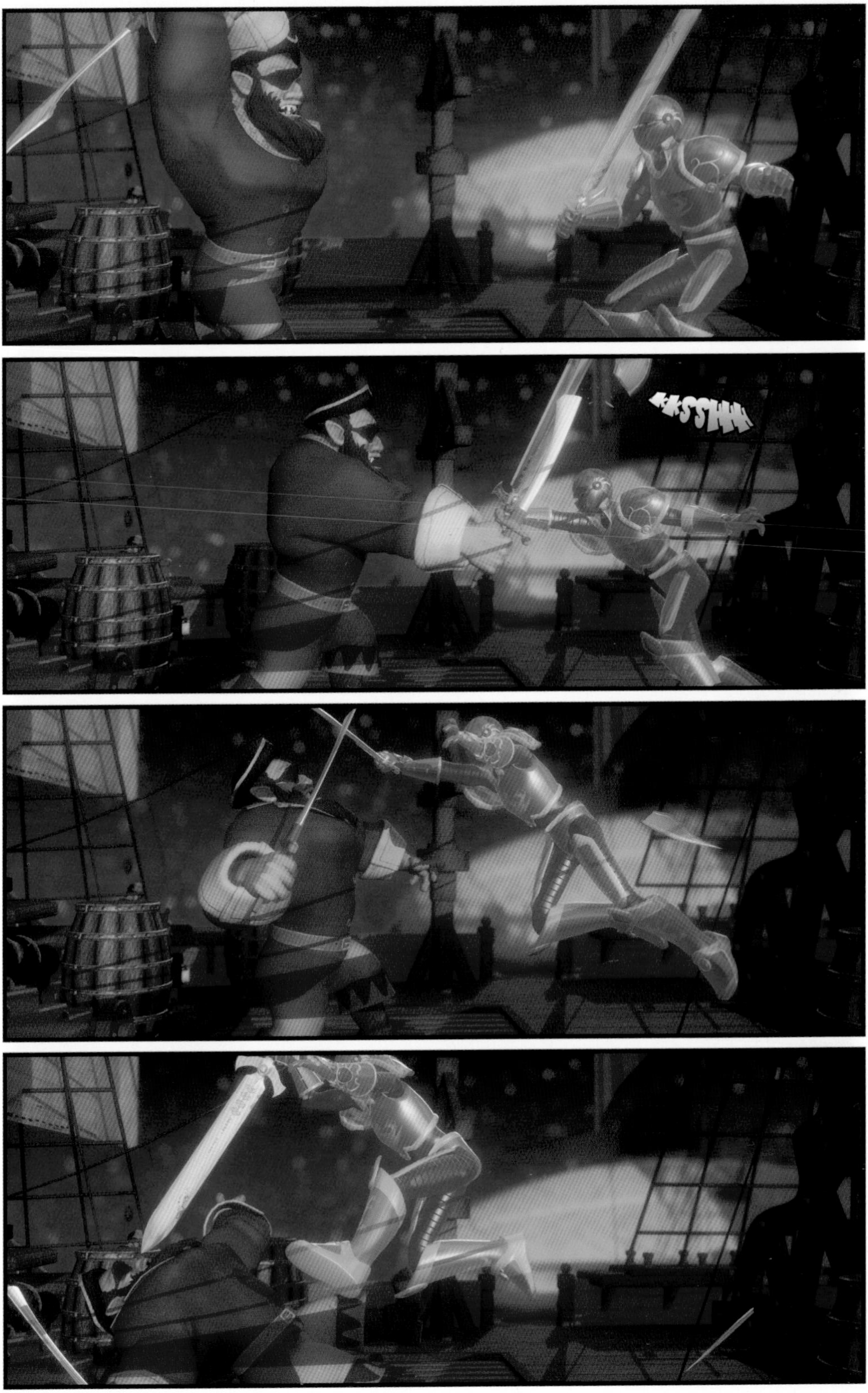
K-K-SSHHH

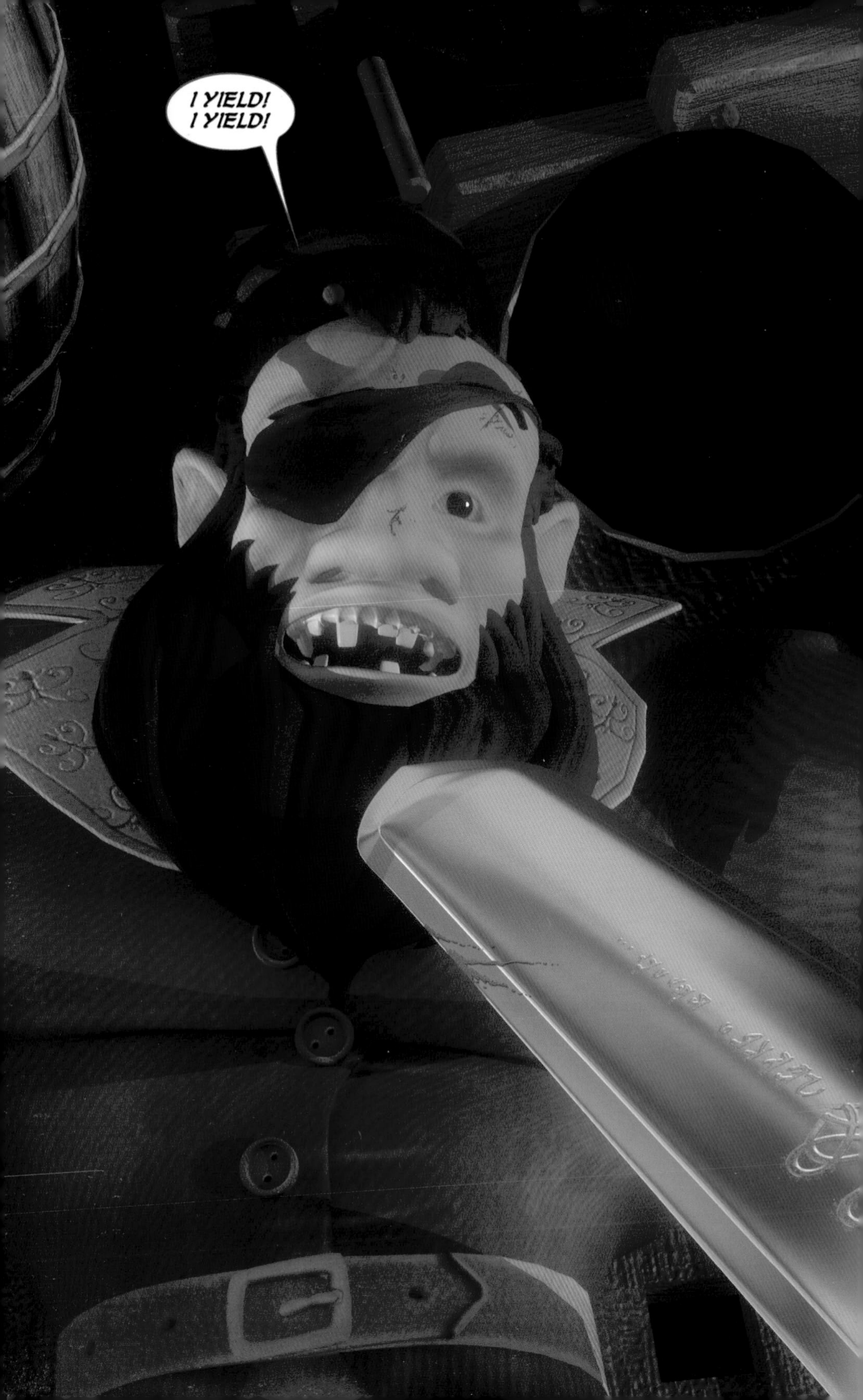
I YIELD!
I YIELD!

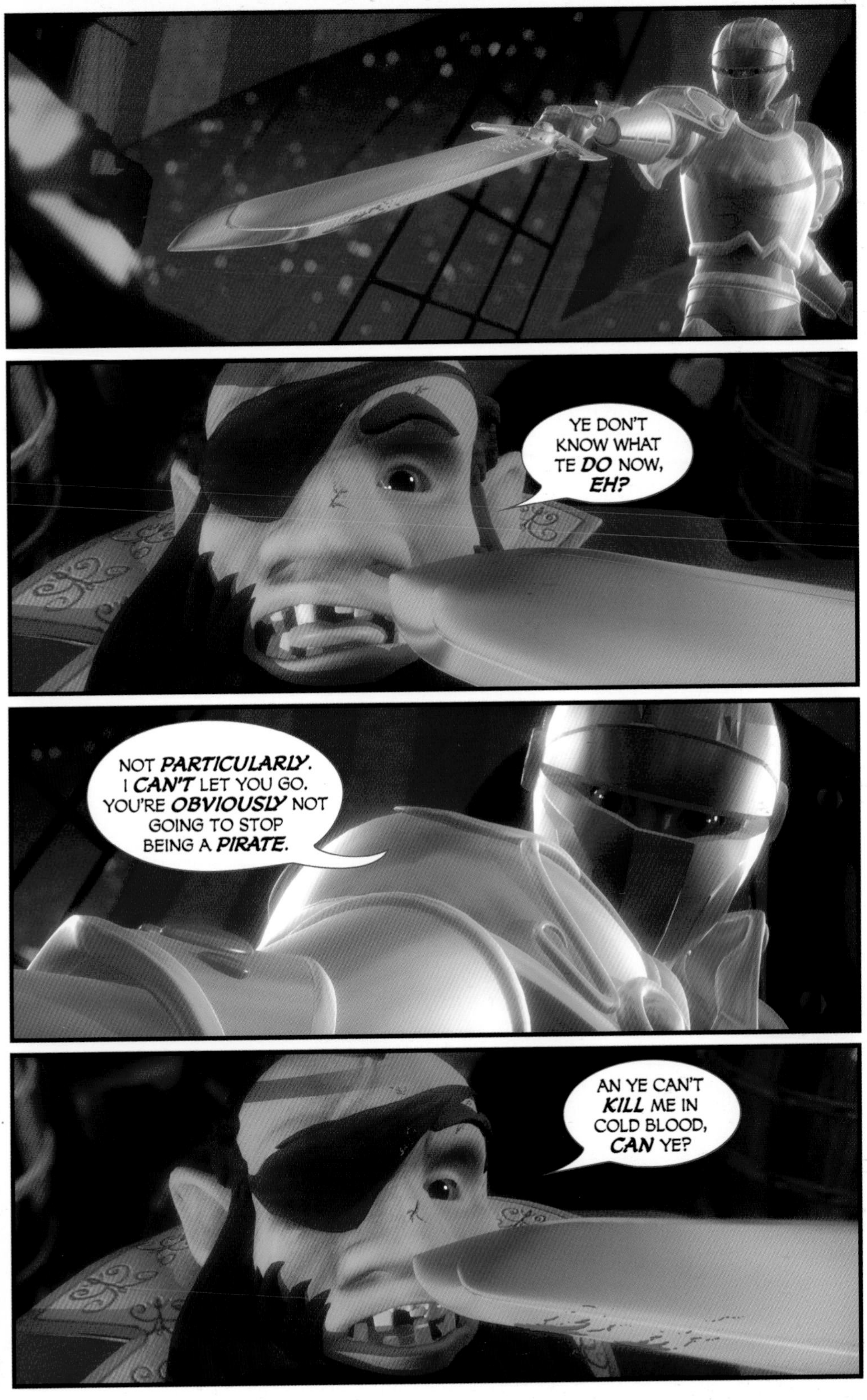
YE DON'T KNOW WHAT TE DO NOW, EH?
NOT PARTICULARLY. I CAN'T LET YOU GO. YOU'RE OBVIOUSLY NOT GOING TO STOP BEING A PIRATE.
AN YE CAN'T KILL ME IN COLD BLOOD, CAN YE?

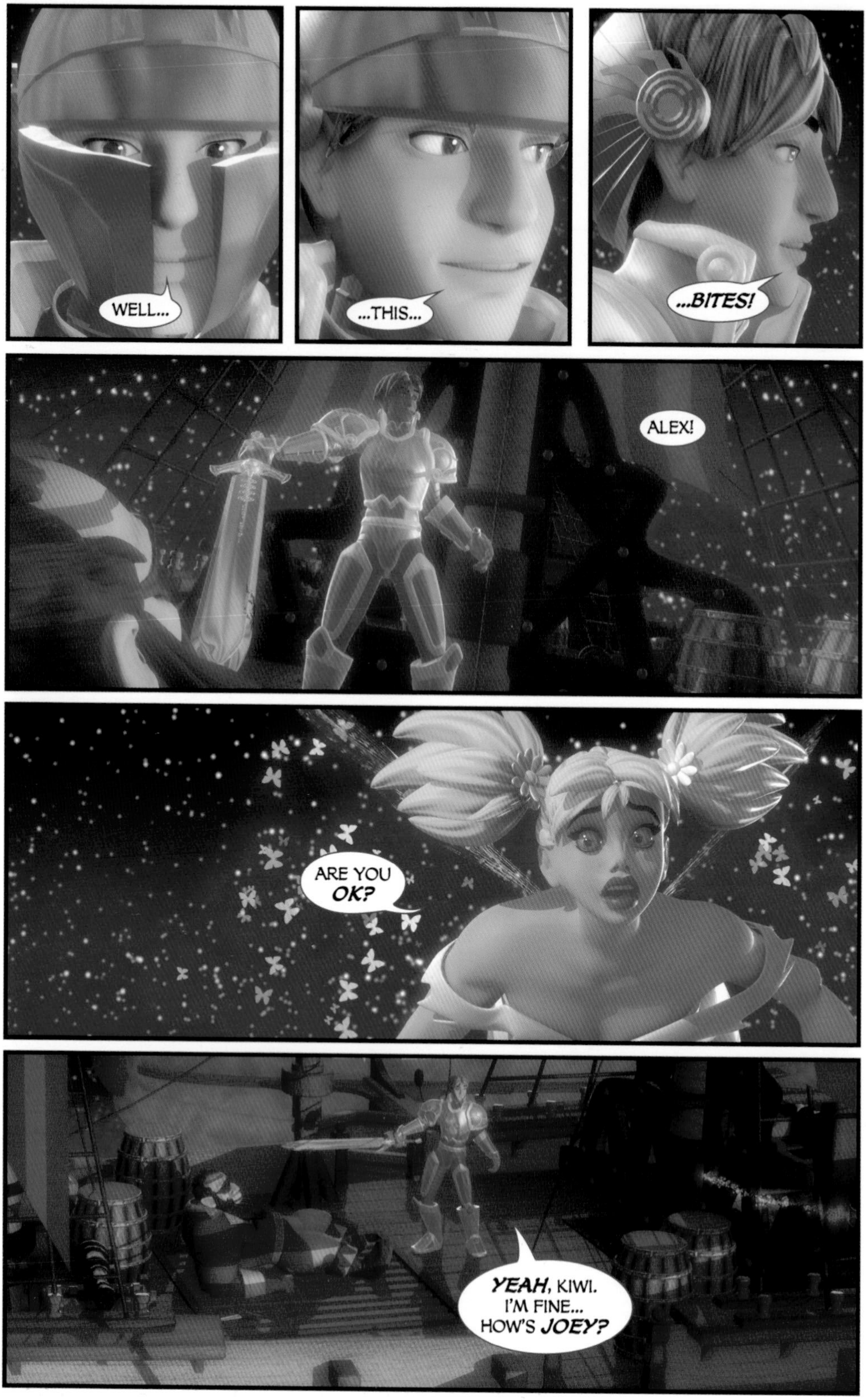
WELL...
...THIS...
...BITES!
ALEX!
ARE YOU OK?
YEAH, KIWI. I'M FINE... HOW'S JOEY?

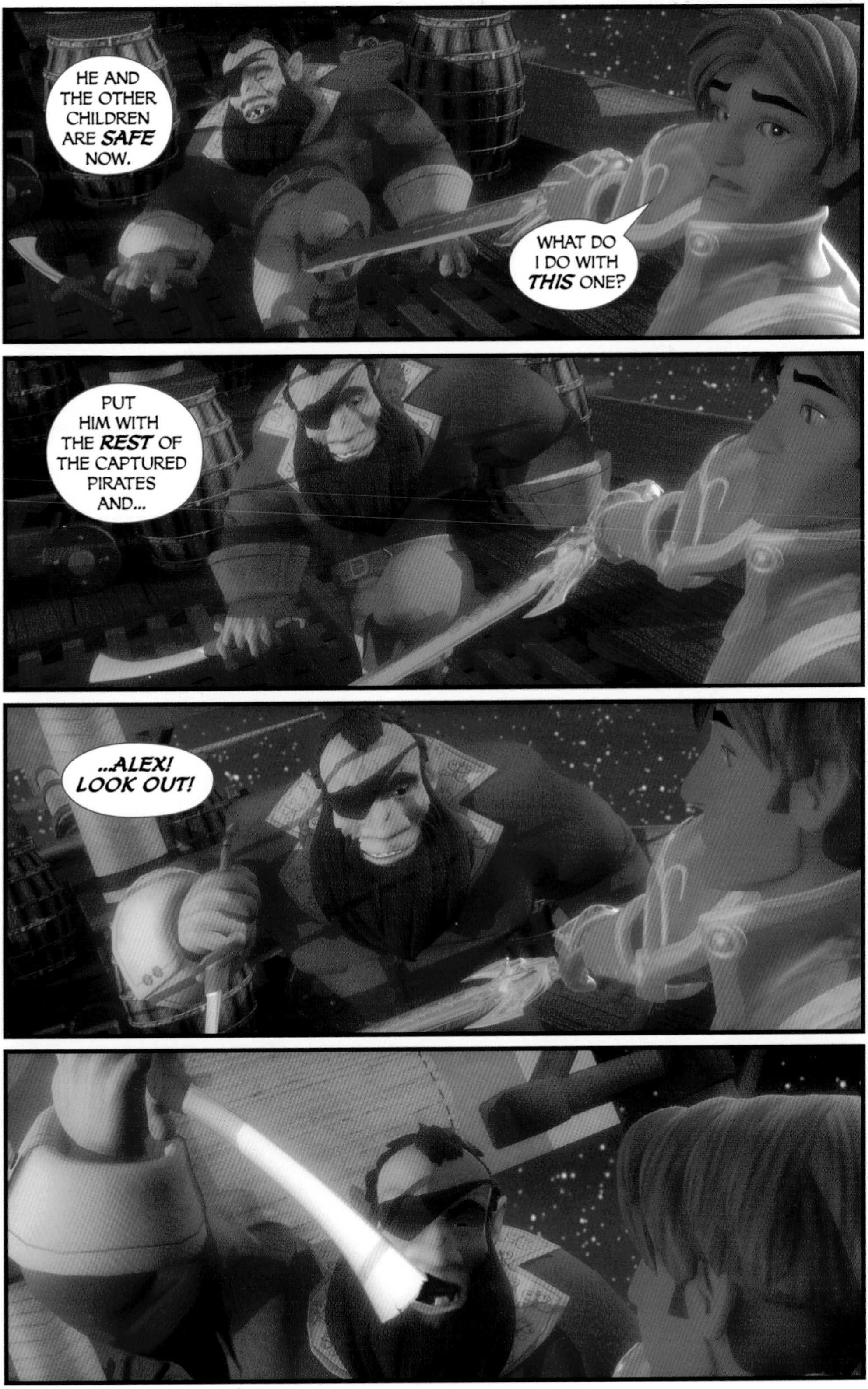
HE AND THE OTHER CHILDREN ARE SAFE NOW.
WHAT DO I DO WITH THIS ONE?
PUT HIM WITH THE REST OF THE CAPTURED PIRATES AND...
...ALEX! LOOK OUT!

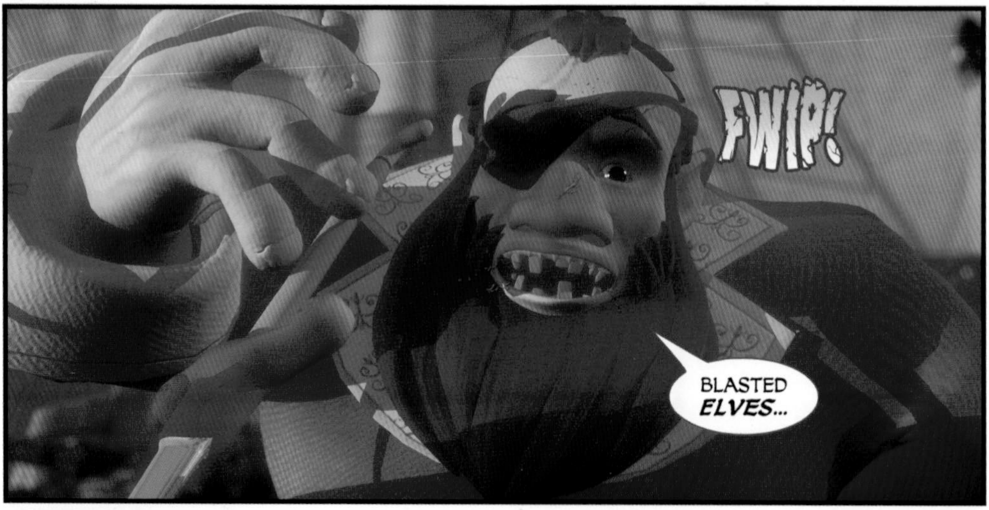
FWIP!
BLASTED ELVES...

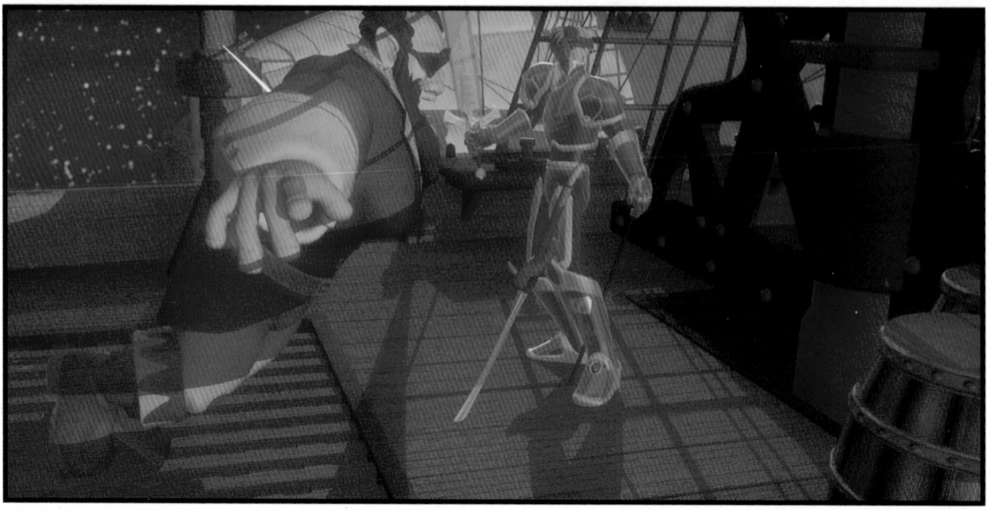

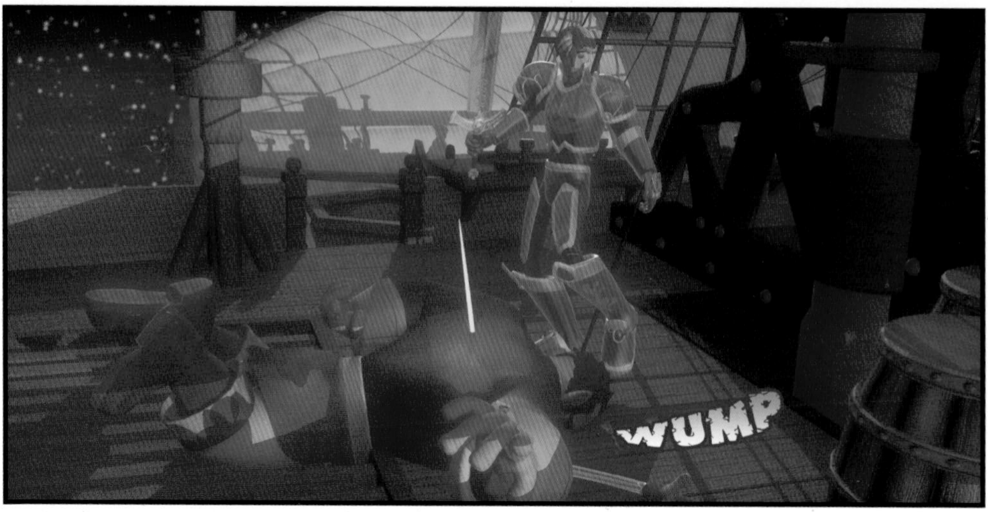
WUMP

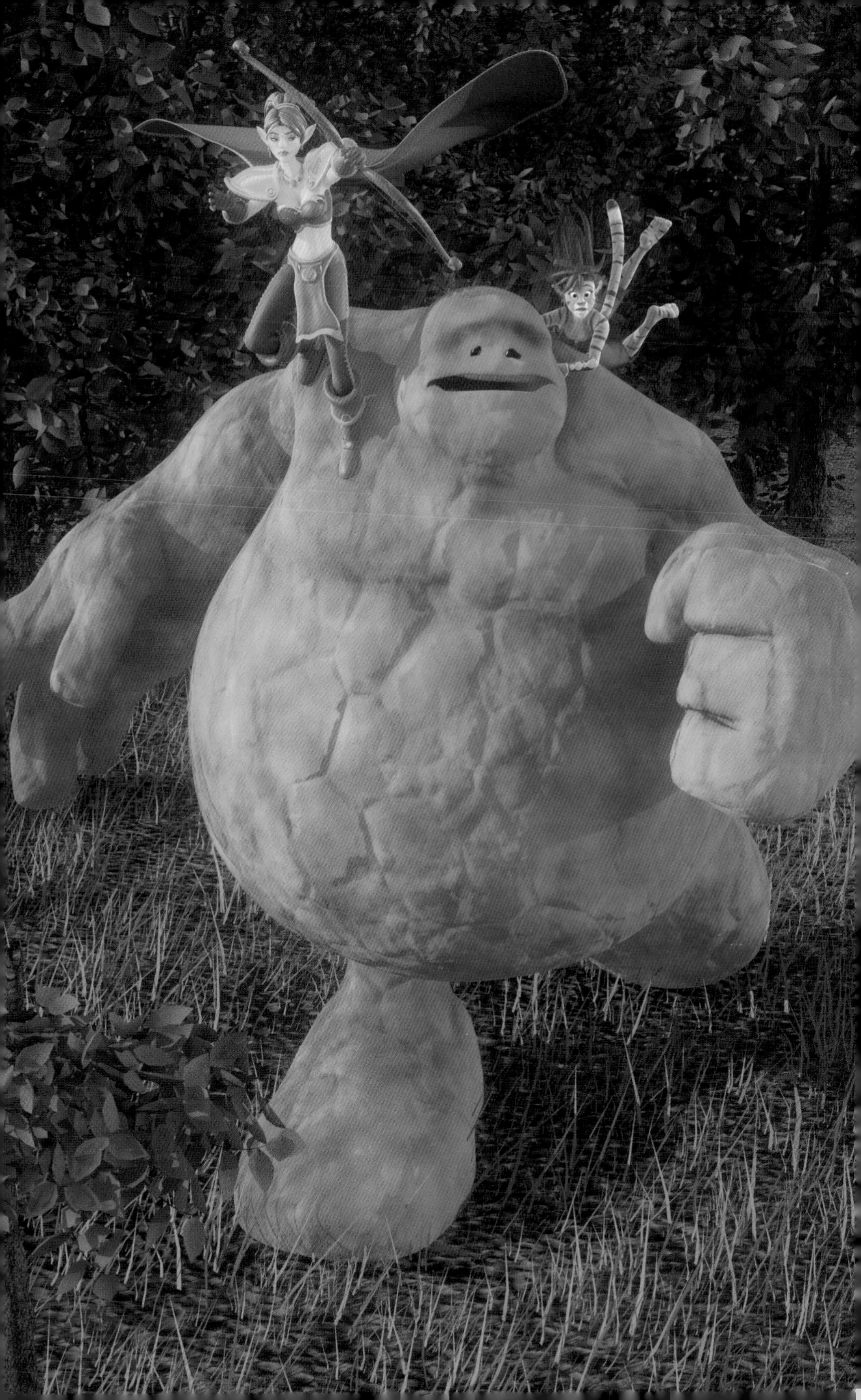

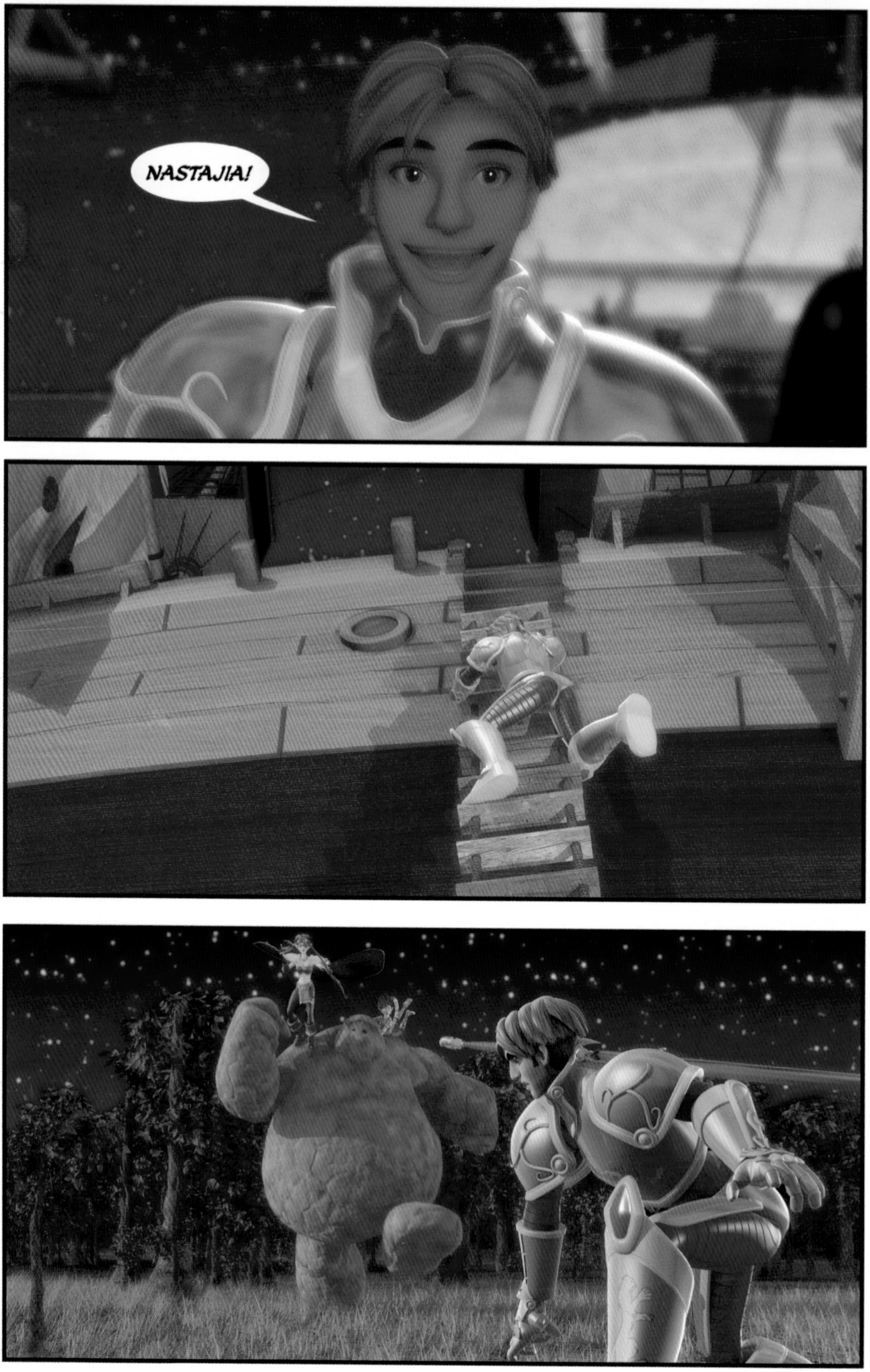
NASTAJIA!

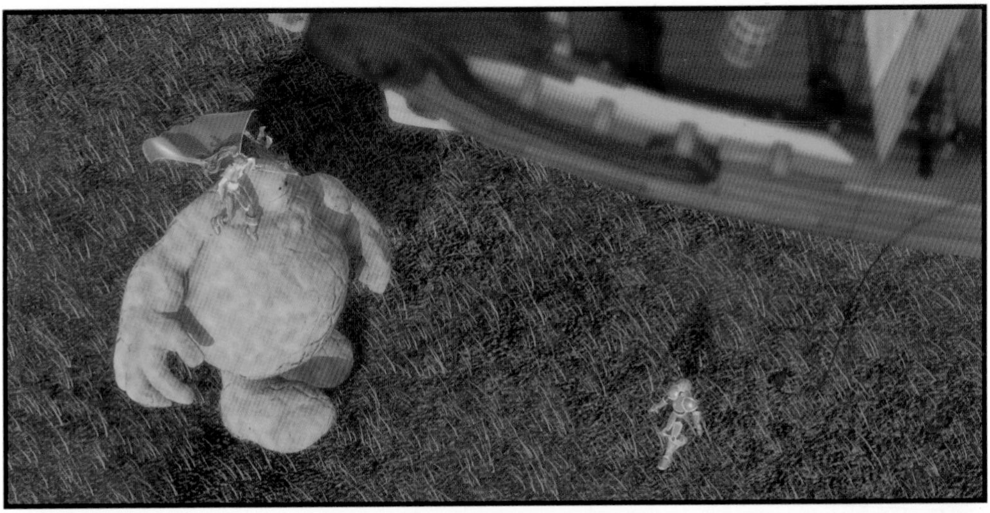

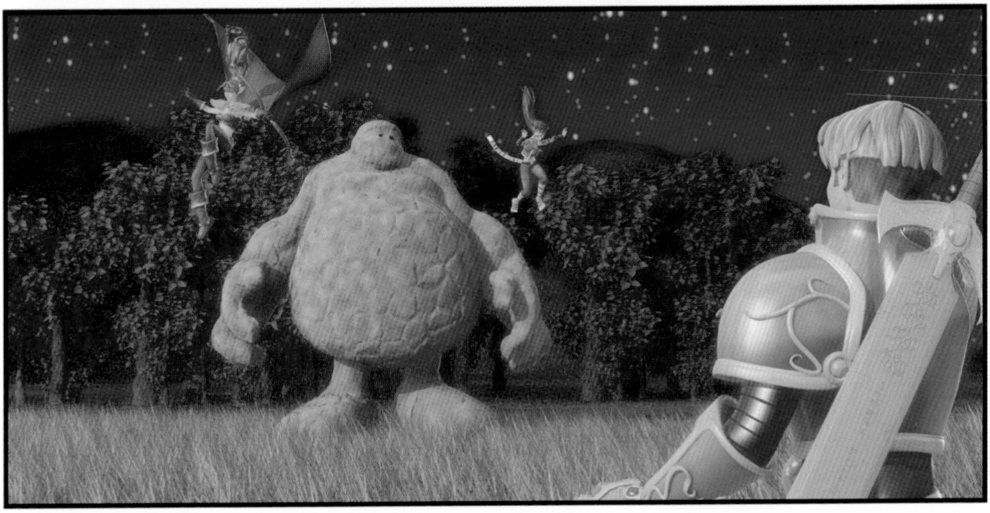

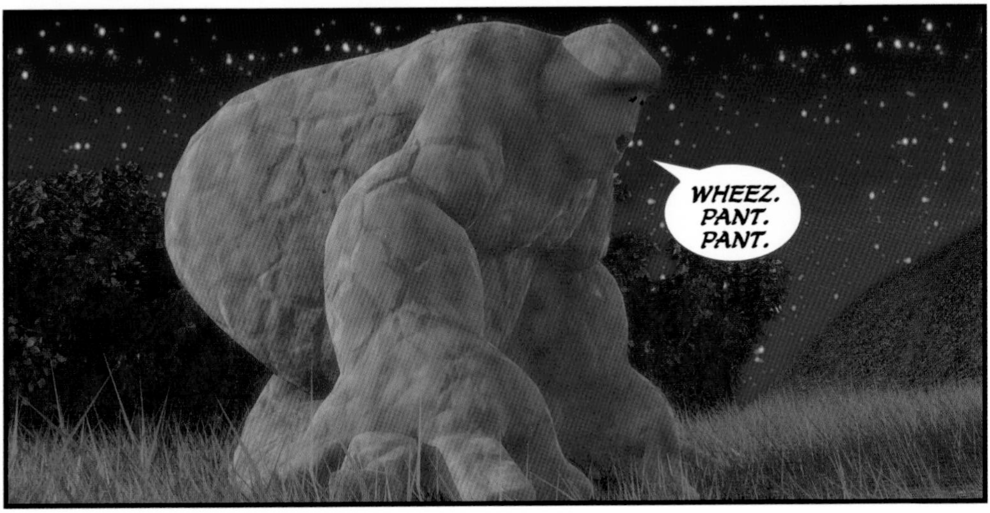
WHEEZ. PANT. PANT.

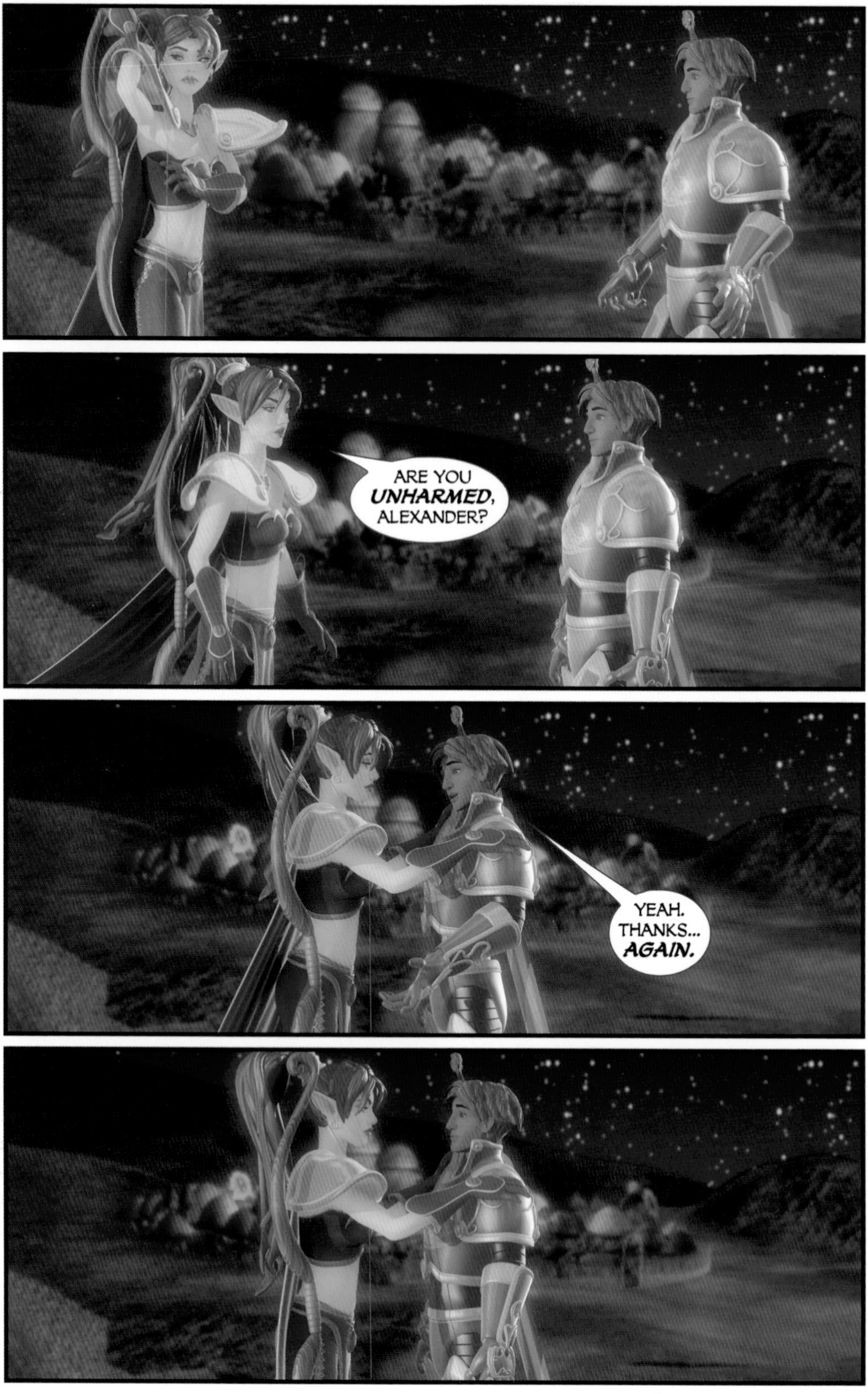
ARE YOU UNHARMED, ALEXANDER?
YEAH. THANKS... AGAIN.

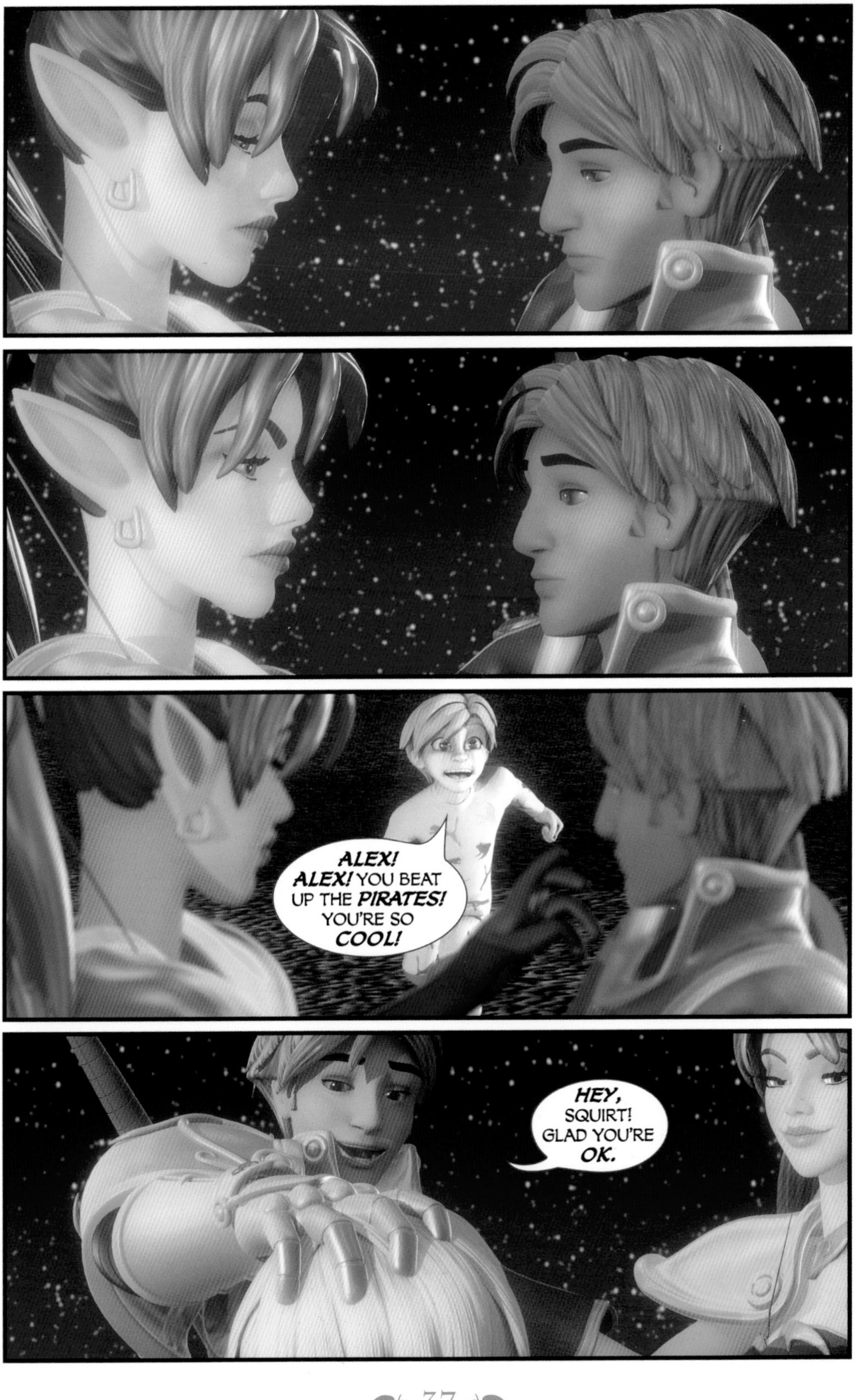
ALEX! ALEX! YOU BEAT UP THE PIRATES! YOU'RE SO COOL!
HEY, SQUIRT! GLAD YOU'RE OK.

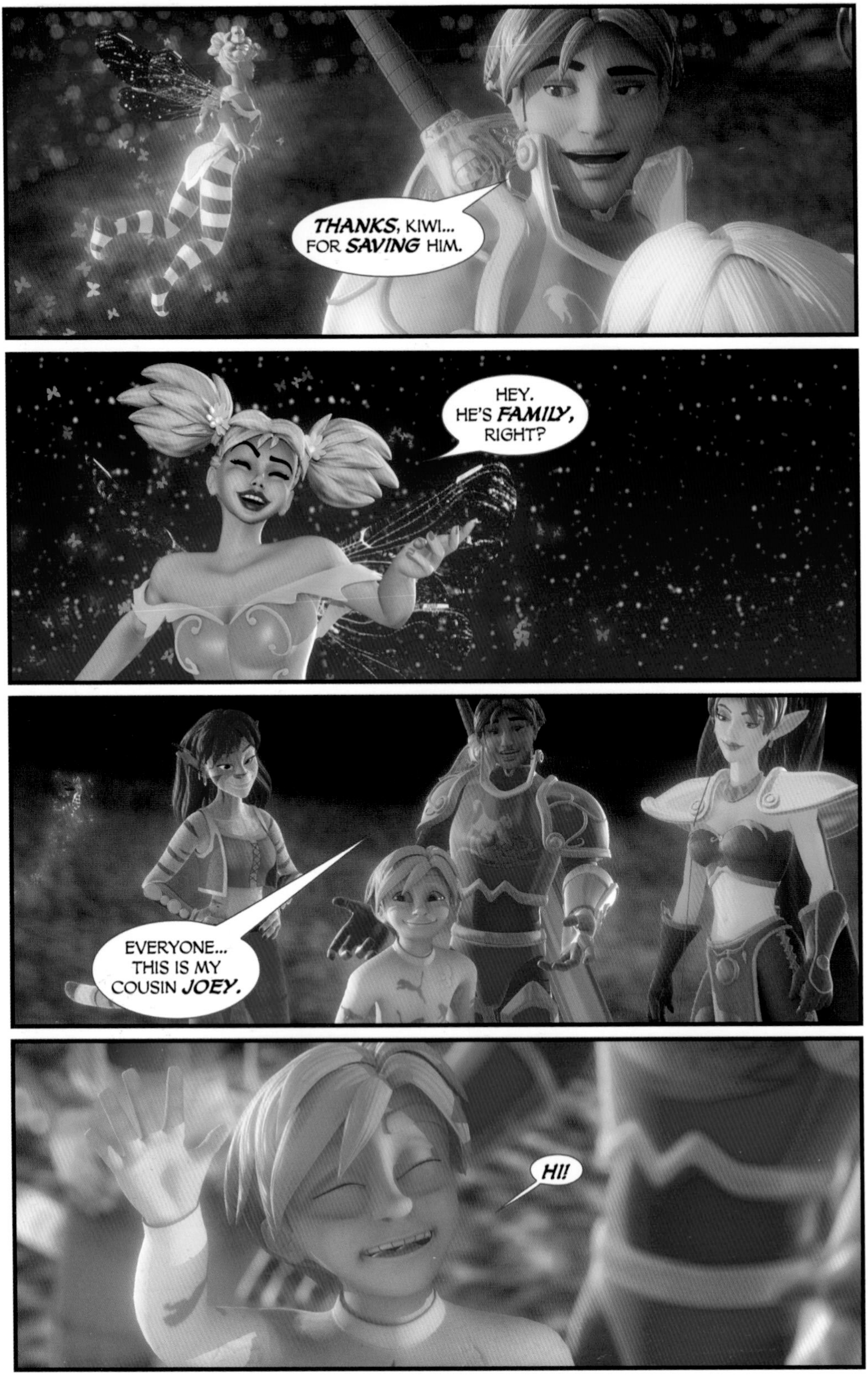
THANKS, KIWI... FOR SAVING HIM.
HEY. HE'S FAMILY, RIGHT?
EVERYONE... THIS IS MY COUSIN JOEY.
HI!

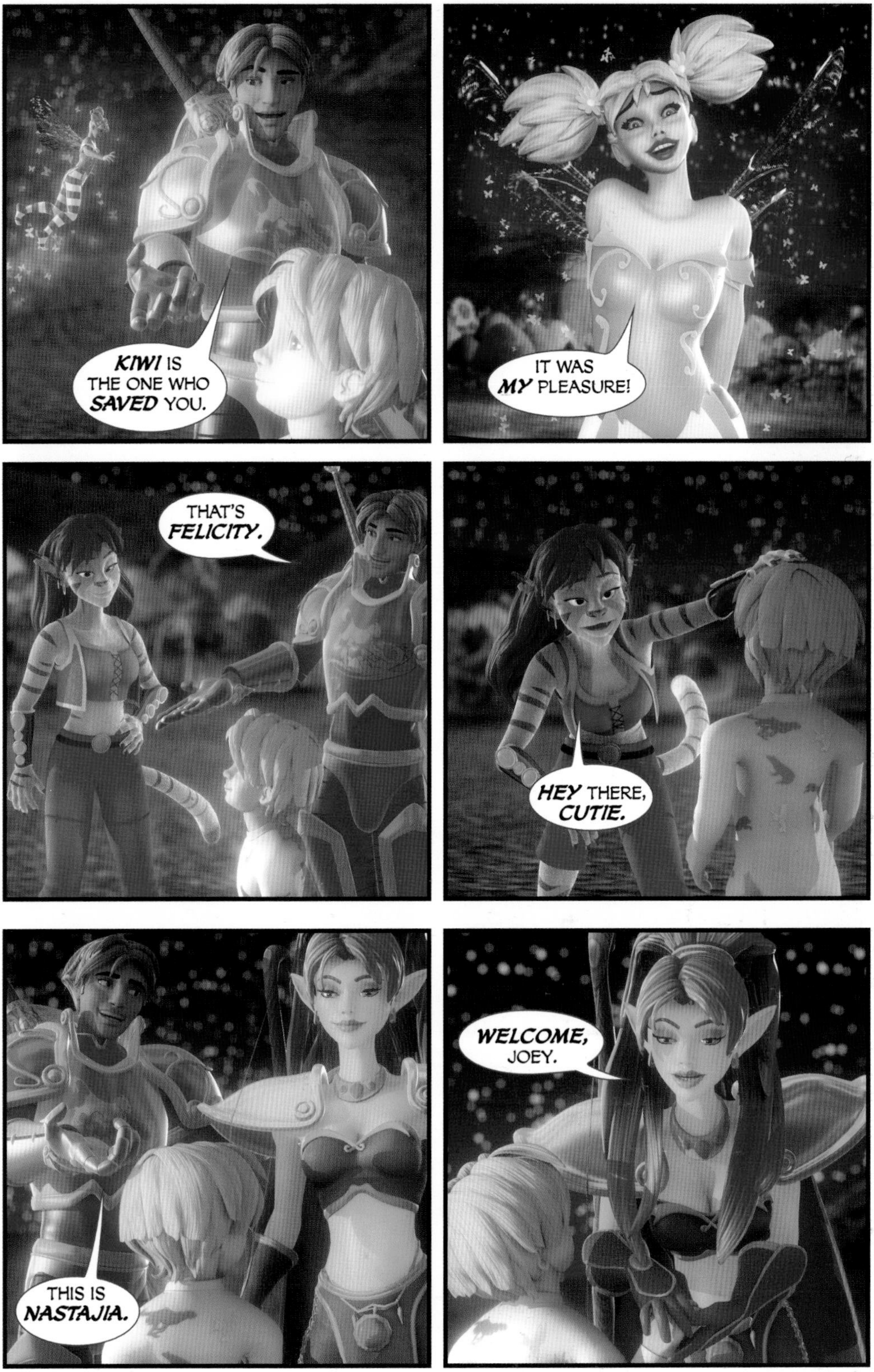
KIWI IS THE ONE WHO SAVED YOU.
IT WAS MY PLEASURE!
THAT'S FELICITY.
HEY THERE, CUTIE.
THIS IS NASTAJIA.
WELCOME, JOEY.

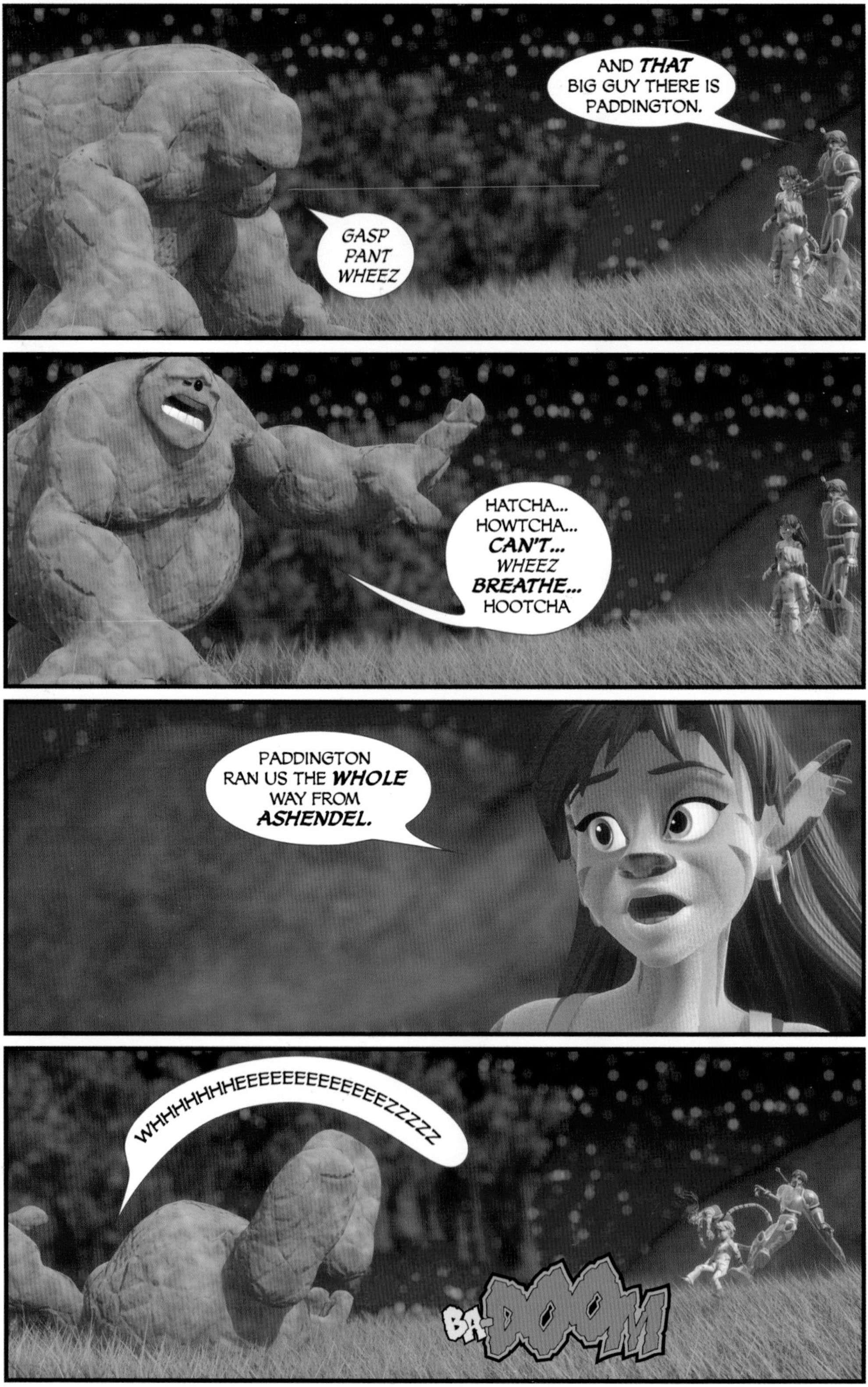
AND ***THAT*** BIG GUY THERE IS PADDINGTON.
GASP PANT WHEEZ
HATCHA... HOWTCHA... ***CAN'T...*** *WHEEZ* ***BREATHE...*** HOOTCHA
PADDINGTON RAN US THE ***WHOLE*** WAY FROM ***ASHENDEL.***
WHHHHHHEEEEEEEEEEEEEEEZZZZZ
BA-DOOM

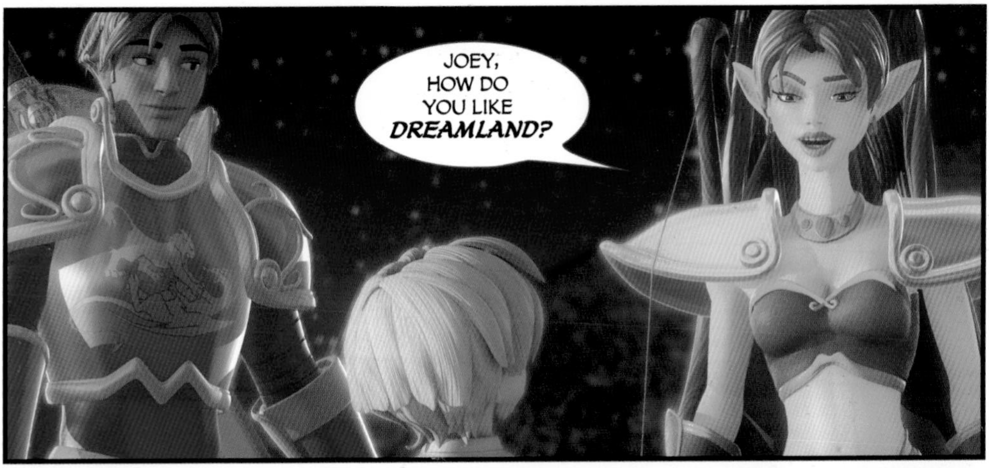
JOEY, HOW DO YOU LIKE *DREAMLAND?*

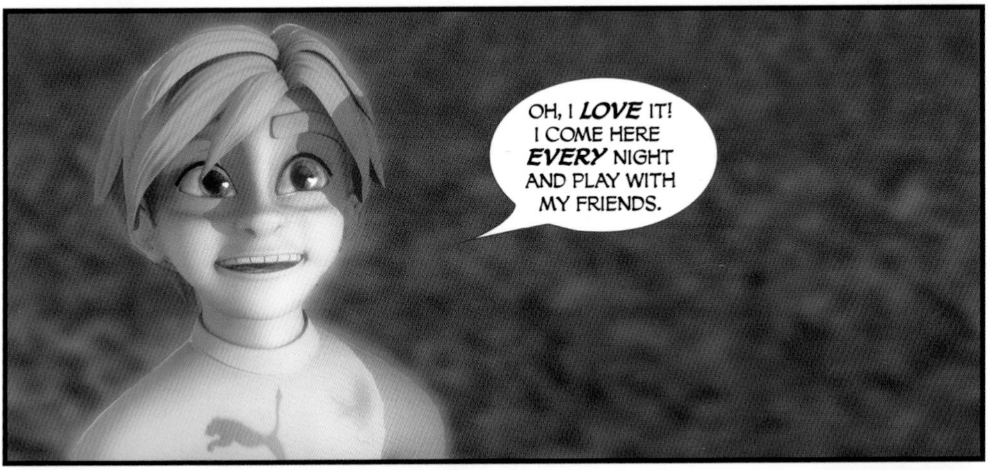
OH, I *LOVE* IT! I COME HERE *EVERY* NIGHT AND PLAY WITH MY FRIENDS.

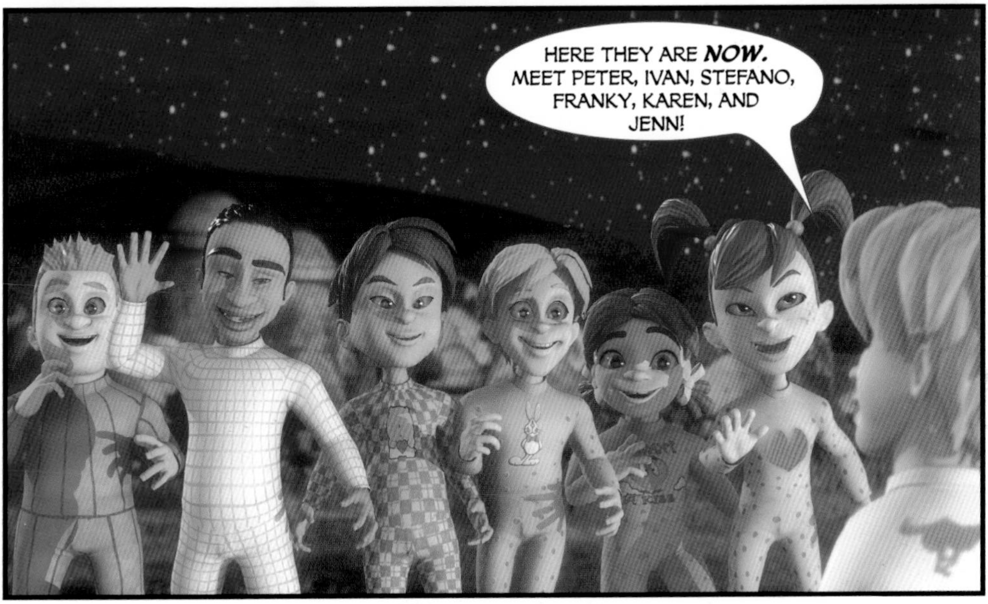
HERE THEY ARE *NOW.* MEET PETER, IVAN, STEFANO, FRANKY, KAREN, AND JENN!

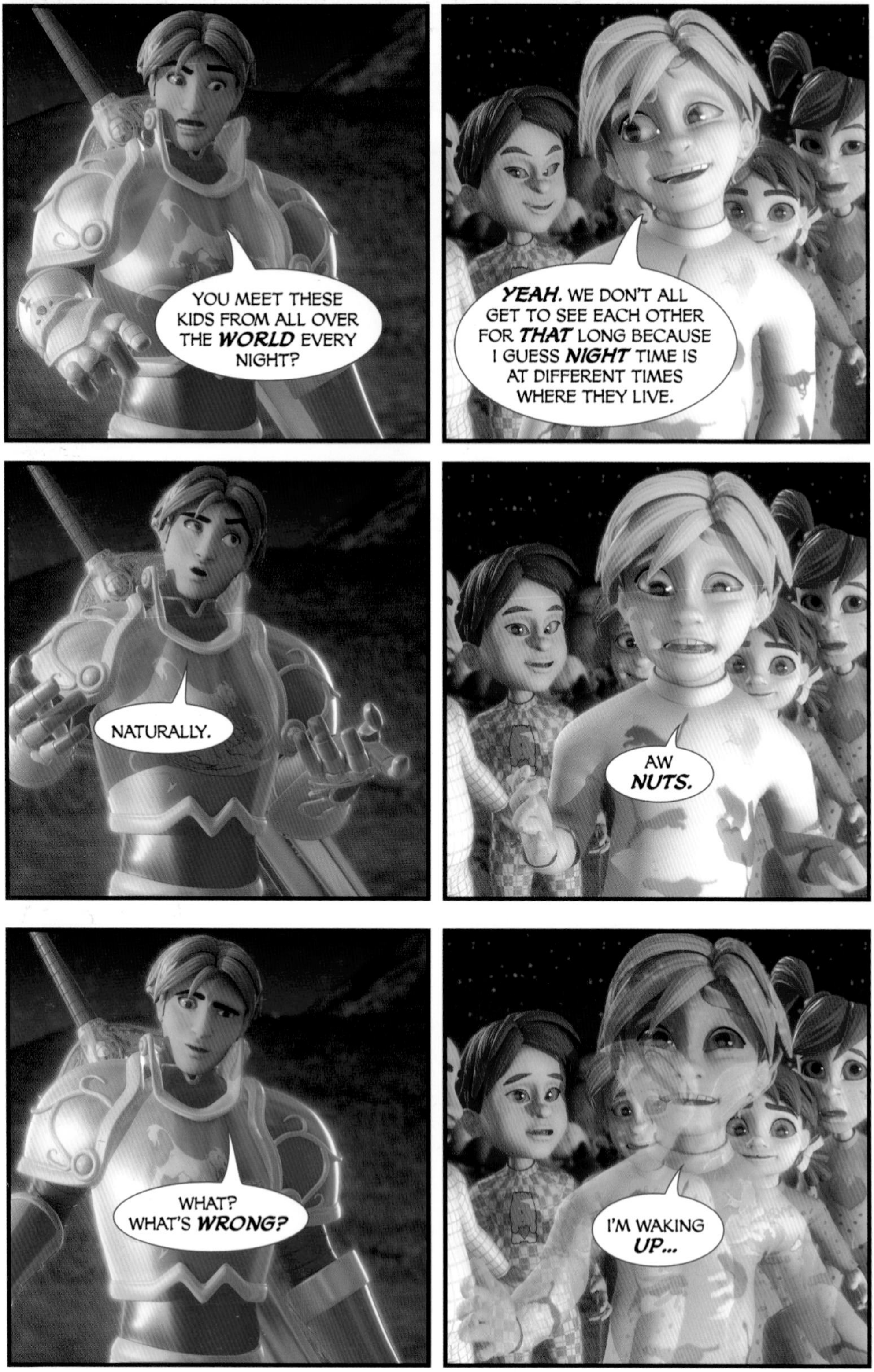
YOU MEET THESE KIDS FROM ALL OVER THE WORLD EVERY NIGHT?
YEAH. WE DON'T ALL GET TO SEE EACH OTHER FOR THAT LONG BECAUSE I GUESS NIGHT TIME IS AT DIFFERENT TIMES WHERE THEY LIVE.
NATURALLY.
AW NUTS.
WHAT? WHAT'S WRONG?
I'M WAKING UP...

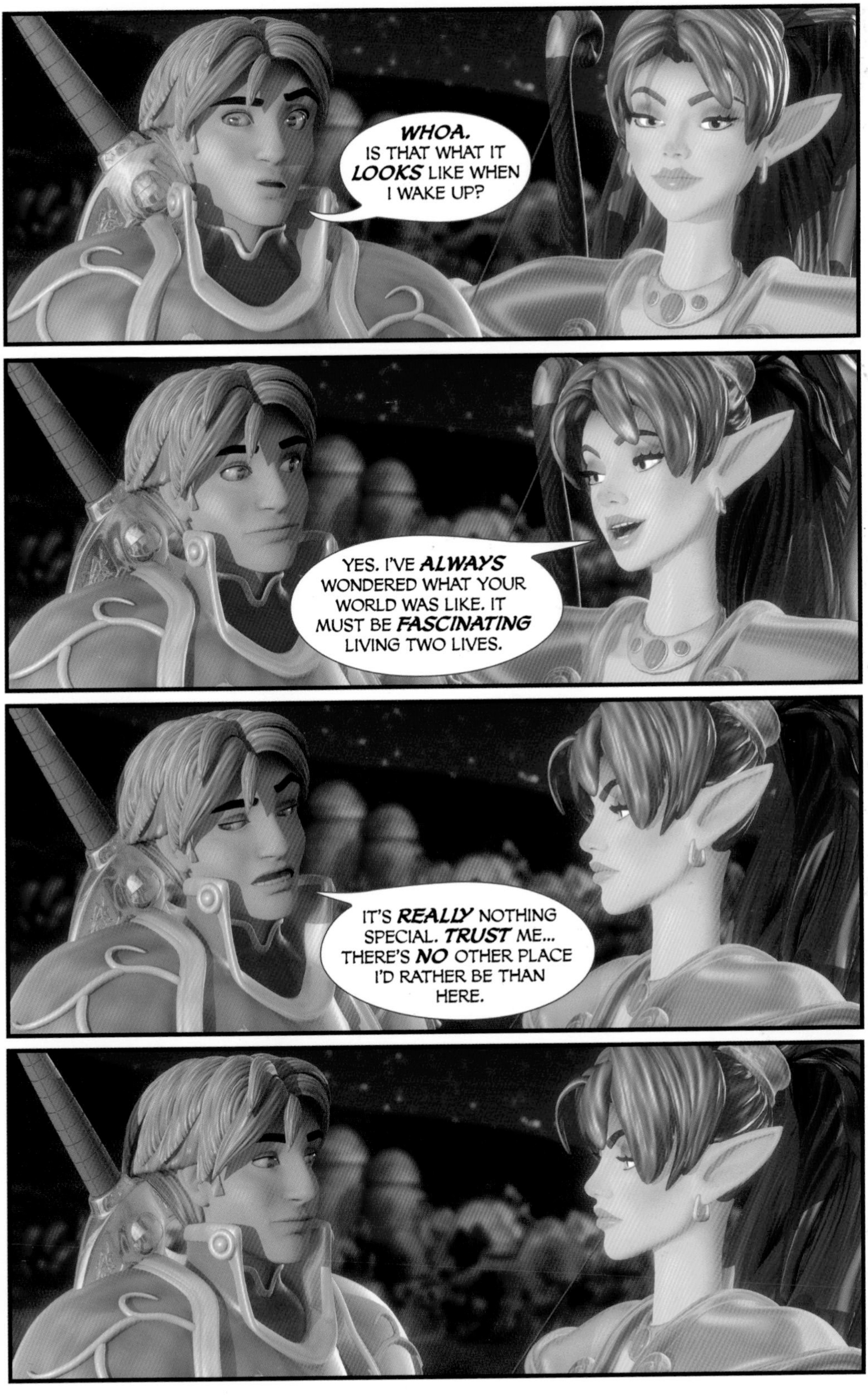
WHOA. IS THAT WHAT IT LOOKS LIKE WHEN I WAKE UP?
YES. I'VE ALWAYS WONDERED WHAT YOUR WORLD WAS LIKE. IT MUST BE FASCINATING LIVING TWO LIVES.
IT'S REALLY NOTHING SPECIAL. TRUST ME... THERE'S NO OTHER PLACE I'D RATHER BE THAN HERE.

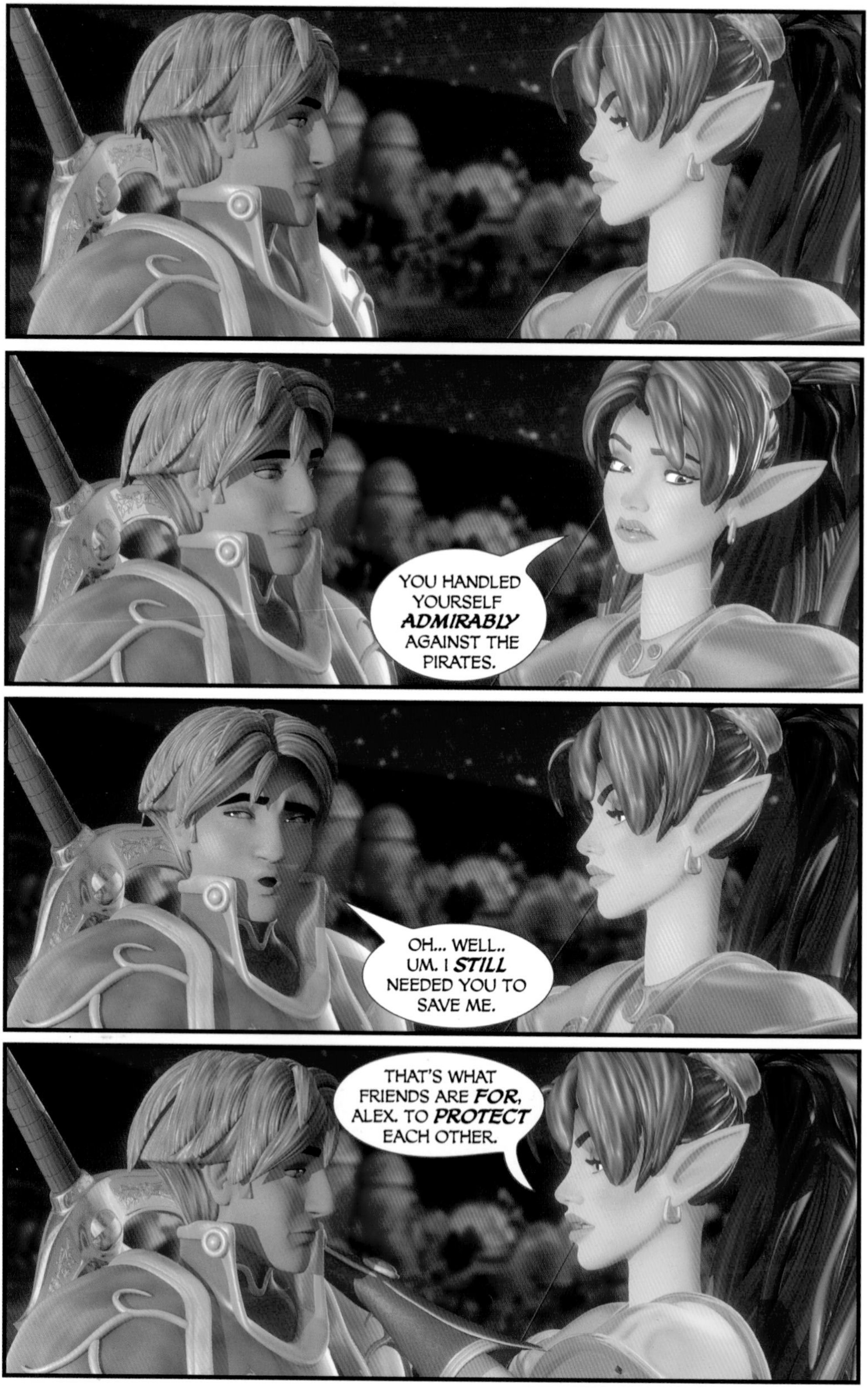
YOU HANDLED YOURSELF ADMIRABLY AGAINST THE PIRATES.
OH... WELL.. UM. I STILL NEEDED YOU TO SAVE ME.
THAT'S WHAT FRIENDS ARE FOR, ALEX. TO PROTECT EACH OTHER.

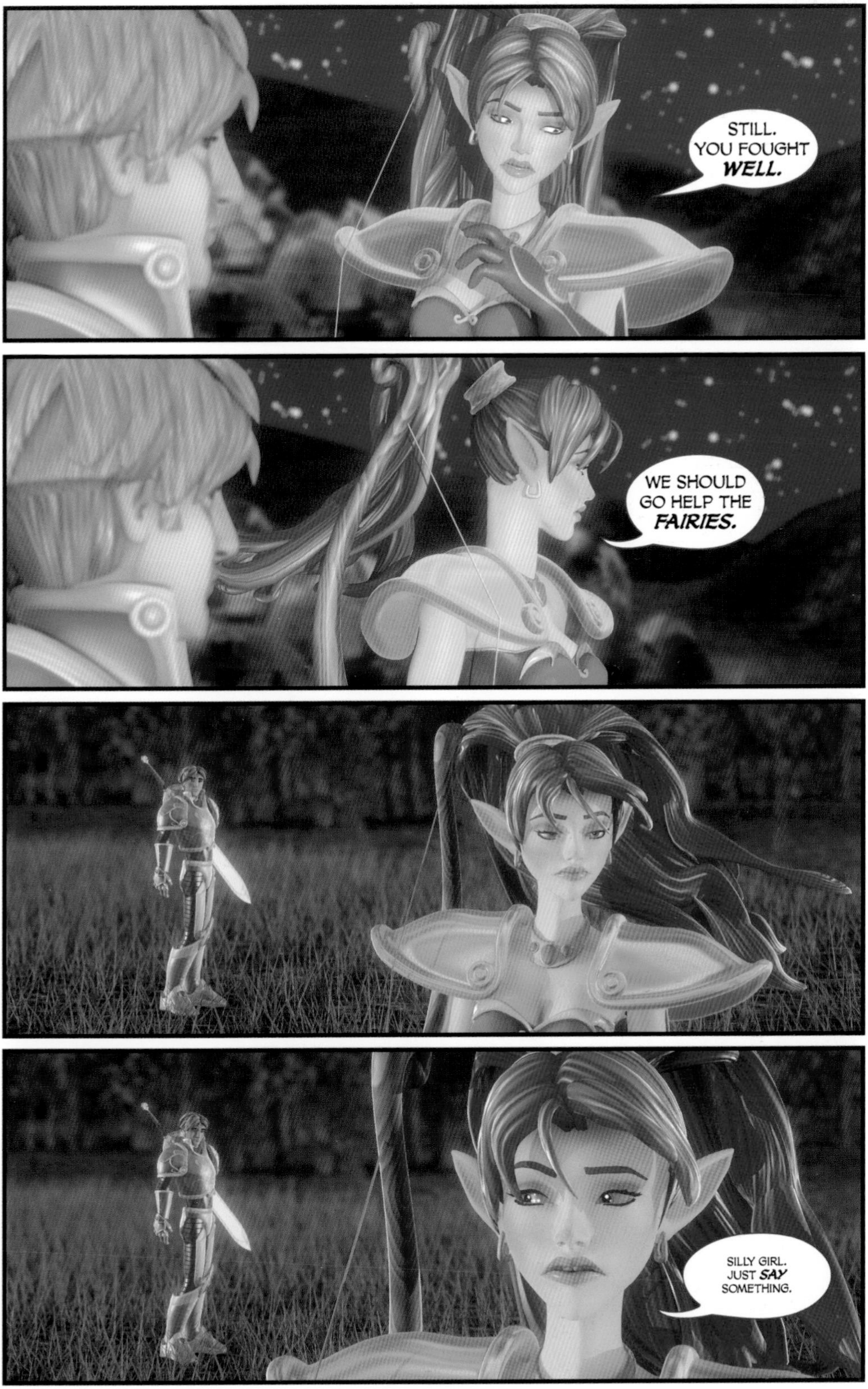
STILL. YOU FOUGHT **WELL.**
WE SHOULD GO HELP THE **FAIRIES.**
SILLY GIRL. JUST **SAY** SOMETHING.

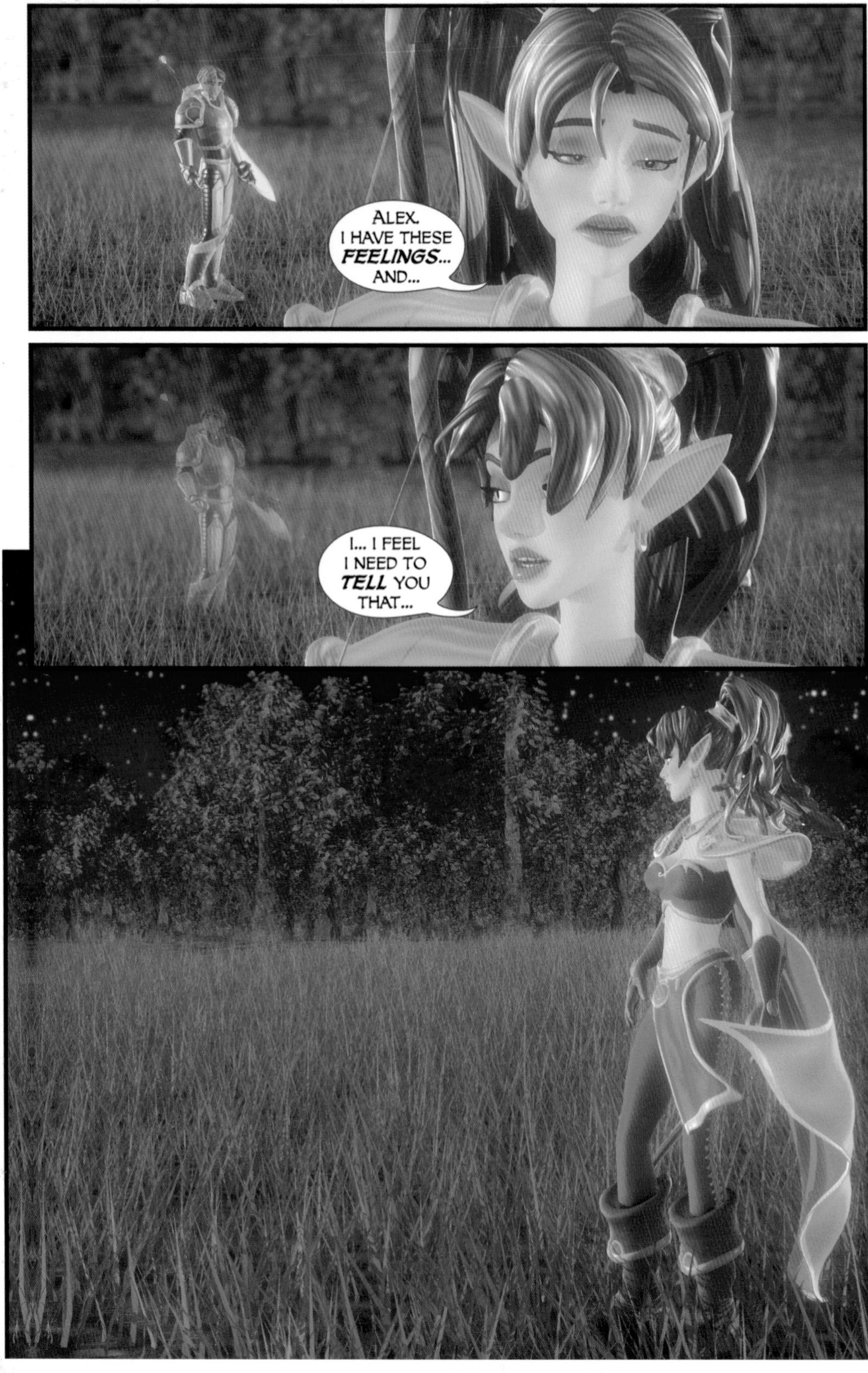
ALEX.
I HAVE THESE
FEELINGS...
AND...
I... I FEEL
I NEED TO
TELL YOU
THAT...

CHAPTER TEN

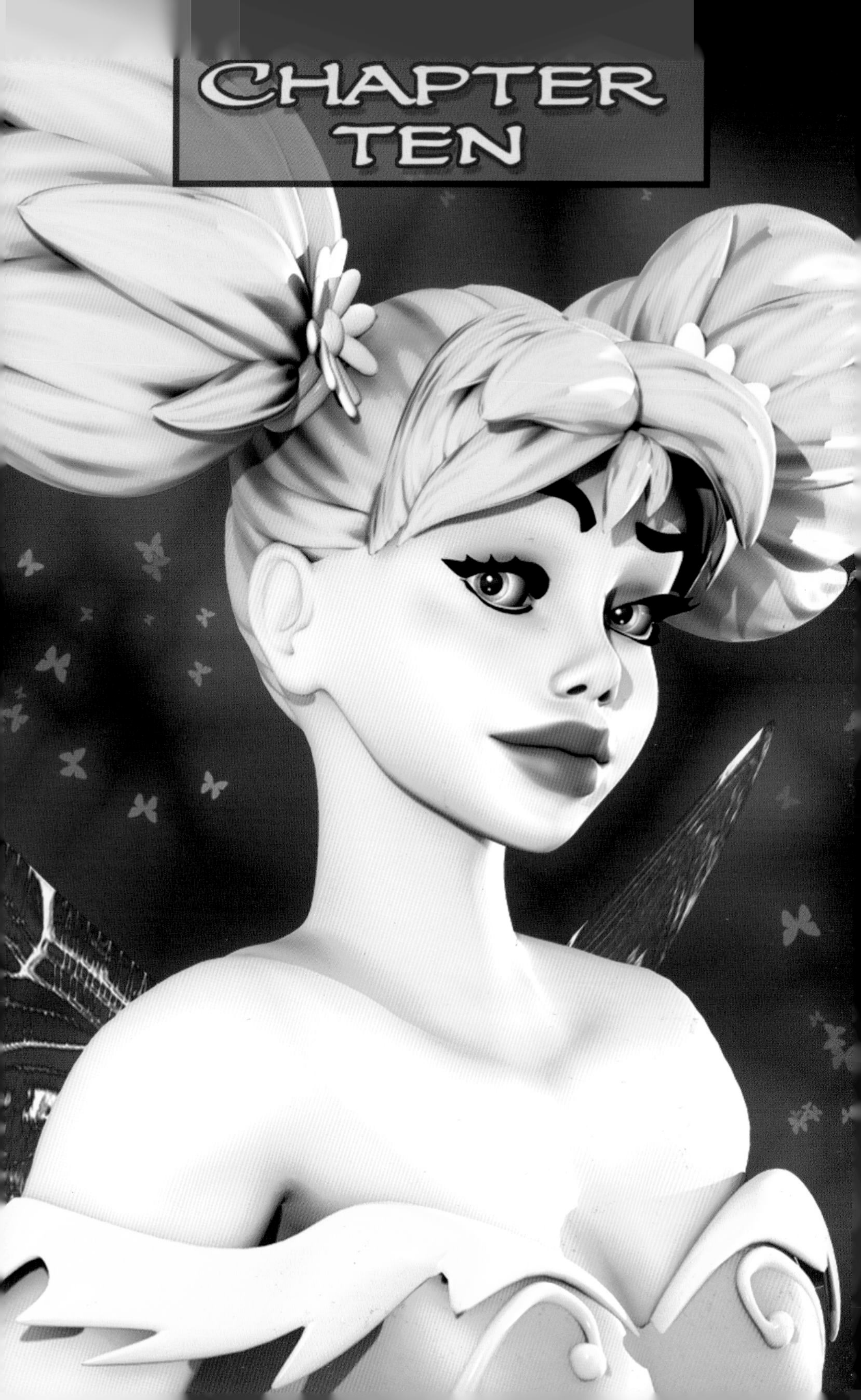

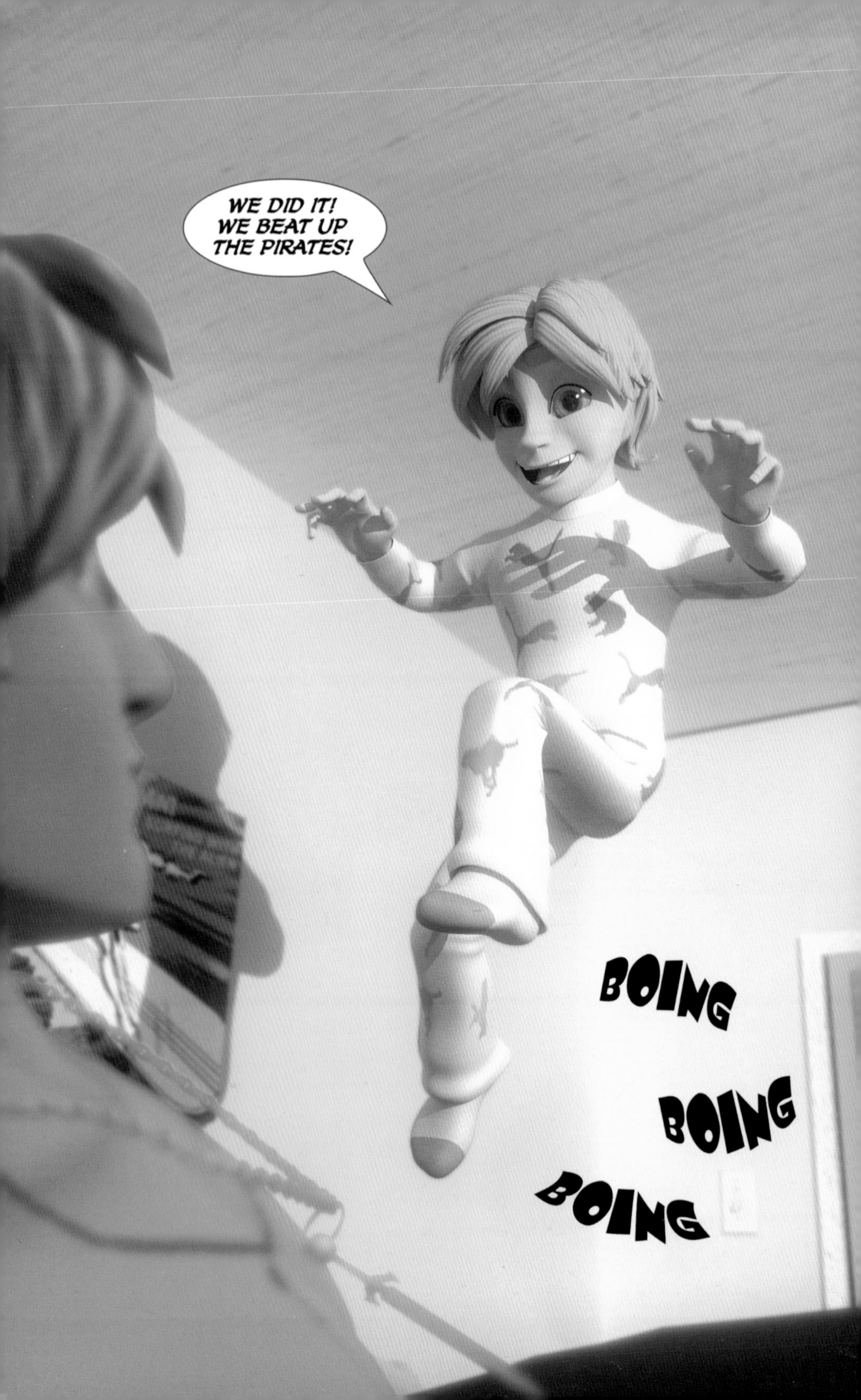
WE DID IT! WE BEAT UP THE PIRATES!
BOING
BOING
BOING

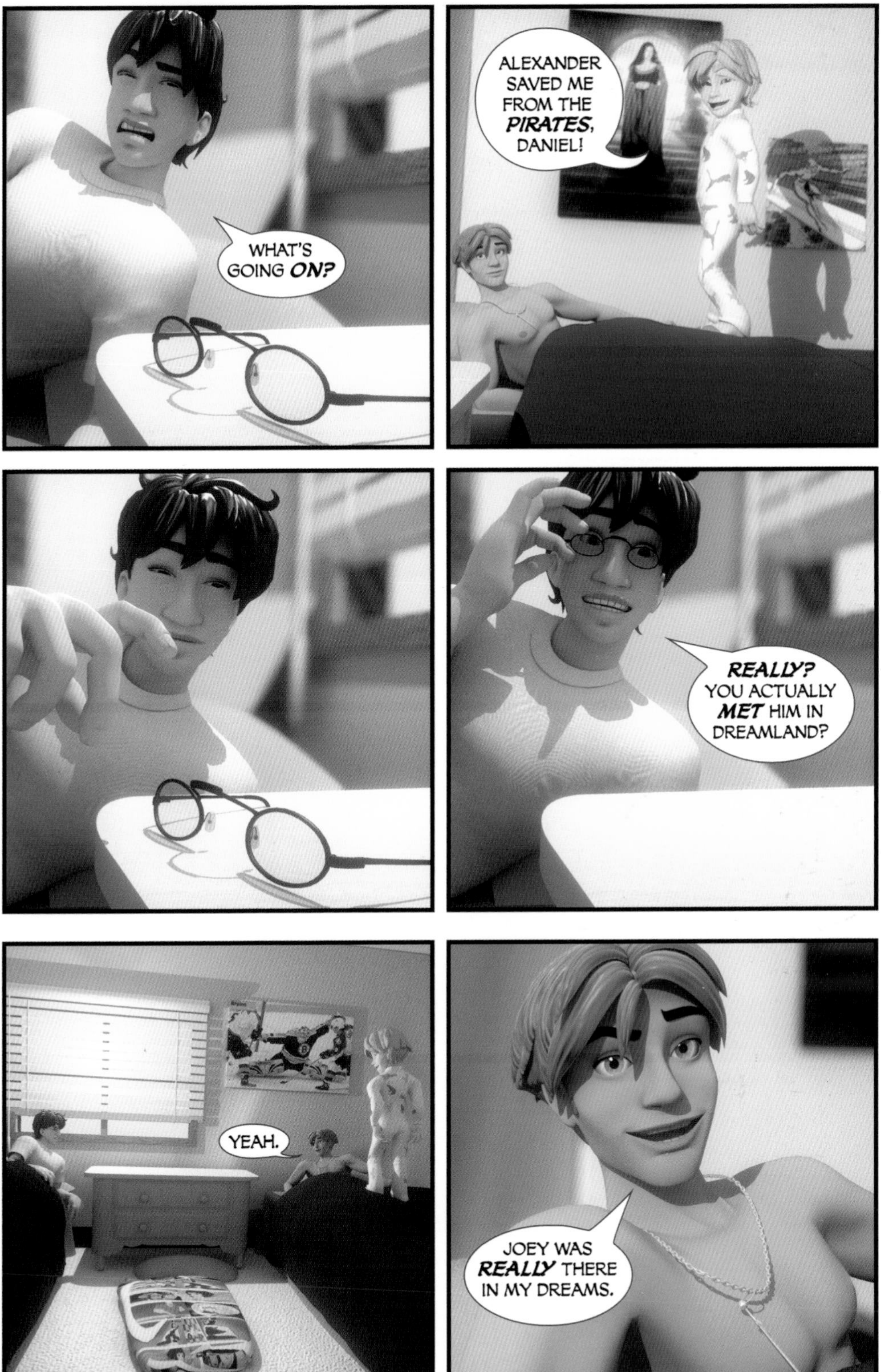
WHAT'S GOING ON?
ALEXANDER SAVED ME FROM THE PIRATES, DANIEL!
REALLY? YOU ACTUALLY MET HIM IN DREAMLAND?
YEAH.
JOEY WAS REALLY THERE IN MY DREAMS.

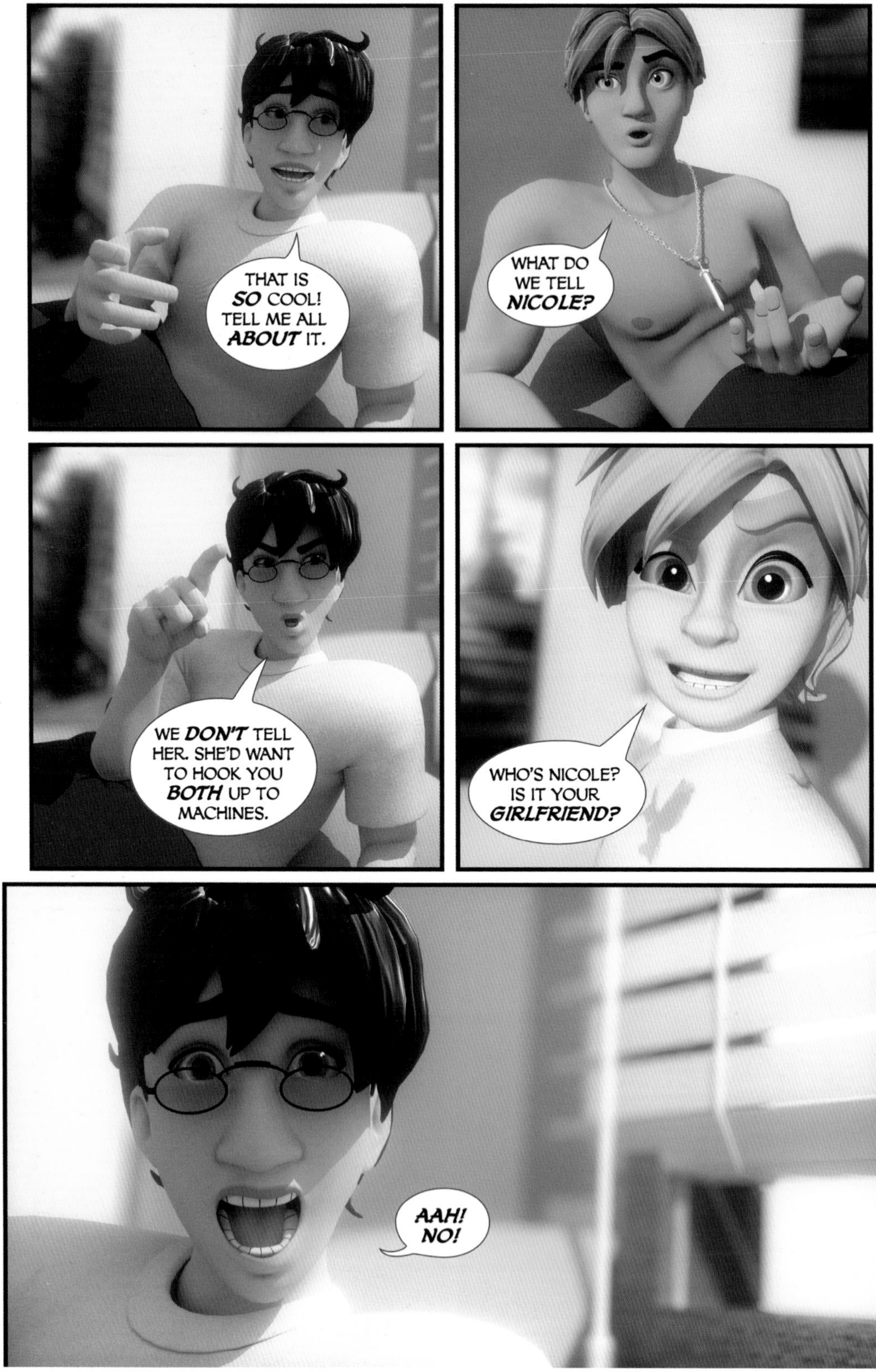
THAT IS SO COOL! TELL ME ALL ABOUT IT.
WHAT DO WE TELL NICOLE?
WE DON'T TELL HER. SHE'D WANT TO HOOK YOU BOTH UP TO MACHINES.
WHO'S NICOLE? IS IT YOUR GIRLFRIEND?
AAH! NO!

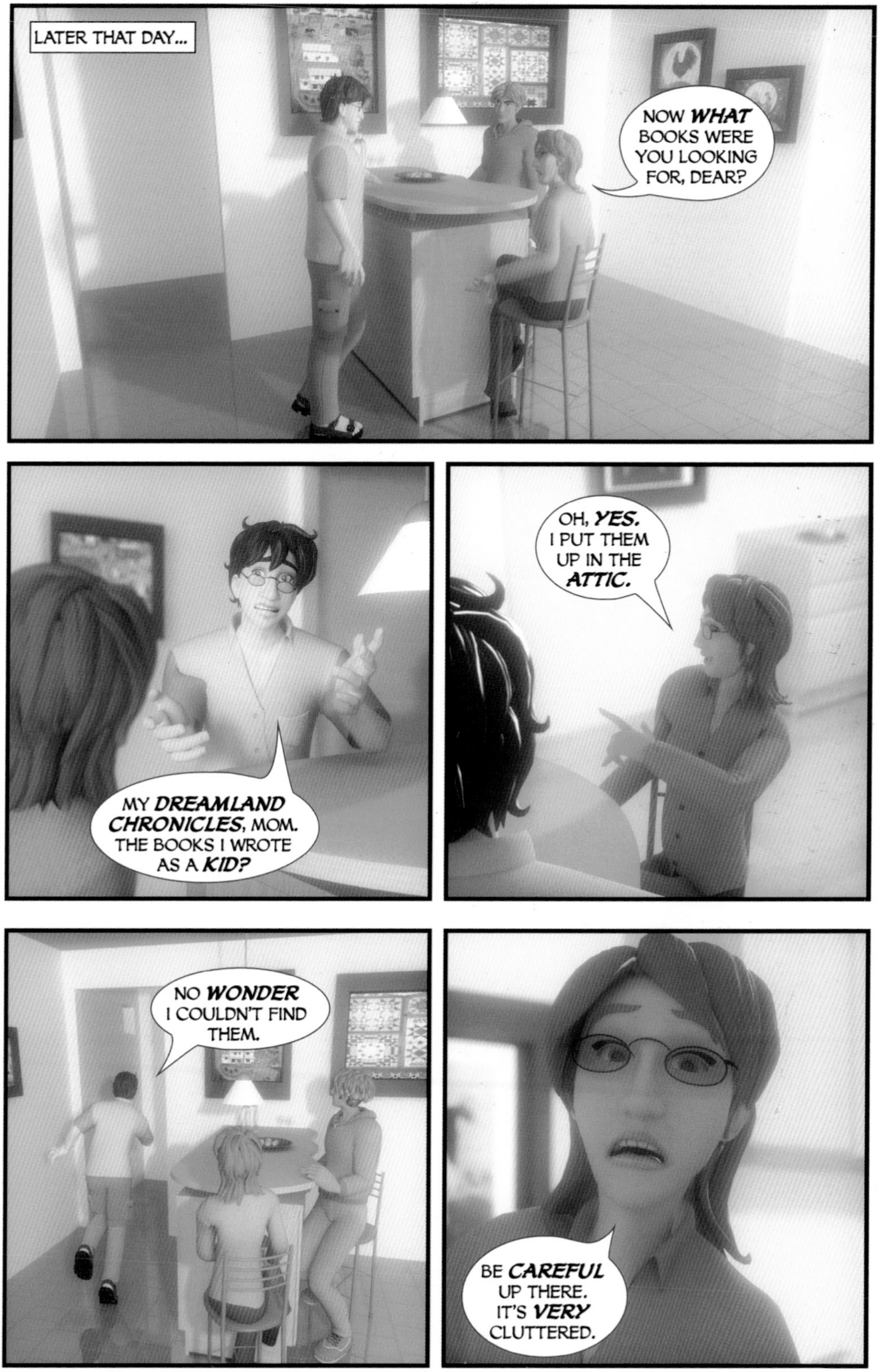
LATER THAT DAY...
NOW WHAT BOOKS WERE YOU LOOKING FOR, DEAR?
MY DREAMLAND CHRONICLES, MOM. THE BOOKS I WROTE AS A KID?
OH, YES. I PUT THEM UP IN THE ATTIC.
NO WONDER I COULDN'T FIND THEM.
BE CAREFUL UP THERE. IT'S VERY CLUTTERED.

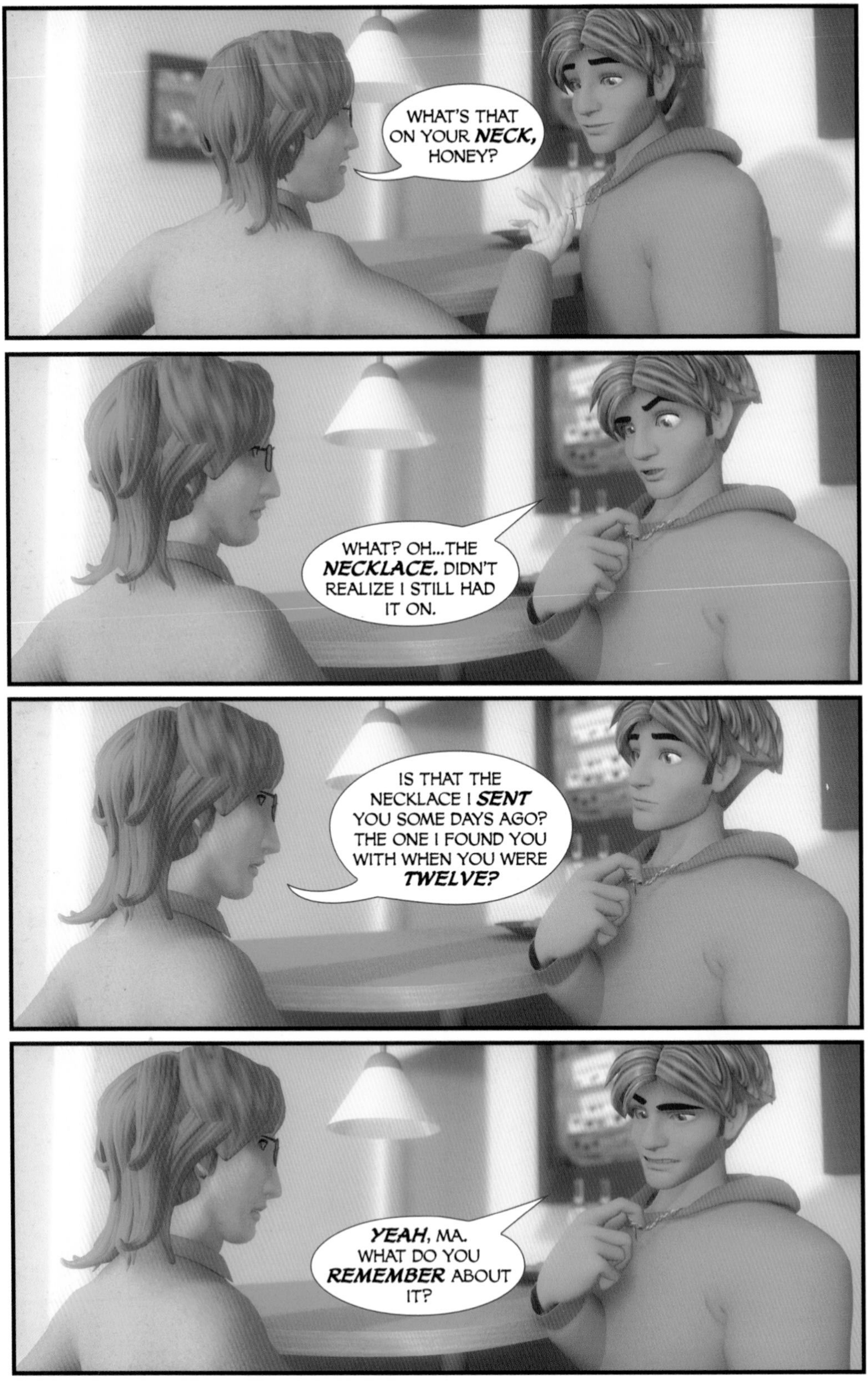
WHAT'S THAT ON YOUR NECK, HONEY?
WHAT? OH...THE NECKLACE. DIDN'T REALIZE I STILL HAD IT ON.
IS THAT THE NECKLACE I SENT YOU SOME DAYS AGO? THE ONE I FOUND YOU WITH WHEN YOU WERE TWELVE?
YEAH, MA. WHAT DO YOU REMEMBER ABOUT IT?

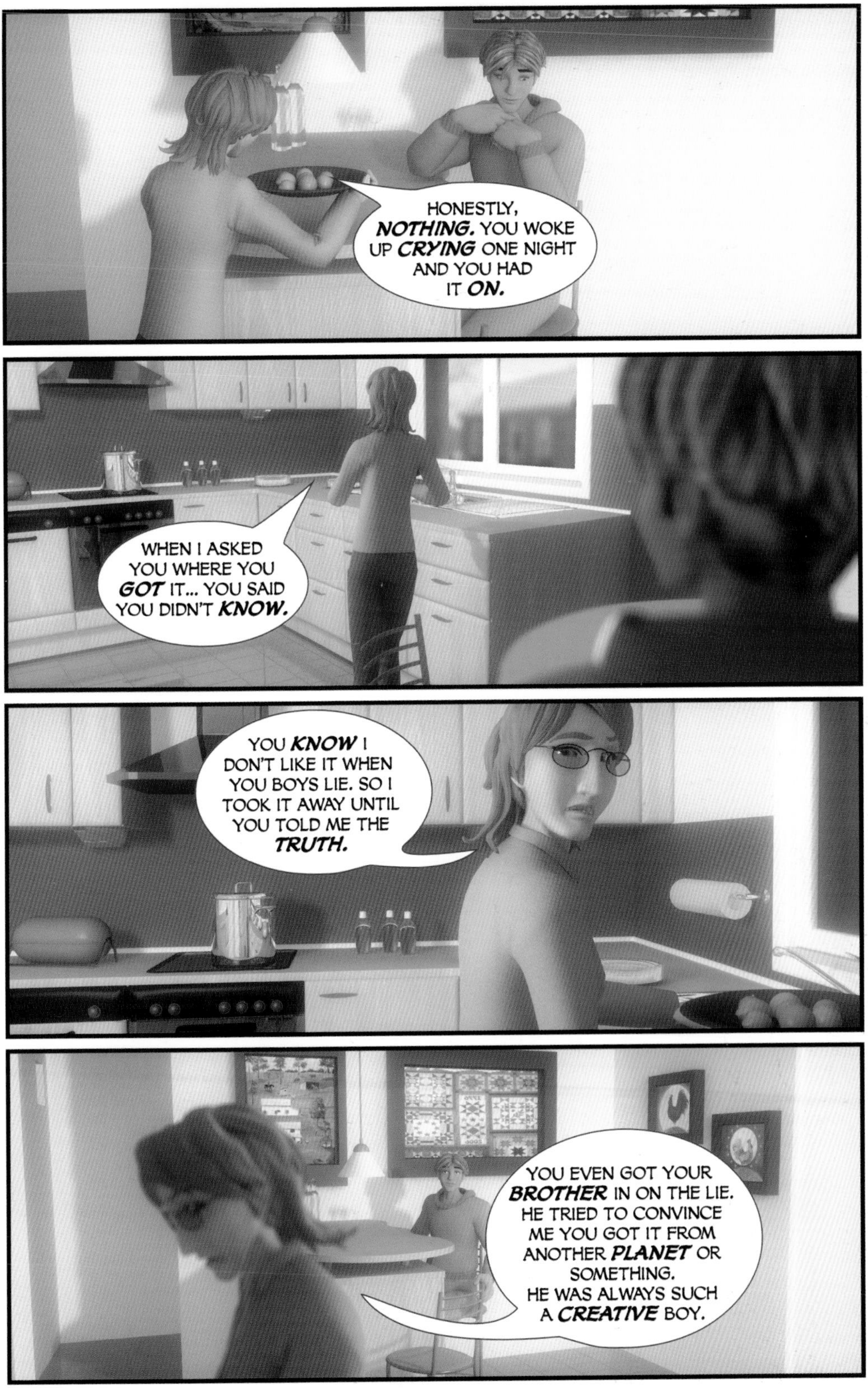
HONESTLY, NOTHING. YOU WOKE UP CRYING ONE NIGHT AND YOU HAD IT ON.
WHEN I ASKED YOU WHERE YOU GOT IT... YOU SAID YOU DIDN'T KNOW.
YOU KNOW I DON'T LIKE IT WHEN YOU BOYS LIE. SO I TOOK IT AWAY UNTIL YOU TOLD ME THE TRUTH.
YOU EVEN GOT YOUR BROTHER IN ON THE LIE. HE TRIED TO CONVINCE ME YOU GOT IT FROM ANOTHER PLANET OR SOMETHING. HE WAS ALWAYS SUCH A CREATIVE BOY.

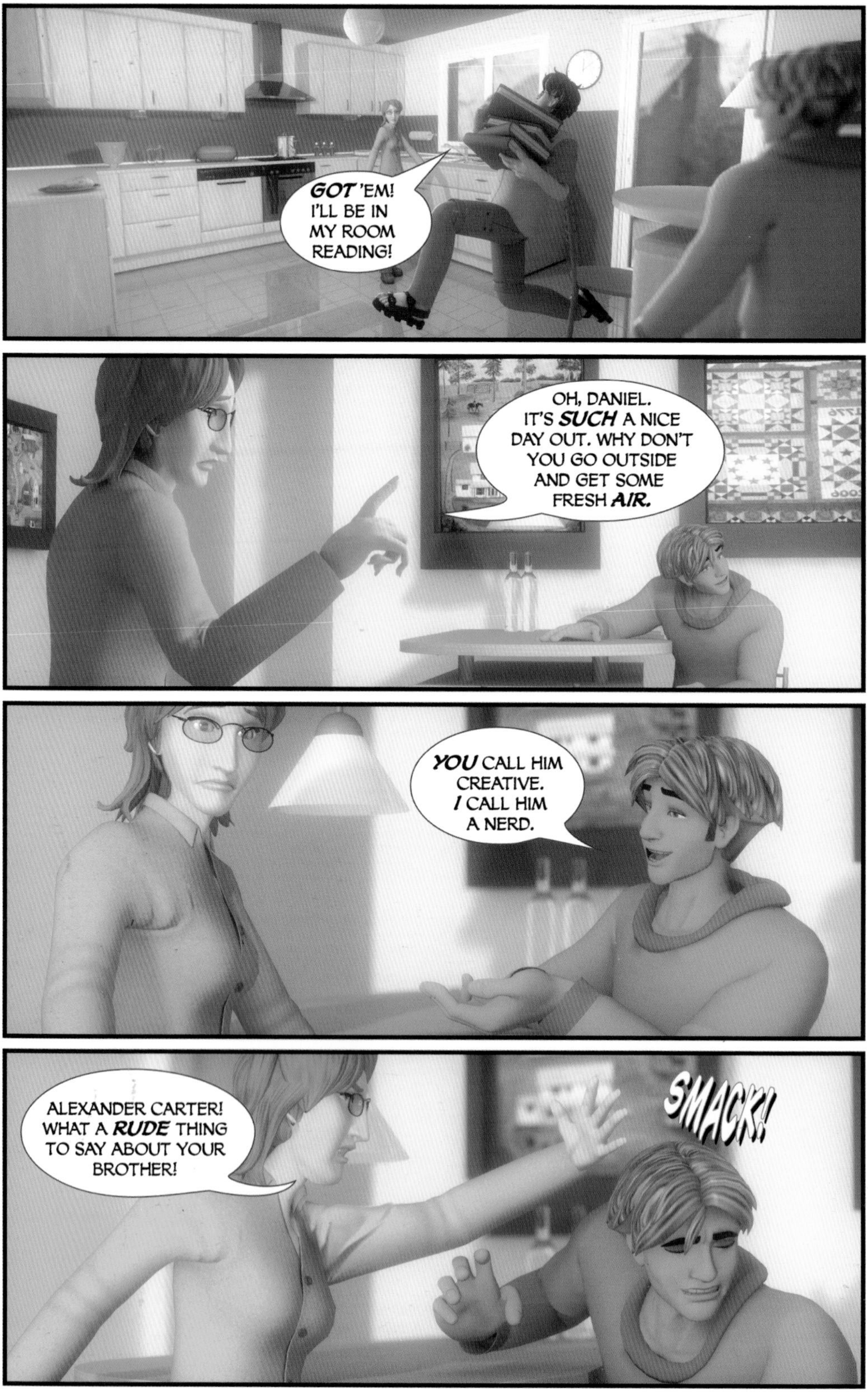
GOT 'EM! I'LL BE IN MY ROOM READING!
OH, DANIEL. IT'S SUCH A NICE DAY OUT. WHY DON'T YOU GO OUTSIDE AND GET SOME FRESH AIR.
YOU CALL HIM CREATIVE. I CALL HIM A NERD.
ALEXANDER CARTER! WHAT A RUDE THING TO SAY ABOUT YOUR BROTHER!
SMACK!

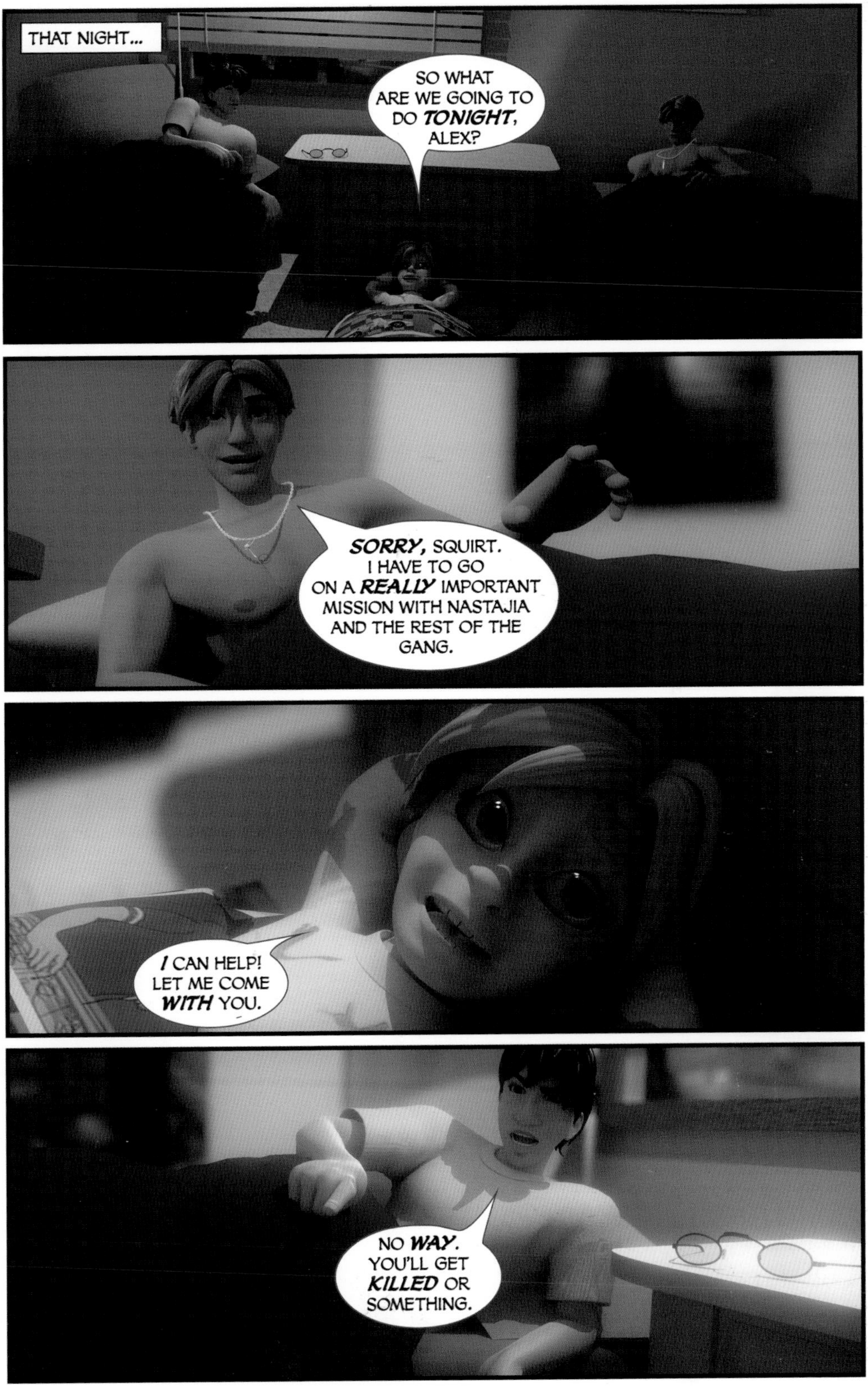
THAT NIGHT...
SO WHAT ARE WE GOING TO DO *TONIGHT*, ALEX?
SORRY, SQUIRT. I HAVE TO GO ON A *REALLY* IMPORTANT MISSION WITH NASTAJIA AND THE REST OF THE GANG.
I CAN HELP! LET ME COME *WITH* YOU.
NO *WAY*. YOU'LL GET *KILLED* OR SOMETHING.

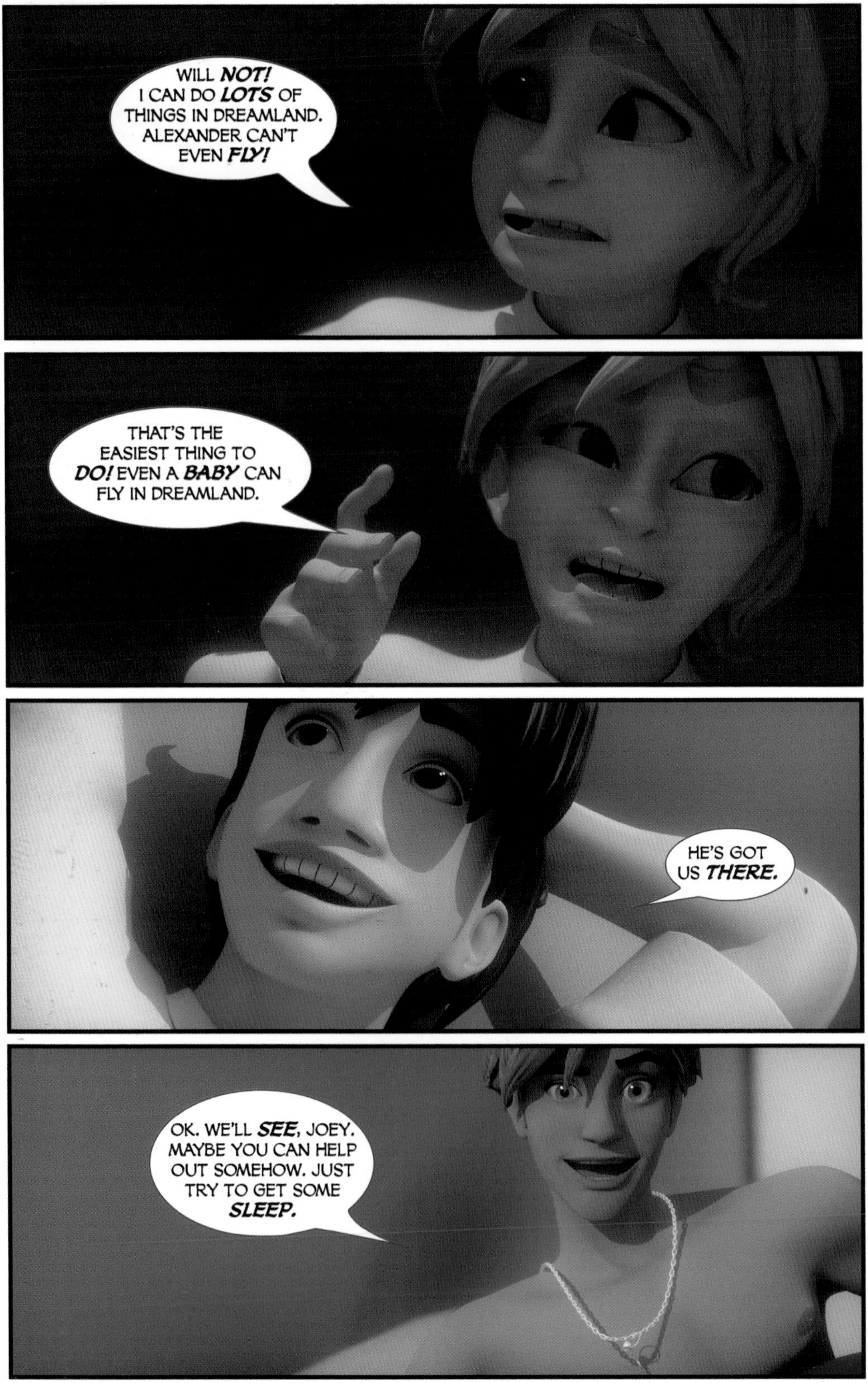
WILL NOT! I CAN DO LOTS OF THINGS IN DREAMLAND. ALEXANDER CAN'T EVEN FLY!
THAT'S THE EASIEST THING TO DO! EVEN A BABY CAN FLY IN DREAMLAND.
HE'S GOT US THERE.
OK. WE'LL SEE, JOEY. MAYBE YOU CAN HELP OUT SOMEHOW. JUST TRY TO GET SOME SLEEP.

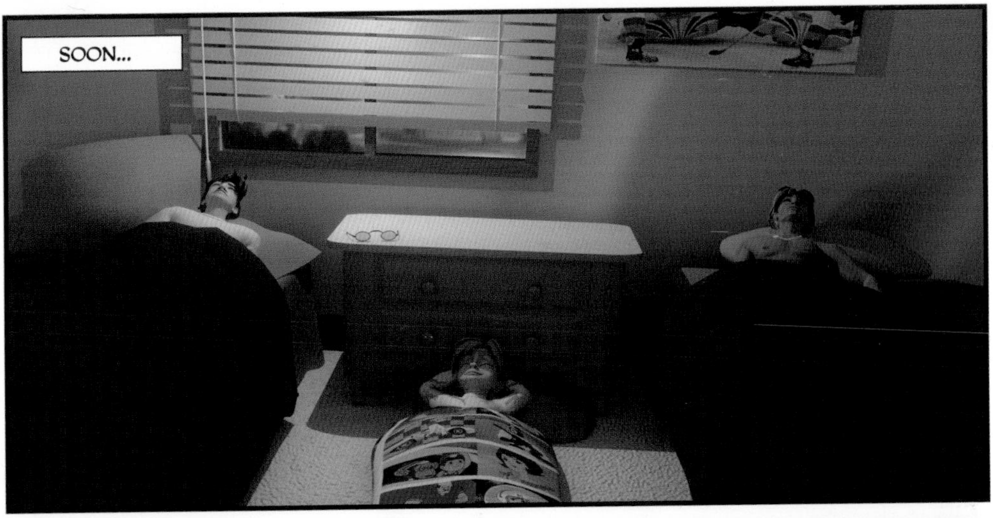
SOON...

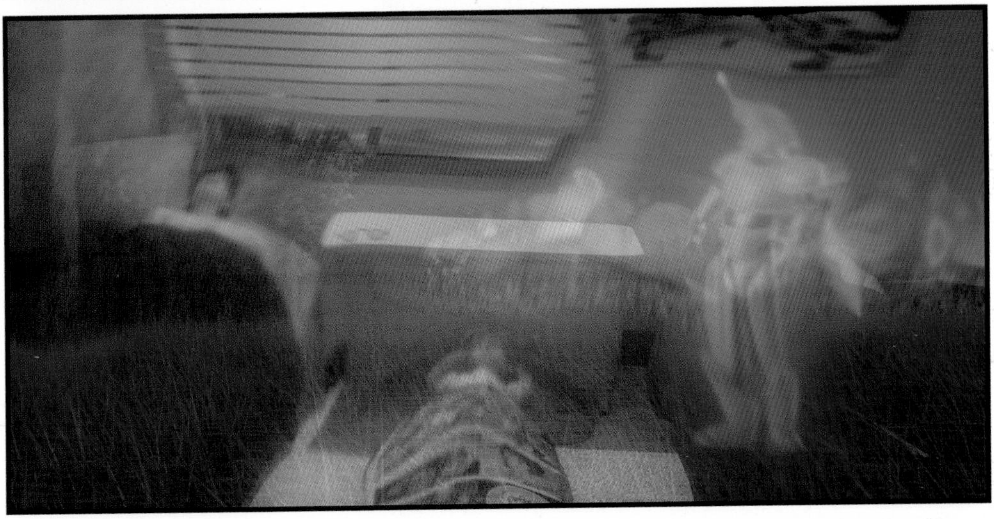

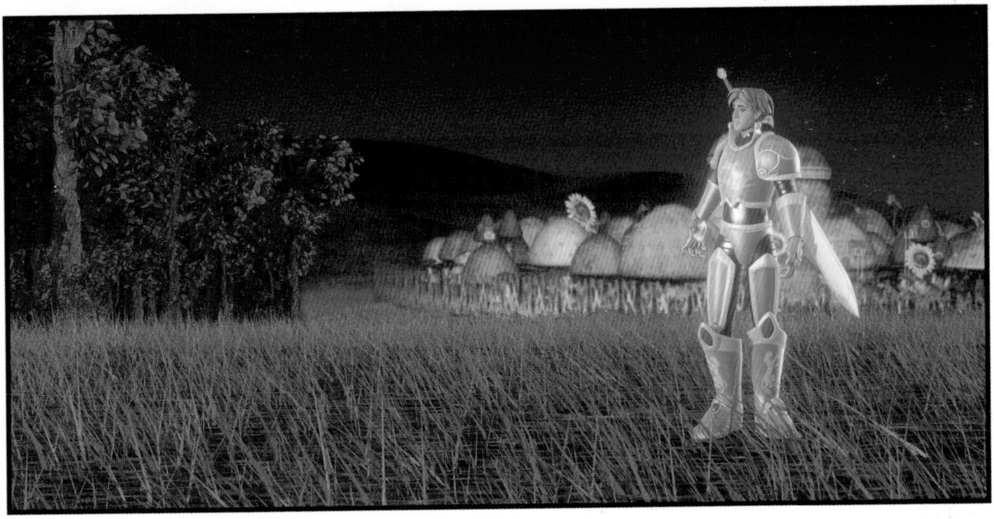

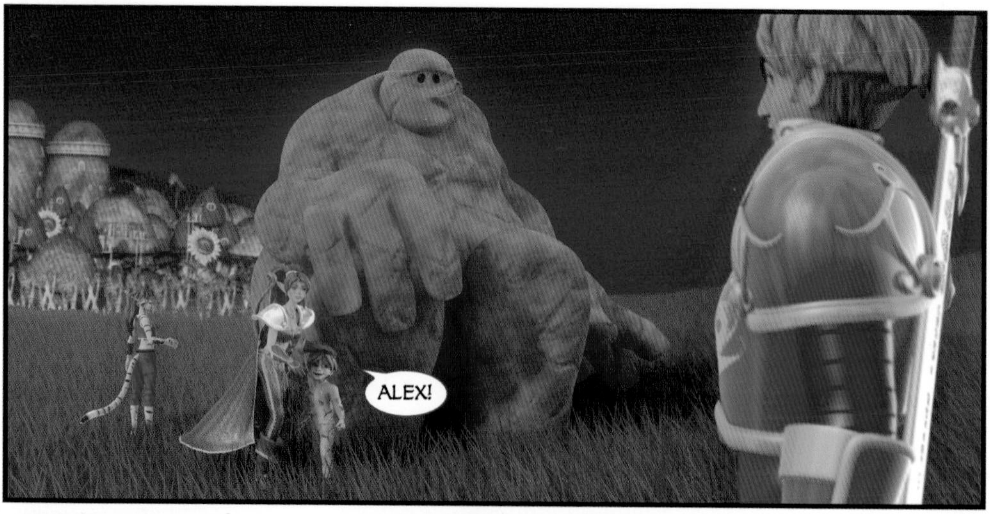
ALEX!

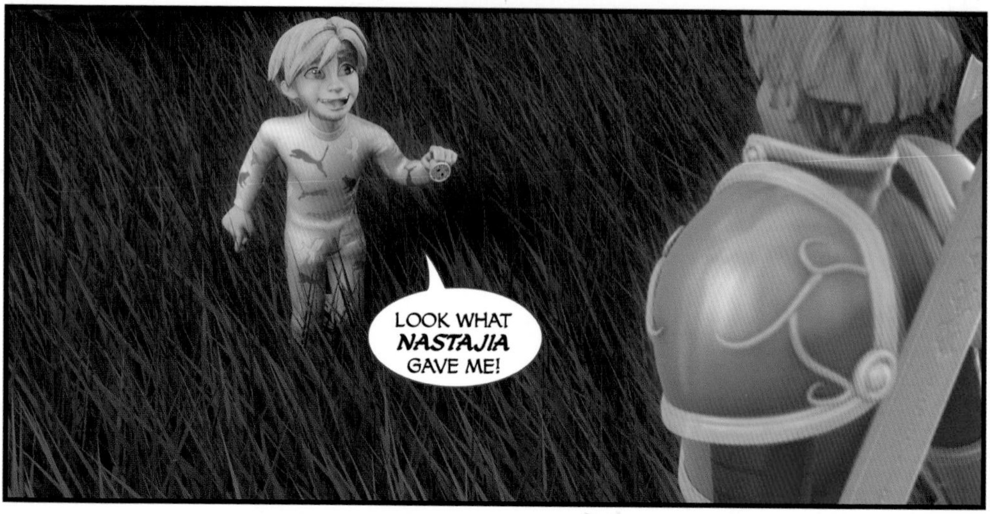
LOOK WHAT **NASTAJIA** GAVE ME!

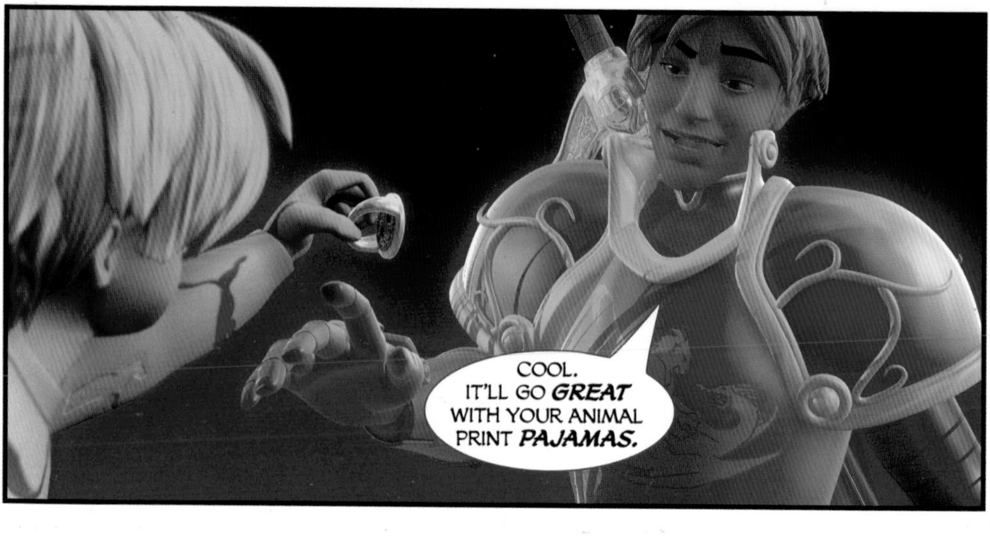
COOL. IT'LL GO **GREAT** WITH YOUR ANIMAL PRINT **PAJAMAS.**

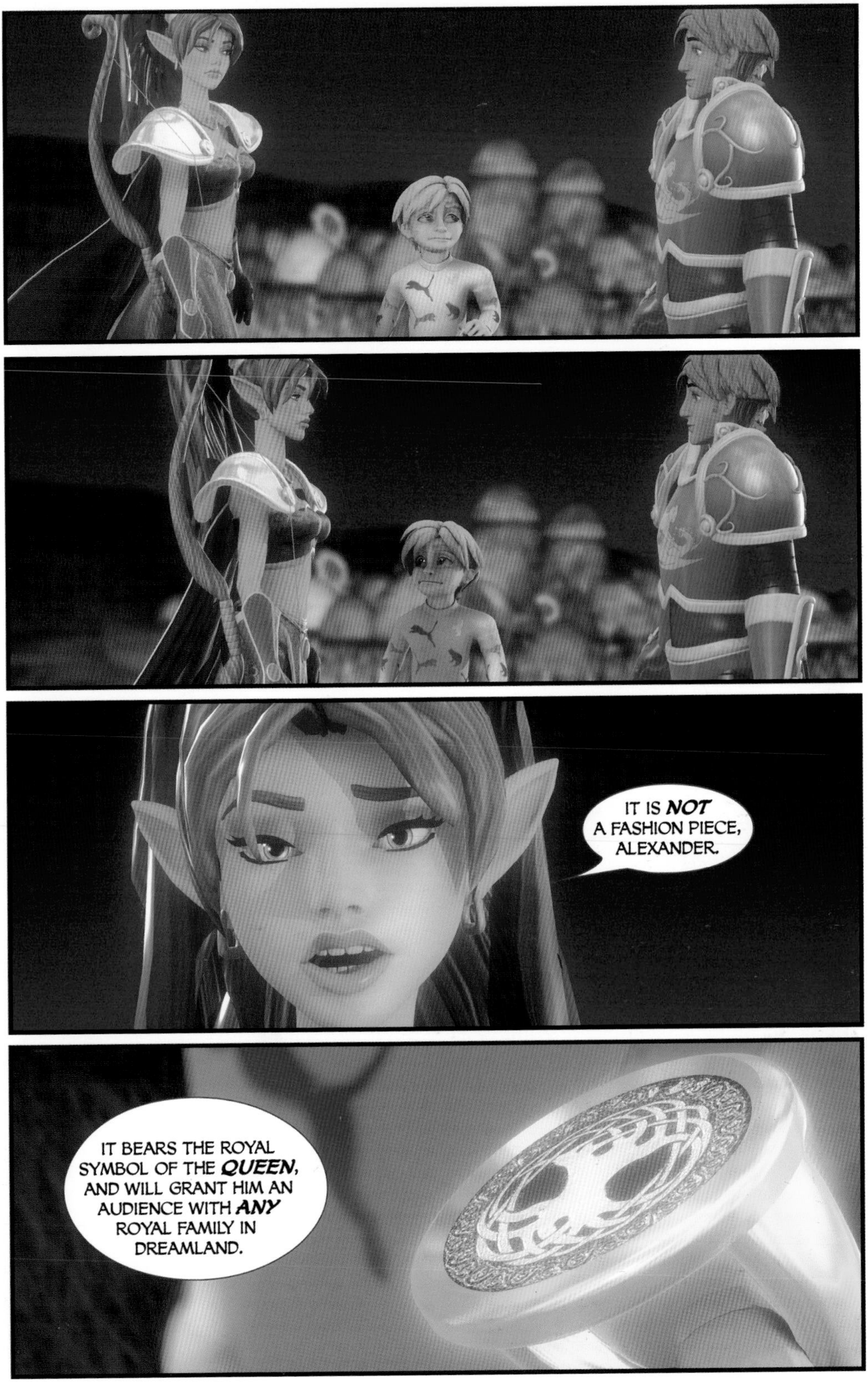
IT IS NOT A FASHION PIECE, ALEXANDER.
IT BEARS THE ROYAL SYMBOL OF THE QUEEN, AND WILL GRANT HIM AN AUDIENCE WITH ANY ROYAL FAMILY IN DREAMLAND.

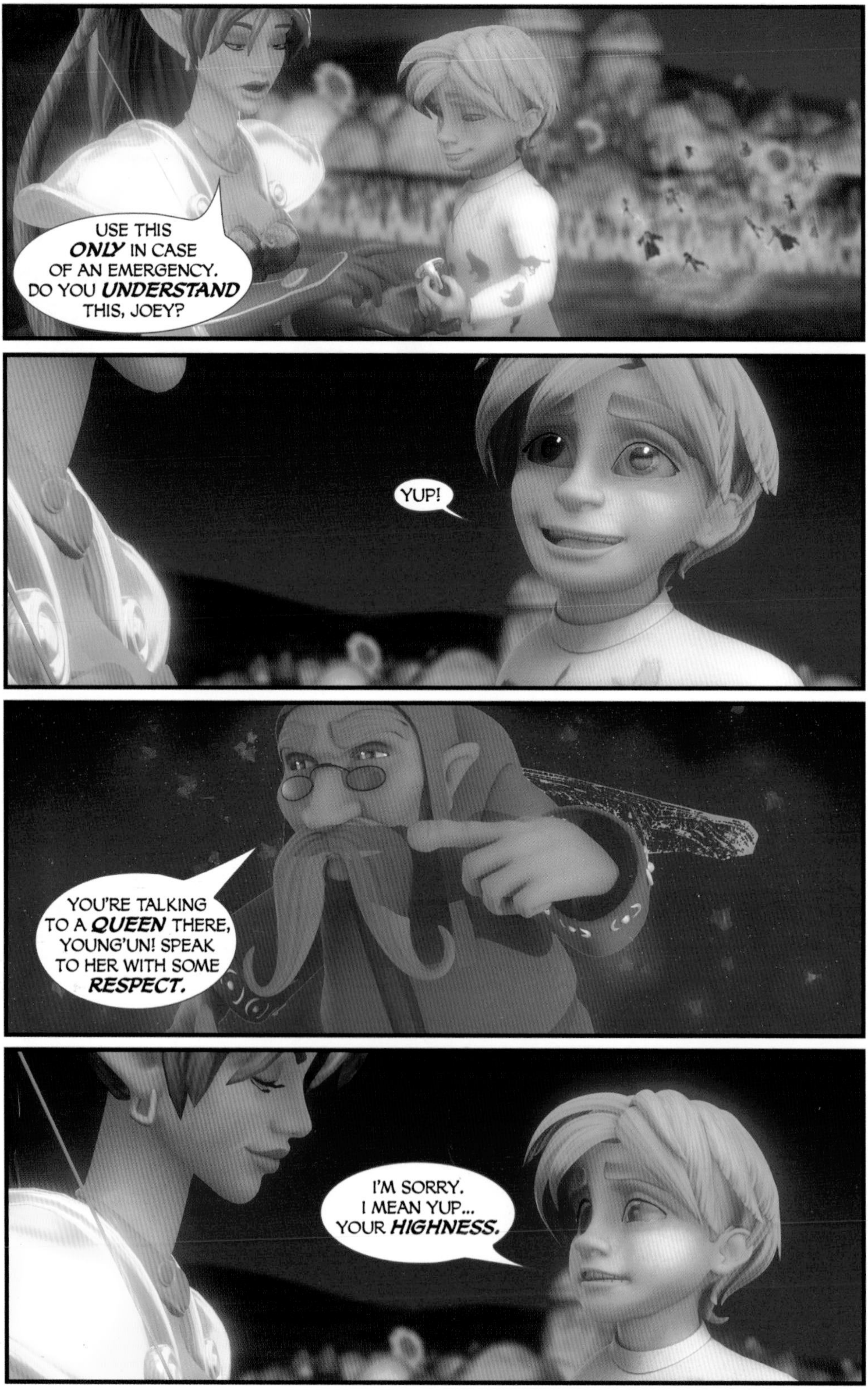
USE THIS ONLY IN CASE OF AN EMERGENCY. DO YOU UNDERSTAND THIS, JOEY?
YUP!
YOU'RE TALKING TO A QUEEN THERE, YOUNG'UN! SPEAK TO HER WITH SOME RESPECT.
I'M SORRY. I MEAN YUP... YOUR HIGHNESS.

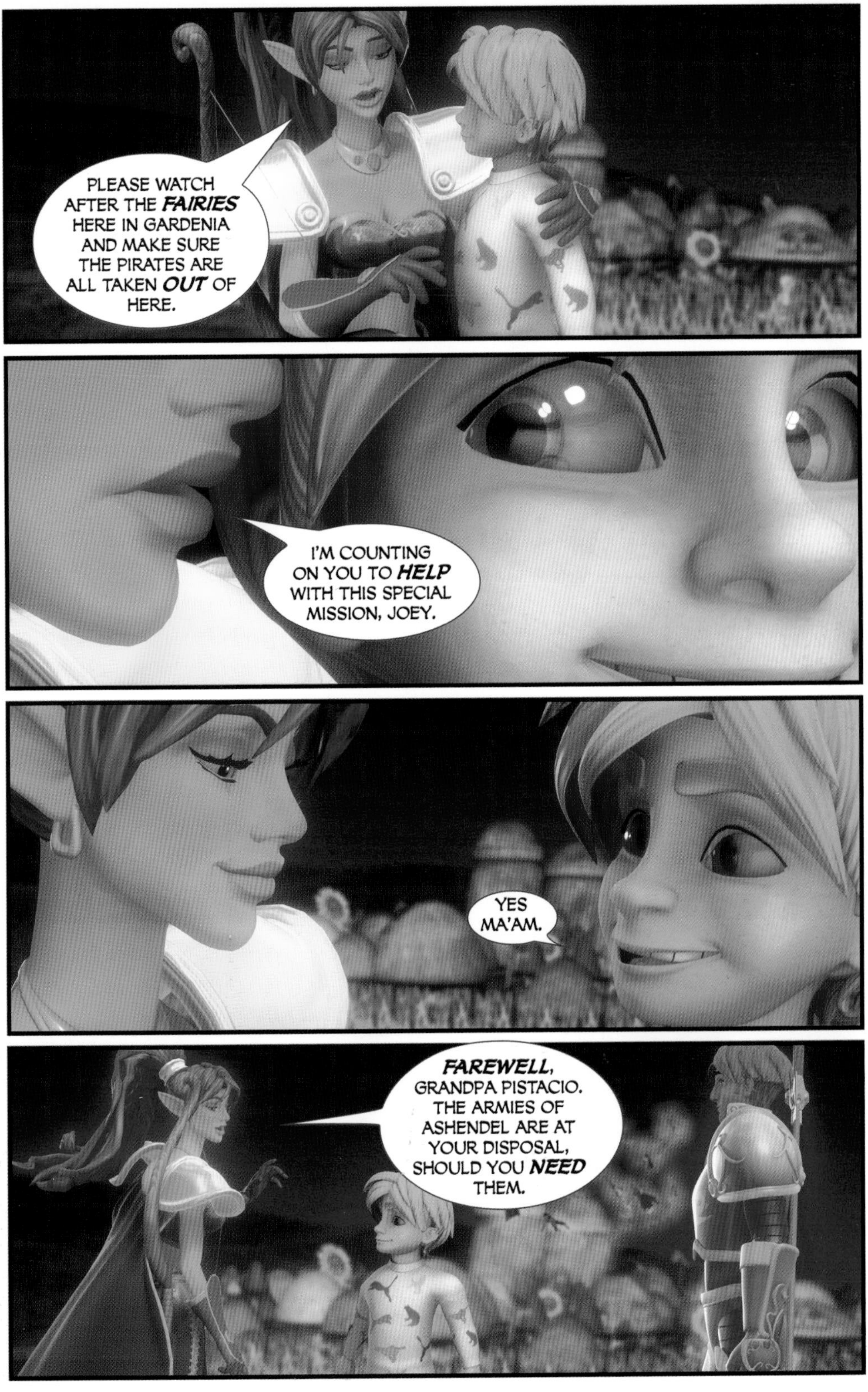
PLEASE WATCH AFTER THE FAIRIES HERE IN GARDENIA AND MAKE SURE THE PIRATES ARE ALL TAKEN OUT OF HERE.
I'M COUNTING ON YOU TO HELP WITH THIS SPECIAL MISSION, JOEY.
YES MA'AM.
FAREWELL, GRANDPA PISTACIO. THE ARMIES OF ASHENDEL ARE AT YOUR DISPOSAL, SHOULD YOU NEED THEM.

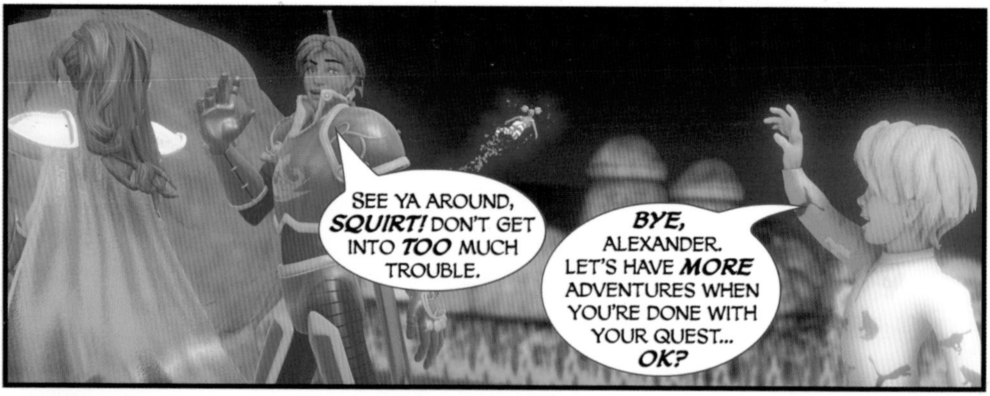
SEE YA AROUND, **SQUIRT!** DON'T GET INTO **TOO** MUCH TROUBLE.
BYE, ALEXANDER. LET'S HAVE **MORE** ADVENTURES WHEN YOU'RE DONE WITH YOUR QUEST... **OK?**

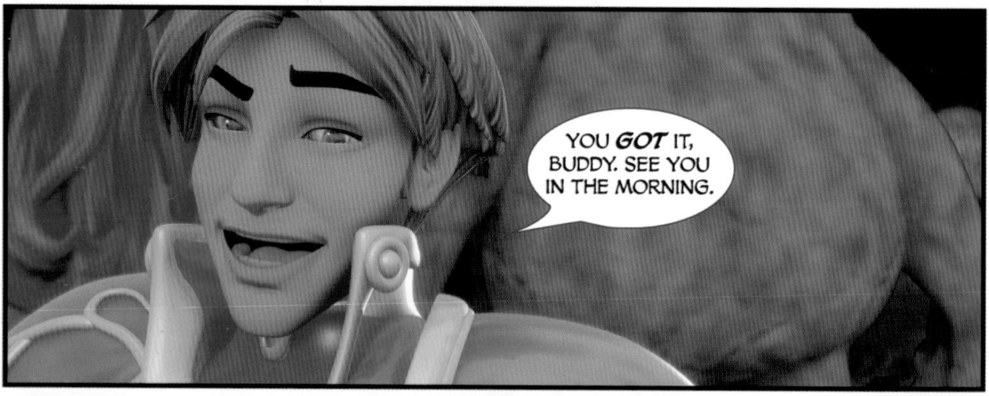
YOU **GOT** IT, BUDDY. SEE YOU IN THE MORNING.

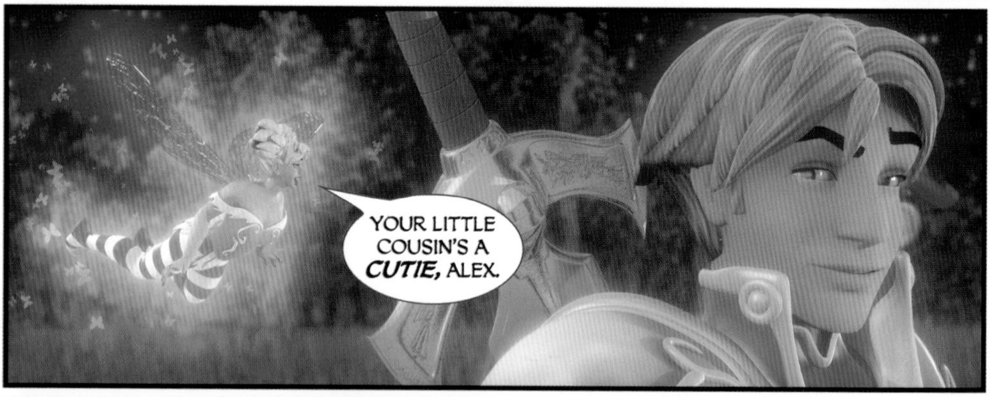
YOUR LITTLE COUSIN'S A **CUTIE,** ALEX.

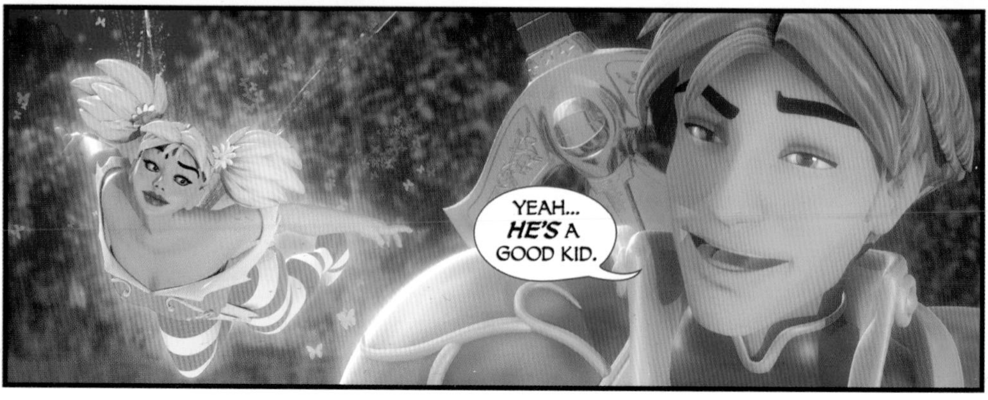
YEAH... **HE'S** A GOOD KID.

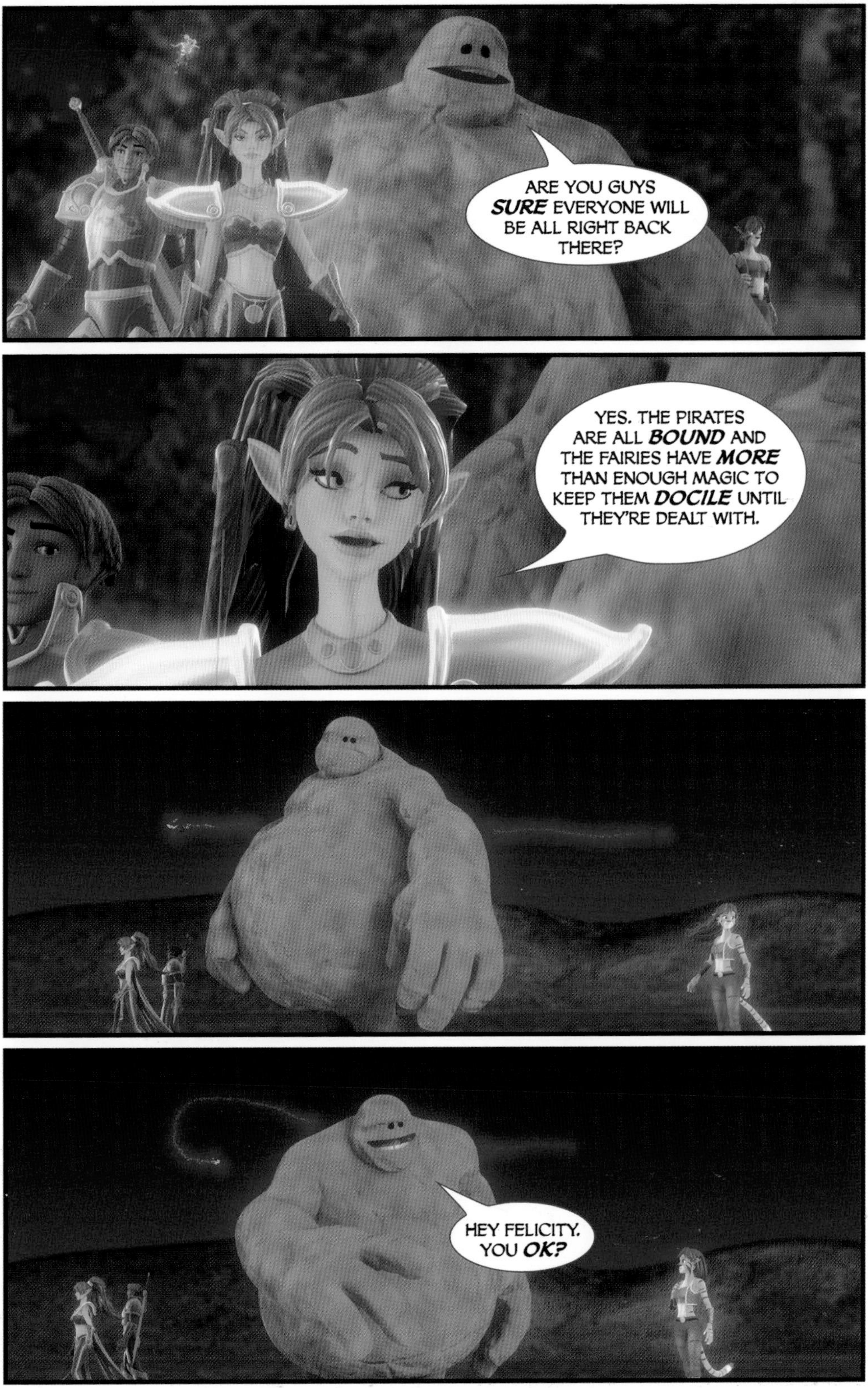
ARE YOU GUYS SURE EVERYONE WILL BE ALL RIGHT BACK THERE?
YES. THE PIRATES ARE ALL BOUND AND THE FAIRIES HAVE MORE THAN ENOUGH MAGIC TO KEEP THEM DOCILE UNTIL THEY'RE DEALT WITH.
HEY FELICITY. YOU OK?

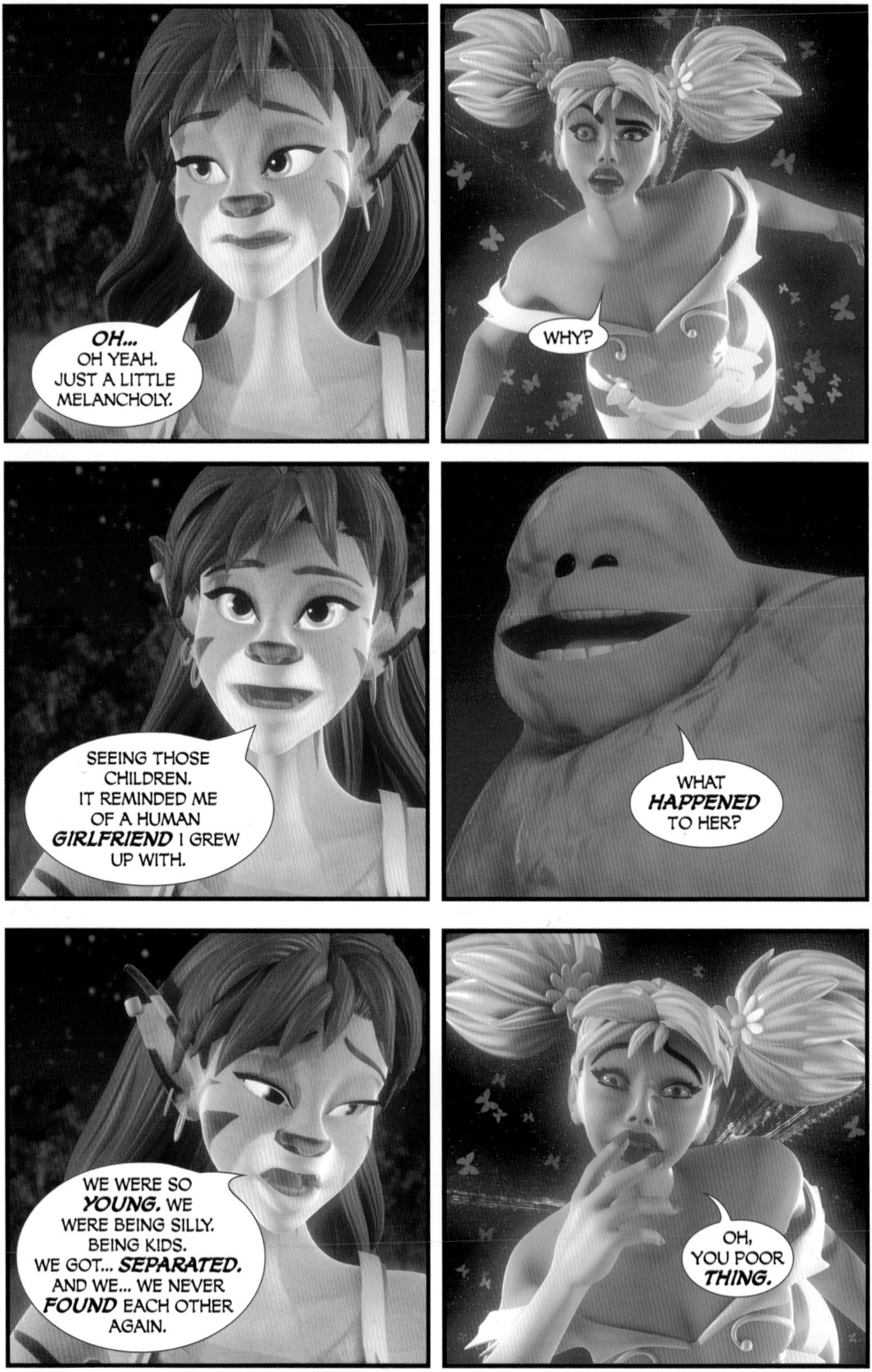
OH... OH YEAH. JUST A LITTLE MELANCHOLY.
WHY?
SEEING THOSE CHILDREN. IT REMINDED ME OF A HUMAN GIRLFRIEND I GREW UP WITH.
WHAT HAPPENED TO HER?
WE WERE SO YOUNG. WE WERE BEING SILLY. BEING KIDS. WE GOT... SEPARATED. AND WE... WE NEVER FOUND EACH OTHER AGAIN.
OH, YOU POOR THING.

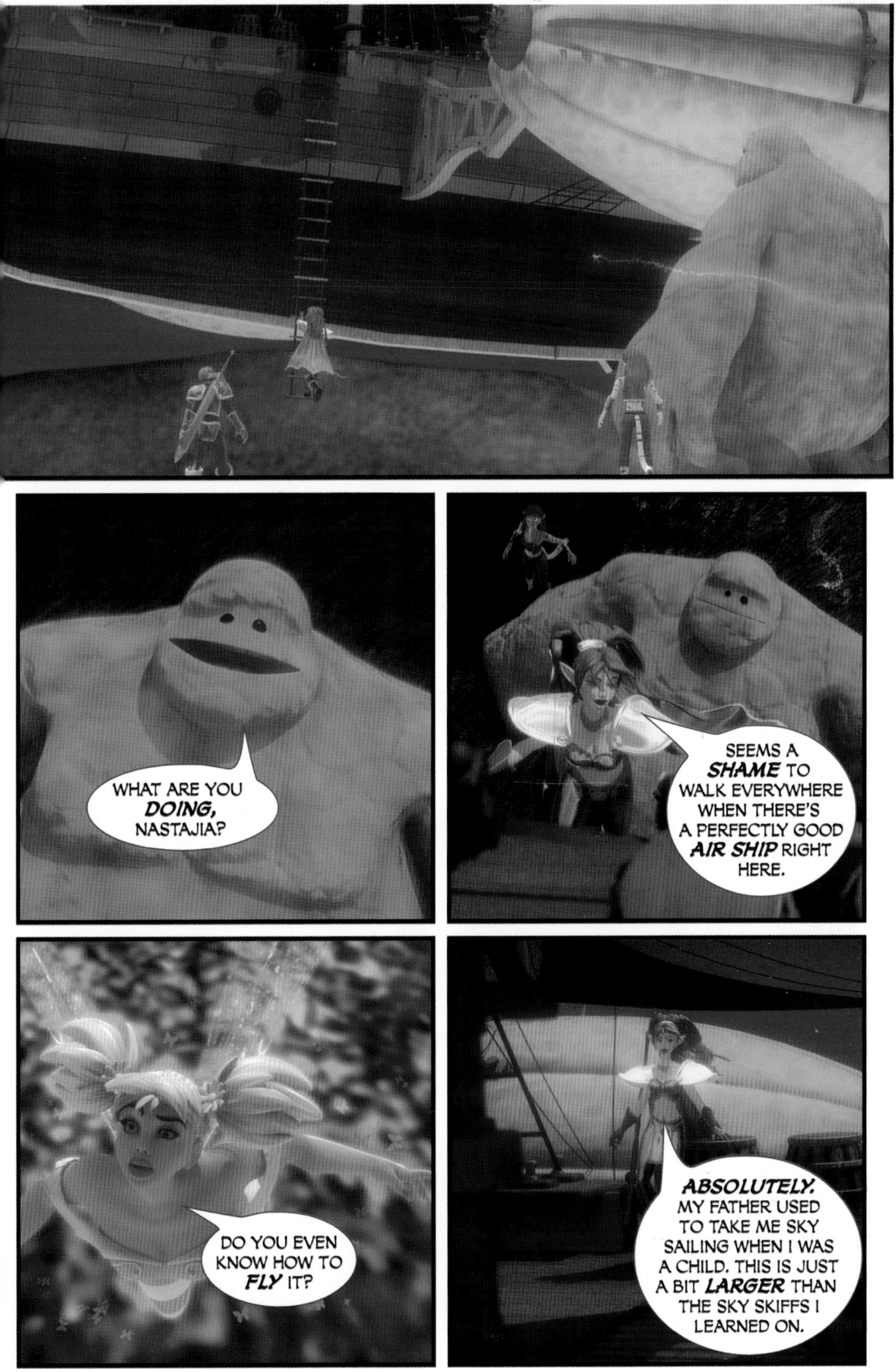
WHAT ARE YOU DOING, NASTAJIA?
SEEMS A SHAME TO WALK EVERYWHERE WHEN THERE'S A PERFECTLY GOOD AIR SHIP RIGHT HERE.
DO YOU EVEN KNOW HOW TO FLY IT?
ABSOLUTELY. MY FATHER USED TO TAKE ME SKY SAILING WHEN I WAS A CHILD. THIS IS JUST A BIT LARGER THAN THE SKY SKIFFS I LEARNED ON.

CREAAAKKK

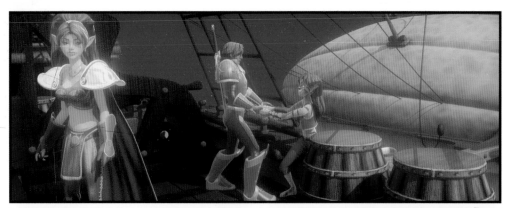

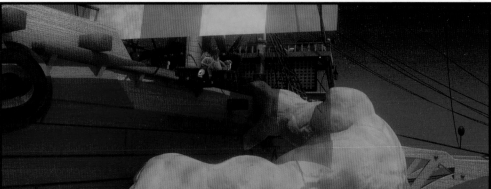

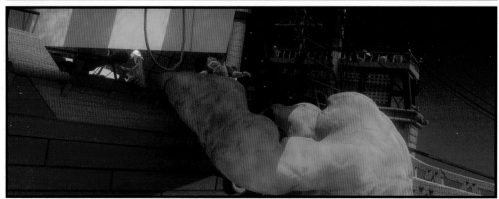

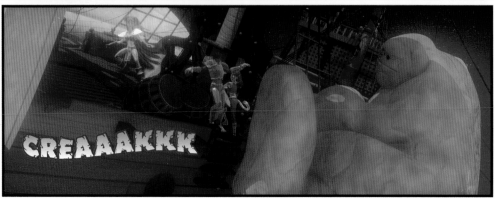

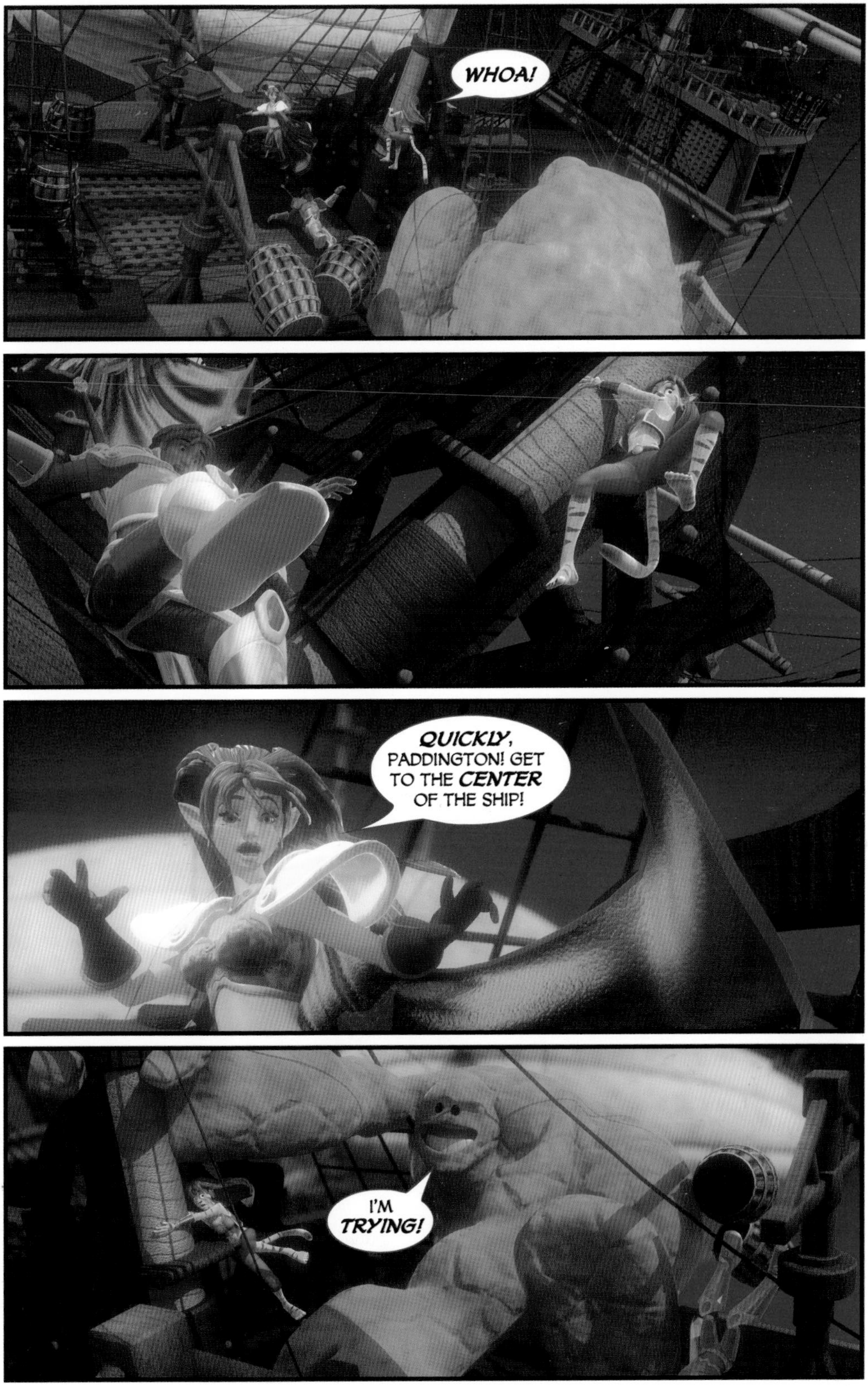
WHOA!
QUICKLY, PADDINGTON! GET TO THE CENTER OF THE SHIP!
I'M TRYING!

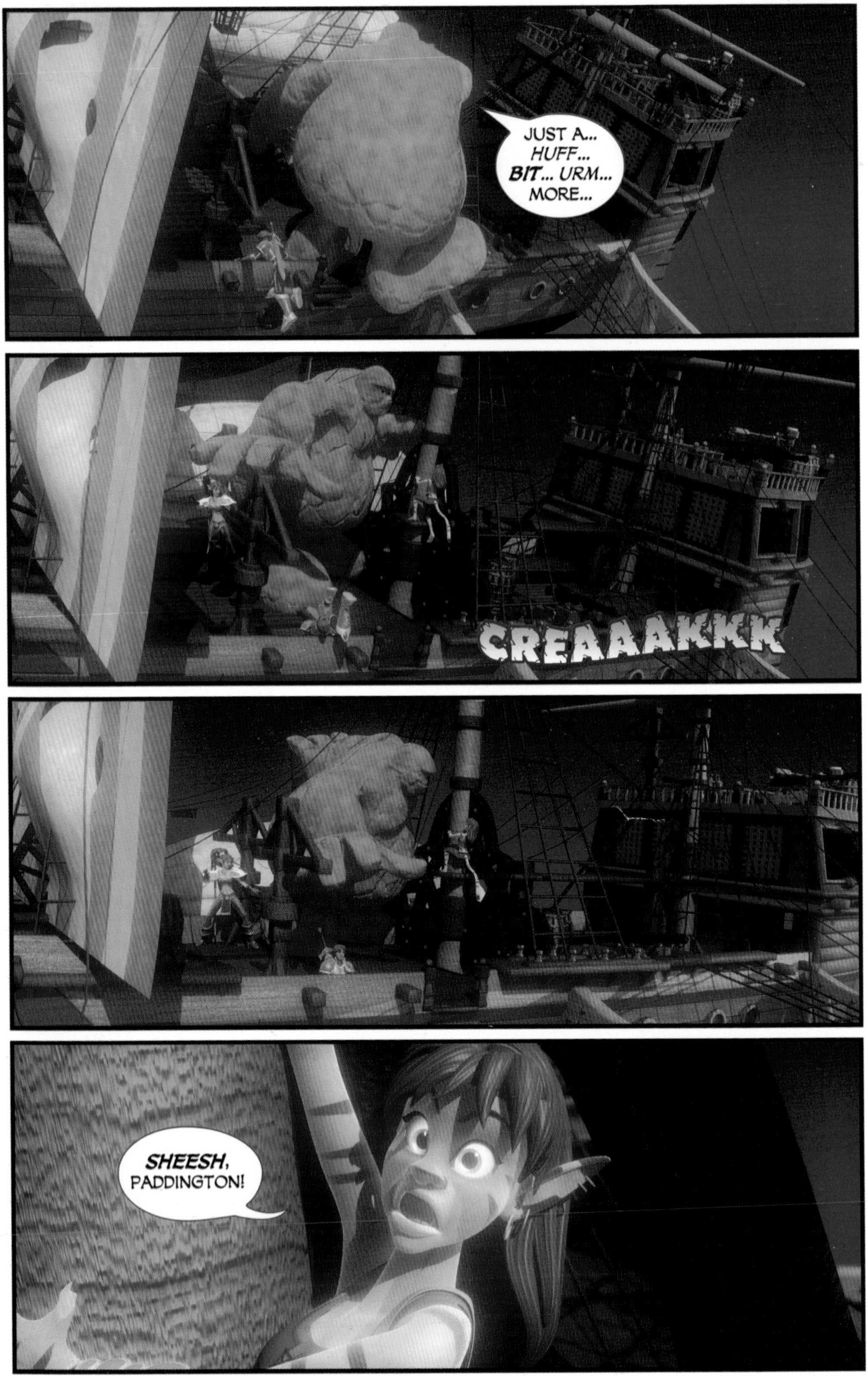
JUST A... HUFF... BIT... URM... MORE...
CREAAAKKK
SHEESH, PADDINGTON!

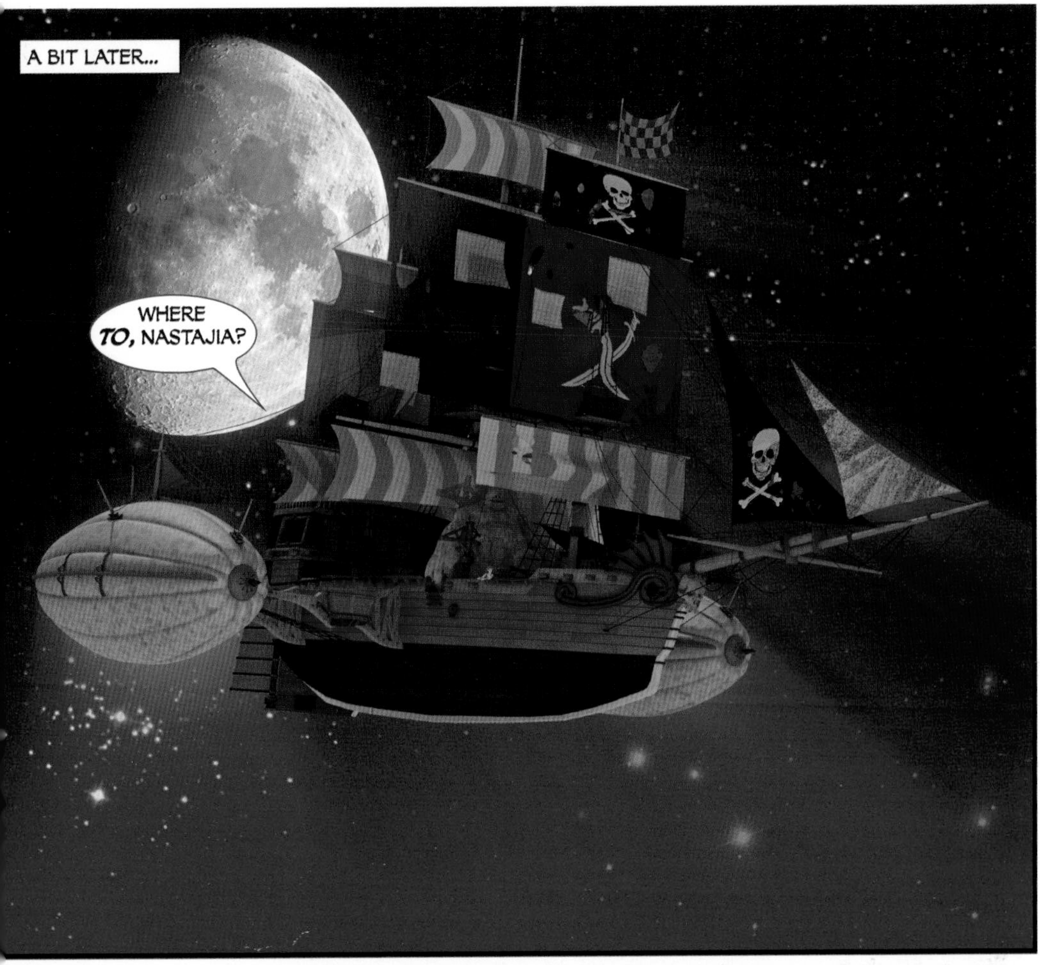
A BIT LATER...
WHERE TO, NASTAJIA?

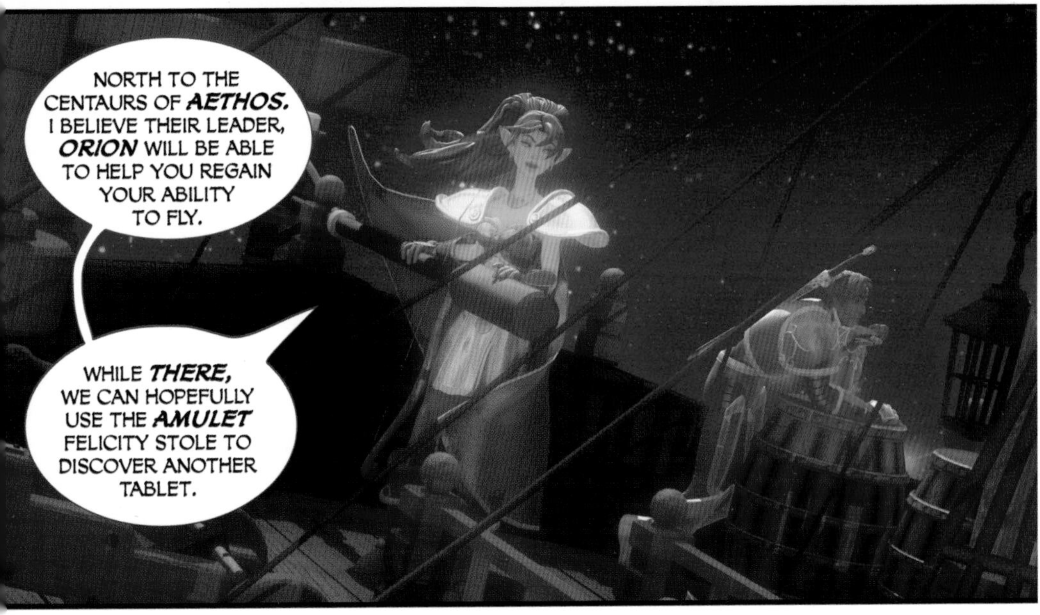
NORTH TO THE CENTAURS OF AETHOS. I BELIEVE THEIR LEADER, ORION WILL BE ABLE TO HELP YOU REGAIN YOUR ABILITY TO FLY.
WHILE THERE, WE CAN HOPEFULLY USE THE AMULET FELICITY STOLE TO DISCOVER ANOTHER TABLET.

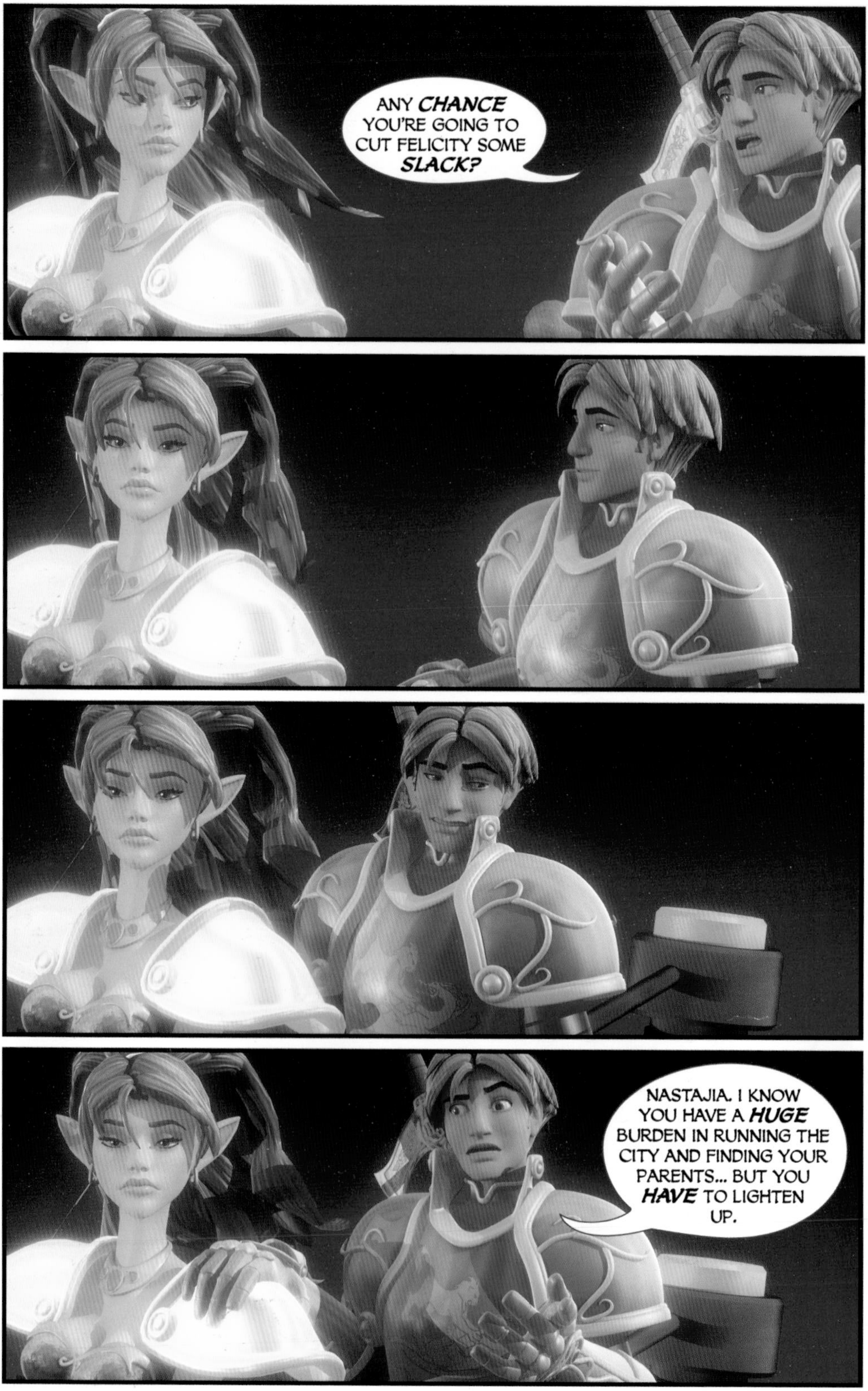
ANY CHANCE YOU'RE GOING TO CUT FELICITY SOME SLACK?
NASTAJIA. I KNOW YOU HAVE A HUGE BURDEN IN RUNNING THE CITY AND FINDING YOUR PARENTS... BUT YOU HAVE TO LIGHTEN UP.

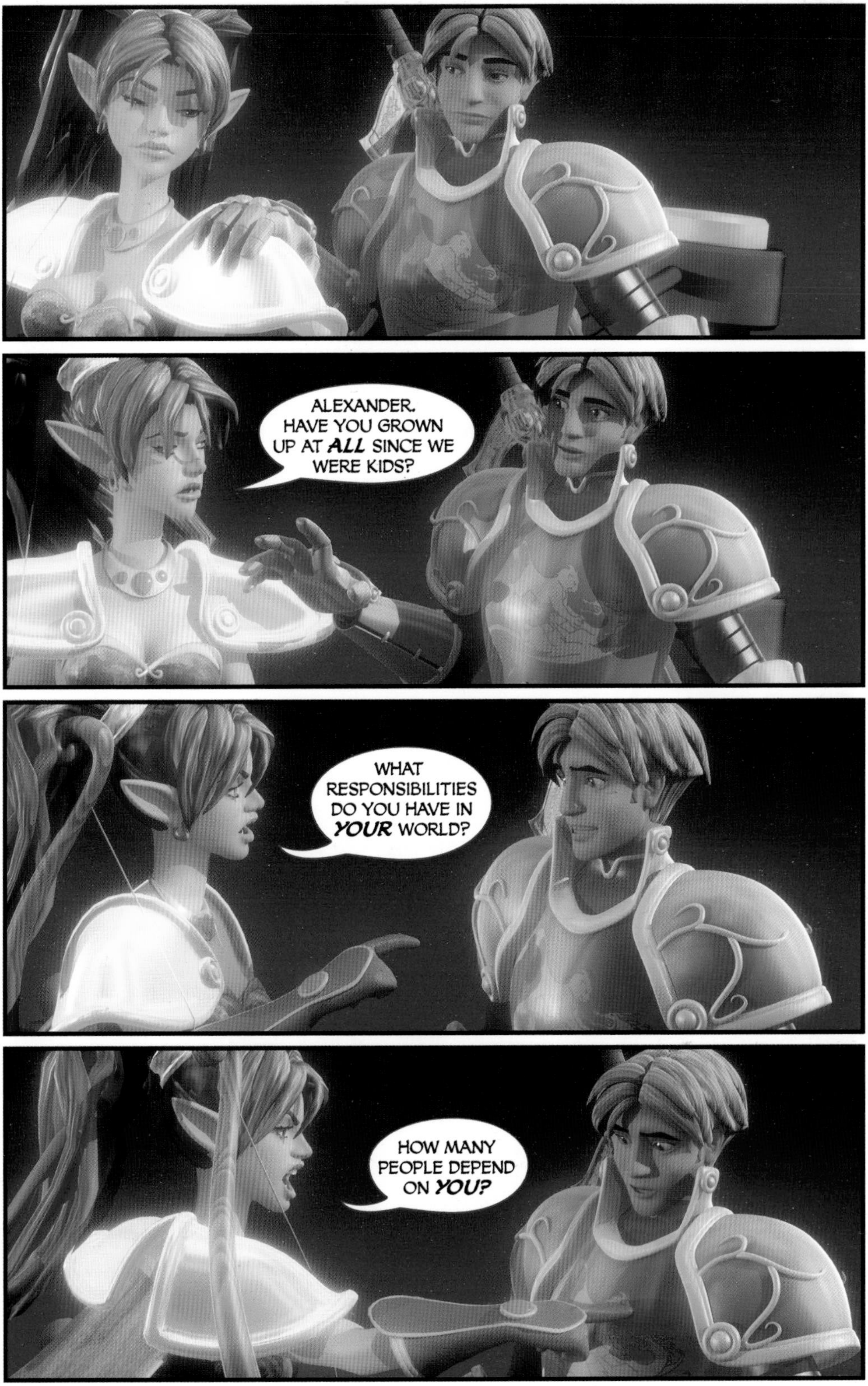
ALEXANDER. HAVE YOU GROWN UP AT ALL SINCE WE WERE KIDS?
WHAT RESPONSIBILITIES DO YOU HAVE IN YOUR WORLD?
HOW MANY PEOPLE DEPEND ON YOU?

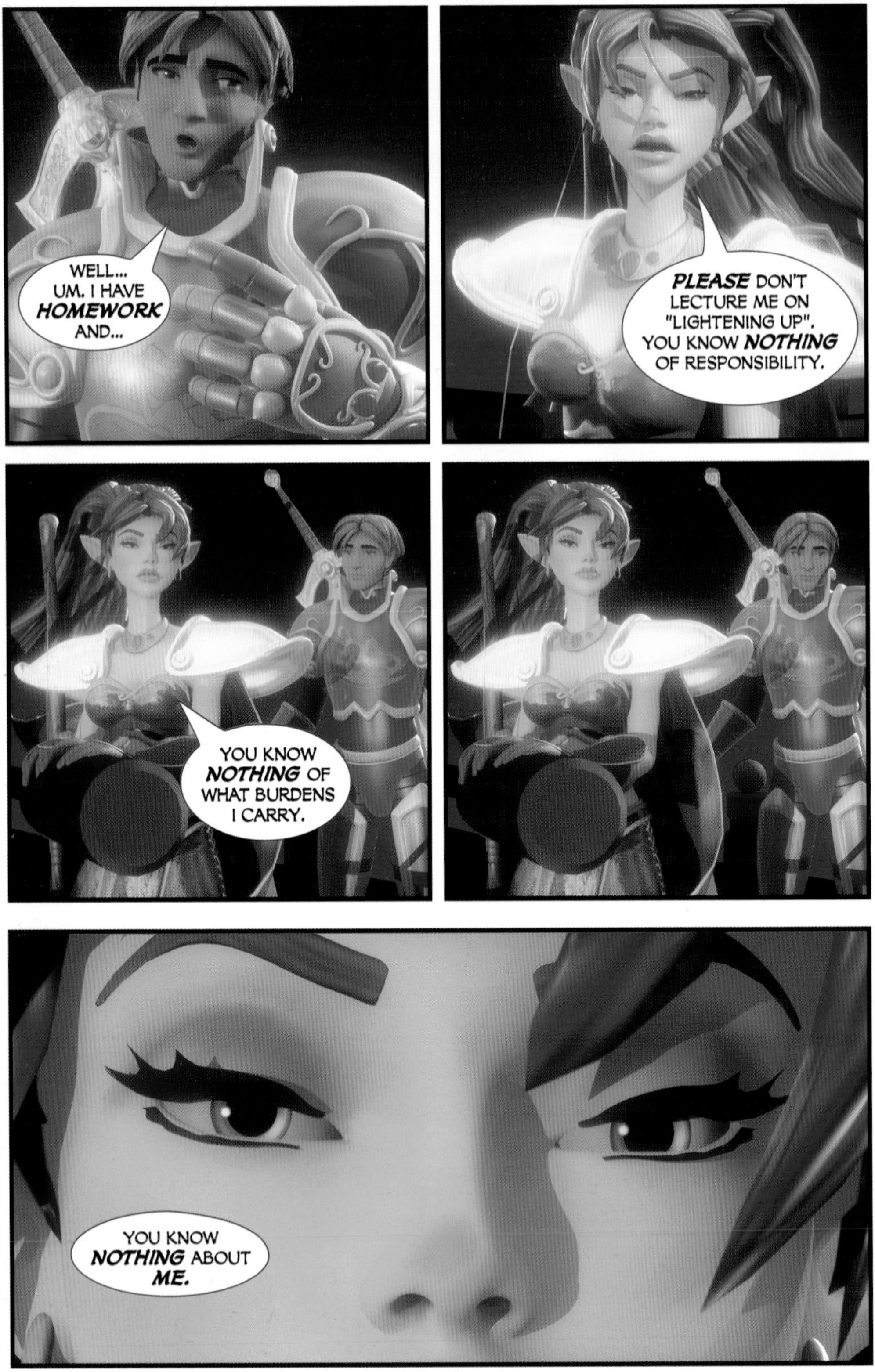
WELL... UM. I HAVE HOMEWORK AND...
PLEASE DON'T LECTURE ME ON "LIGHTENING UP". YOU KNOW NOTHING OF RESPONSIBILITY.
YOU KNOW NOTHING OF WHAT BURDENS I CARRY.
YOU KNOW NOTHING ABOUT ME.

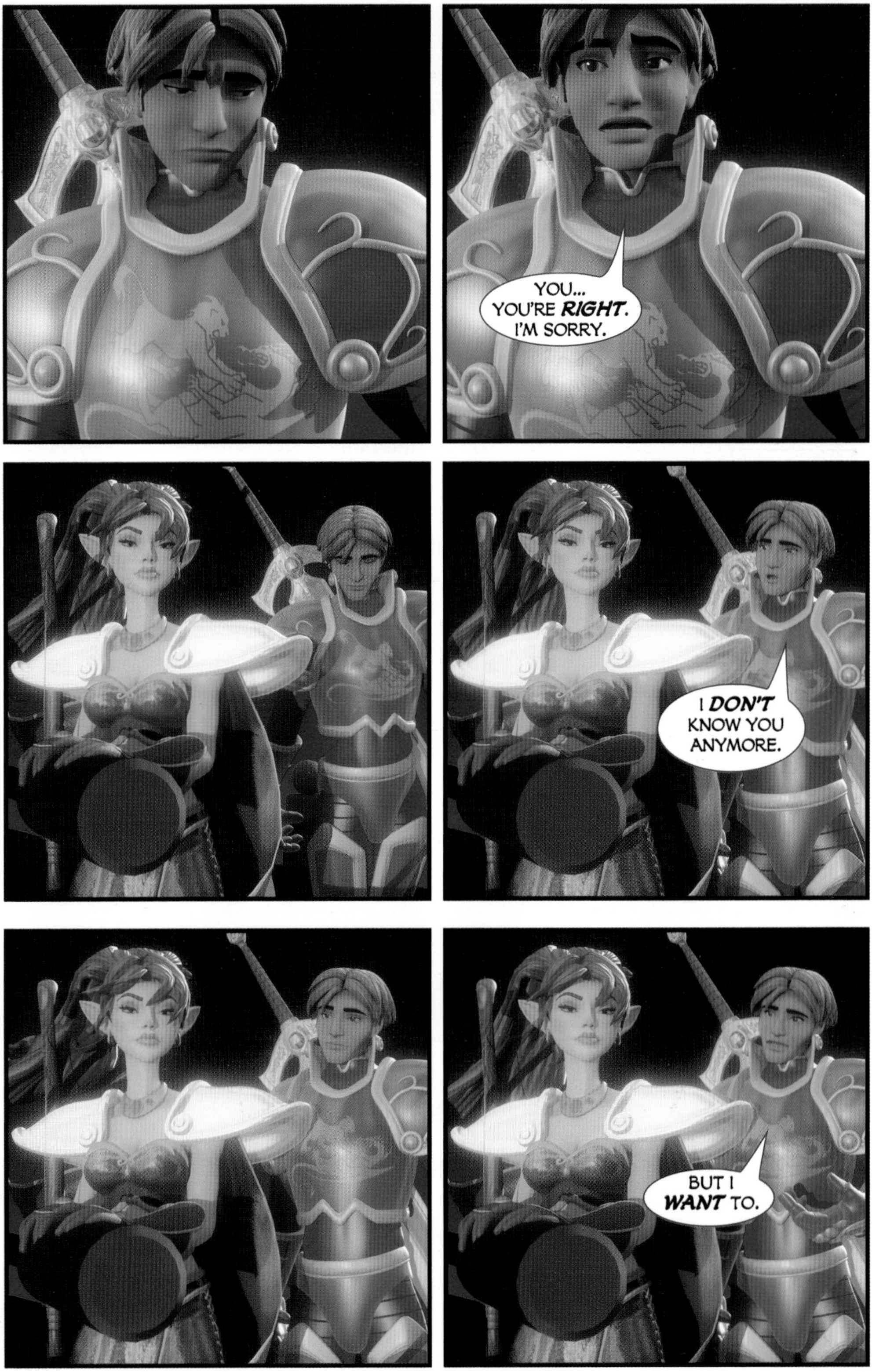
YOU...
YOU'RE RIGHT.
I'M SORRY.
I DON'T
KNOW YOU
ANYMORE.
BUT I
WANT TO.

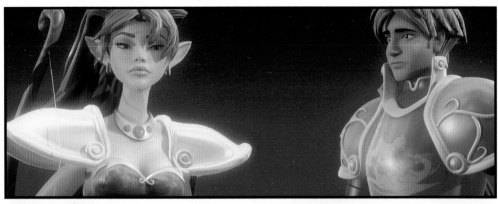

MY BROTHER DAN AND I WERE *READING* ABOUT WHEN WE WERE KIDS. WE HAD A PICNIC WITH YOUR *PARENTS.*

THEY WERE *KIND* PEOPLE, NASTAJIA.

THEY WERE *GREAT PARENTS.*

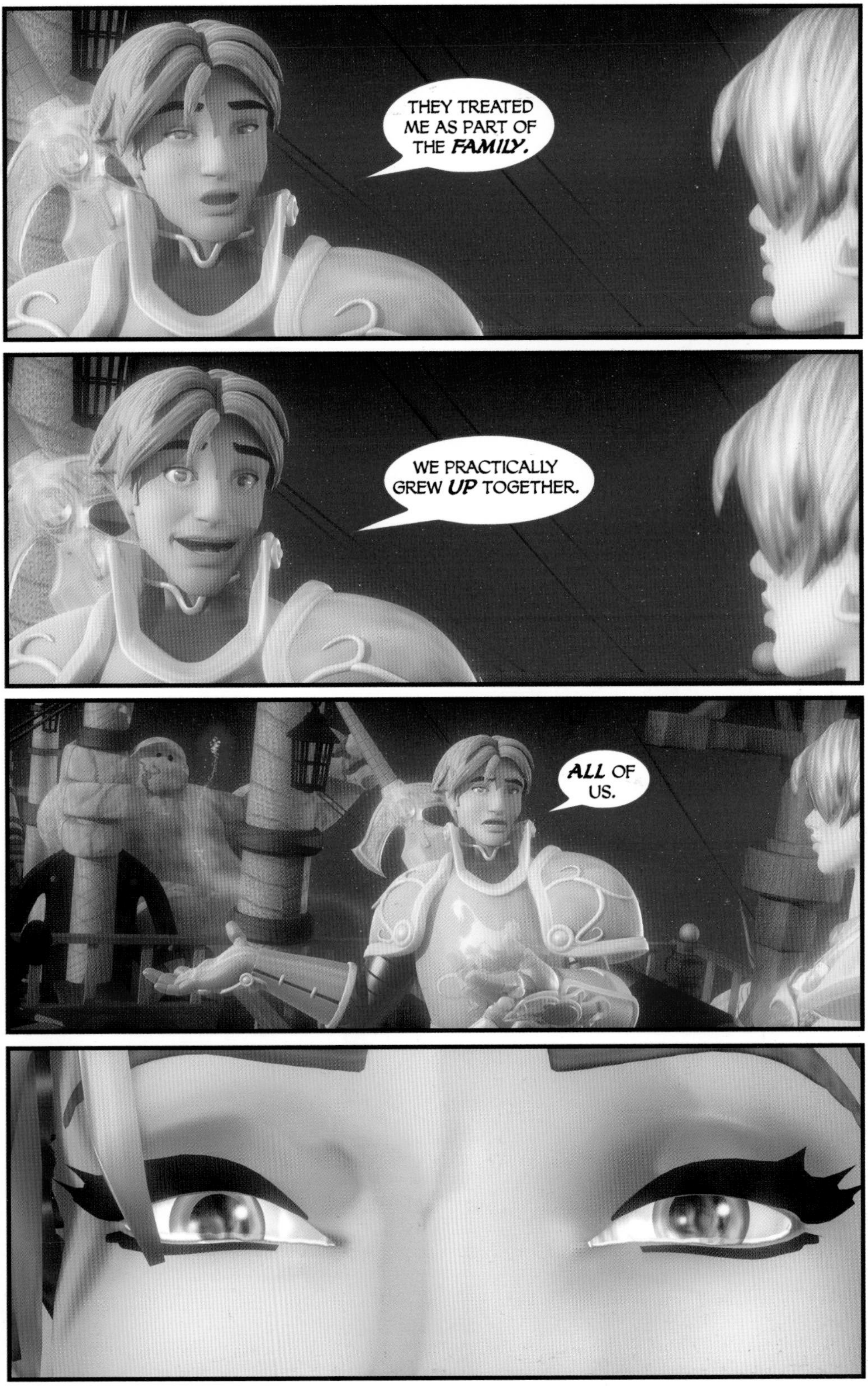
THEY TREATED ME AS PART OF THE FAMILY.
WE PRACTICALLY GREW UP TOGETHER.
ALL OF US.

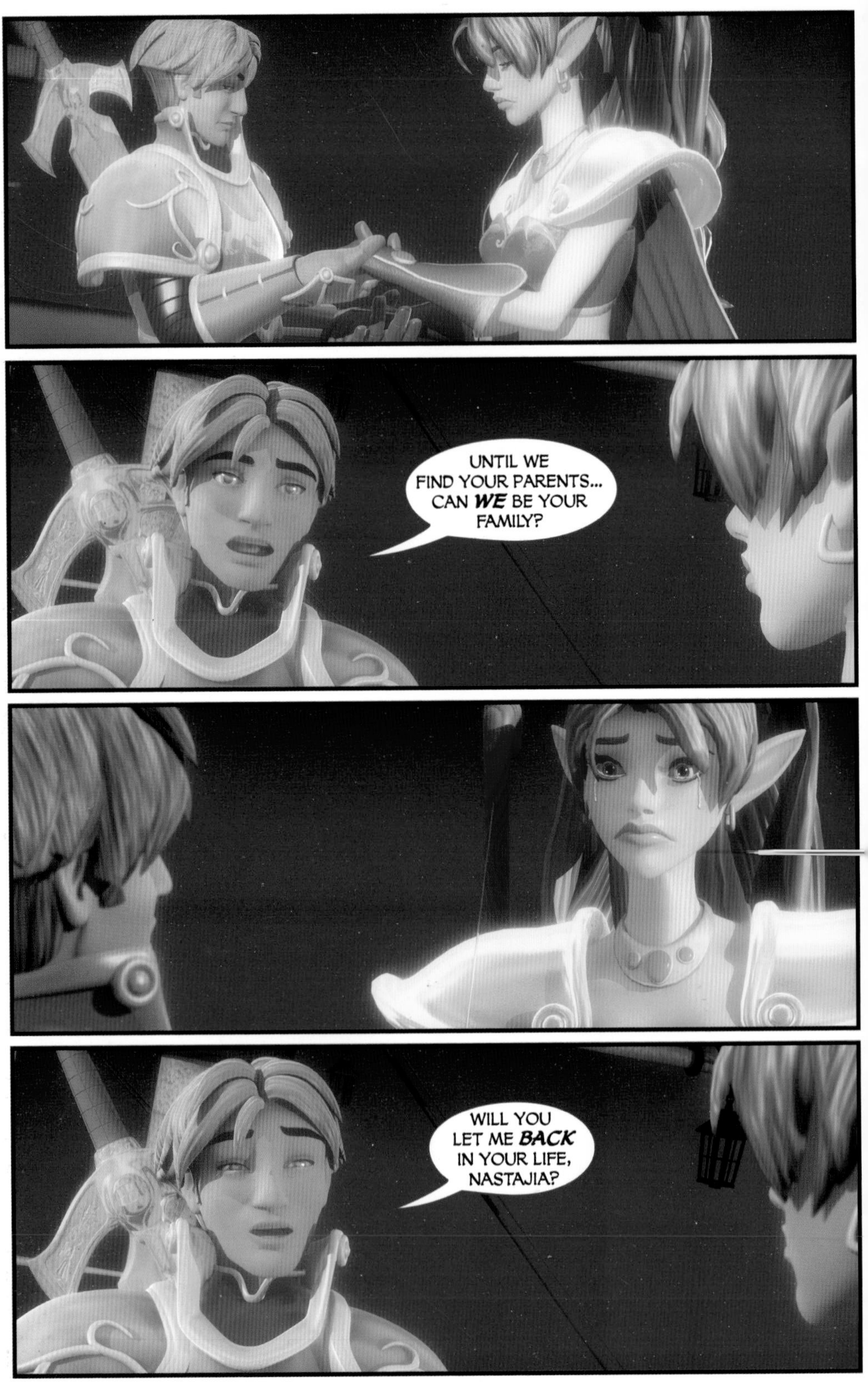
UNTIL WE FIND YOUR PARENTS... CAN WE BE YOUR FAMILY?
WILL YOU LET ME BACK IN YOUR LIFE, NASTAJIA?

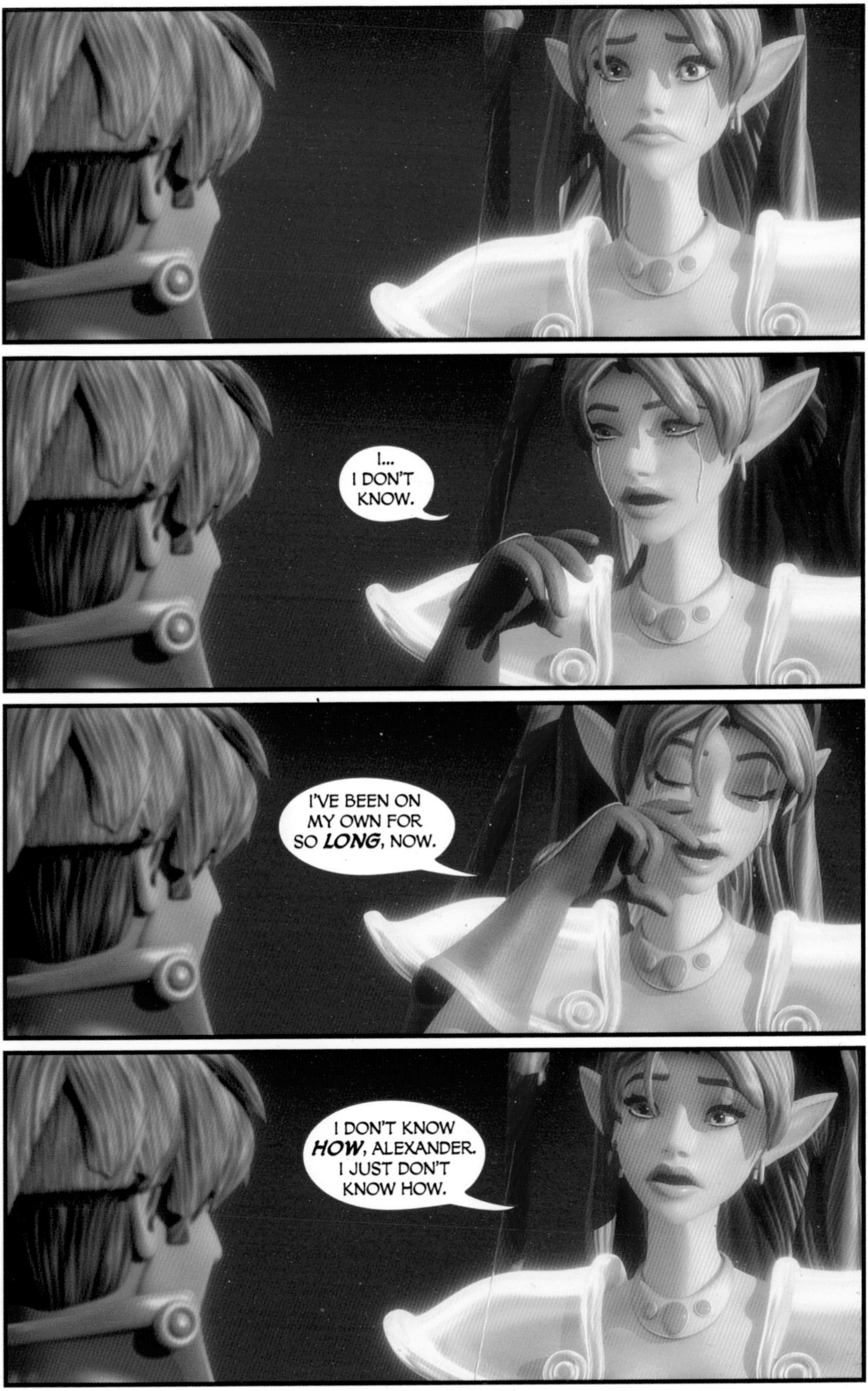
I...
I DON'T KNOW.
I'VE BEEN ON MY OWN FOR SO *LONG*, NOW.
I DON'T KNOW *HOW*, ALEXANDER. I JUST DON'T KNOW HOW.

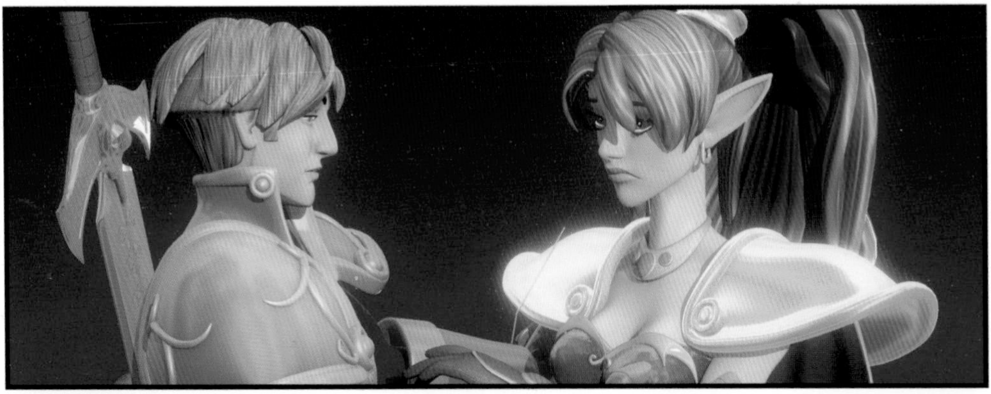

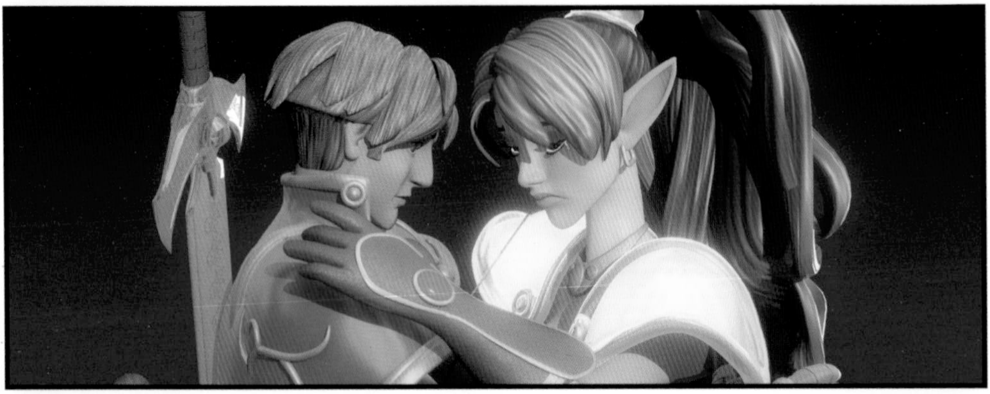

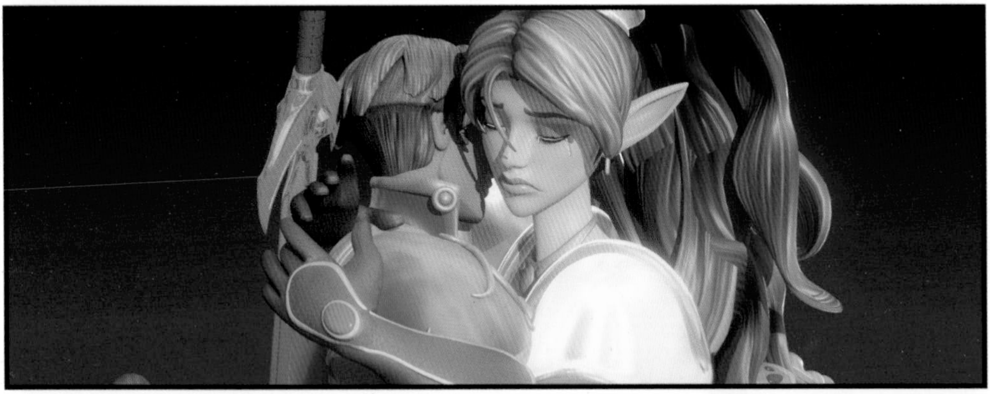

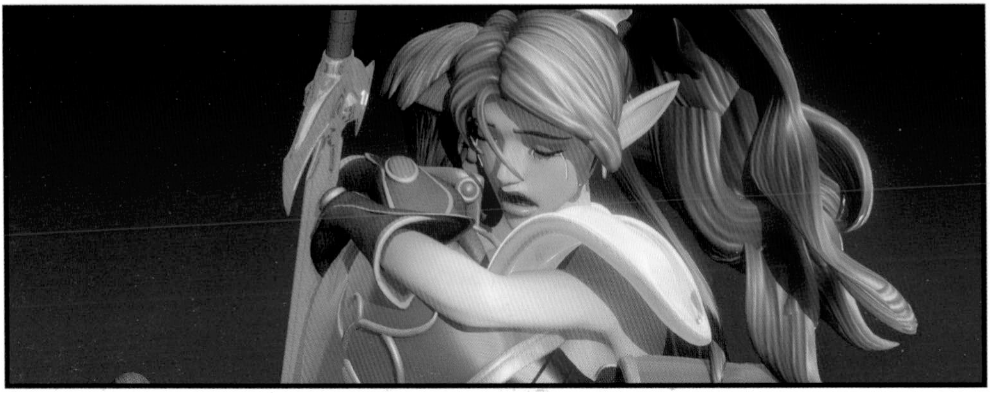

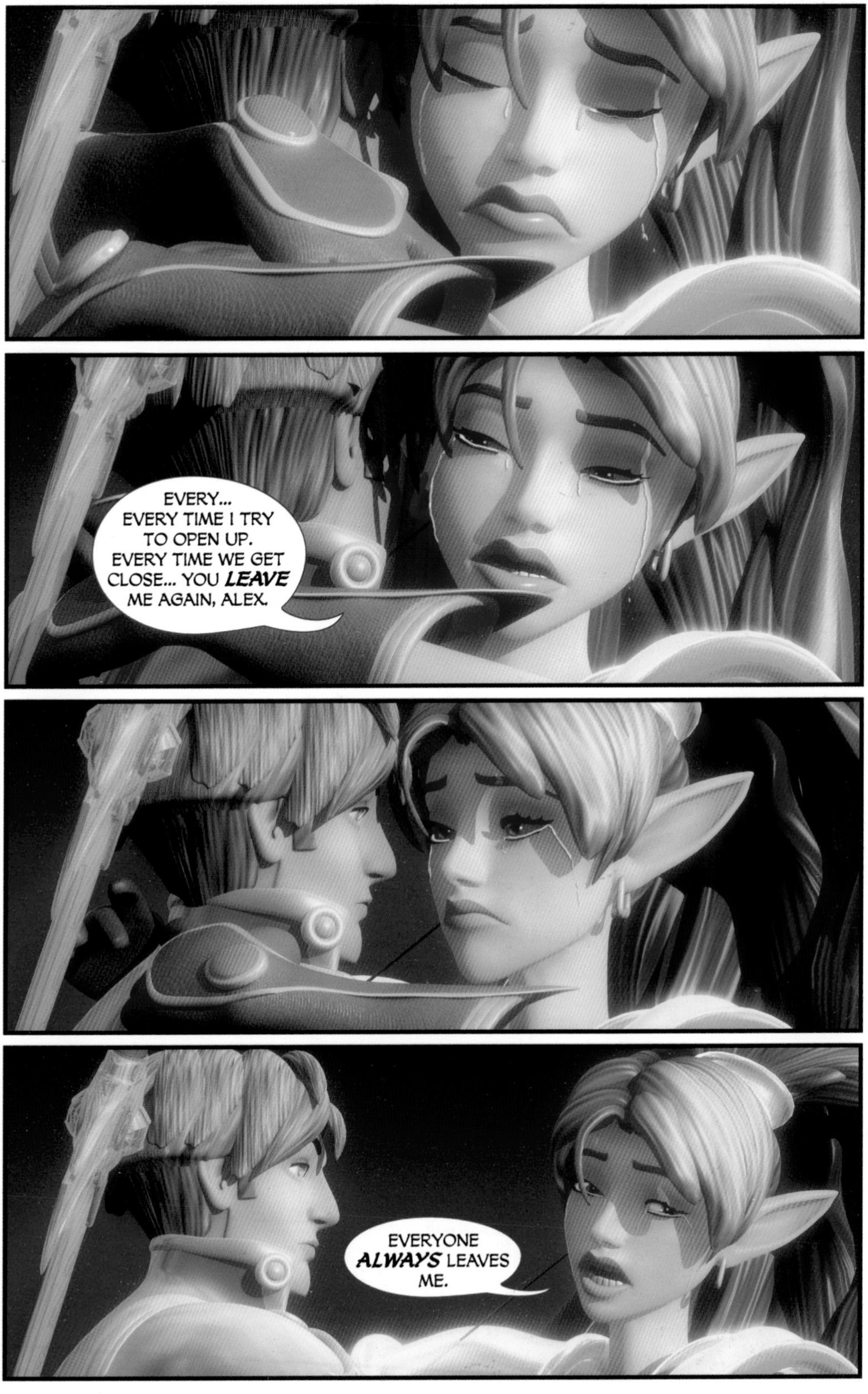
EVERY... EVERY TIME I TRY TO OPEN UP. EVERY TIME WE GET CLOSE... YOU LEAVE ME AGAIN, ALEX.
EVERYONE ALWAYS LEAVES ME.

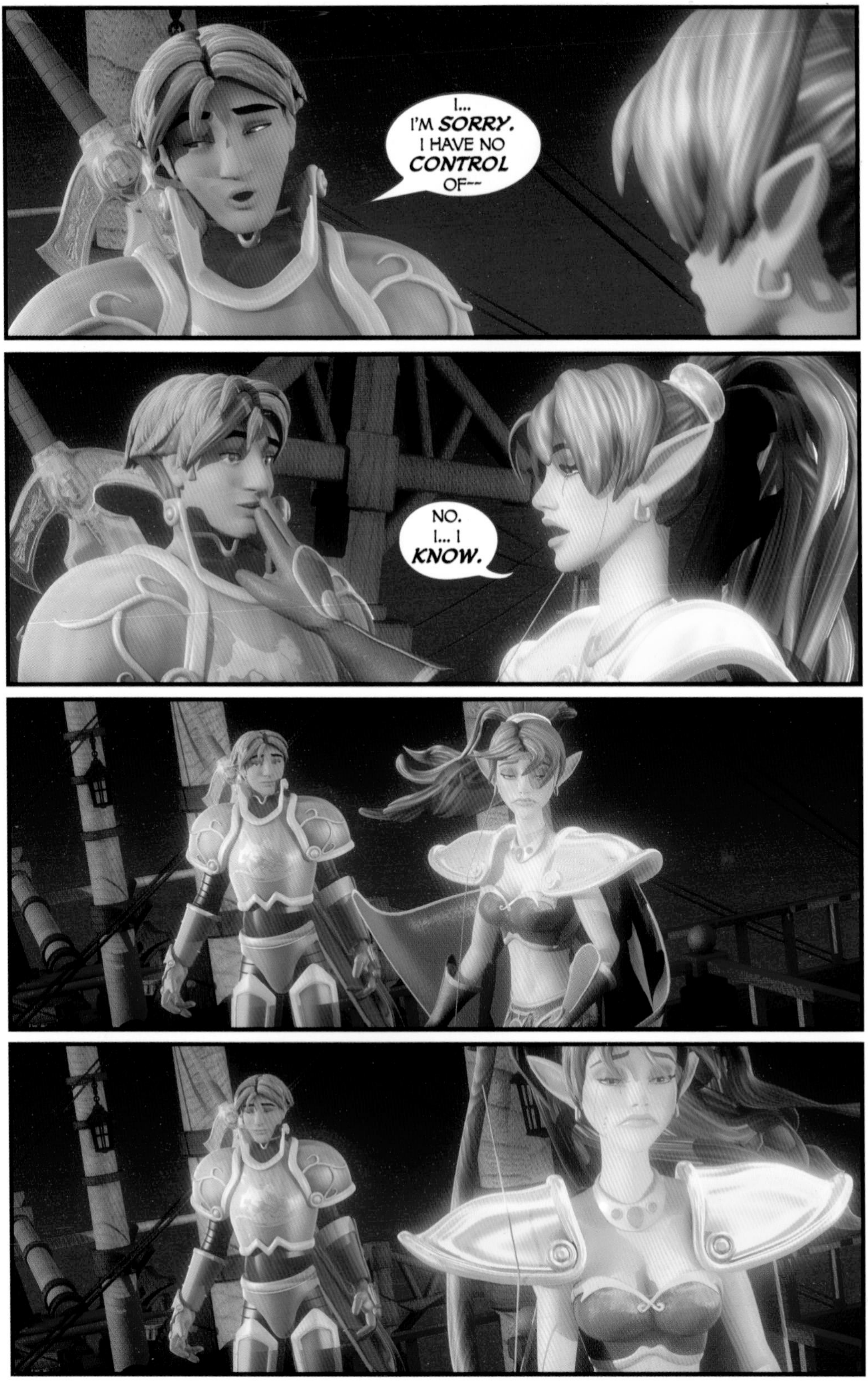
I... I'M SORRY. I HAVE NO CONTROL OF--
NO. I... I KNOW.

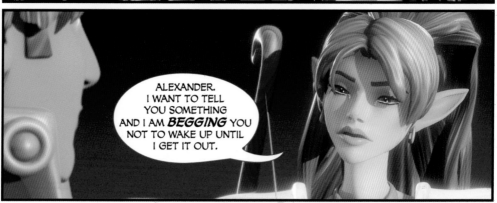

ALEXANDER.
I WANT TO TELL
YOU SOMETHING
AND I AM *BEGGING* YOU
NOT TO WAKE UP UNTIL
I GET IT OUT.

OH... OKAY...

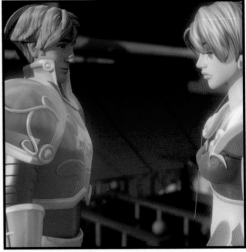

HAVING YOU *BACK... SEEING* YOU AGAIN...

...FEELINGS FROM MY *CHILDHOOD*...

...MEMORIES OF A *HAPPIER* TIME, WHEN MY PARENTS WERE AROUND. WHEN WE WERE FREE TO FLY ACROSS DREAMLAND WITHOUT A *CARE* IN THE WORLD.

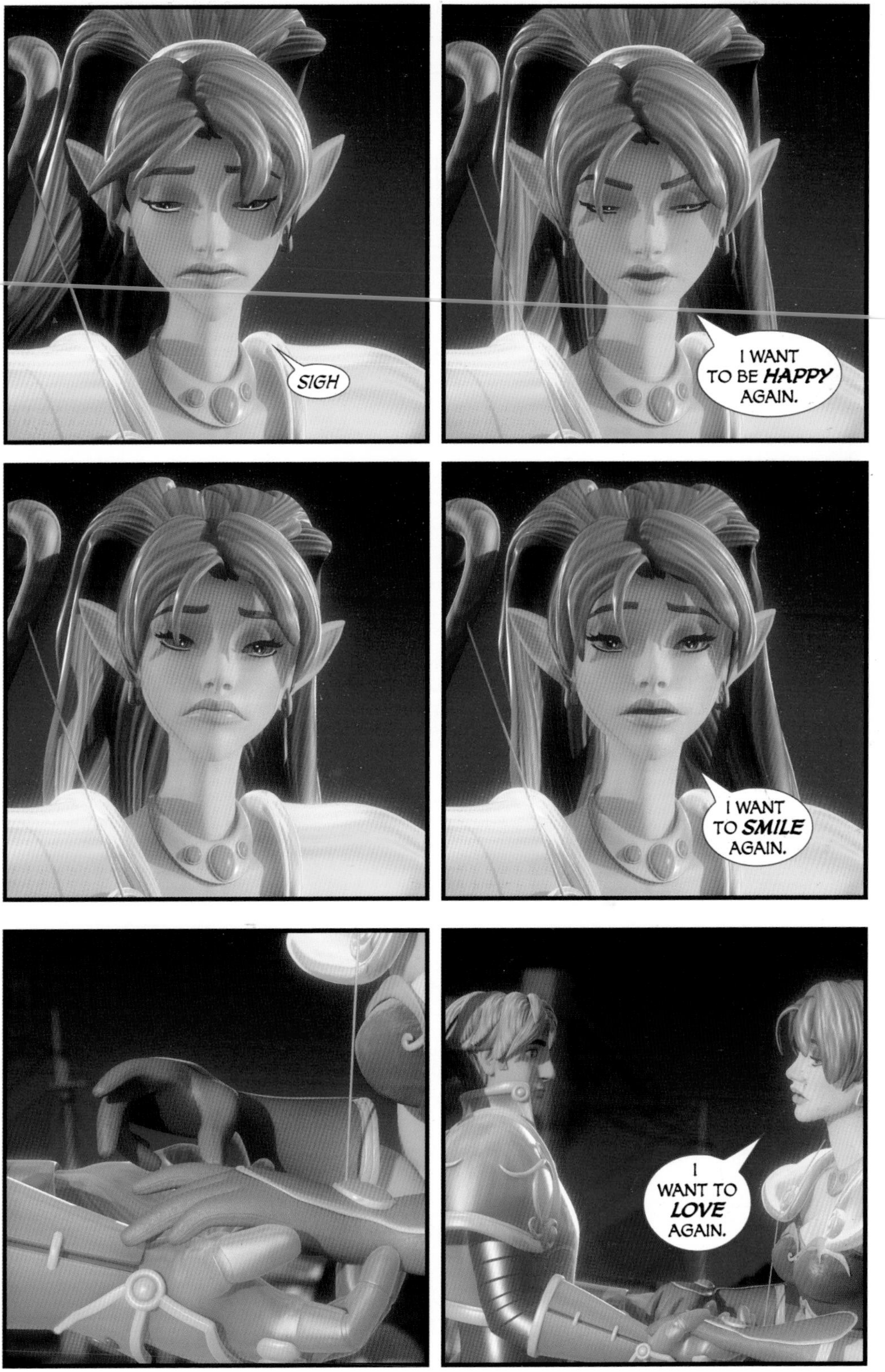
SIGH
I WANT TO BE HAPPY AGAIN.
I WANT TO SMILE AGAIN.
I WANT TO LOVE AGAIN.

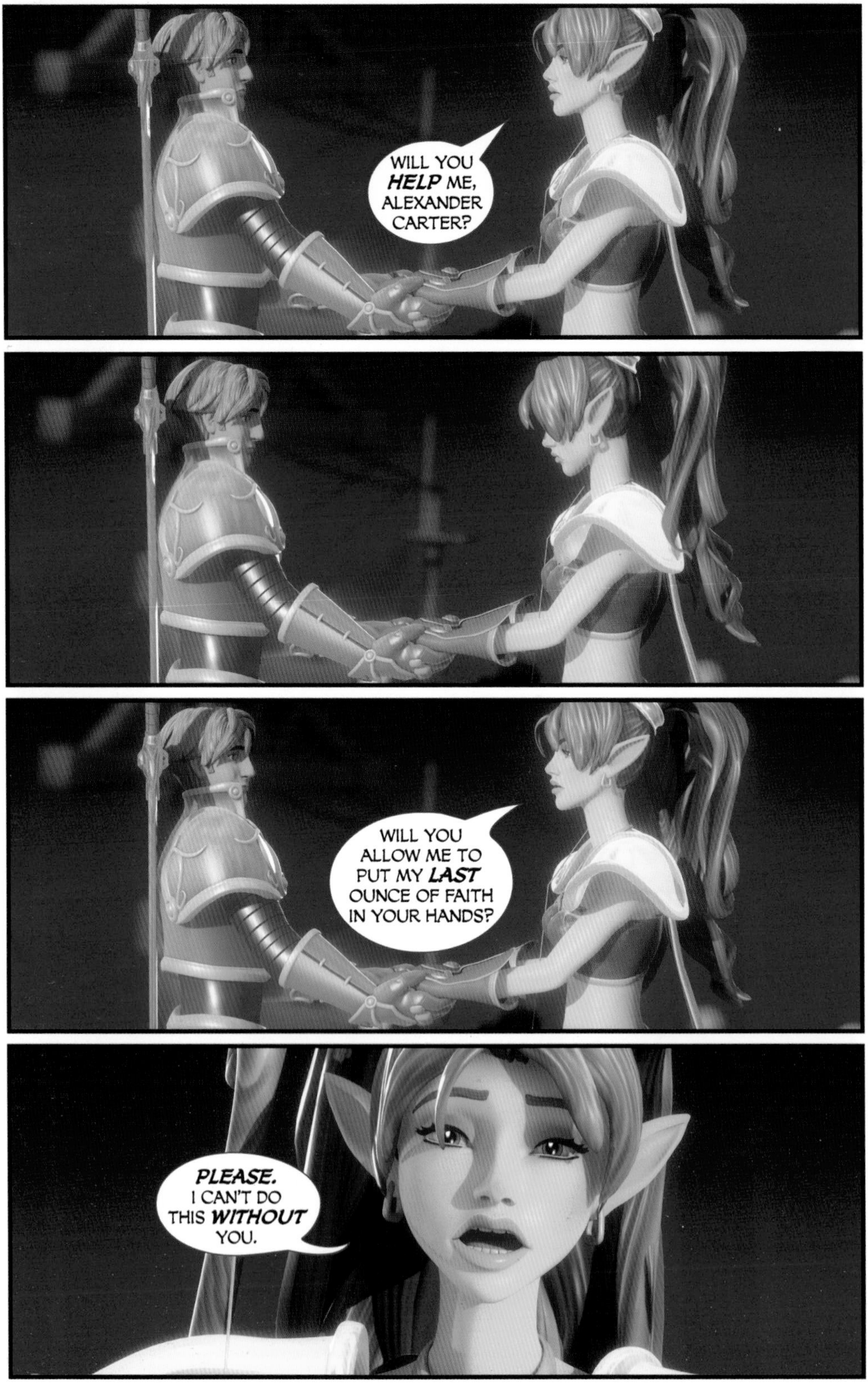
WILL YOU HELP ME, ALEXANDER CARTER?
WILL YOU ALLOW ME TO PUT MY LAST OUNCE OF FAITH IN YOUR HANDS?
PLEASE. I CAN'T DO THIS WITHOUT YOU.

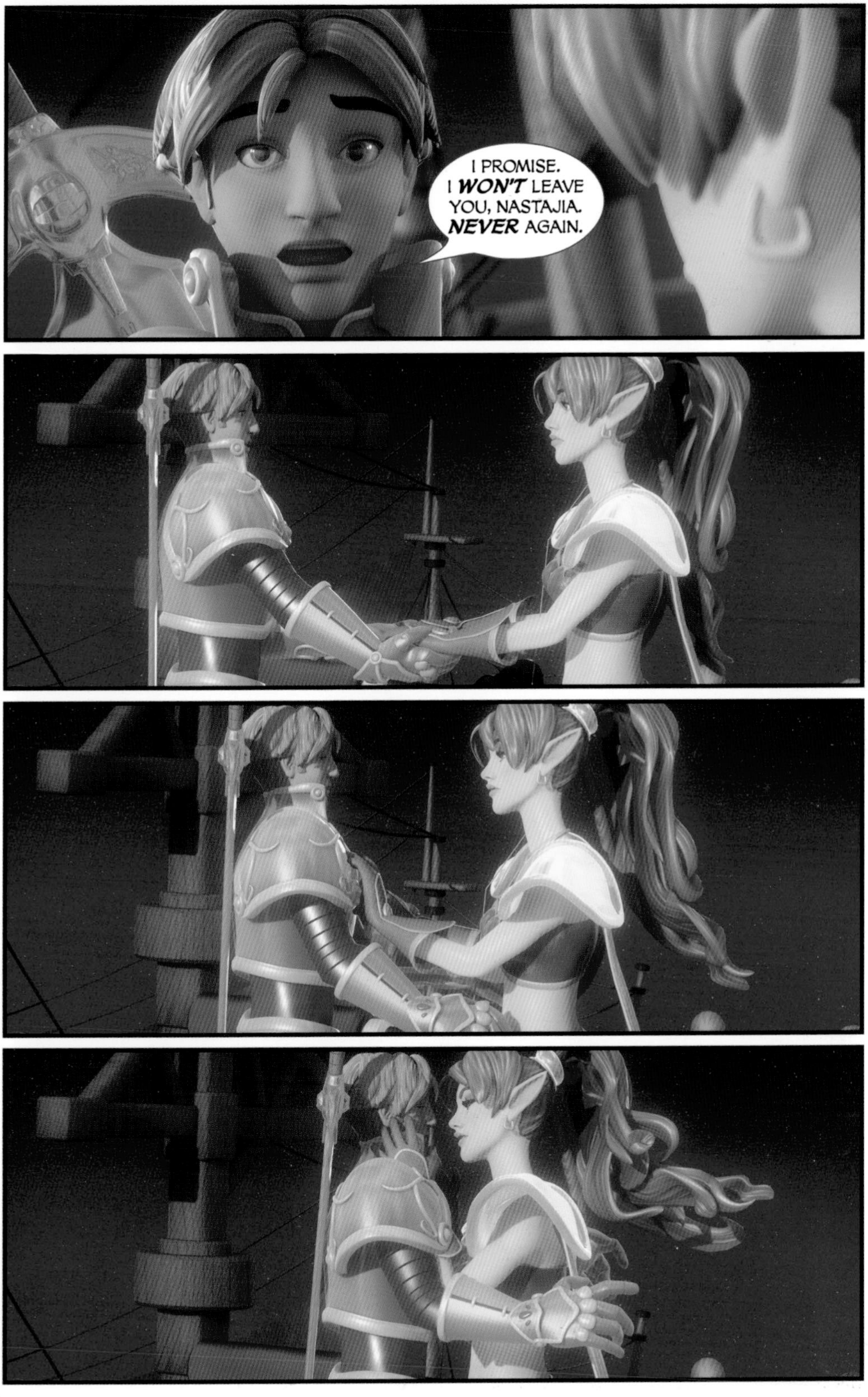
I PROMISE. I WON'T LEAVE YOU, NASTAJIA. NEVER AGAIN.

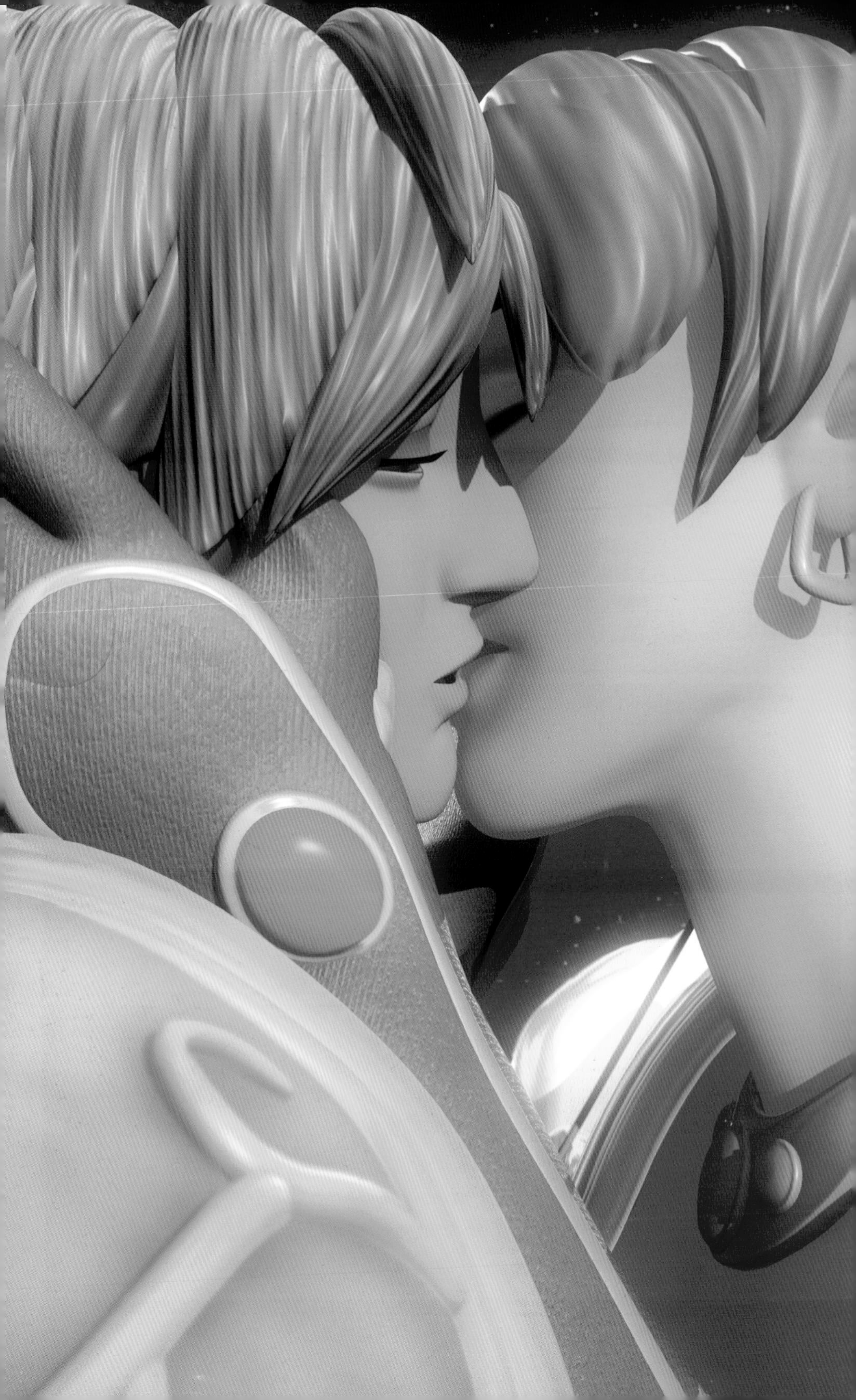

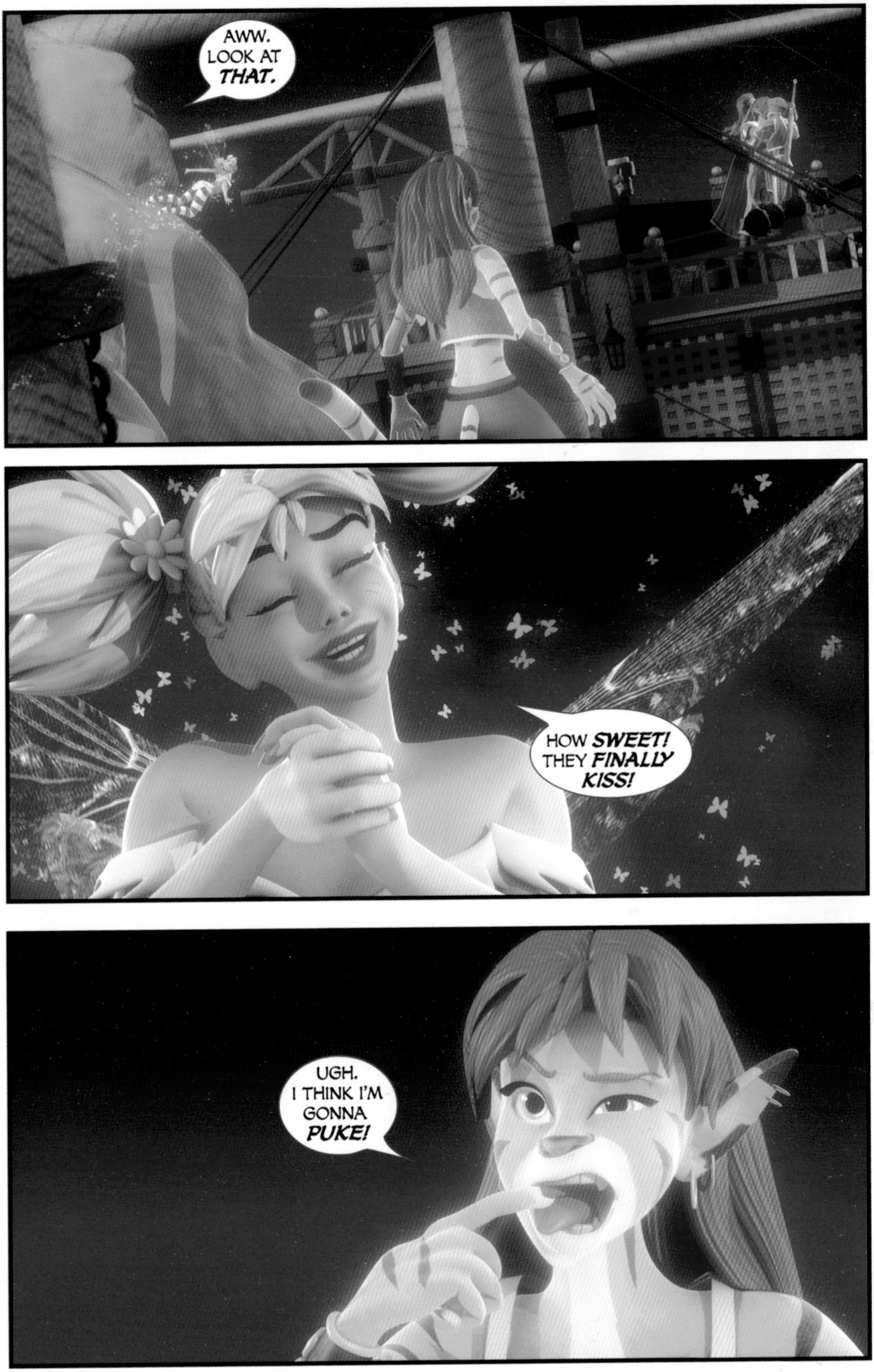
AWW. LOOK AT *THAT.*
HOW *SWEET!* THEY *FINALLY KISS!*
UGH. I THINK I'M GONNA *PUKE!*

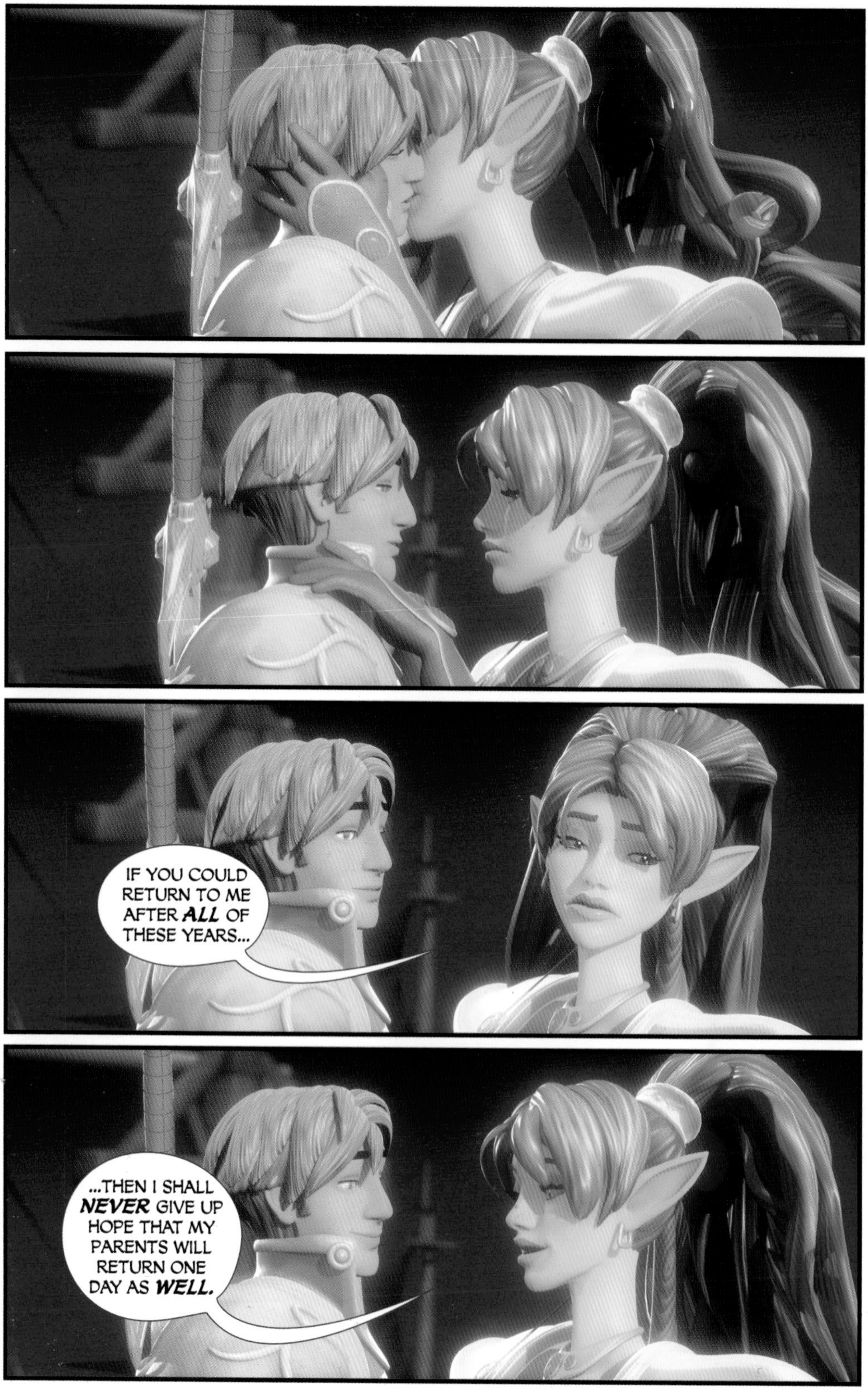
IF YOU COULD RETURN TO ME AFTER ALL OF THESE YEARS...
...THEN I SHALL NEVER GIVE UP HOPE THAT MY PARENTS WILL RETURN ONE DAY AS WELL.

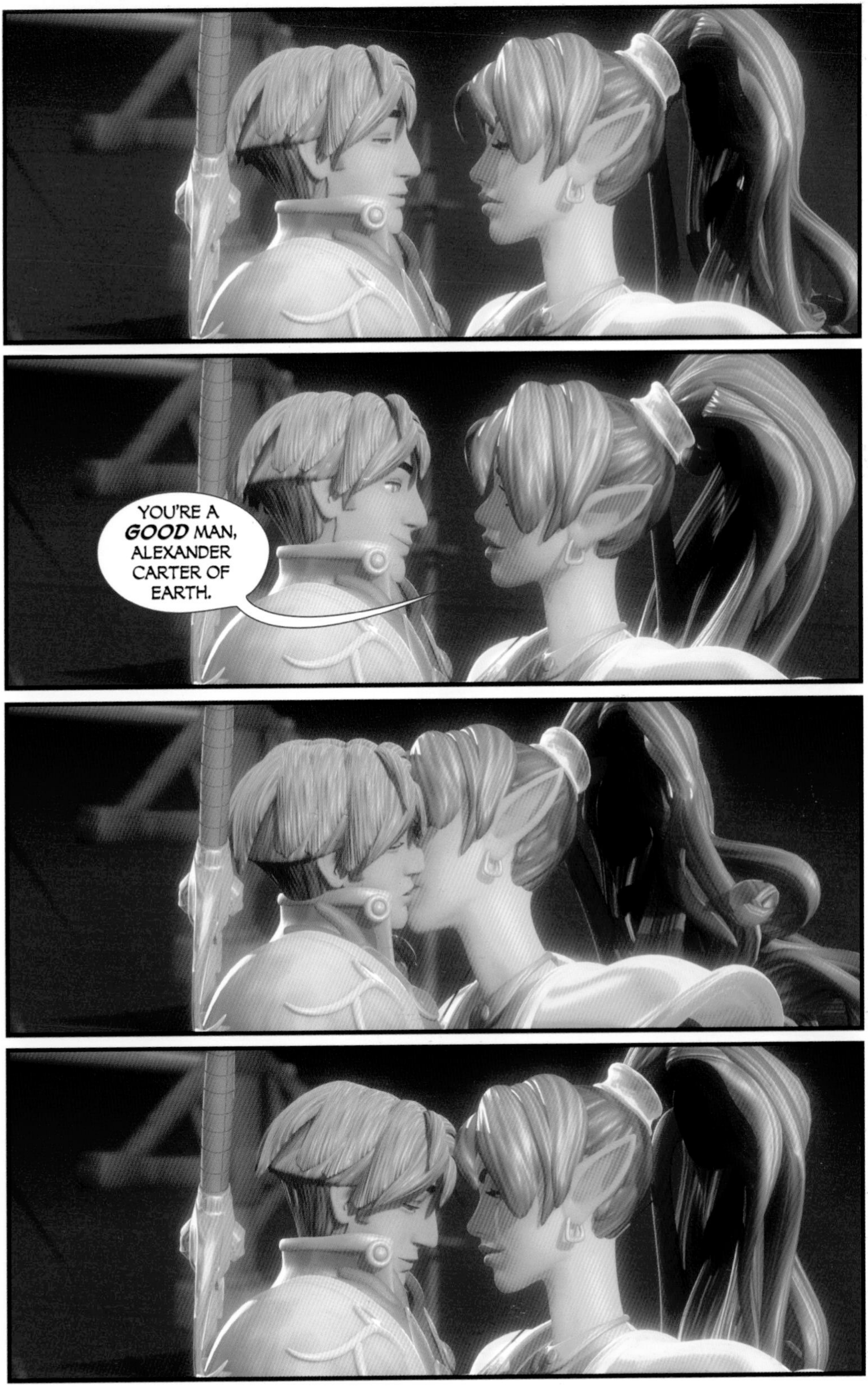
YOU'RE A GOOD MAN, ALEXANDER CARTER OF EARTH.

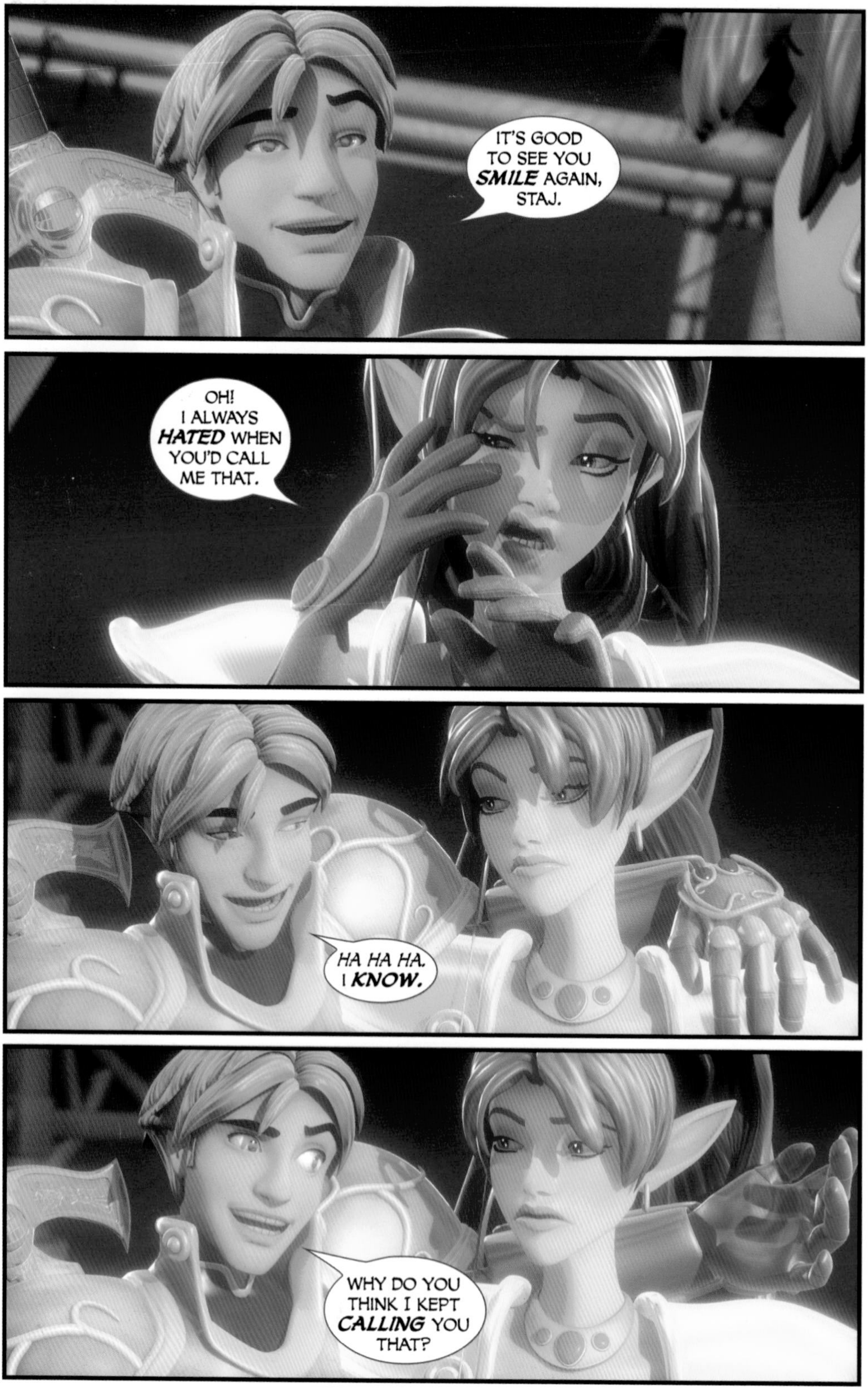
IT'S GOOD TO SEE YOU *SMILE* AGAIN, STAJ.
OH! I ALWAYS *HATED* WHEN YOU'D CALL ME THAT.
HA HA HA. I *KNOW.*
WHY DO YOU THINK I KEPT *CALLING* YOU THAT?

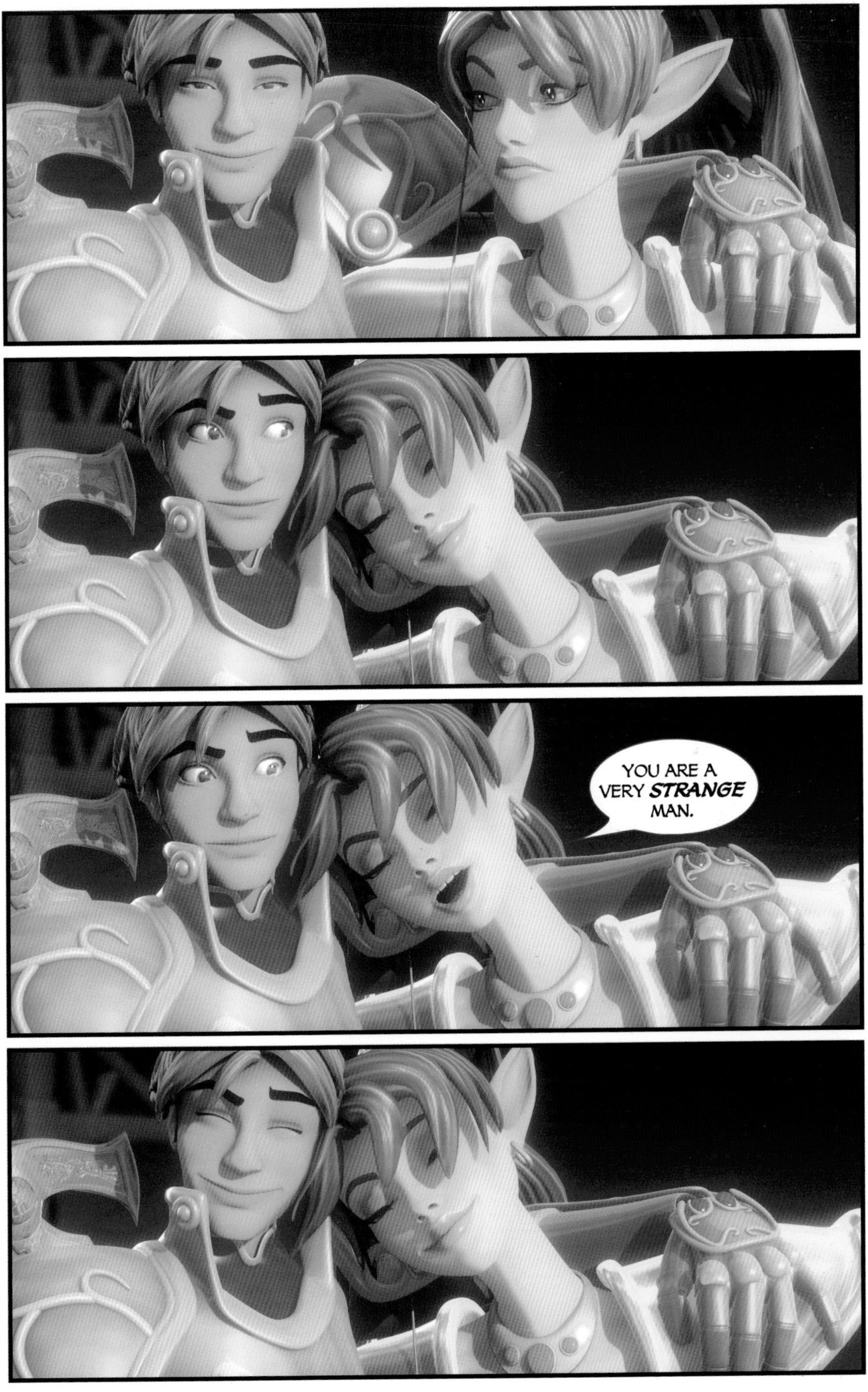
YOU ARE A VERY *STRANGE* MAN.

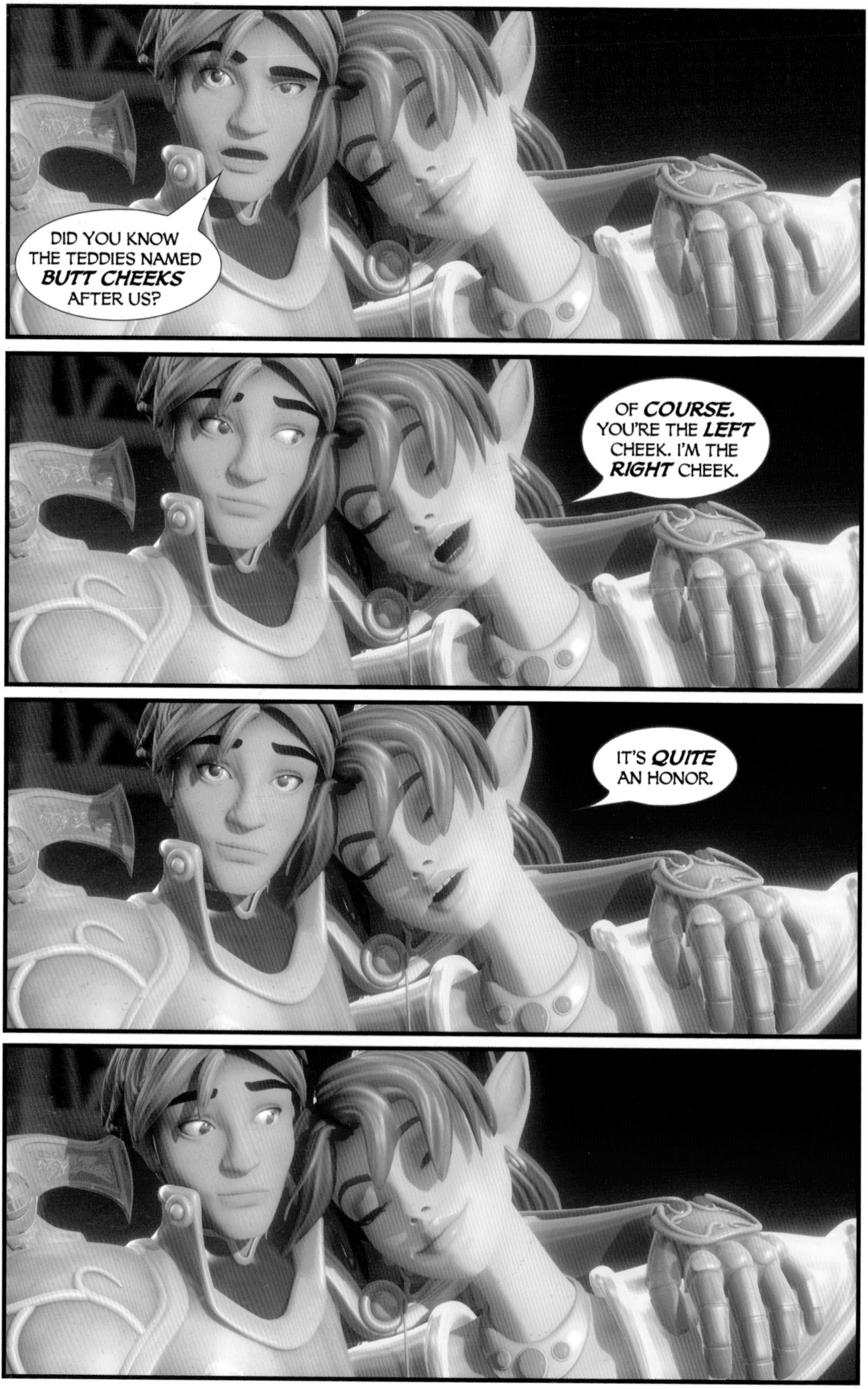
DID YOU KNOW THE TEDDIES NAMED BUTT CHEEKS AFTER US?
OF COURSE. YOU'RE THE LEFT CHEEK. I'M THE RIGHT CHEEK.
IT'S QUITE AN HONOR.

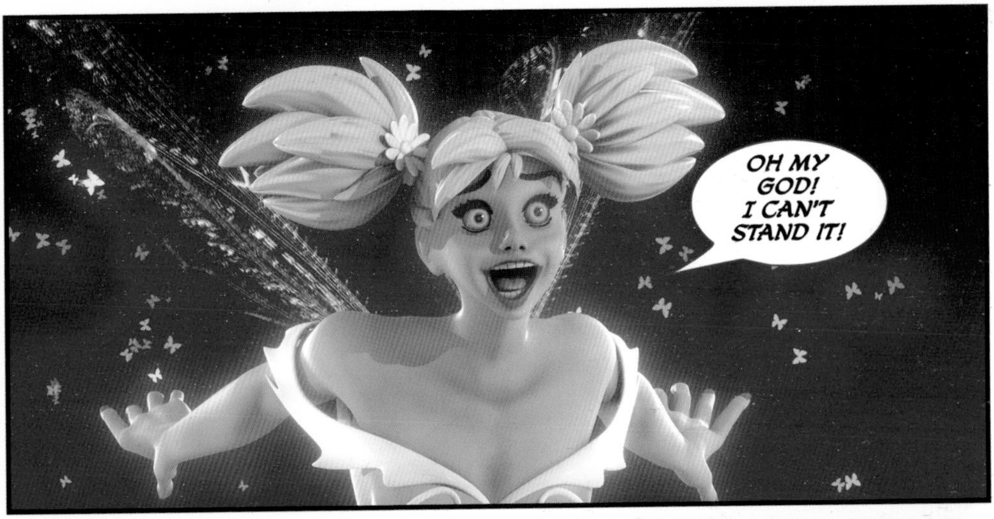
OH MY GOD! I CAN'T STAND IT!

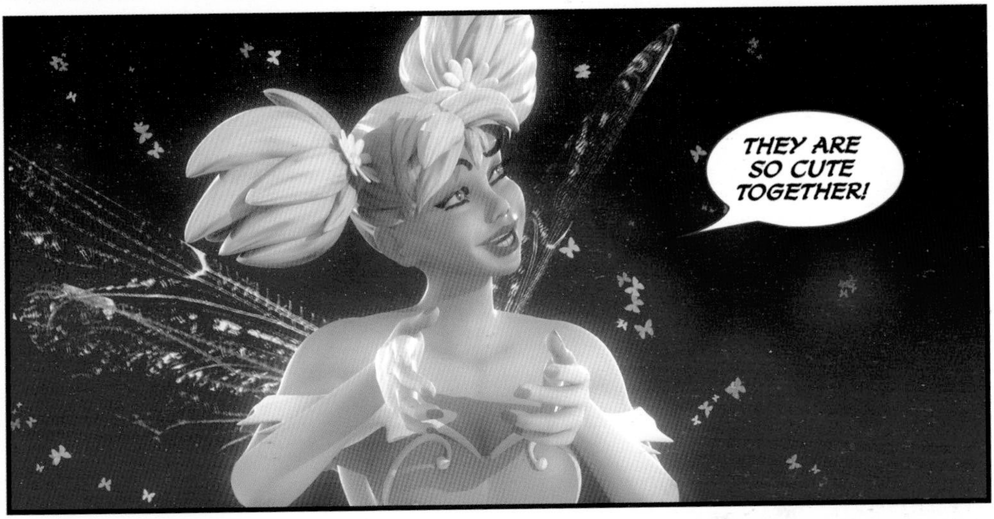
THEY ARE SO CUTE TOGETHER!

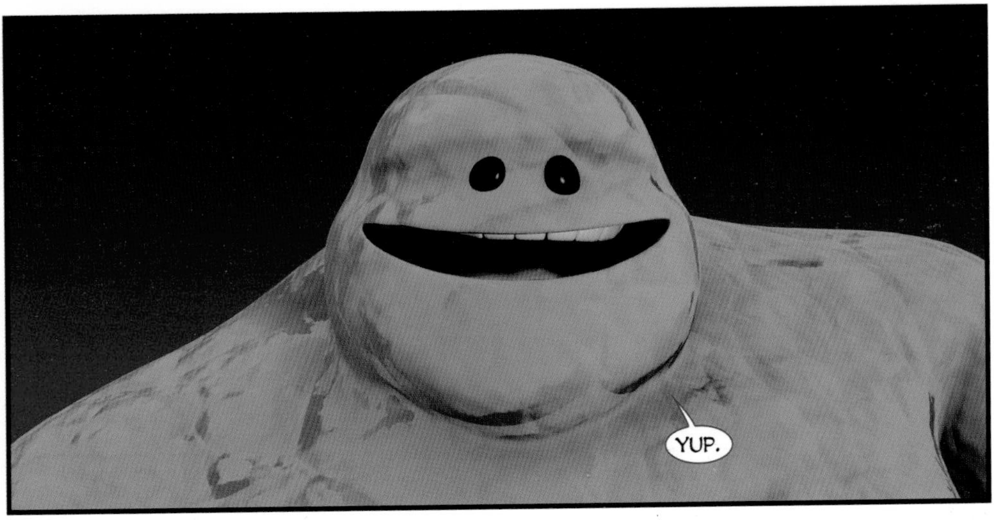
YUP.

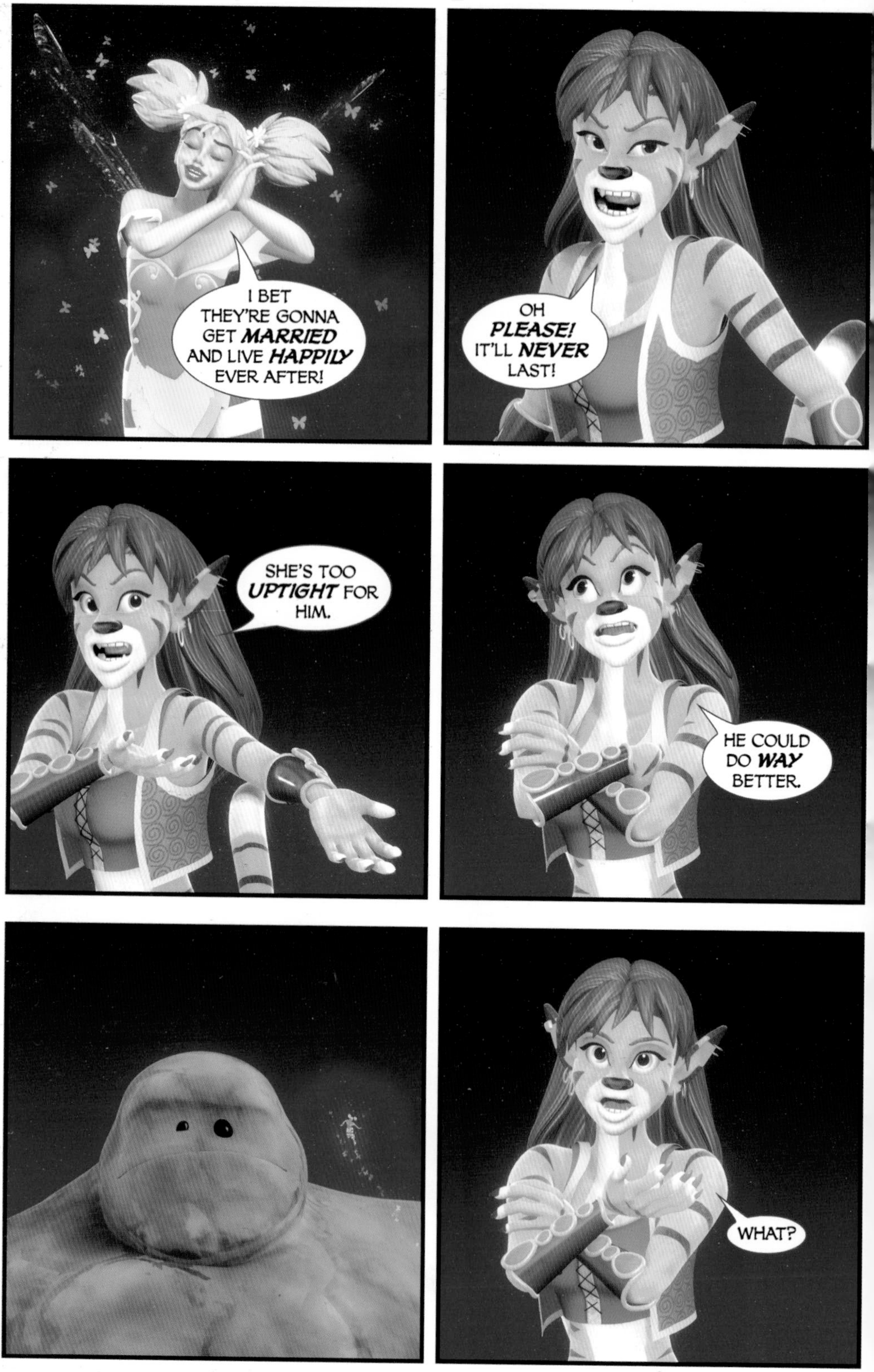
I BET THEY'RE GONNA GET MARRIED AND LIVE HAPPILY EVER AFTER!
OH PLEASE! IT'LL NEVER LAST!
SHE'S TOO UPTIGHT FOR HIM.
HE COULD DO WAY BETTER.
WHAT?

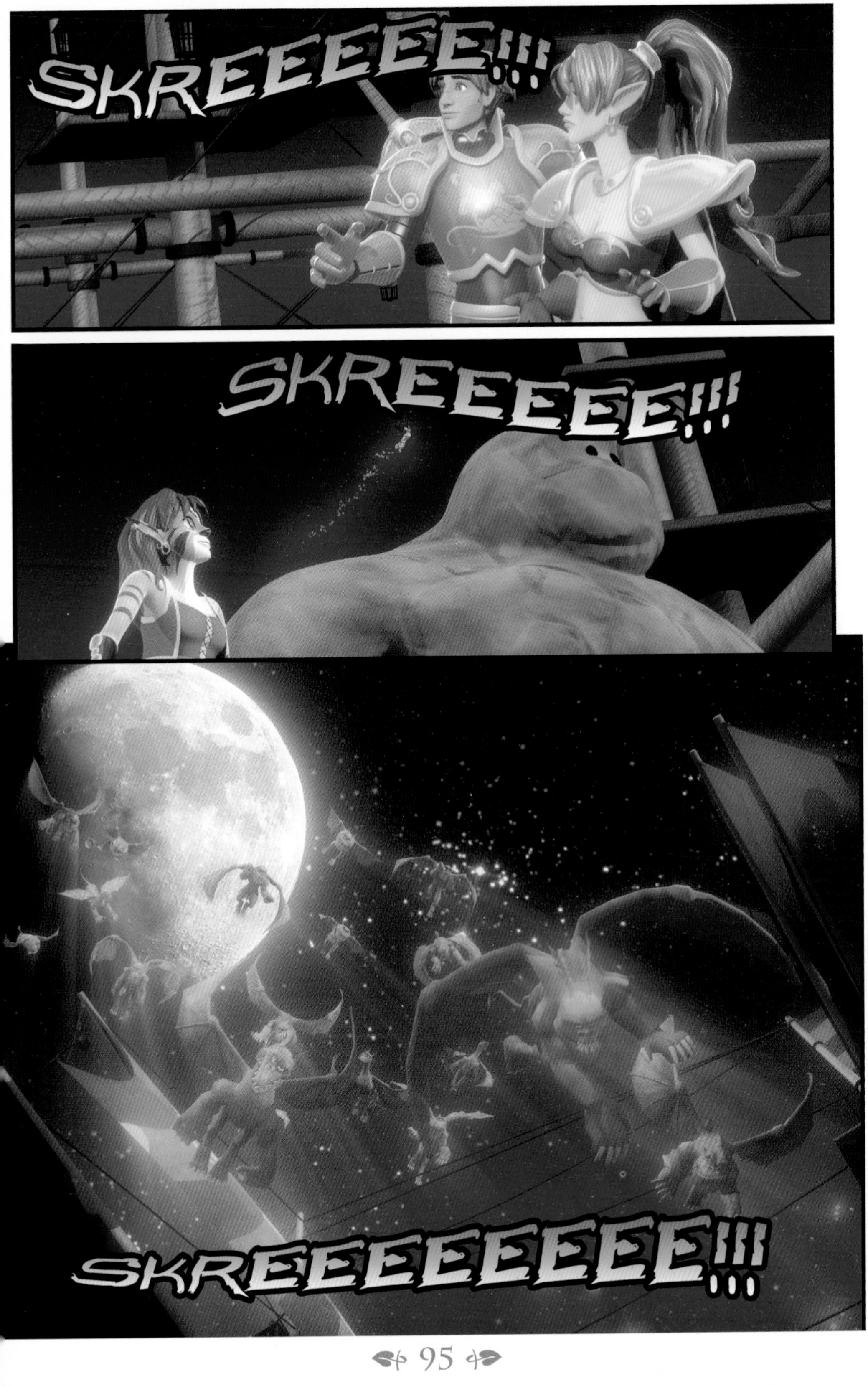
SKREEEEEE!!!
SKREEEEEE!!!
SKREEEEEEEEEE!!!

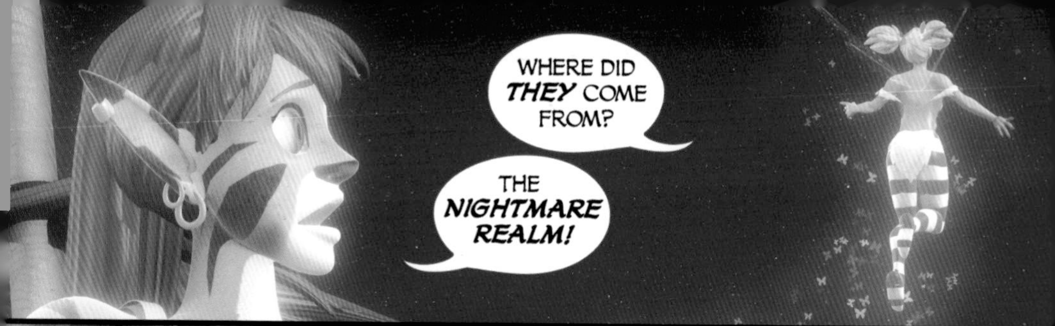
WHERE DID THEY COME FROM?
THE NIGHTMARE REALM!

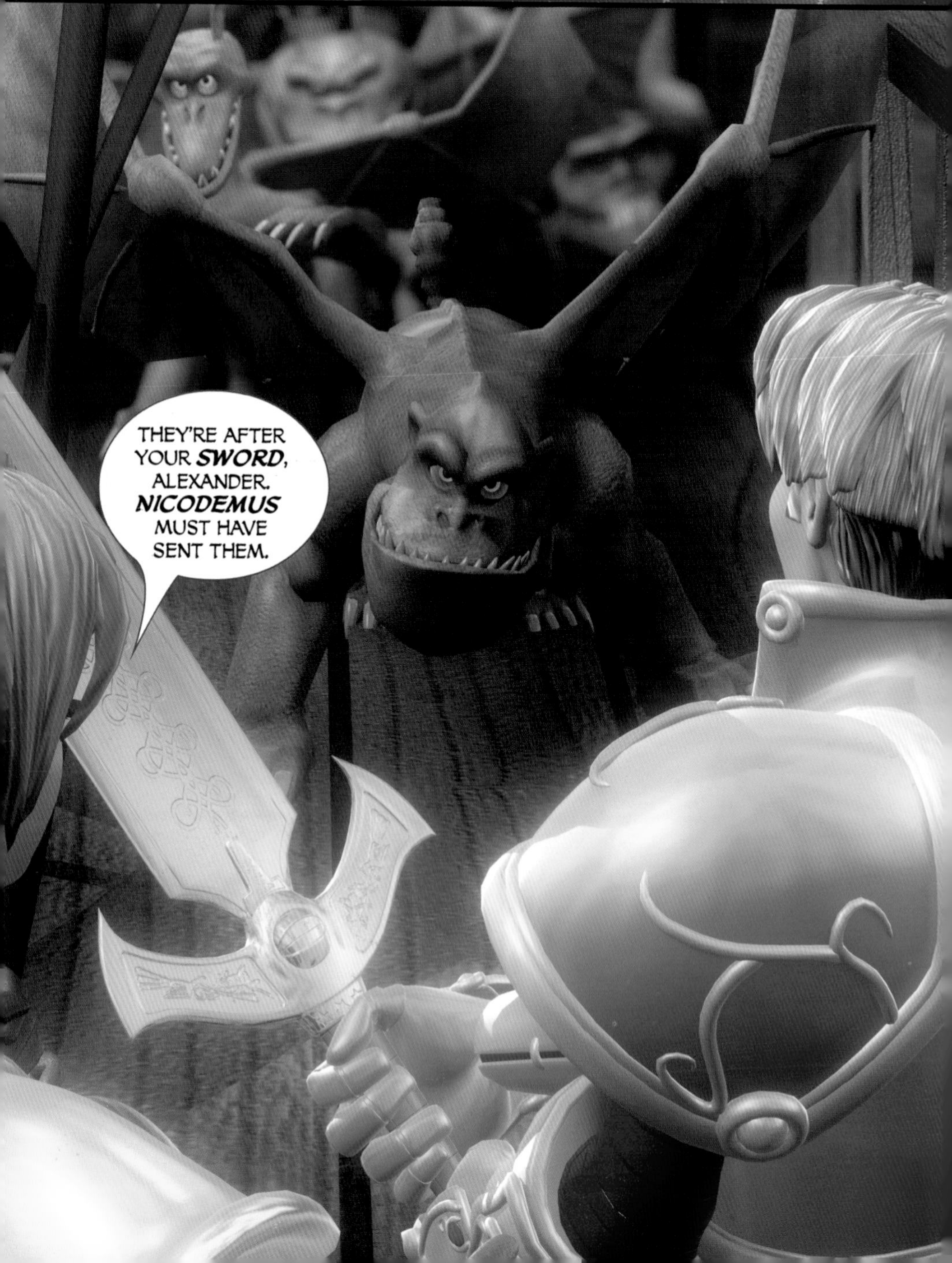
THEY'RE AFTER YOUR SWORD, ALEXANDER. NICODEMUS MUST HAVE SENT THEM.

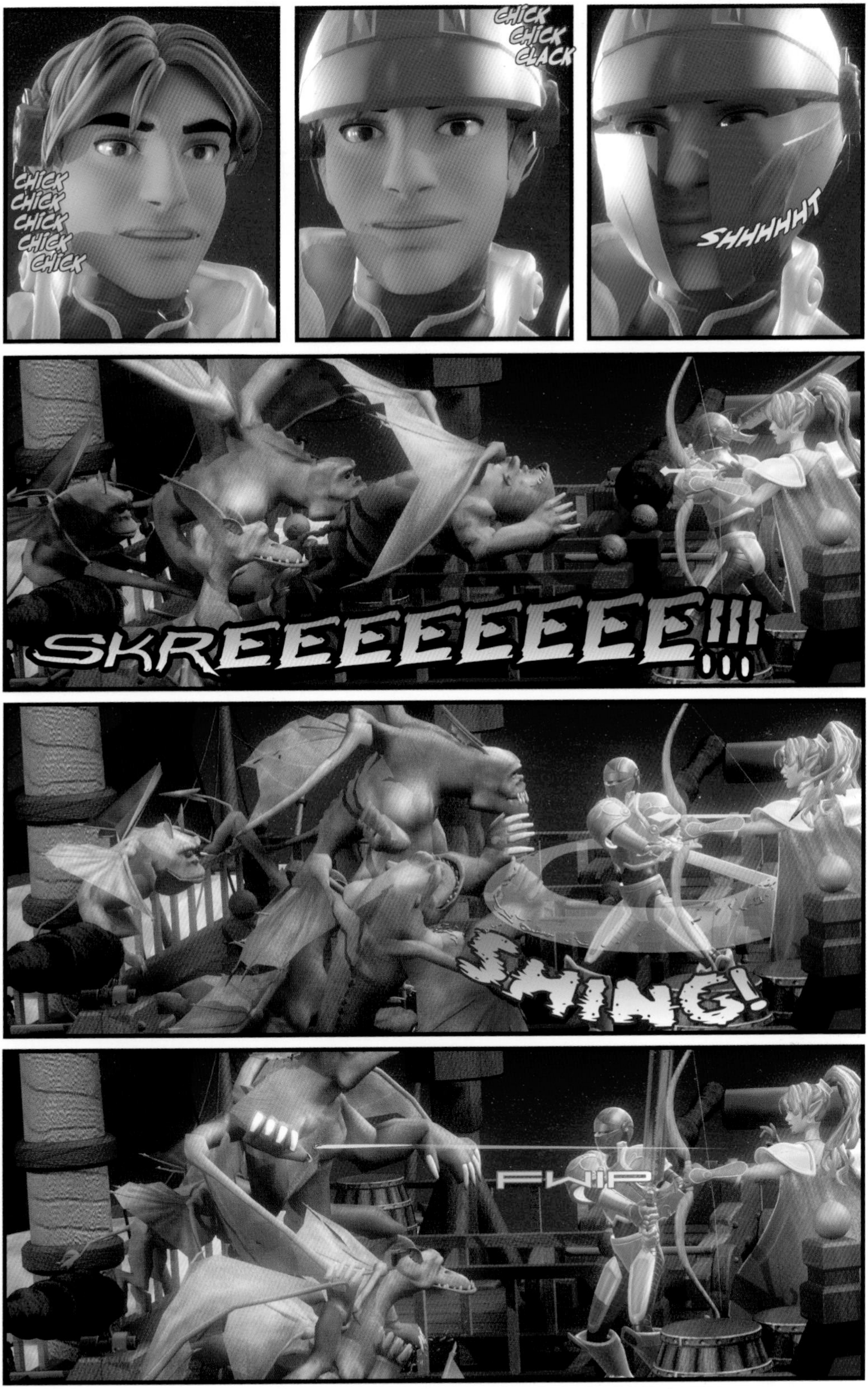
CHICK
CHICK
CHICK
CHICK
CHICK
CHICK
CHICK
CLACK
SHHHHHT
SKREEEEEEEE!!!
SHING!
FWIP

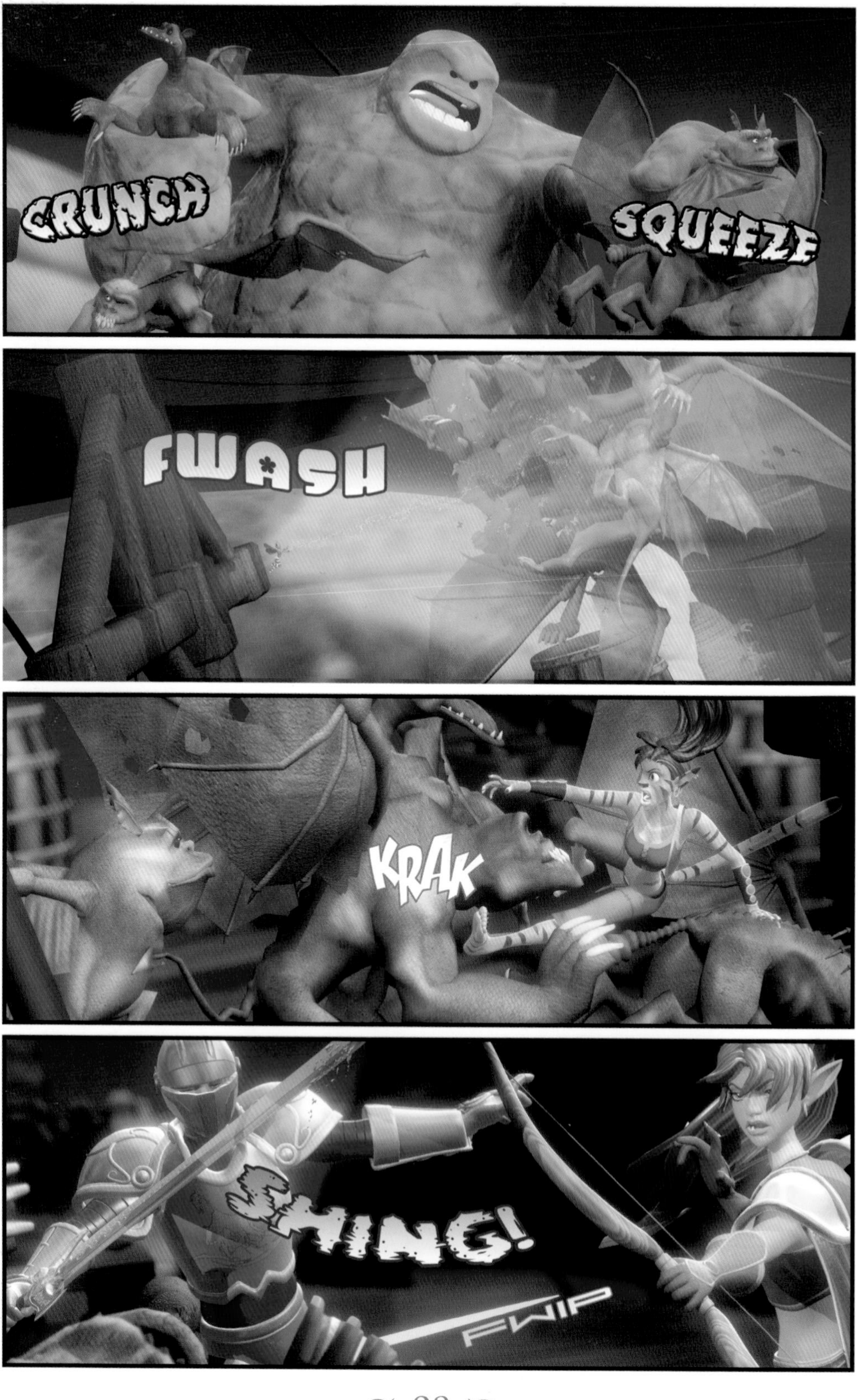
CRUNCH
SQUEEZE
FWASH
KRAK
SHING!
FWIP

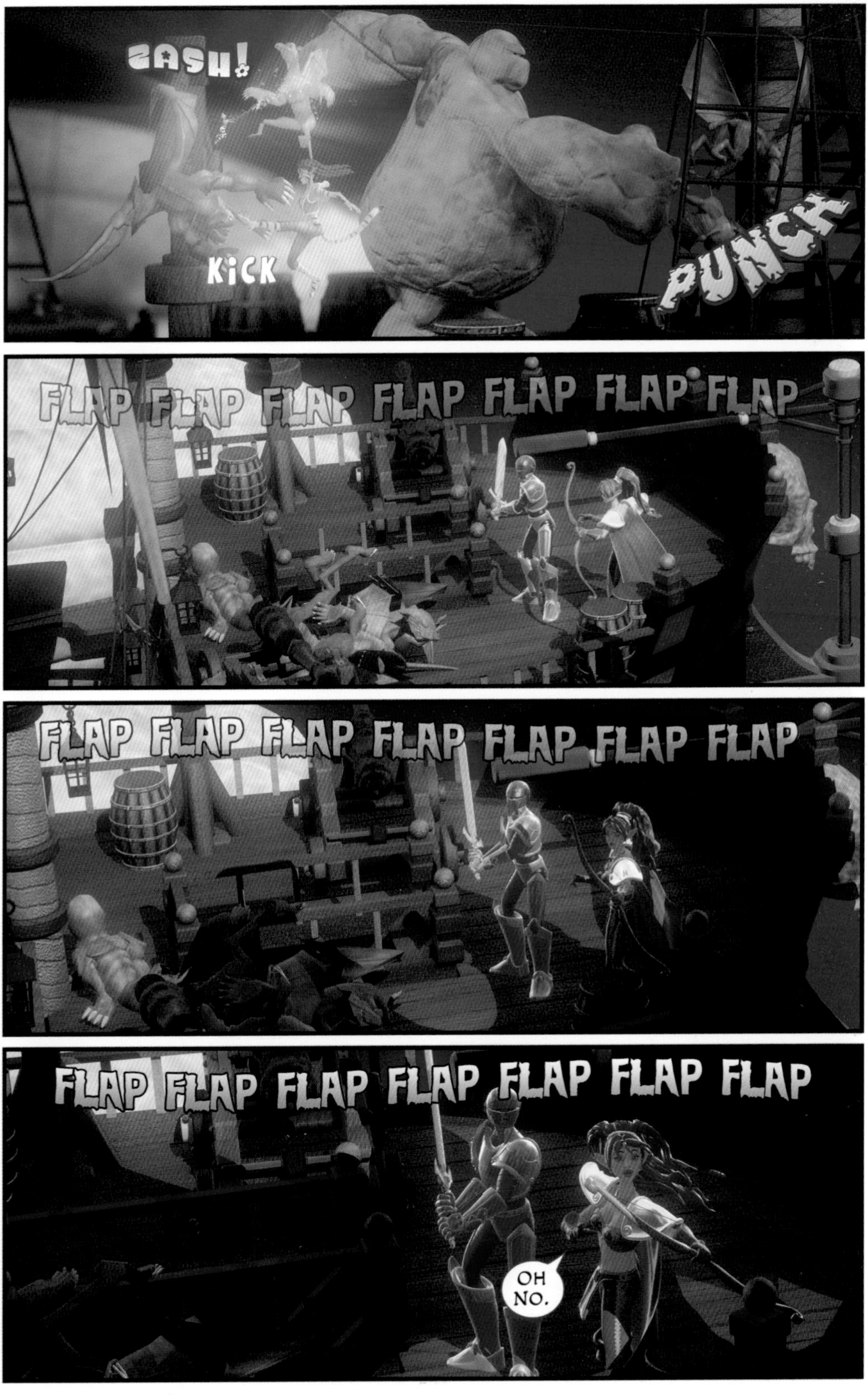
ZASH!
KICK
PUNCH
FLAP FLAP FLAP FLAP FLAP FLAP FLAP
FLAP FLAP FLAP FLAP FLAP FLAP FLAP
FLAP FLAP FLAP FLAP FLAP FLAP FLAP
OH NO.

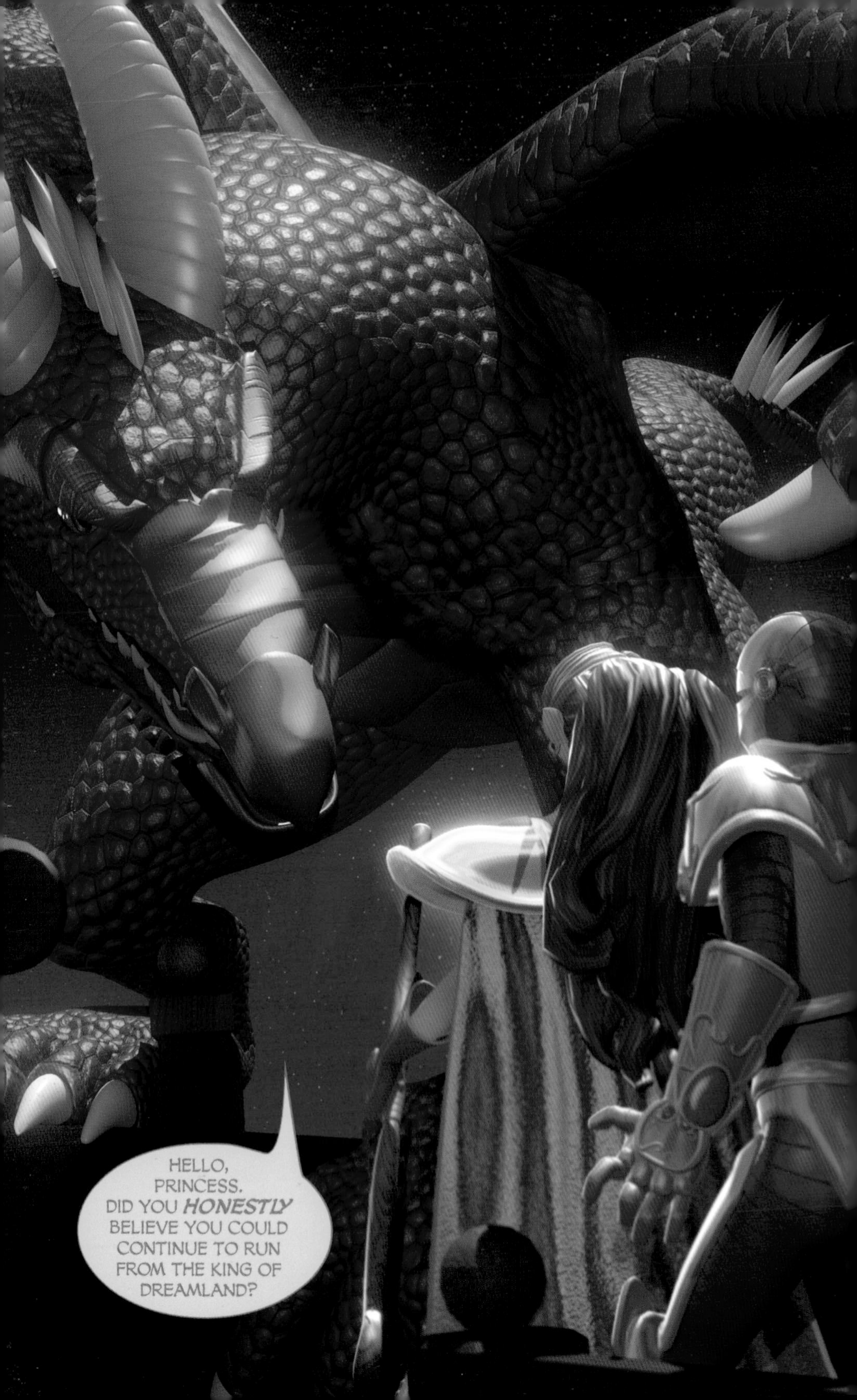
HELLO, PRINCESS. DID YOU HONESTLY BELIEVE YOU COULD CONTINUE TO RUN FROM THE KING OF DREAMLAND?

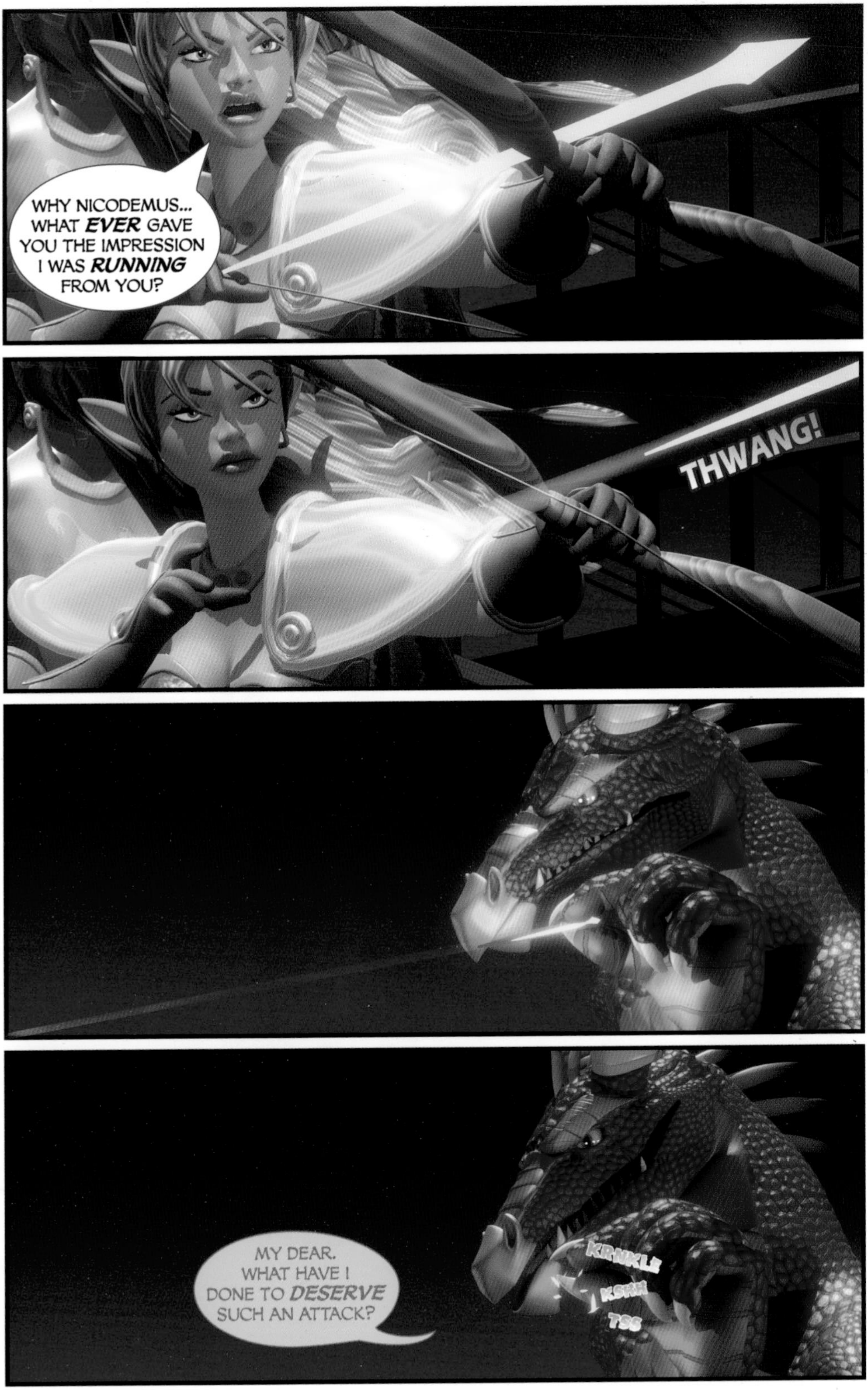
WHY NICODEMUS... WHAT EVER GAVE YOU THE IMPRESSION I WAS RUNNING FROM YOU?
THWANG!
MY DEAR. WHAT HAVE I DONE TO DESERVE SUCH AN ATTACK?
KRNKLE
KSHH
TSS

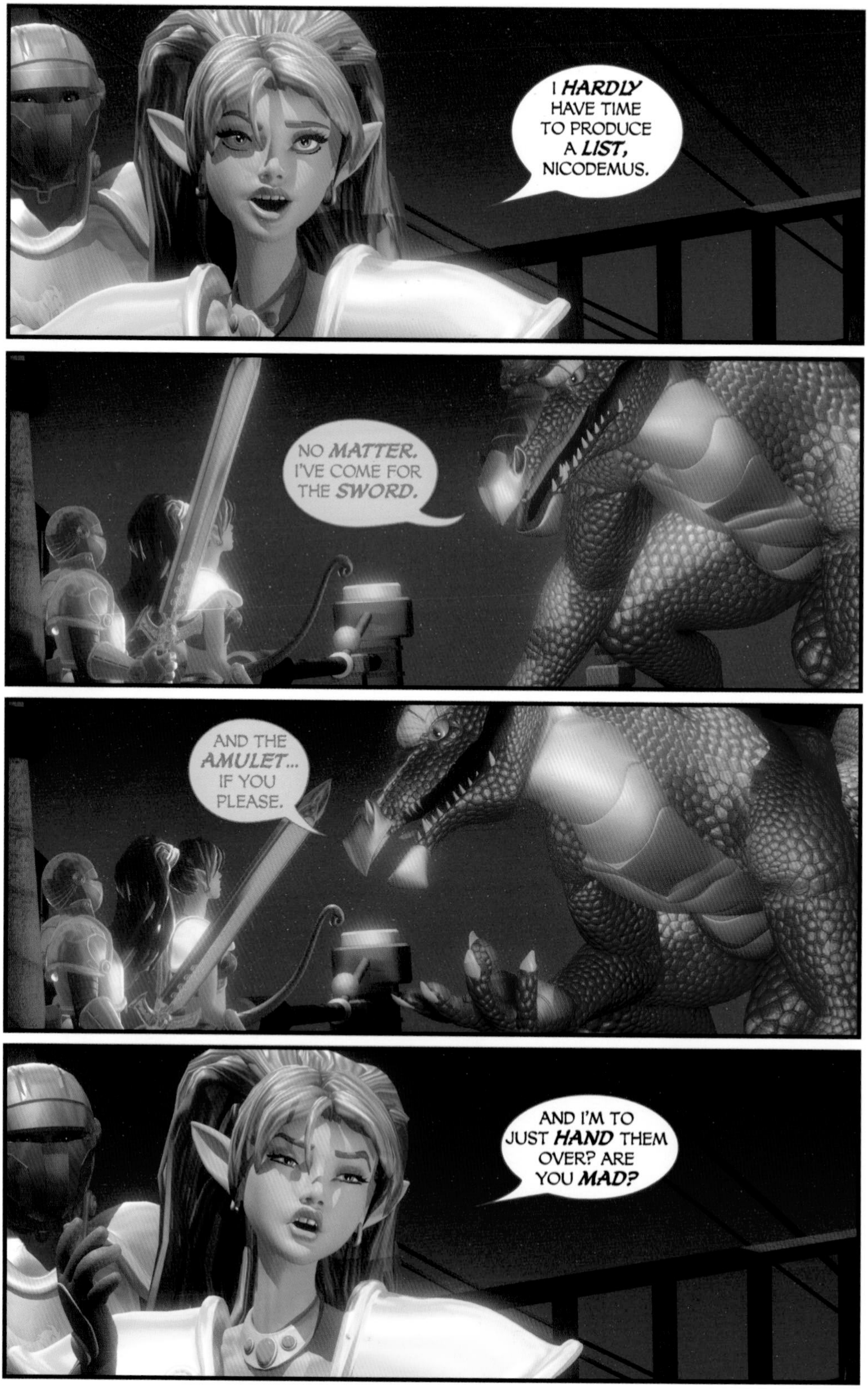
I HARDLY HAVE TIME TO PRODUCE A LIST, NICODEMUS.
NO MATTER. I'VE COME FOR THE SWORD.
AND THE AMULET... IF YOU PLEASE.
AND I'M TO JUST HAND THEM OVER? ARE YOU MAD?

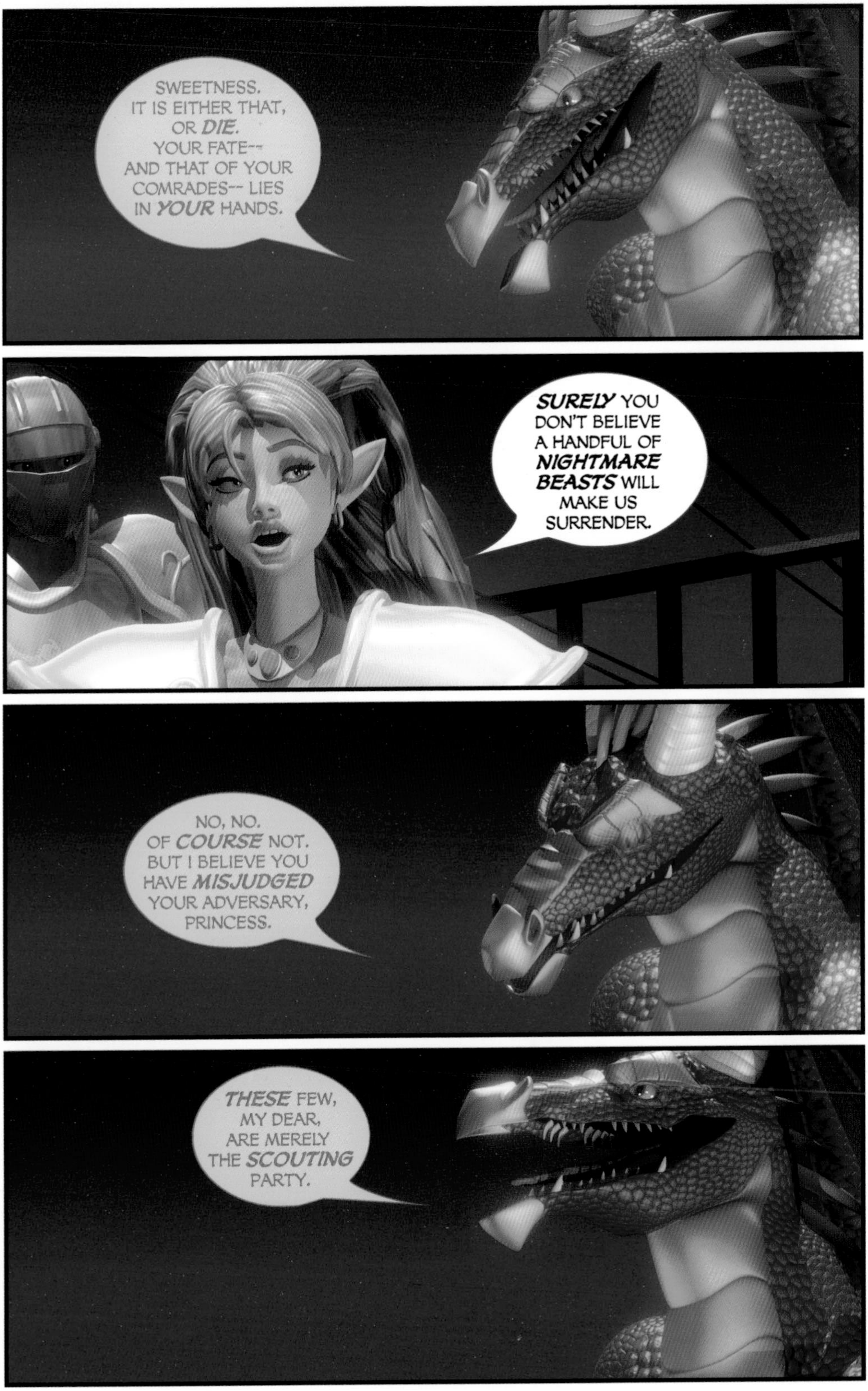
SWEETNESS. IT IS EITHER THAT, OR DIE. YOUR FATE-- AND THAT OF YOUR COMRADES-- LIES IN YOUR HANDS.
SURELY YOU DON'T BELIEVE A HANDFUL OF NIGHTMARE BEASTS WILL MAKE US SURRENDER.
NO, NO. OF COURSE NOT. BUT I BELIEVE YOU HAVE MISJUDGED YOUR ADVERSARY, PRINCESS.
THESE FEW, MY DEAR, ARE MERELY THE SCOUTING PARTY.

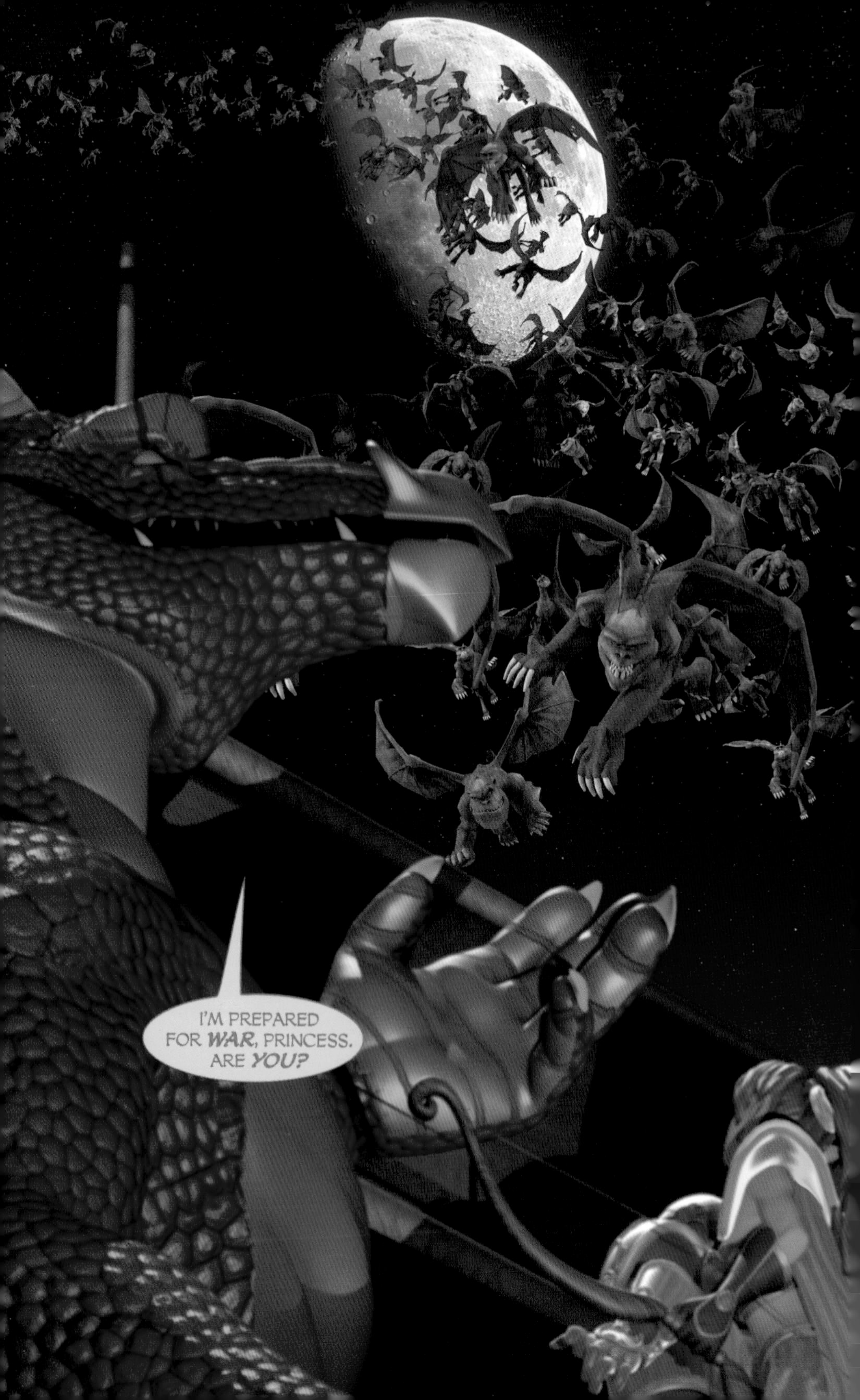
I'M PREPARED FOR WAR, PRINCESS. ARE YOU?

CHAPTER ELEVEN

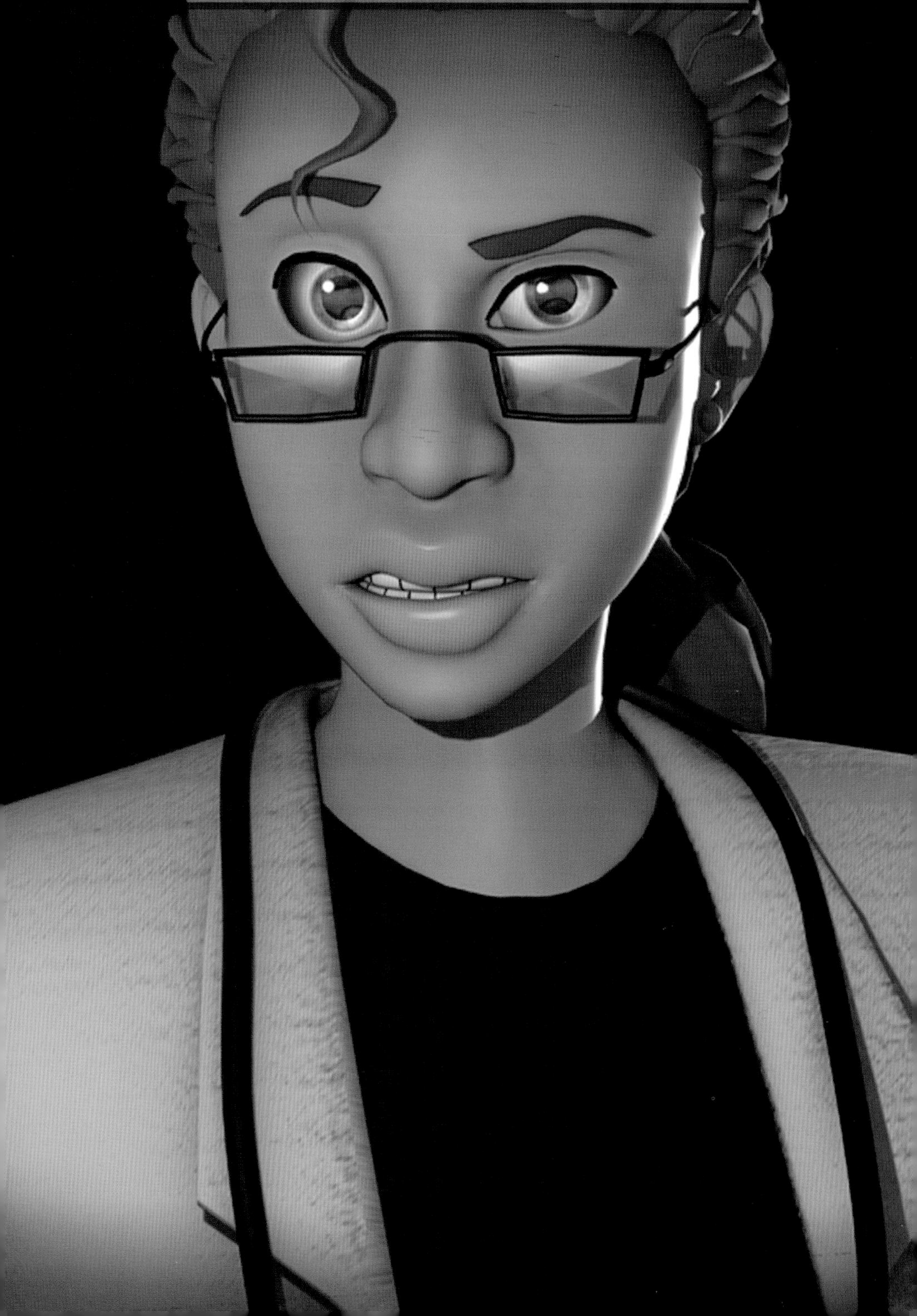

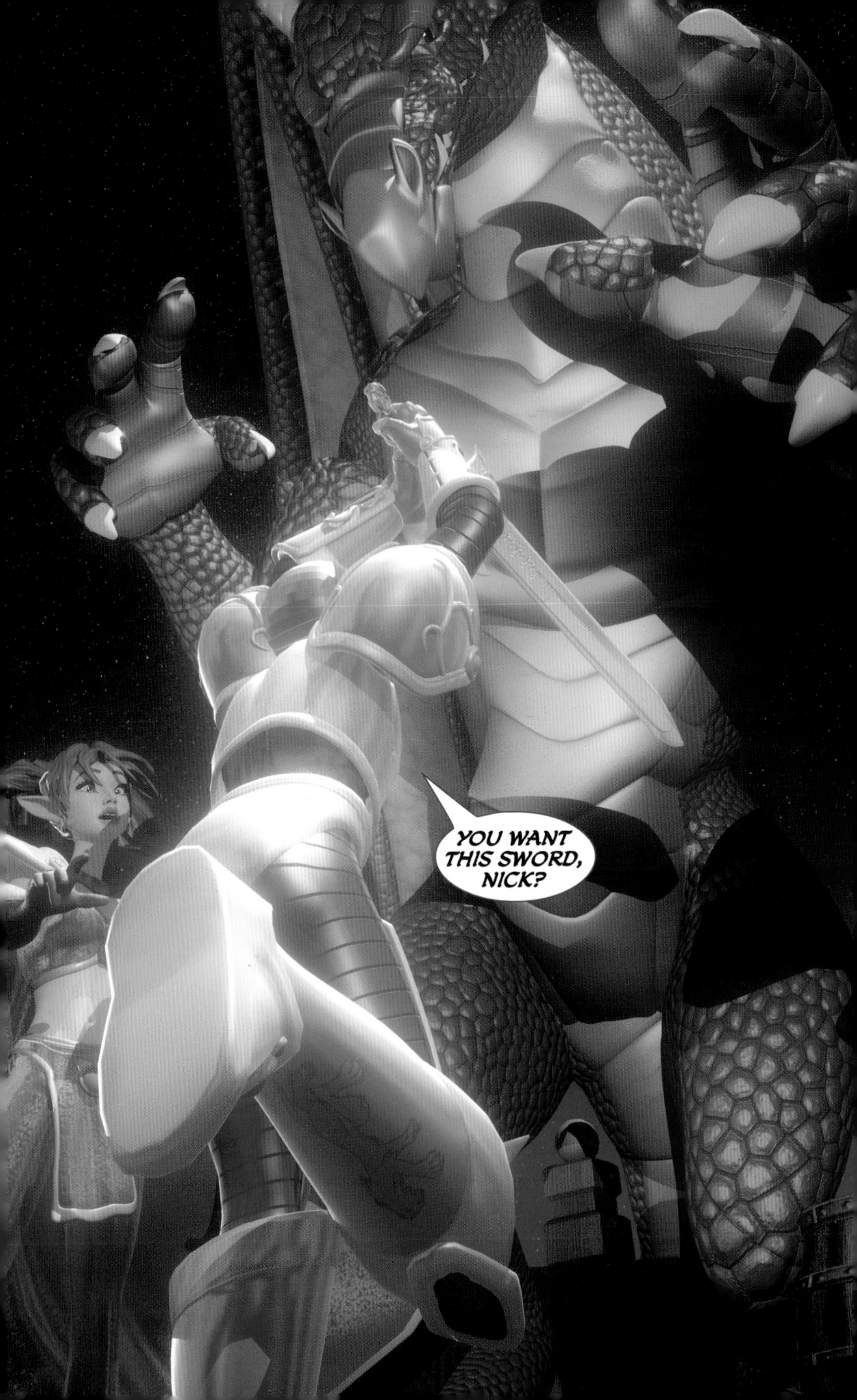
YOU WANT THIS SWORD, NICK?

TAKE IT!
SHUNK!
RAAAAR!
WRETCHED CREATURE!
WHAT MUST I DO TO END THIS RELENTLESS PLAGUE OF HUMANKIND FROM MY DOMAIN?

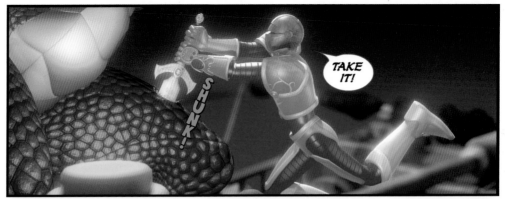

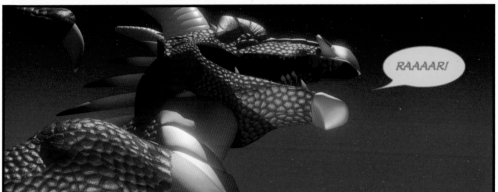

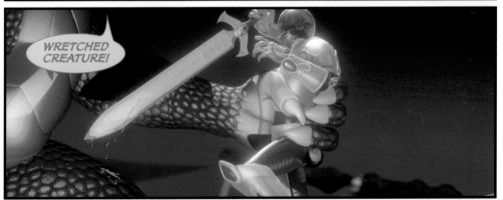

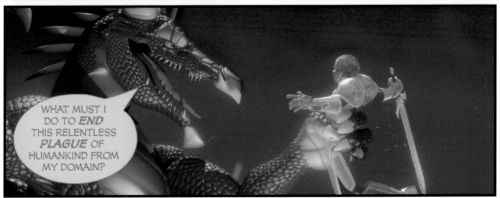

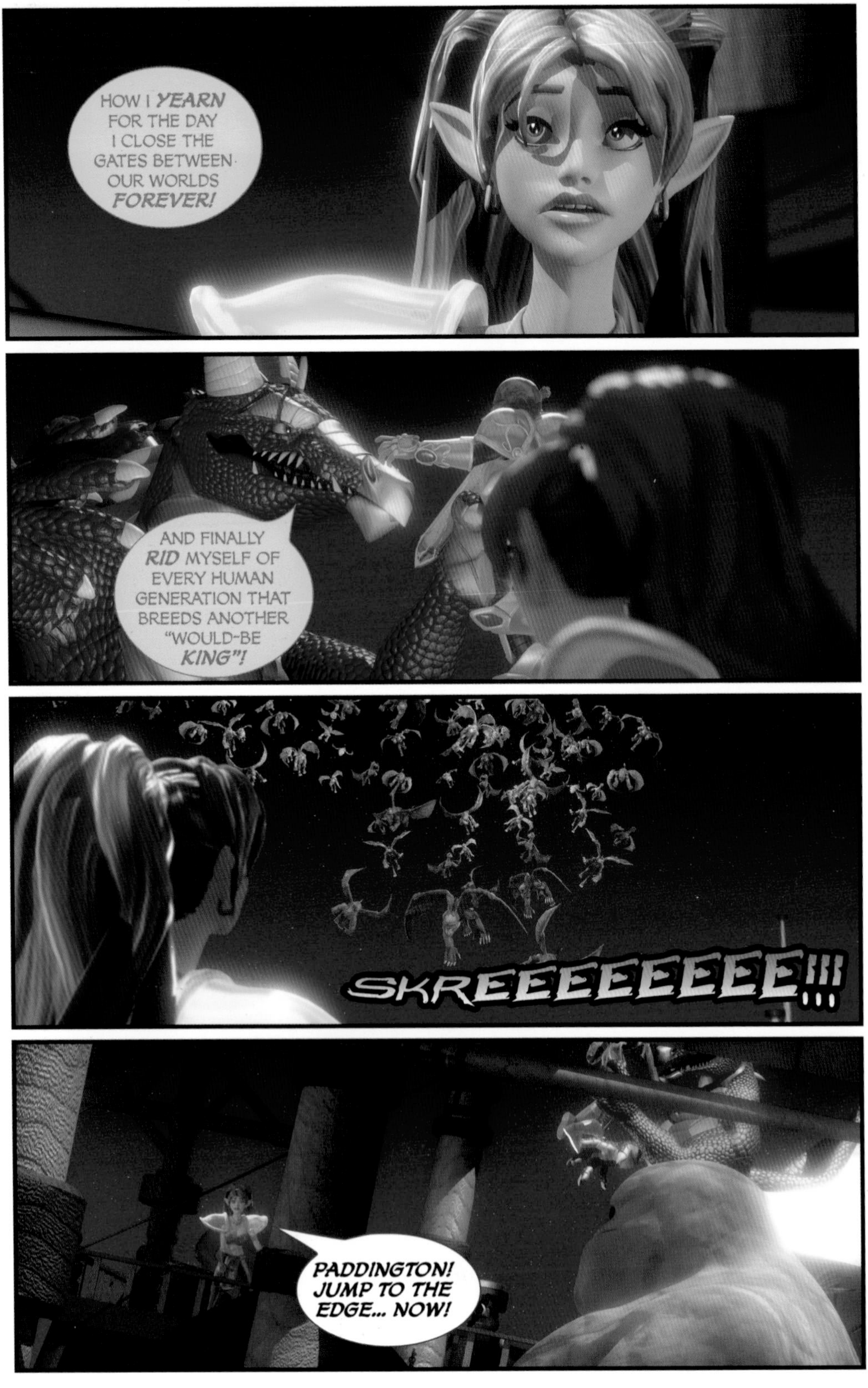
HOW I YEARN FOR THE DAY I CLOSE THE GATES BETWEEN OUR WORLDS FOREVER!
AND FINALLY RID MYSELF OF EVERY HUMAN GENERATION THAT BREEDS ANOTHER "WOULD-BE KING"!
SKREEEEEEEEEE!!!
PADDINGTON! JUMP TO THE EDGE... NOW!

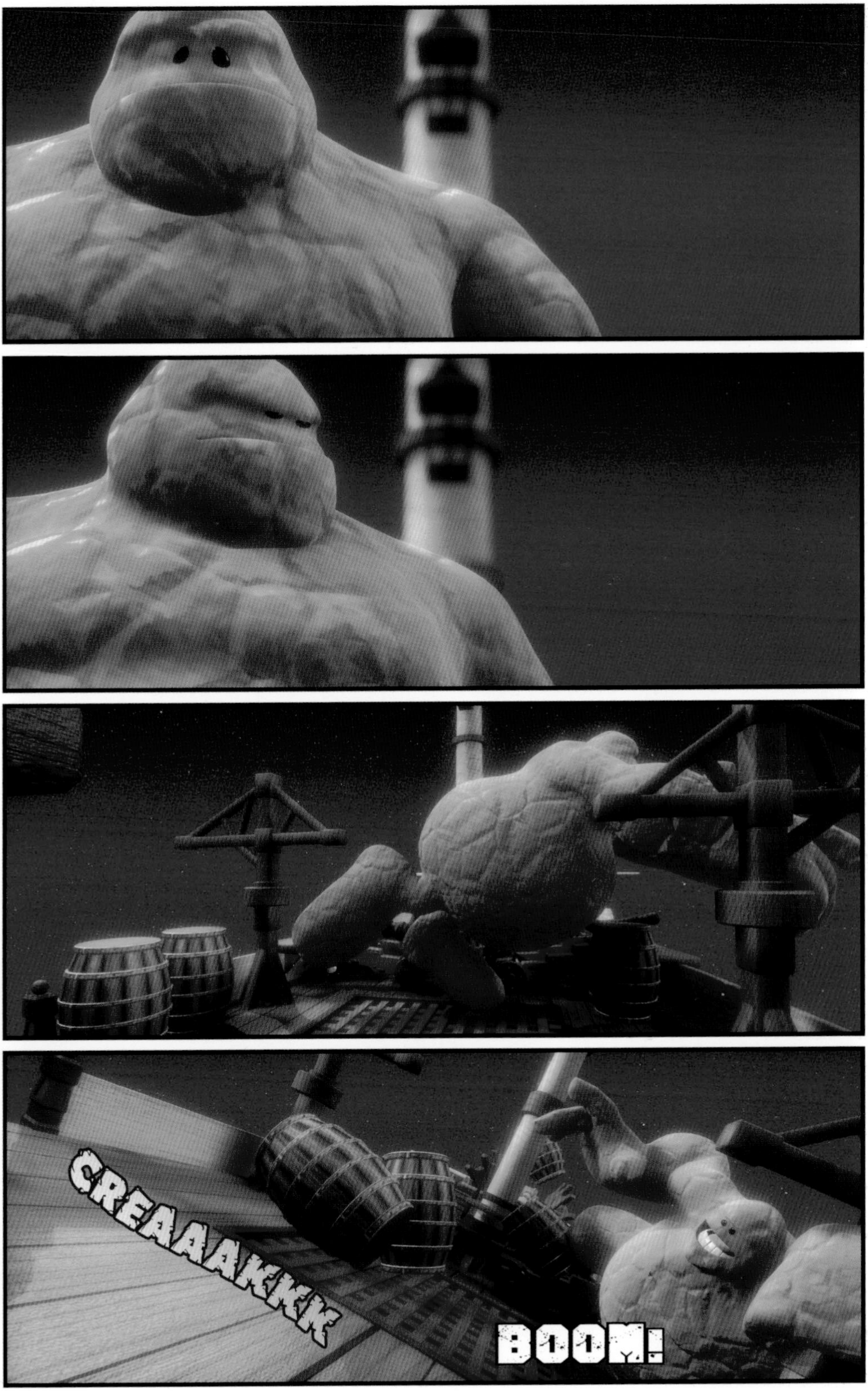
CREAAAAKKKK
BOOM!

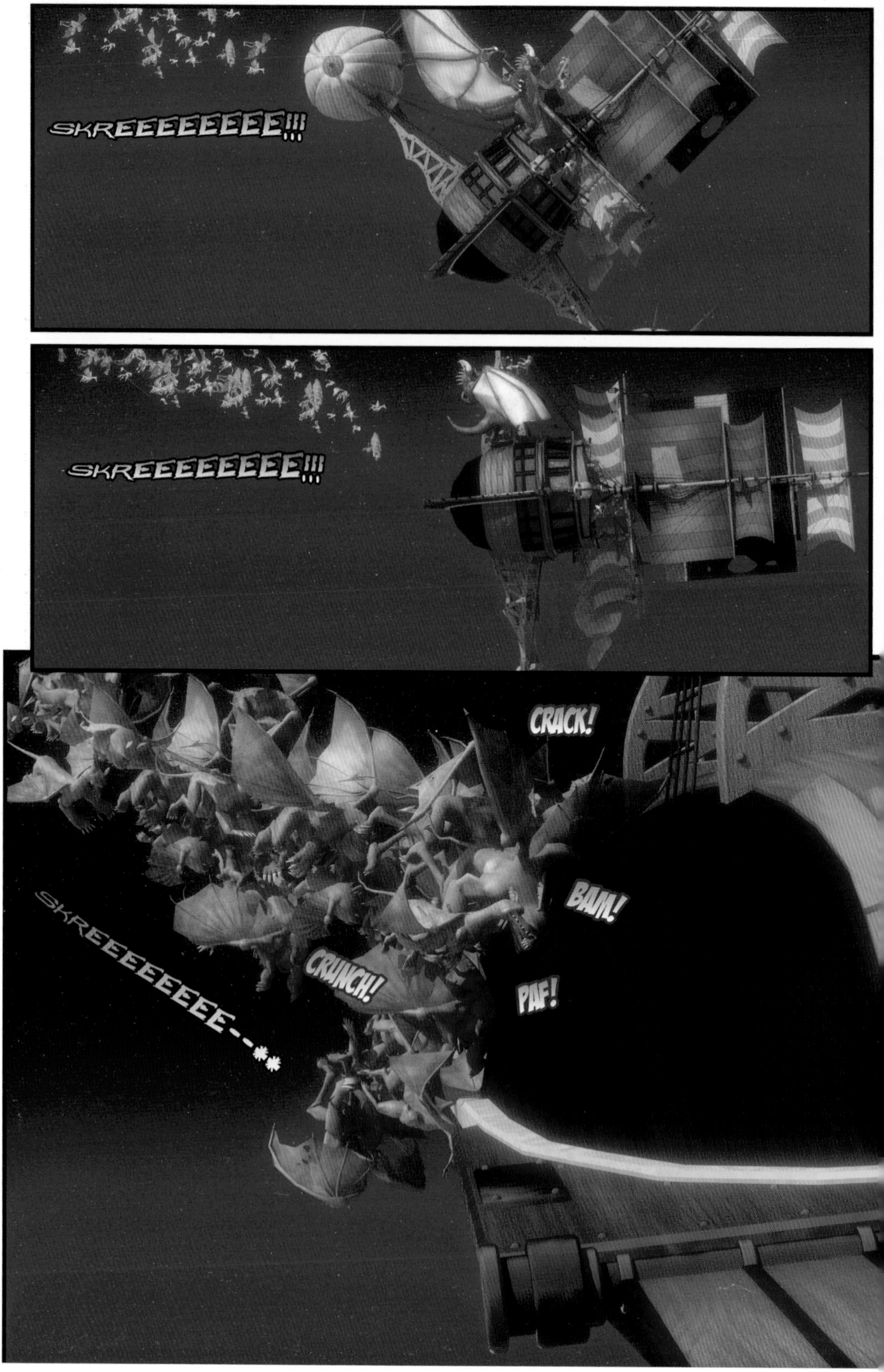
SKREEEEEEEEE!!!
SKREEEEEEEEE!!!
CRACK!
BAM!
CRUNCH!
PAF!
SKREEEEEEEEE--**

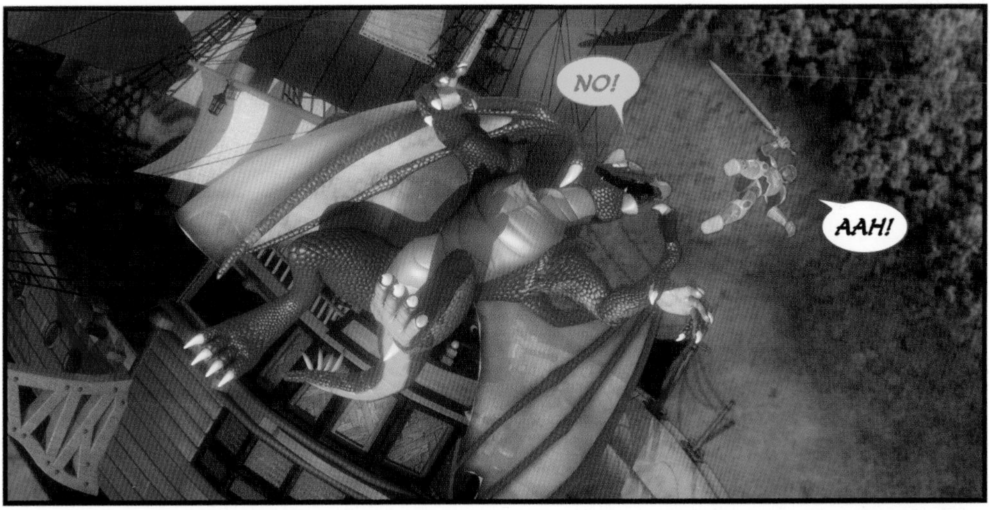
NO!
AAH!

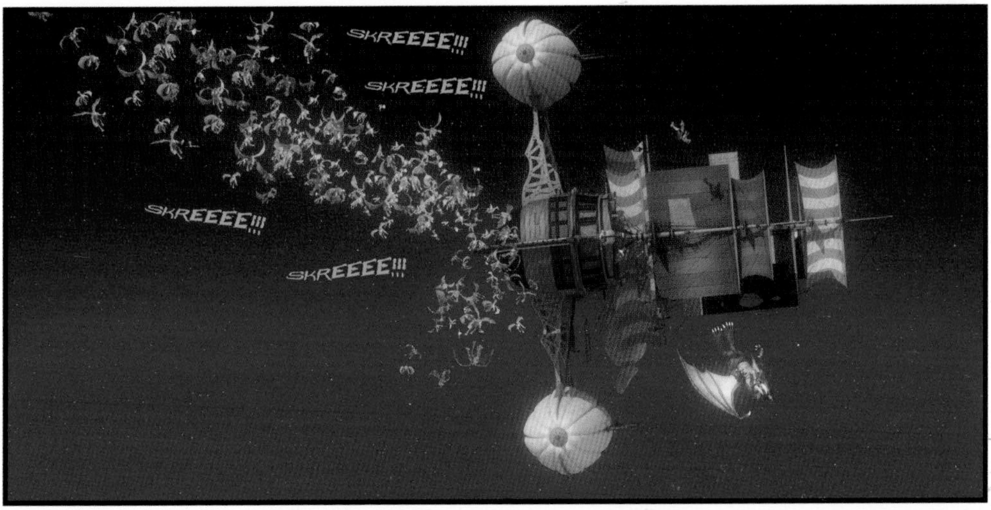
SKREEEE!!!
SKREEEE!!!
SKREEEE!!!
SKREEEE!!!

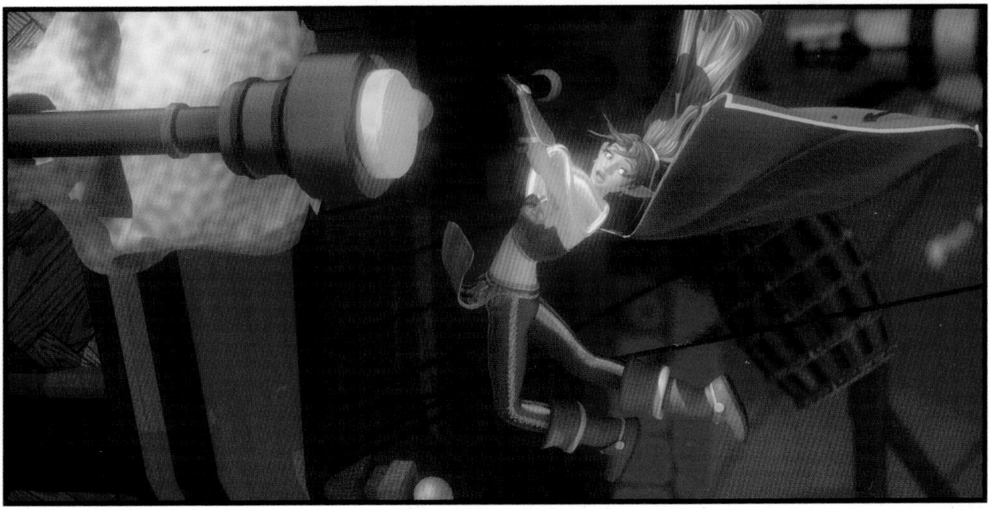

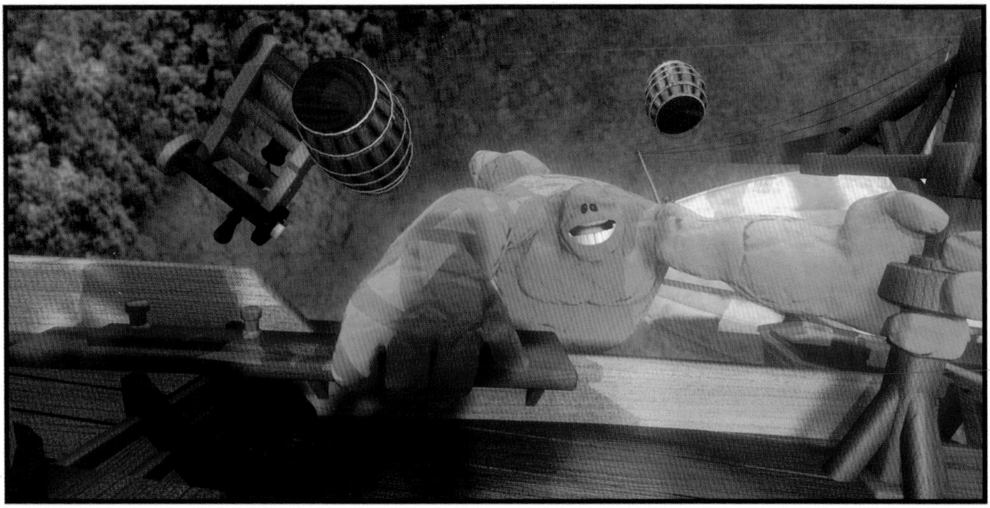

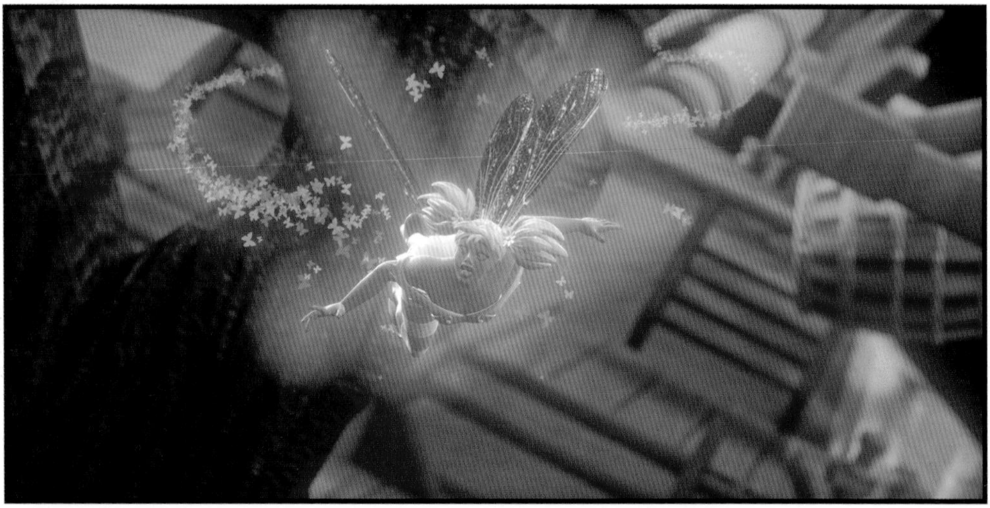

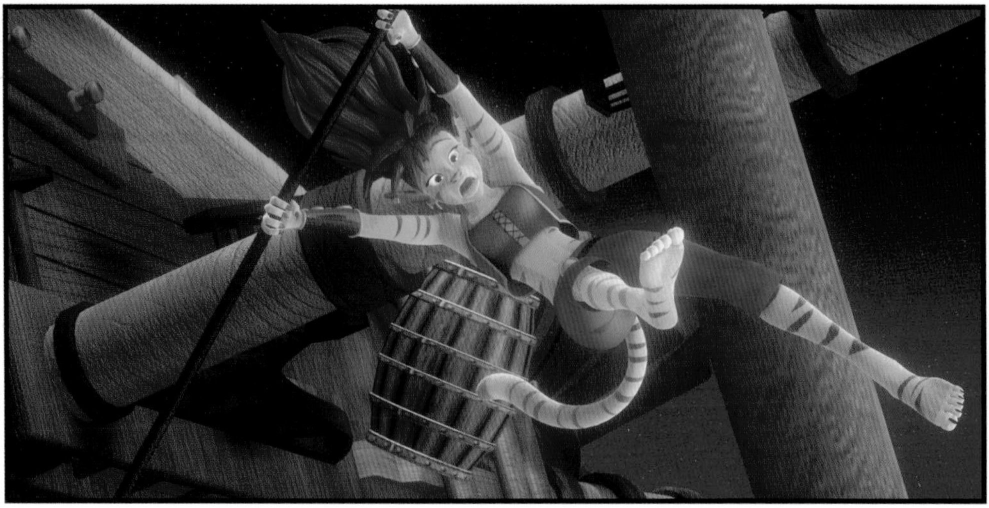

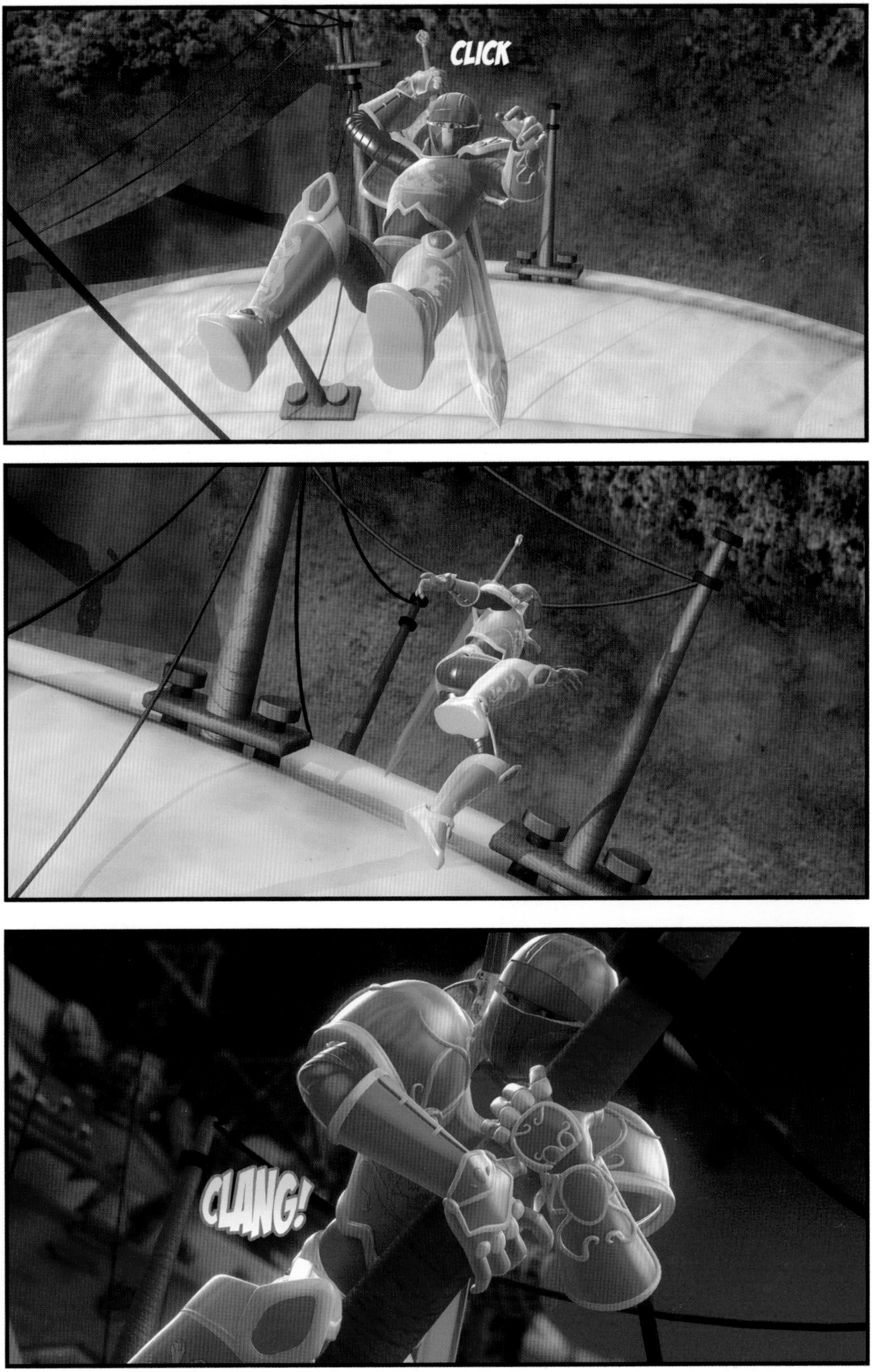
CLICK
CLANG!

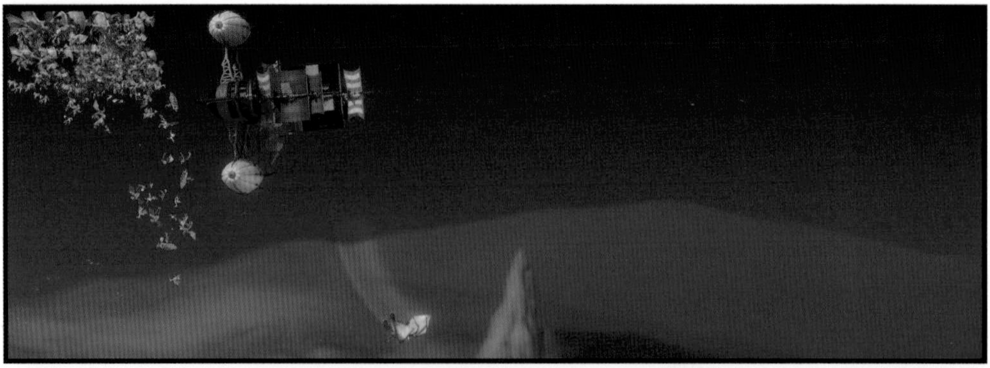

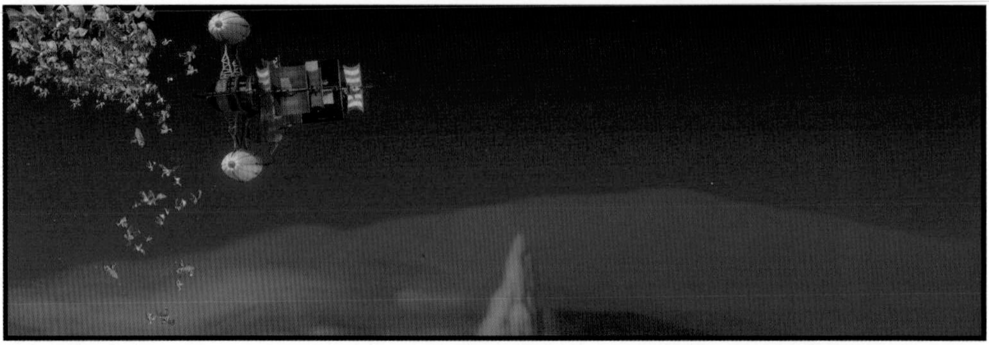

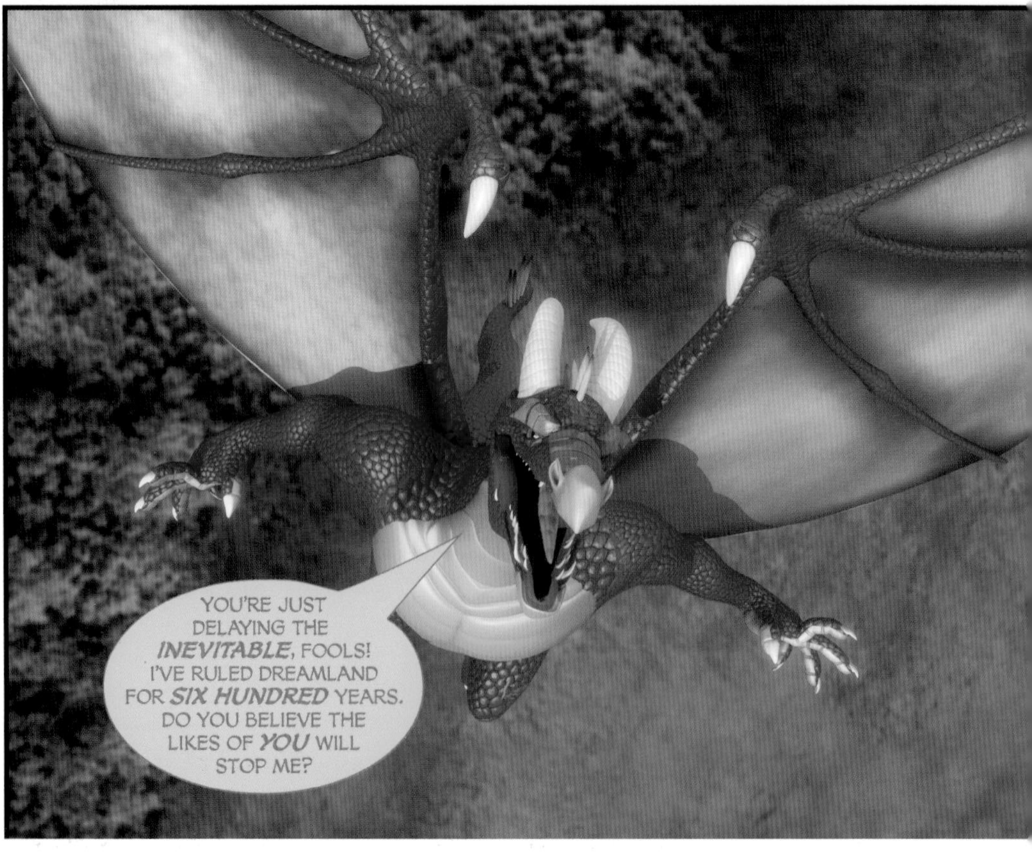
YOU'RE JUST DELAYING THE INEVITABLE, FOOLS! I'VE RULED DREAMLAND FOR SIX HUNDRED YEARS. DO YOU BELIEVE THE LIKES OF YOU WILL STOP ME?

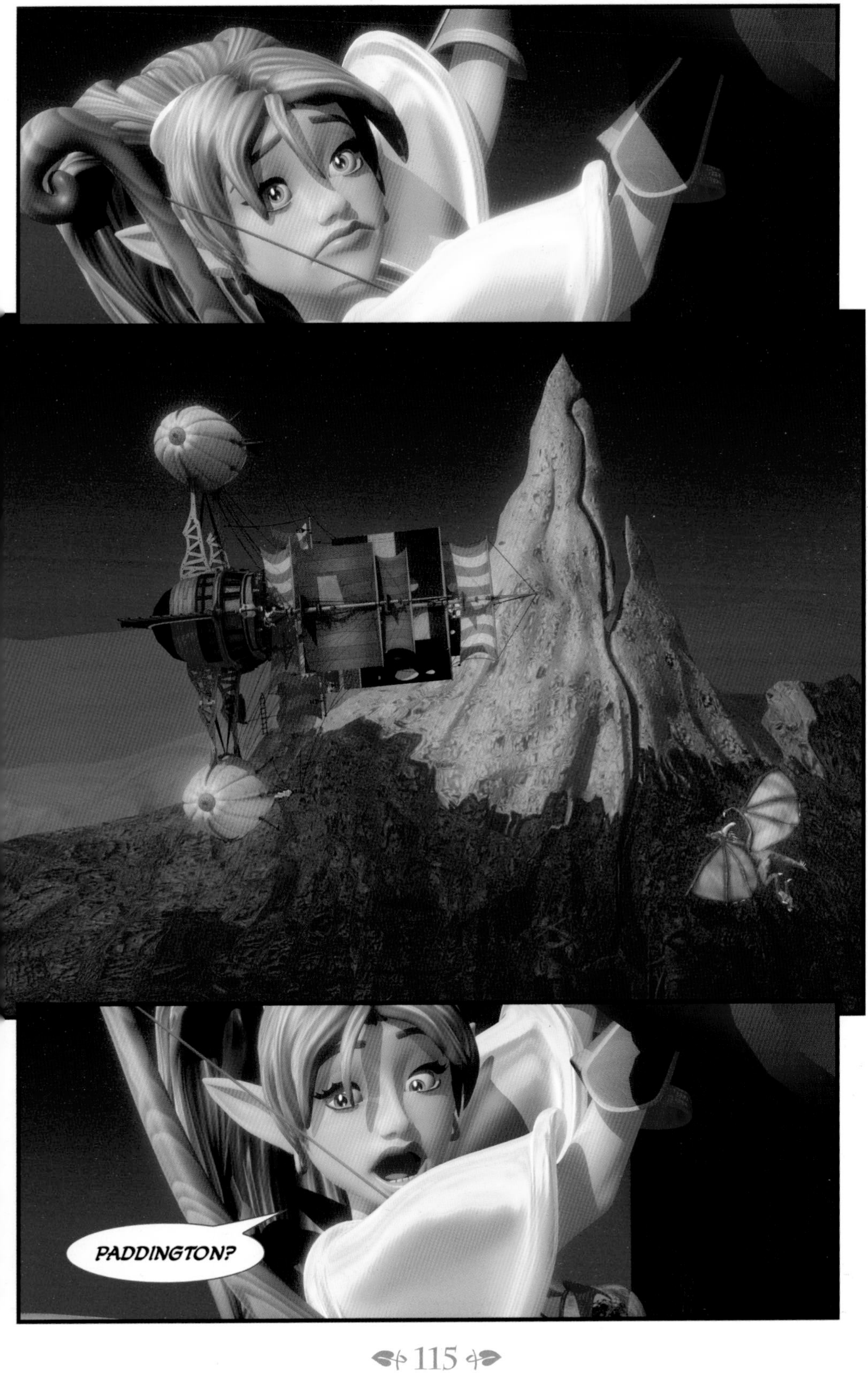
PADDINGTON?

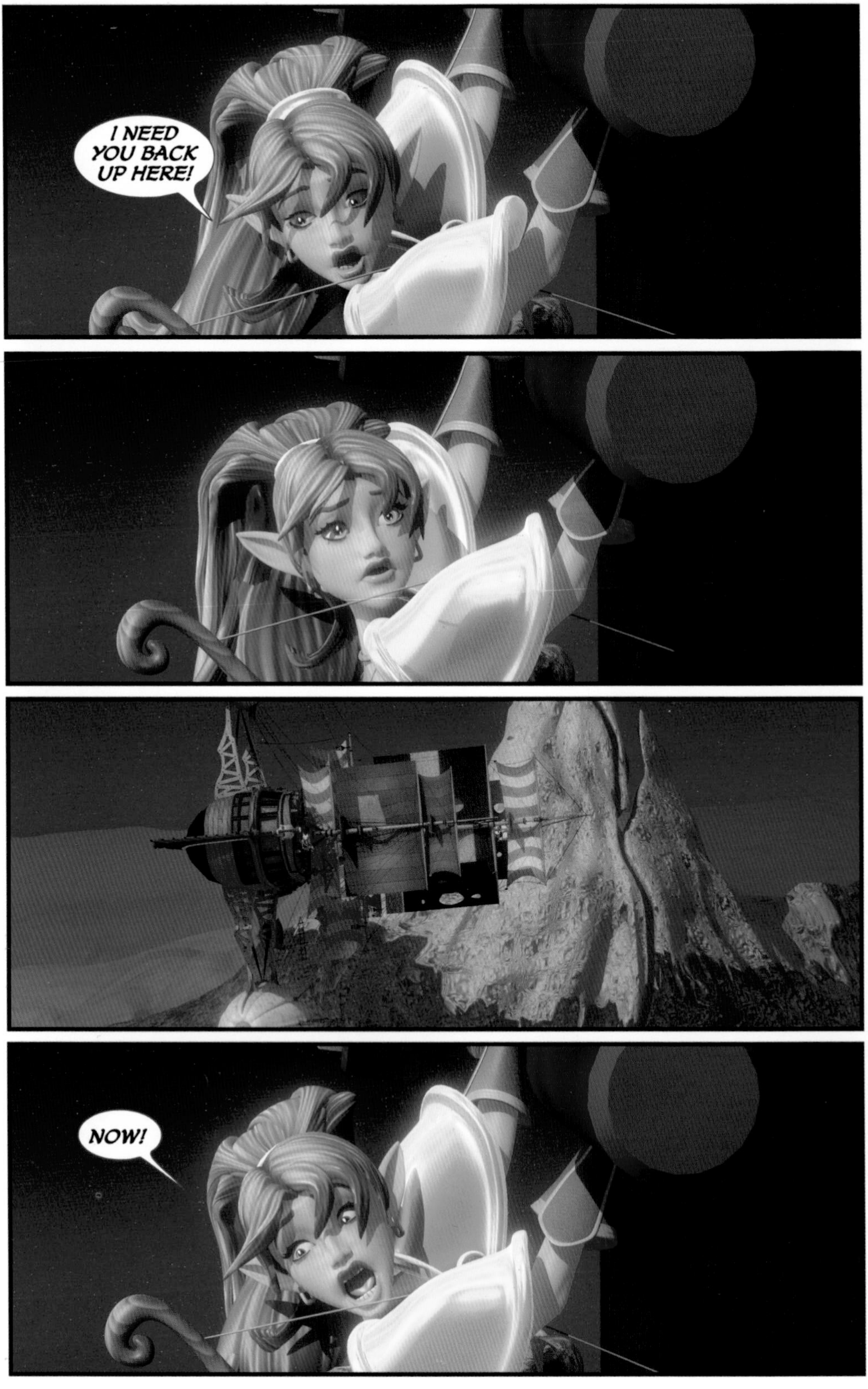
I NEED YOU BACK UP HERE!
NOW!

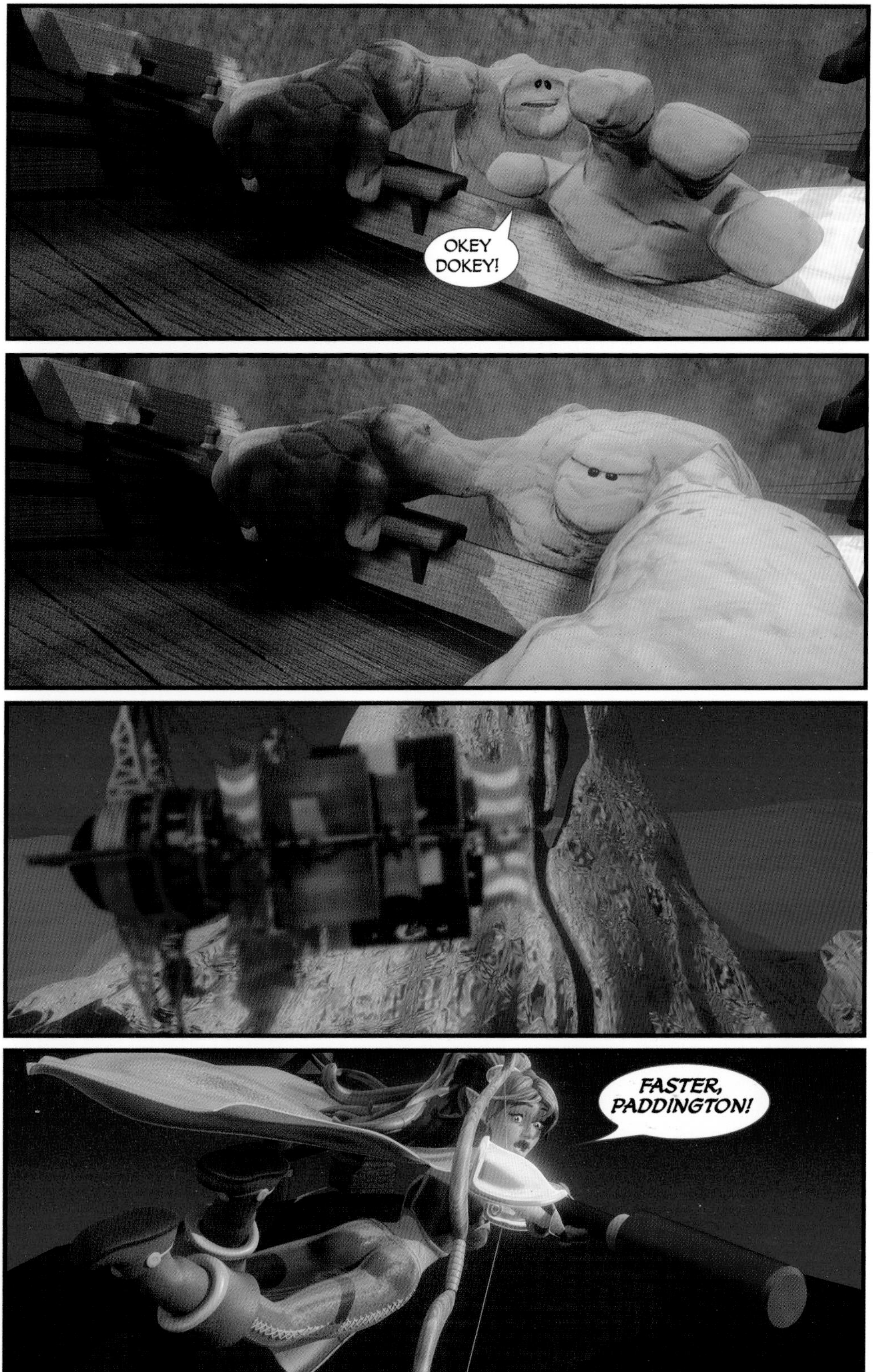
OKEY DOKEY!
FASTER, PADDINGTON!

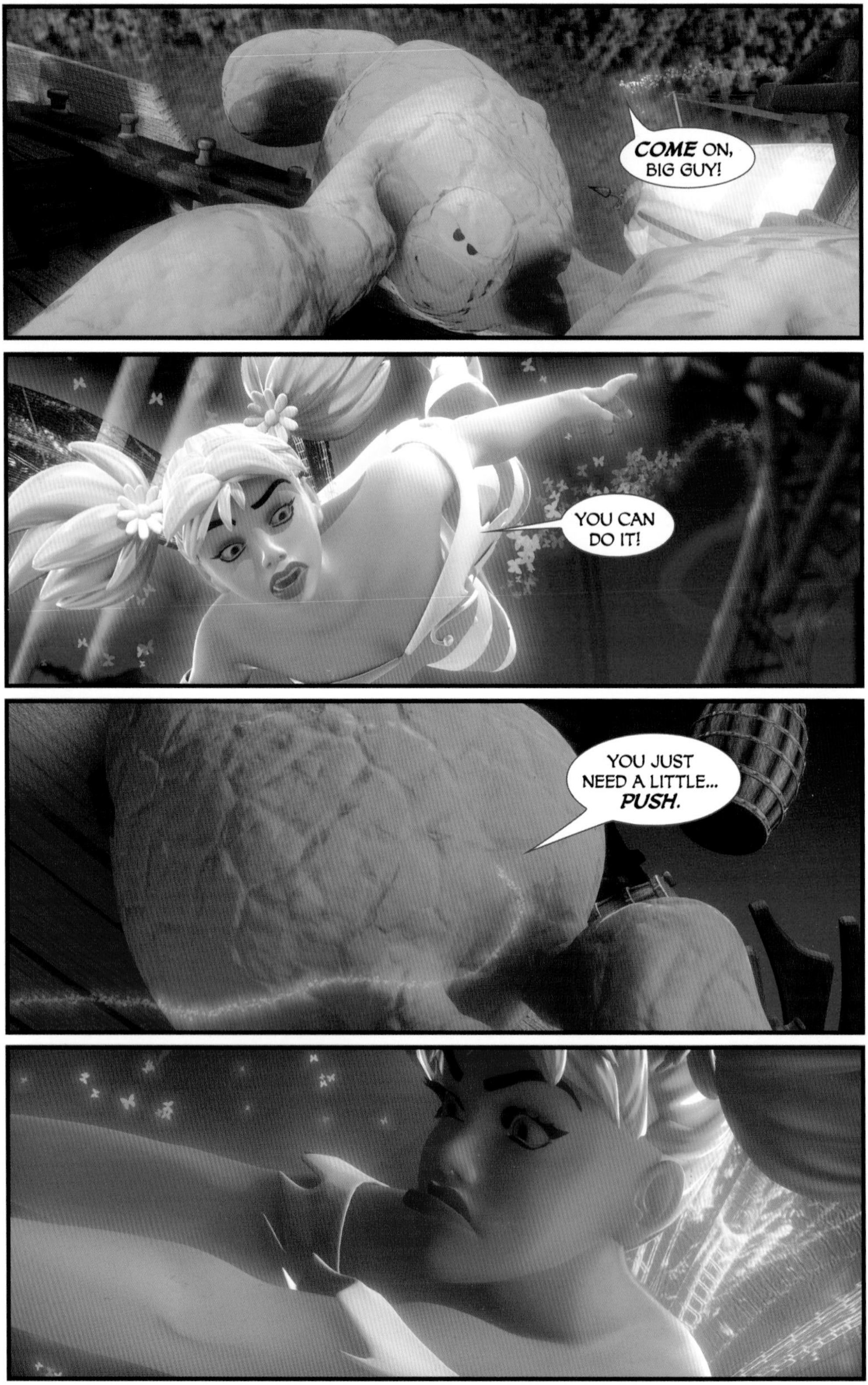
COME ON, BIG GUY!
YOU CAN DO IT!
YOU JUST NEED A LITTLE... PUSH.

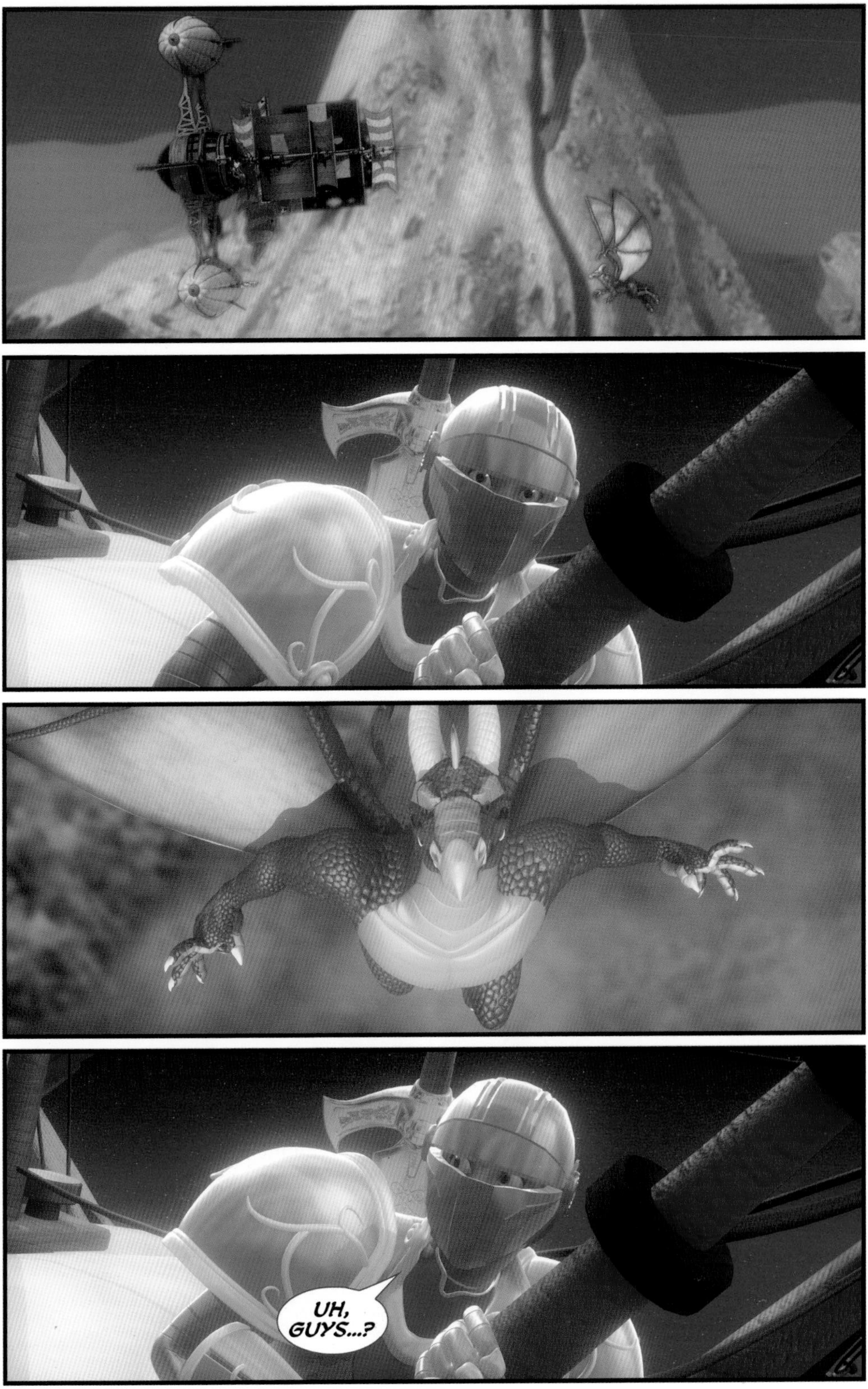
UH, GUYS...?

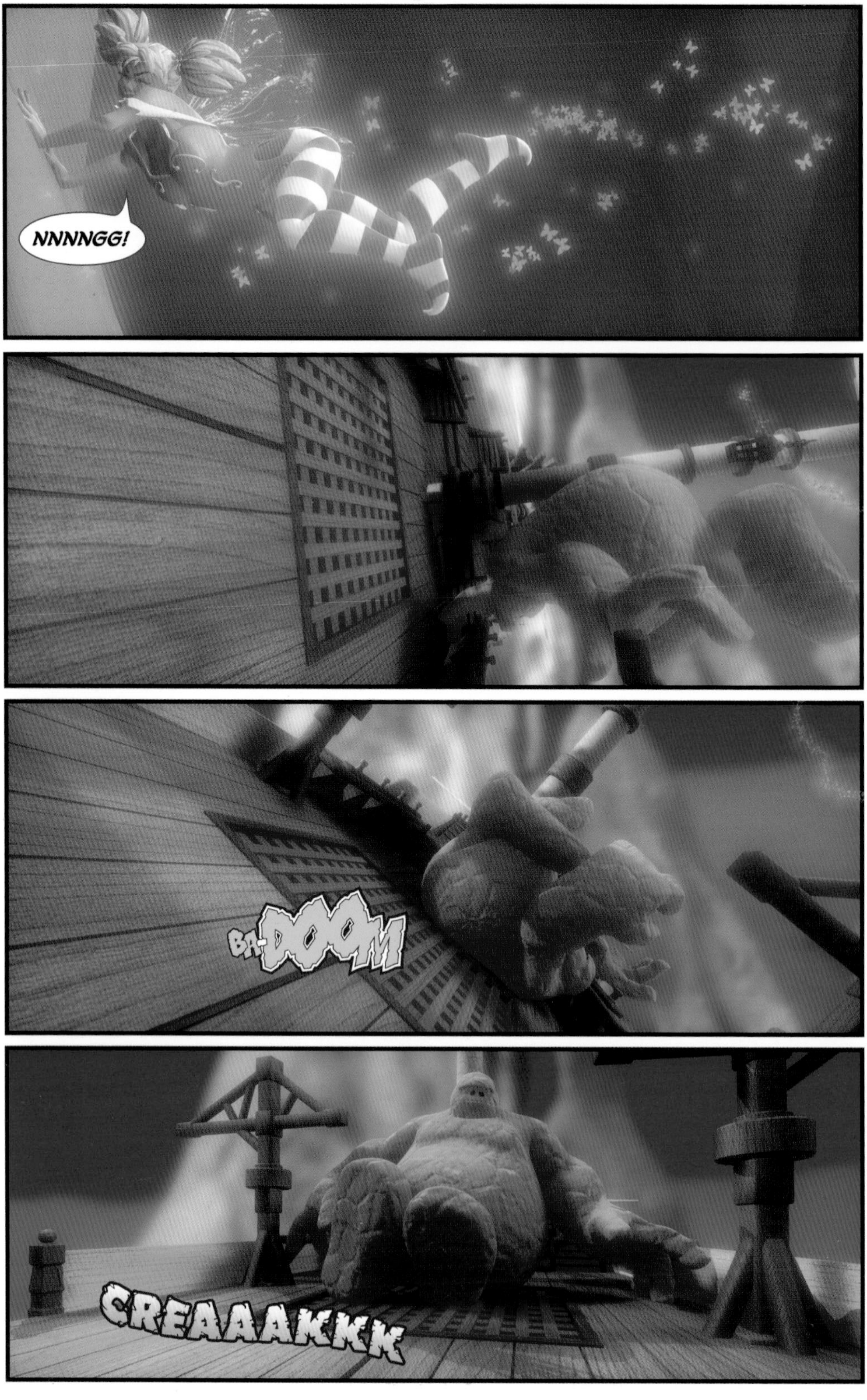
NNNNGG!
BA-DOOM
CREAAAKKK

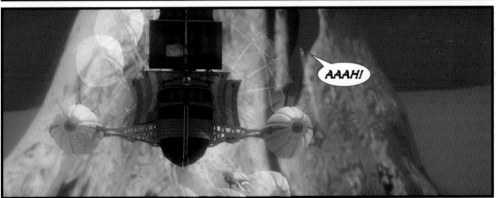

AAAH!

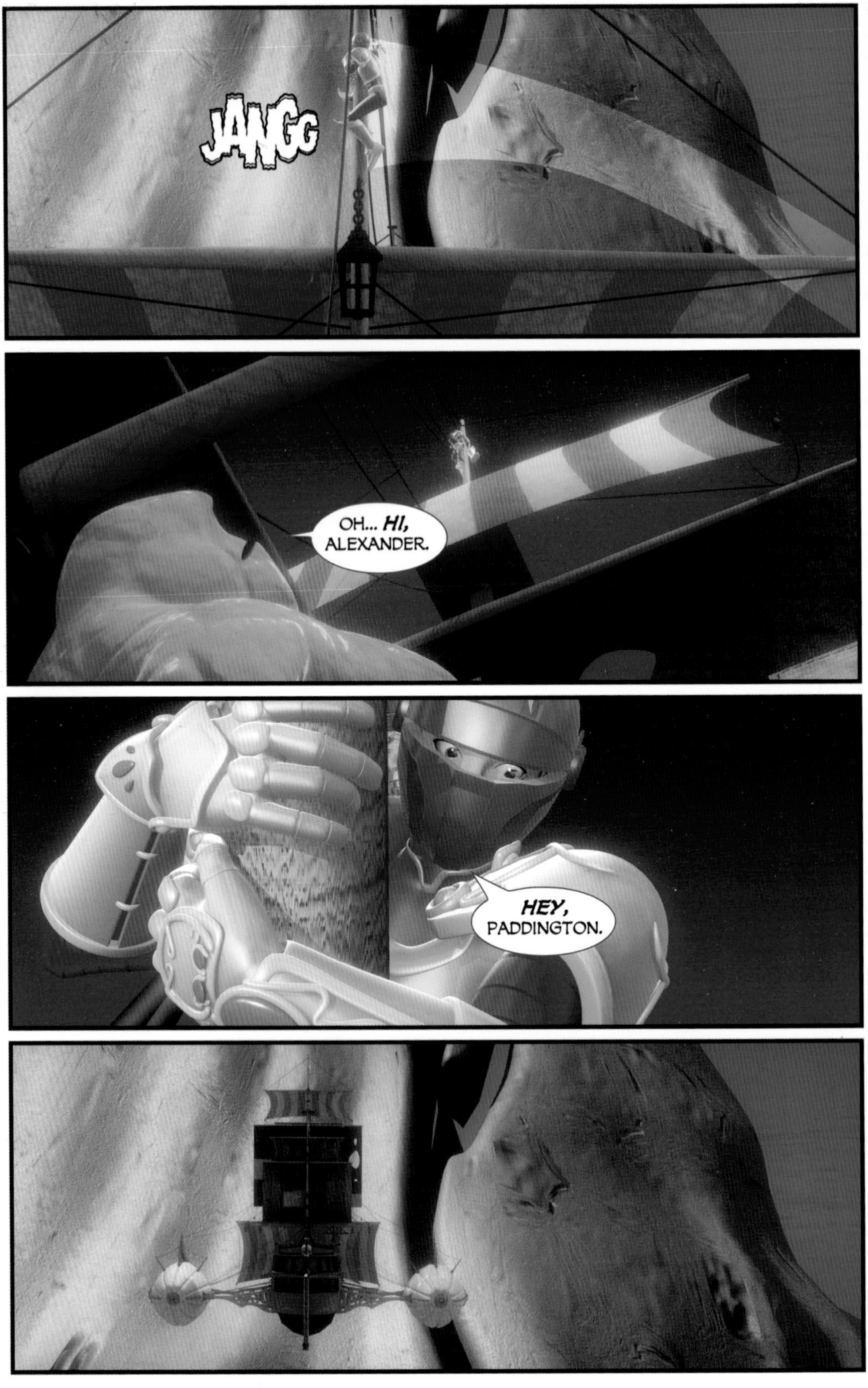
JANGG
OH... HI, ALEXANDER.
HEY, PADDINGTON.

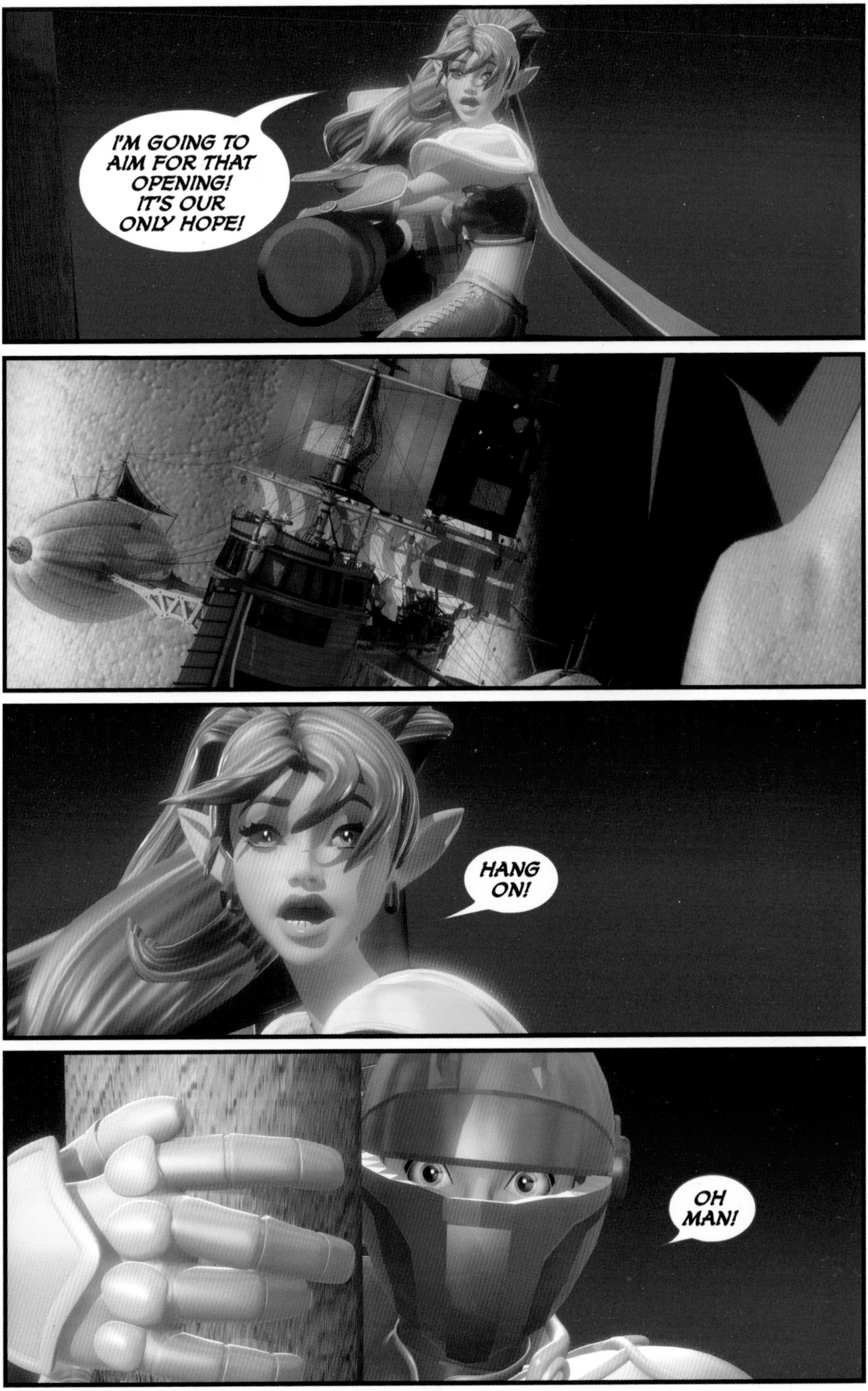
I'M GOING TO AIM FOR THAT OPENING! IT'S OUR ONLY HOPE!
HANG ON!
OH MAN!

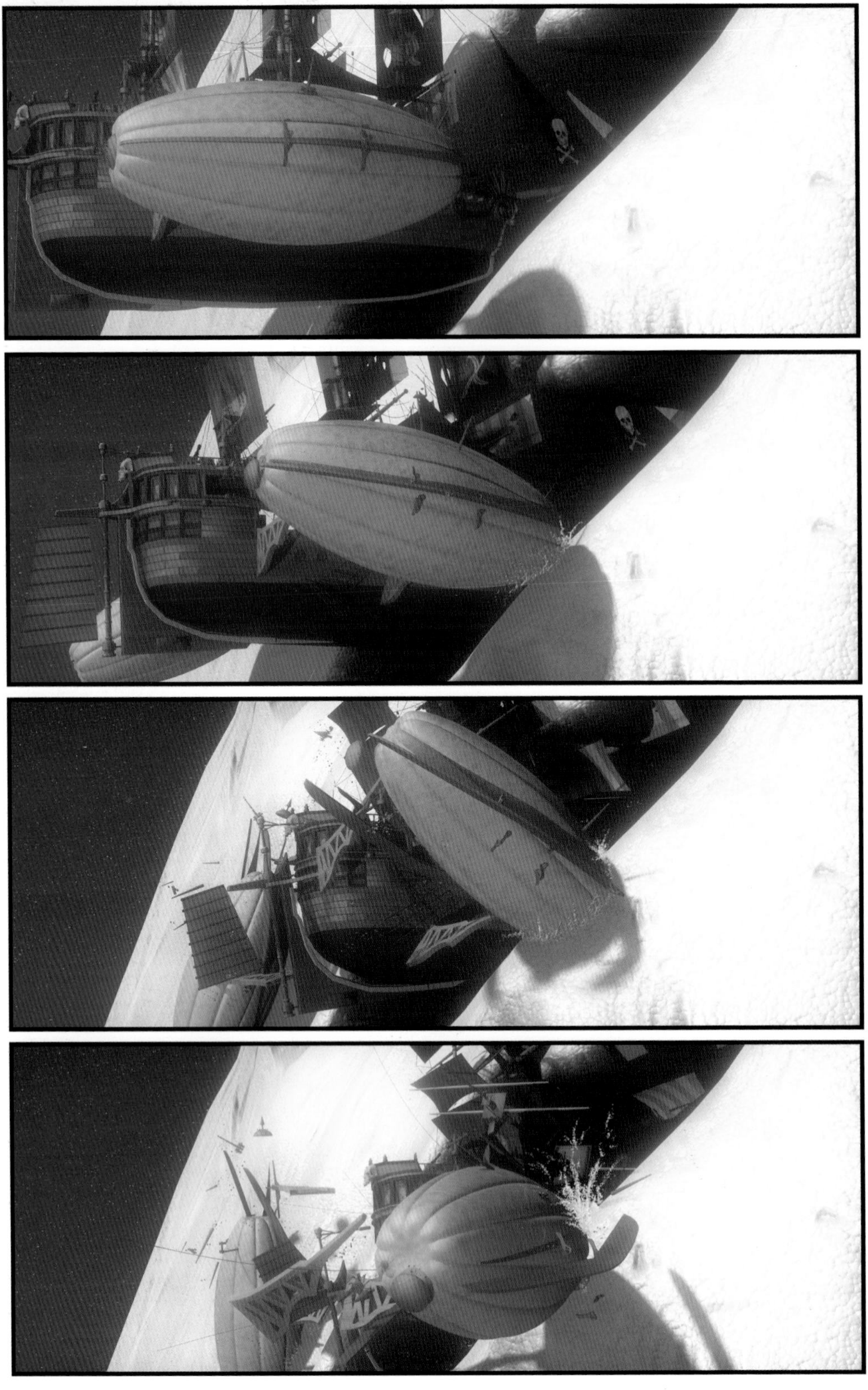

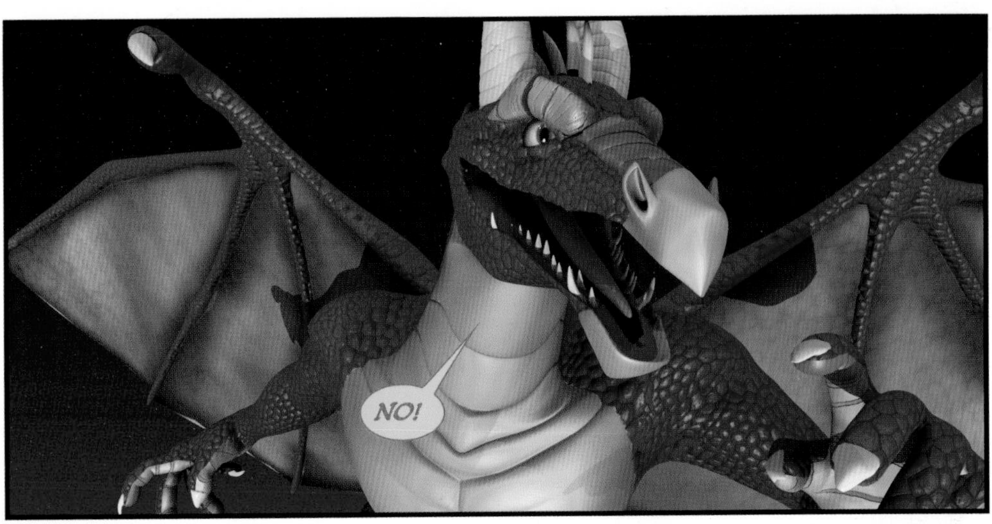
NO!

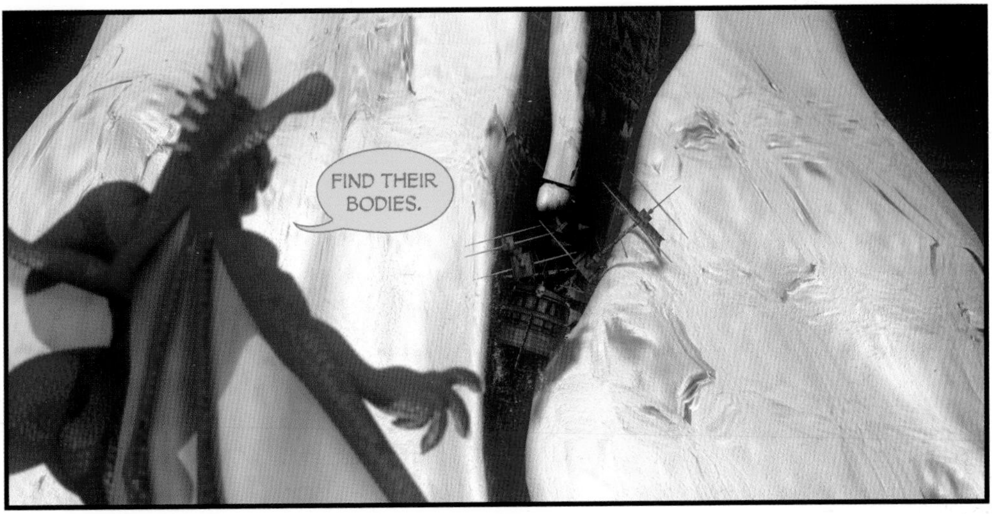
FIND THEIR BODIES.

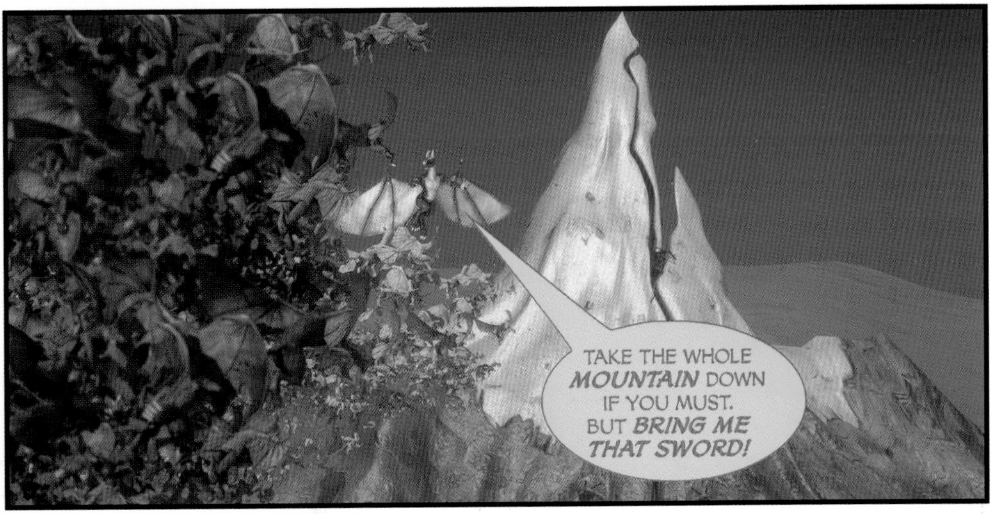
TAKE THE WHOLE MOUNTAIN DOWN IF YOU MUST. BUT BRING ME THAT SWORD!

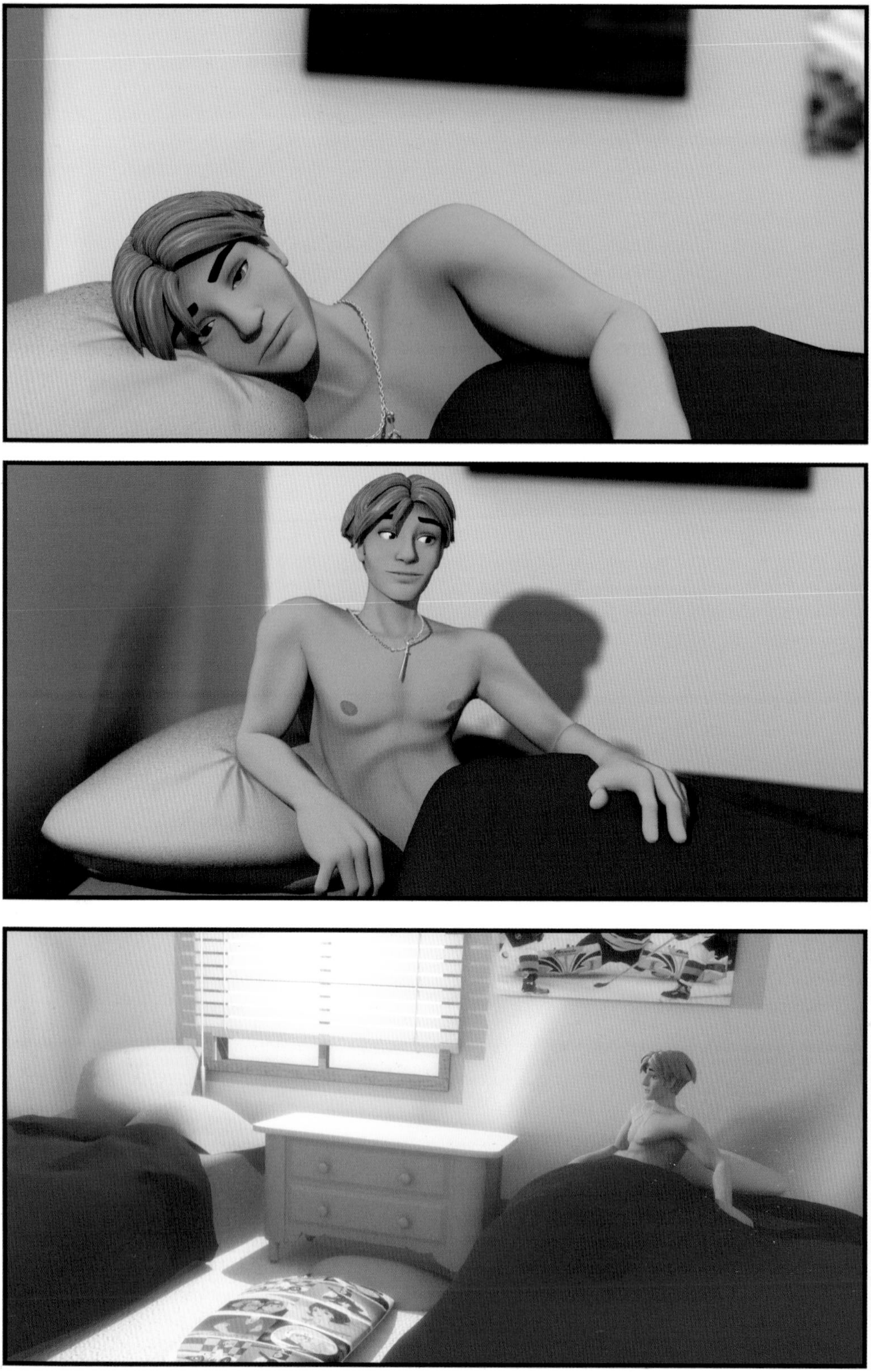

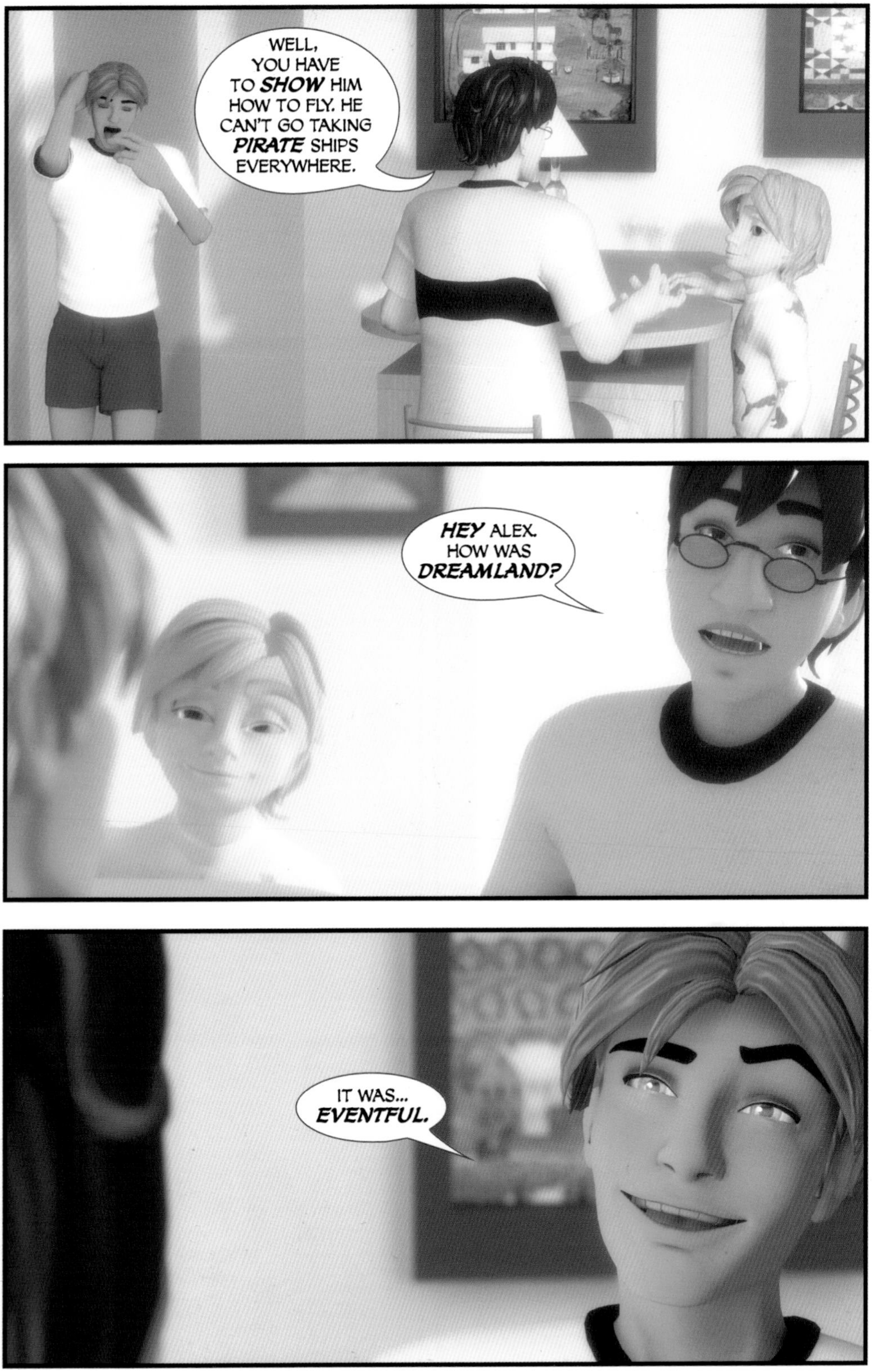
WELL, YOU HAVE TO SHOW HIM HOW TO FLY. HE CAN'T GO TAKING PIRATE SHIPS EVERYWHERE.
HEY ALEX. HOW WAS DREAMLAND?
IT WAS... EVENTFUL.

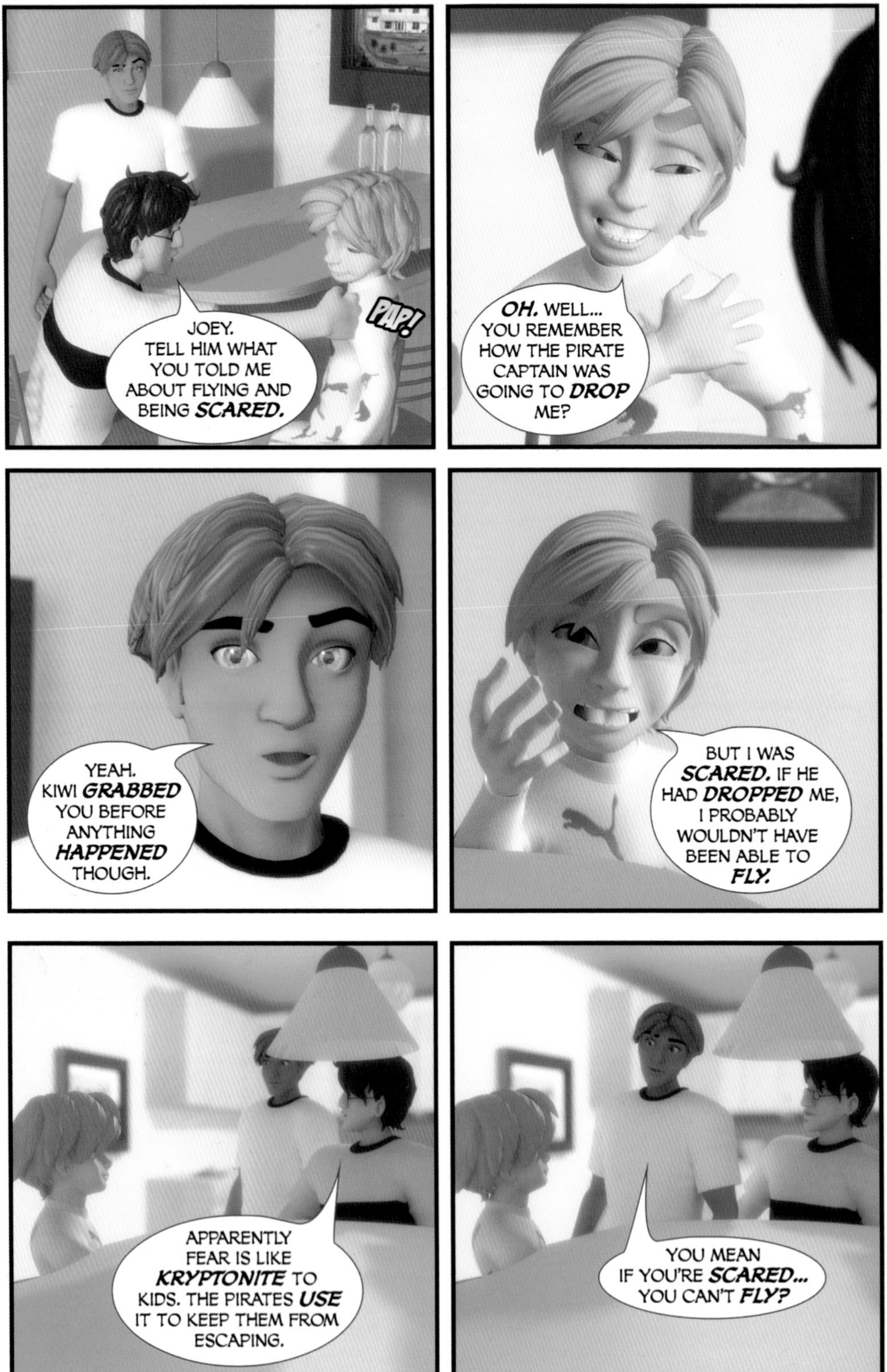
PAP!
JOEY. TELL HIM WHAT YOU TOLD ME ABOUT FLYING AND BEING SCARED.
OH. WELL... YOU REMEMBER HOW THE PIRATE CAPTAIN WAS GOING TO DROP ME?
YEAH. KIWI GRABBED YOU BEFORE ANYTHING HAPPENED THOUGH.
BUT I WAS SCARED. IF HE HAD DROPPED ME, I PROBABLY WOULDN'T HAVE BEEN ABLE TO FLY.
APPARENTLY FEAR IS LIKE KRYPTONITE TO KIDS. THE PIRATES USE IT TO KEEP THEM FROM ESCAPING.
YOU MEAN IF YOU'RE SCARED... YOU CAN'T FLY?

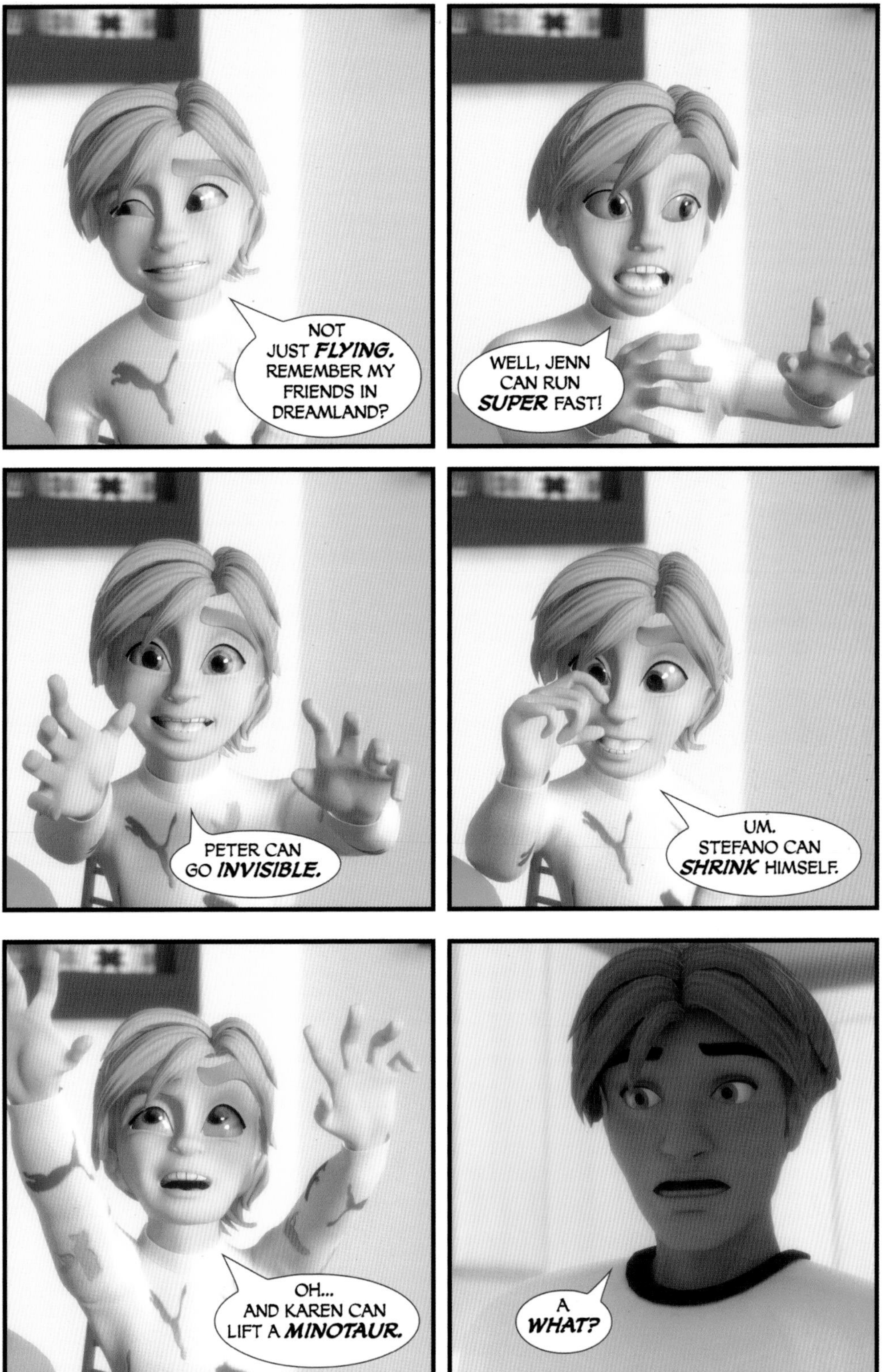
NOT JUST FLYING. REMEMBER MY FRIENDS IN DREAMLAND?
WELL, JENN CAN RUN SUPER FAST!
PETER CAN GO INVISIBLE.
UM. STEFANO CAN SHRINK HIMSELF.
OH... AND KAREN CAN LIFT A MINOTAUR.
A WHAT?

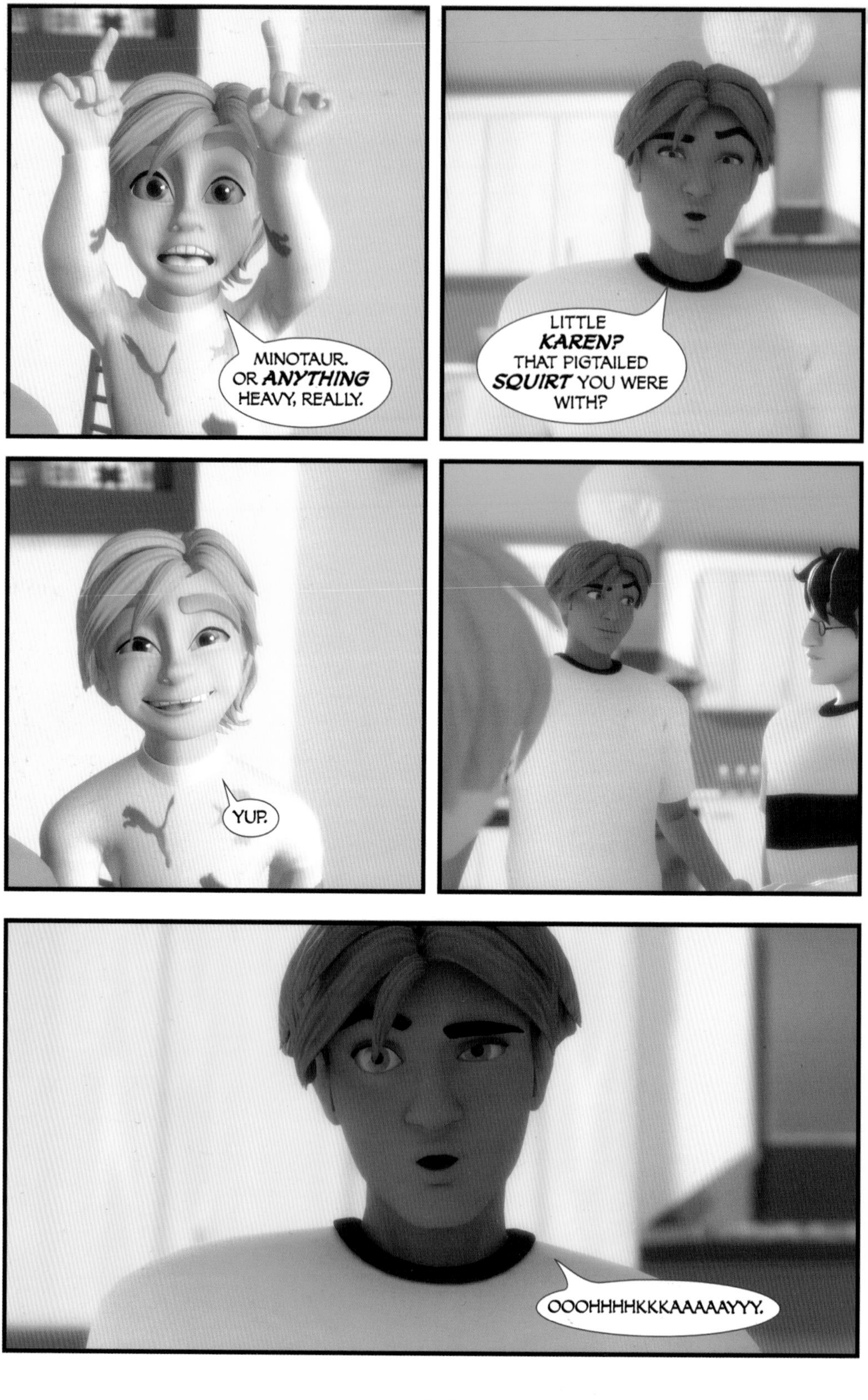
MINOTAUR. OR ANYTHING HEAVY, REALLY.
LITTLE KAREN? THAT PIGTAILED SQUIRT YOU WERE WITH?
YUP.
OOOHHHHKKKAAAAAYYY.

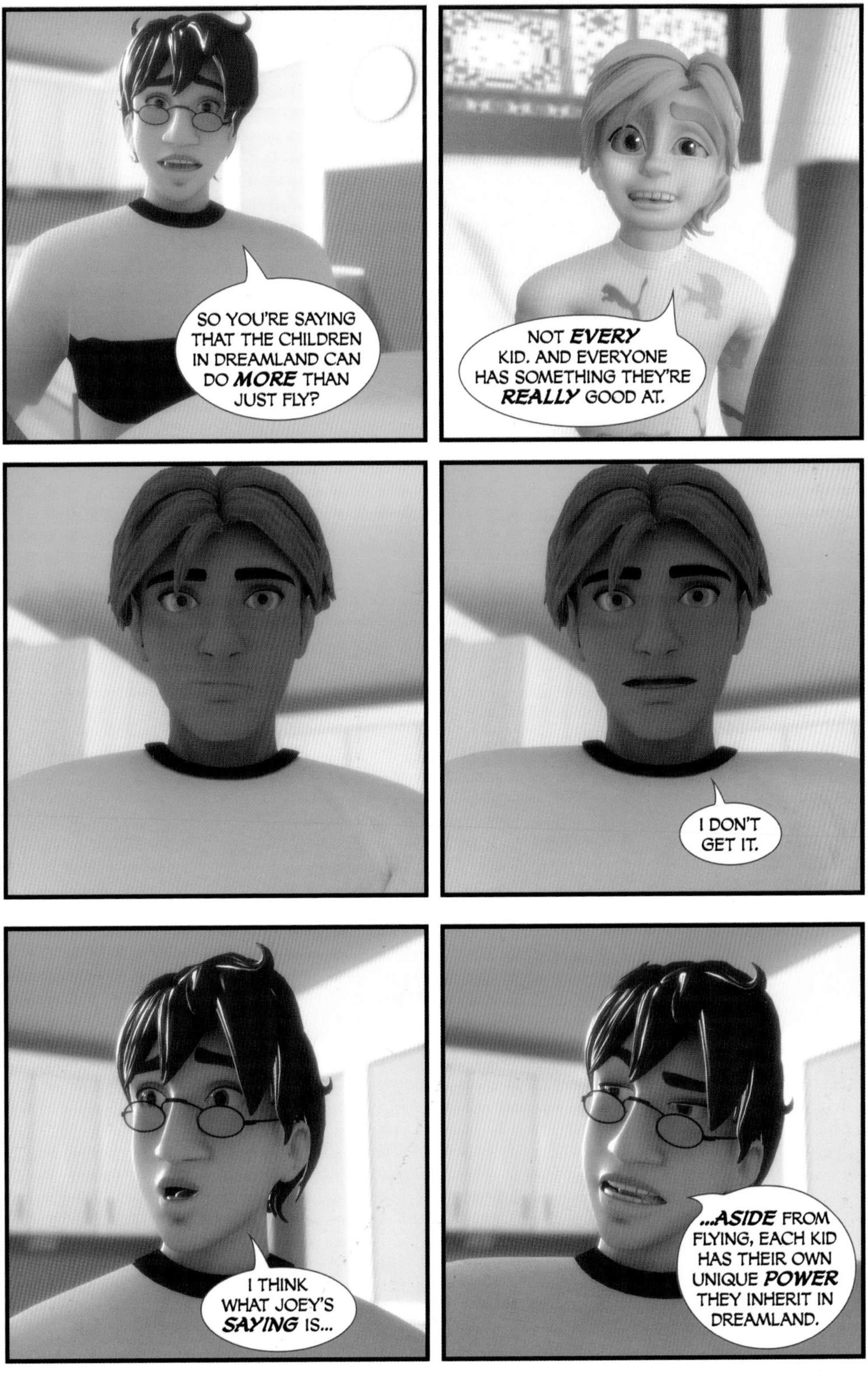
SO YOU'RE SAYING THAT THE CHILDREN IN DREAMLAND CAN DO MORE THAN JUST FLY?
NOT EVERY KID. AND EVERYONE HAS SOMETHING THEY'RE REALLY GOOD AT.
I DON'T GET IT.
I THINK WHAT JOEY'S SAYING IS...
...ASIDE FROM FLYING, EACH KID HAS THEIR OWN UNIQUE POWER THEY INHERIT IN DREAMLAND.

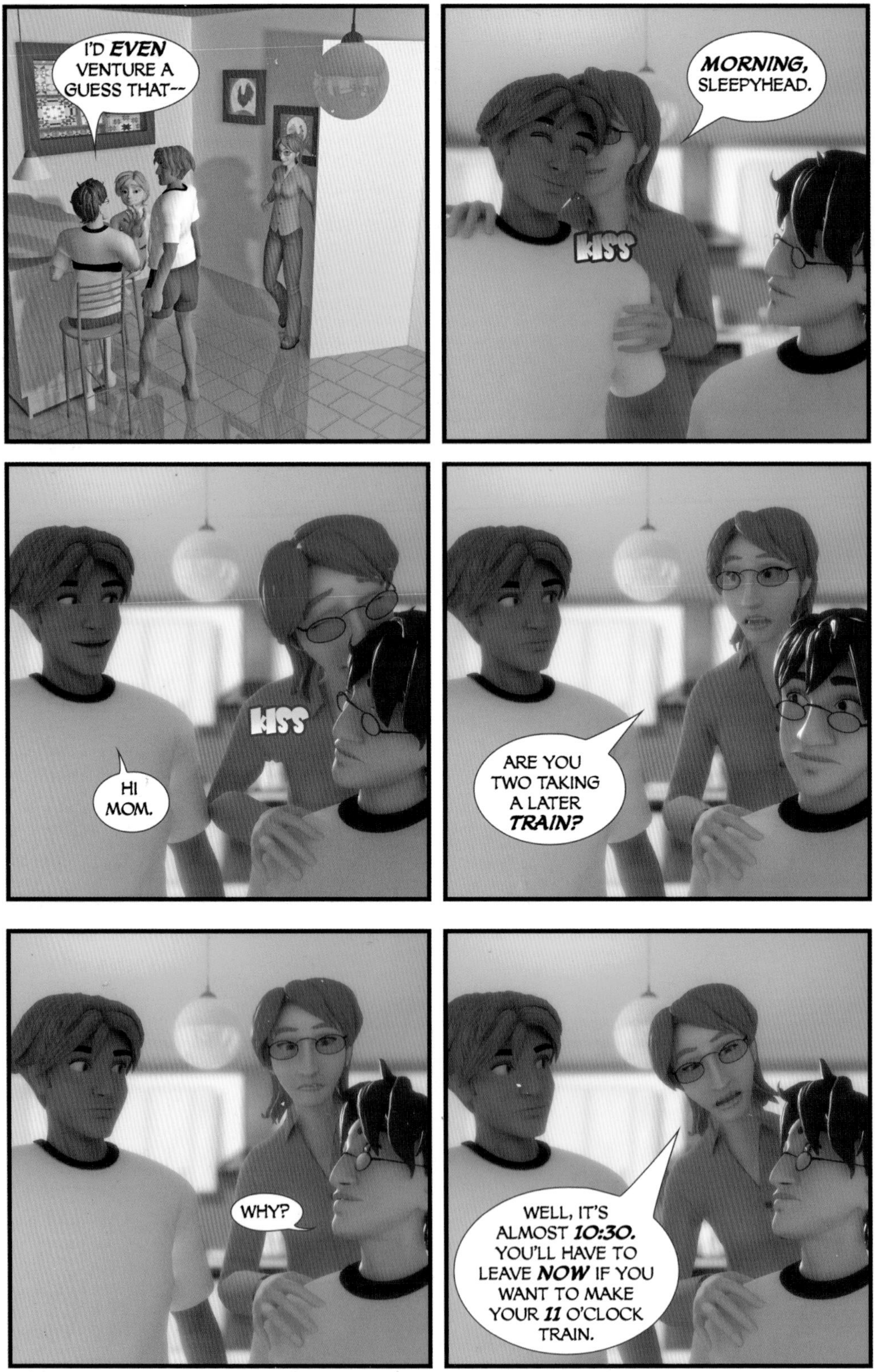
I'D EVEN VENTURE A GUESS THAT--
MORNING, SLEEPYHEAD.
KISS
KISS
HI MOM.
ARE YOU TWO TAKING A LATER TRAIN?
WHY?
WELL, IT'S ALMOST 10:30. YOU'LL HAVE TO LEAVE NOW IF YOU WANT TO MAKE YOUR 11 O'CLOCK TRAIN.

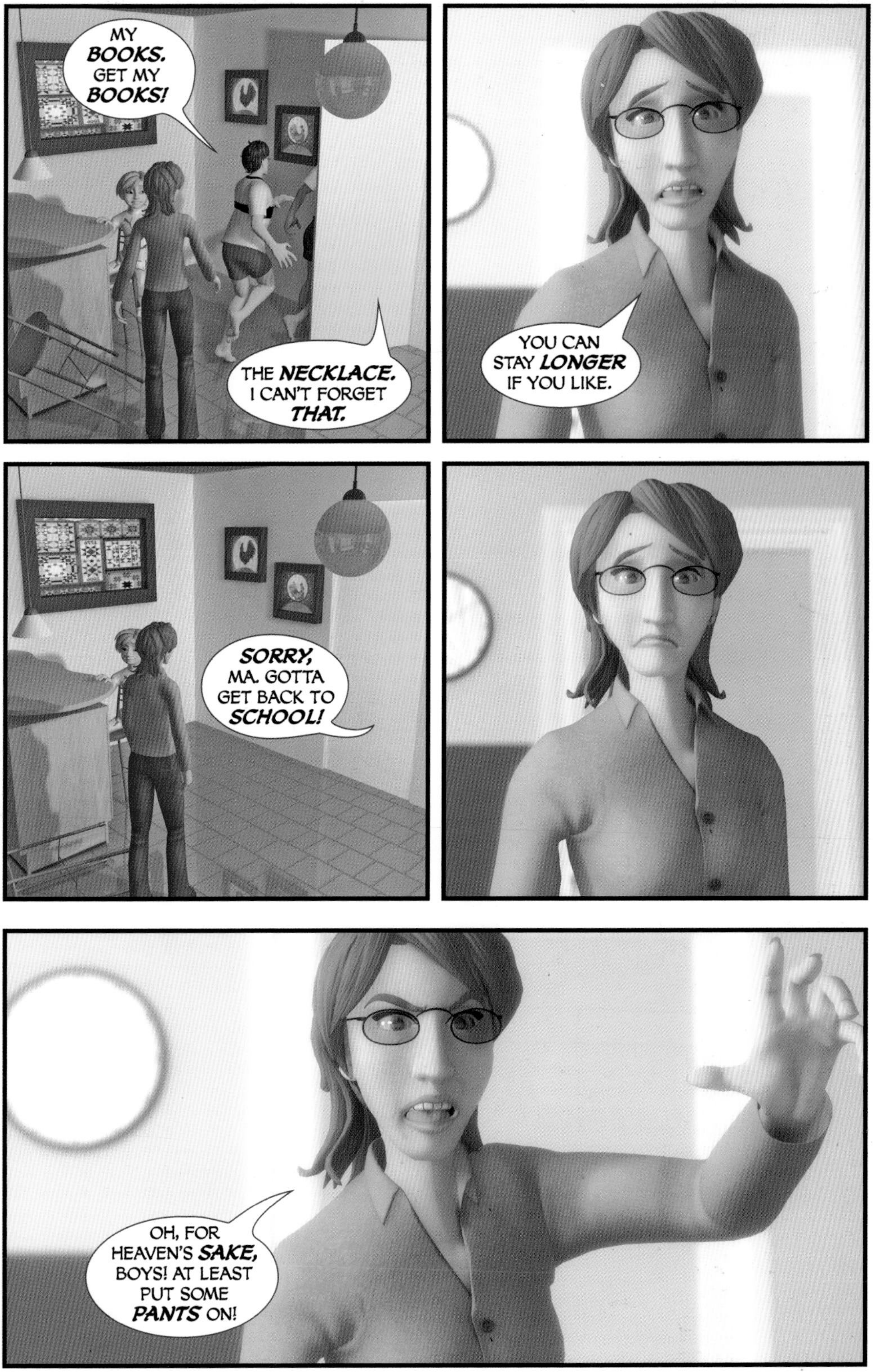
MY BOOKS. GET MY BOOKS!
THE NECKLACE. I CAN'T FORGET THAT.
YOU CAN STAY LONGER IF YOU LIKE.
SORRY, MA. GOTTA GET BACK TO SCHOOL!
OH, FOR HEAVEN'S SAKE, BOYS! AT LEAST PUT SOME PANTS ON!

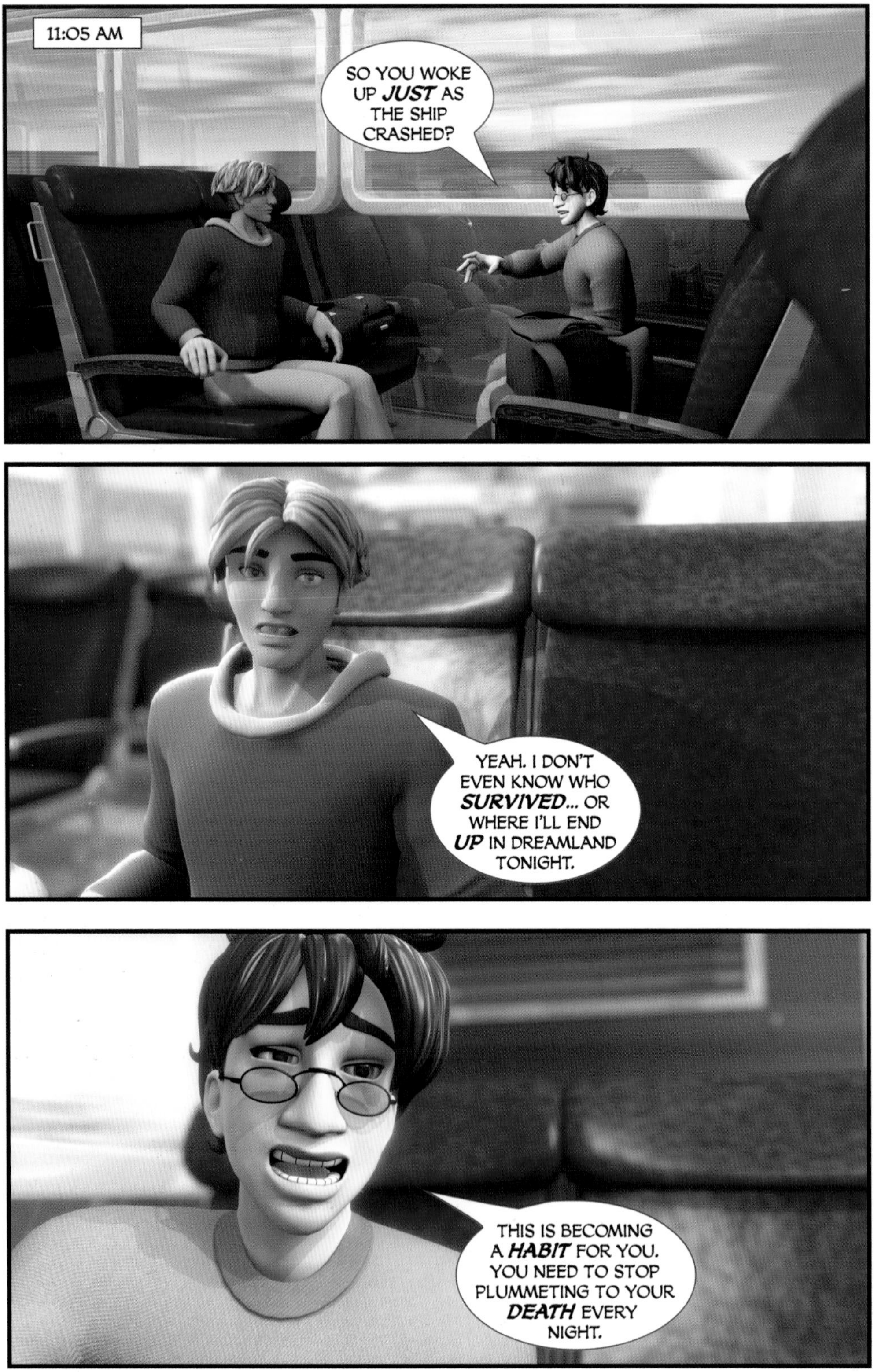
11:05 AM
SO YOU WOKE UP JUST AS THE SHIP CRASHED?
YEAH. I DON'T EVEN KNOW WHO SURVIVED... OR WHERE I'LL END UP IN DREAMLAND TONIGHT.
THIS IS BECOMING A HABIT FOR YOU. YOU NEED TO STOP PLUMMETING TO YOUR DEATH EVERY NIGHT.

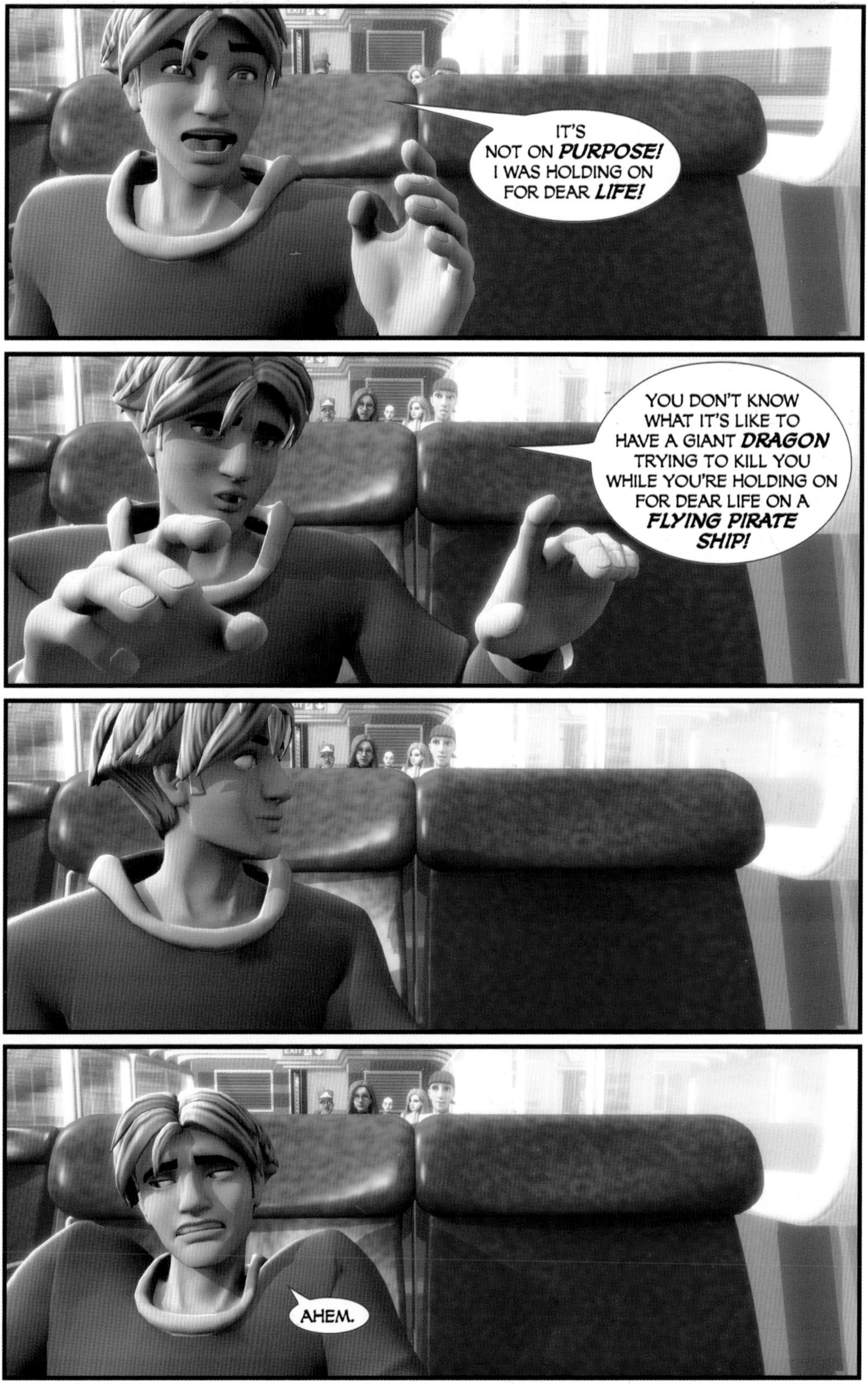
IT'S NOT ON PURPOSE! I WAS HOLDING ON FOR DEAR LIFE!
YOU DON'T KNOW WHAT IT'S LIKE TO HAVE A GIANT DRAGON TRYING TO KILL YOU WHILE YOU'RE HOLDING ON FOR DEAR LIFE ON A FLYING PIRATE SHIP!
AHEM.

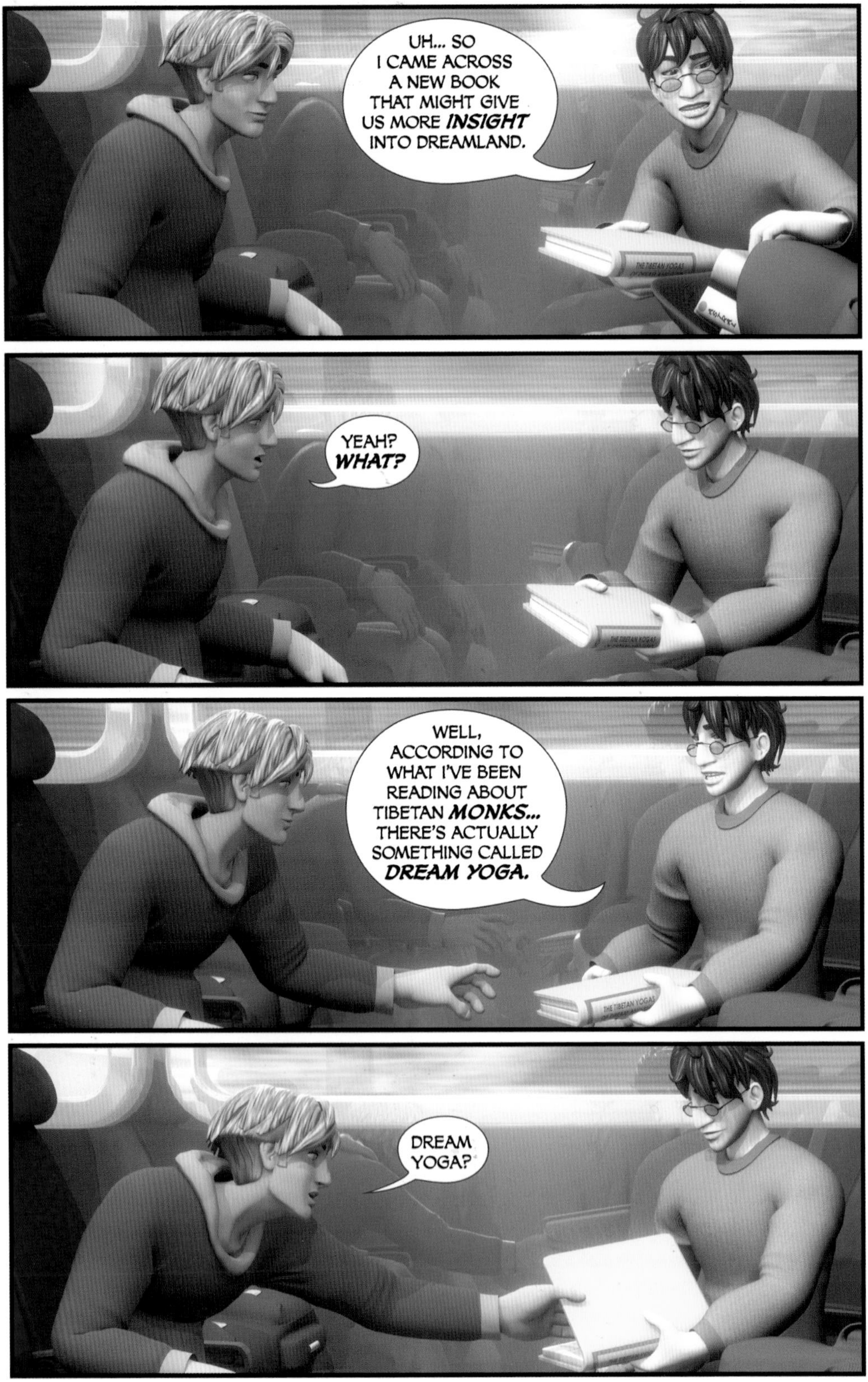
UH... SO I CAME ACROSS A NEW BOOK THAT MIGHT GIVE US MORE **INSIGHT** INTO DREAMLAND.
YEAH? **WHAT?**
WELL, ACCORDING TO WHAT I'VE BEEN READING ABOUT TIBETAN **MONKS...** THERE'S ACTUALLY SOMETHING CALLED **DREAM YOGA.**
DREAM YOGA?

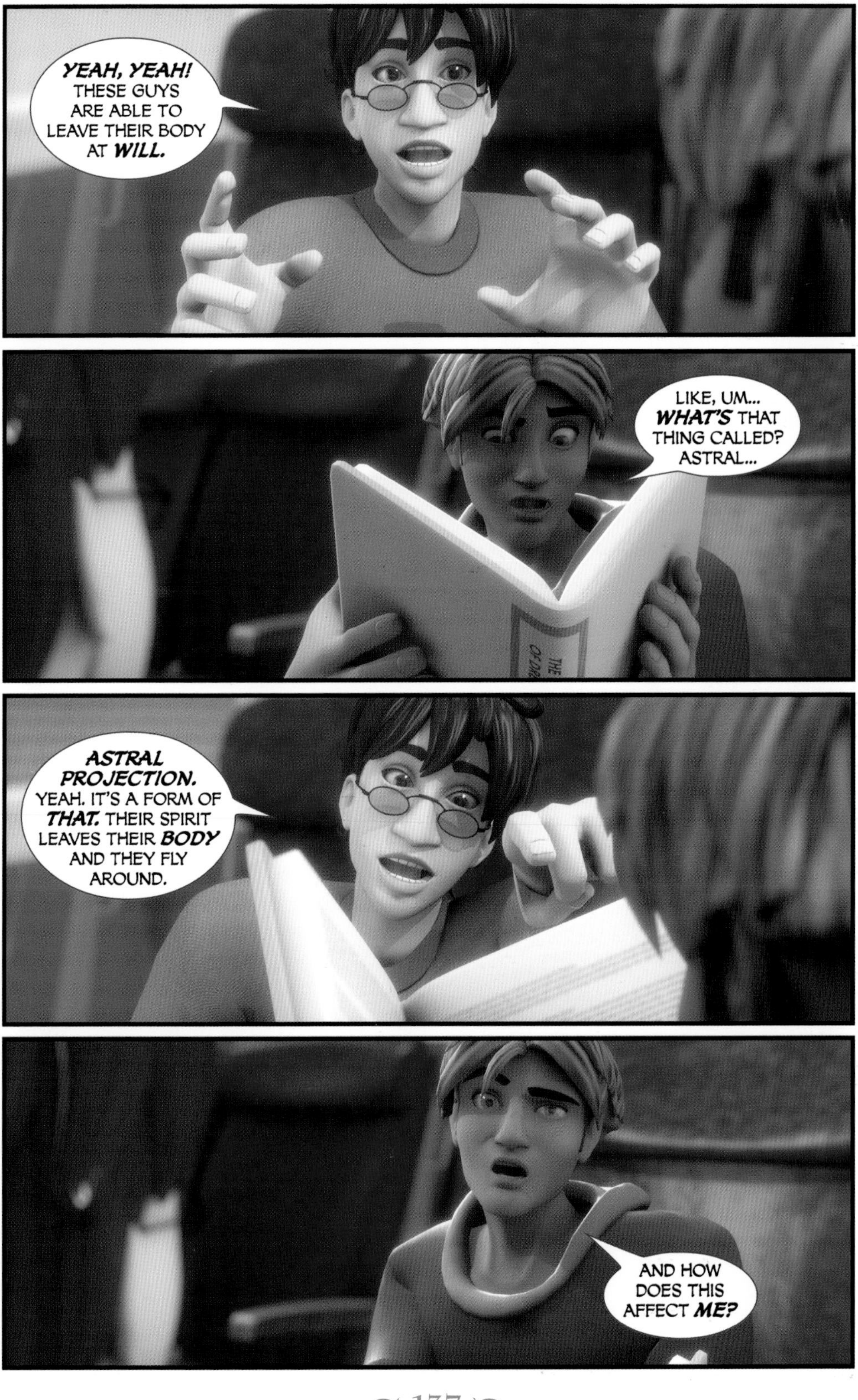
YEAH, YEAH! THESE GUYS ARE ABLE TO LEAVE THEIR BODY AT WILL.
LIKE, UM... WHAT'S THAT THING CALLED? ASTRAL...
ASTRAL PROJECTION. YEAH. IT'S A FORM OF THAT. THEIR SPIRIT LEAVES THEIR BODY AND THEY FLY AROUND.
AND HOW DOES THIS AFFECT ME?

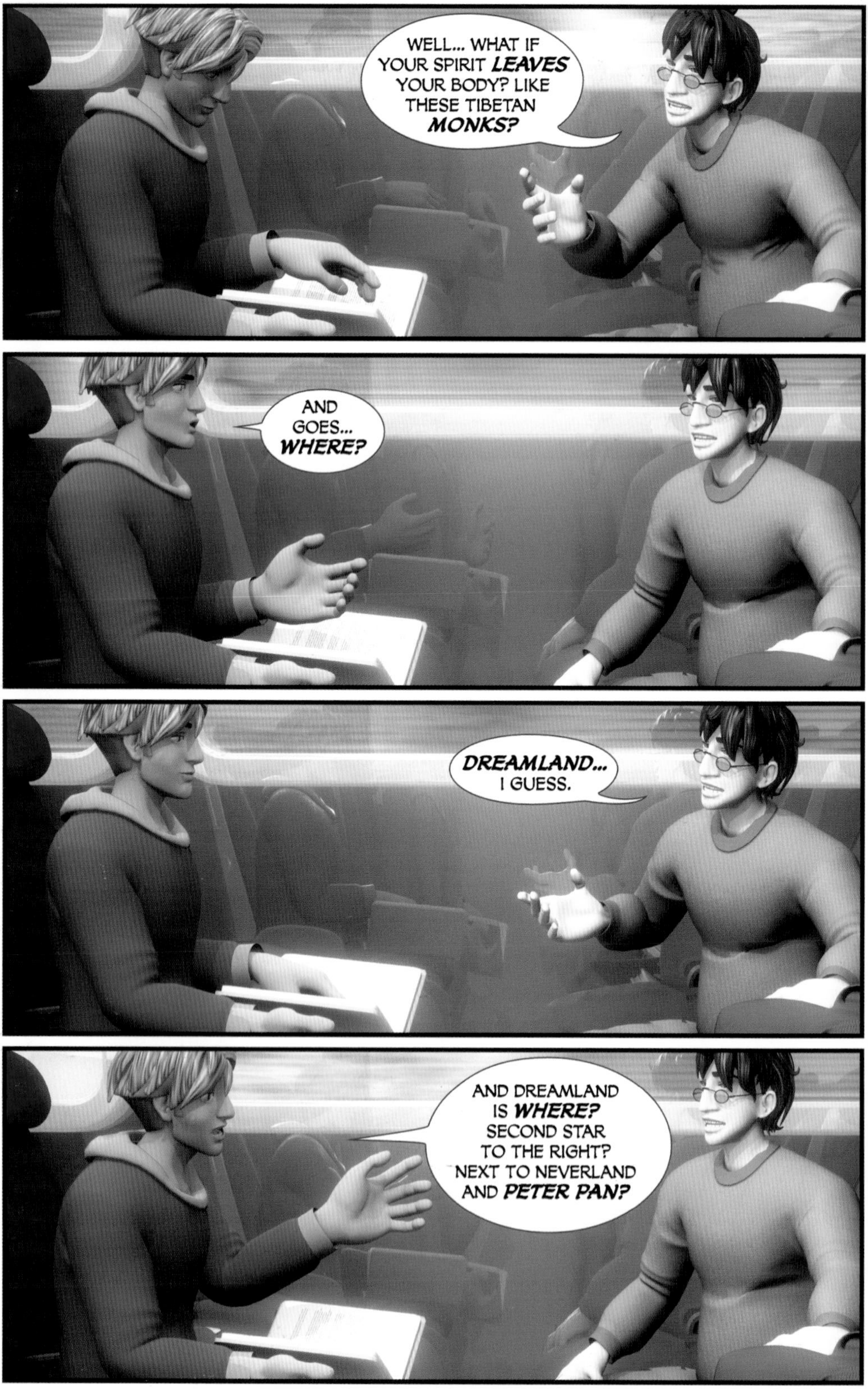
WELL... WHAT IF YOUR SPIRIT ***LEAVES*** YOUR BODY? LIKE THESE TIBETAN ***MONKS?***
AND GOES... ***WHERE?***
DREAMLAND... I GUESS.
AND DREAMLAND IS ***WHERE?*** SECOND STAR TO THE RIGHT? NEXT TO NEVERLAND AND ***PETER PAN?***

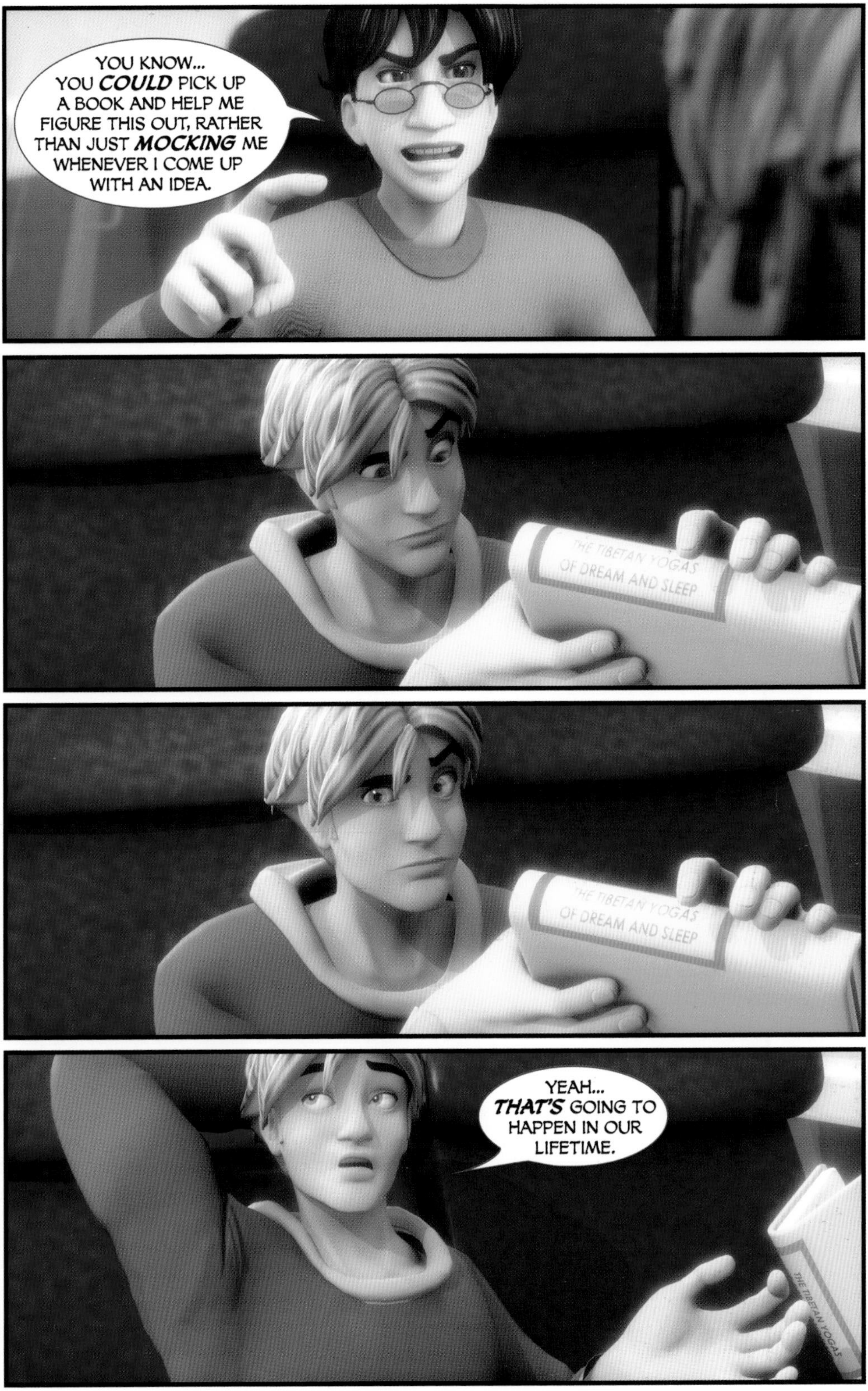
YOU KNOW... YOU COULD PICK UP A BOOK AND HELP ME FIGURE THIS OUT, RATHER THAN JUST MOCKING ME WHENEVER I COME UP WITH AN IDEA.
THE TIBETAN YOGAS OF DREAM AND SLEEP
THE TIBETAN YOGAS OF DREAM AND SLEEP
YEAH... THAT'S GOING TO HAPPEN IN OUR LIFETIME.
THE TIBETAN YOGAS

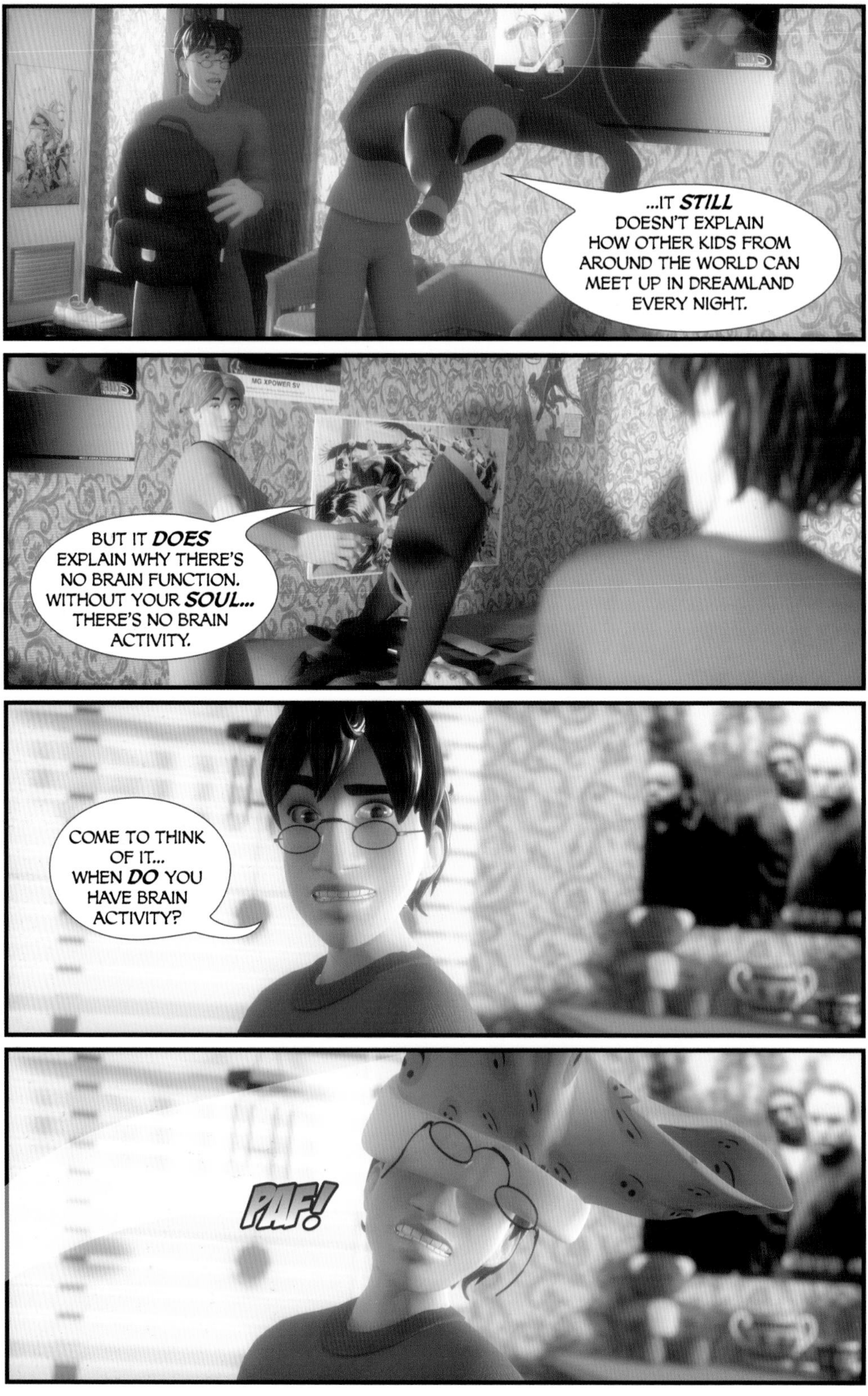
...IT STILL DOESN'T EXPLAIN HOW OTHER KIDS FROM AROUND THE WORLD CAN MEET UP IN DREAMLAND EVERY NIGHT.
MG XPOWER SV
BUT IT DOES EXPLAIN WHY THERE'S NO BRAIN FUNCTION. WITHOUT YOUR SOUL... THERE'S NO BRAIN ACTIVITY.
COME TO THINK OF IT... WHEN DO YOU HAVE BRAIN ACTIVITY?
PAF!

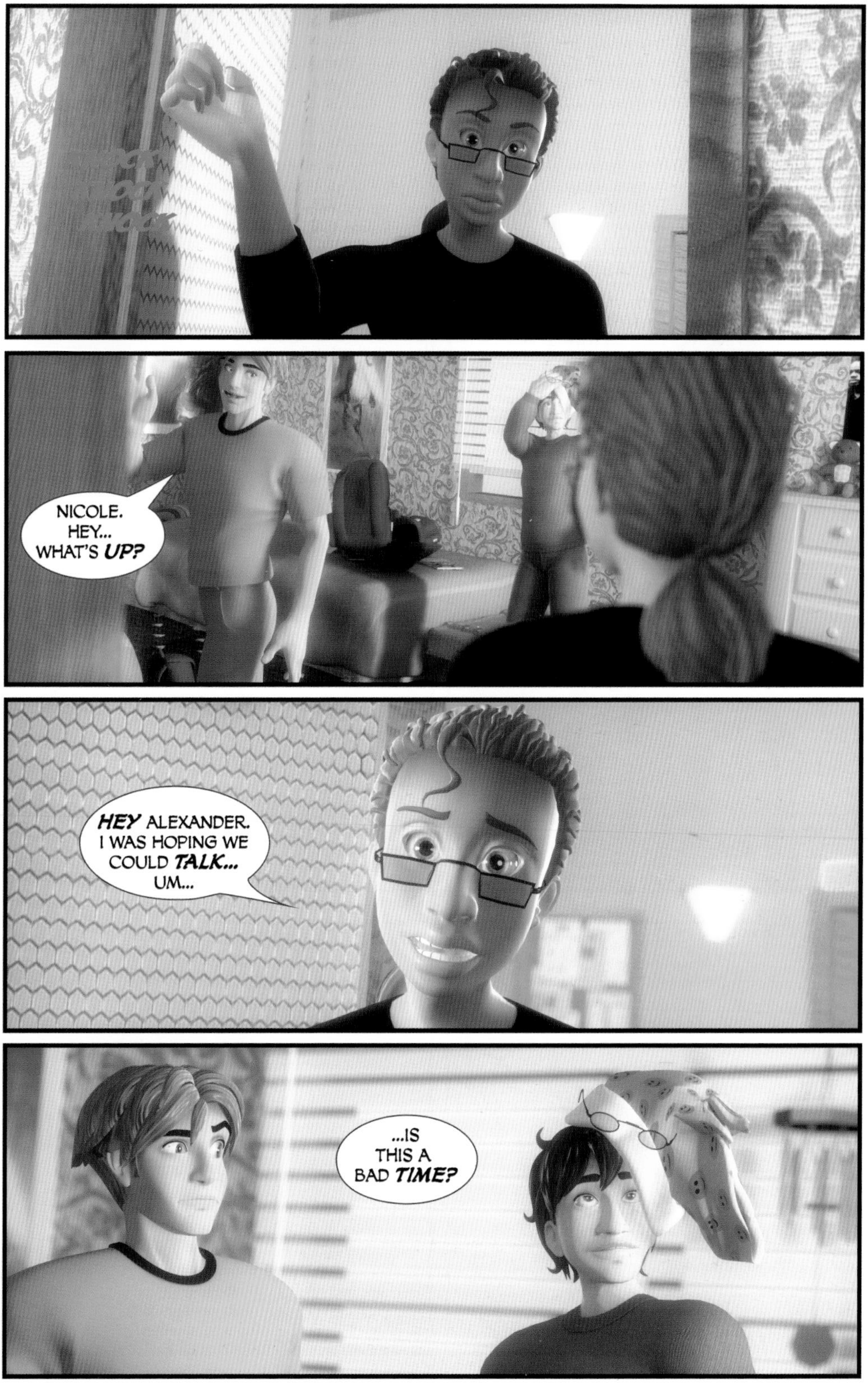
NICOLE. HEY... WHAT'S UP?
HEY ALEXANDER. I WAS HOPING WE COULD TALK... UM...
...IS THIS A BAD TIME?

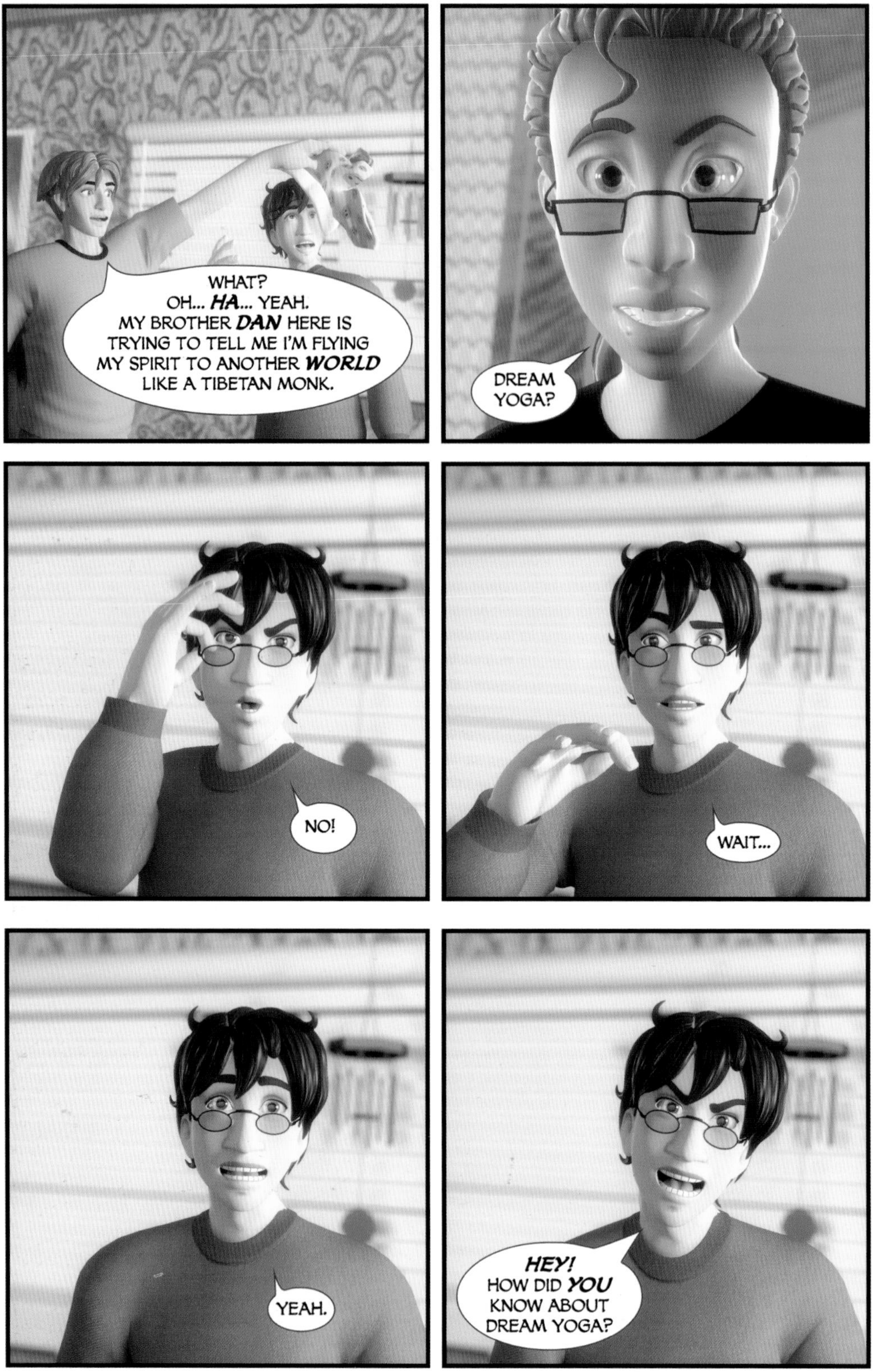
WHAT? OH... HA... YEAH. MY BROTHER DAN HERE IS TRYING TO TELL ME I'M FLYING MY SPIRIT TO ANOTHER WORLD LIKE A TIBETAN MONK.
DREAM YOGA?
NO!
WAIT...
YEAH.
HEY! HOW DID YOU KNOW ABOUT DREAM YOGA?

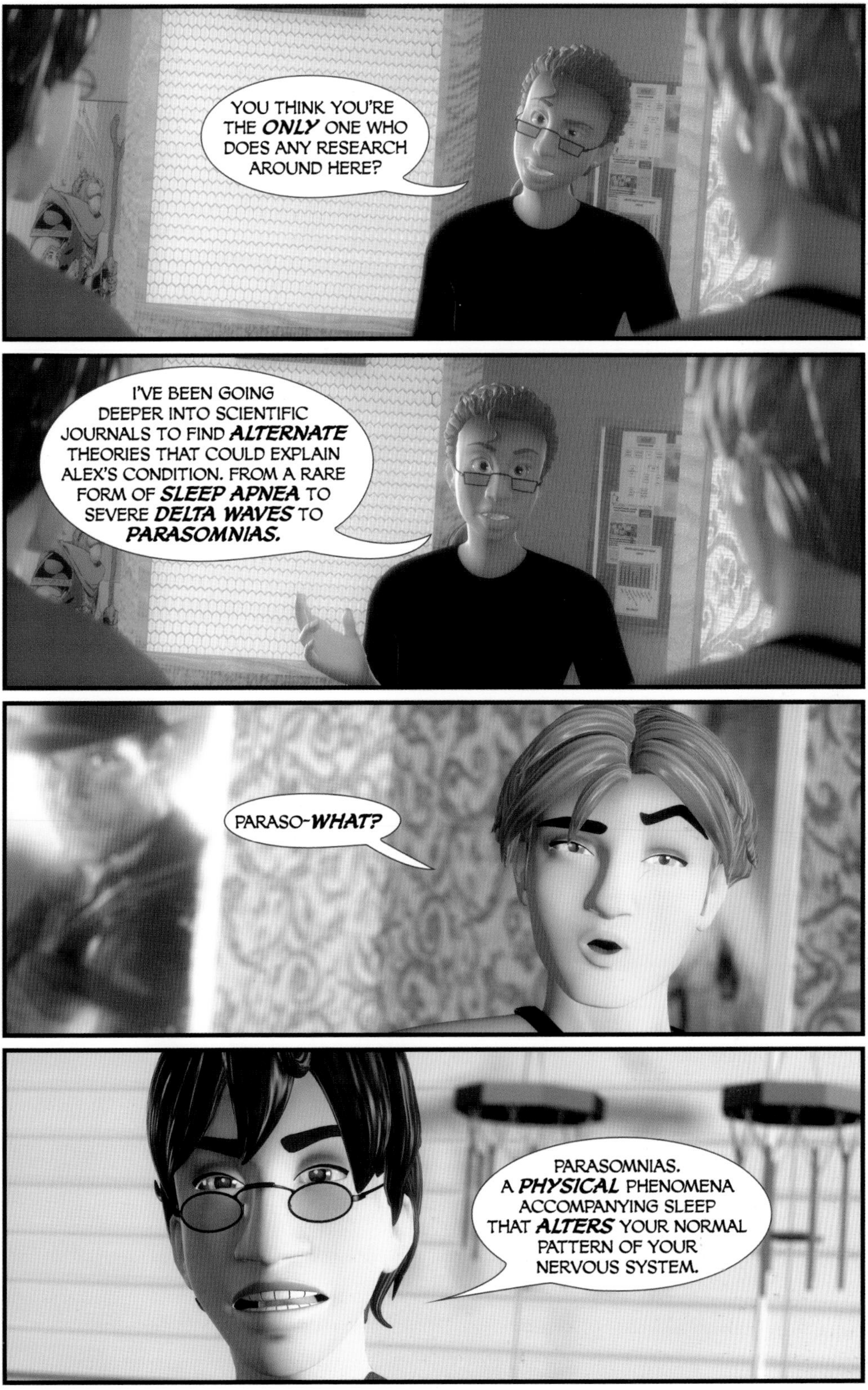
YOU THINK YOU'RE THE ONLY ONE WHO DOES ANY RESEARCH AROUND HERE?
I'VE BEEN GOING DEEPER INTO SCIENTIFIC JOURNALS TO FIND ALTERNATE THEORIES THAT COULD EXPLAIN ALEX'S CONDITION. FROM A RARE FORM OF SLEEP APNEA TO SEVERE DELTA WAVES TO PARASOMNIAS.
PARASO-WHAT?
PARASOMNIAS. A PHYSICAL PHENOMENA ACCOMPANYING SLEEP THAT ALTERS YOUR NORMAL PATTERN OF YOUR NERVOUS SYSTEM.

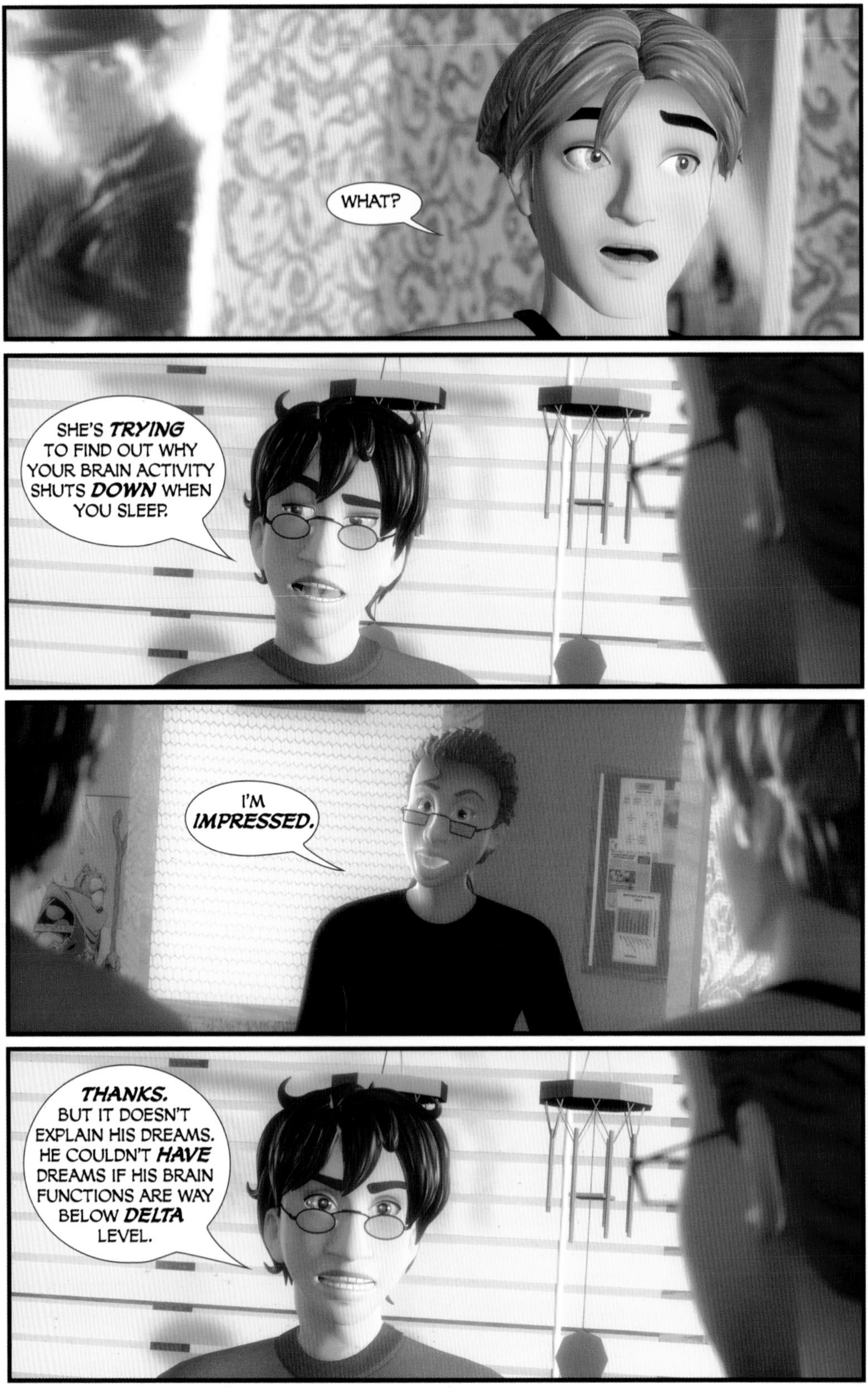
WHAT?
SHE'S TRYING TO FIND OUT WHY YOUR BRAIN ACTIVITY SHUTS DOWN WHEN YOU SLEEP.
I'M IMPRESSED.
THANKS. BUT IT DOESN'T EXPLAIN HIS DREAMS. HE COULDN'T HAVE DREAMS IF HIS BRAIN FUNCTIONS ARE WAY BELOW DELTA LEVEL.

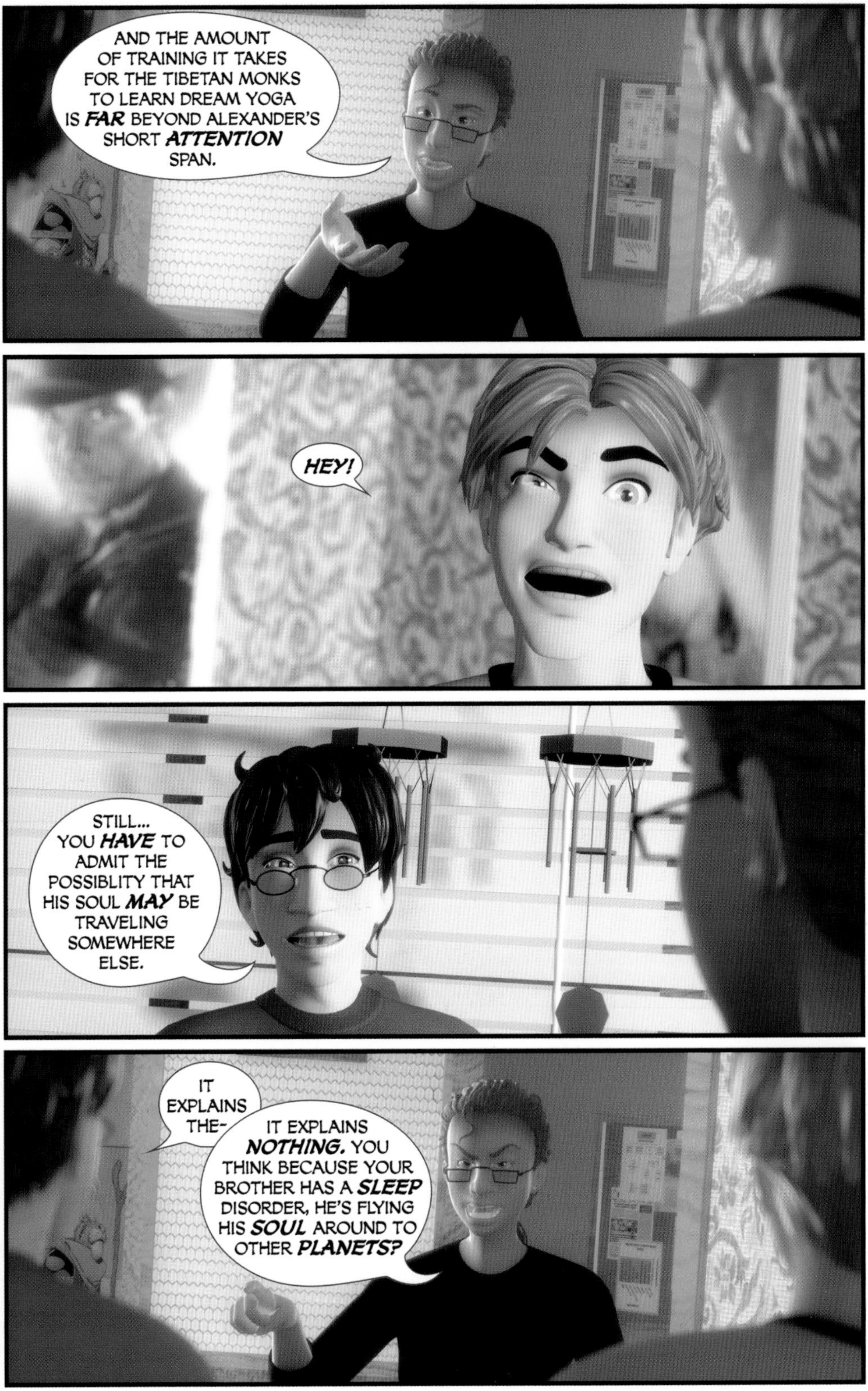
AND THE AMOUNT OF TRAINING IT TAKES FOR THE TIBETAN MONKS TO LEARN DREAM YOGA IS *FAR* BEYOND ALEXANDER'S SHORT *ATTENTION* SPAN.
HEY!
STILL... YOU *HAVE* TO ADMIT THE POSSIBLITY THAT HIS SOUL *MAY* BE TRAVELING SOMEWHERE ELSE.
IT EXPLAINS THE-
IT EXPLAINS *NOTHING.* YOU THINK BECAUSE YOUR BROTHER HAS A *SLEEP* DISORDER, HE'S FLYING HIS *SOUL* AROUND TO OTHER *PLANETS?*

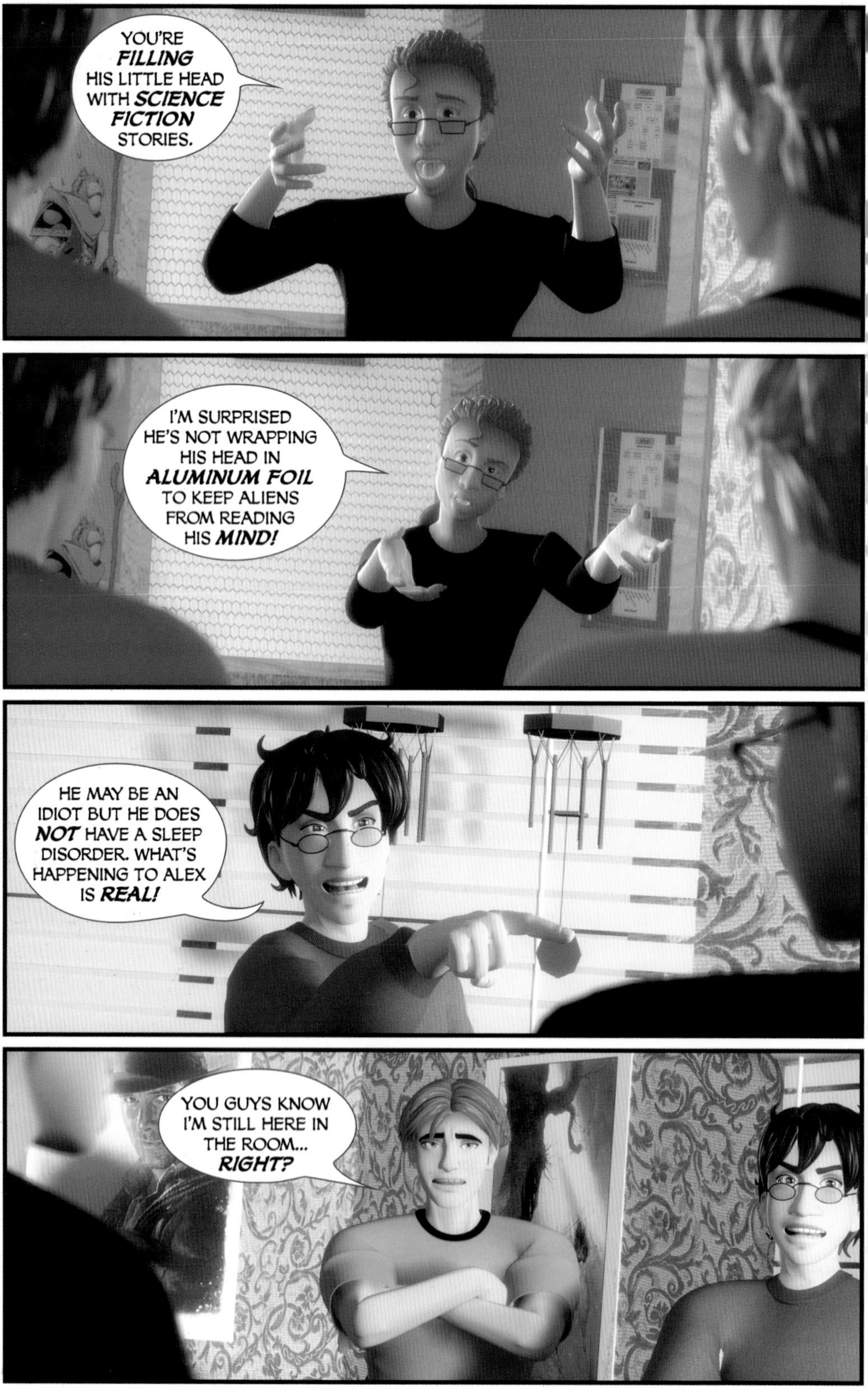
YOU'RE FILLING HIS LITTLE HEAD WITH SCIENCE FICTION STORIES.
I'M SURPRISED HE'S NOT WRAPPING HIS HEAD IN ALUMINUM FOIL TO KEEP ALIENS FROM READING HIS MIND!
HE MAY BE AN IDIOT BUT HE DOES NOT HAVE A SLEEP DISORDER. WHAT'S HAPPENING TO ALEX IS REAL!
YOU GUYS KNOW I'M STILL HERE IN THE ROOM... RIGHT?

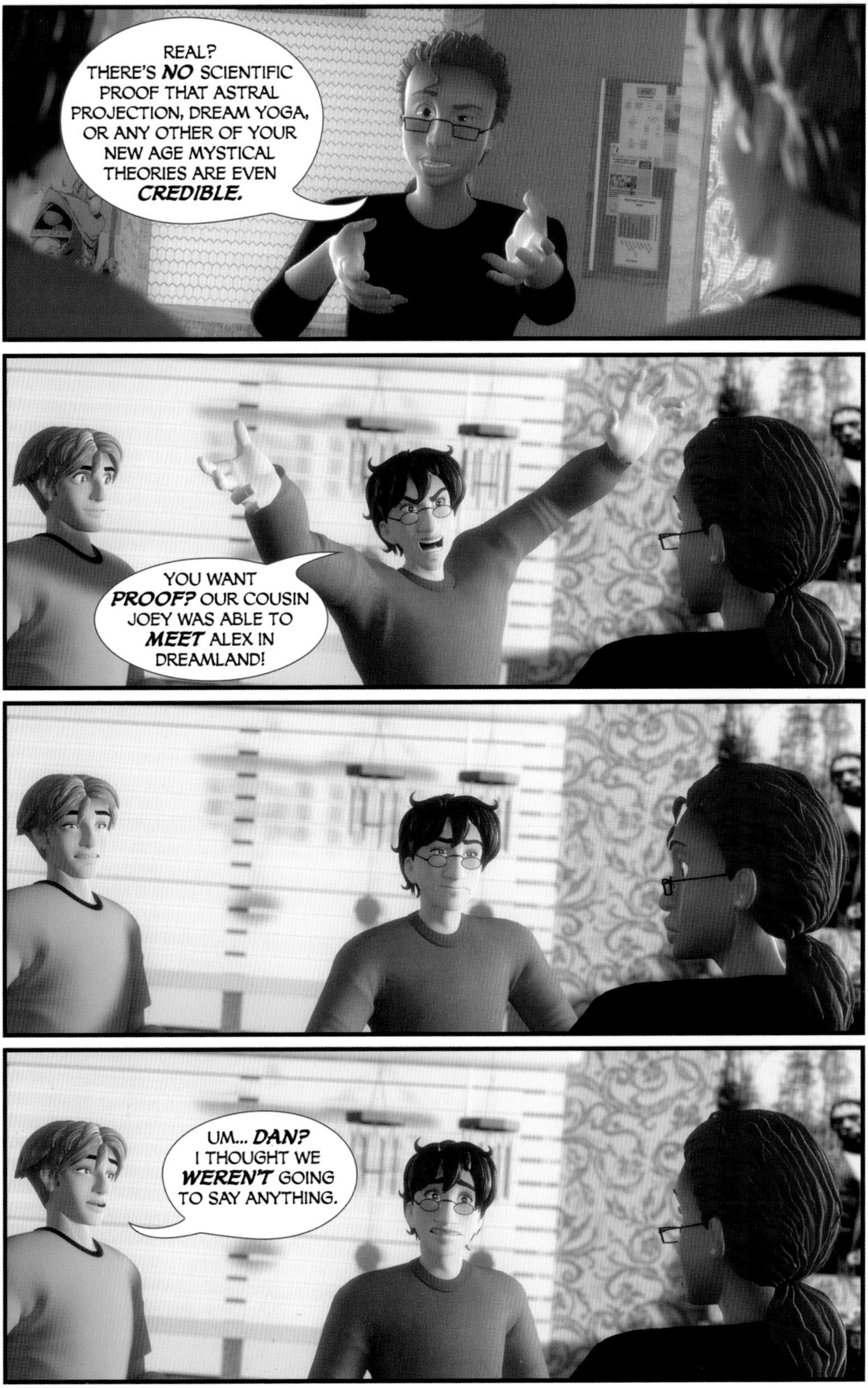
REAL? THERE'S **NO** SCIENTIFIC PROOF THAT ASTRAL PROJECTION, DREAM YOGA, OR ANY OTHER OF YOUR NEW AGE MYSTICAL THEORIES ARE EVEN ***CREDIBLE.***
YOU WANT ***PROOF?*** OUR COUSIN JOEY WAS ABLE TO ***MEET*** ALEX IN DREAMLAND!
UM... ***DAN?*** I THOUGHT WE ***WEREN'T*** GOING TO SAY ANYTHING.

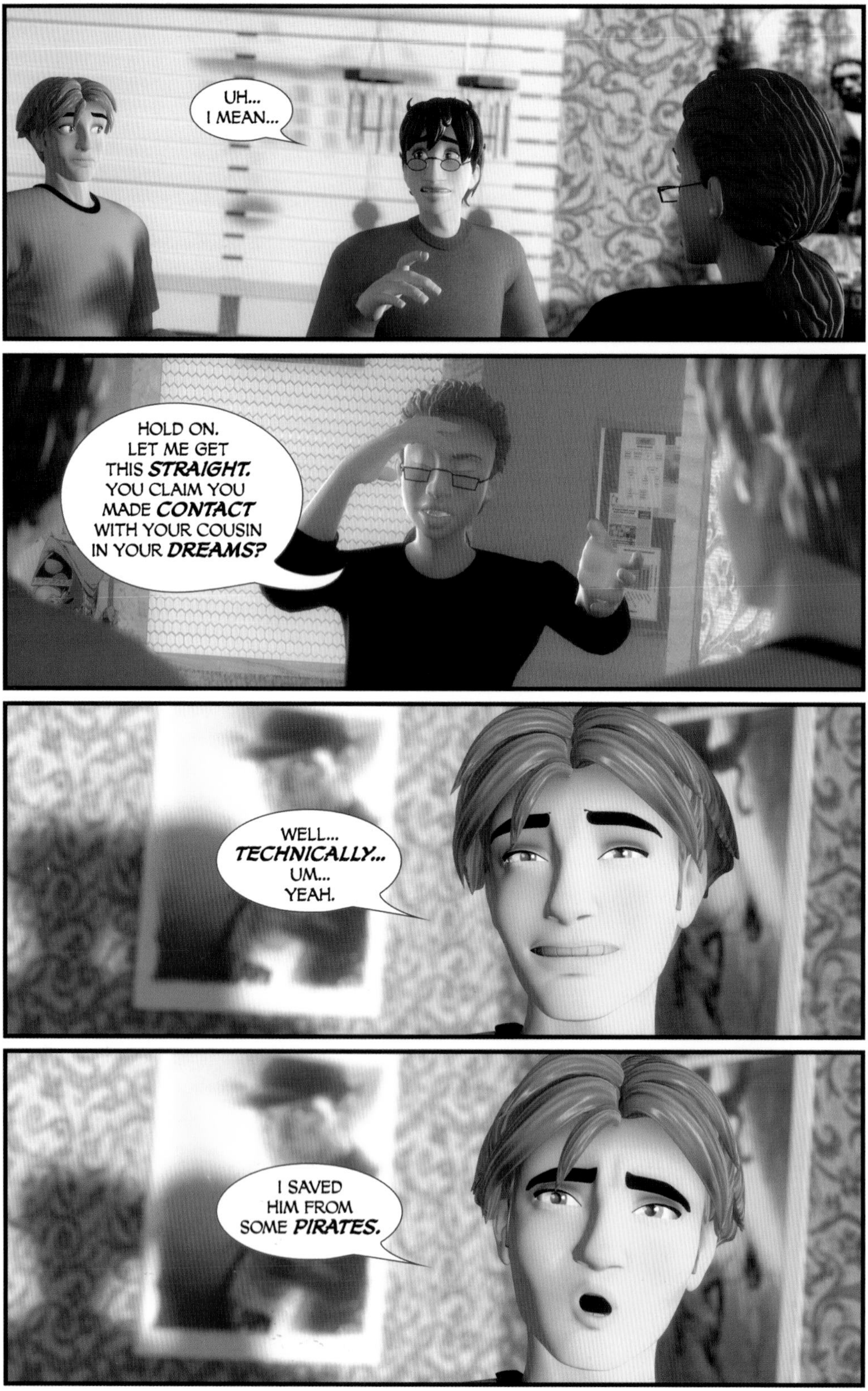
UH... I MEAN...
HOLD ON. LET ME GET THIS *STRAIGHT.* YOU CLAIM YOU MADE *CONTACT* WITH YOUR COUSIN IN YOUR *DREAMS?*
WELL... *TECHNICALLY...* UM... YEAH.
I SAVED HIM FROM SOME *PIRATES.*

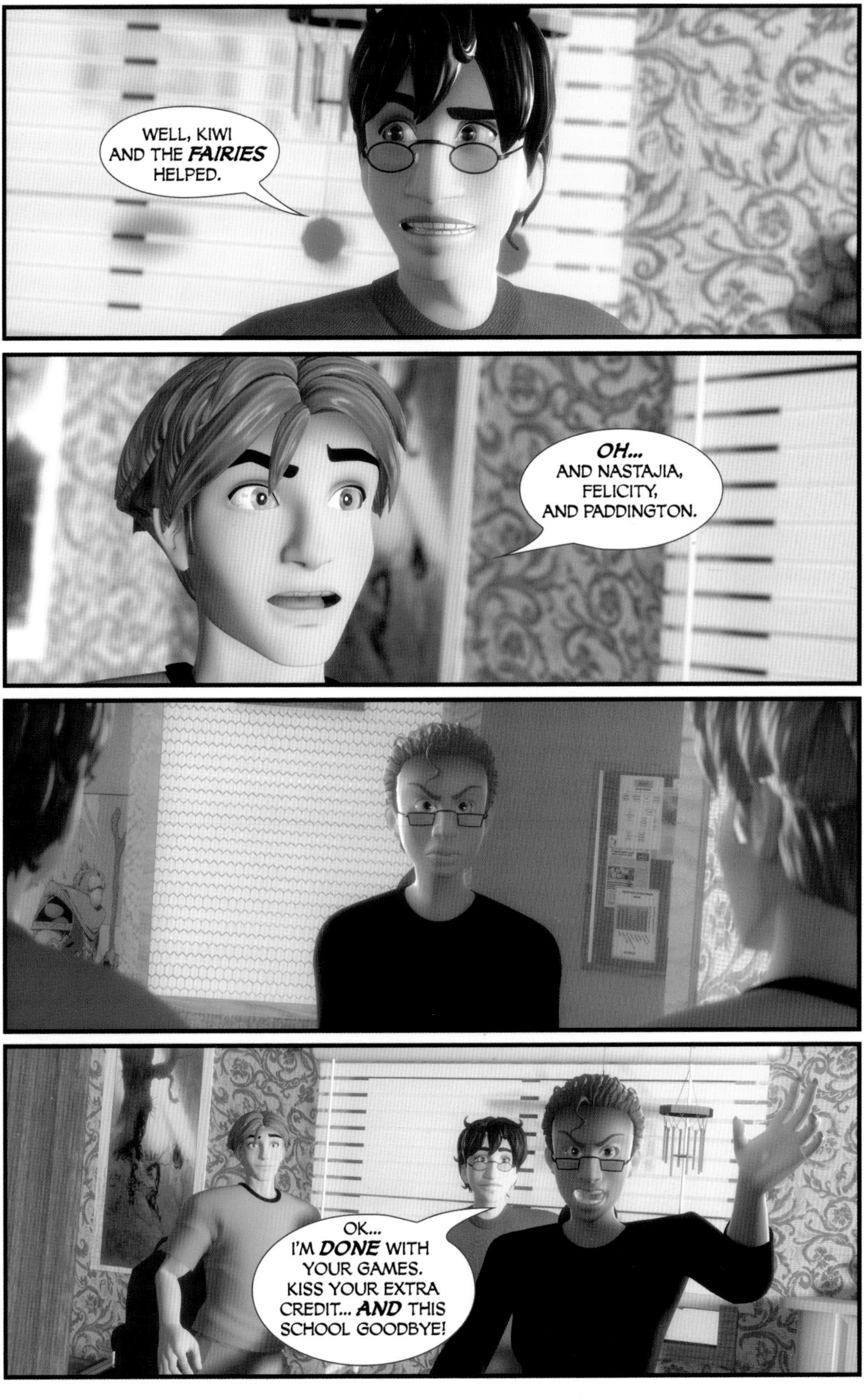
WELL, KIWI AND THE FAIRIES HELPED.
OH... AND NASTAJIA, FELICITY, AND PADDINGTON.
OK... I'M DONE WITH YOUR GAMES. KISS YOUR EXTRA CREDIT... AND THIS SCHOOL GOODBYE!

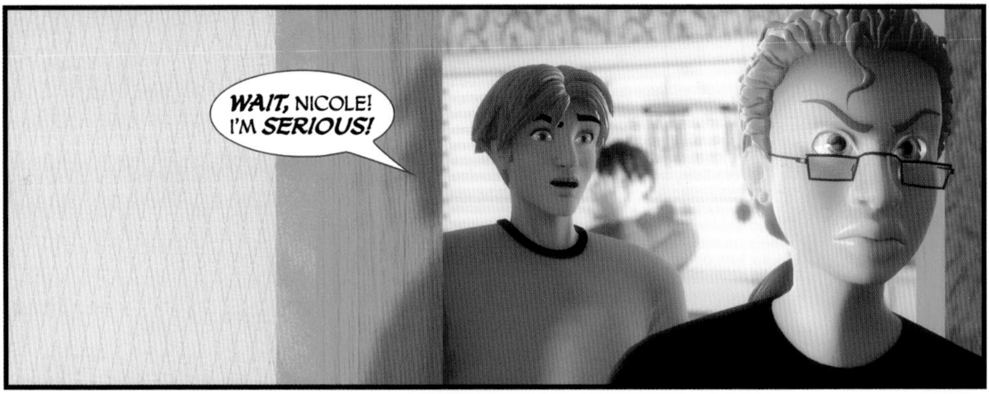
WAIT, NICOLE! I'M SERIOUS!

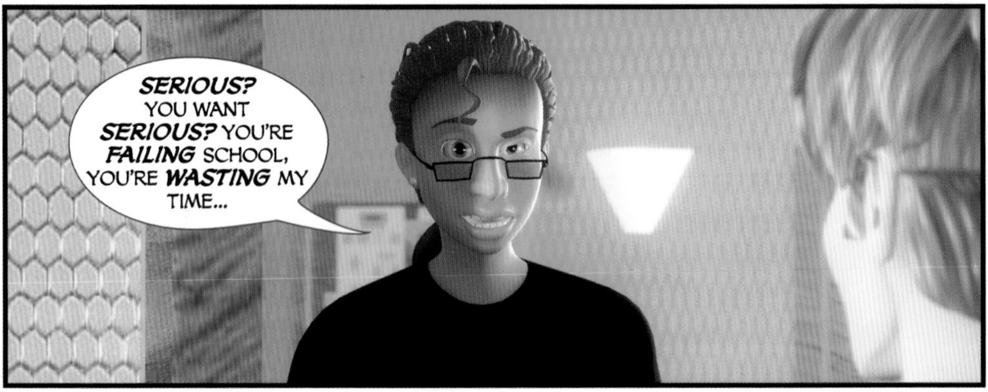
SERIOUS? YOU WANT SERIOUS? YOU'RE FAILING SCHOOL, YOU'RE WASTING MY TIME...

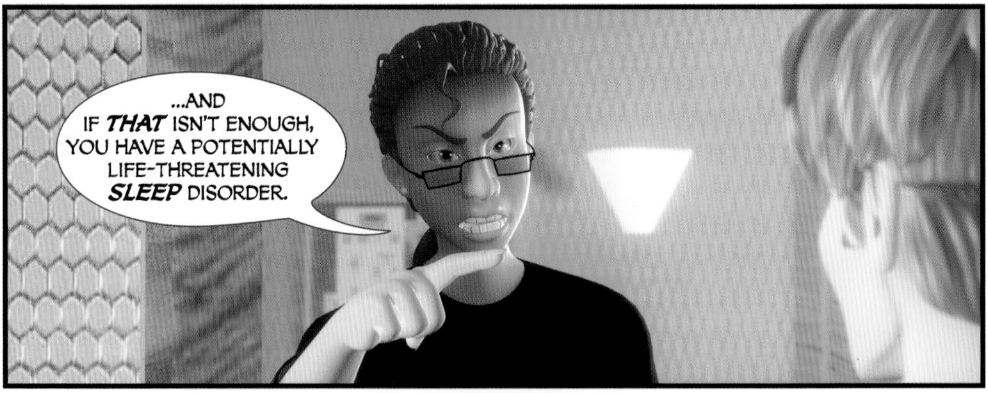
...AND IF THAT ISN'T ENOUGH, YOU HAVE A POTENTIALLY LIFE-THREATENING SLEEP DISORDER.

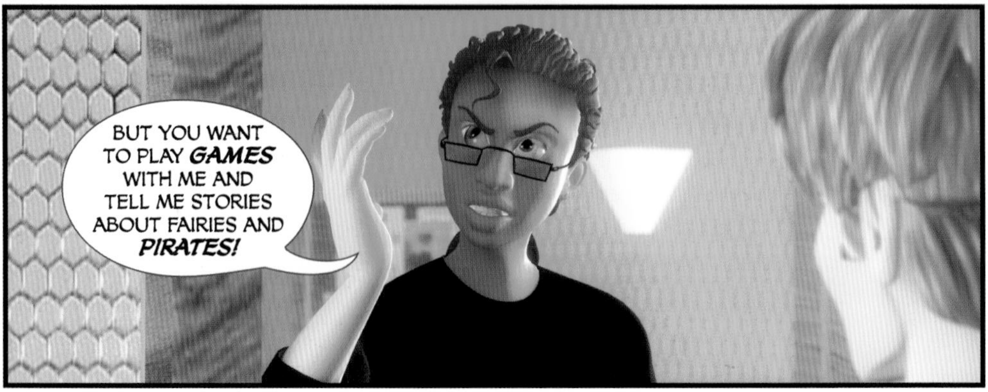
BUT YOU WANT TO PLAY GAMES WITH ME AND TELL ME STORIES ABOUT FAIRIES AND PIRATES!

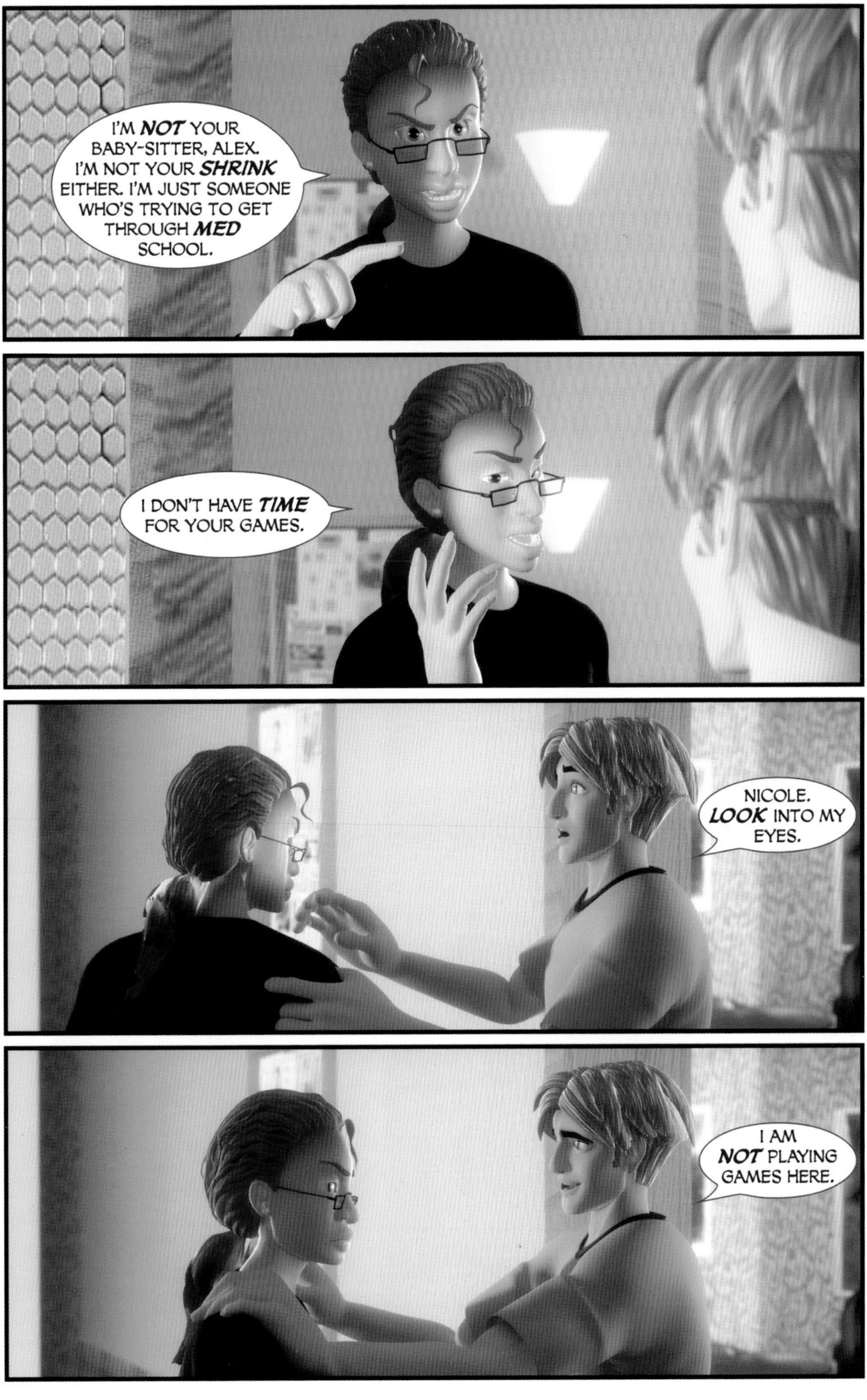
I'M NOT YOUR BABY-SITTER, ALEX. I'M NOT YOUR SHRINK EITHER. I'M JUST SOMEONE WHO'S TRYING TO GET THROUGH MED SCHOOL.
I DON'T HAVE TIME FOR YOUR GAMES.
NICOLE. LOOK INTO MY EYES.
I AM NOT PLAYING GAMES HERE.

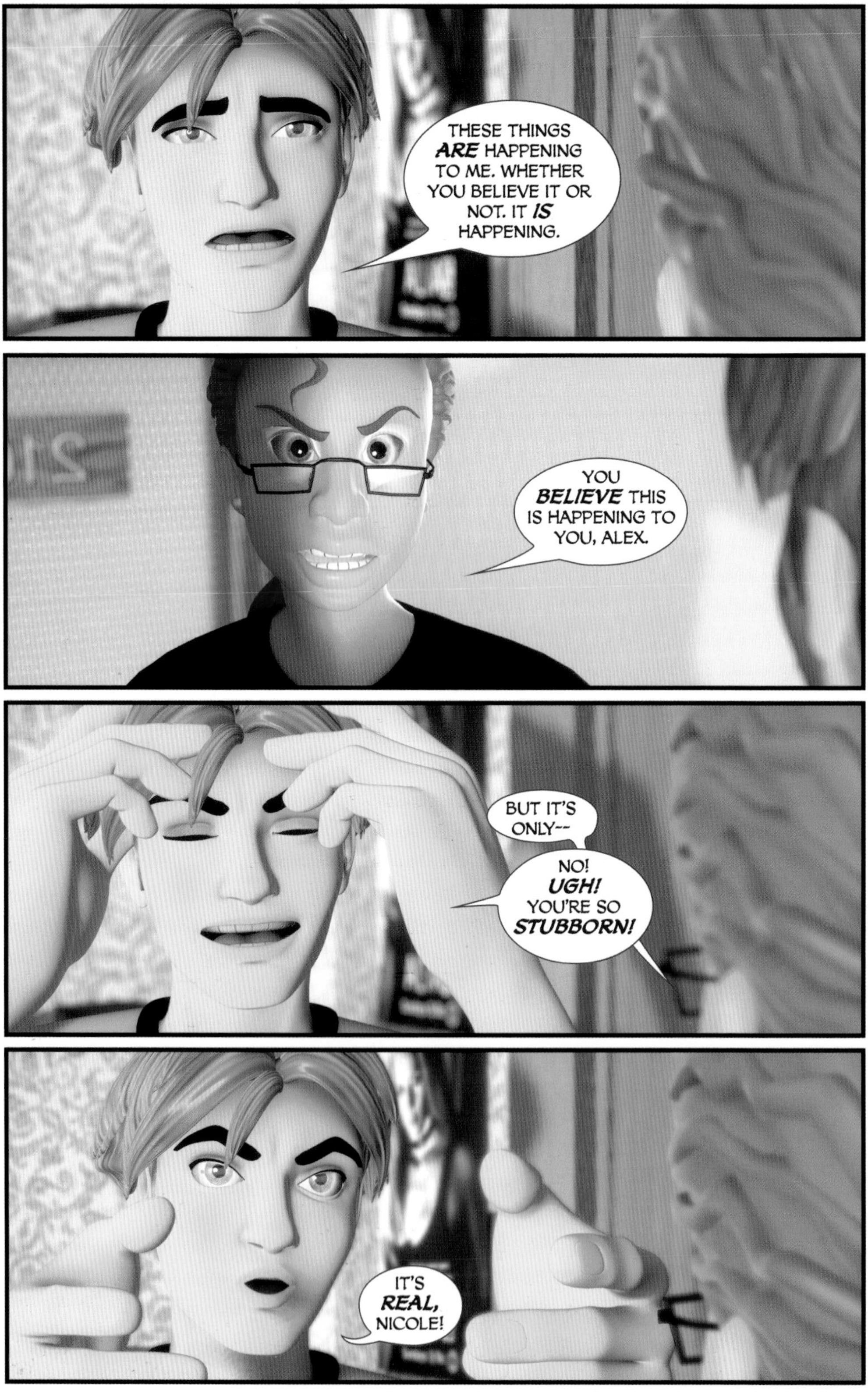
THESE THINGS ARE HAPPENING TO ME. WHETHER YOU BELIEVE IT OR NOT. IT IS HAPPENING.
YOU BELIEVE THIS IS HAPPENING TO YOU, ALEX.
BUT IT'S ONLY--
NO! UGH! YOU'RE SO STUBBORN!
IT'S REAL, NICOLE!

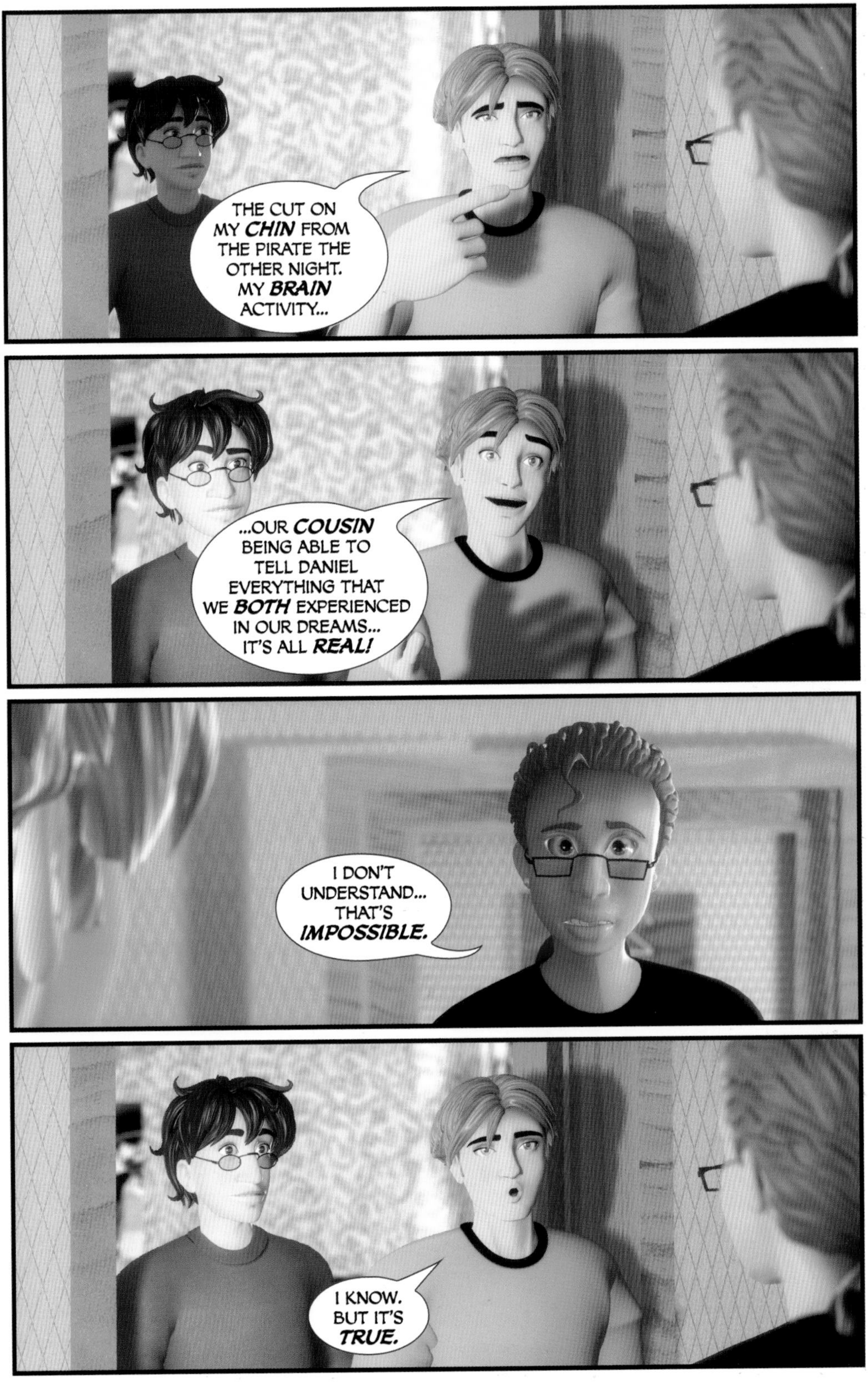
THE CUT ON MY CHIN FROM THE PIRATE THE OTHER NIGHT. MY BRAIN ACTIVITY...
...OUR COUSIN BEING ABLE TO TELL DANIEL EVERYTHING THAT WE BOTH EXPERIENCED IN OUR DREAMS... IT'S ALL REAL!
I DON'T UNDERSTAND... THAT'S IMPOSSIBLE.
I KNOW. BUT IT'S TRUE.

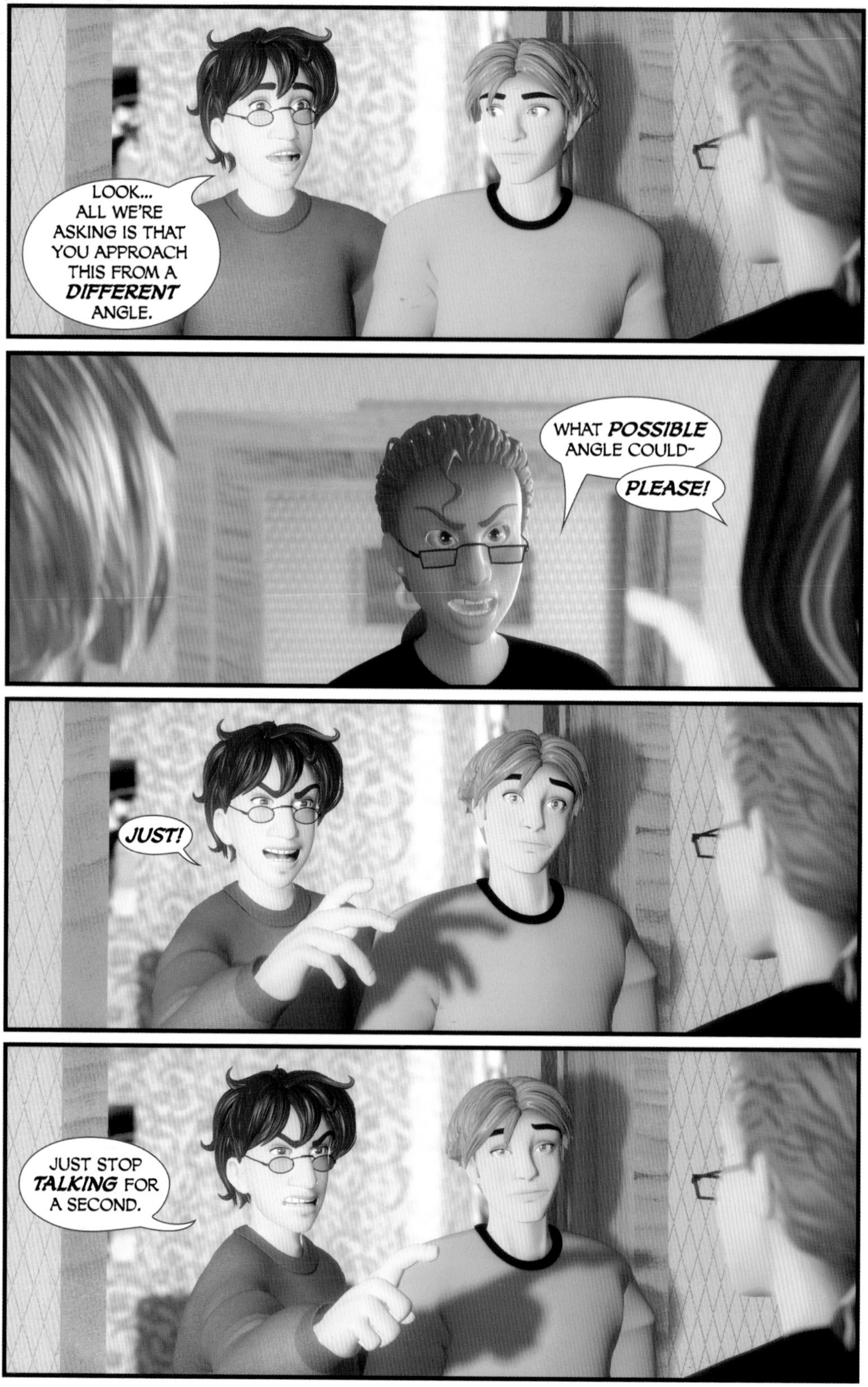
LOOK... ALL WE'RE ASKING IS THAT YOU APPROACH THIS FROM A DIFFERENT ANGLE.
WHAT POSSIBLE ANGLE COULD-
PLEASE!
JUST!
JUST STOP TALKING FOR A SECOND.

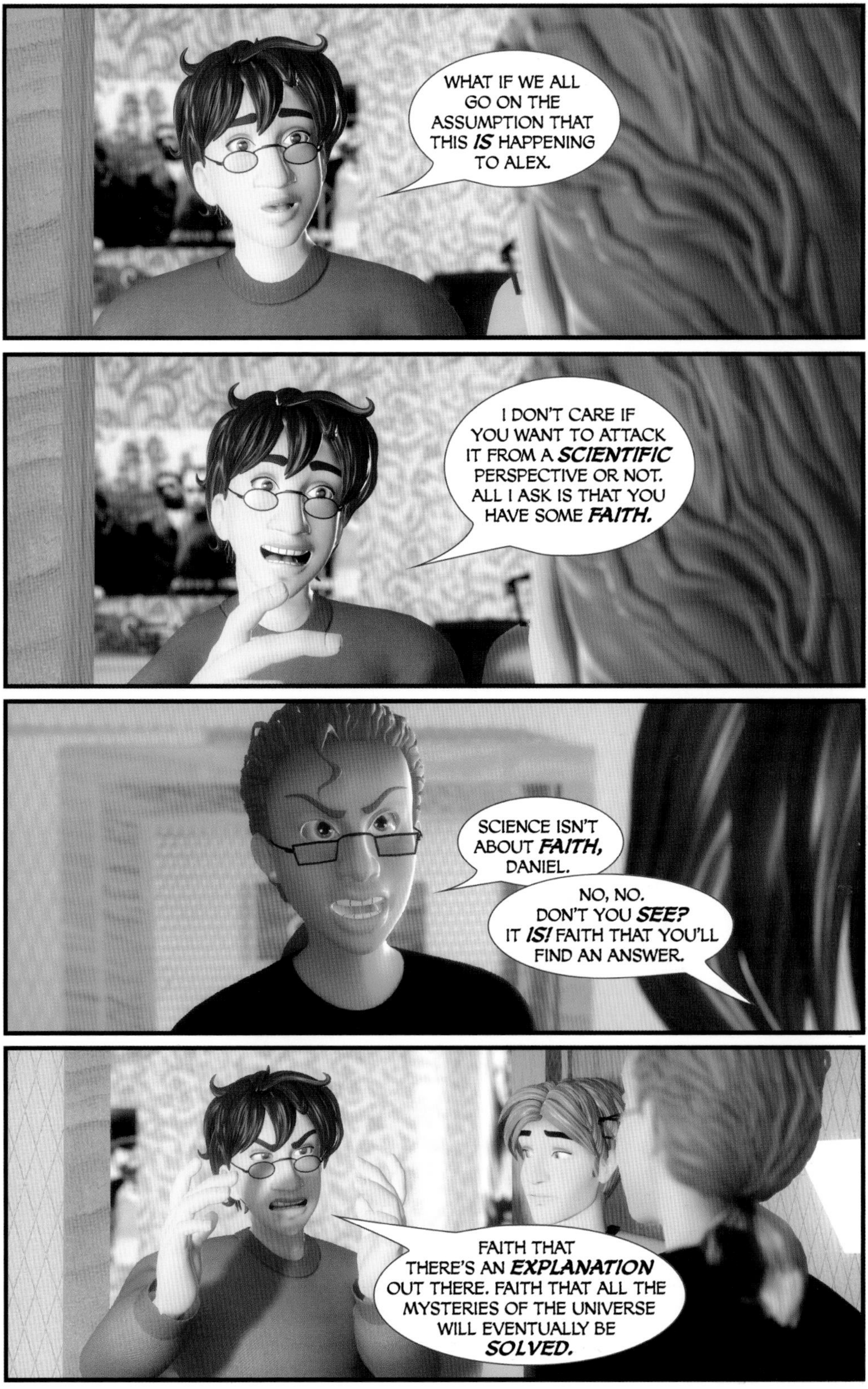
WHAT IF WE ALL GO ON THE ASSUMPTION THAT THIS IS HAPPENING TO ALEX.
I DON'T CARE IF YOU WANT TO ATTACK IT FROM A SCIENTIFIC PERSPECTIVE OR NOT. ALL I ASK IS THAT YOU HAVE SOME FAITH.
SCIENCE ISN'T ABOUT FAITH, DANIEL.
NO, NO. DON'T YOU SEE? IT IS! FAITH THAT YOU'LL FIND AN ANSWER.
FAITH THAT THERE'S AN EXPLANATION OUT THERE. FAITH THAT ALL THE MYSTERIES OF THE UNIVERSE WILL EVENTUALLY BE SOLVED.

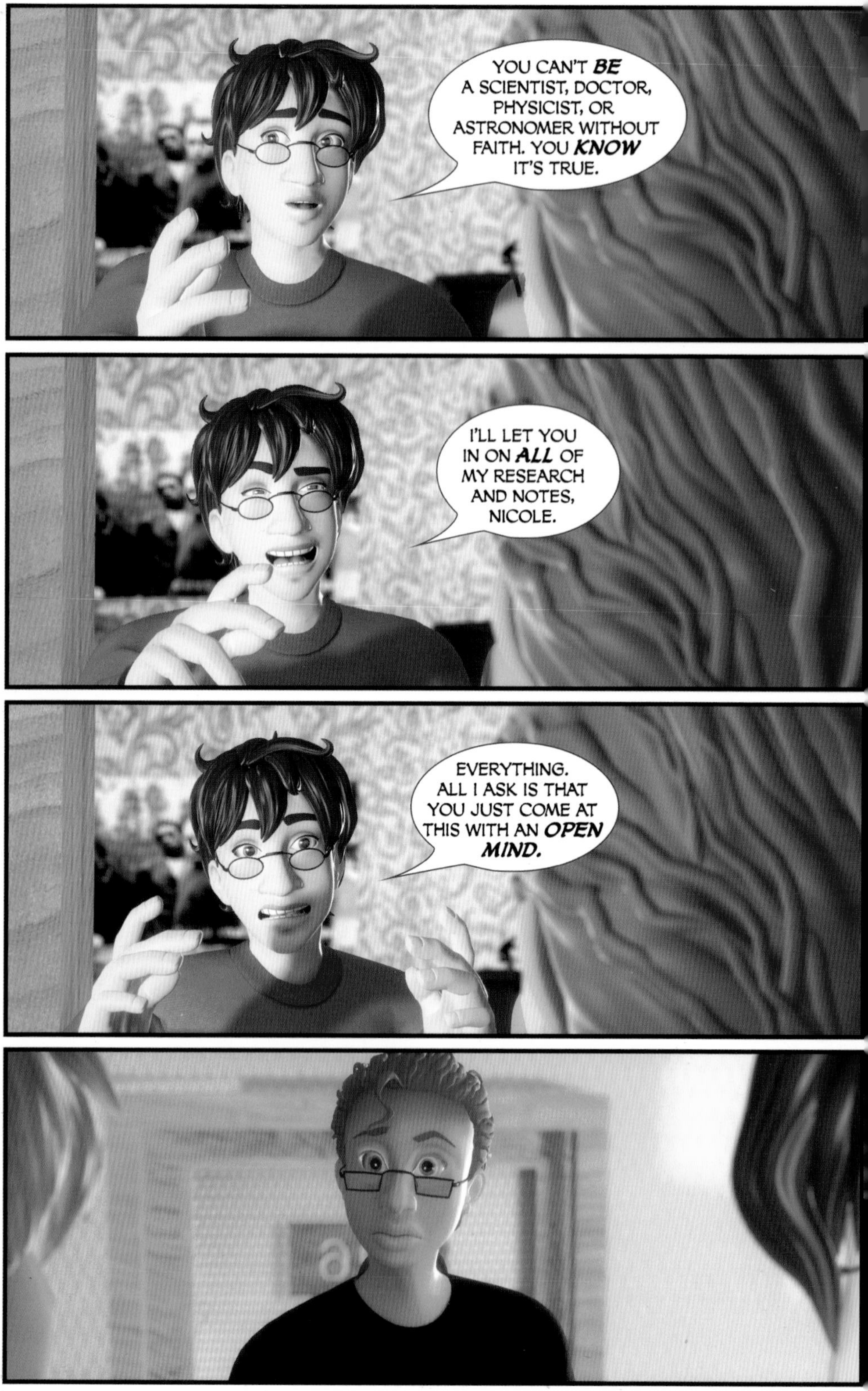
YOU CAN'T *BE* A SCIENTIST, DOCTOR, PHYSICIST, OR ASTRONOMER WITHOUT FAITH. YOU *KNOW* IT'S TRUE.
I'LL LET YOU IN ON *ALL* OF MY RESEARCH AND NOTES, NICOLE.
EVERYTHING. ALL I ASK IS THAT YOU JUST COME AT THIS WITH AN *OPEN MIND.*

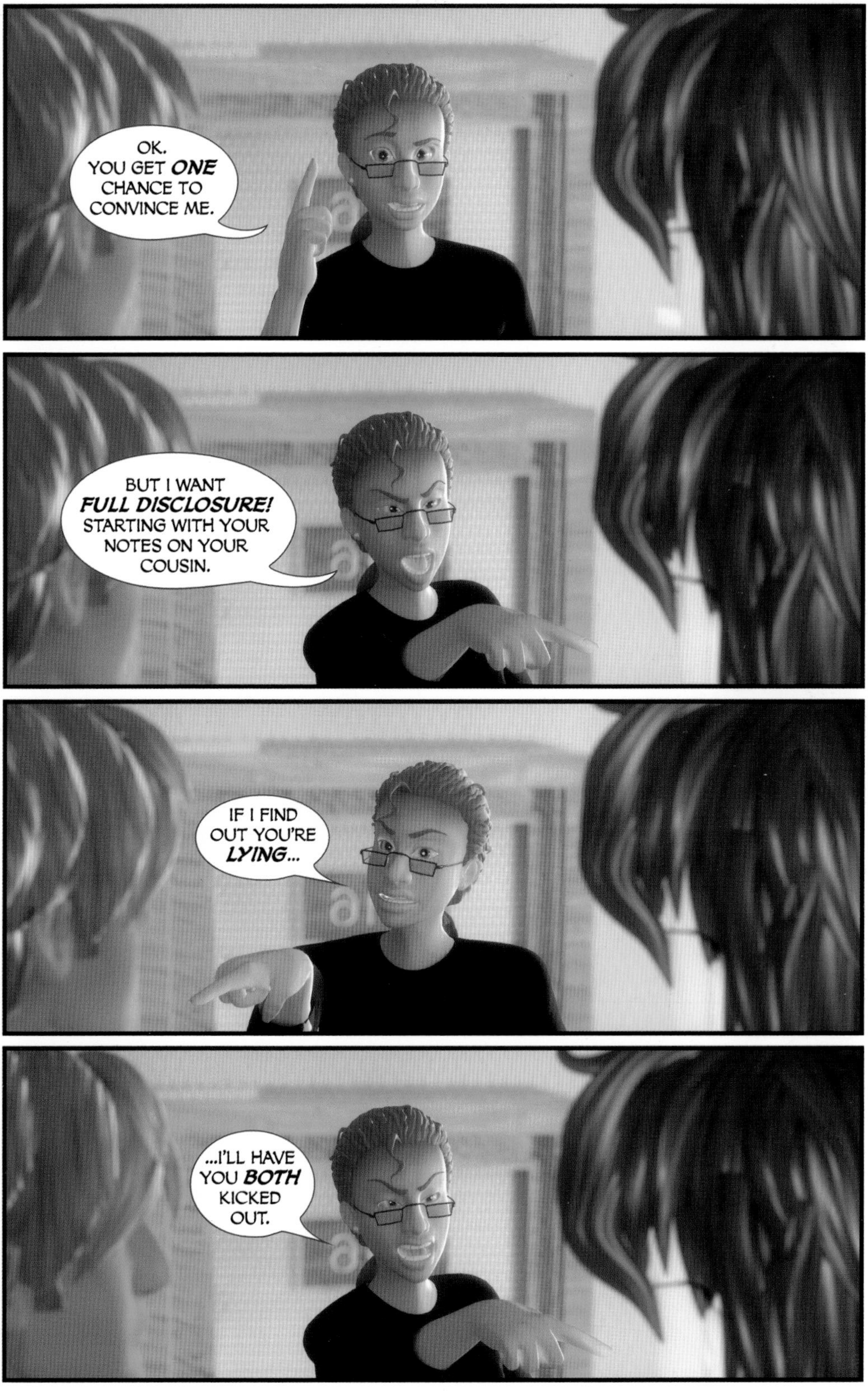
OK. YOU GET ONE CHANCE TO CONVINCE ME.
BUT I WANT FULL DISCLOSURE! STARTING WITH YOUR NOTES ON YOUR COUSIN.
IF I FIND OUT YOU'RE LYING...
...I'LL HAVE YOU BOTH KICKED OUT.

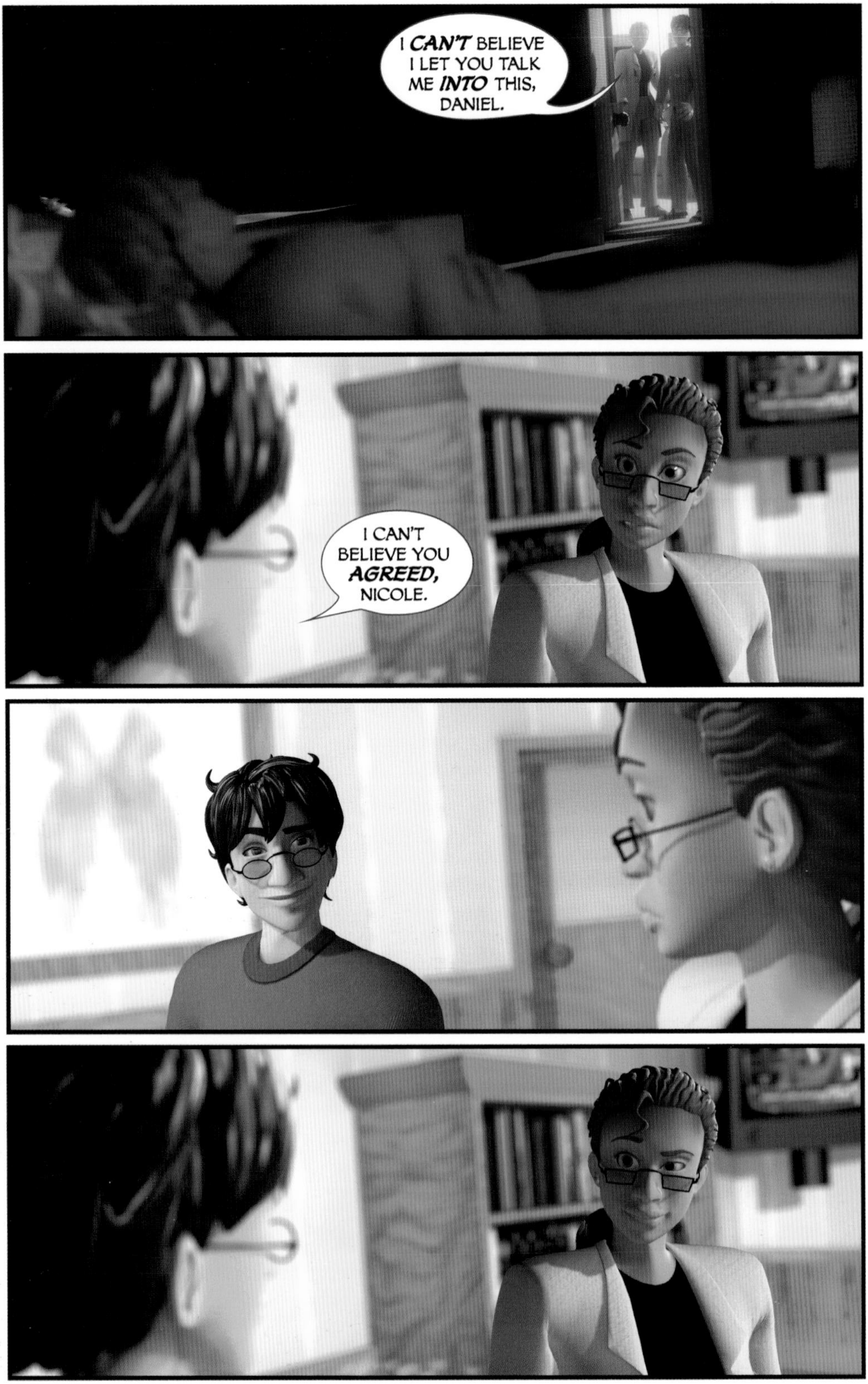
I CAN'T BELIEVE I LET YOU TALK ME INTO THIS, DANIEL.
I CAN'T BELIEVE YOU AGREED, NICOLE.

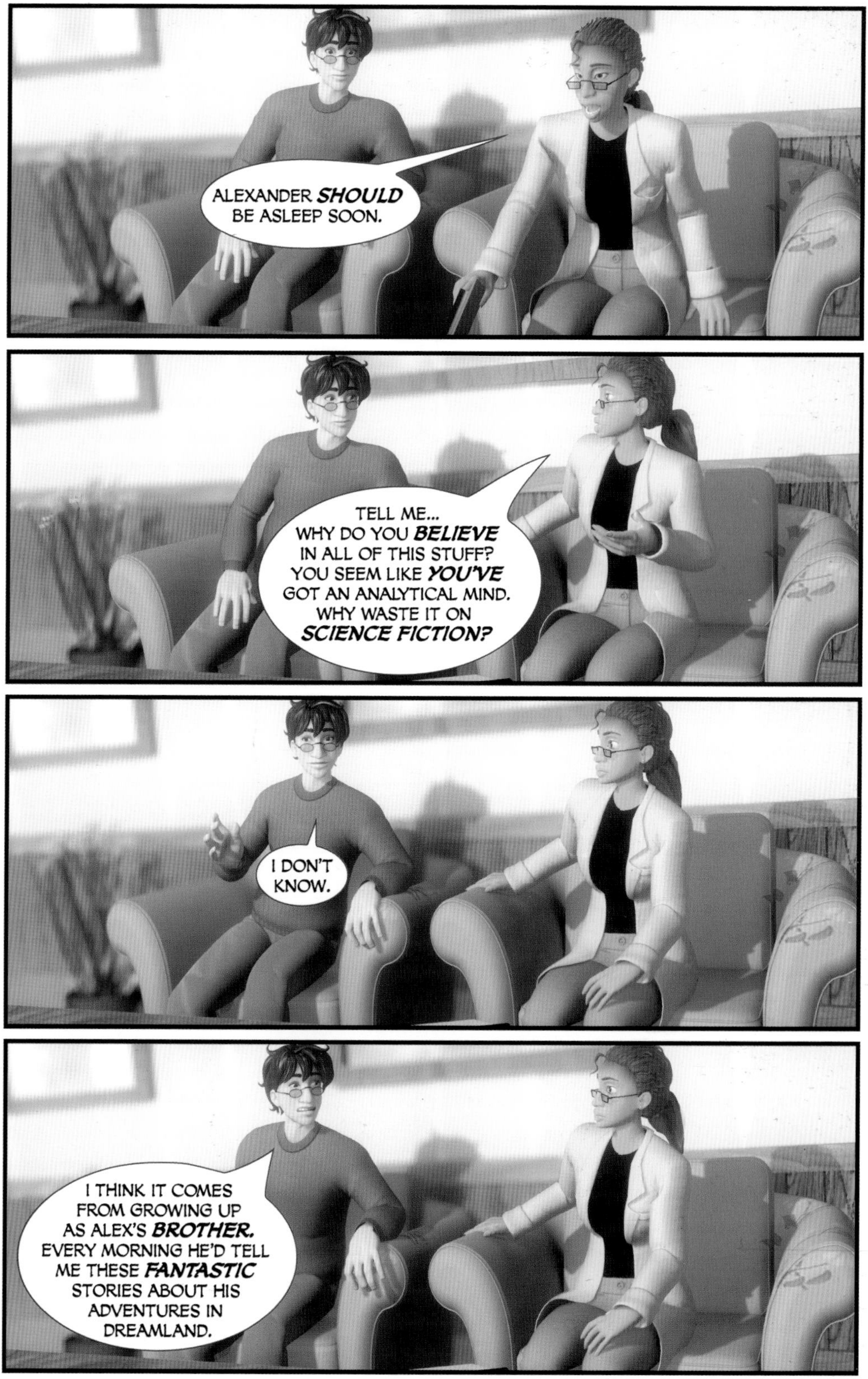
ALEXANDER *SHOULD* BE ASLEEP SOON.
TELL ME... WHY DO YOU *BELIEVE* IN ALL OF THIS STUFF? YOU SEEM LIKE *YOU'VE* GOT AN ANALYTICAL MIND. WHY WASTE IT ON *SCIENCE FICTION?*
I DON'T KNOW.
I THINK IT COMES FROM GROWING UP AS ALEX'S *BROTHER.* EVERY MORNING HE'D TELL ME THESE *FANTASTIC* STORIES ABOUT HIS ADVENTURES IN DREAMLAND.

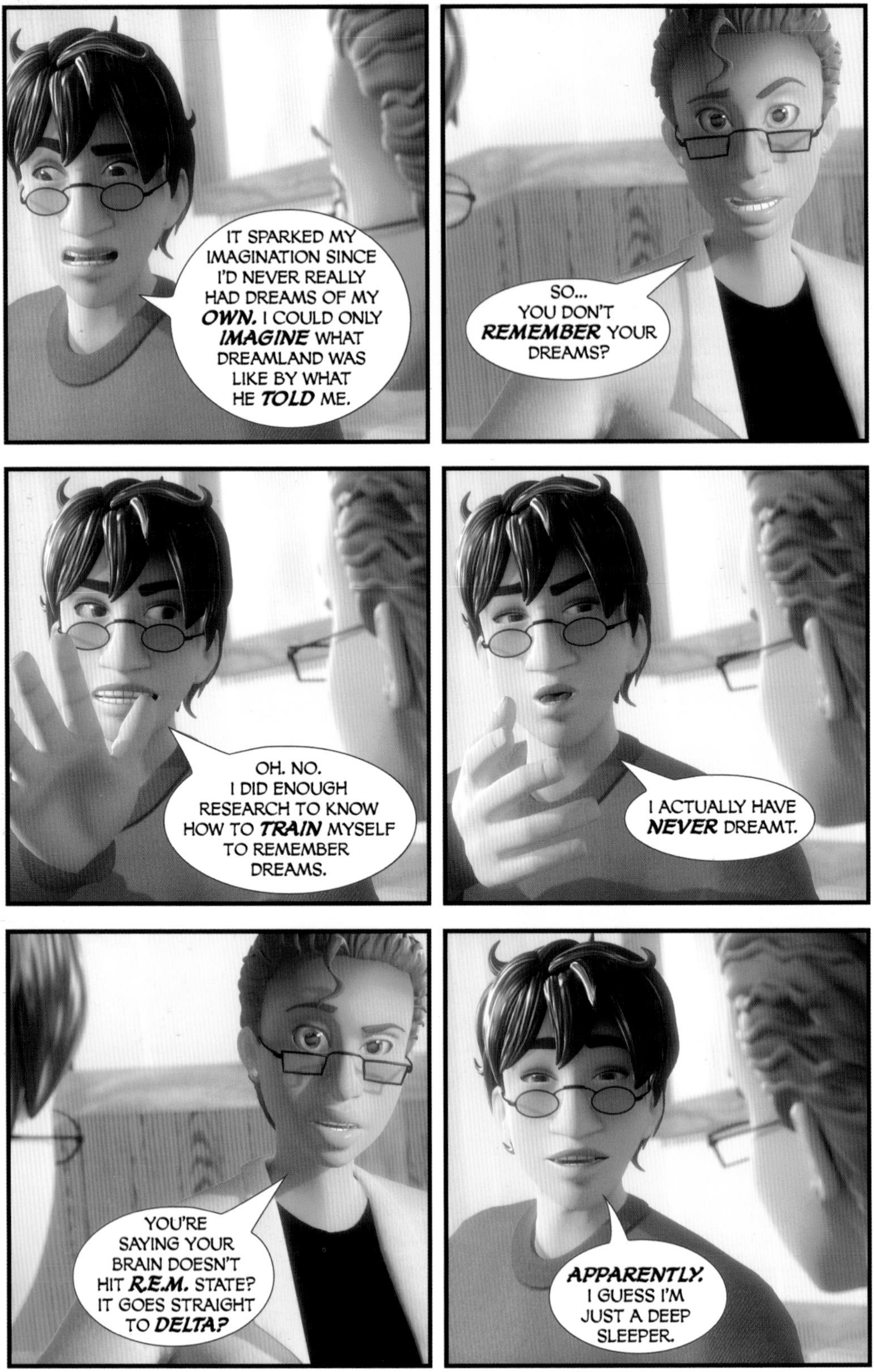
IT SPARKED MY IMAGINATION SINCE I'D NEVER REALLY HAD DREAMS OF MY OWN. I COULD ONLY IMAGINE WHAT DREAMLAND WAS LIKE BY WHAT HE TOLD ME.
SO... YOU DON'T REMEMBER YOUR DREAMS?
OH. NO. I DID ENOUGH RESEARCH TO KNOW HOW TO TRAIN MYSELF TO REMEMBER DREAMS.
I ACTUALLY HAVE NEVER DREAMT.
YOU'RE SAYING YOUR BRAIN DOESN'T HIT R.E.M. STATE? IT GOES STRAIGHT TO DELTA?
APPARENTLY. I GUESS I'M JUST A DEEP SLEEPER.

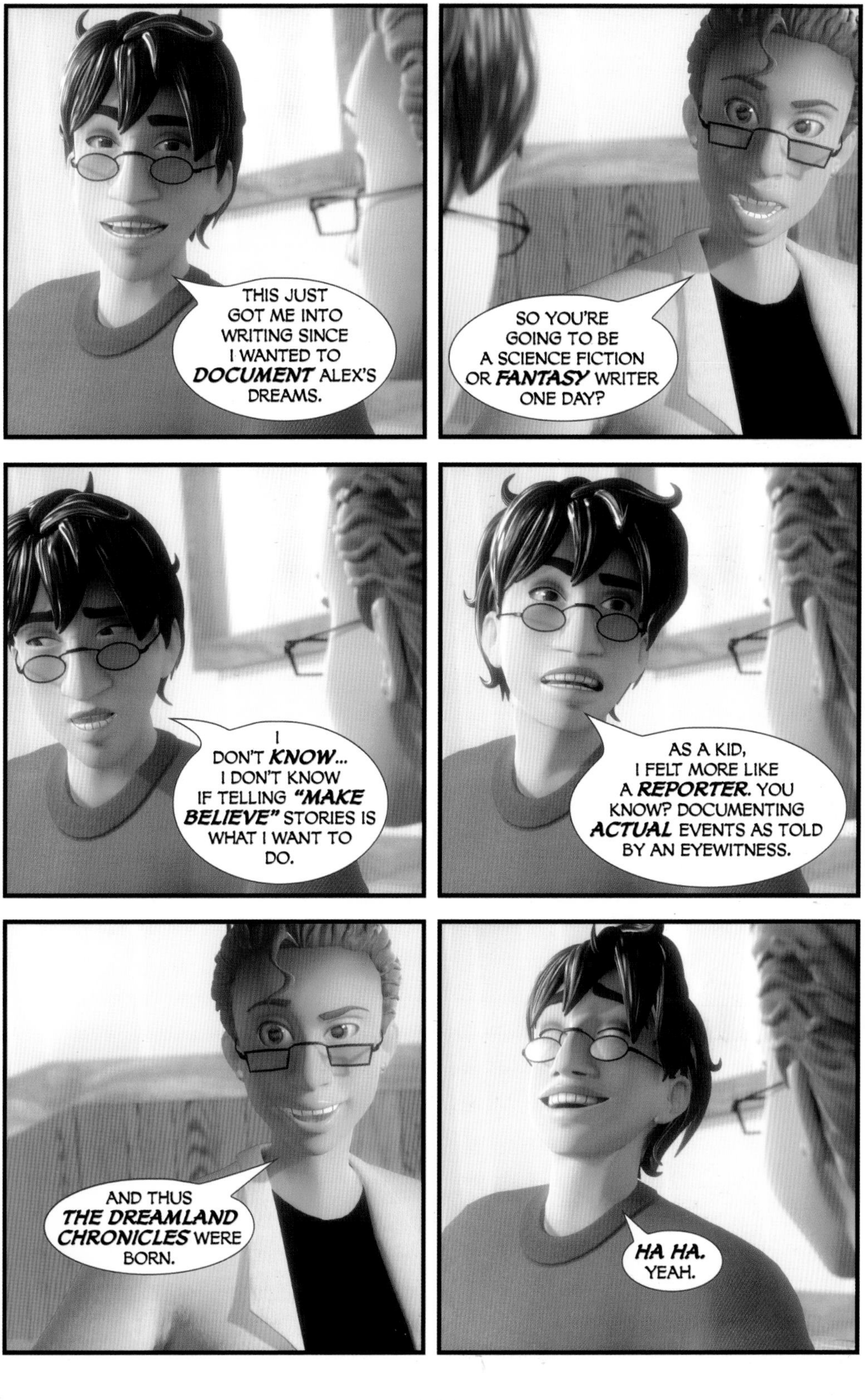
THIS JUST GOT ME INTO WRITING SINCE I WANTED TO DOCUMENT ALEX'S DREAMS.
SO YOU'RE GOING TO BE A SCIENCE FICTION OR FANTASY WRITER ONE DAY?
I DON'T KNOW... I DON'T KNOW IF TELLING "MAKE BELIEVE" STORIES IS WHAT I WANT TO DO.
AS A KID, I FELT MORE LIKE A REPORTER. YOU KNOW? DOCUMENTING ACTUAL EVENTS AS TOLD BY AN EYEWITNESS.
AND THUS THE DREAMLAND CHRONICLES WERE BORN.
HA HA. YEAH.

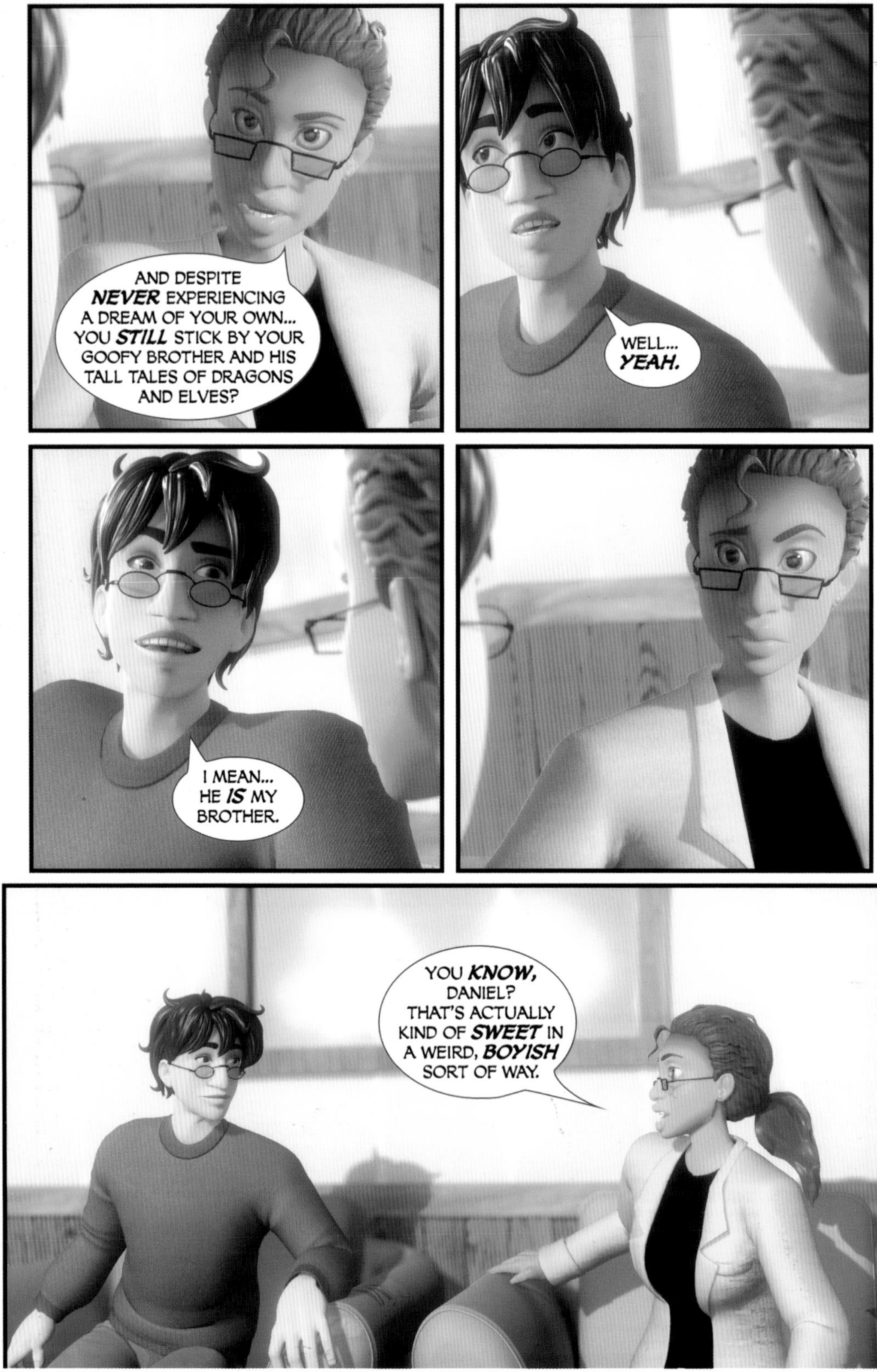
AND DESPITE NEVER EXPERIENCING A DREAM OF YOUR OWN... YOU STILL STICK BY YOUR GOOFY BROTHER AND HIS TALL TALES OF DRAGONS AND ELVES?
WELL... YEAH.
I MEAN... HE IS MY BROTHER.
YOU KNOW, DANIEL? THAT'S ACTUALLY KIND OF SWEET IN A WEIRD, BOYISH SORT OF WAY.

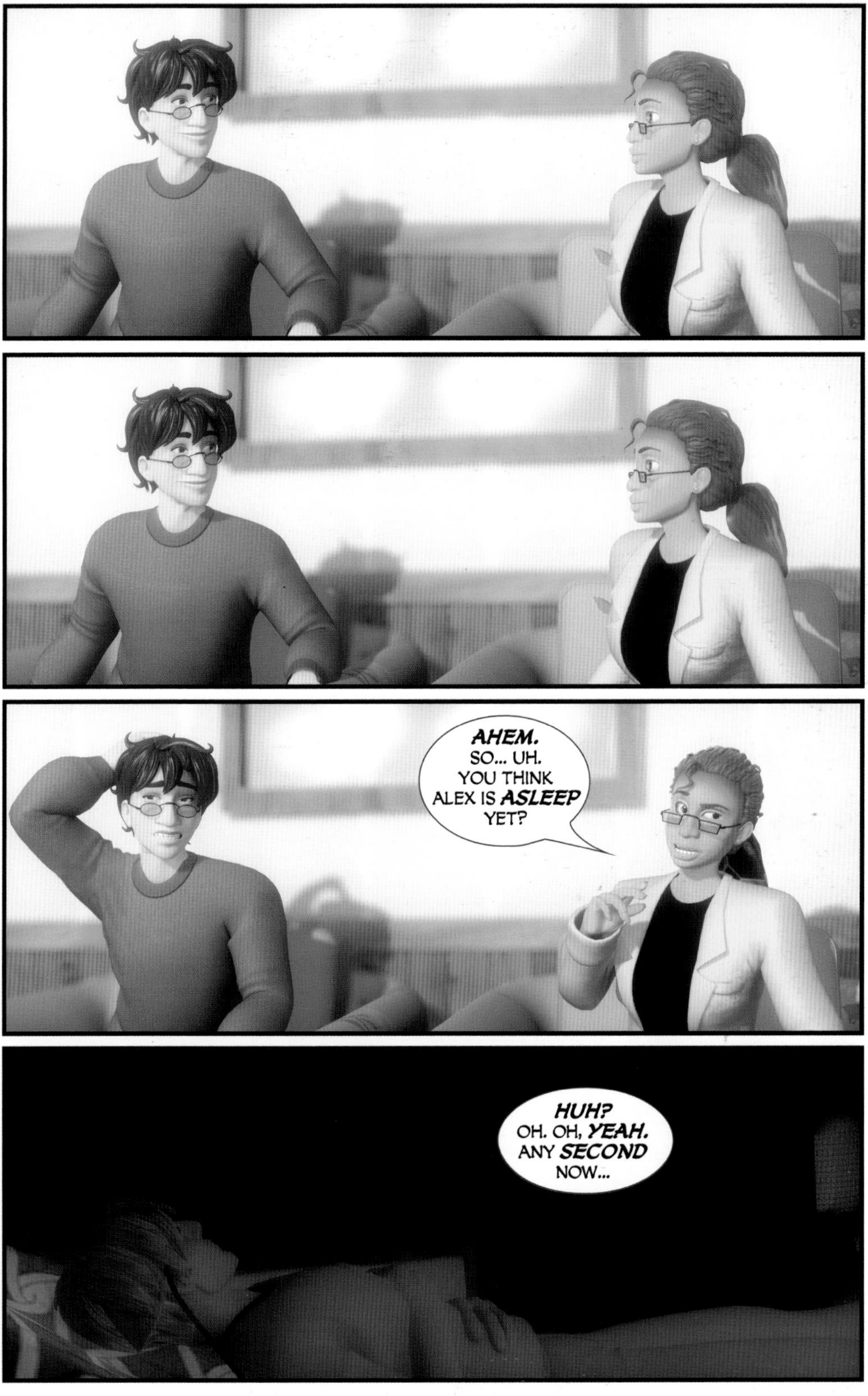
AHEM. SO... UH. YOU THINK ALEX IS ASLEEP YET?
HUH? OH. OH, YEAH. ANY SECOND NOW...

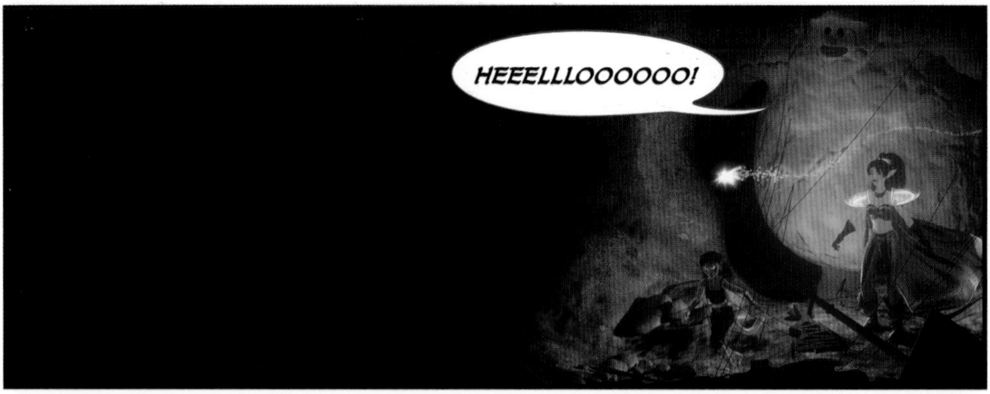
HEEELLLOOOOOO!

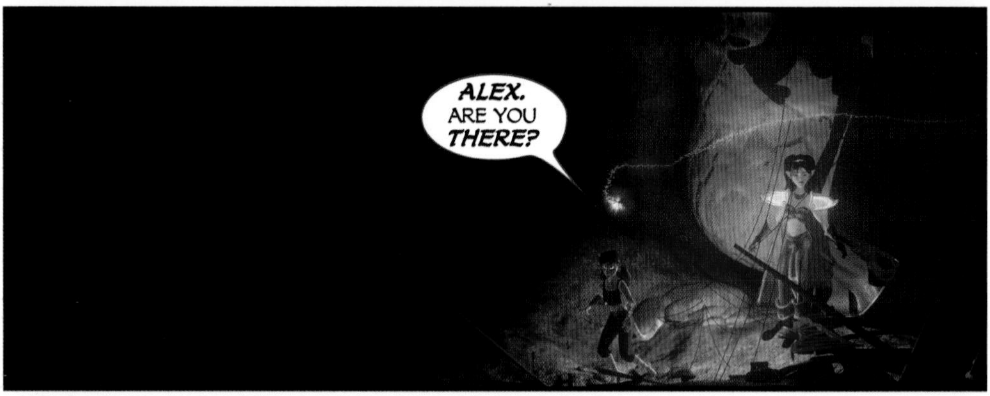
ALEX. ARE YOU THERE?

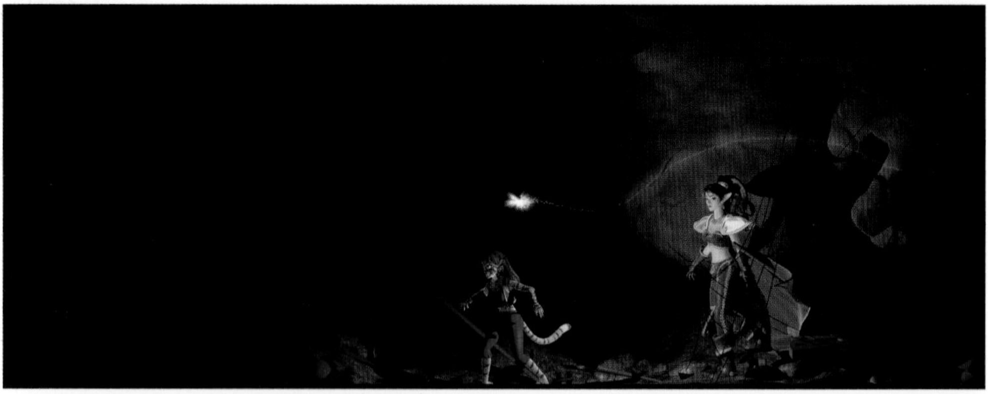

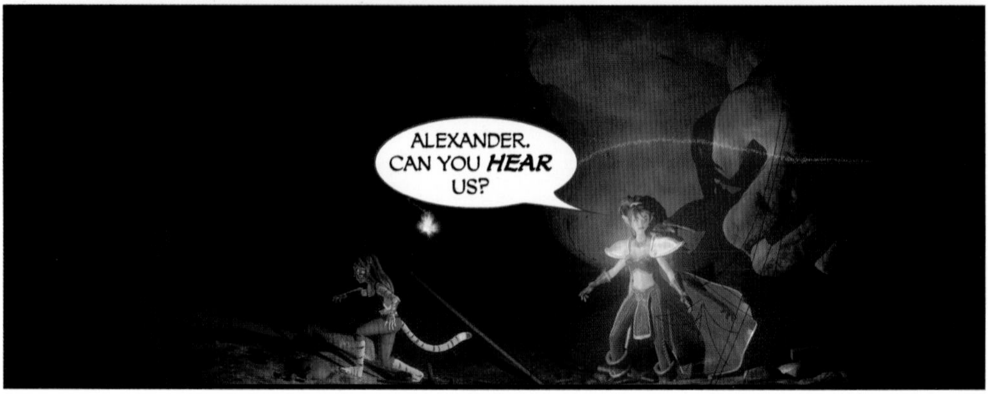
ALEXANDER. CAN YOU HEAR US?

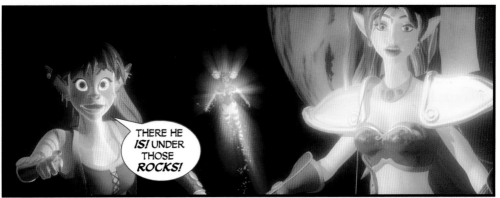

THERE HE *IS!* UNDER THOSE *ROCKS!*

HEY, GUYS.

UGH.

I'M... UH... I'M *STUCK.*

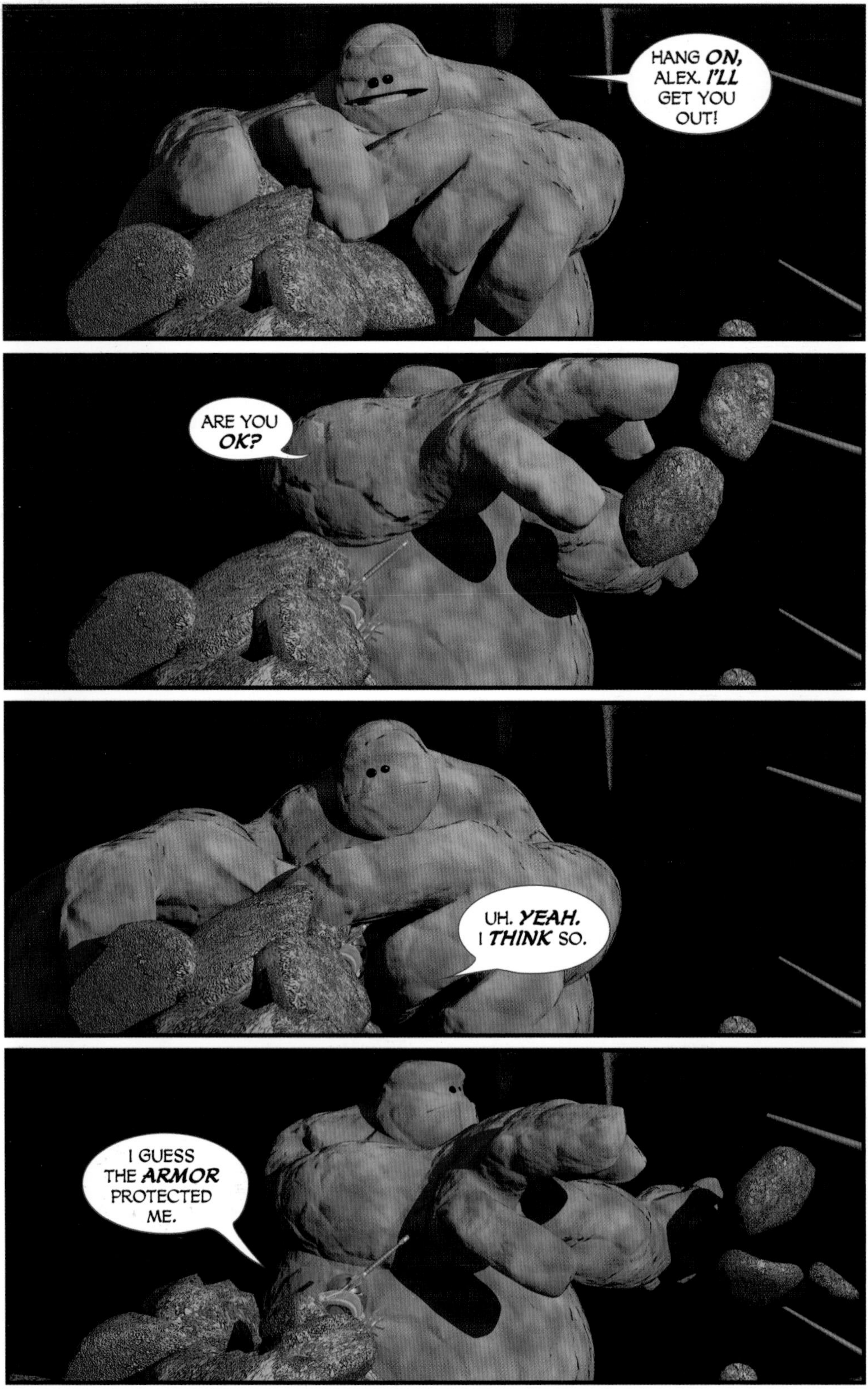
HANG ON, ALEX. I'LL GET YOU OUT!
ARE YOU OK?
UH. YEAH. I THINK SO.
I GUESS THE ARMOR PROTECTED ME.

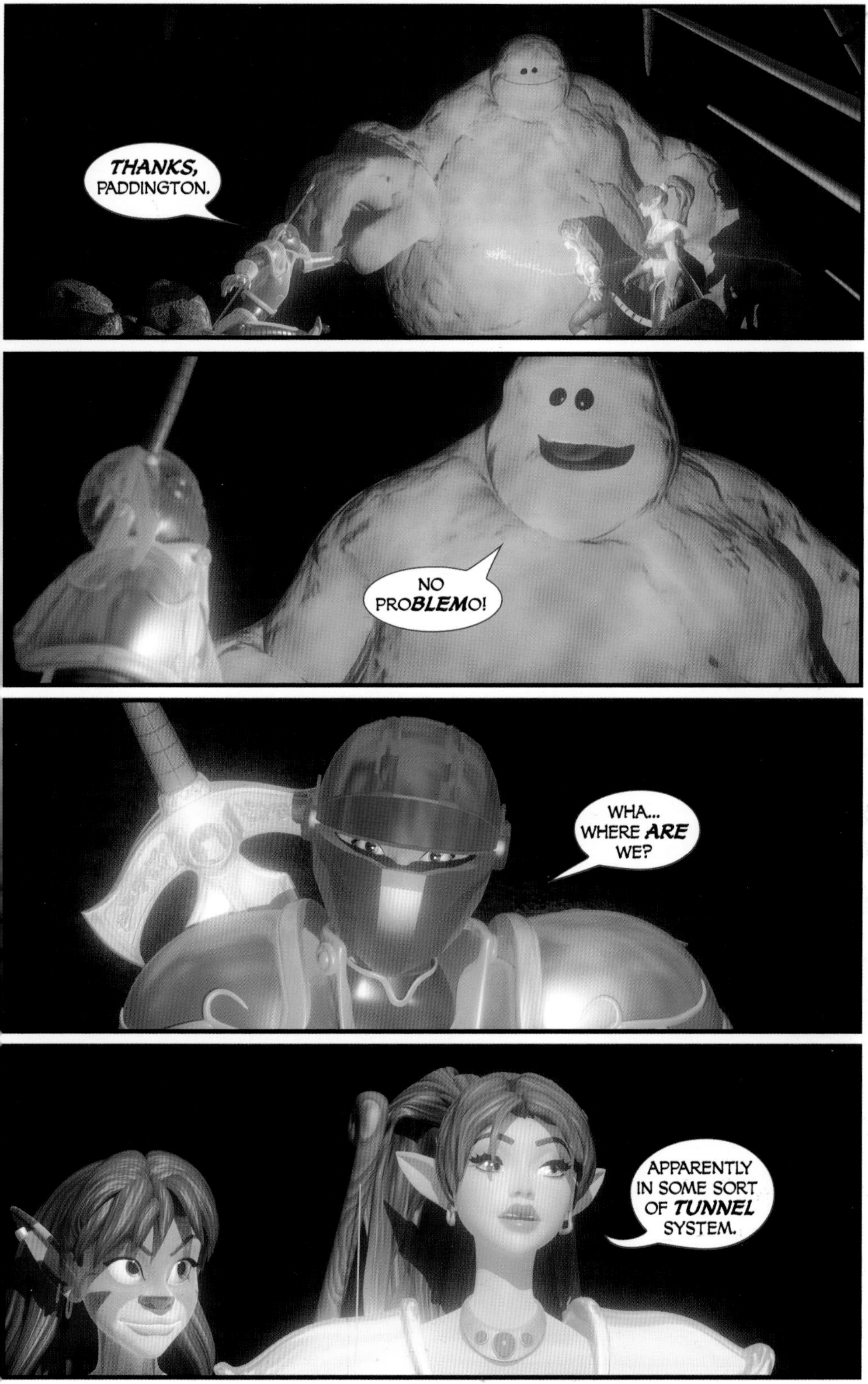
THANKS, PADDINGTON.
NO PROBLEMO!
WHA... WHERE ARE WE?
APPARENTLY IN SOME SORT OF TUNNEL SYSTEM.

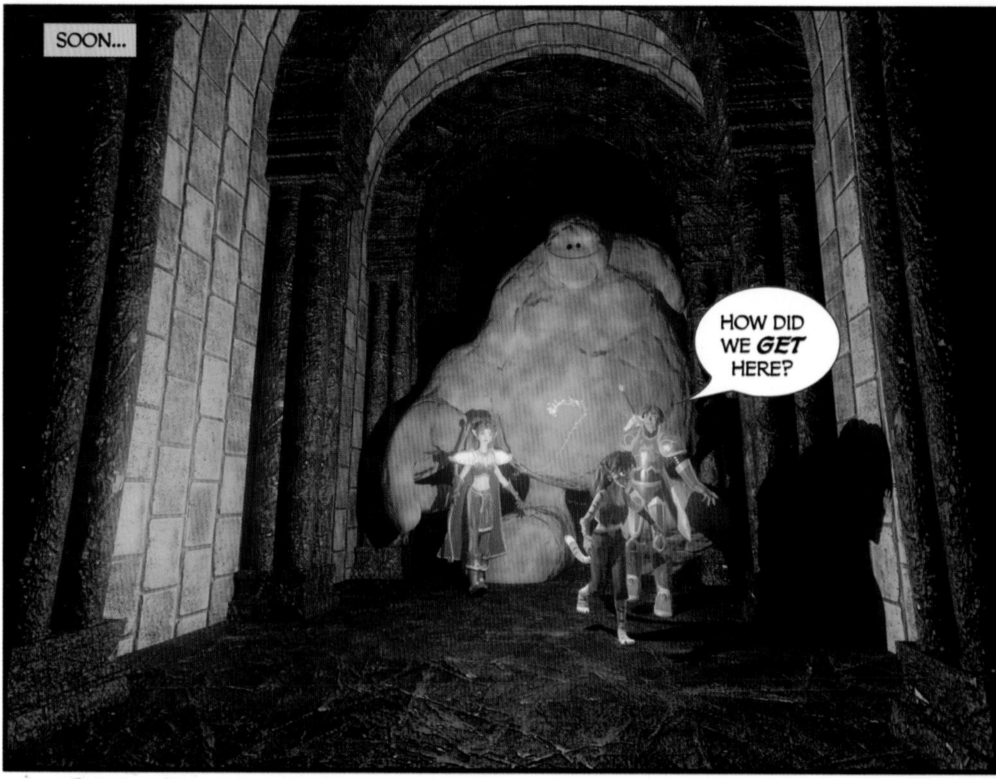
SOON...
HOW DID WE GET HERE?

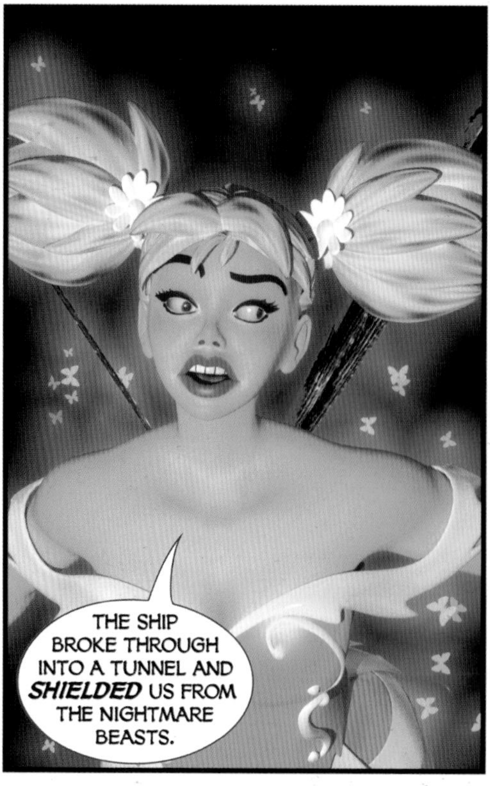
THE SHIP BROKE THROUGH INTO A TUNNEL AND SHIELDED US FROM THE NIGHTMARE BEASTS.

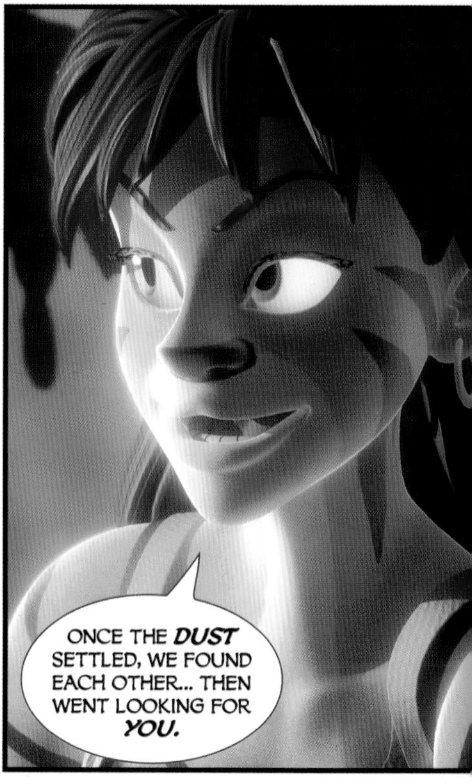
ONCE THE DUST SETTLED, WE FOUND EACH OTHER... THEN WENT LOOKING FOR YOU.

OK.
THEN I GUESS WE JUST FIND OUT WHERE *HERE* IS?
AND HOPEFULLY *SOON*. MY BACK IS *KILLING* ME.

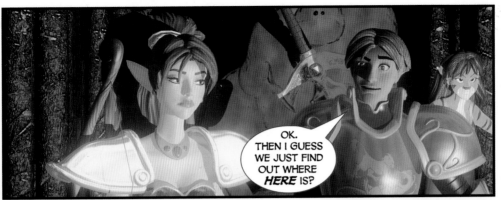

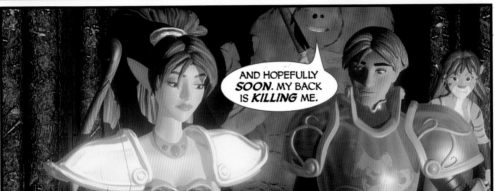

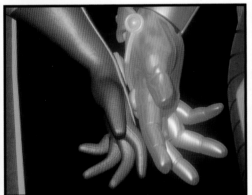

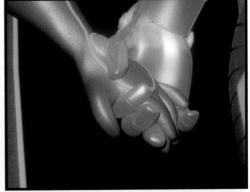

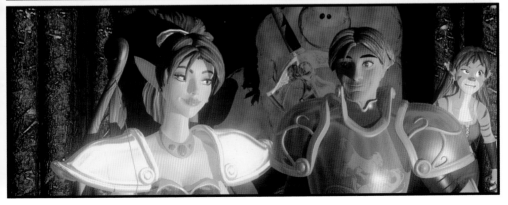

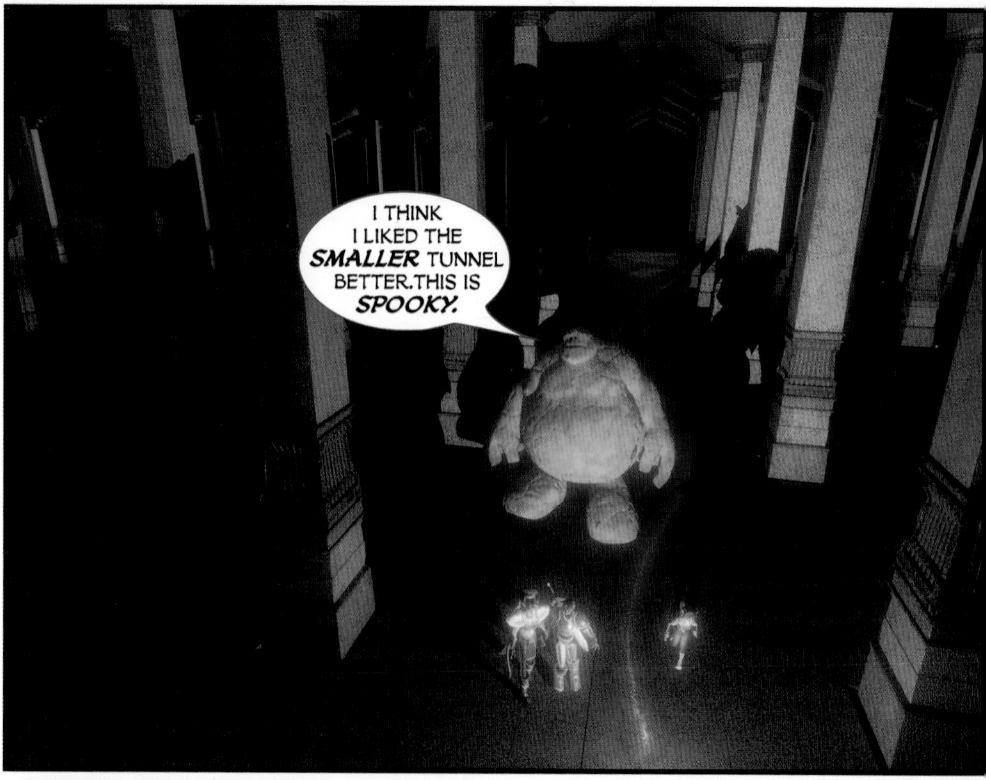
I THINK I LIKED THE SMALLER TUNNEL BETTER.THIS IS SPOOKY.

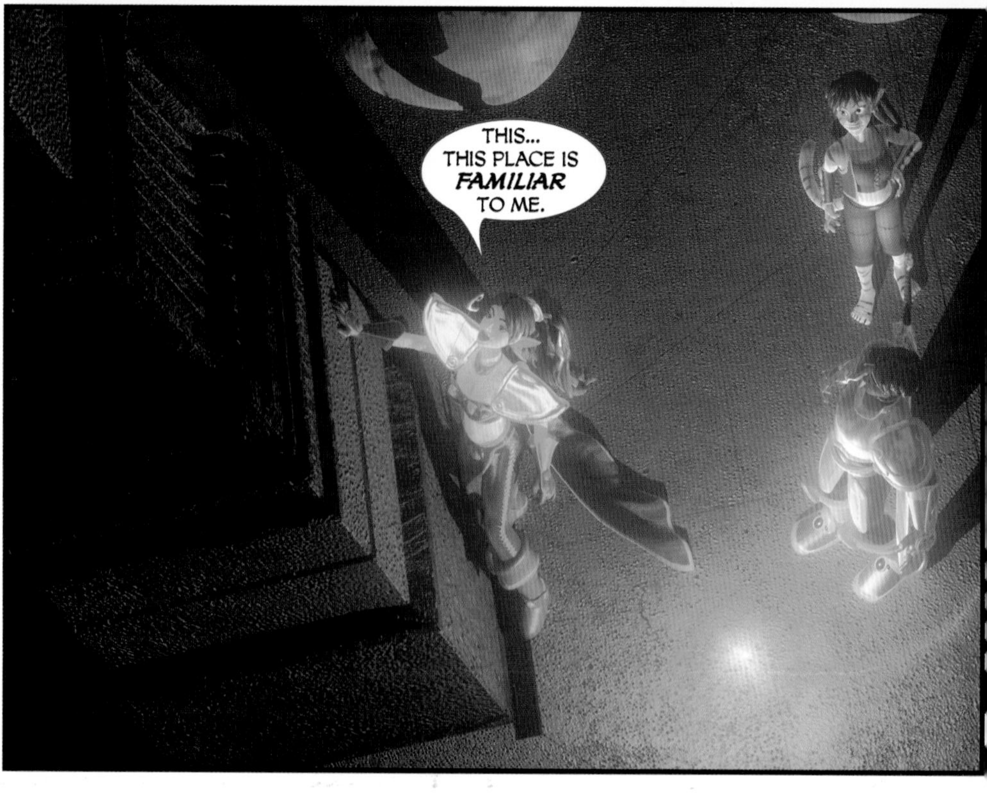
THIS... THIS PLACE IS FAMILIAR TO ME.

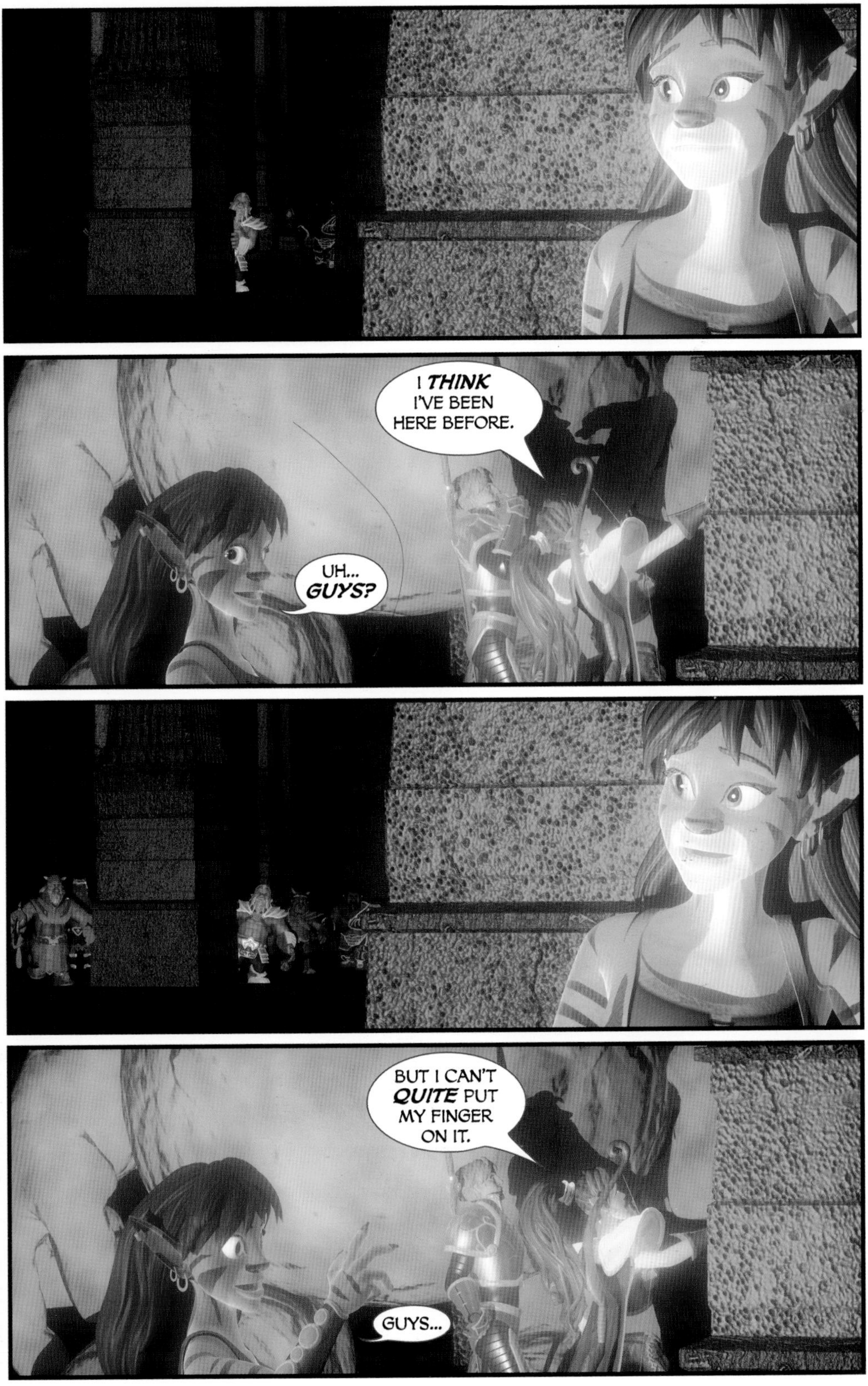
I THINK I'VE BEEN HERE BEFORE.
UH... GUYS?
BUT I CAN'T QUITE PUT MY FINGER ON IT.
GUYS...

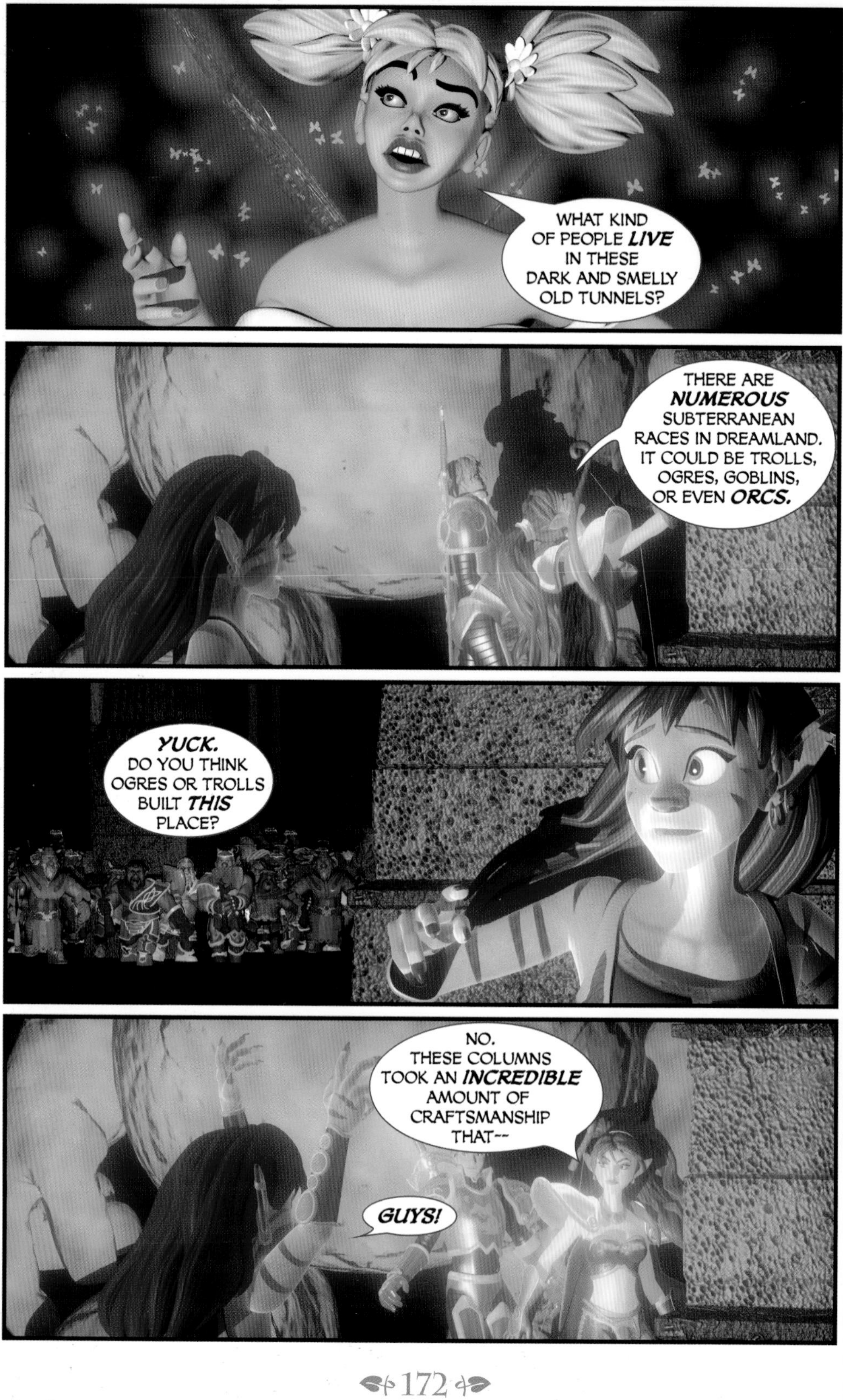
WHAT KIND OF PEOPLE *LIVE* IN THESE DARK AND SMELLY OLD TUNNELS?
THERE ARE *NUMEROUS* SUBTERRANEAN RACES IN DREAMLAND. IT COULD BE TROLLS, OGRES, GOBLINS, OR EVEN *ORCS.*
YUCK. DO YOU THINK OGRES OR TROLLS BUILT *THIS* PLACE?
NO. THESE COLUMNS TOOK AN *INCREDIBLE* AMOUNT OF CRAFTSMANSHIP THAT--
GUYS!

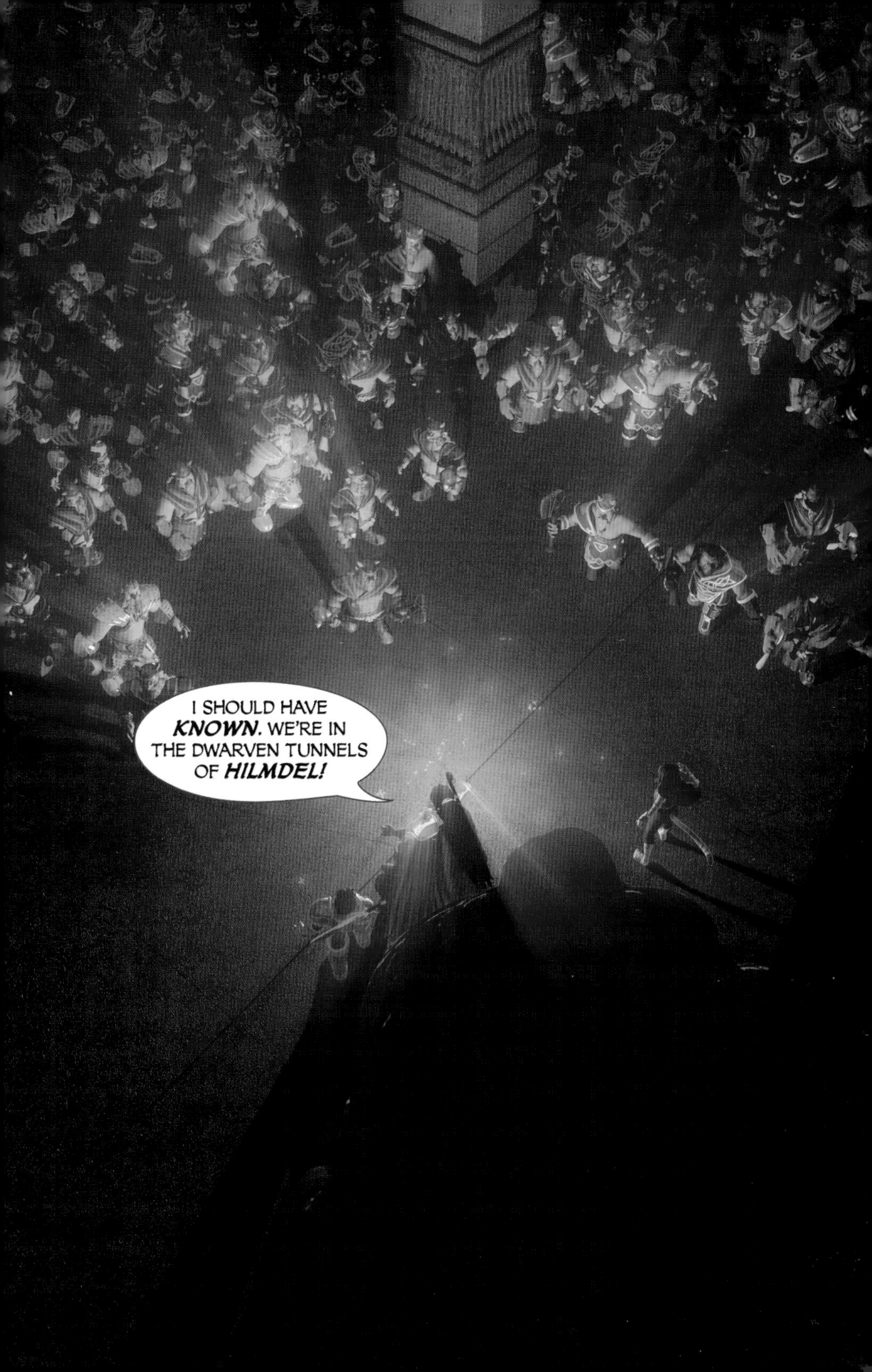
I SHOULD HAVE **KNOWN**. WE'RE IN THE DWARVEN TUNNELS OF **HILMDEL!**

CHAPTER TWELVE

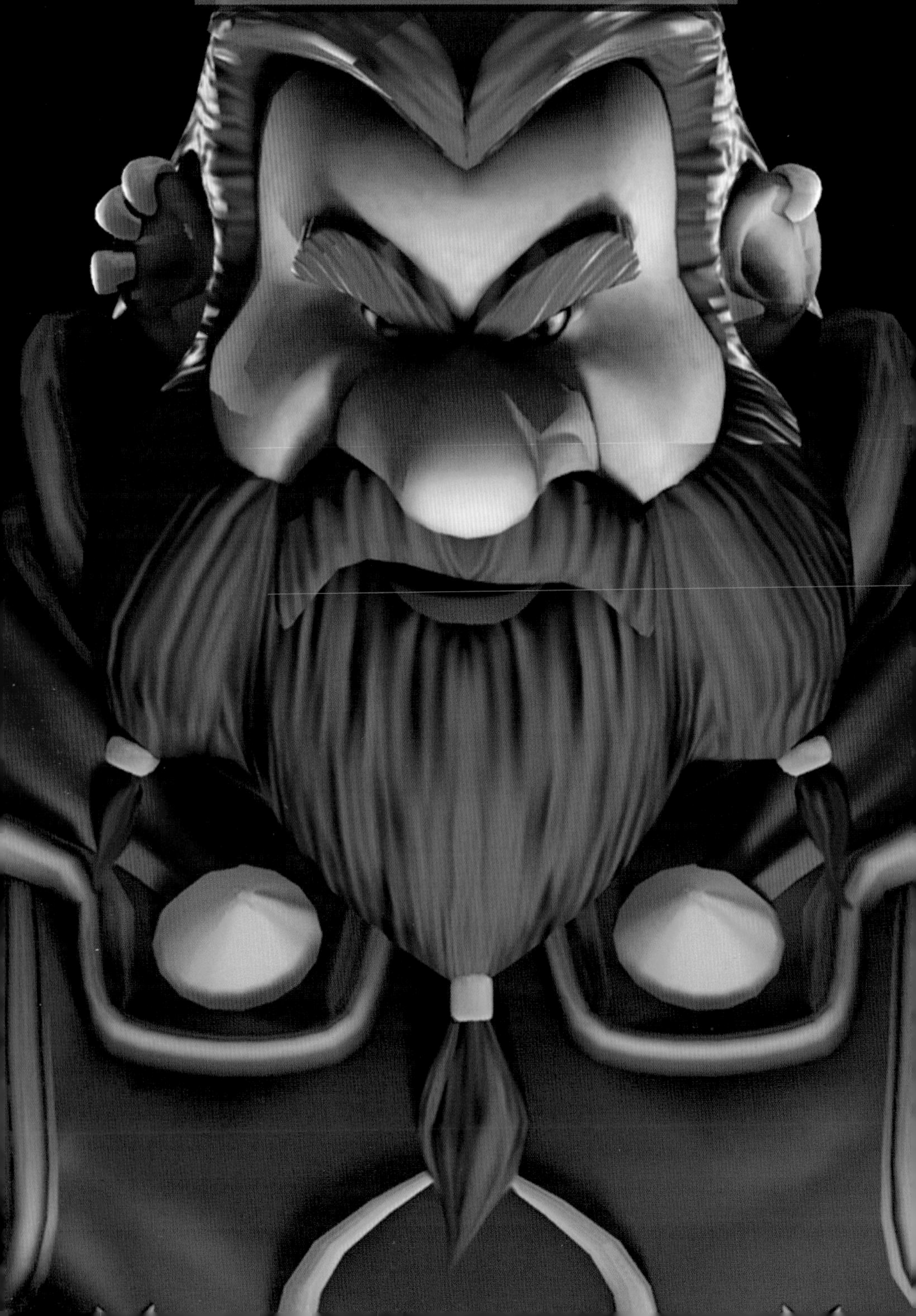

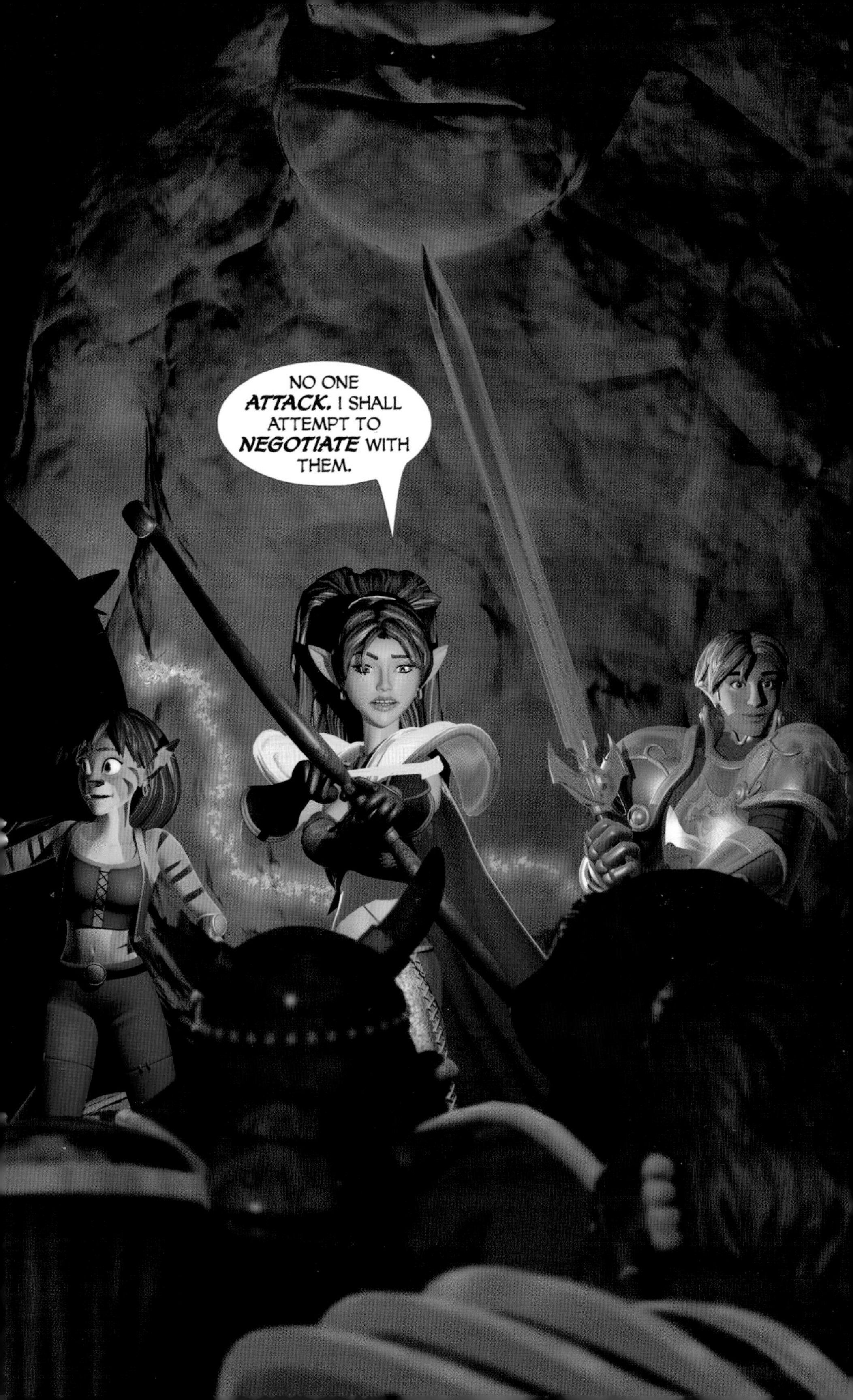
NO ONE ATTACK. I SHALL ATTEMPT TO NEGOTIATE WITH THEM.

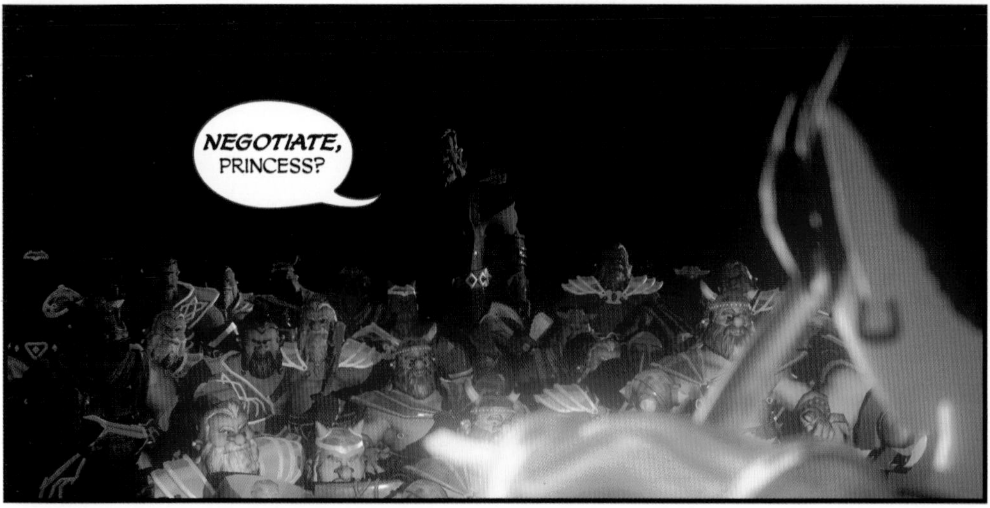
NEGOTIATE, PRINCESS?

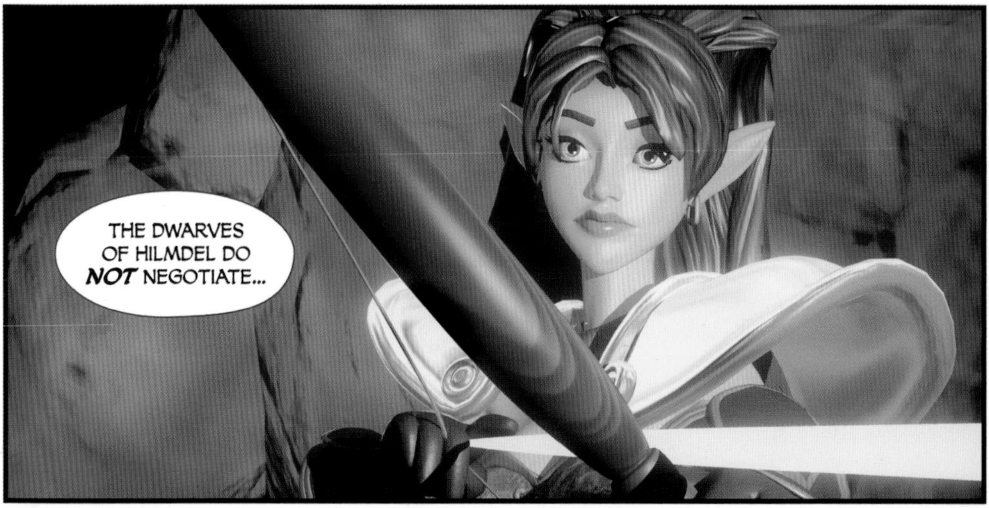
THE DWARVES OF HILMDEL DO **NOT** NEGOTIATE...

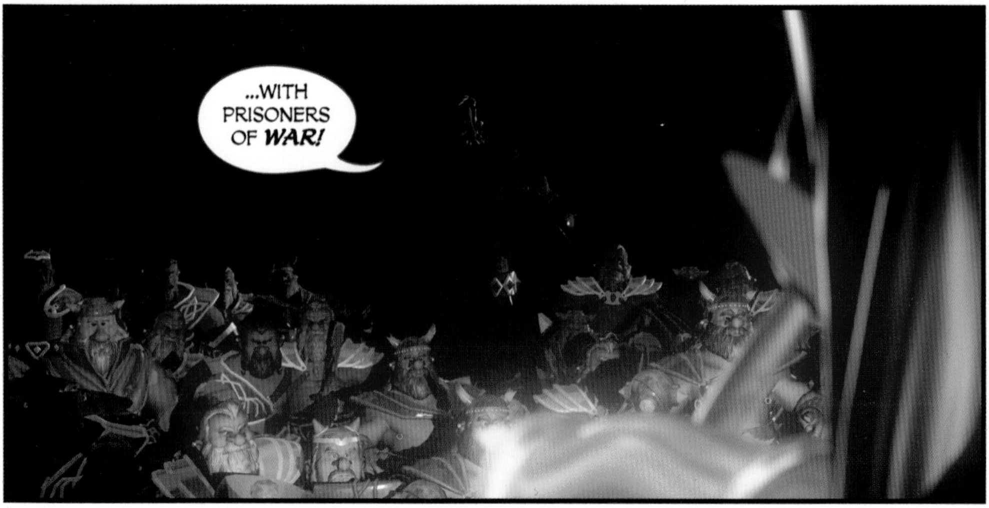
...WITH PRISONERS OF **WAR!**

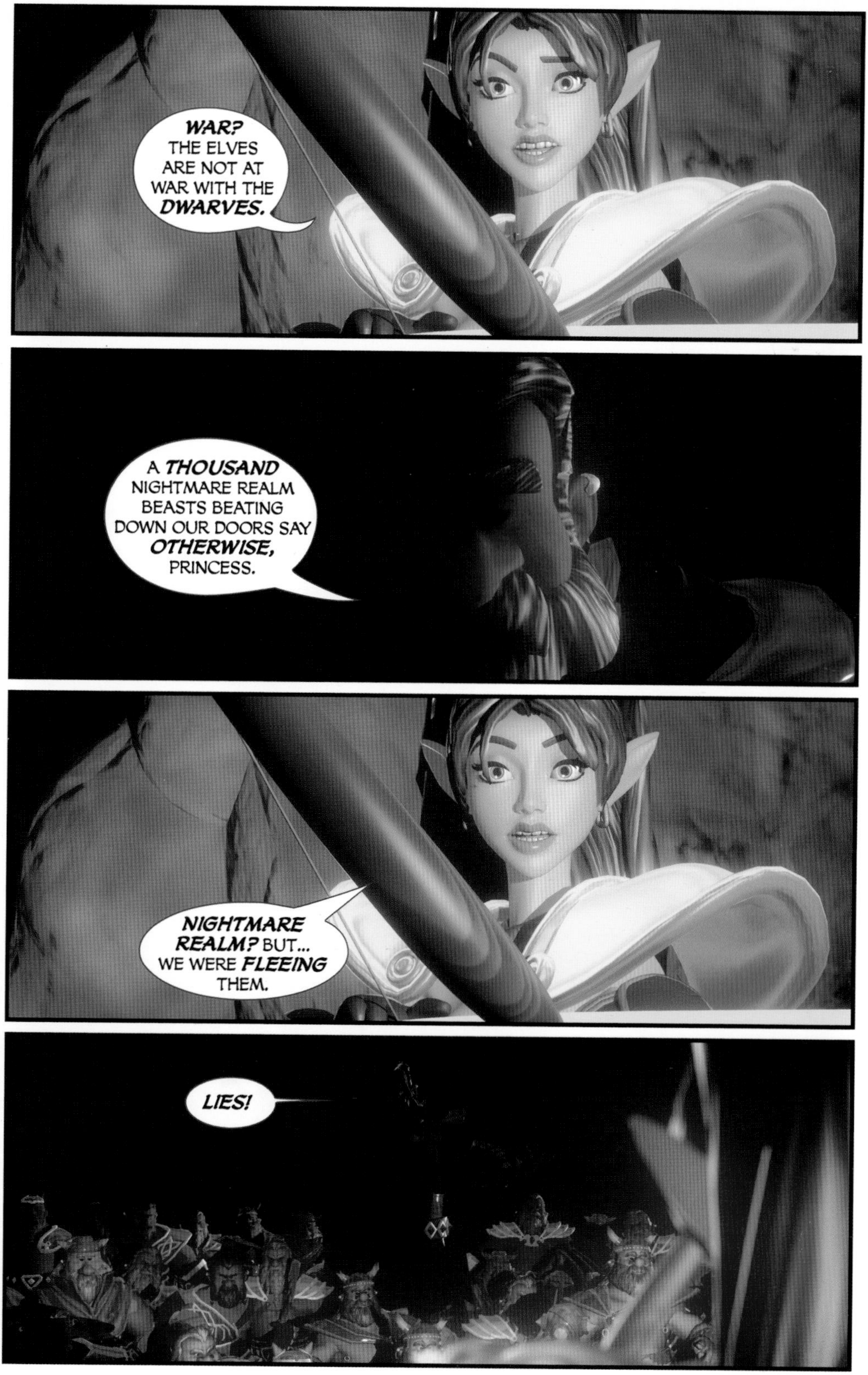
WAR? THE ELVES ARE NOT AT WAR WITH THE DWARVES.
A THOUSAND NIGHTMARE REALM BEASTS BEATING DOWN OUR DOORS SAY OTHERWISE, PRINCESS.
NIGHTMARE REALM? BUT... WE WERE FLEEING THEM.
LIES!

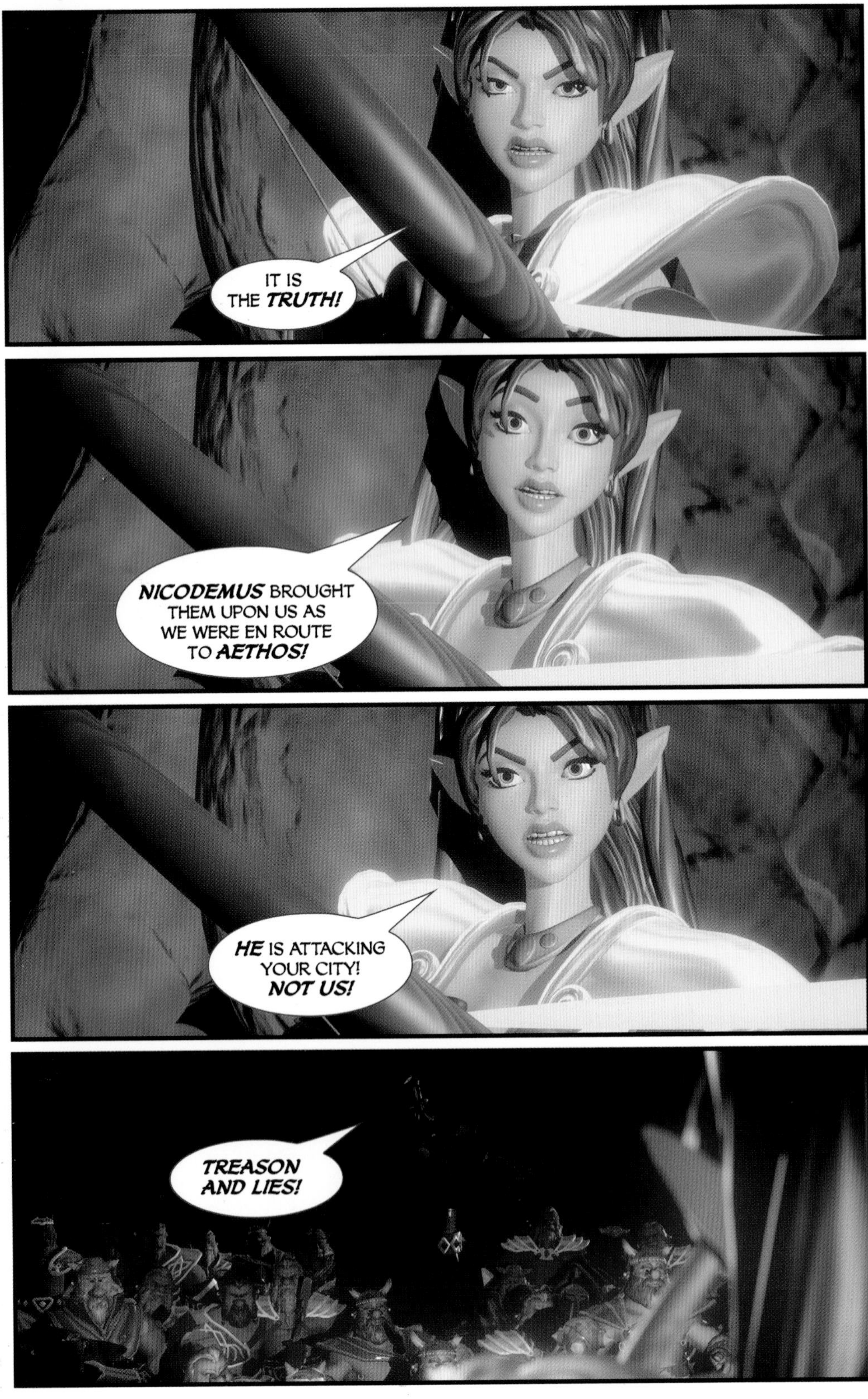
IT IS THE TRUTH!
NICODEMUS BROUGHT THEM UPON US AS WE WERE EN ROUTE TO AETHOS!
HE IS ATTACKING YOUR CITY! NOT US!
TREASON AND LIES!

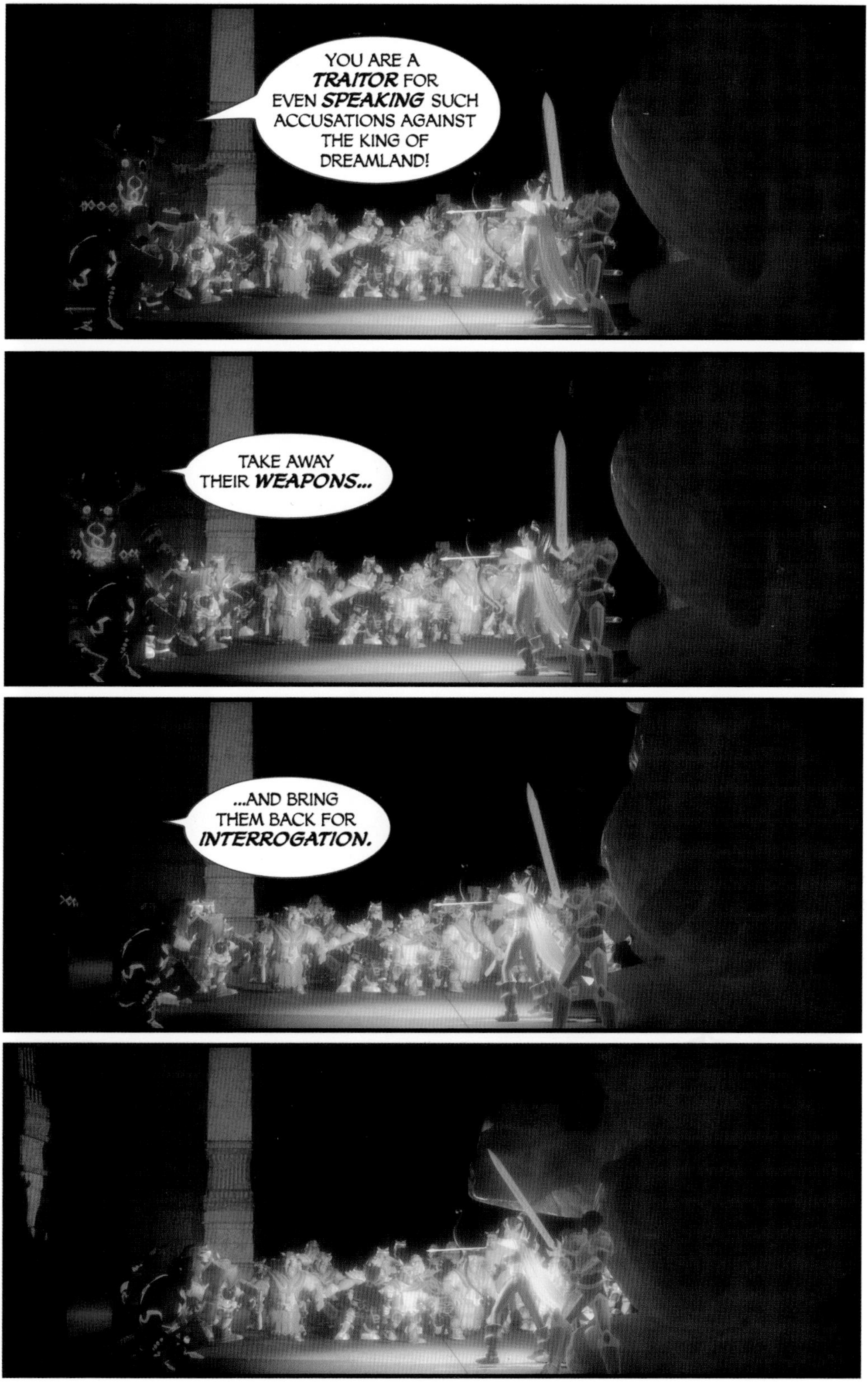
YOU ARE A *TRAITOR* FOR EVEN *SPEAKING* SUCH ACCUSATIONS AGAINST THE KING OF DREAMLAND!
TAKE AWAY THEIR *WEAPONS...*
...AND BRING THEM BACK FOR *INTERROGATION.*

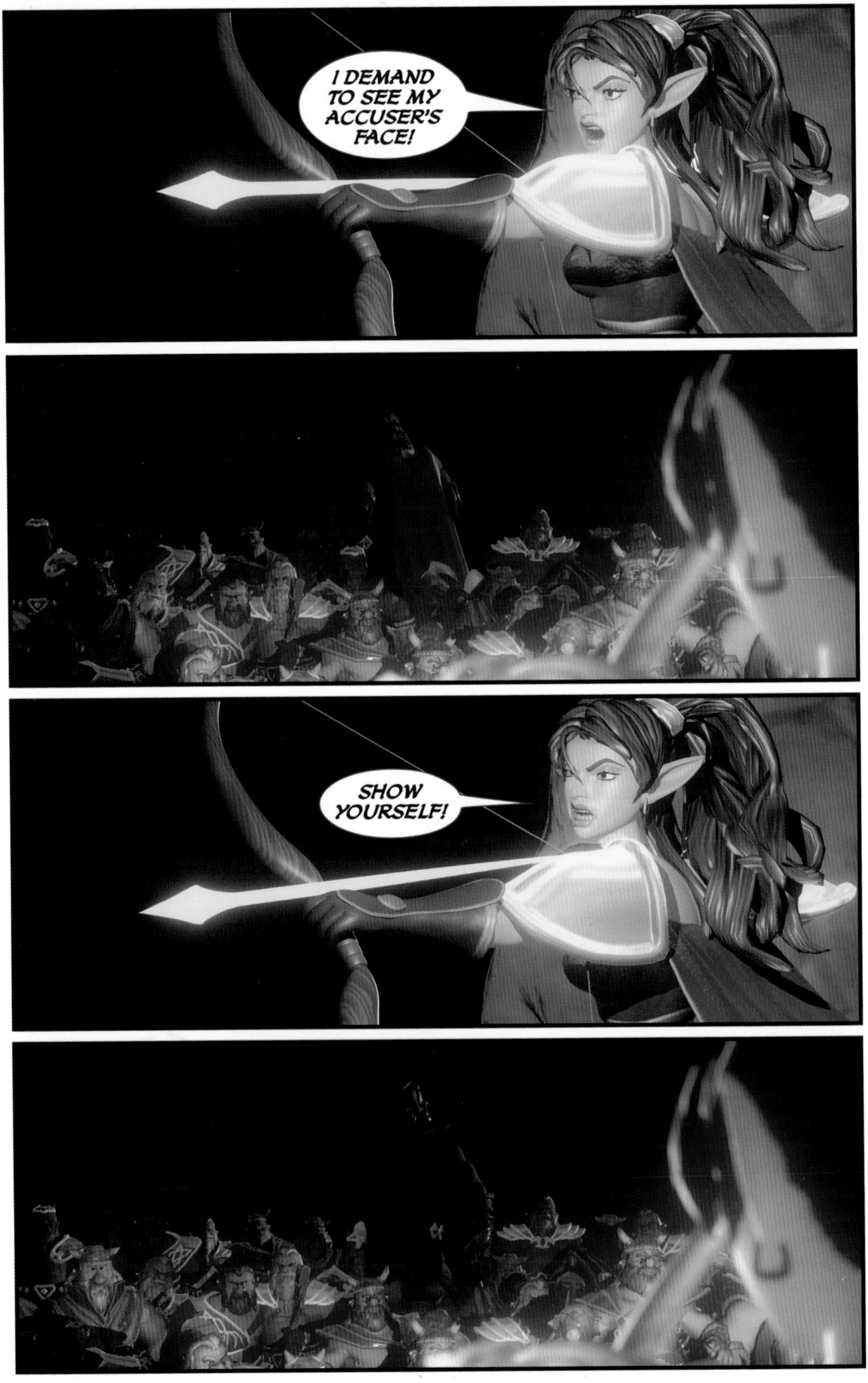
I DEMAND TO SEE MY ACCUSER'S FACE!
SHOW YOURSELF!

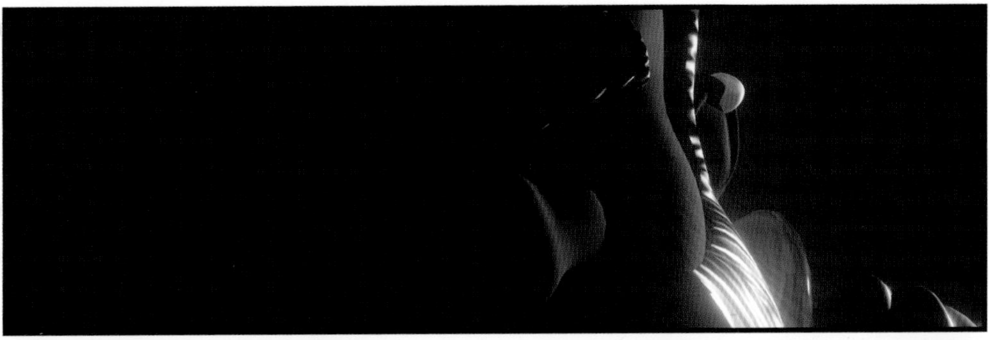

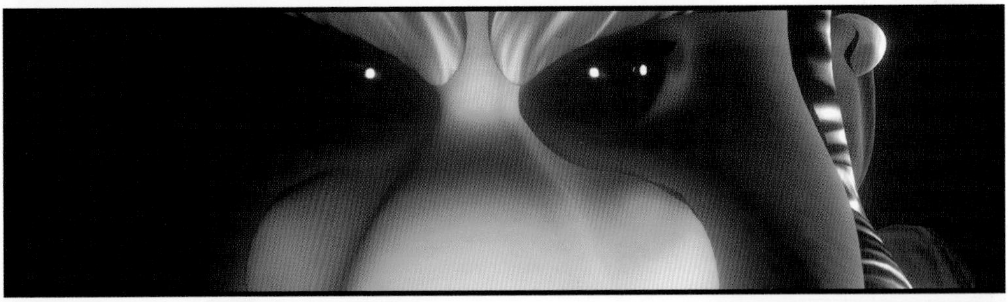

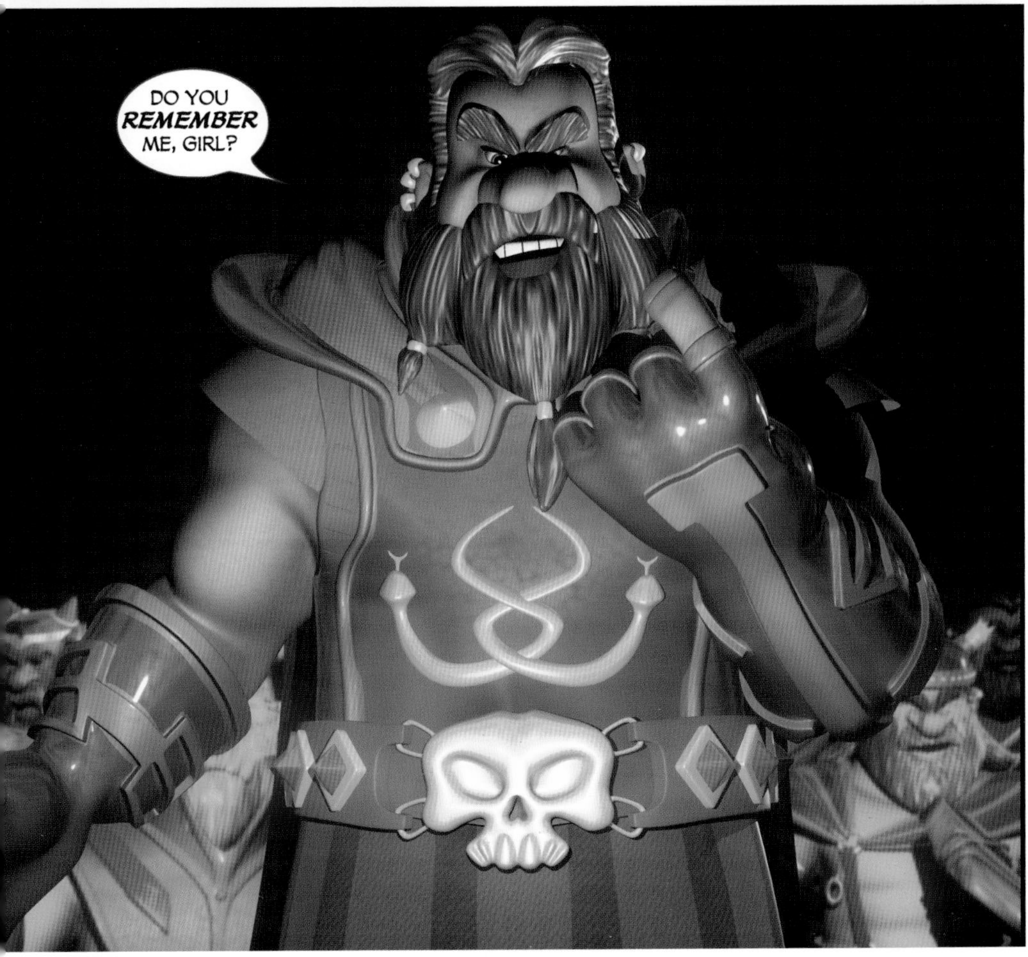
DO YOU **REMEMBER** ME, GIRL?

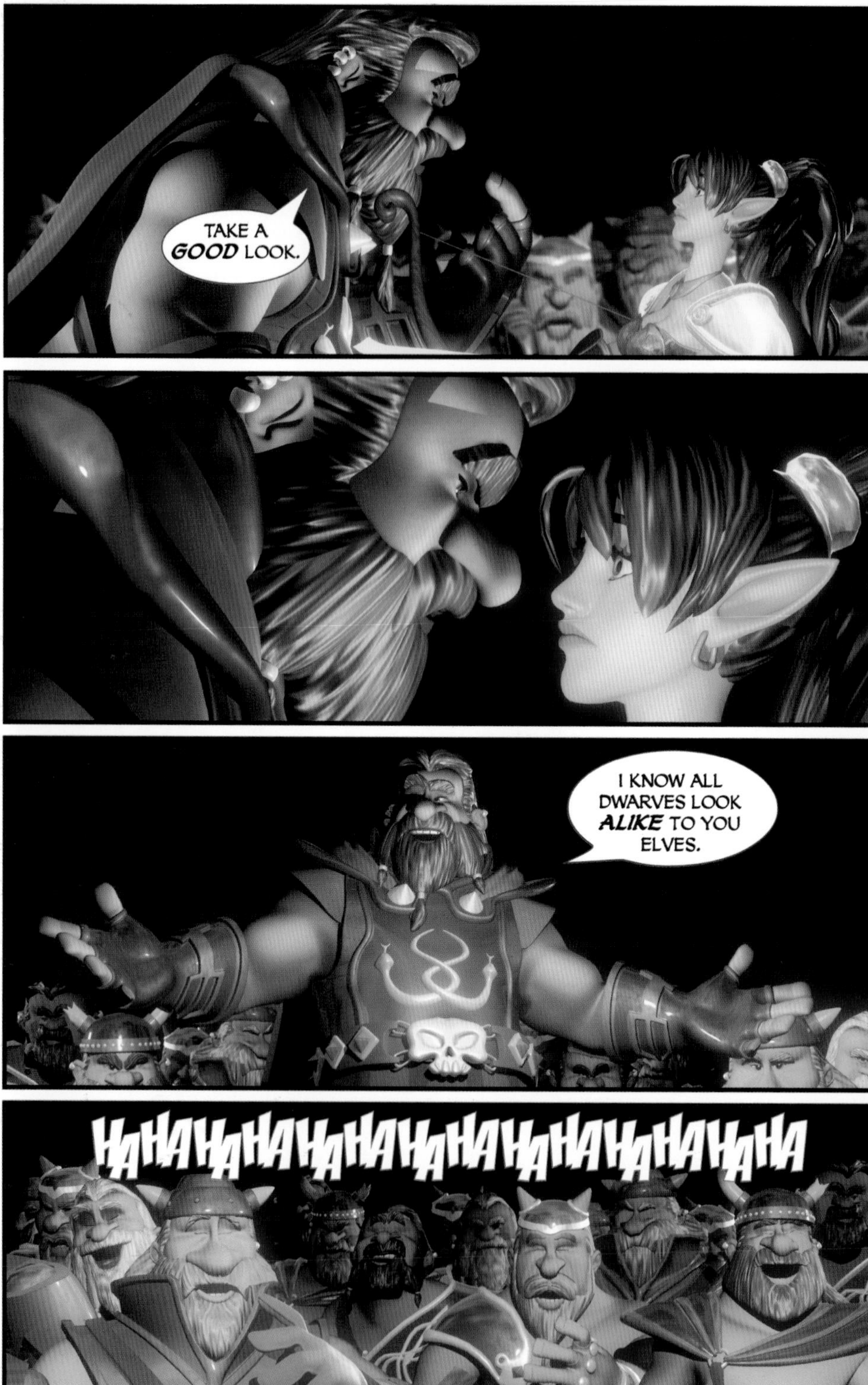
TAKE A GOOD LOOK.
I KNOW ALL DWARVES LOOK ALIKE TO YOU ELVES.
HAHAHAHAHAHAHAHAHAHAHAHAHAHAHAHAHAHA

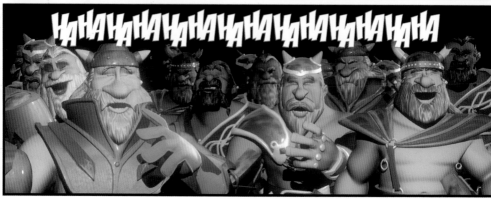

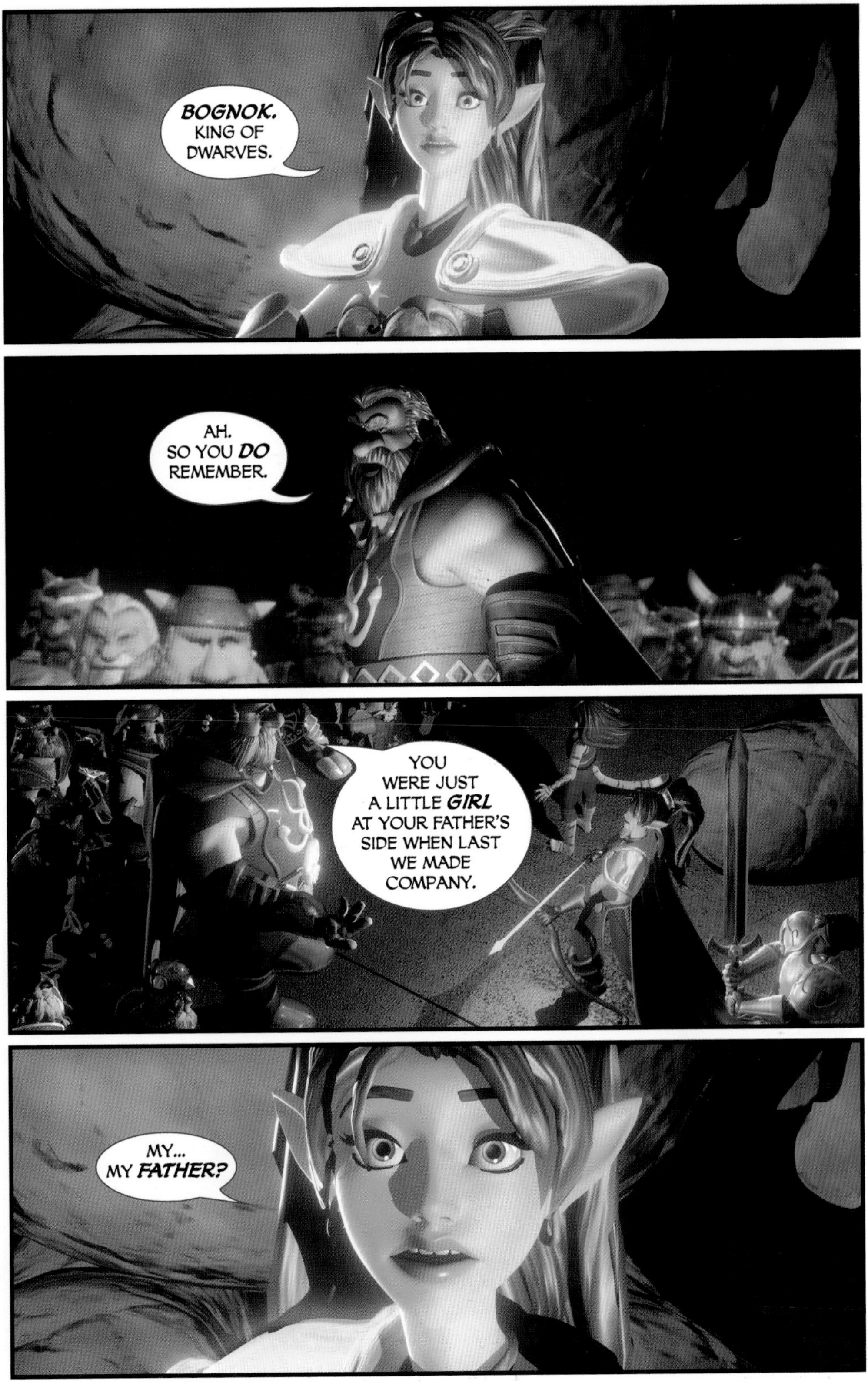
BOGNOK. KING OF DWARVES.
AH. SO YOU DO REMEMBER.
YOU WERE JUST A LITTLE GIRL AT YOUR FATHER'S SIDE WHEN LAST WE MADE COMPANY.
MY... MY FATHER?

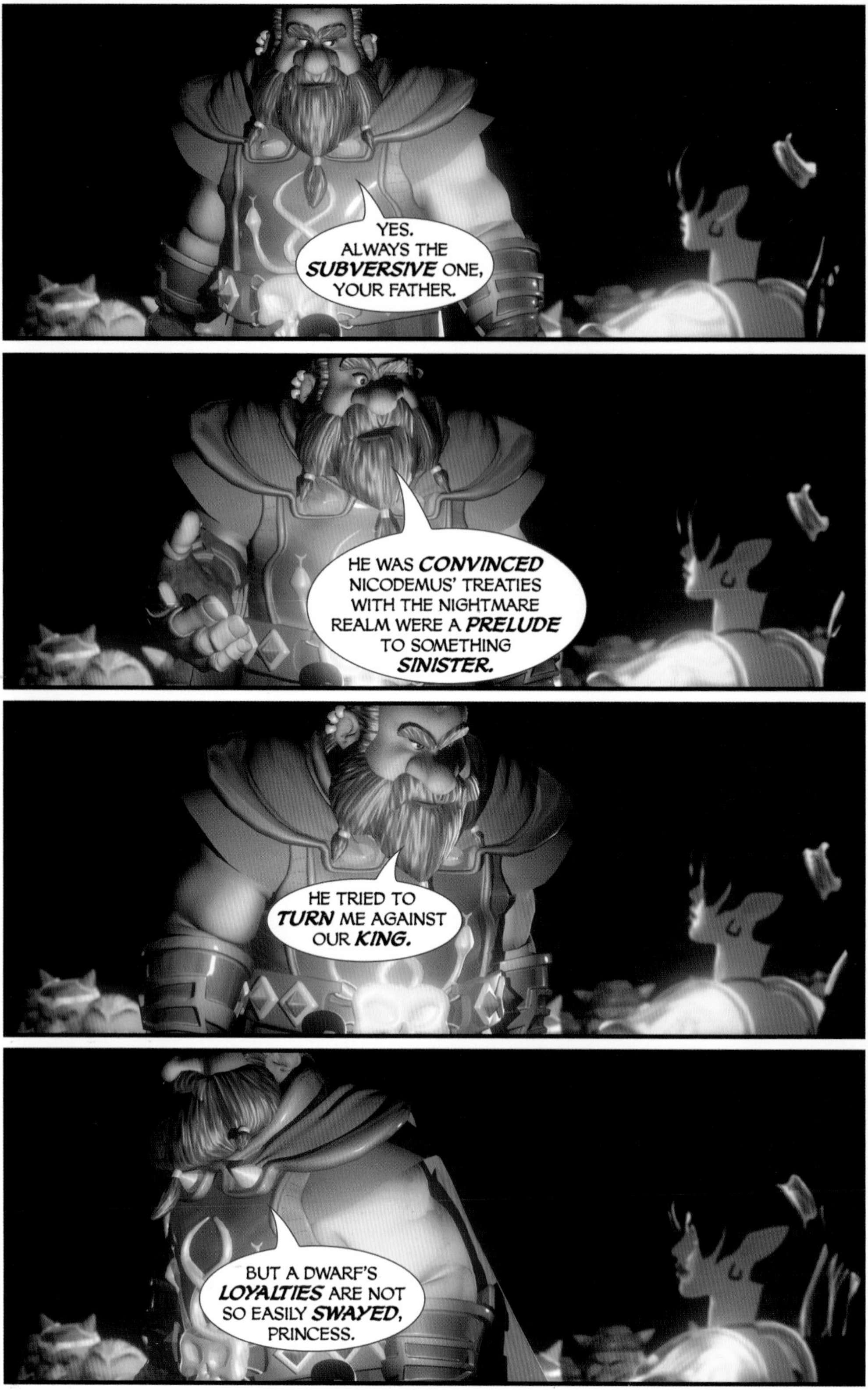
YES. ALWAYS THE SUBVERSIVE ONE, YOUR FATHER.
HE WAS CONVINCED NICODEMUS' TREATIES WITH THE NIGHTMARE REALM WERE A PRELUDE TO SOMETHING SINISTER.
HE TRIED TO TURN ME AGAINST OUR KING.
BUT A DWARF'S LOYALTIES ARE NOT SO EASILY SWAYED, PRINCESS.

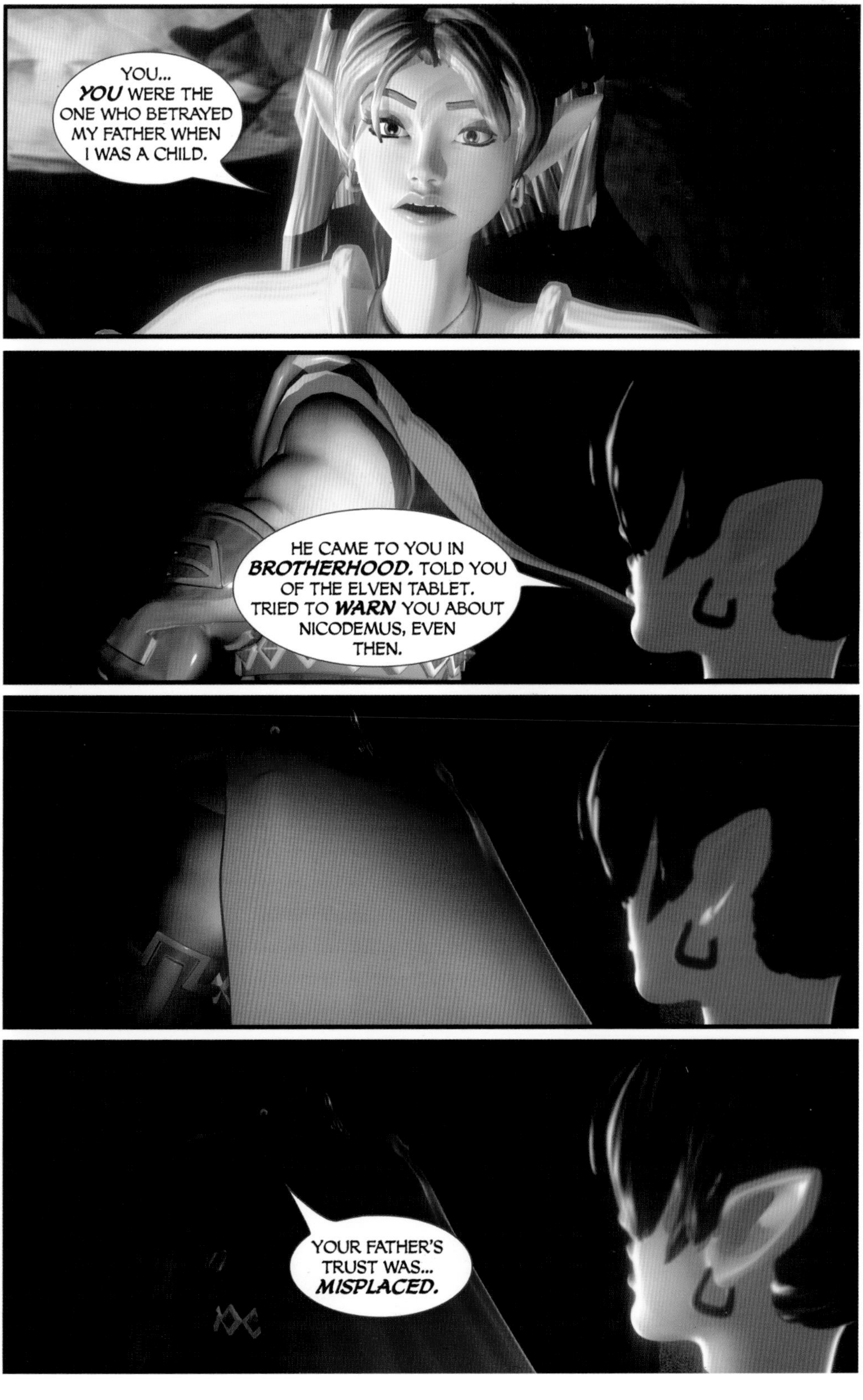
YOU...
YOU WERE THE ONE WHO BETRAYED MY FATHER WHEN I WAS A CHILD.
HE CAME TO YOU IN BROTHERHOOD. TOLD YOU OF THE ELVEN TABLET. TRIED TO WARN YOU ABOUT NICODEMUS, EVEN THEN.
YOUR FATHER'S TRUST WAS... MISPLACED.

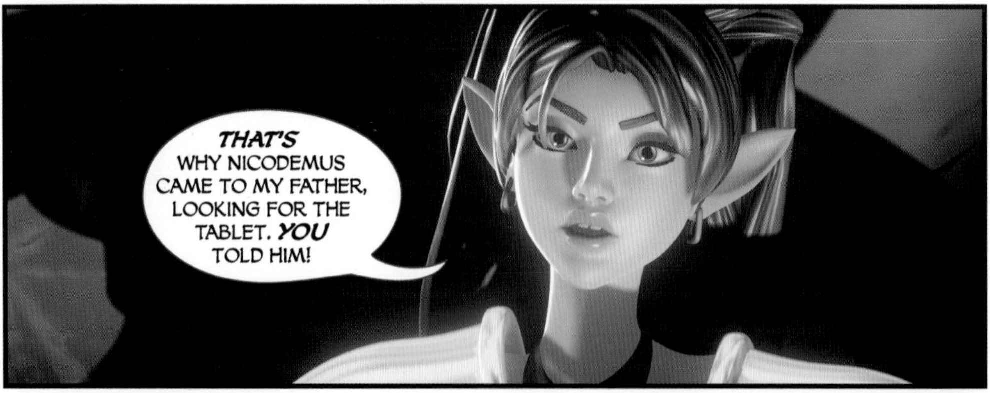
THAT'S WHY NICODEMUS CAME TO MY FATHER, LOOKING FOR THE TABLET. YOU TOLD HIM!

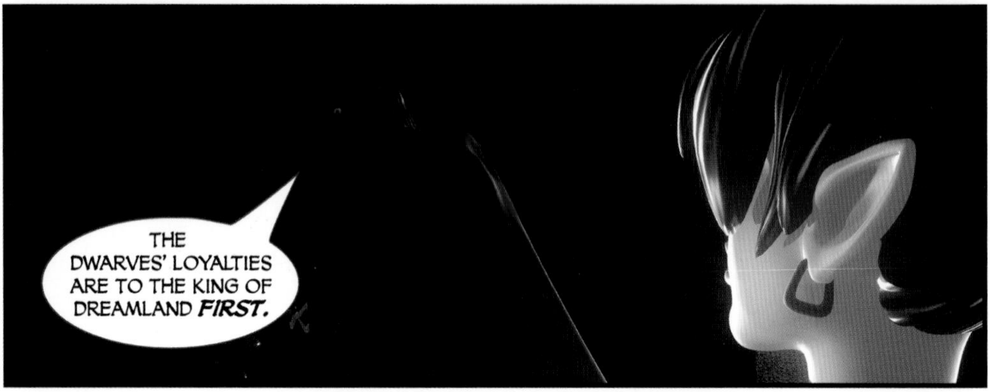
THE DWARVES' LOYALTIES ARE TO THE KING OF DREAMLAND FIRST.

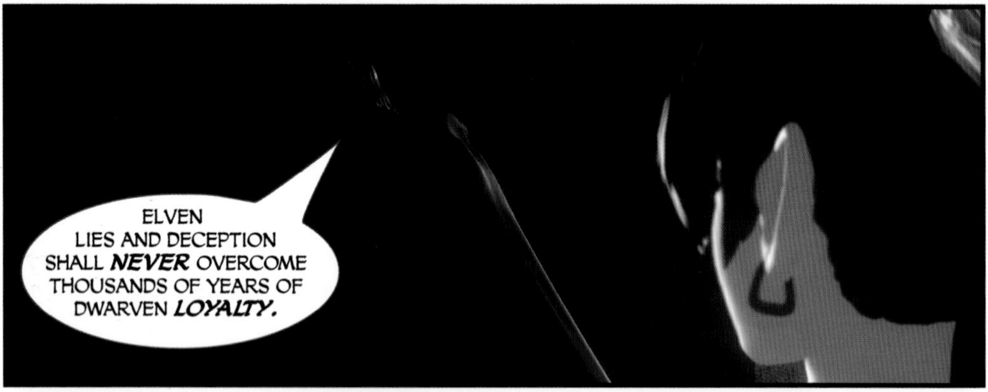
ELVEN LIES AND DECEPTION SHALL NEVER OVERCOME THOUSANDS OF YEARS OF DWARVEN LOYALTY.

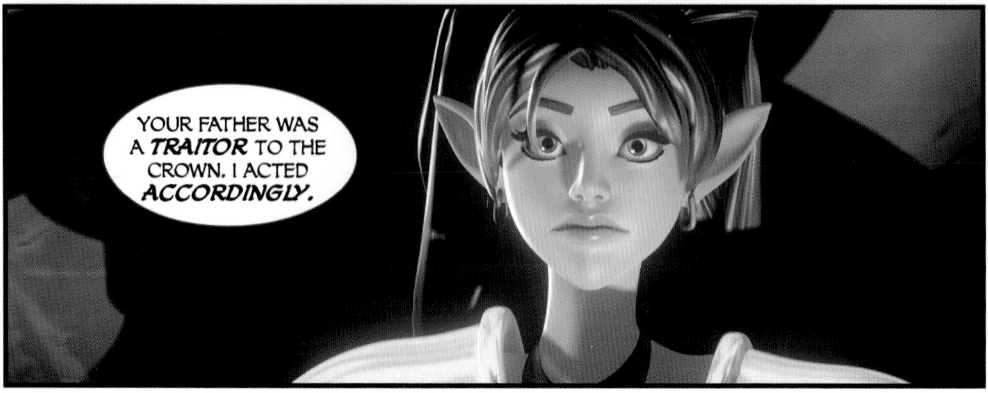
YOUR FATHER WAS A TRAITOR TO THE CROWN. I ACTED ACCORDINGLY.

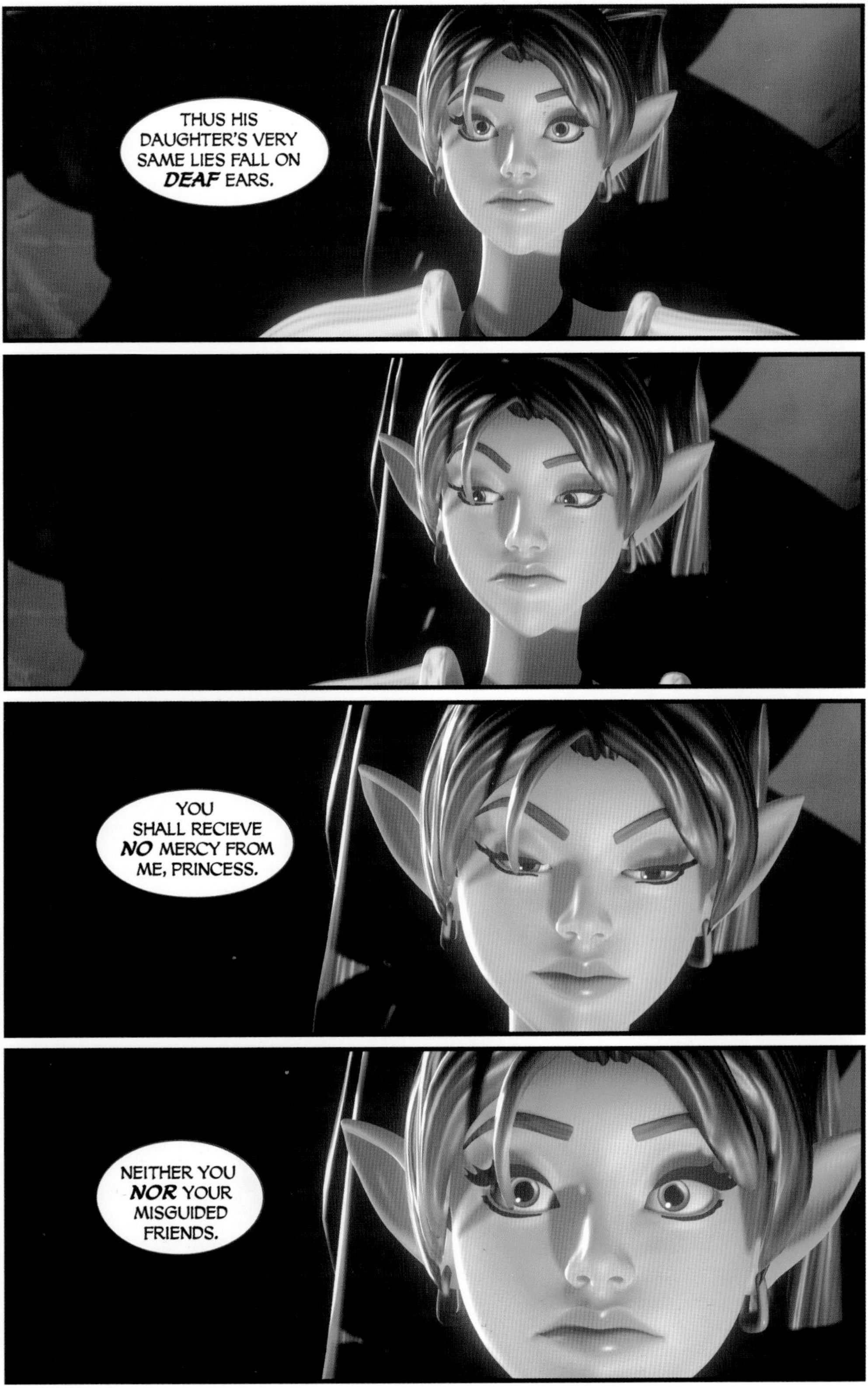
THUS HIS DAUGHTER'S VERY SAME LIES FALL ON *DEAF* EARS.
YOU SHALL RECIEVE *NO* MERCY FROM ME, PRINCESS.
NEITHER YOU *NOR* YOUR MISGUIDED FRIENDS.

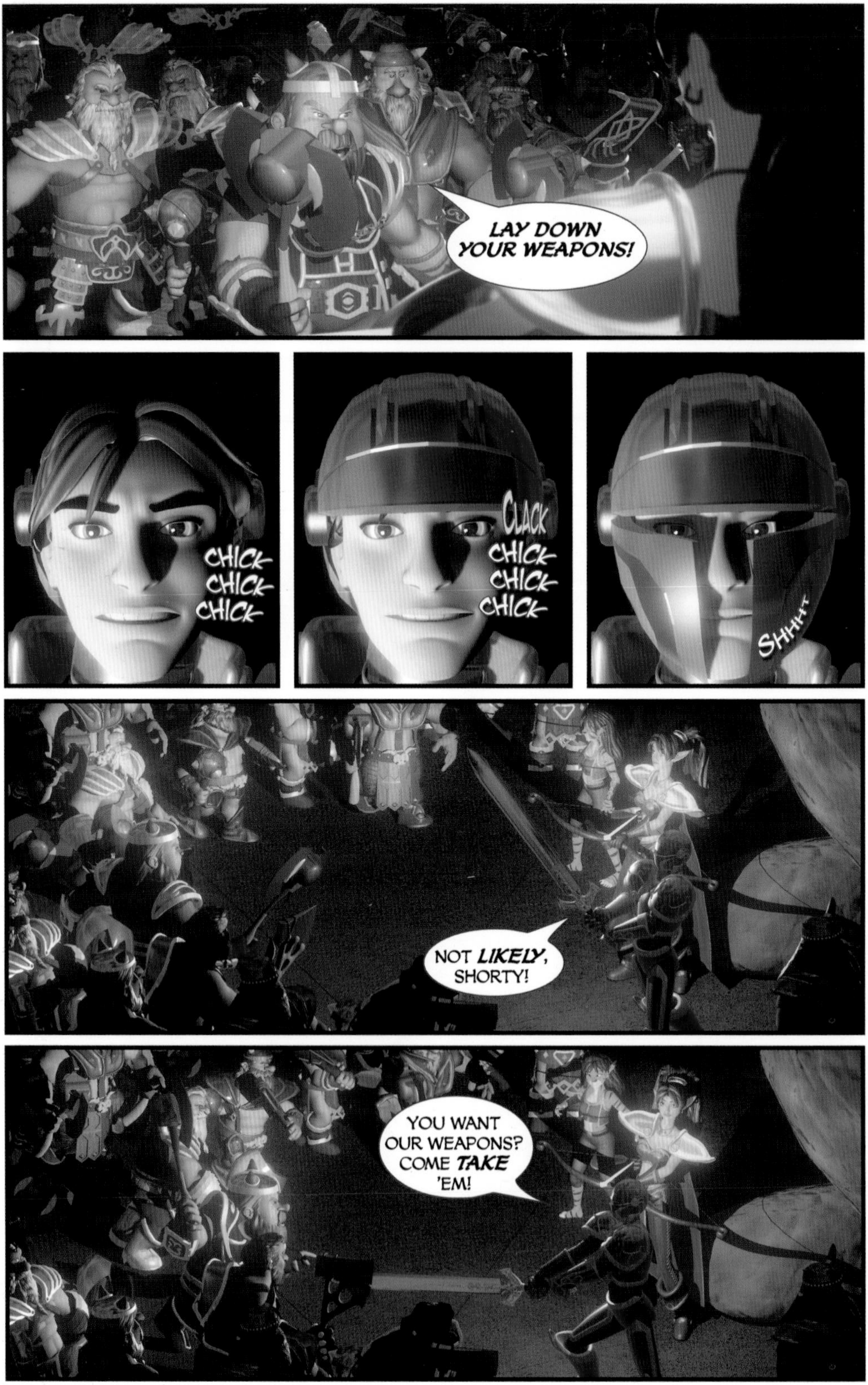
LAY DOWN YOUR WEAPONS!
CHICK CHICK CHICK
CLACK CHICK CHICK CHICK
SHHHT
NOT LIKELY, SHORTY!
YOU WANT OUR WEAPONS? COME TAKE 'EM!

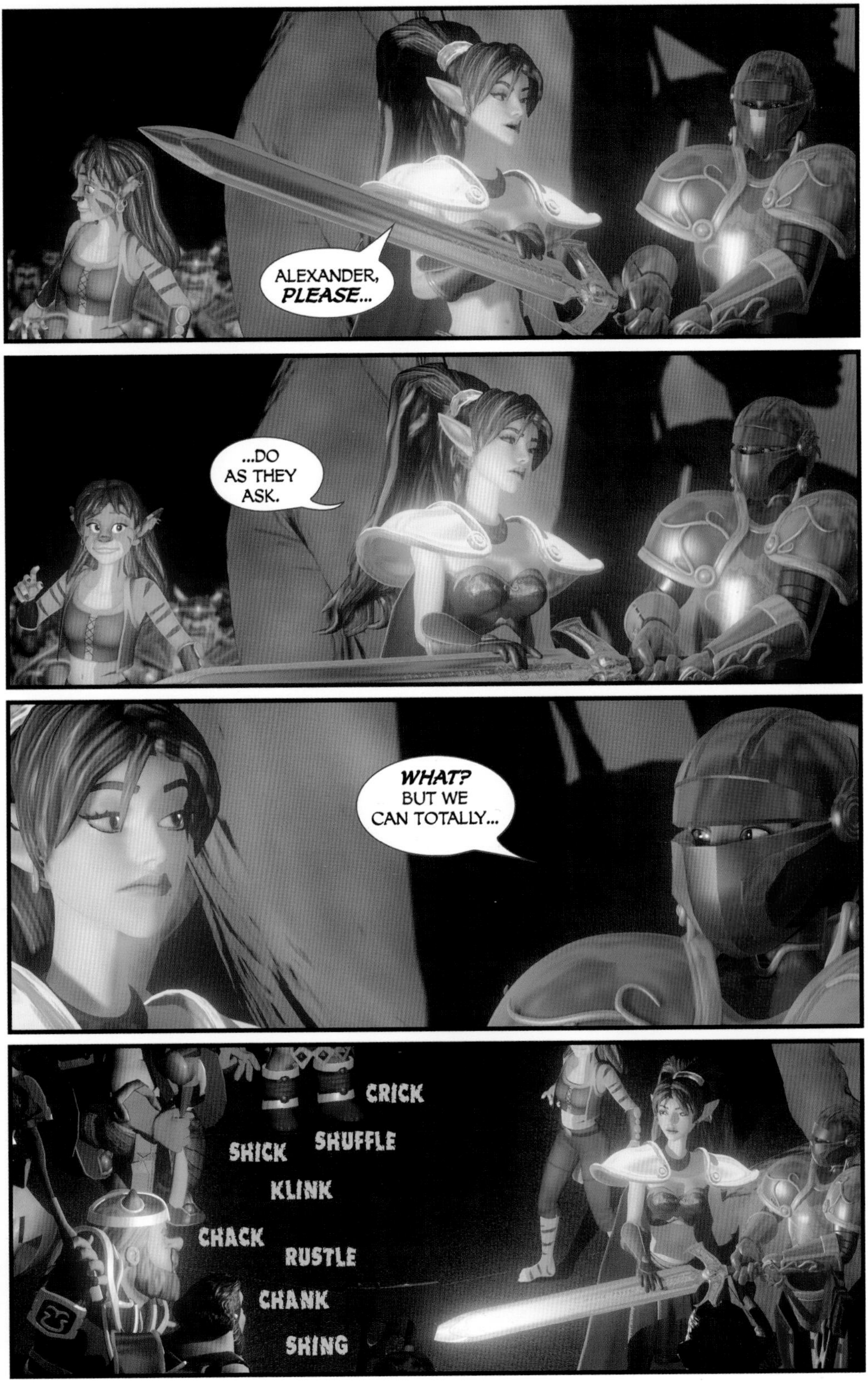
ALEXANDER, PLEASE...
...DO AS THEY ASK.
WHAT? BUT WE CAN TOTALLY...
CRICK
SHUFFLE
SHICK
KLINK
CHACK
RUSTLE
CHANK
SHING

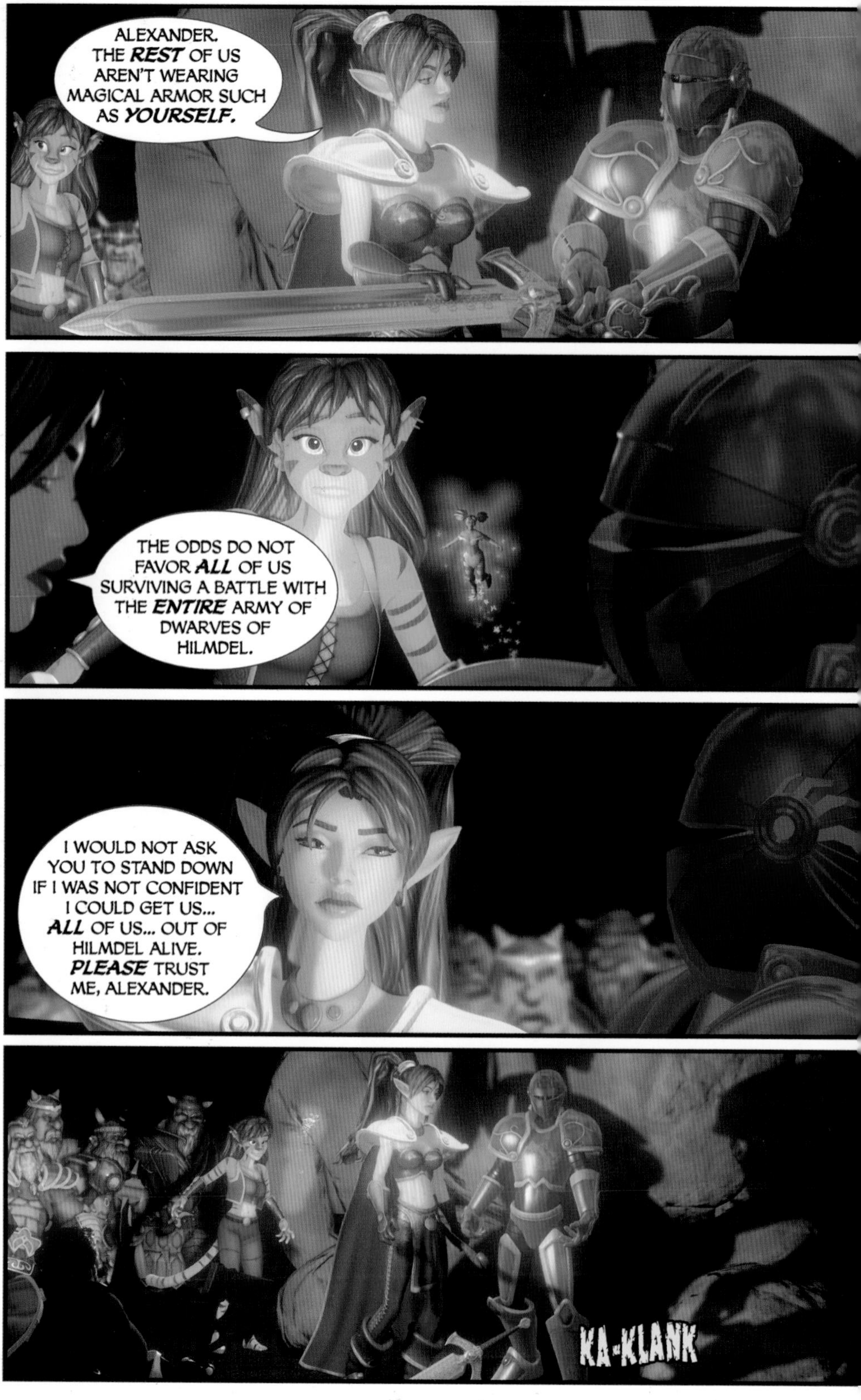
ALEXANDER. THE REST OF US AREN'T WEARING MAGICAL ARMOR SUCH AS YOURSELF.
THE ODDS DO NOT FAVOR ALL OF US SURVIVING A BATTLE WITH THE ENTIRE ARMY OF DWARVES OF HILMDEL.
I WOULD NOT ASK YOU TO STAND DOWN IF I WAS NOT CONFIDENT I COULD GET US... ALL OF US... OUT OF HILMDEL ALIVE. PLEASE TRUST ME, ALEXANDER.
KA-KLANK

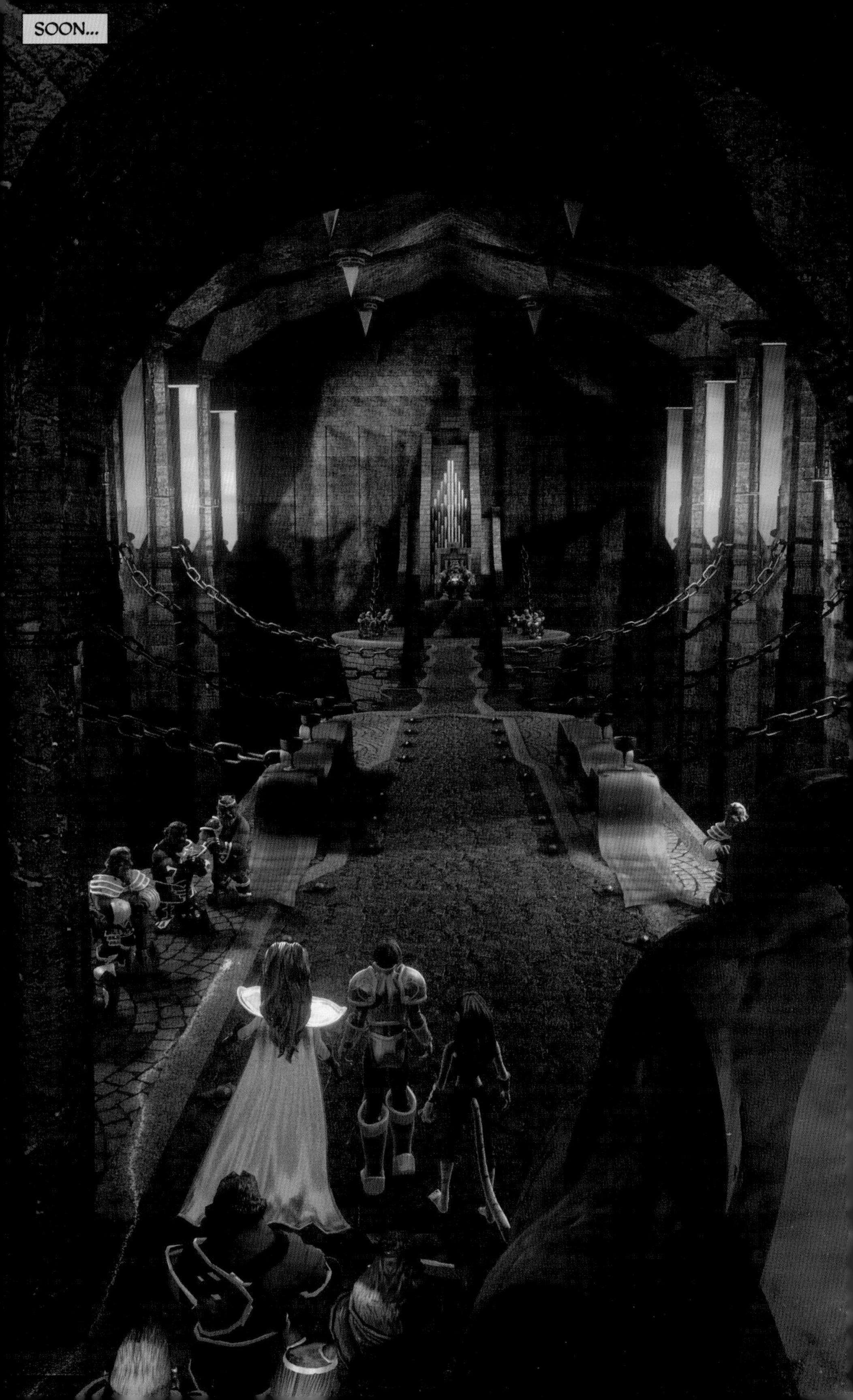
SOON...

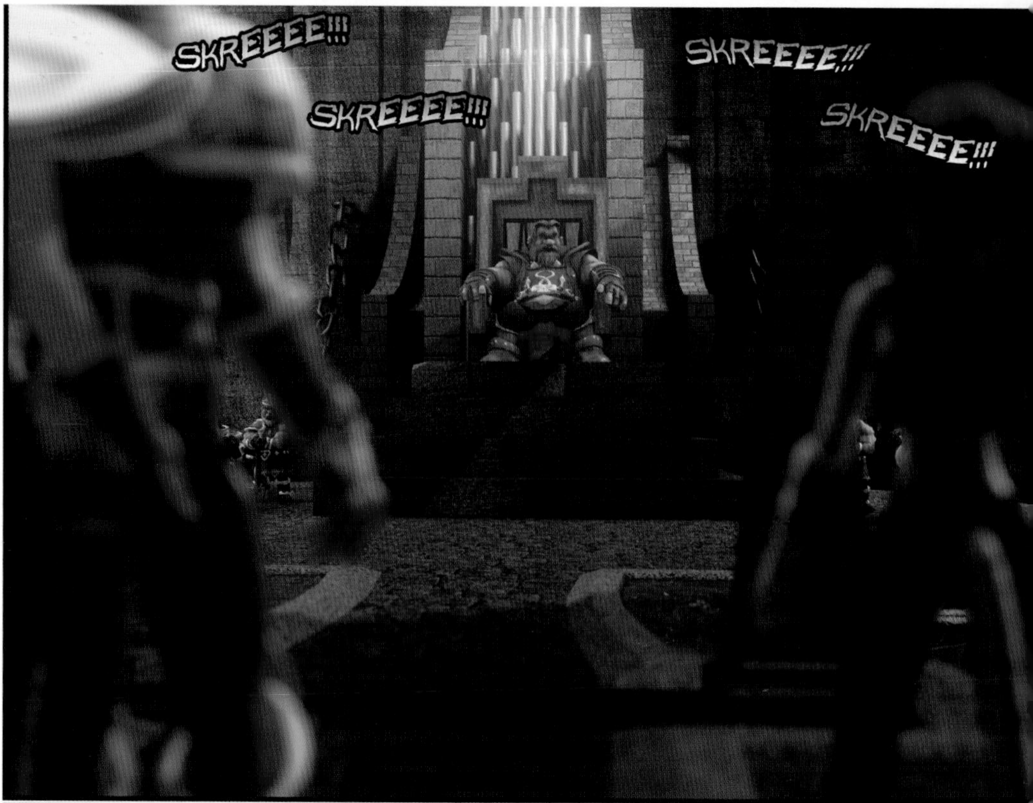
SKREEEE!!!
SKREEEE!!!
SKREEEE!!!
SKREEEE!!!

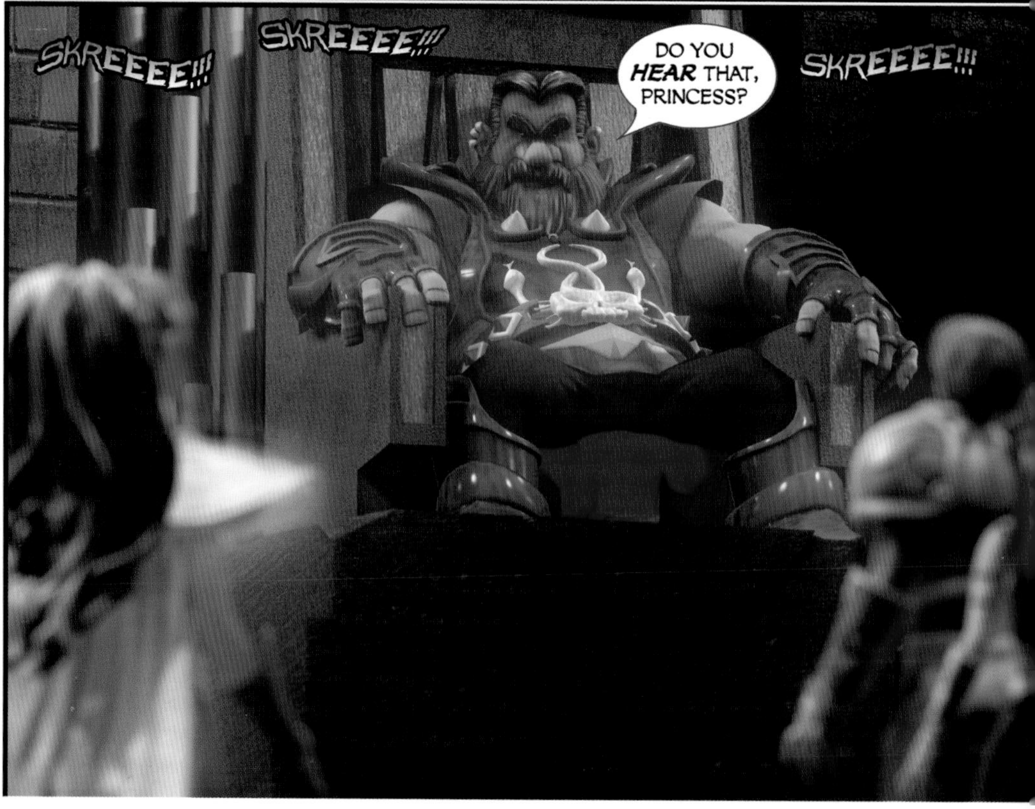
SKREEEE!!!
SKREEEE!!!
DO YOU HEAR THAT, PRINCESS?
SKREEEE!!!

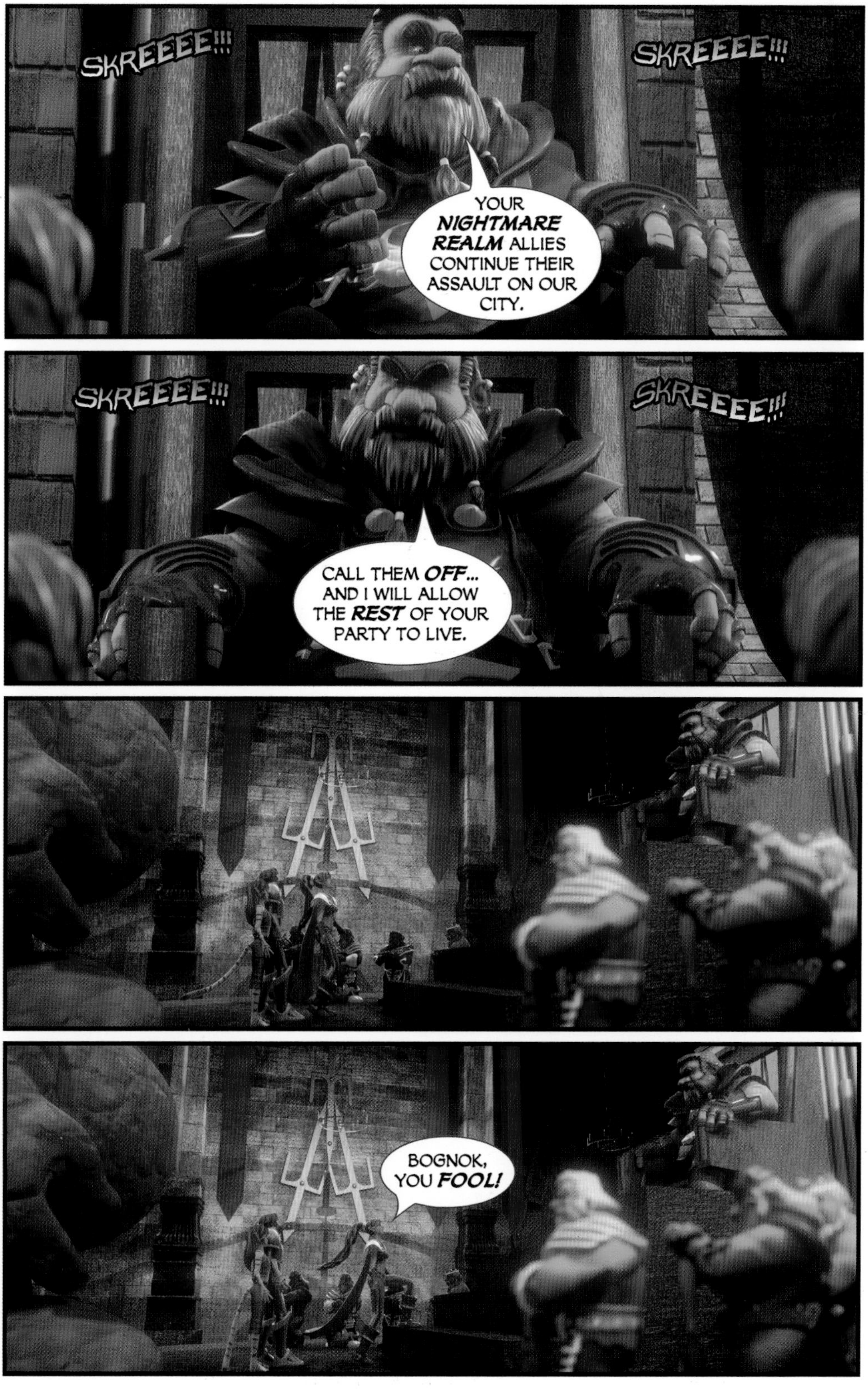
SKREEEE!!!
SKREEEE!!!
YOUR NIGHTMARE REALM ALLIES CONTINUE THEIR ASSAULT ON OUR CITY.
SKREEEE!!!
SKREEEE!!!
CALL THEM OFF... AND I WILL ALLOW THE REST OF YOUR PARTY TO LIVE.
BOGNOK, YOU FOOL!

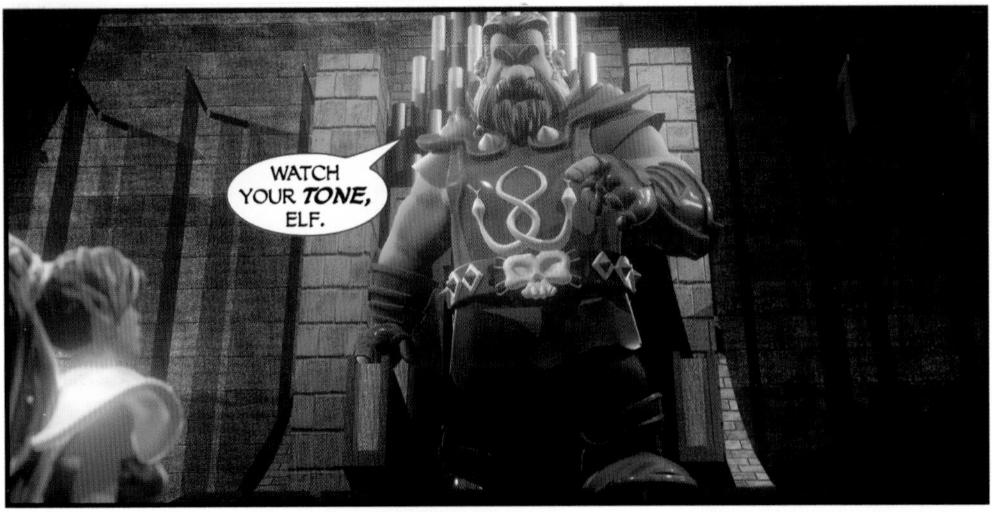
WATCH YOUR ***TONE,*** ELF.

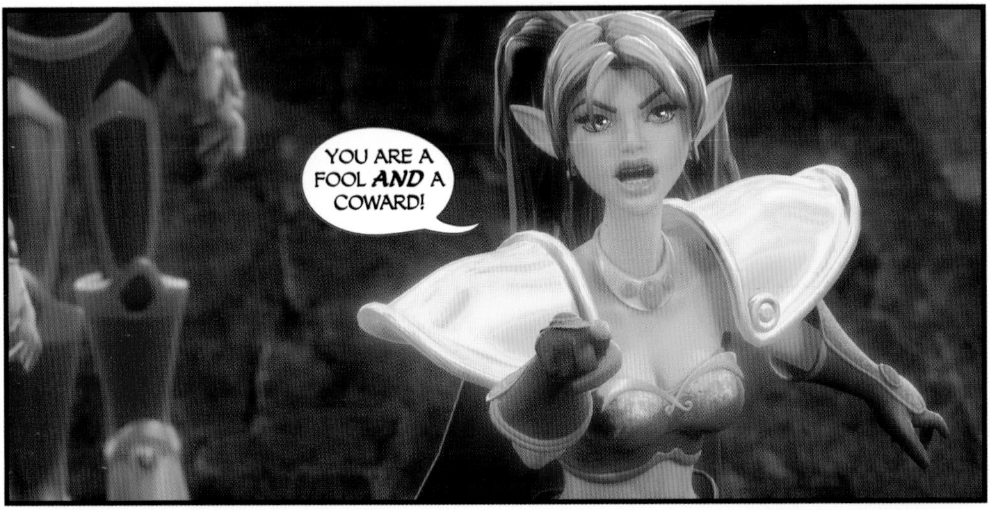
YOU ARE A FOOL ***AND*** A COWARD!

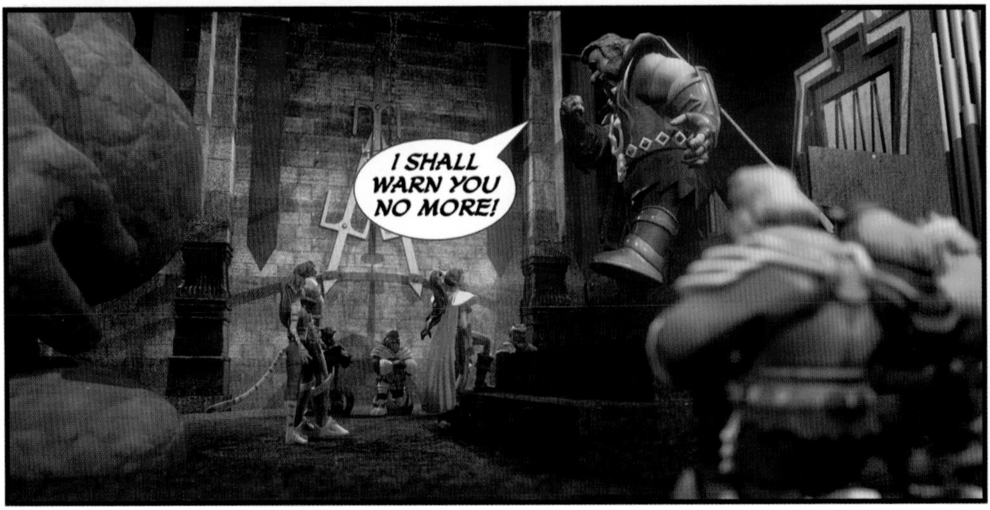
I SHALL WARN YOU NO MORE!

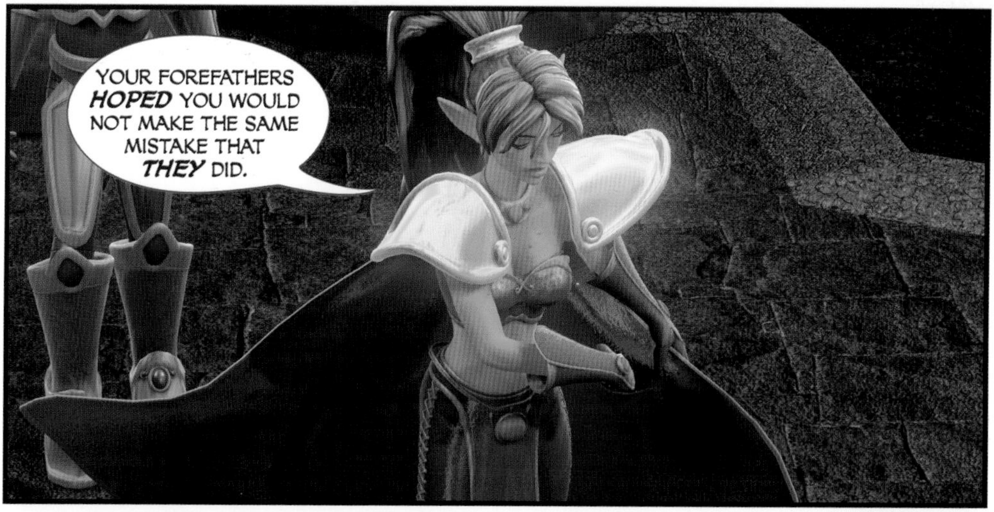
YOUR FOREFATHERS **HOPED** YOU WOULD NOT MAKE THE SAME MISTAKE THAT **THEY** DID.

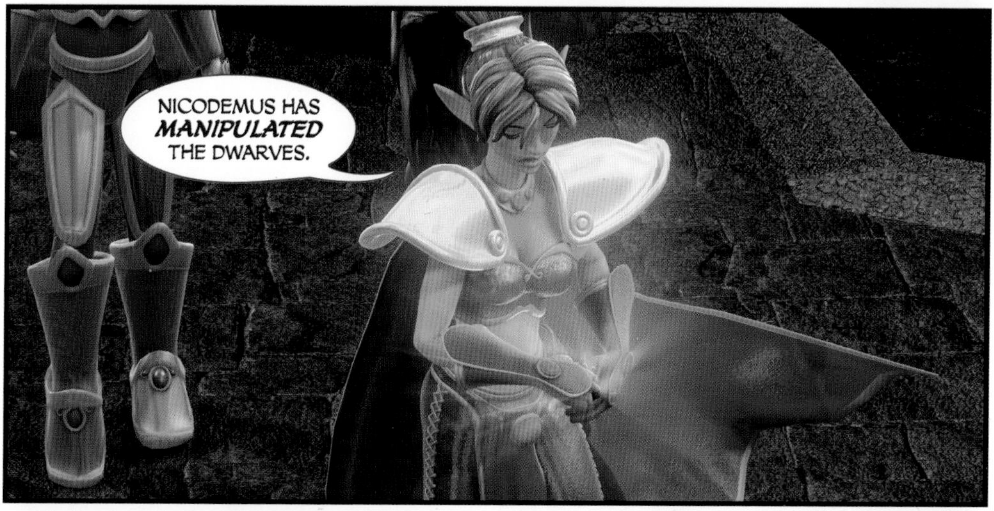
NICODEMUS HAS **MANIPULATED** THE DWARVES.

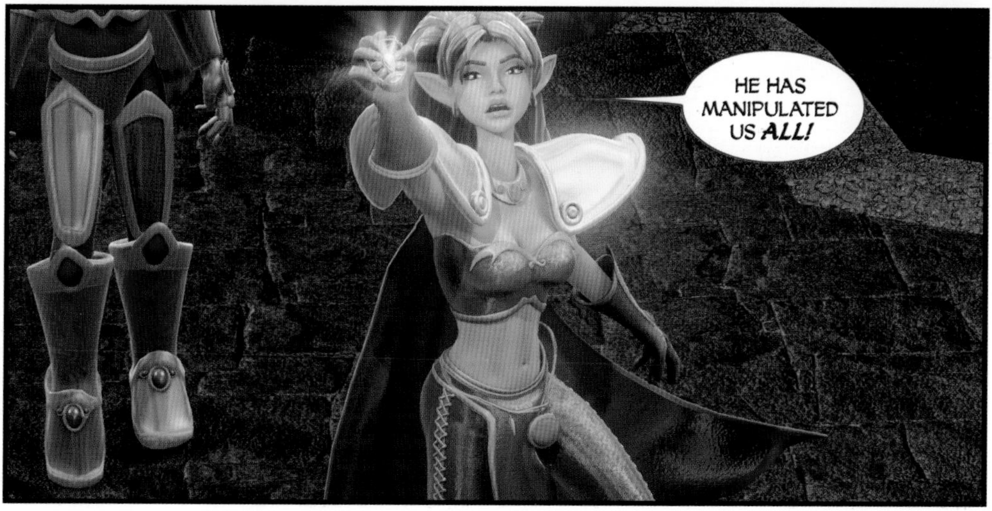
HE HAS MANIPULATED US **ALL!**

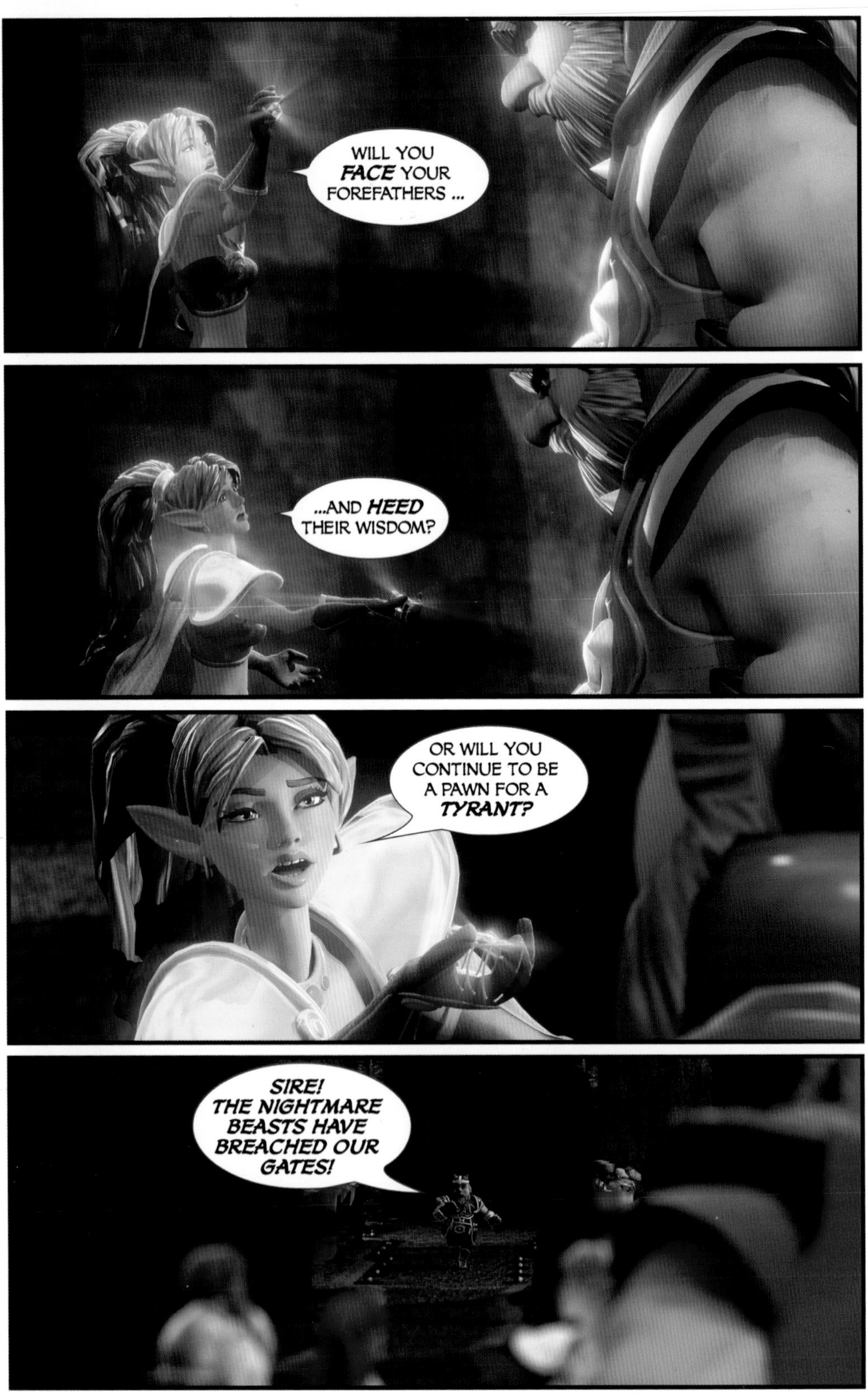
WILL YOU FACE YOUR FOREFATHERS ...
...AND HEED THEIR WISDOM?
OR WILL YOU CONTINUE TO BE A PAWN FOR A TYRANT?
SIRE! THE NIGHTMARE BEASTS HAVE BREACHED OUR GATES!

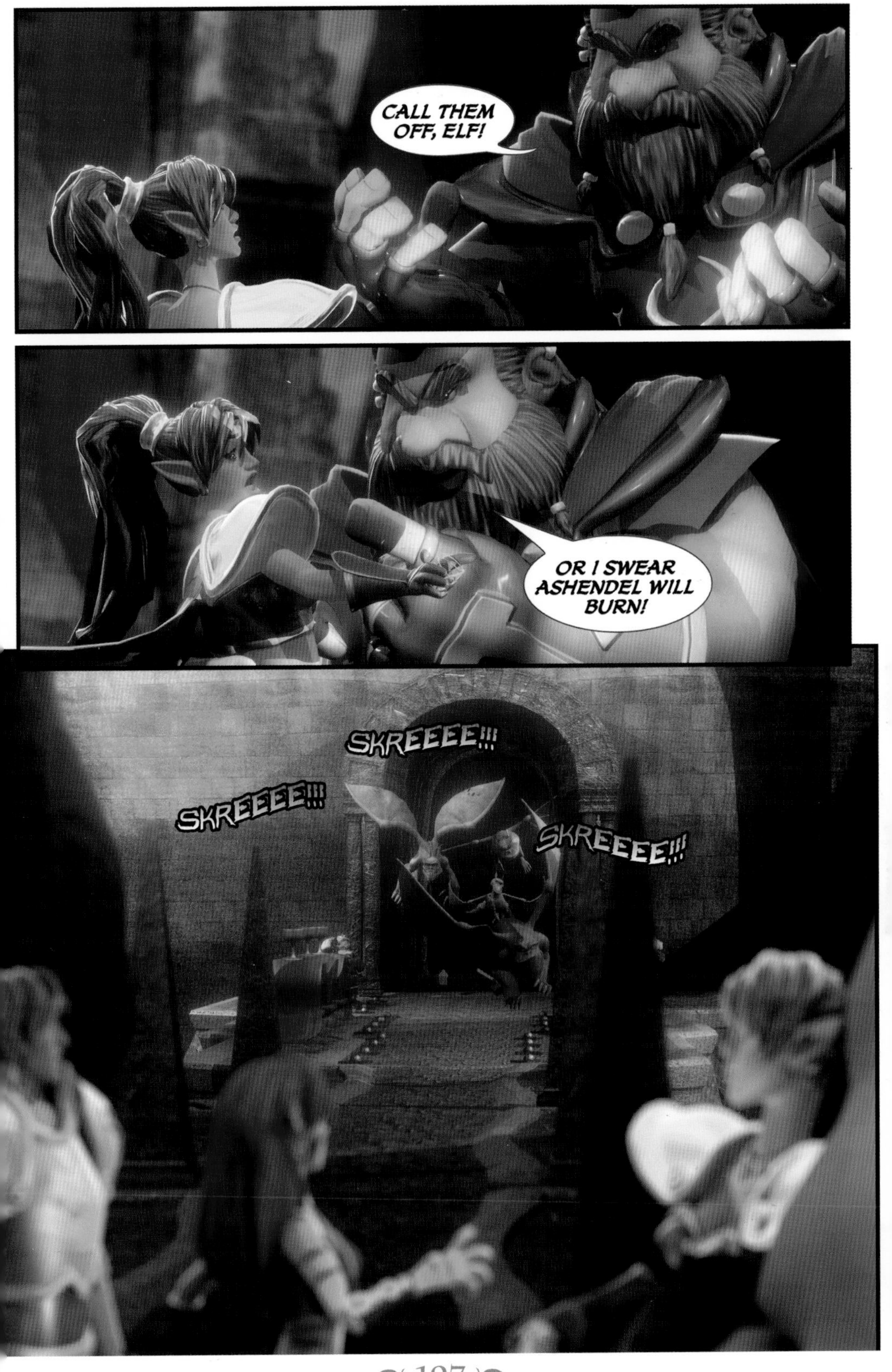
CALL THEM OFF, ELF!
OR I SWEAR ASHENDEL WILL BURN!
SKREEEEE!!!
SKREEEEE!!!
SKREEEEE!!!

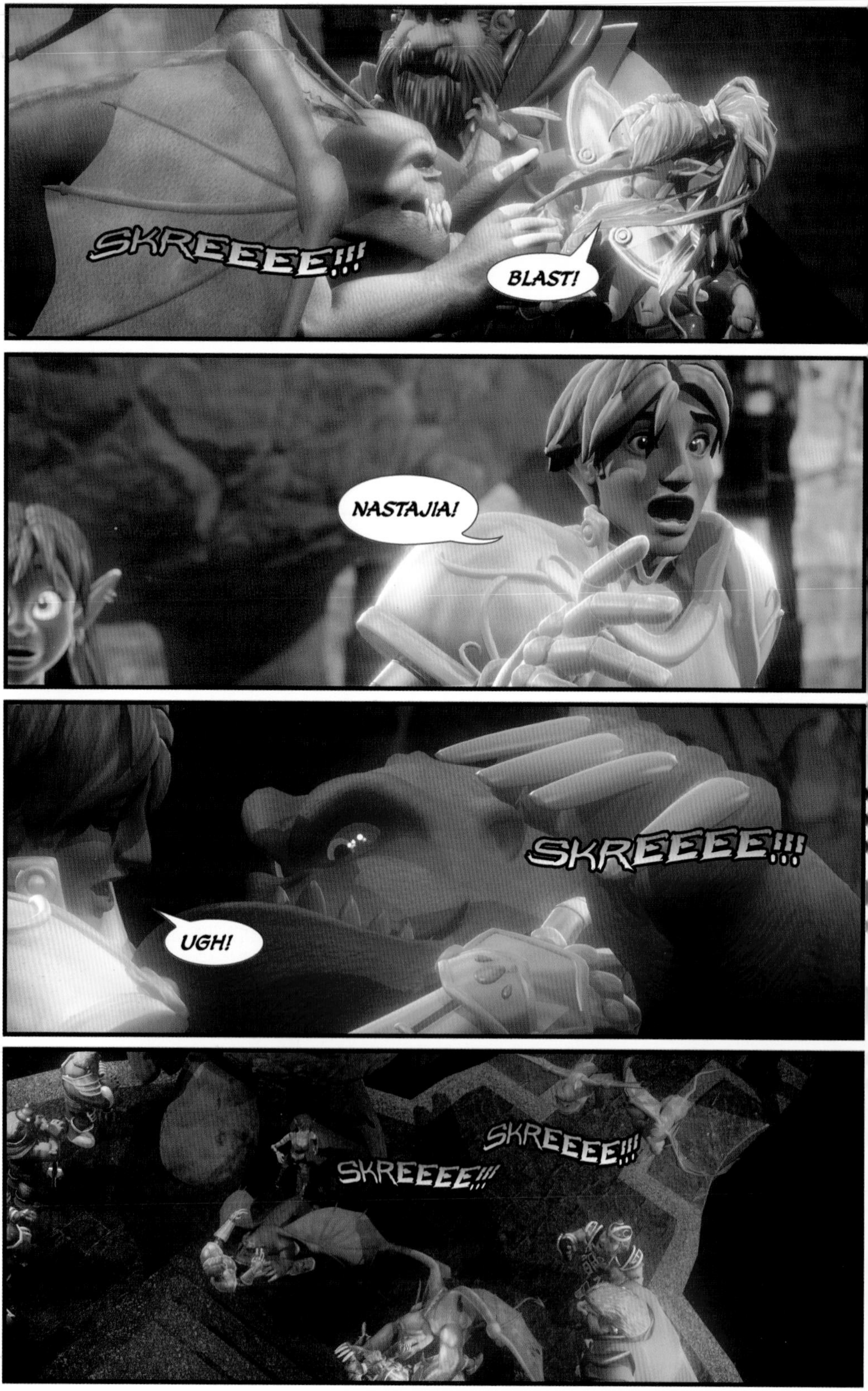
SKREEEEE!!!
BLAST!
NASTAJIA!
SKREEEEE!!!
UGH!
SKREEEE!!!
SKREEEE!!!

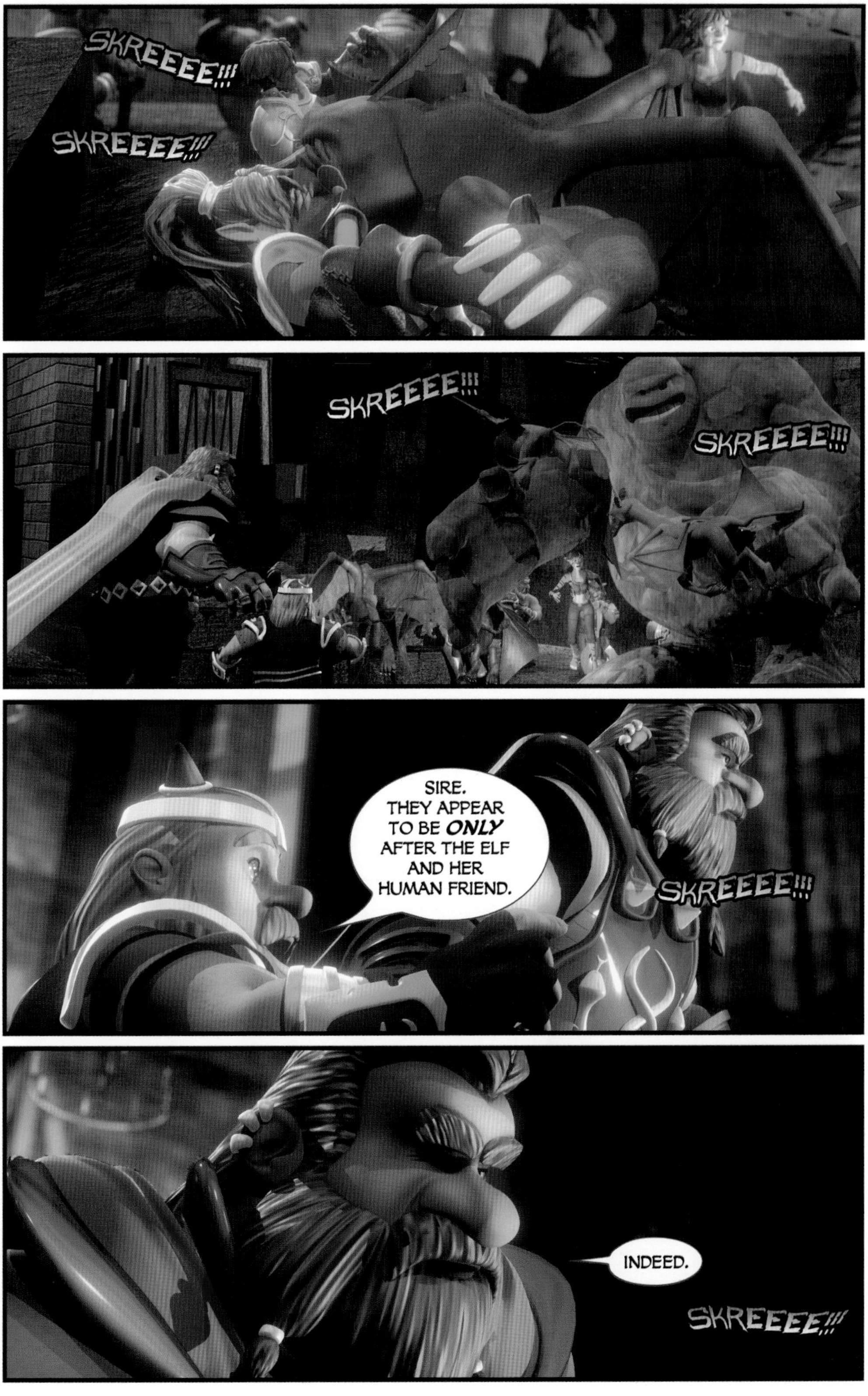
SKREEEE!!!
SKREEEE!!!
SKREEEE!!!
SKREEEE!!!
SIRE. THEY APPEAR TO BE *ONLY* AFTER THE ELF AND HER HUMAN FRIEND.
SKREEEE!!!
INDEED.
SKREEEE!!!

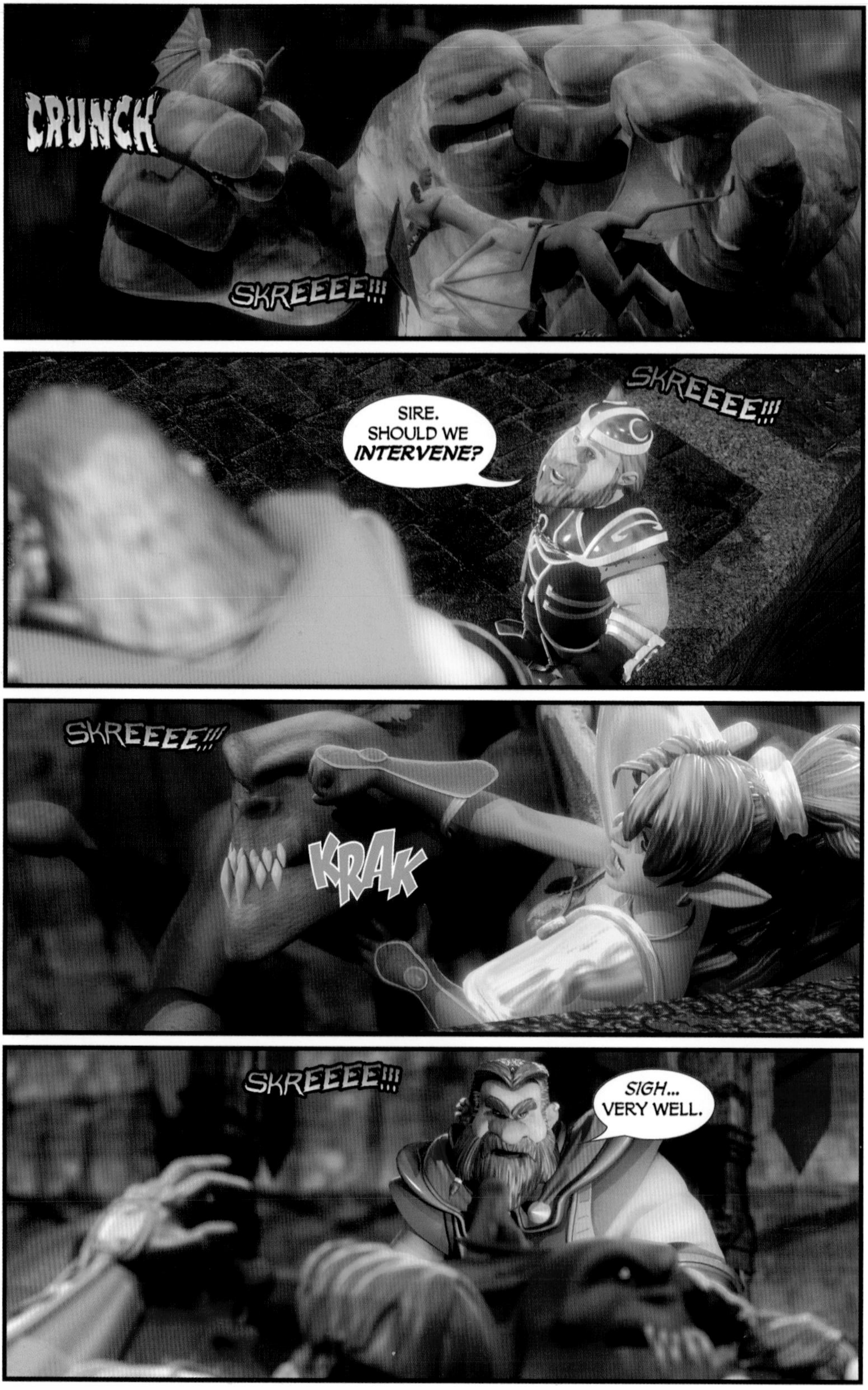
CRUNCH
SKREEEE!!!
SKREEEE!!!
SIRE. SHOULD WE INTERVENE?
SKREEEE!!!
KRAK
SKREEEE!!!
SIGH... VERY WELL.

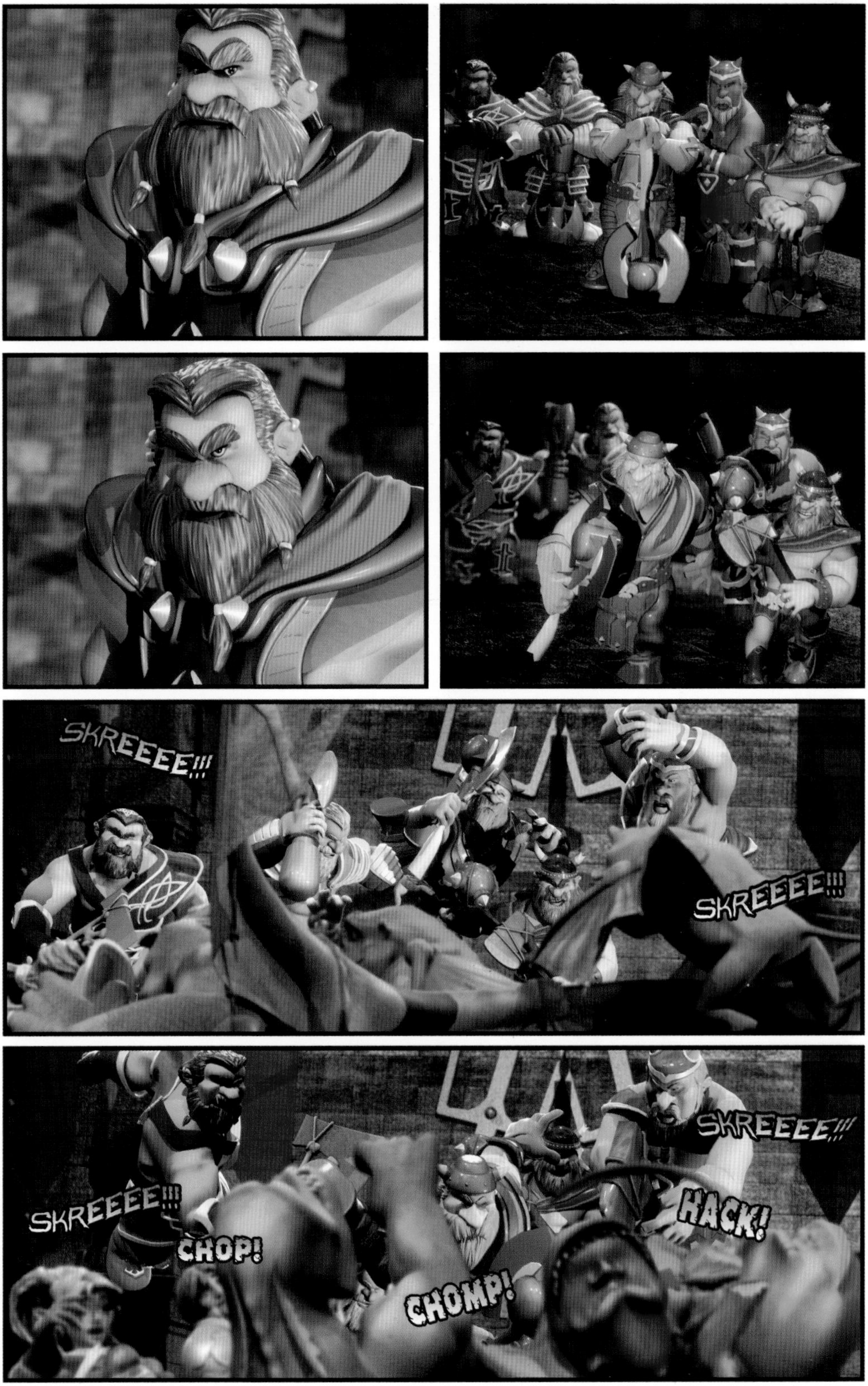
SKREEEEE!!!
SKREEEEE!!!
SKREEEEE!!!
CHOP!
SKREEEEE!!!
HACK!
CHOMP!

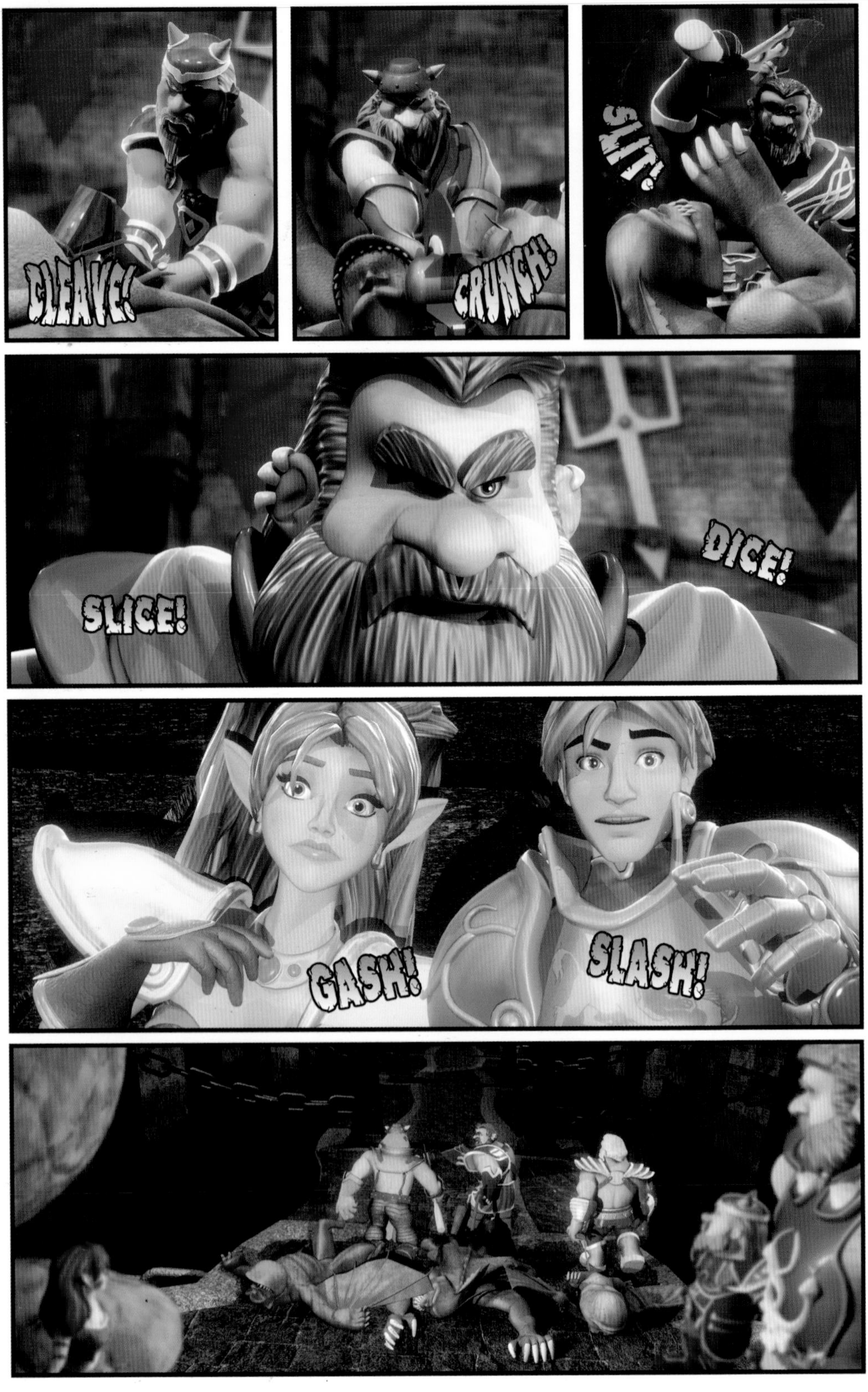
CLEAVE!
CRUNCH!
SLIT!
SLICE!
DICE!
GASH!
SLASH!

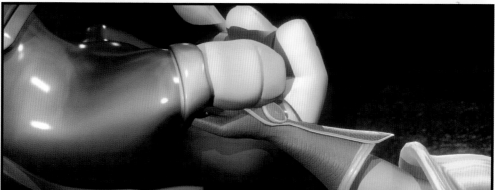

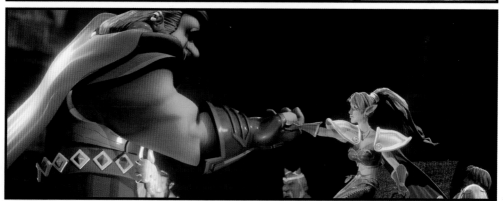

EXPLAIN.

SIX HUNDRED YEARS AGO, **BOTH** OF OUR FOREFATHERS SET OUT TO **WRITE** DOWN OUR HISTORY.

IT WAS **INTENTIONALLY** KEPT FROM NICODEMUS.

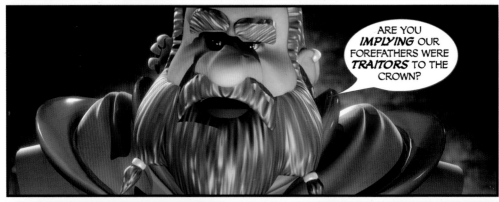

ARE YOU **IMPLYING** OUR FOREFATHERS WERE **TRAITORS** TO THE CROWN?

HARDLY. IN FACT... THE **OPPOSITE**, I WOULD PRESUME.

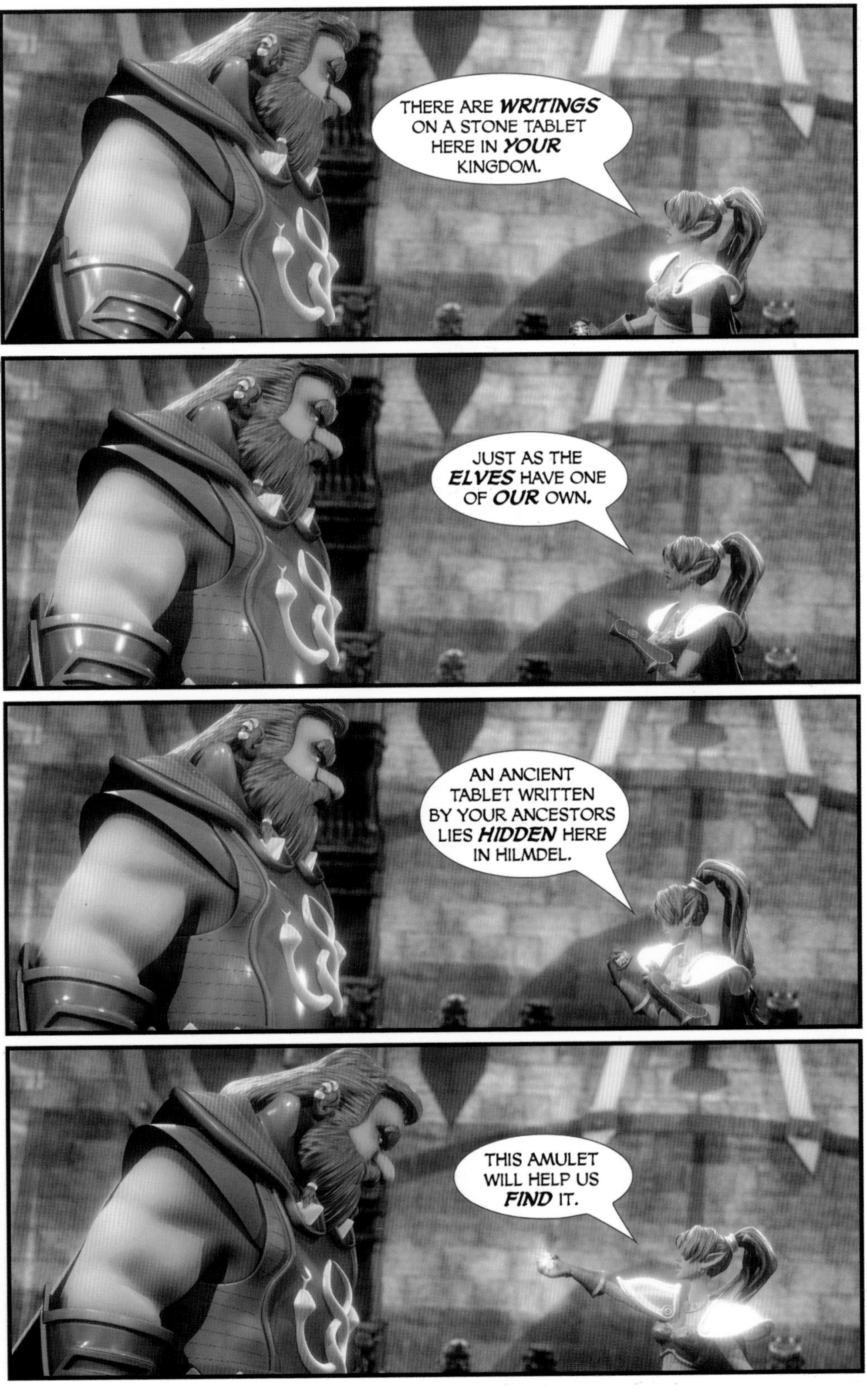
THERE ARE WRITINGS ON A STONE TABLET HERE IN YOUR KINGDOM.
JUST AS THE ELVES HAVE ONE OF OUR OWN.
AN ANCIENT TABLET WRITTEN BY YOUR ANCESTORS LIES HIDDEN HERE IN HILMDEL.
THIS AMULET WILL HELP US FIND IT.

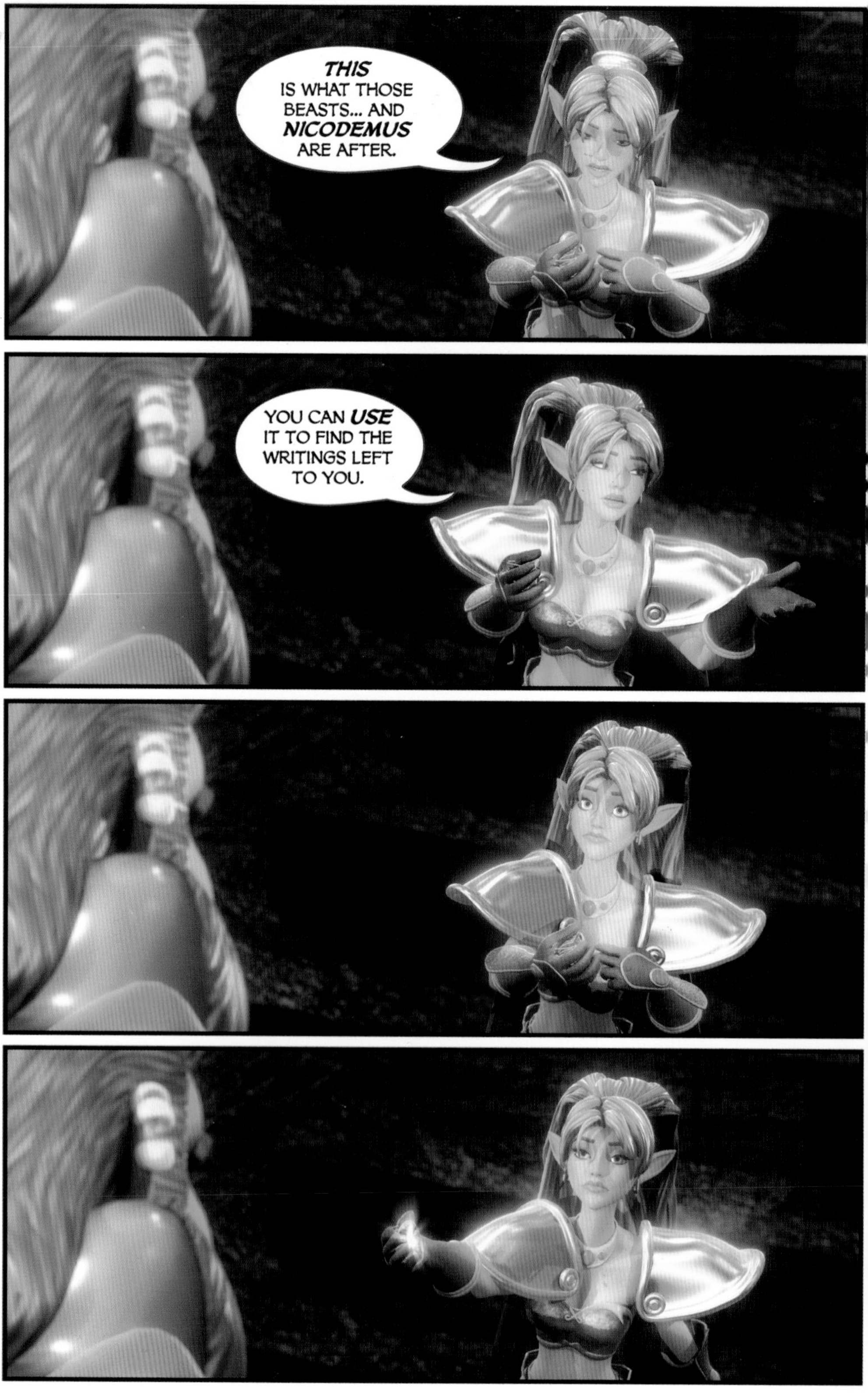
THIS IS WHAT THOSE BEASTS... AND NICODEMUS ARE AFTER.
YOU CAN USE IT TO FIND THE WRITINGS LEFT TO YOU.

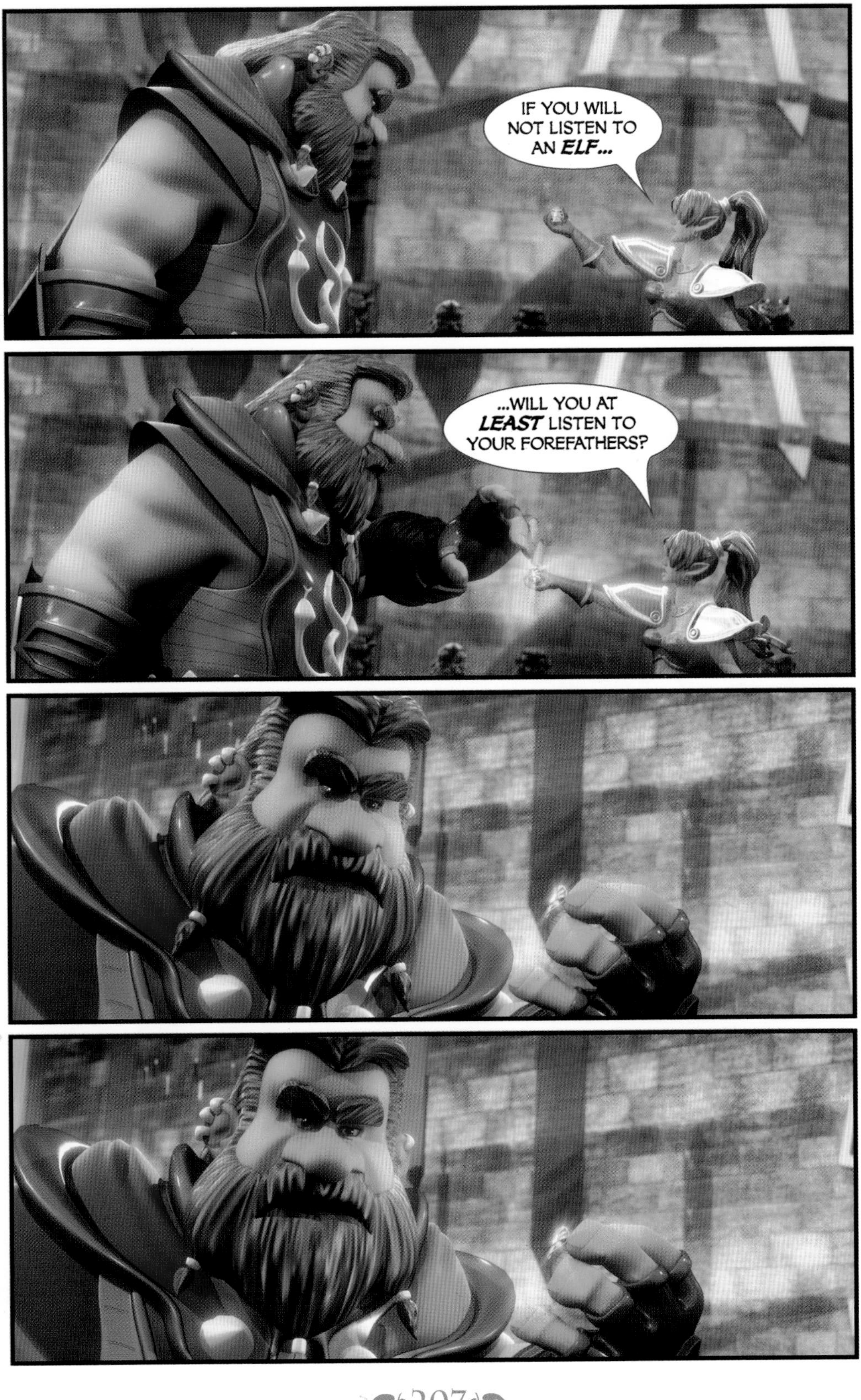
IF YOU WILL NOT LISTEN TO AN ELF...
...WILL YOU AT LEAST LISTEN TO YOUR FOREFATHERS?

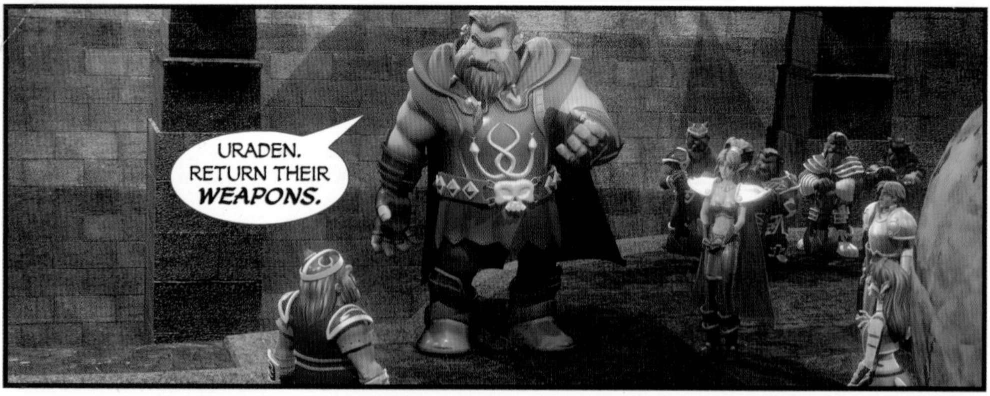
URADEN. RETURN THEIR *WEAPONS.*

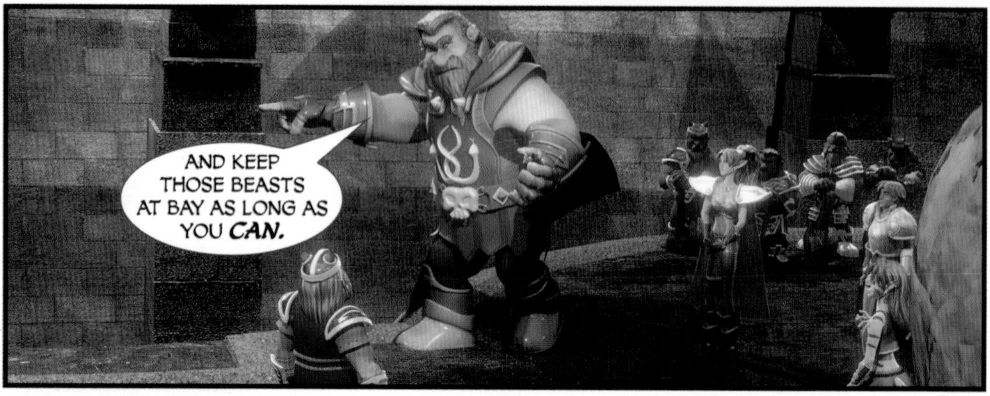
AND KEEP THOSE BEASTS AT BAY AS LONG AS YOU *CAN.*

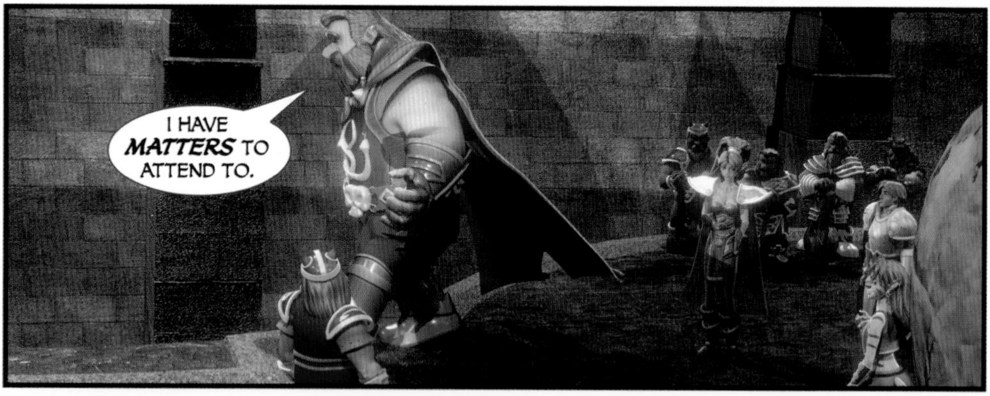
I HAVE *MATTERS* TO ATTEND TO.

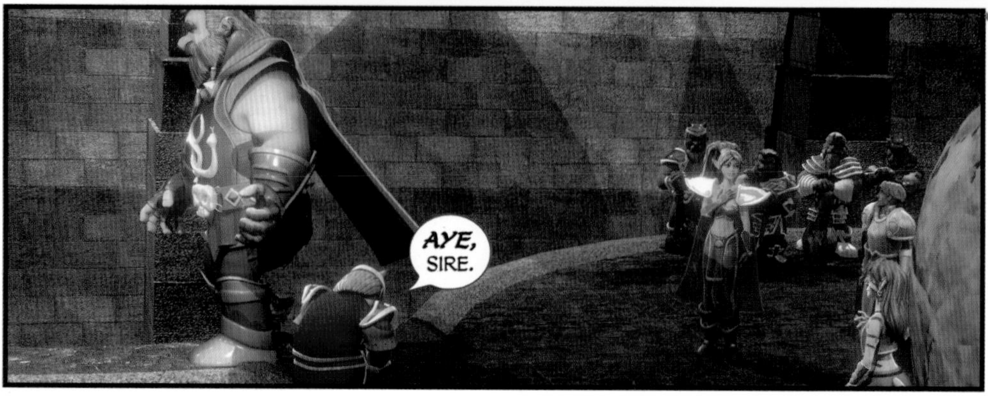
AYE, SIRE.

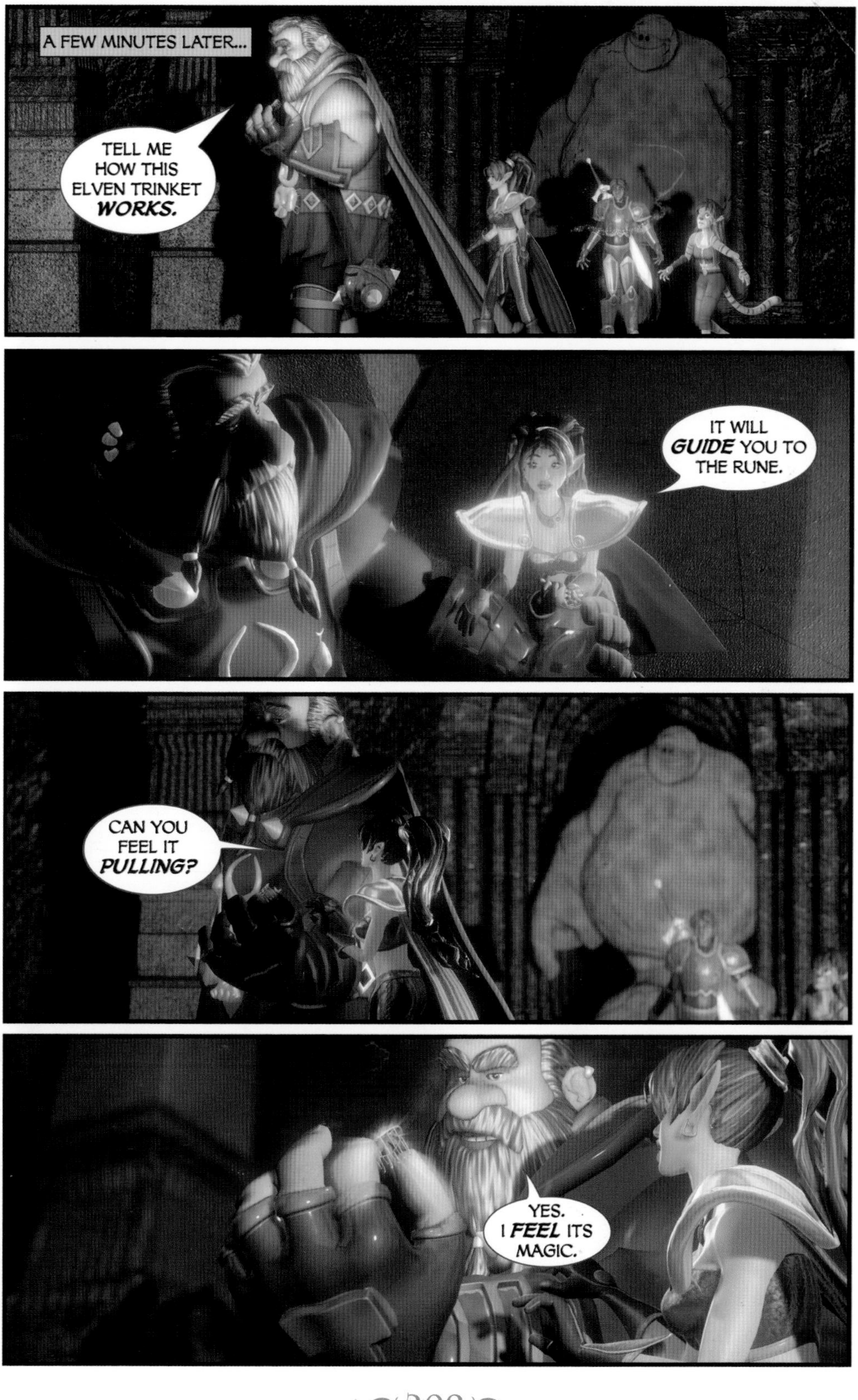
A FEW MINUTES LATER...
TELL ME HOW THIS ELVEN TRINKET WORKS.
IT WILL GUIDE YOU TO THE RUNE.
CAN YOU FEEL IT PULLING?
YES. I FEEL ITS MAGIC.

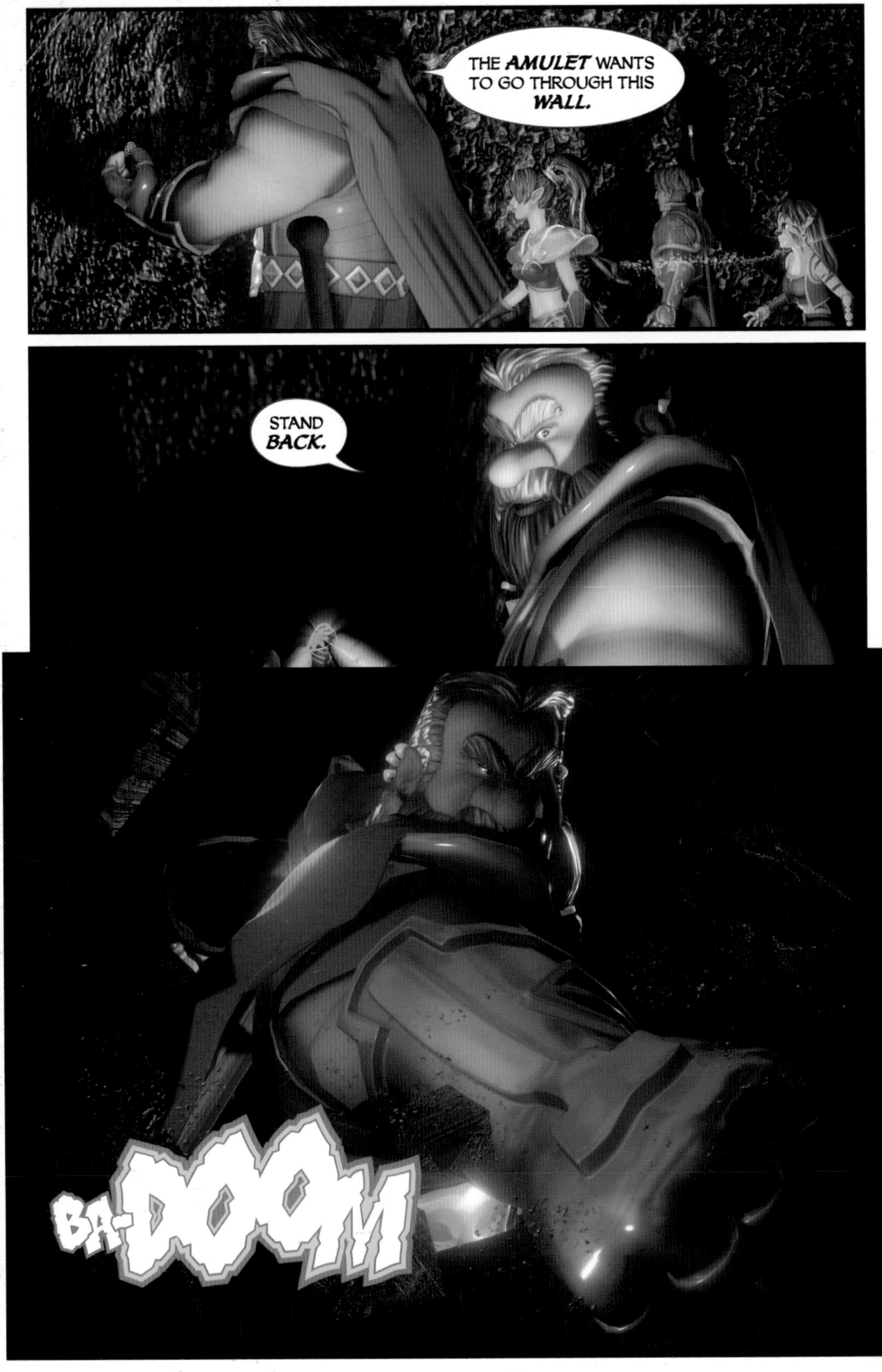
THE AMULET WANTS TO GO THROUGH THIS WALL.
STAND BACK.
BA-DOOM

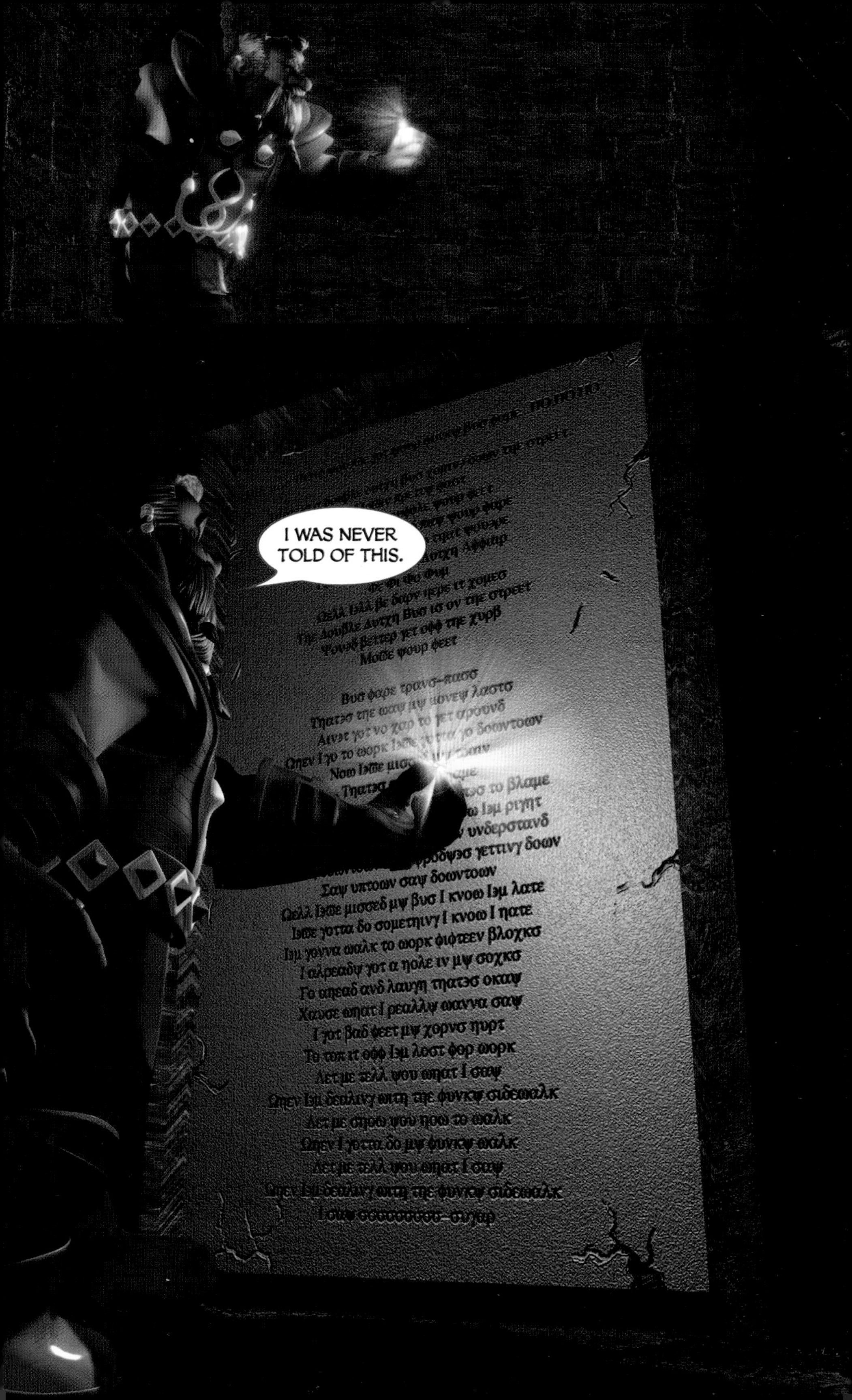
I WAS NEVER TOLD OF THIS.

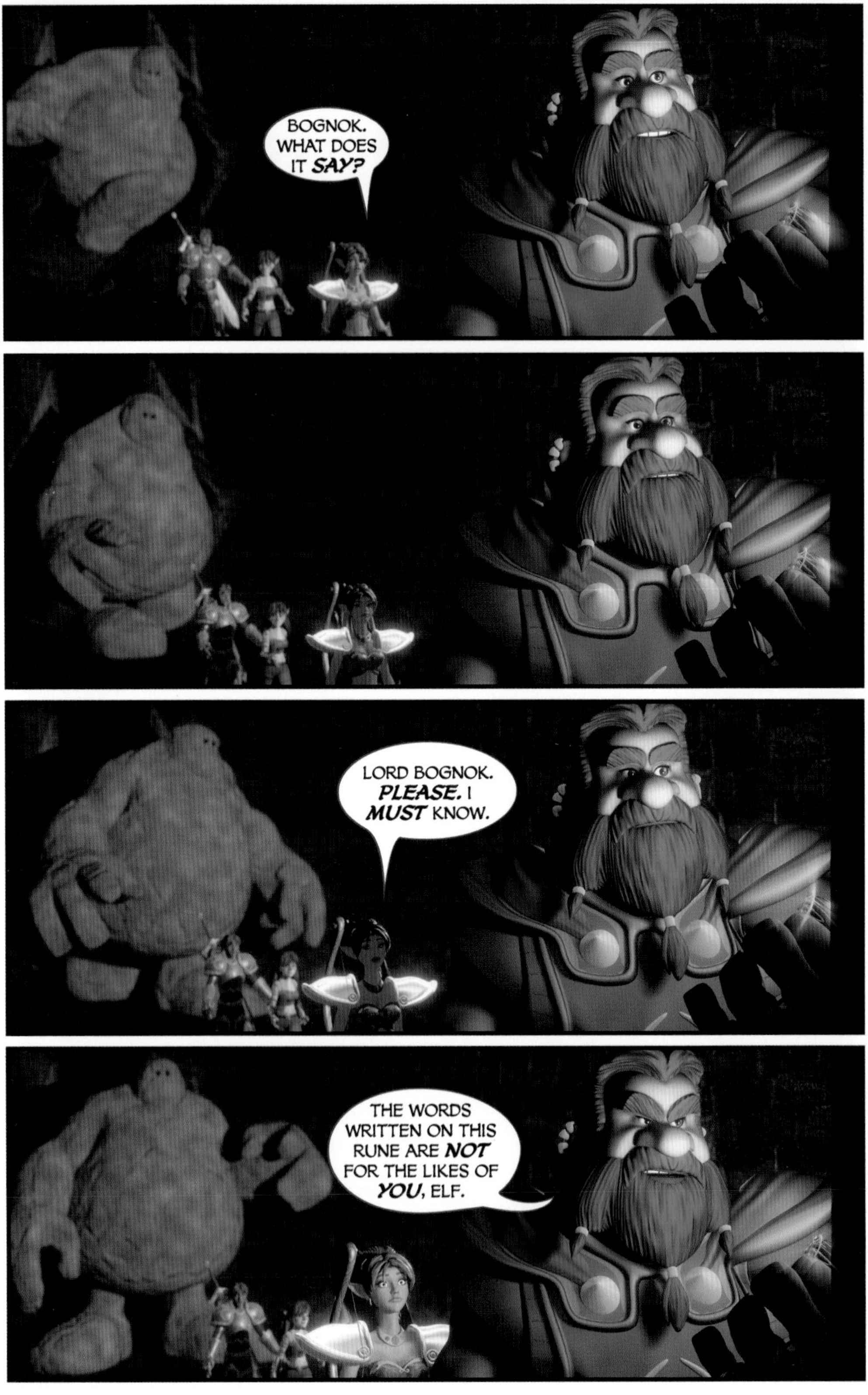
BOGNOK. WHAT DOES IT *SAY?*
LORD BOGNOK. *PLEASE.* I *MUST* KNOW.
THE WORDS WRITTEN ON THIS RUNE ARE *NOT* FOR THE LIKES OF *YOU*, ELF.

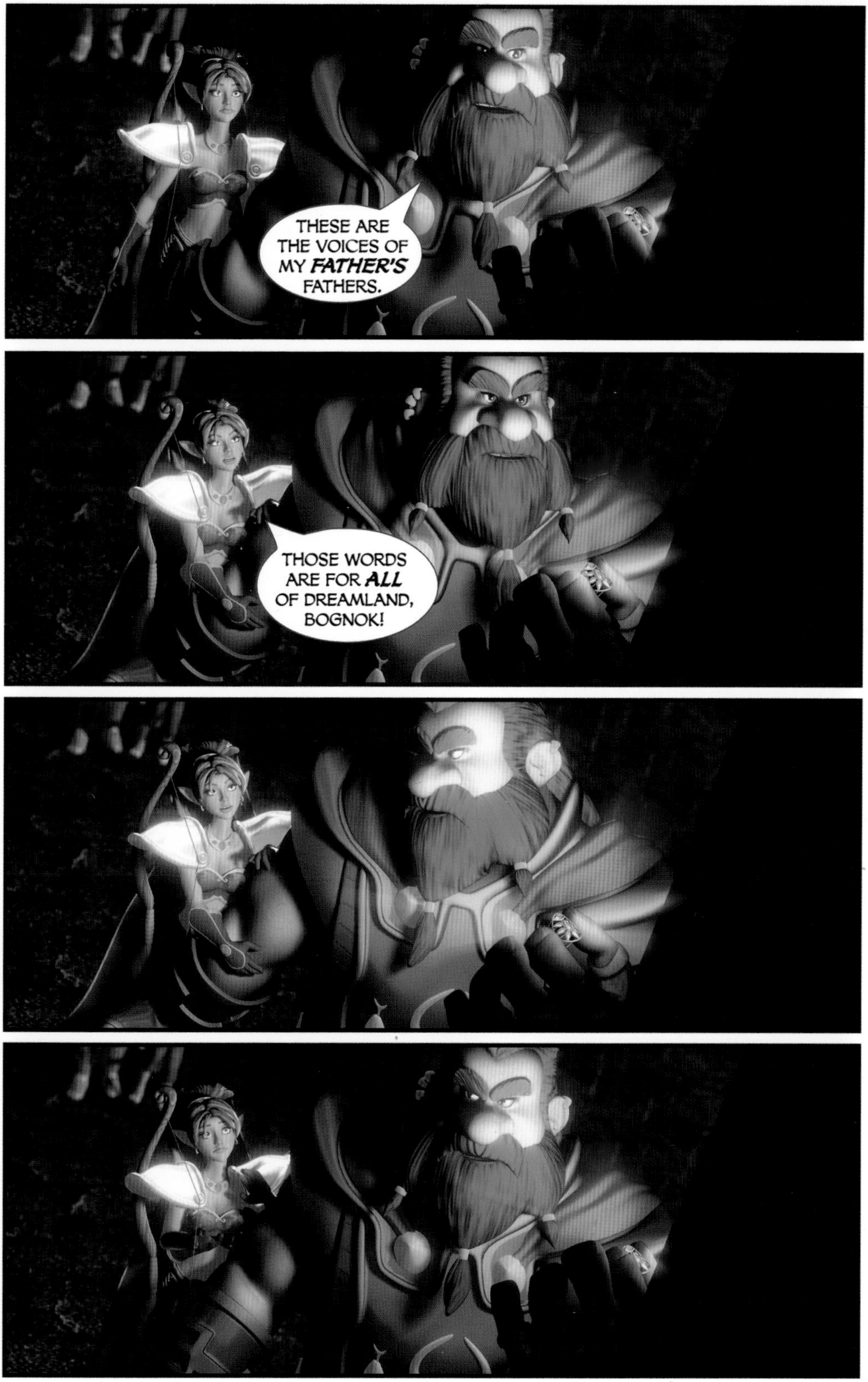
THESE ARE THE VOICES OF MY *FATHER'S* FATHERS.
THOSE WORDS ARE FOR *ALL* OF DREAMLAND, BOGNOK!

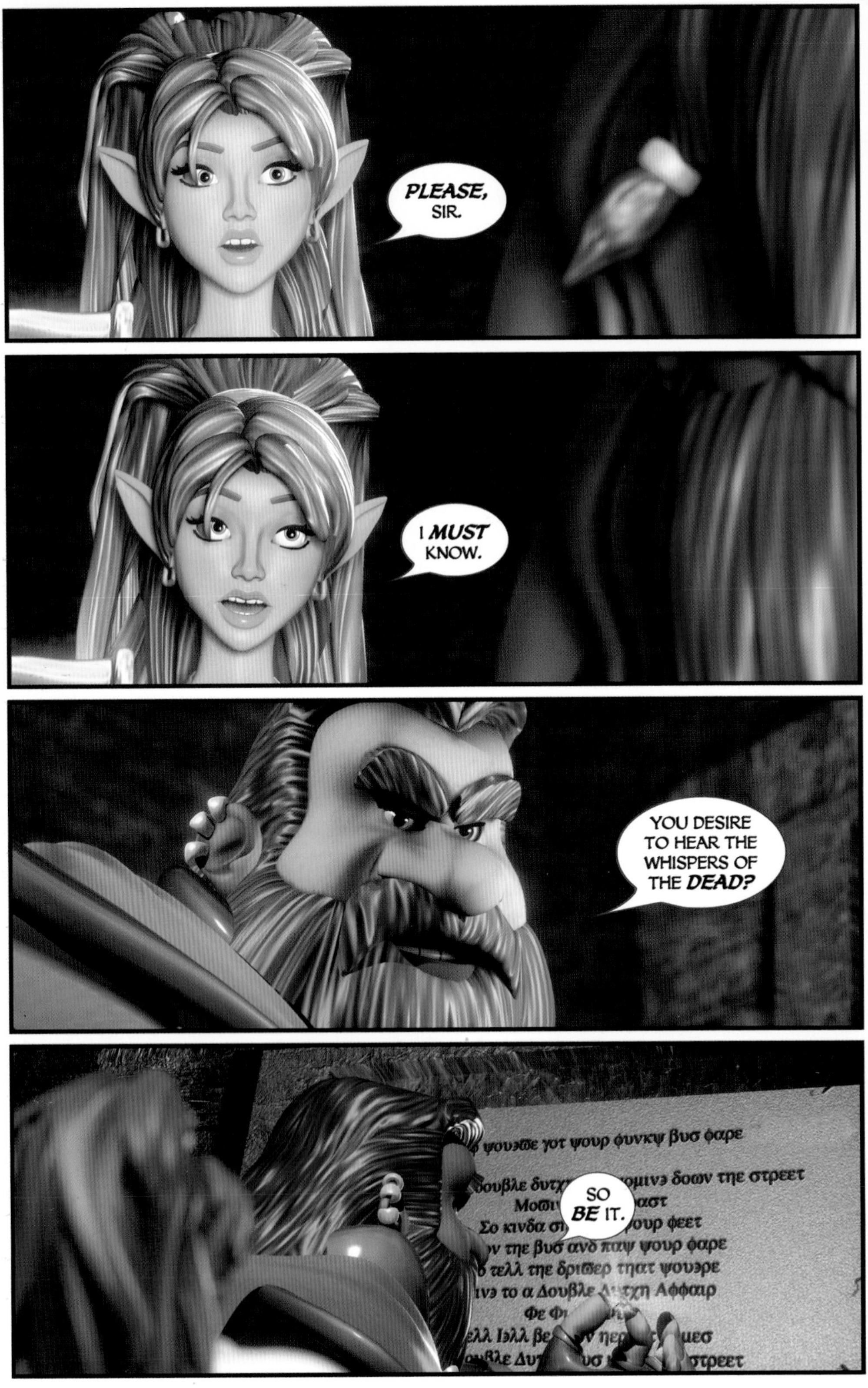

PLEASE, SIR.
I *MUST* KNOW.
YOU DESIRE TO HEAR THE WHISPERS OF THE *DEAD?*
SO *BE* IT.

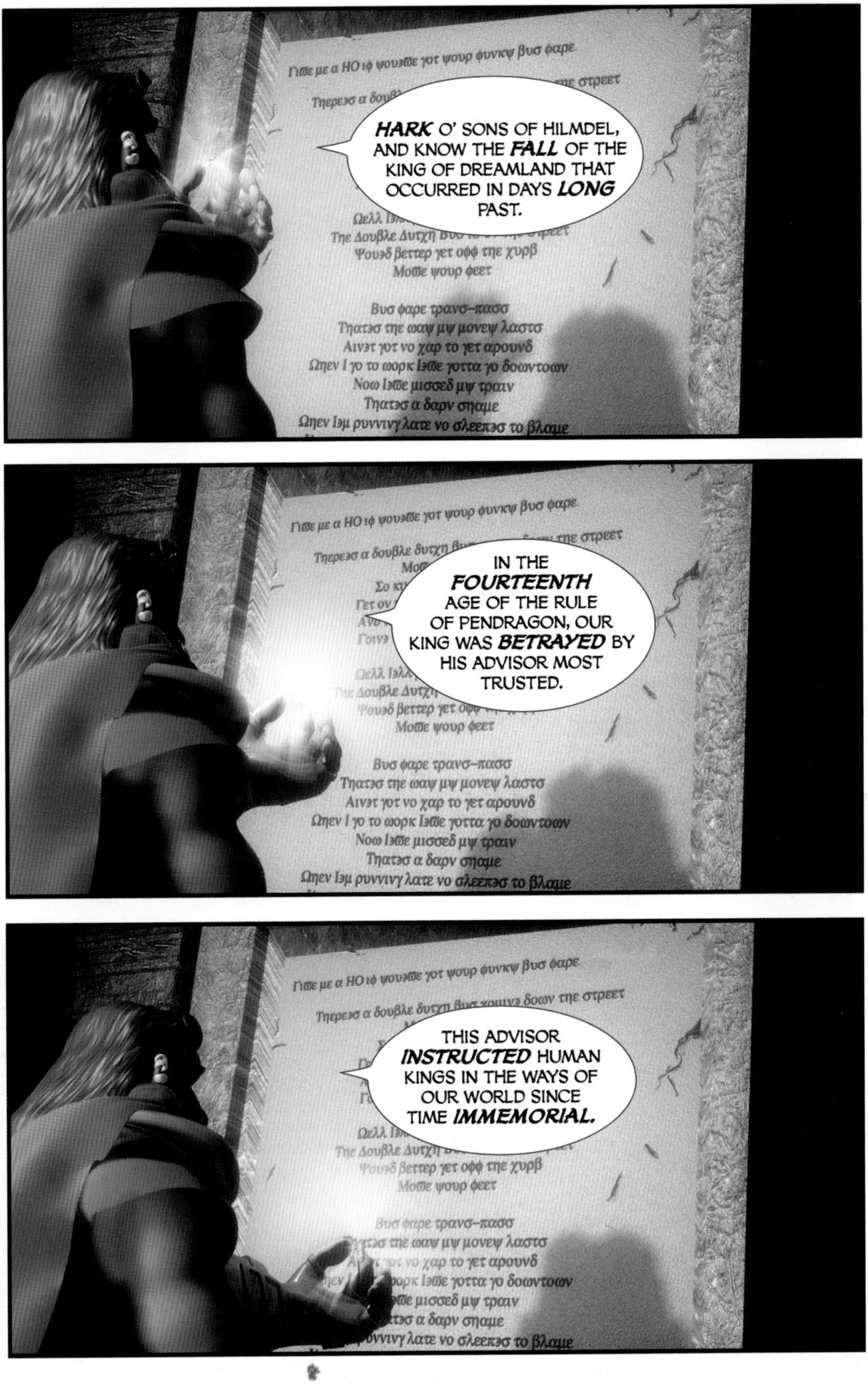
HARK O' SONS OF HILMDEL, AND KNOW THE FALL OF THE KING OF DREAMLAND THAT OCCURRED IN DAYS LONG PAST.
IN THE FOURTEENTH AGE OF THE RULE OF PENDRAGON, OUR KING WAS BETRAYED BY HIS ADVISOR MOST TRUSTED.
THIS ADVISOR INSTRUCTED HUMAN KINGS IN THE WAYS OF OUR WORLD SINCE TIME IMMEMORIAL.

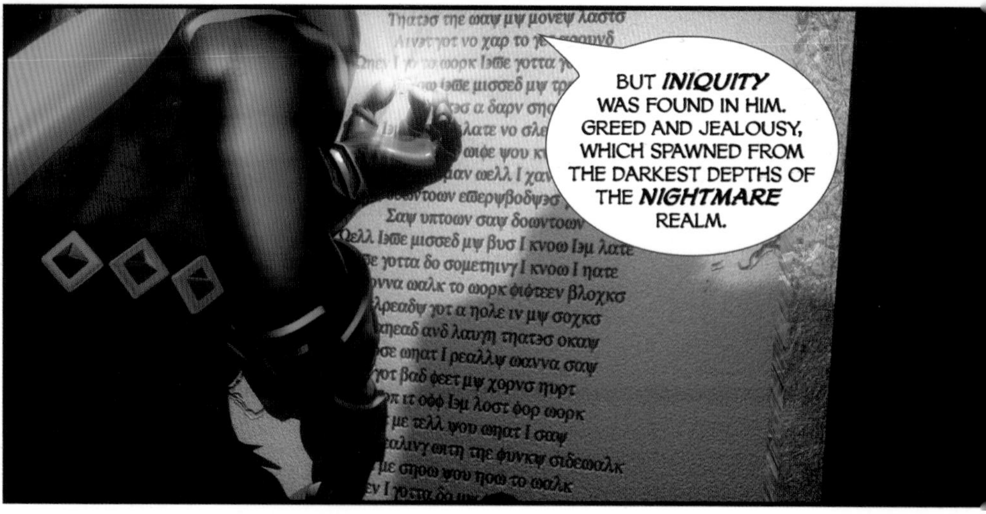
BUT *INIQUITY* WAS FOUND IN HIM. GREED AND JEALOUSY, WHICH SPAWNED FROM THE DARKEST DEPTHS OF THE *NIGHTMARE* REALM.

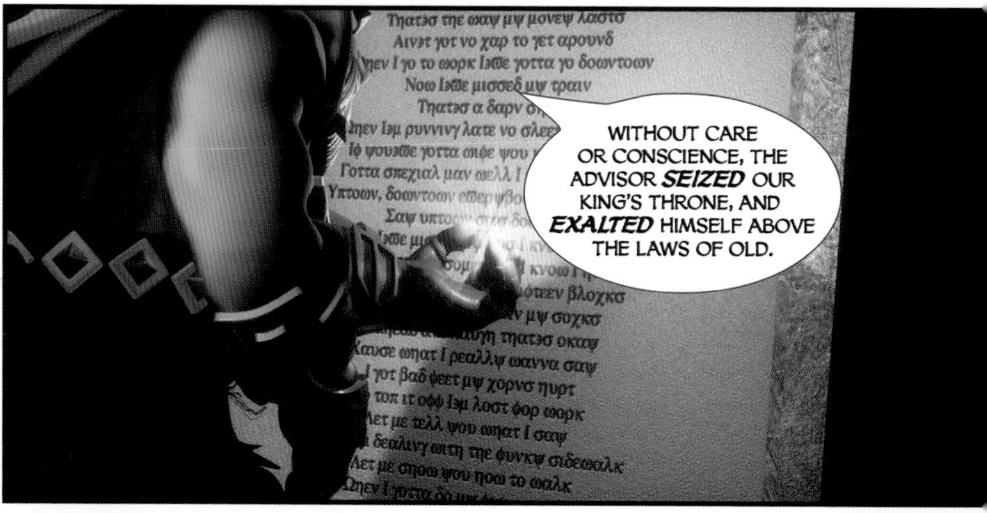
WITHOUT CARE OR CONSCIENCE, THE ADVISOR *SEIZED* OUR KING'S THRONE, AND *EXALTED* HIMSELF ABOVE THE LAWS OF OLD.

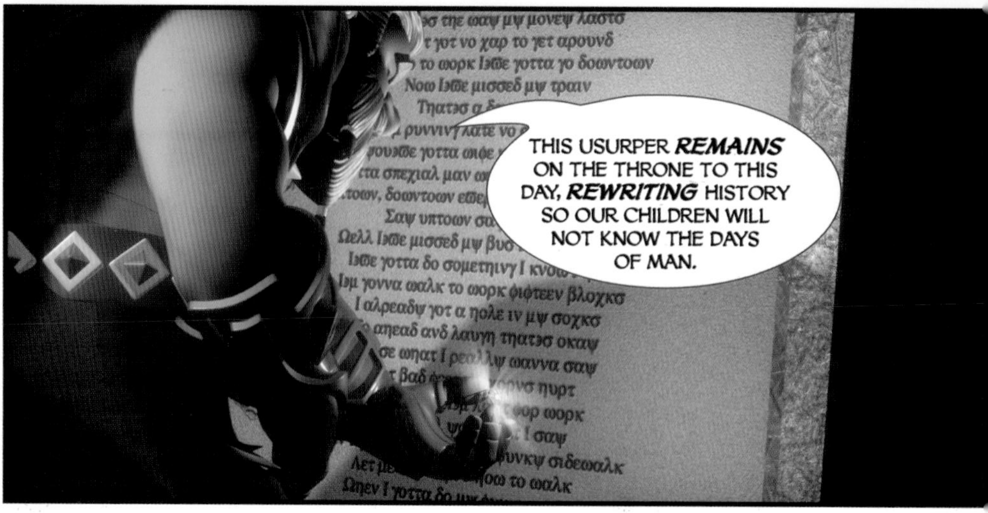
THIS USURPER *REMAINS* ON THE THRONE TO THIS DAY, *REWRITING* HISTORY SO OUR CHILDREN WILL NOT KNOW THE DAYS OF MAN.

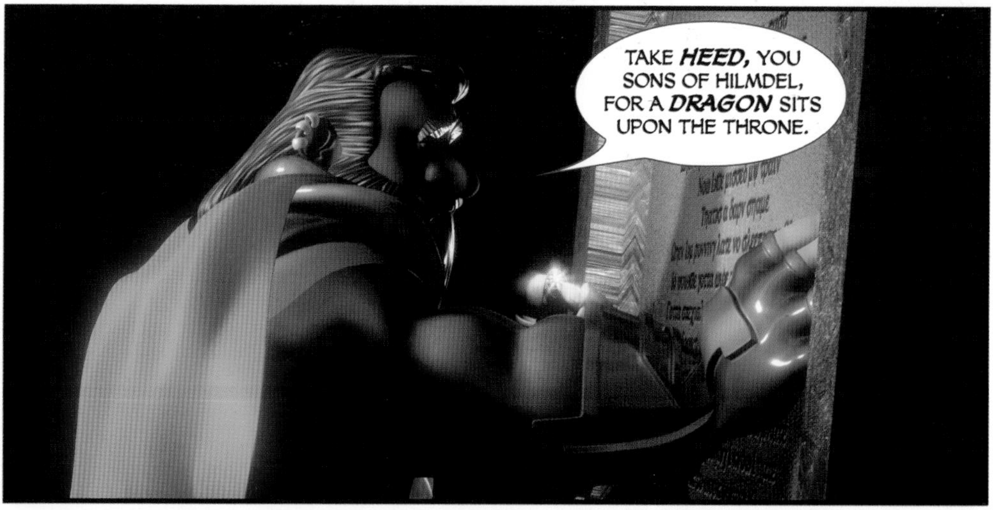
TAKE HEED, YOU SONS OF HILMDEL, FOR A DRAGON SITS UPON THE THRONE.

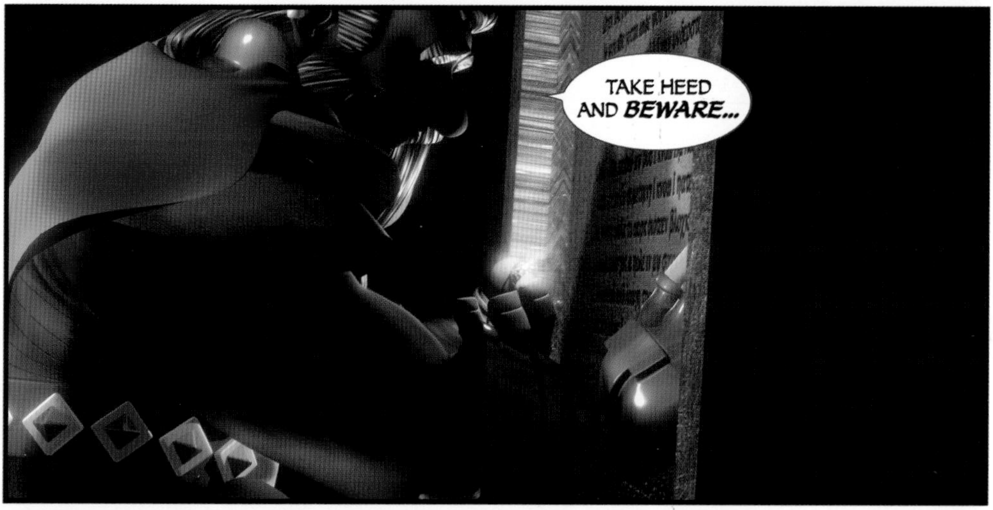
TAKE HEED AND BEWARE...

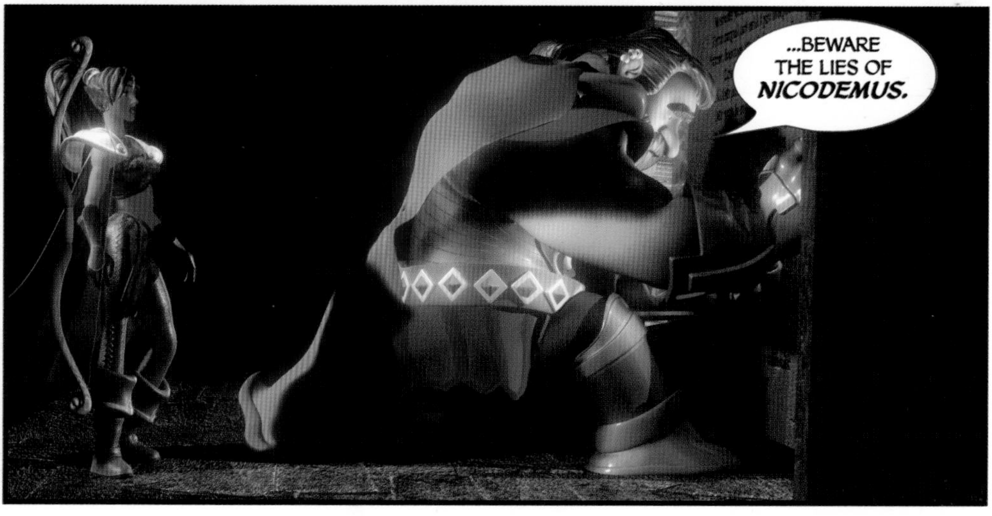
...BEWARE THE LIES OF NICODEMUS.

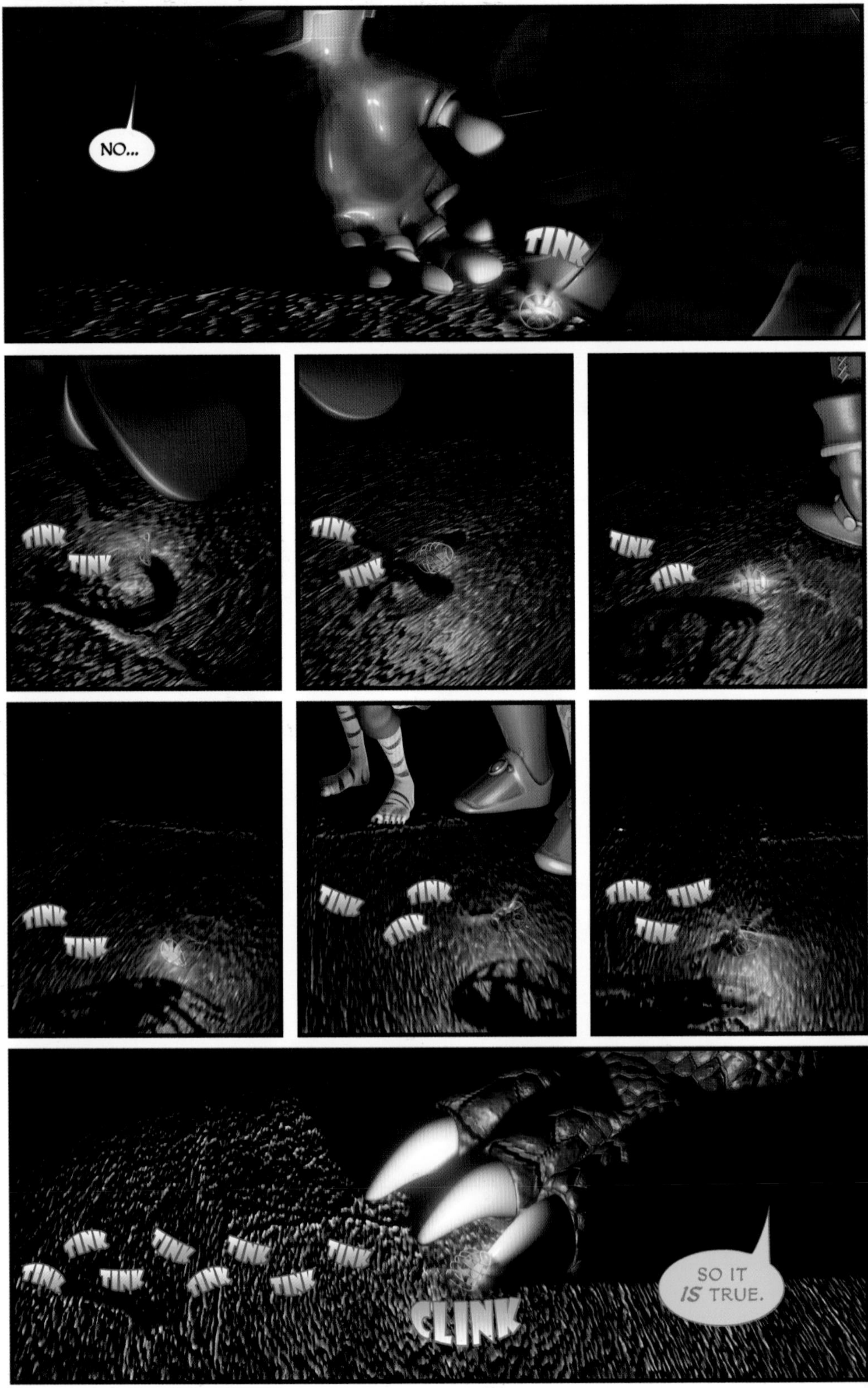
NO...
TINK
TINK
TINK
TINK
TINK
TINK
TINK
TINK
TINK
TINK
TINK
TINK
TINK
TINK
TINK
TINK
TINK
TINK
TINK
TINK
TINK
TINK
TINK
CLINK
SO IT *IS* TRUE.

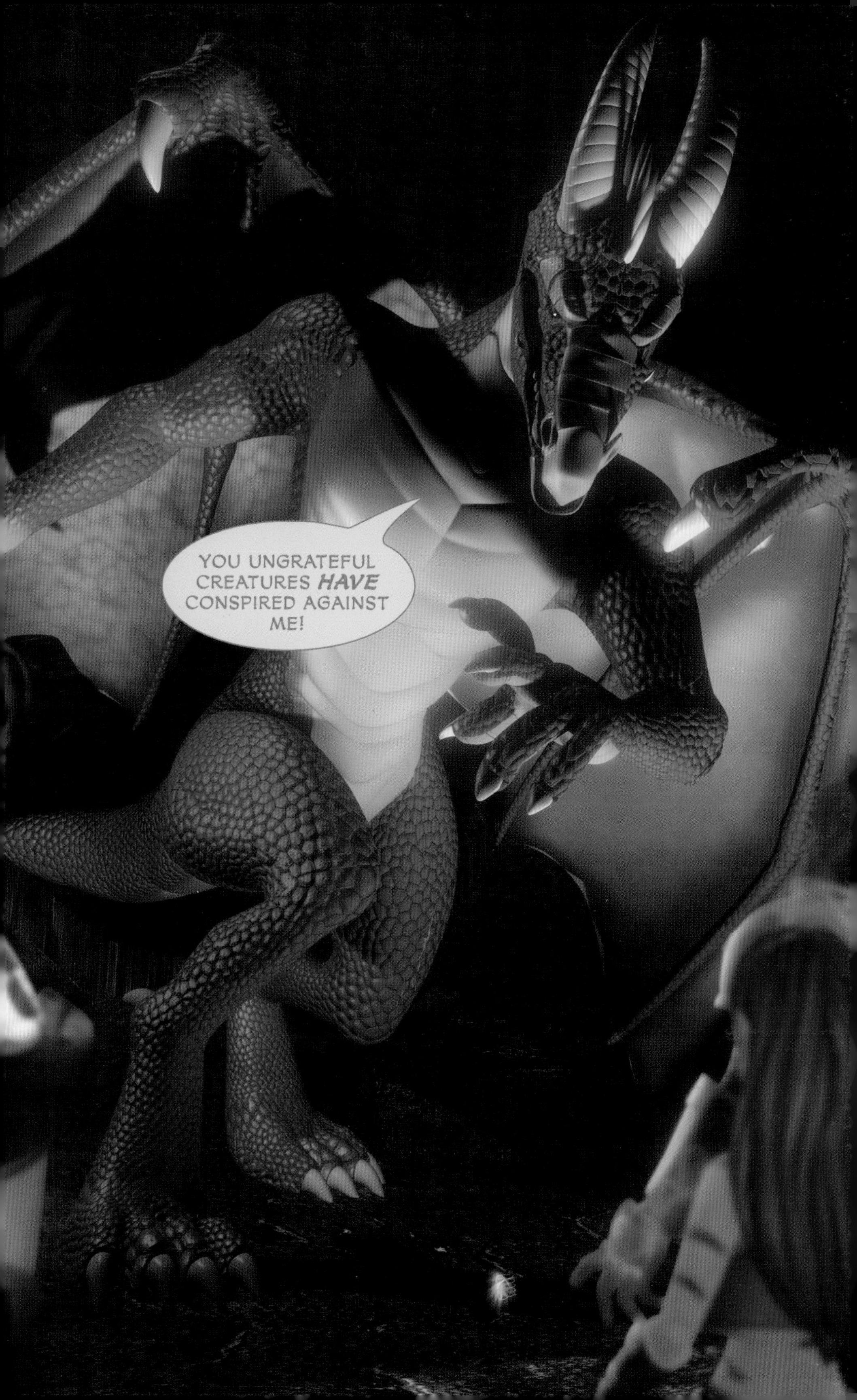
YOU UNGRATEFUL CREATURES HAVE CONSPIRED AGAINST ME!

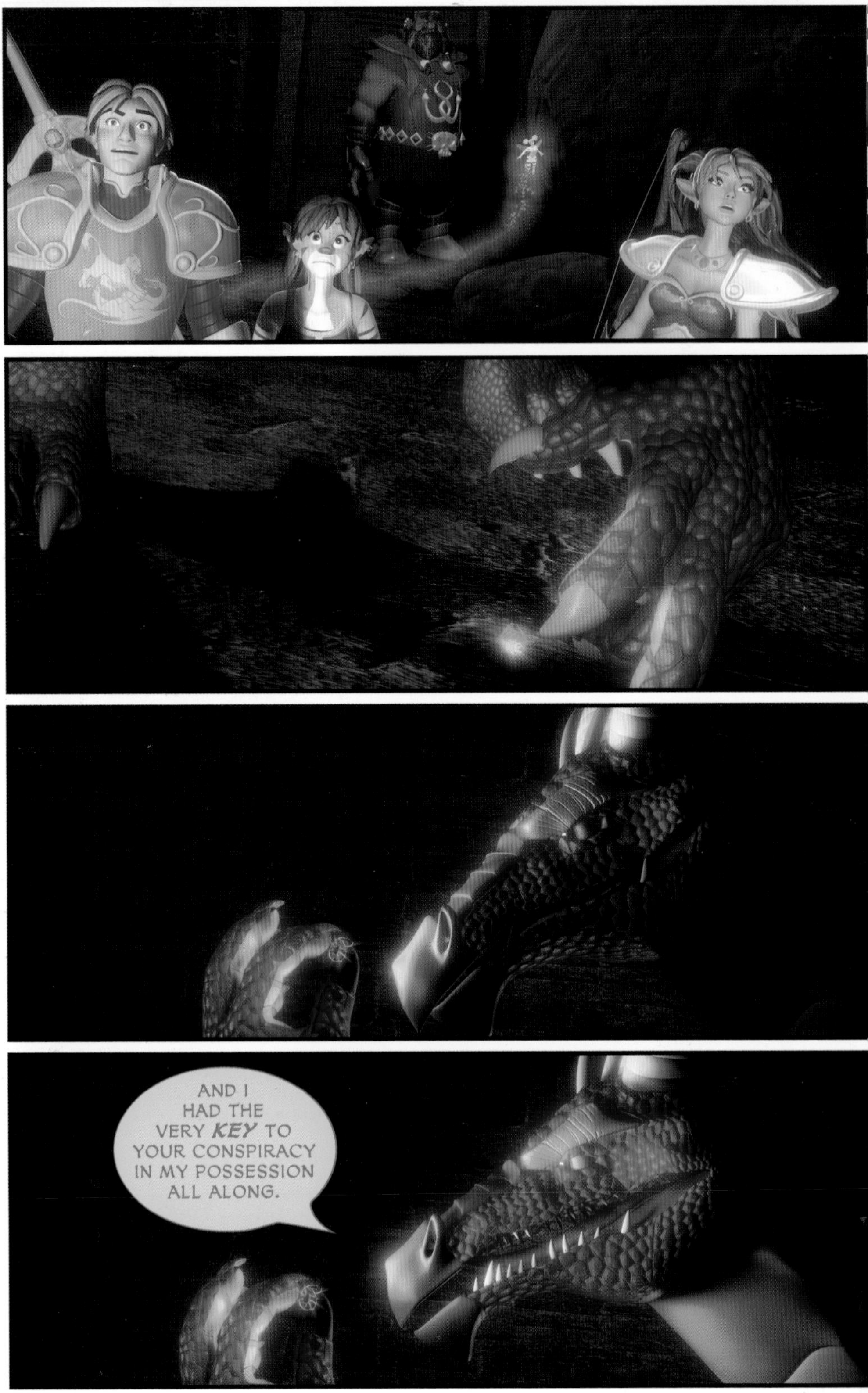
AND I HAD THE VERY *KEY* TO YOUR CONSPIRACY IN MY POSSESSION ALL ALONG.

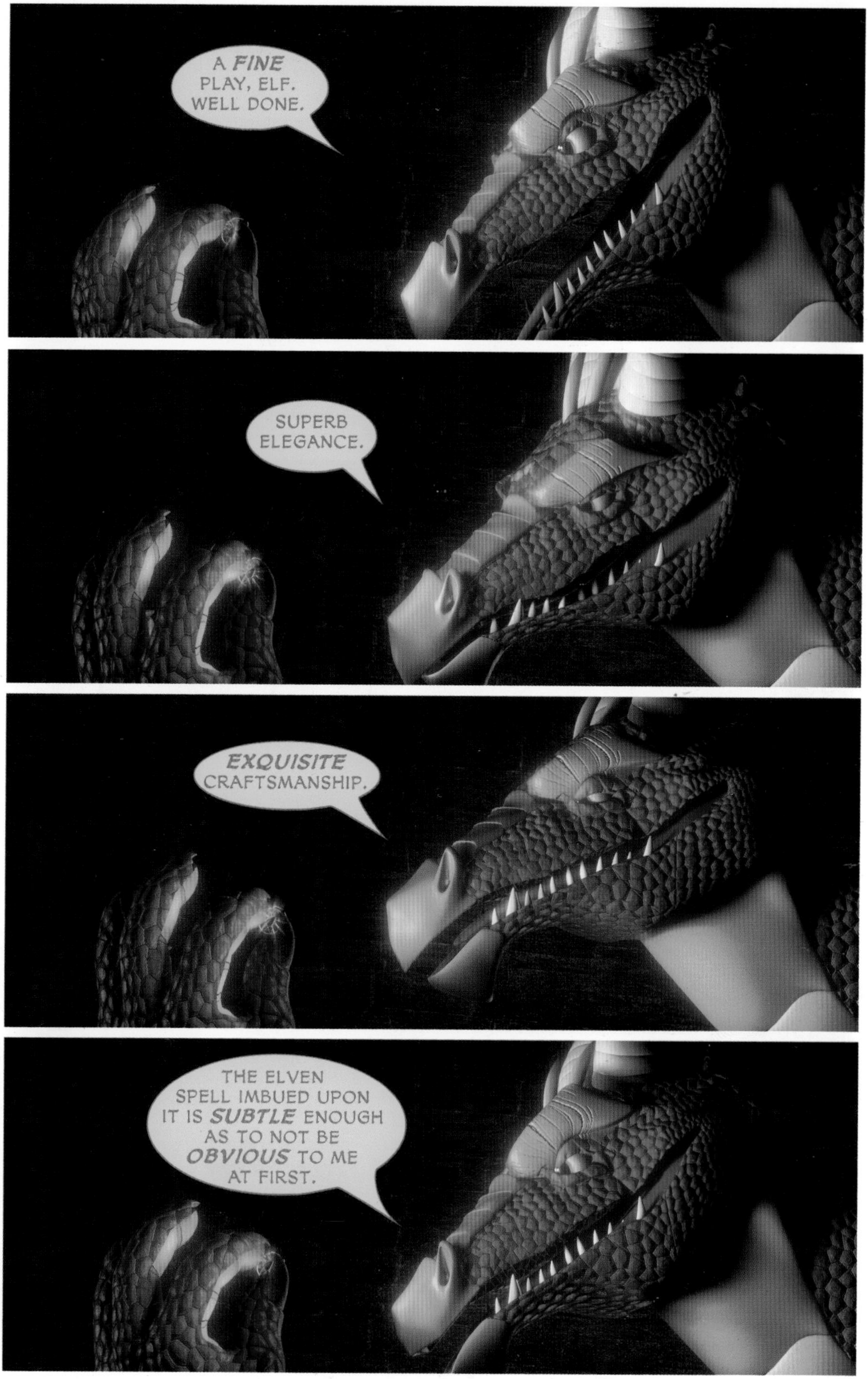
A FINE PLAY, ELF. WELL DONE.
SUPERB ELEGANCE.
EXQUISITE CRAFTSMANSHIP.
THE ELVEN SPELL IMBUED UPON IT IS SUBTLE ENOUGH AS TO NOT BE OBVIOUS TO ME AT FIRST.

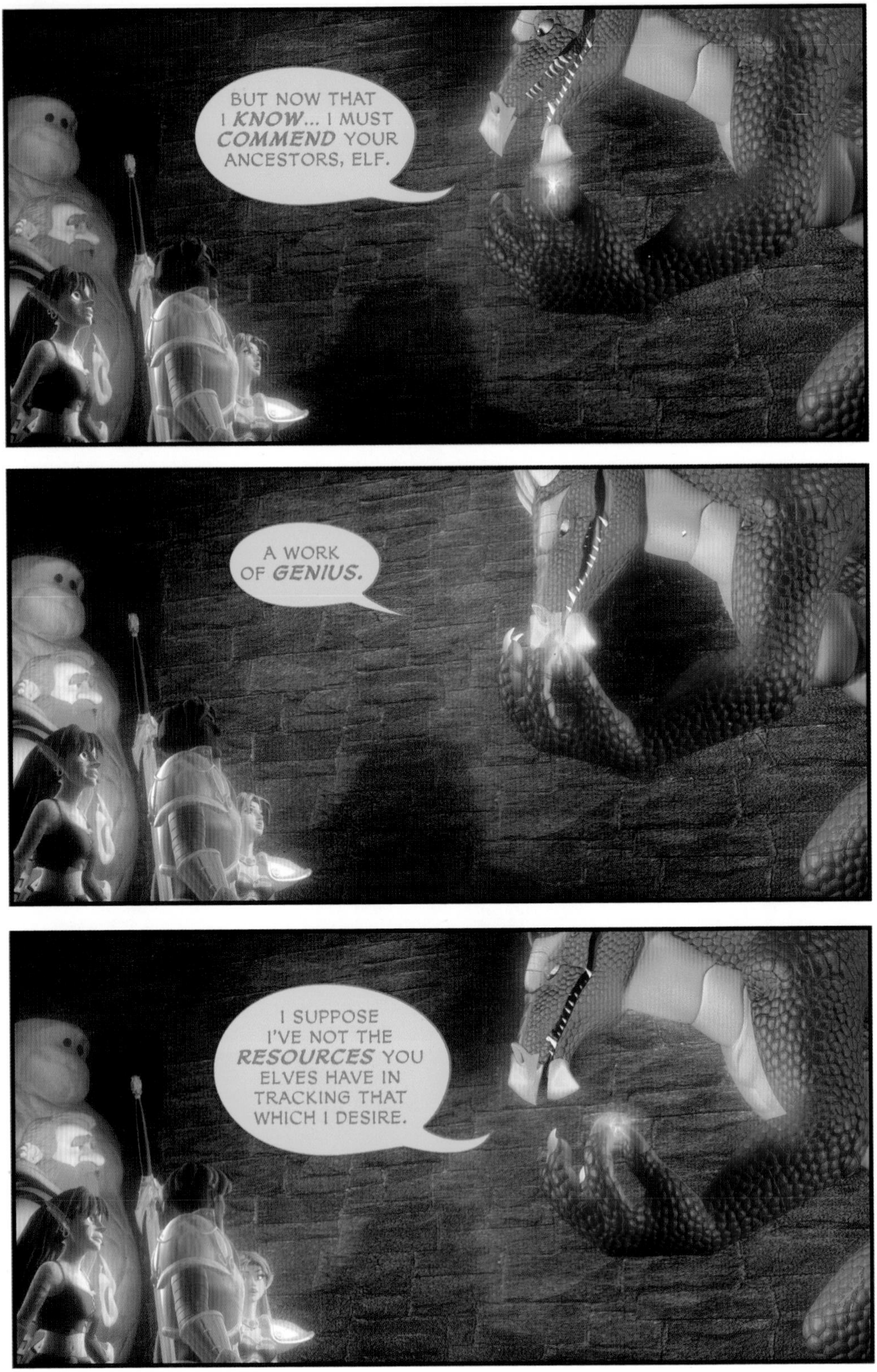
BUT NOW THAT I KNOW... I MUST COMMEND YOUR ANCESTORS, ELF.
A WORK OF GENIUS.
I SUPPOSE I'VE NOT THE RESOURCES YOU ELVES HAVE IN TRACKING THAT WHICH I DESIRE.

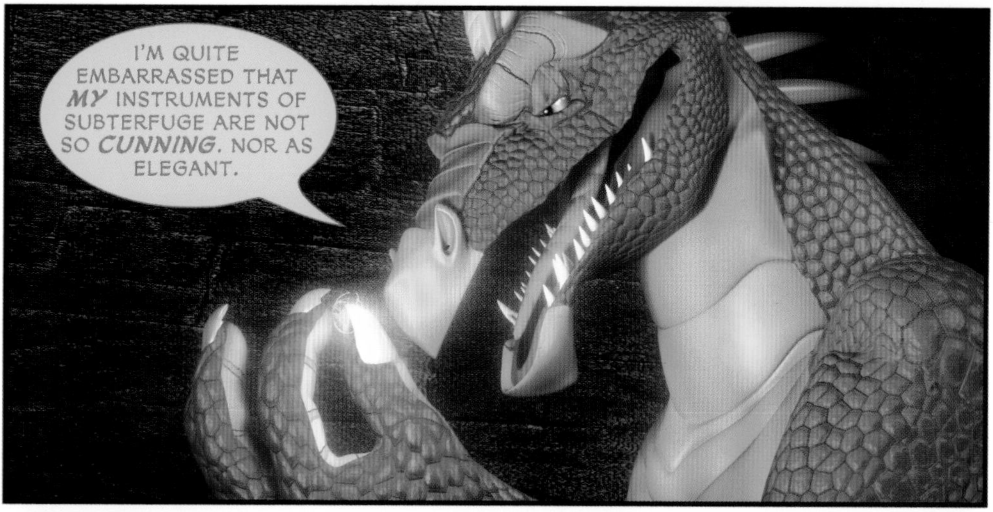
I'M QUITE EMBARRASSED THAT *MY* INSTRUMENTS OF SUBTERFUGE ARE NOT SO *CUNNING*. NOR AS ELEGANT.

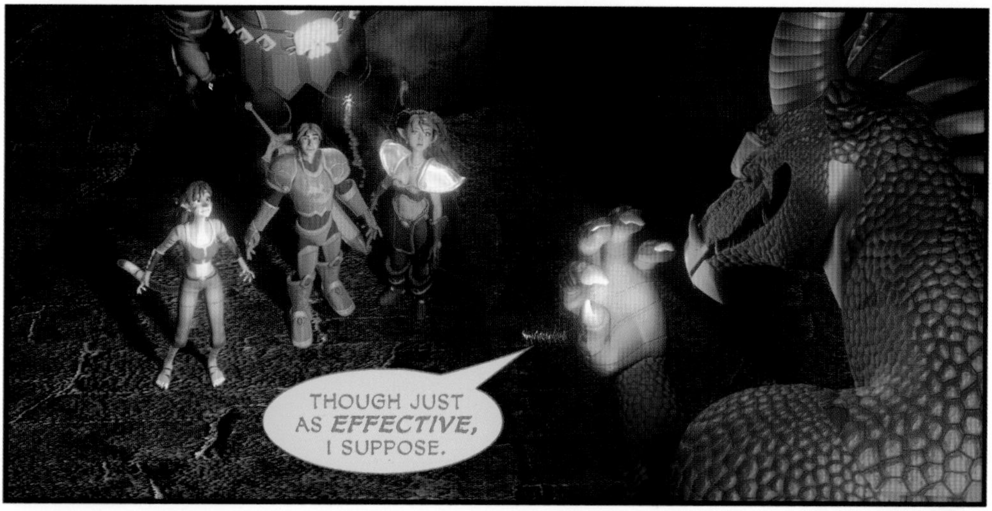
THOUGH JUST AS *EFFECTIVE*, I SUPPOSE.

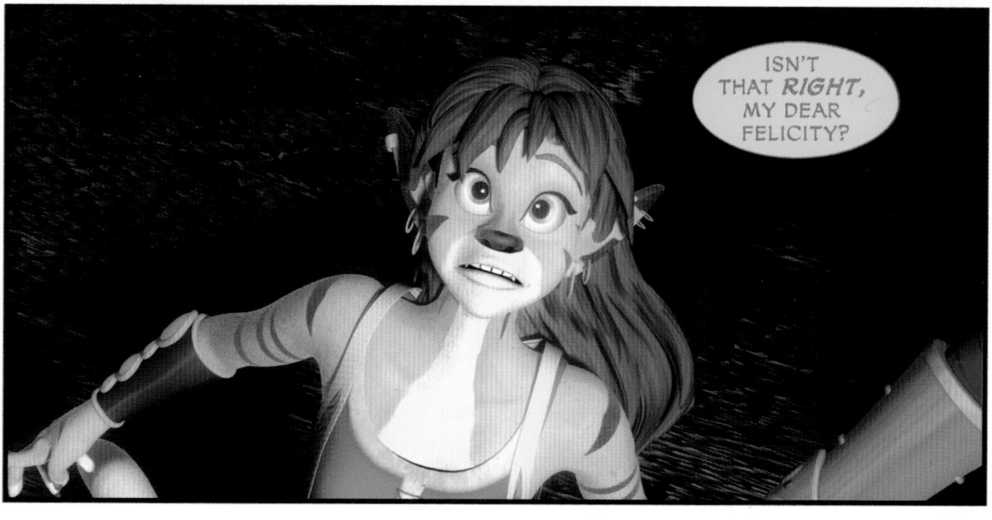
ISN'T THAT *RIGHT*, MY DEAR FELICITY?

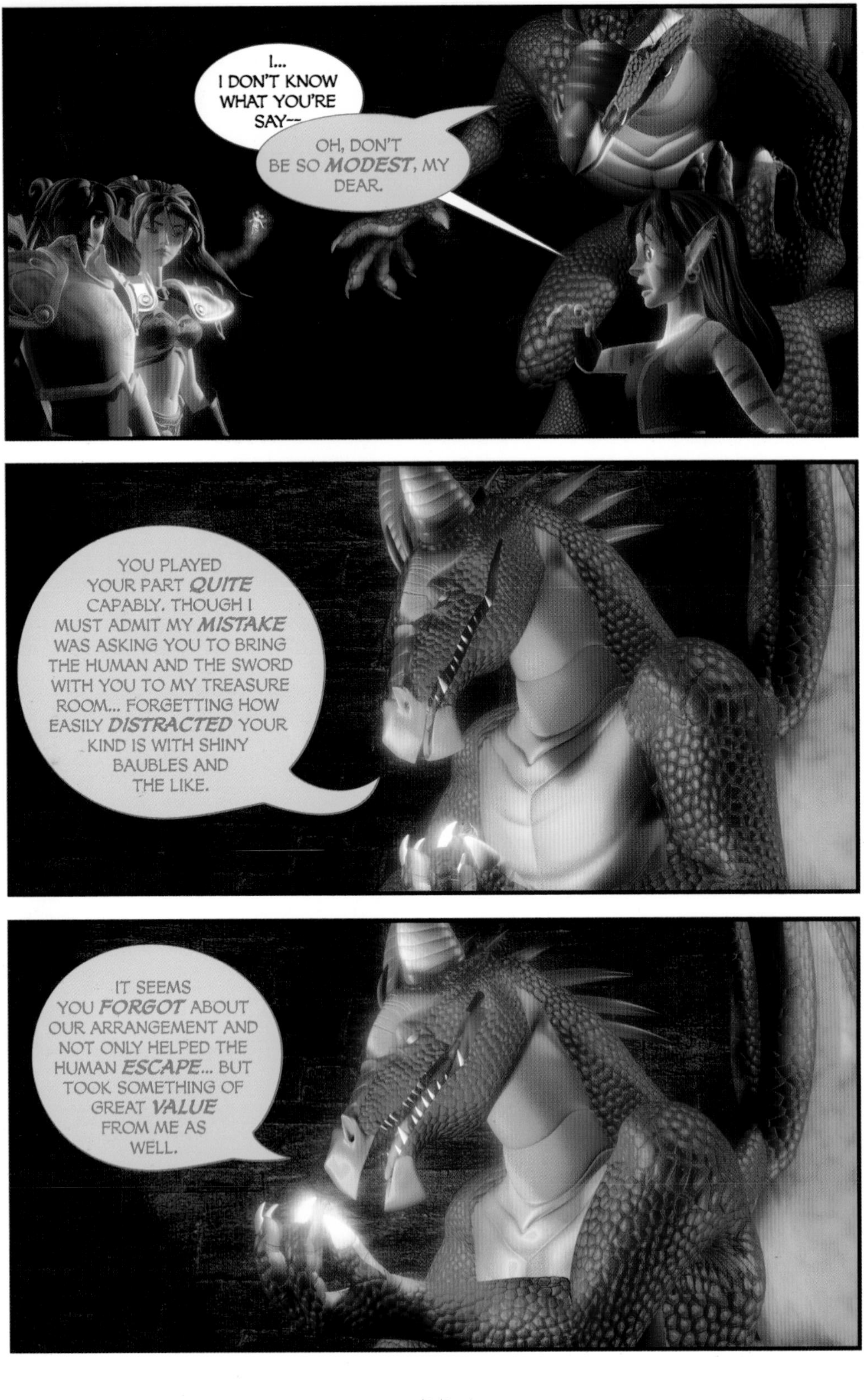
I... I DON'T KNOW WHAT YOU'RE SAY--
OH, DON'T BE SO MODEST, MY DEAR.
YOU PLAYED YOUR PART QUITE CAPABLY. THOUGH I MUST ADMIT MY MISTAKE WAS ASKING YOU TO BRING THE HUMAN AND THE SWORD WITH YOU TO MY TREASURE ROOM... FORGETTING HOW EASILY DISTRACTED YOUR KIND IS WITH SHINY BAUBLES AND THE LIKE.
IT SEEMS YOU FORGOT ABOUT OUR ARRANGEMENT AND NOT ONLY HELPED THE HUMAN ESCAPE... BUT TOOK SOMETHING OF GREAT VALUE FROM ME AS WELL.

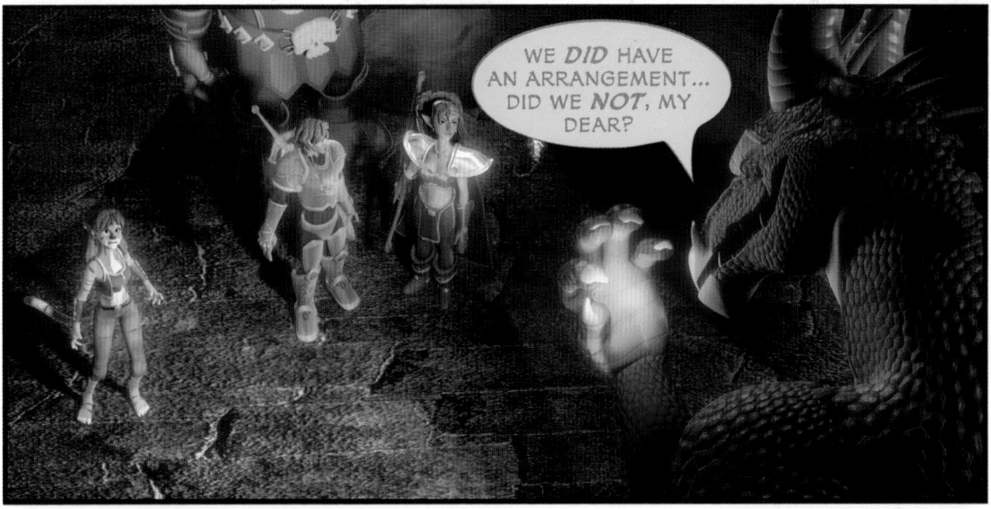
WE *DID* HAVE AN ARRANGEMENT... DID WE *NOT*, MY DEAR?

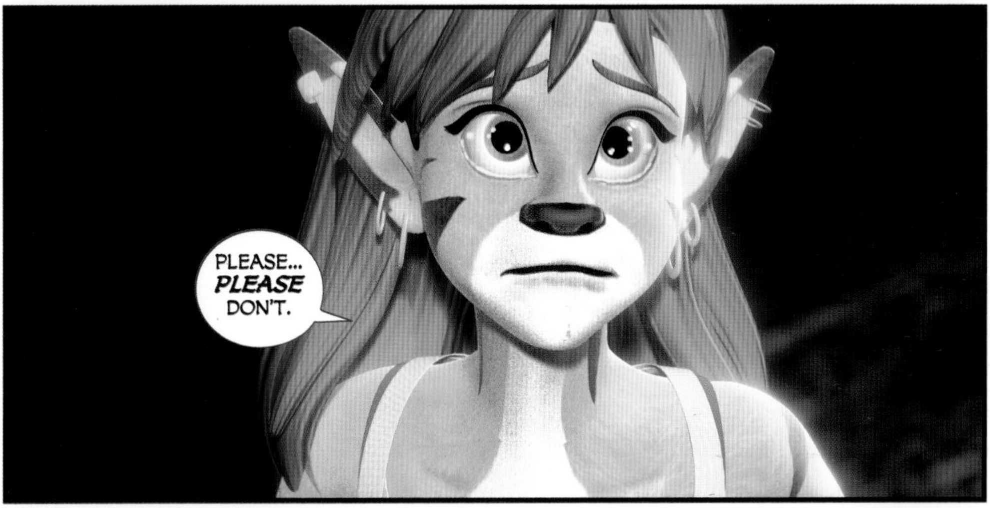
PLEASE... *PLEASE* DON'T.

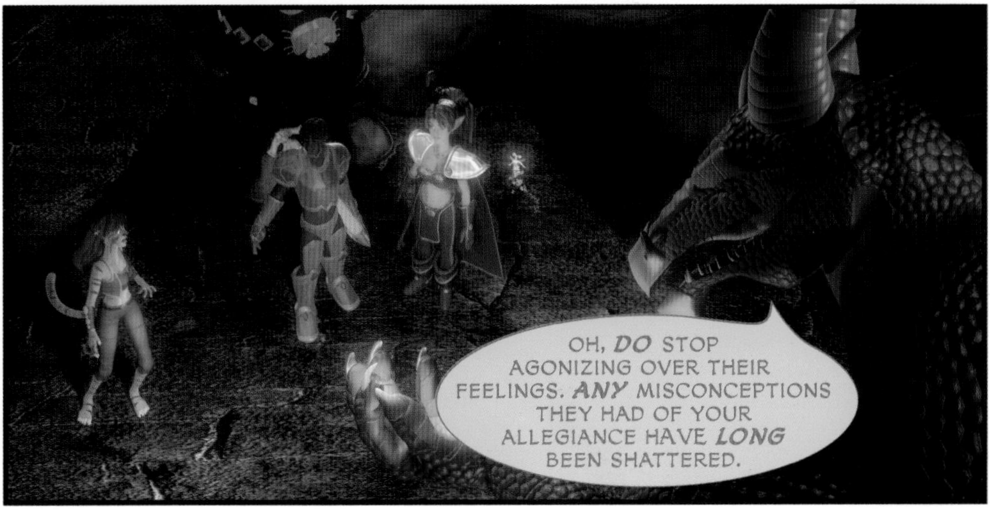
OH, *DO* STOP AGONIZING OVER THEIR FEELINGS. *ANY* MISCONCEPTIONS THEY HAD OF YOUR ALLEGIANCE HAVE *LONG* BEEN SHATTERED.

NOTHING? VERY WELL THEN.

BUT... SO YOU HAVE NO ILLUSIONS TO THE *CONTRARY*... YOU ARE NO LONGER IN MY SERVICE. YOUR PARDON IS HEREBY *RESCINDED.* YOU ARE ONCE AGAIN A WANTED CRIMINAL!

YOU SHOULD BE *THANKING* ME, HUMAN. SHE BETRAYED *ME*, AND ALL THE KING OF DREAMLAND COULD OFFER HER. GIVEN THE OPPORTUNITY, SHE WOULD *SURELY* HAVE BETRAYED YOU AS WELL.

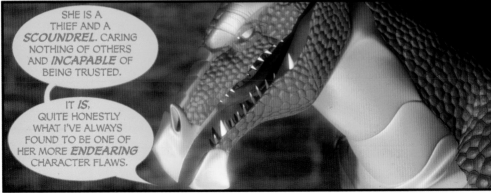

SHE IS A THIEF AND A *SCOUNDREL.* CARING NOTHING OF OTHERS AND *INCAPABLE* OF BEING TRUSTED.

IT *IS*, QUITE HONESTLY WHAT I'VE ALWAYS FOUND TO BE ONE OF HER MORE *ENDEARING* CHARACTER FLAWS.

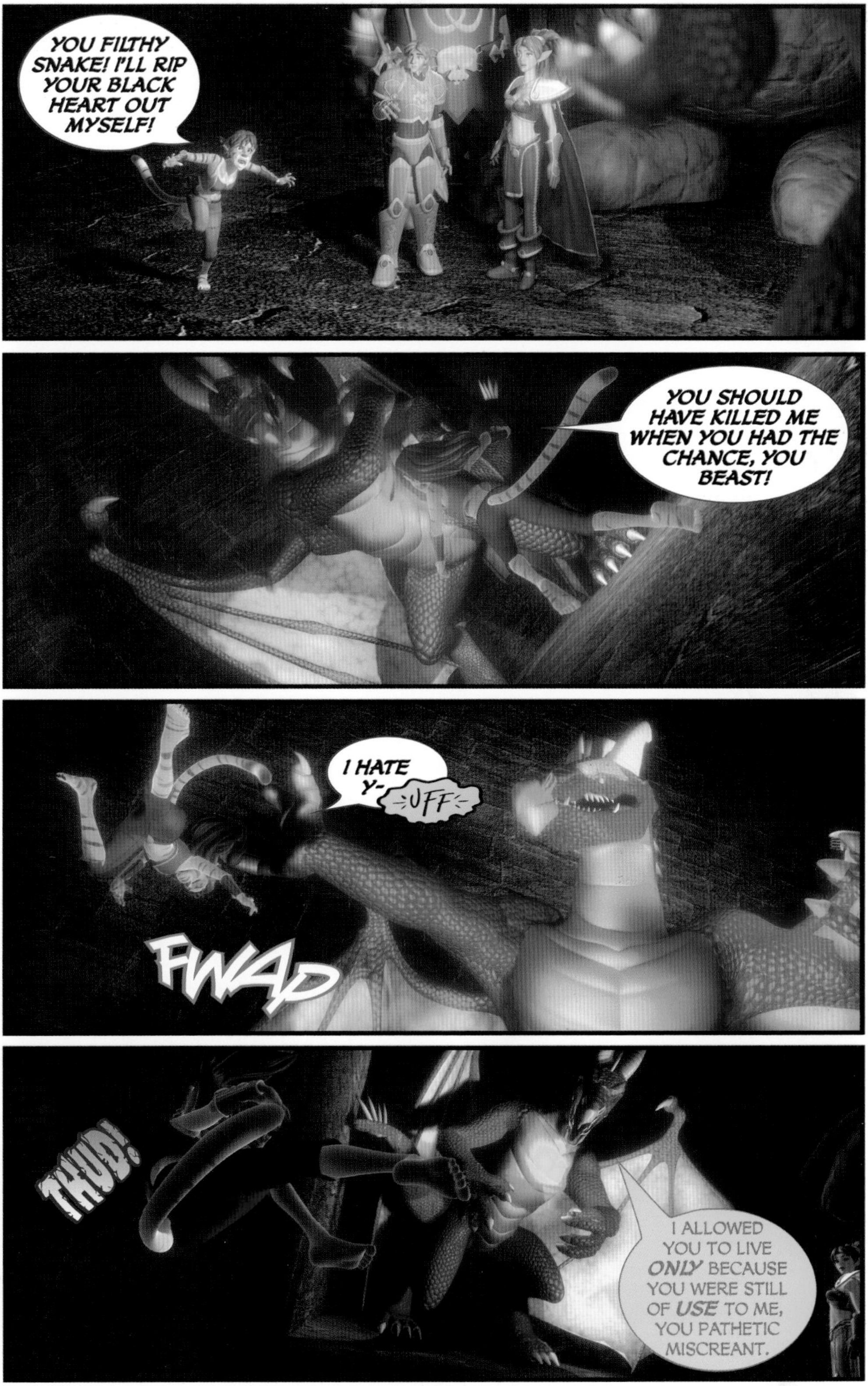
YOU FILTHY SNAKE! I'LL RIP YOUR BLACK HEART OUT MYSELF!
YOU SHOULD HAVE KILLED ME WHEN YOU HAD THE CHANCE, YOU BEAST!
I HATE Y-
UFF
FWAP
THUD!
I ALLOWED YOU TO LIVE ONLY BECAUSE YOU WERE STILL OF USE TO ME, YOU PATHETIC MISCREANT.

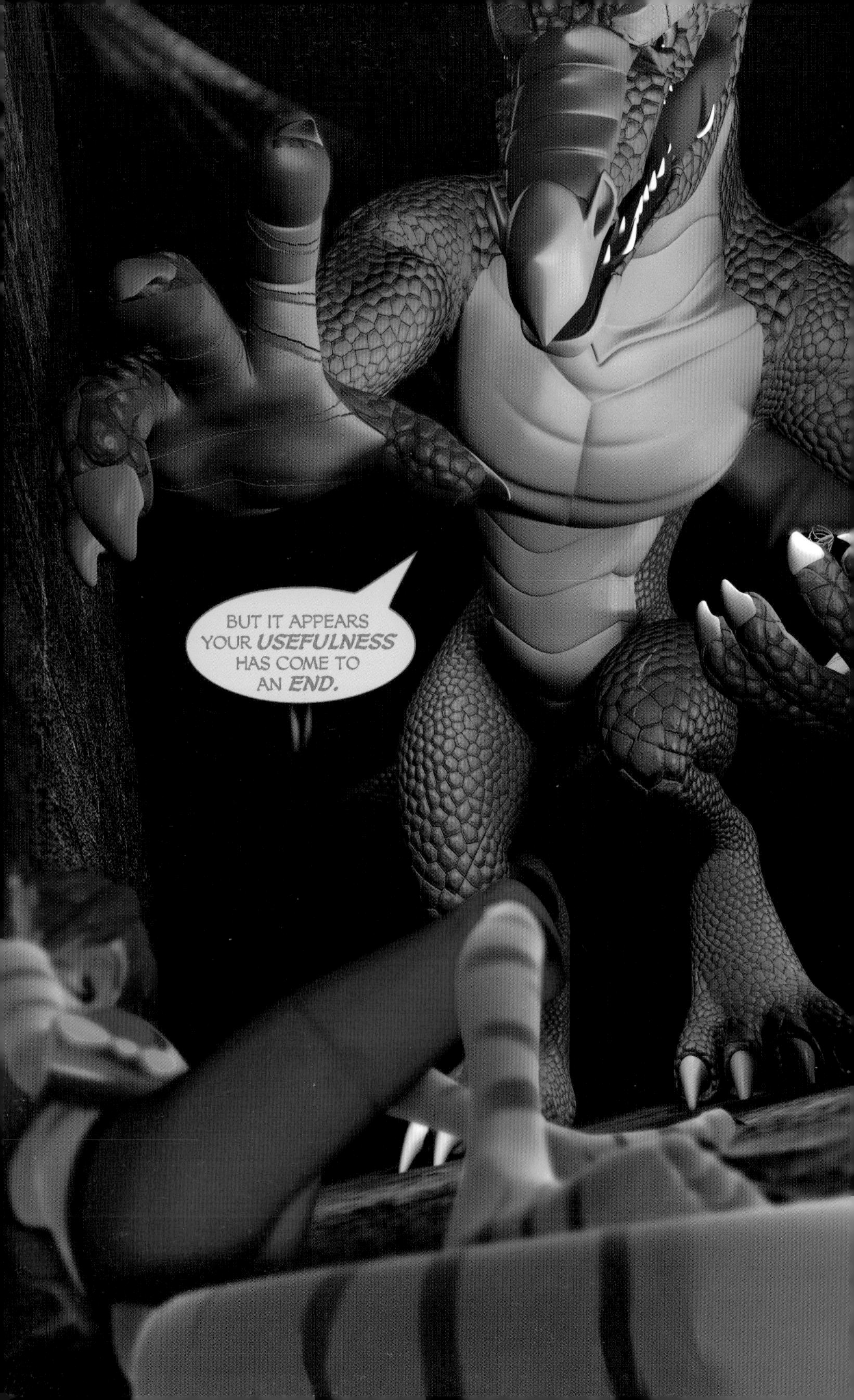
BUT IT APPEARS YOUR *USEFULNESS* HAS COME TO AN *END.*

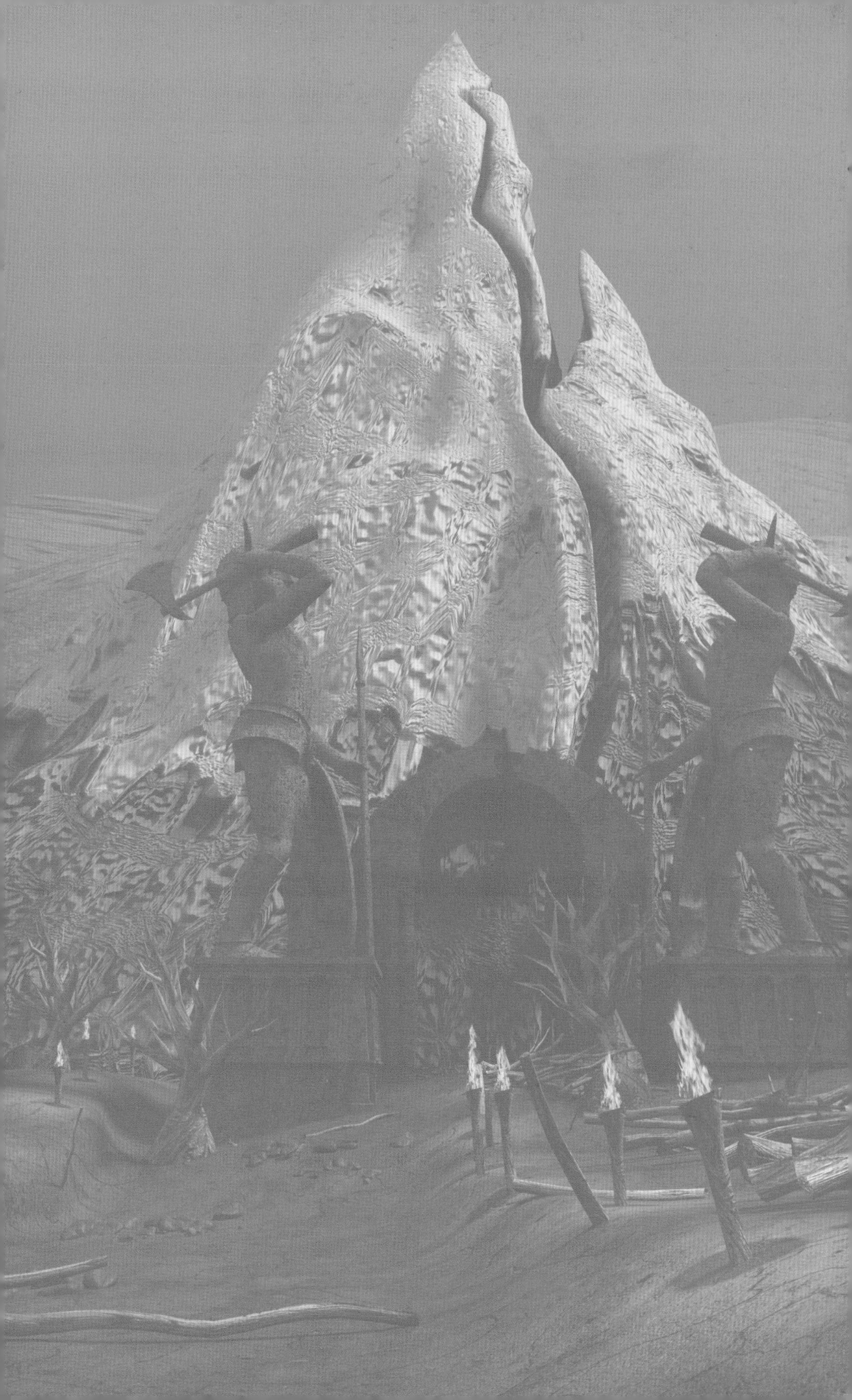

BRINGING DREAMLAND TO LIFE

THANK YOU FOR READING BOOK THREE OF THE DREAMLAND CHRONICLES.

AS IN THE FIRST TWO BOOKS... I'D LIKE TO SHOW YOU A BIT OF WHAT GOES INTO THIS EPIC FANTASY STORY.

SO MUCH IS DONE TO CREATE THE LOOK OF DREAMLAND. JUST LIKE YOUR FAVORITE ANIMATED MOVIE... A TEAM OF ARTISTS AND FRIENDS HELP ME CREATE THE WORLD OF DREAMLAND AND ITS INHABITANTS.

THE FOLLOWING PAGES WILL SHOW OFF SOME OF THE INCREDIBLE AMOUNT OF TALENT AND DETAIL THAT WENT INTO BRINGING DREAMLAND TO LIFE.

WHILE KAREN KRAJENBRINK DID THE BULK OF THE CHARACTER DESIGNS FOR DREAMLAND... AND CONTINUES TO DO SO TO THIS DAY...

ROBIN MITCHELL STEPPED IN TO HELP OUT WITH SOME DESIGNS FOR OBERON, THE DWARVES, AND THE NIGHTMARE BEASTS.

I THOUGHT YOU'D ENJOY SEEING SOME OF HIS WONDERFUL WORK...

DWARVES. DWARVES. DWARVES. ROBIN HAD A GREAT TAKE ON THESE STOCKY WARRIORS. I LOVE THE COSTUMES AND WEAPONS.

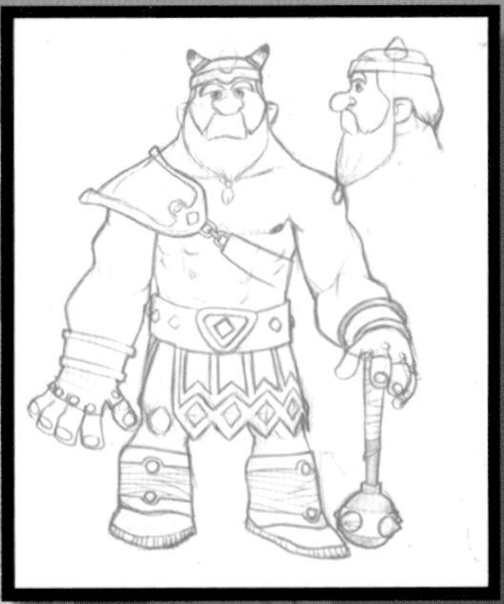

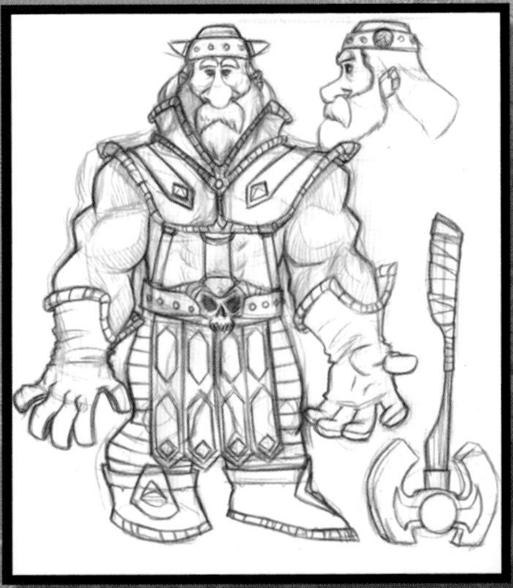

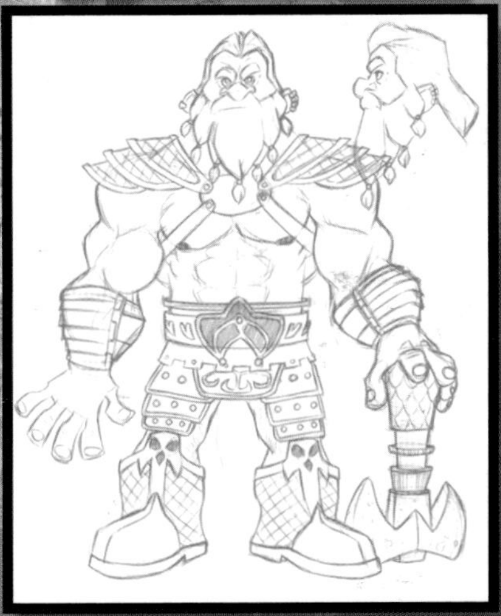

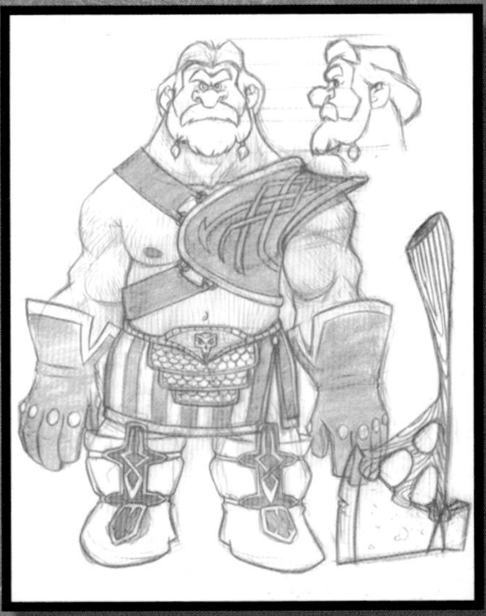

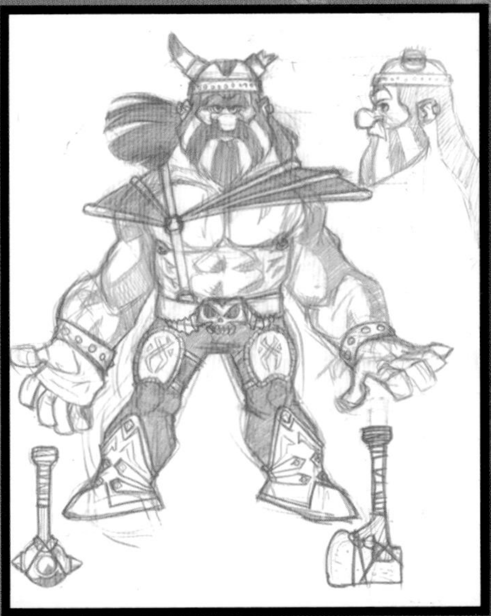

NOT EVERY CHARACTER IS PERFECT THE FIRST TIME OUT. NO MATTER HOW TALENTED THE ARTIST MAY BE... THEY'RE NOT MIND READERS.
I USUALLY HAVE AN IDEA IN MY MIND WHEN WRITING THESE CHARACTERS, SO SOMETIMES I HAVE TO GET THAT IDEA ACROSS WITH NOTES.

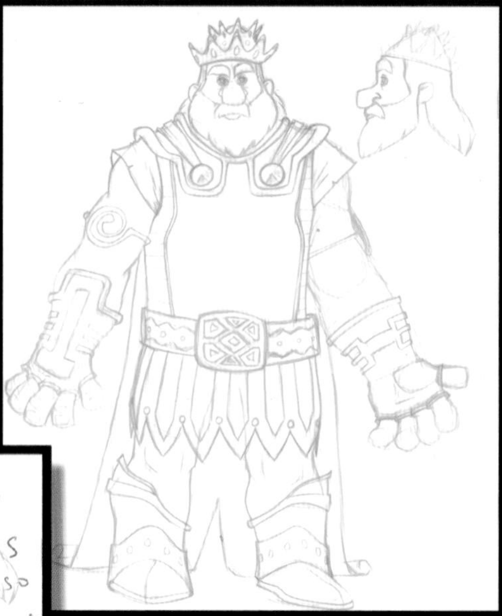

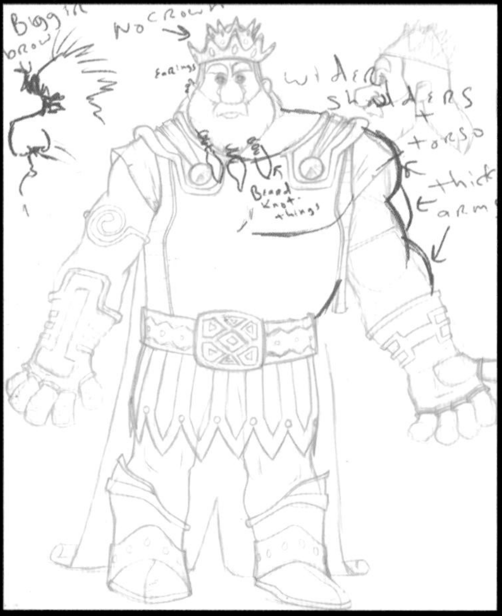
No Crown
wider shoulders + torso
thick arms

BOGNOK NEEDED MORE MASS AND MORE "MEAN-NESS". SO I DID SOME SCRIBBLES OVER ROBIN'S INITIAL DESIGN.

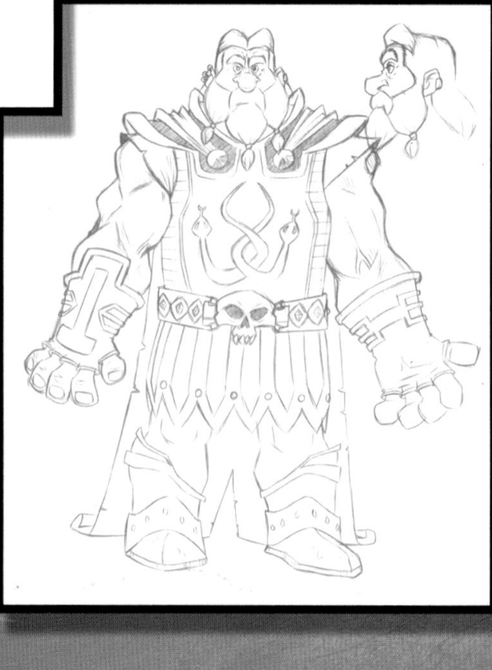

SECOND TIME OUT... HE'S PERFECT! LOVE HIM!

KAREN WOULD GO THROUGH
SEVERAL DESIGNS UNTIL
WE FOUND SOMETHING THAT
WORKED.

HERE WE SEE ALEX AND
DAN'S MOM. OLDER, YOUNGER,
BUSINESS WOMAN, AND FINALLY
THE ONE WE WENT WITH.

SOME OF THE ARTISTS WERE DEPICTED AS JOEY'S FRIENDS IN THE BOOK.

HERE WE SEE STEFANO, PETER, KAREN, AND JENN.

IT WAS SO FUN TO SEE KAREN COME UP WITH CARTOON VERSIONS OF THE REST OF THE CREW... AS WELL AS HERSELF.

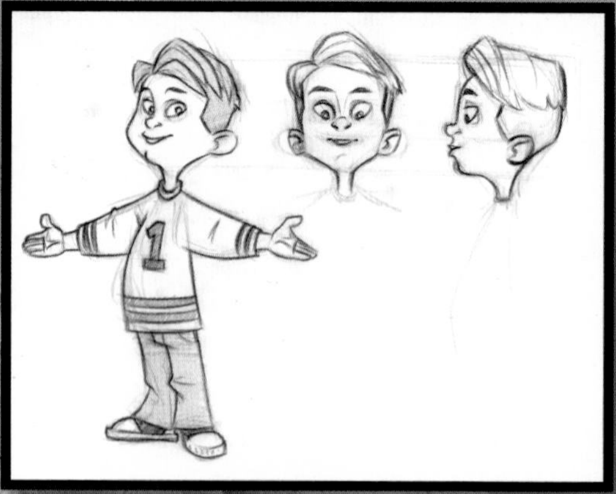

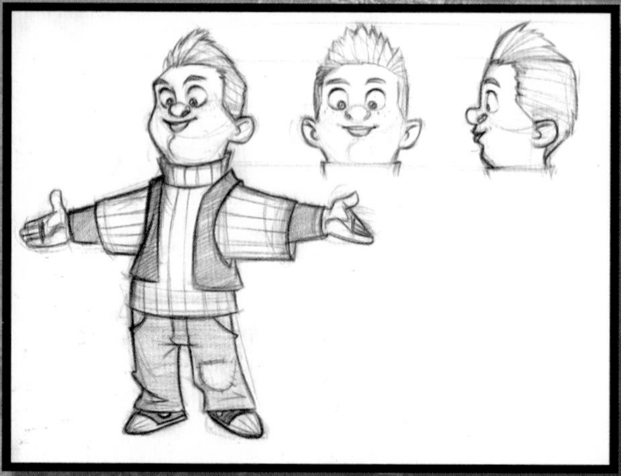

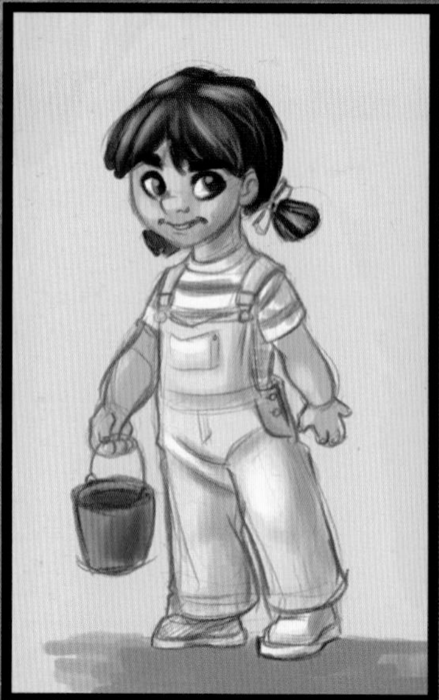

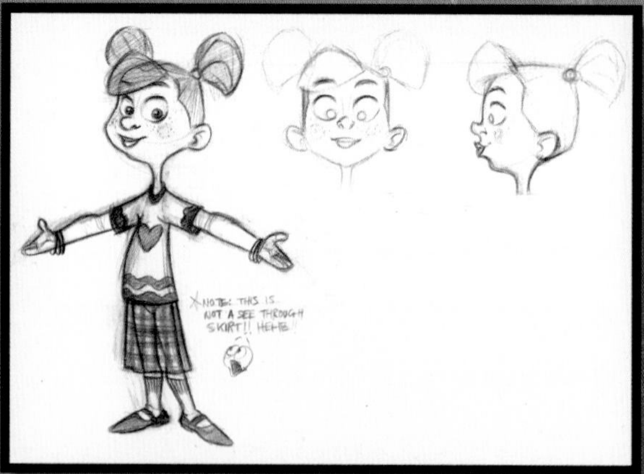
NOTE: THIS IS NOT A SEE THROUGH SKIRT!! HEHE!!

IVAN'S JOB THIS TIME AROUND
SEEMED TO FOCUS ON PEOPLE
UNDER FIVE FEET TALL.

FROM NIGHTMARE BEASTS
TO DWARVES TO CHILDREN...
IVAN DIGITALLY SCULPTED
THE CHARACTERS TO
PERFECTION.

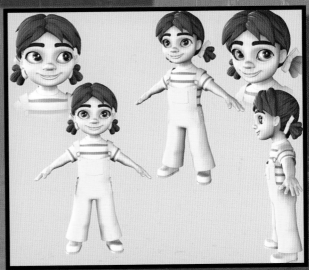

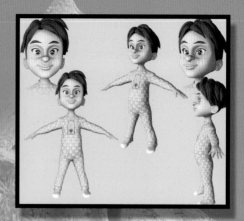

IT REALLY WAS A FUN
TREAT TO SEE 3D CARTOON
KID VERSIONS OF THE TEAM
IN THE COMIC.

I THINK IVAN AND KAREN
BOTH TOOK A BIT OF JOY
IN CARACATURING THEMSELVES
IN THEIR RESPECTIVE MEDIUMS.

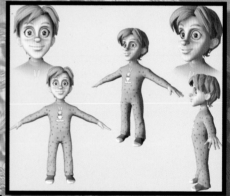

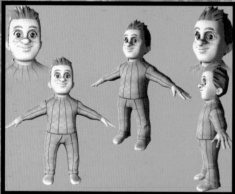

BY THE WAY...
THAT'S 3D IVAN.
:)

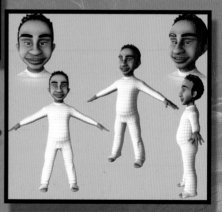

AND OF COURSE, WHAT WOULD WE DO WITHOUT STEFANO AND HIS LOVELY ENVIRONMENTS?

I FOUND SOME UNSEEN DESIGNS OF ASHENDEL'S ELVEN CITY AND SOME OF THE DETAILS OF HOW IT WORKS...

ENJOY.

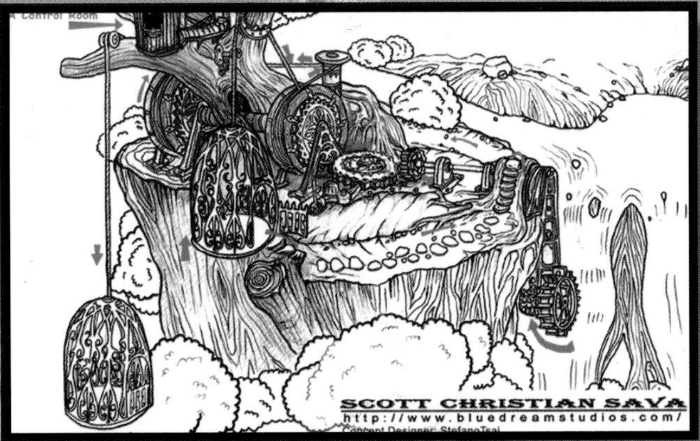

Control Room
SCOTT CHRISTIAN SAVA
http://www.bluedreamstudios.com/

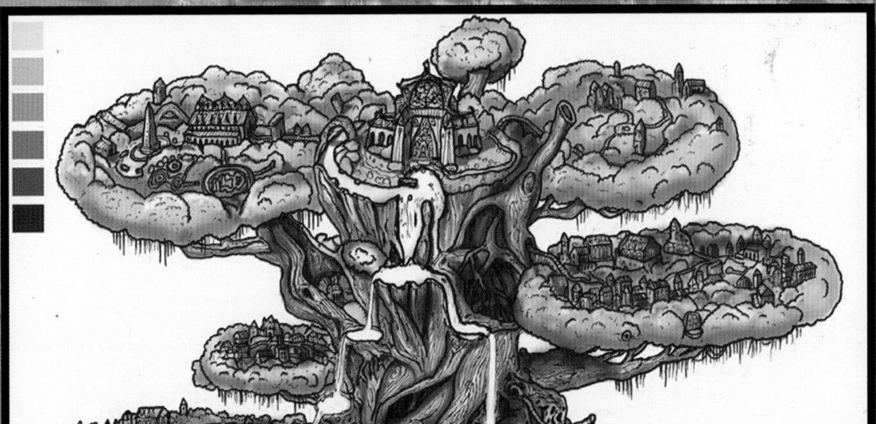

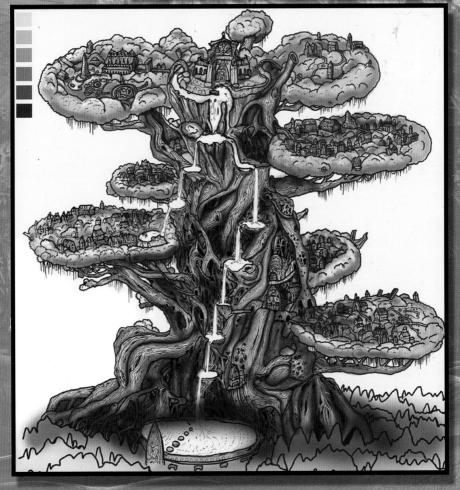

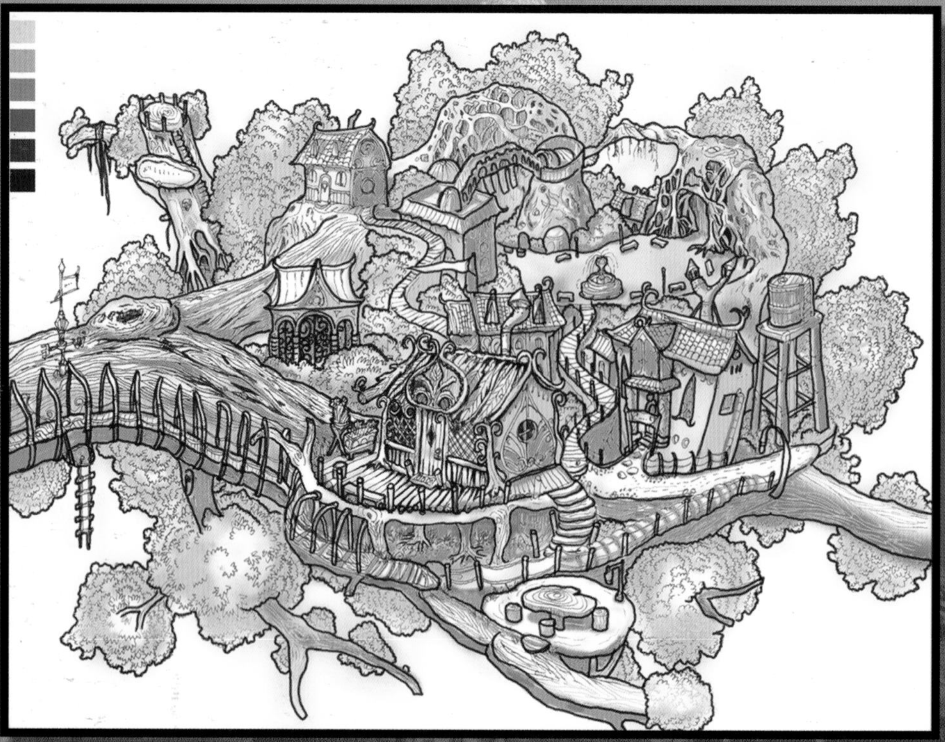

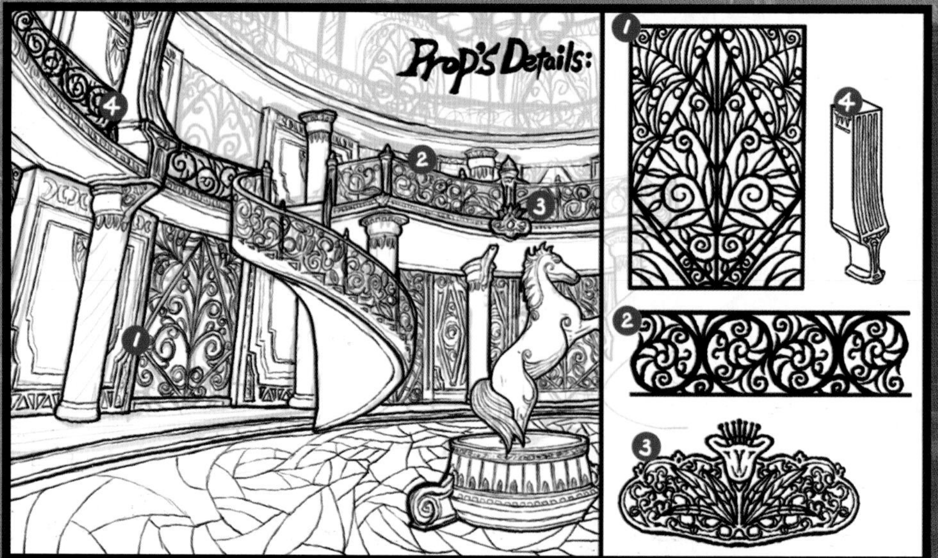

Prop's Details:
1
2
3
4

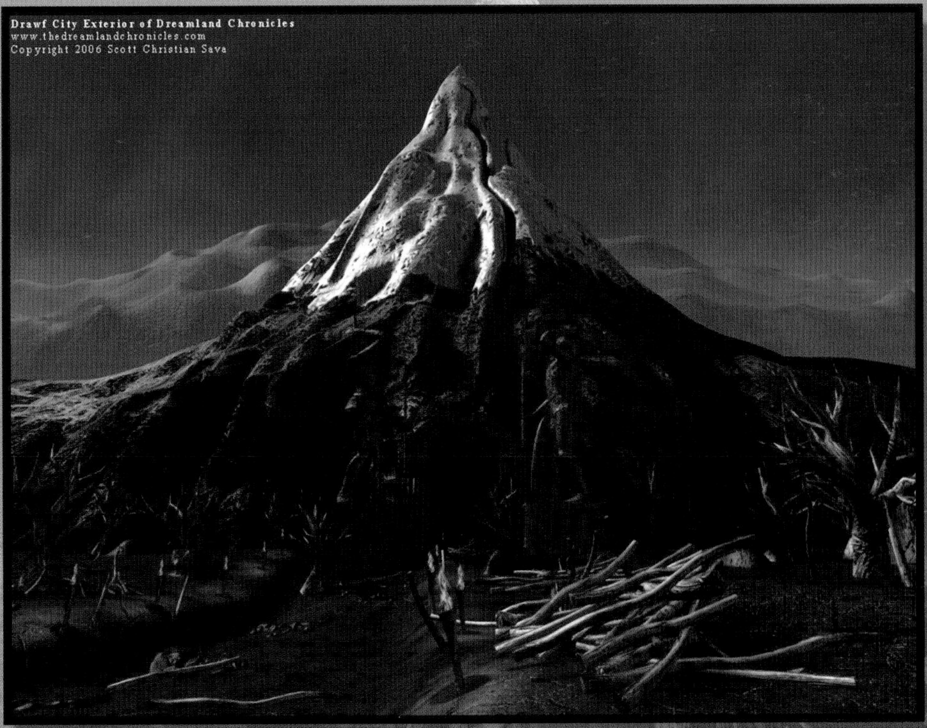
Drawf City Exterior of Dreamland Chronicles
www.thedreamlandchronicles.com
Copyright 2006 Scott Christian Sava

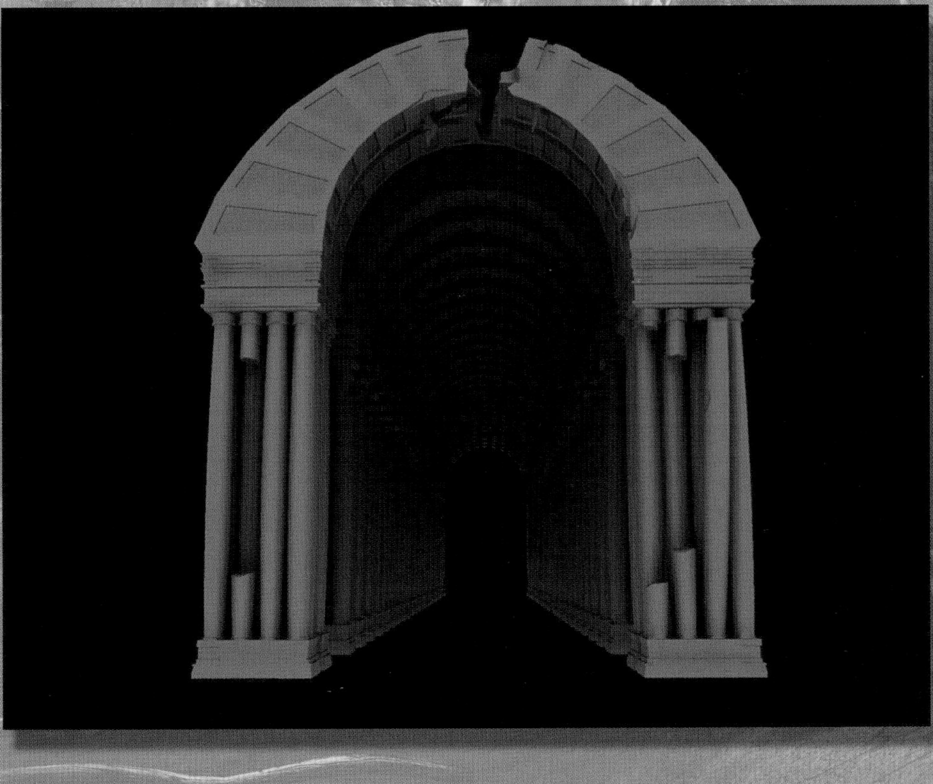

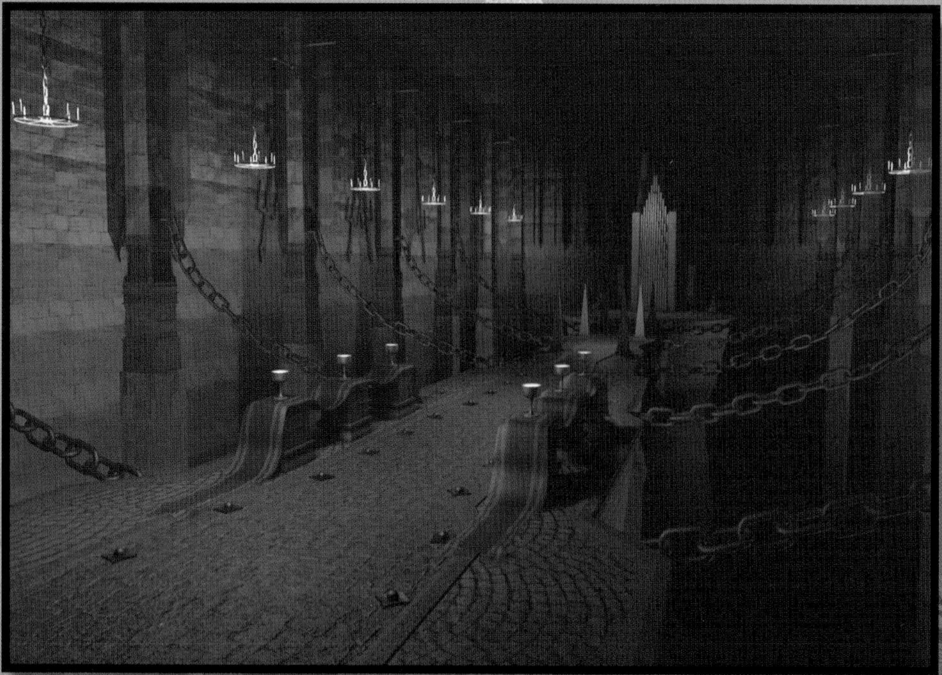

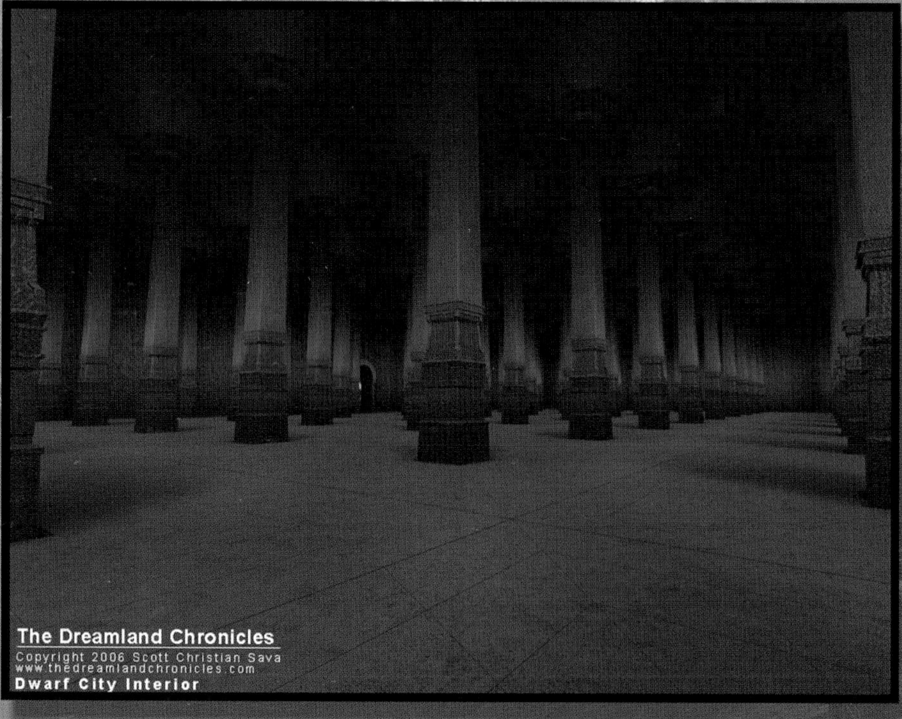
The Dreamland Chronicles
Copyright 2006 Scott Christian Sava
www.thedreamlandchronicles.com
Dwarf City Interior

SCENES FROM THE DREAMLAND ARCHIVES...

BACK IN 2002-2003, WE WERE WORKING ON THE INITIAL ASSETS TO DREAMLAND.

THE CHARACTERS AND ENVIRONMENTS WERE STARTING TO COME TOGETHER.

I WAS REALLY EXCITED TO SHOW THEM OFF. SO FOR THE SAN DIEGO COMIC-CON... I PUT TOGETHER A COUPLE PAGES TO SHOW EVERYONE.

I'D JUST FINISHED SPIDER-MAN AND WANTED TO "FLEX MY 3D MUSCLES" AND SEE HOW FAR I COULD PUSH THE MEDIUM.

THIS IS WHAT I CAME UP WITH.

THIS IS MY FIRST FIRST TIME PLAYING WITH THE DREAMLAND CHARACTERS AND ITS WORLD.

NO DIALOGUE...

I JUST WANTED TO PLAY AROUND WITH THE CHARACTERS.

JUST TAKE THEM FOR A WALK...

I THINK PADDINGTON LOOKS A BIT MORE LIKE A BROWN PAPER BAG THAN HE DOES ROCK.

KIWI... GOOFY AS EVER, THOUGH.

NOTICE... I HADN'T DEVELOPED HER GLOW AND HER BUTTERFLY TRAIL YET.

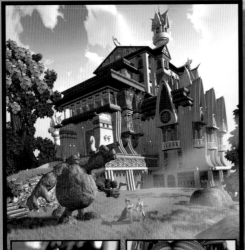

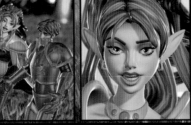

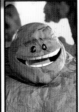

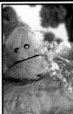

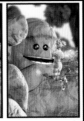

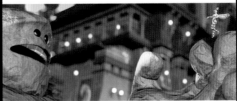

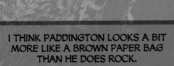

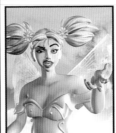

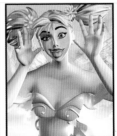

FAN ART AND SUCH

THIS YEAR, WHEN I FINISHED UP THIS BOOK... I TOOK A COUPLE WEEKS OFF FROM UPDATING THE WEBSITE.

RATHER THAN HAVING NOTHING ON THE SITE... MY FELLOW WEB COMIC CREATORS AND READERS TOOK IT UPON THEMSELVES TO HELP ME OUT BY OFFERING THEIR TALENT AND TIME TO CREATE PIN-UPS, FAN FICTION, AND GUEST PAGES.

THE FOLLOWING ARE SOME OF THE MANY WONDERFUL PIECES OF ART I RECEIVED.

THANK YOU ALL SO MUCH!

YOU GUYS ARE FANTASTIC!

BY COLM LAWLOR

BY MEGAN FERNANDO

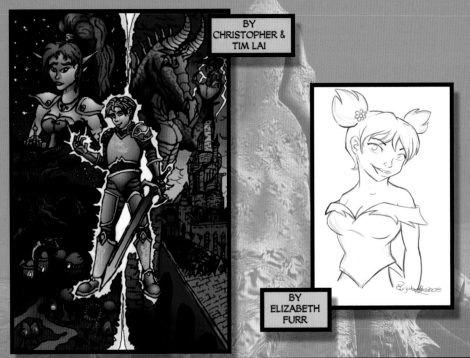

BY
CHRISTOPHER &
TIM LAI

BY
ELIZABETH
FURR

WHAT HAPPENS
WHEN ALEX FALLS ASLEEP IN CLASS

BY
ZACHARY
HUBL

FOLLOWING GENERAL
LEE'S SURRENDER AT
THE

ELVEN CAPITOL,
MOTHER AND FATHER

HAD TO RATIFY THE
AMMENDMENT,
FREEING

ALL THE DWARVES OF
HILMDEL, THEN
NICODEMUS

BECAME PRESIDENT.
HE WAS LATER
ASSASINATED, AND

WE NEED THE RIGHTFUL
KING! ALEX!

ARE YOU LISTENING

BY
RALPH
CASTON II

ALRIGHT, PADDINGTON.
LET'S GET 'EM!

Alexander and Paddington by Wingus
http://theguycalledwingus.deviantart.com

BY
HENRIKE
DIJKSTRA

'For a dreamer, night's the only time of day.'

the Dreamland Chronicles © Scott Christian Sava
dreamlandchronicles.com

The Dreamland Chronicles © Scott Christian Sava

GuestArt by Nicolás K Vergara

BY
NICOLAS K.
VERGARA

DREAMLAND CHRONICLES TRY OUT:
ROLE OF FELICITY

THPPPT!

CATEGORY:
BALANCE

CATEGORY:
COORDINATION

CATEGORY:
QUICK DECISION MAKING

OFFER OFFER OFFER
UNBELIEVABLE OFFER
OFFER MONEY OFFER

I'LL DO IT!

UH...

WOW GIN.
I DIDN'T
KNOW PEOPLE
COULD BEND
THAT WAY.

MAYBE IT WASN'T
SUCH A BAD THING
TO LOSE, AFTERALL.

DREAMLAND CHRONICLES, FELICITY & NICODEMUS © SCOTT CHRISTIAN SAVA
GINPU & EDWIN © MICHELLE VZ - HTTP://WWW.GINPU.US

BY
MICHELLE
VZ

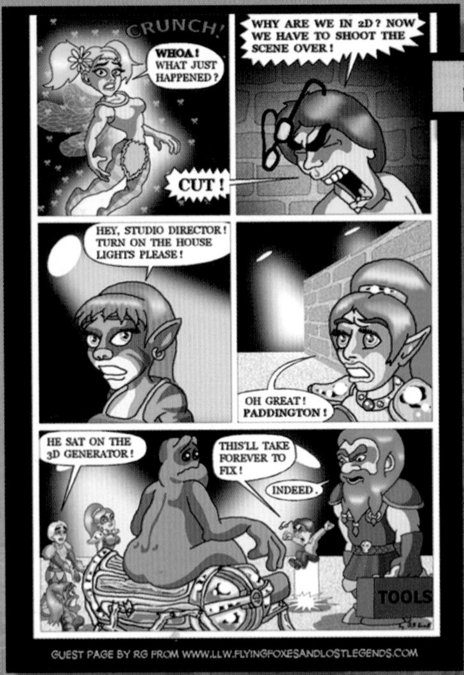

CRUNCH!
WHOA! WHAT JUST HAPPENED?
WHY ARE WE IN 2D? NOW WE HAVE TO SHOOT THE SCENE OVER!
CUT!
HEY, STUDIO DIRECTOR! TURN ON THE HOUSE LIGHTS PLEASE!
OH GREAT! PADDINGTON!
HE SAT ON THE 3D GENERATOR!
THIS'LL TAKE FOREVER TO FIX!
INDEED.
TOOLS

GUEST PAGE BY RG FROM WWW.LLW.FLYINGFOXESANDLOSTLEGENDS.COM

BY RG

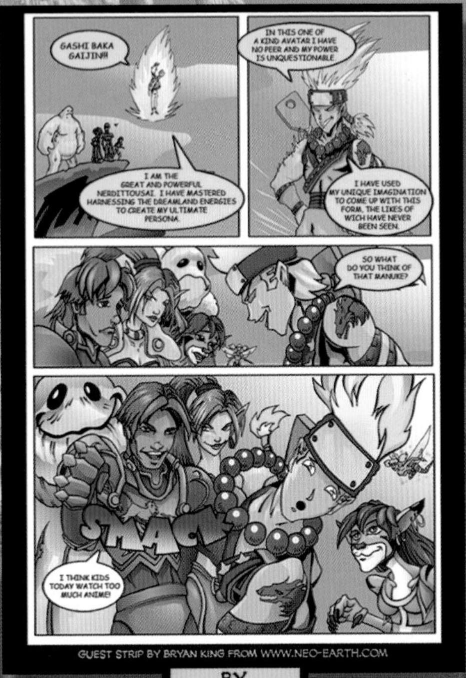

GASHI BAKA GAIJIN!!!
I AM THE GREAT AND POWERFUL NERDITTOUSAI. I HAVE MASTERED HARNESSING THE DREAMLAND ENERGIES TO CREATE MY ULTIMATE PERSONA.
IN THIS ONE OF A KIND AVATAR I HAVE NO PEER AND MY POWER IS UNQUESTIONABLE.
I HAVE USED MY UNIQUE IMAGINATION TO COME UP WITH THIS FORM, THE LIKES OF WICH HAVE NEVER BEEN SEEN.
SO WHAT DO YOU THINK OF THAT MANUKE?
SMACK
I THINK KIDS TODAY WATCH TOO MUCH ANIME!

GUEST STRIP BY BRYAN KING FROM WWW.NEO-EARTH.COM

BY BRYAN KING

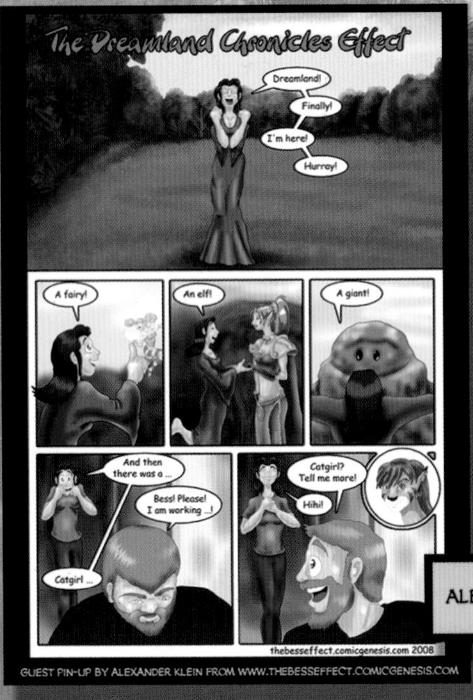

The Dreamland Chronicles Effect
Dreamland!
Finally!
I'm here!
Hurray!
A fairy!
An elf!
A giant!
And then there was a ...
Bess! Please! I am working ...!
Catgirl ...
Catgirl? Tell me more!
Hihi!
thebesseffect.comicgenesis.com 2008

GUEST PIN-UP BY ALEXANDER KLEIN FROM WWW.THEBESSEFFECT.COMICGENESIS.COM

BY ALEXANDER KLEIN

BY RYAN ESTRADA

UNEXPECTED APPEARANCE
A DREAMLAND CHRONICLES GUEST STRIP
WHAT DO YOU THINK HAPPENS WHEN WE DREAM? IS THERE SOME DREAMWORLD-WITHIN-A-DREAM WORLD THAT WE GO TO?
I DON'T DREAM.
I HAD THIS DREAM ONCE WHERE I SHOWED UP TO WORK IN MY UNDERWEAR.
THAT WASN'T A DREAM.
ALL RIGHT, MY SHIFT'S OVER. DON'T LET ANY NEAR THE CASTLE.
SLEEPY TIME!!!!
GYHAUGH!
AH! GET IT OFF!
PUPPY PUPPY!
ROOF! ROOF!
GEEZ, DON'T YOU THINGS USUALLY APPEAR IN MUSHROOM MOUNTAIN, OR FAERIE FOUNTAIN OR SOMETHING EQUALLY STORYBOOKY...?
CAN YOU AT LEAST WAKE UP, AND THEN FALL ASLEEP DURING SOMEONE ELSE'S SHIFT?
COME ON, WAKE UP!
SLEEPY SLEEPY!
GO TO YOUR HOUSE!
THERE'S ICE CREAM IN YOUR HOUSE!
DON'T YOU LIKE ICE CREAM?!?!

GUEST PIN-UP BY RYAN ESTRADA FROM WWW.RYANESTRADA.COM

BY JOY TRUJILLO

Dreamland Chronicles © Scott Christian Sava
You can fly to Forever Land!
All you need is hope,
trust,
and pixie dus--
Grab!!
Watch it Tinker!!
This is my turf!
Now Kiwi, what did we discuss about playing nice with the other pixies?
Sorry Peter, Alex is with us. You're in the wrong story.
2008

GUEST STRIP BY JOY TRUJILLO FROM WWW.SAFYREJET.DEVIANTART.COM

BY SIMONE

JUST BEFORE SAYING I DO...
WELL, THIS SUCKS!
Alex decides to wake up. lol

GUEST PAGE BY SIMONE FROM WWW.AURA-ALORA.DEVIANTART.COM

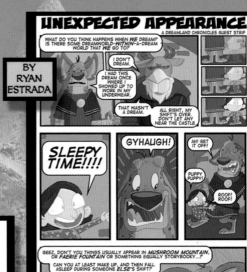

BY
KAEZRER
&
GARKUDION

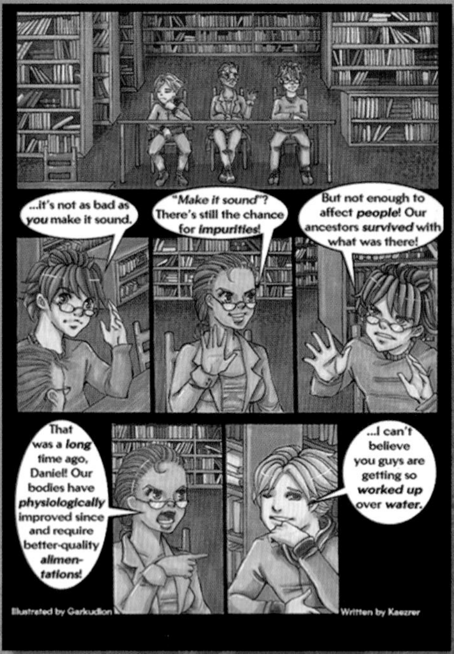
...it's not as bad as *you* make it sound.
"*Make it sound*"? There's still the chance for *impurities*!
But not enough to affect *people*! Our ancestors *survived* with what was there!
That was a *long* time ago, Daniel! Our bodies have *physiologically* improved since and require better-quality *alimentations*!
...I can't believe you guys are getting so *worked up* over *water*.
Illustrated by Garkudion
Written by Kaezrer

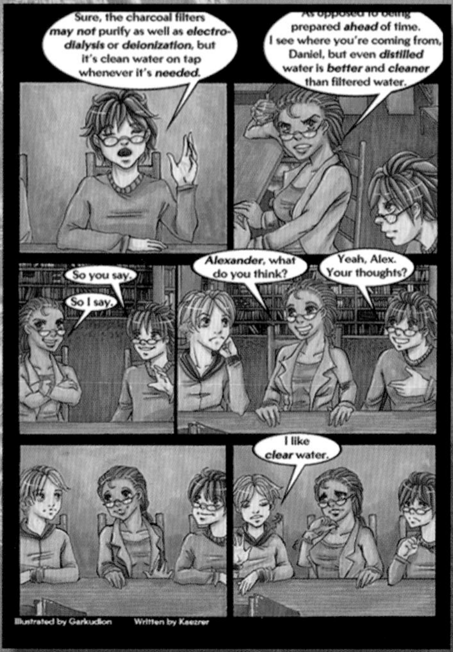
Sure, the charcoal filters *may not* purify as well as *electrodialysis* or *deionization*, but it's clean water on tap whenever it's *needed*.
As opposed to being prepared *ahead* of time. I see where you're coming from, Daniel, but even *distilled* water is *better* and *cleaner* than filtered water.
So you say.
So I say.
Alexander, what do you think?
Yeah, Alex. Your thoughts?
I like *clear* water.
Illustrated by Garkudion
Written by Kaezrer

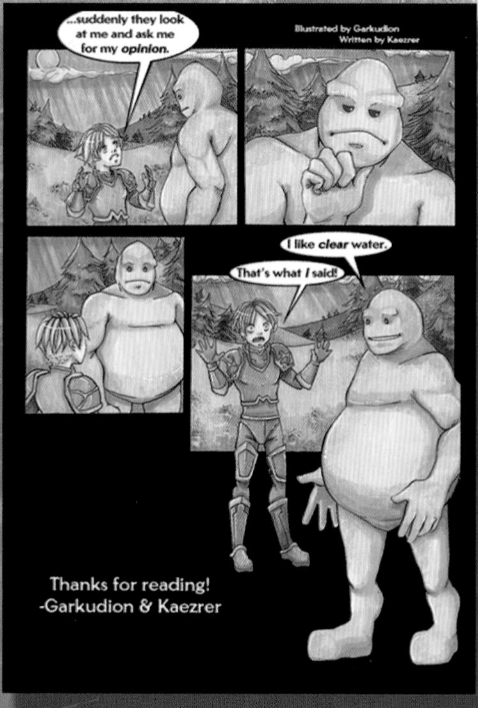
...suddenly they look at me and ask me for my *opinion*.
Illustrated by Garkudion
Written by Kaezrer
I like *clear* water.
That's what *I* said!
Thanks for reading!
-Garkudion & Kaezrer

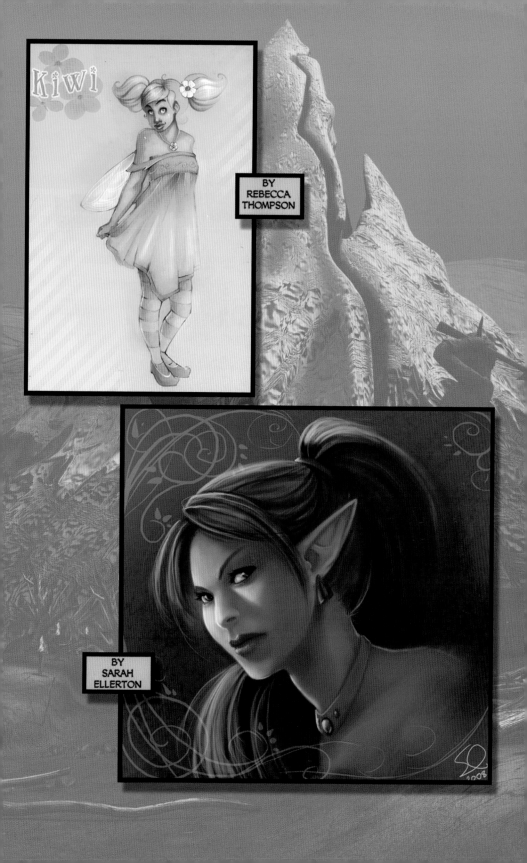

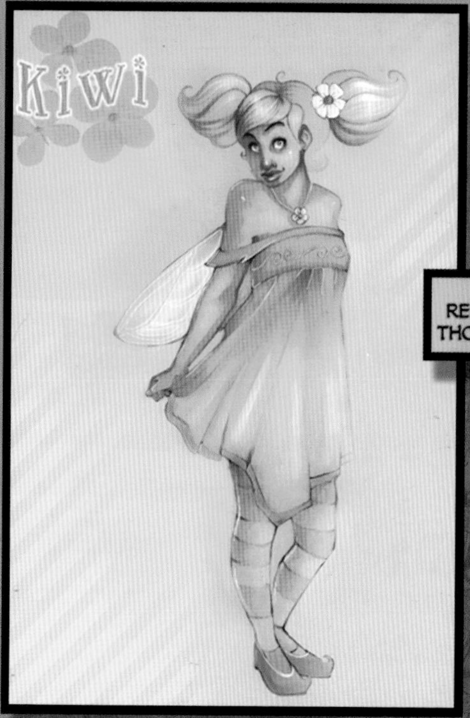
Kiwi

BY REBECCA THOMPSON

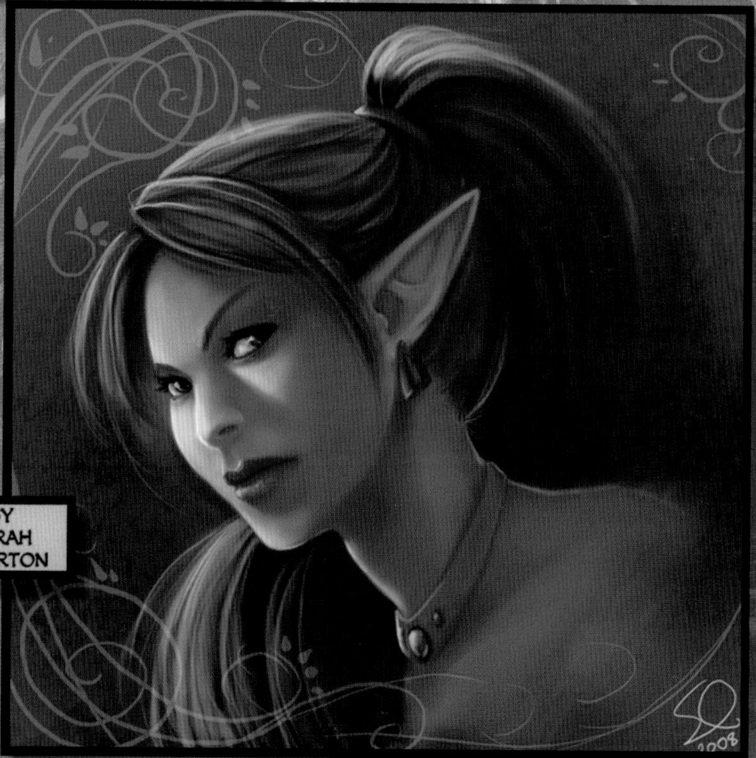

BY SARAH ELLERTON

THE SUPERIFIC SPECTACULAR
DREAMLAND CHRONICLES GUEST WEEK!
WHAT IF...
WHAT IS THIS PLACE?
!
STOP!
GREETINGS. I AM NASTAJIA, QUEEN OF THE ELVES OF ASHENDALE. MAY I PLEASE INQUIRE AS TO WHICH COUNTRY I AM IN?
JUST SHUT UP
EXCUSE ME?
AND DIE.
NOT IF I CAN TAKE YOU DOWN FIRST!
NASTAJIA?
ALEX!
NOOO. WHAT HAPPENED TO THE TV?!
GUEST PAGE BY SHADILYN FROM WWW.KEY.SHADILYN.COM

BY
SHADILYN

YOU HAVE NERVE, BOY, TALKING TO THE KING OF DREAMLAND IN SUCH A DIS-RESPECTFUL MANNER!
I'VE HAD IT! YOU WANT THIS SWORD? YOU CAN PRY IT FROM MY DEAD HAND, NICODEMUS!
HE'S RIGHT ALEX! WHAT ARE YOU DOING?
IT'S OK KIRA. I HAVE A PLAN.
GETTING KILLED IS NOT A PLAN ALEX!
IF I CAN CONTRL THIS SUIT TO PROTECT ME, THEN MAYBE I CAN MAKE THE SUIT DO MORE...
PREPARE TO MEET YOUR DOOM, YOUNG ALEXANDER!
PLEASE, LET THIS WORK!
AAAAARGH!
NOOOOOOOO!

BY
JON
RIGGLE

IS ALEX ALIVE STILL?
PLEASE, LET ALEX BE OK...
HE HAS TO BE ALIVE... I HOPE.
You called down the thunder Nicodemus...
Now you have it. Prepare for your doom!
FINALLY, I RECLAIM THAT WHICH IS RIGHTFULLY MINE!
RUMMMMMMMMMBLE
DRAGON SLAYER MODE ACTIVATED.
WHAT?!
LET'S PLAY!

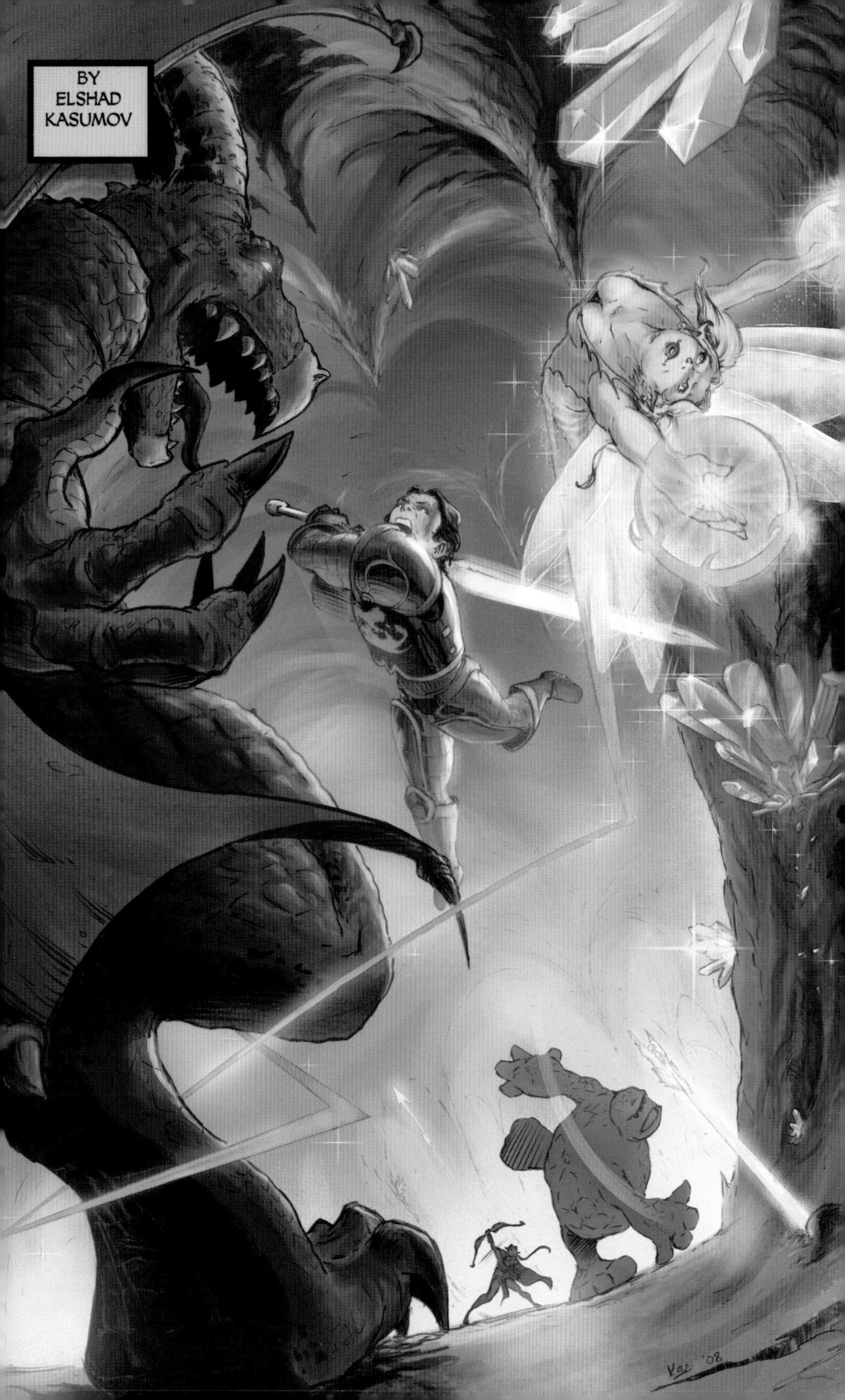
BY ELSHAD KASUMOV

SOMETHING WONDERFUL THAT
I LOVE SEEING ON THE FORUMS
IS FAN FICTION.

THIS GIVES THOSE WHO HAVE A GIFT
FOR WRITING TO TELL STORIES
AND POEMS THAT ADD TO
THE EXISTING WORLD AND
THE CHARACTERS IN IT.

PREPARE TO BE "WOWED"...

BY
ROBERT K.
BROWN

A POEM ABOUT
FELICITY...

"TOO MUCH TO ASK?"

SO NOW THEY KNOW
I GUESS IT WAS UNAVOIDABLE
THAT THEY FIND OUT THE TRUTH
I JUST WISH IT HAD BEEN ON
MY TIME AND WITH
MY VOICE AND NOT
FROM THE ONE WHO THEY HAVE
BEEN TRYING TO DEFEAT THIS
WHOLE TIME
EVEN WITH ALL I HAVE DONE
IN MY LIFE
I HAVE TO KNOW
WAS IT SIMPLY
TOO MUCH TO ASK?

ALL THIS COULD HAVE BEEN DIFFERENT
HAD THEY ALL TRUSTED ME
I WOULD HAVE TOLD THEM ALL
FROM THE OUTSET
AND WE WOULD NOT BE HERE
RIGHT NOW
I KNOW ALEX DID
EVEN IF HE NO LONGER DOES
KIWI AND PADDINGTON
WERE WILLING TO GIVE ME A CHANCE
BUT THE PRINCESS COULD
NEVER SEE PAST HER OWN SUSPICIONS
TO THE TRUTH OF WHAT I WAS
TRYING TO DO
THE HELP I WAS
TRYING TO GIVE
I COULD NOT
PROVE HER RIGHT
NOT WHEN SHE HAD THE POWER
TO TAKE EVERYTHING THAT HAD COME
TO MEAN SOMETHING TO ME
AWAY
EVEN AS A THIEF
WAS A LITTLE BIT OF TRUST JUST
TOO MUCH TO ASK?

I WASN'T ALWAYS THIS WAY
YOU KNOW
WHEN I WAS YOUNGER I HAD
A FRIEND
A REAL AND TRUE FRIEND
HUMAN LIKE ALEX BUT
FEMALE LIKE ME
WE DID SO MUCH
TOGETHER
FRIENDS TILL THE END
BUT THE END CAME SOONER
THAN EITHER OF US KNEW
SHE GREW UP AND CAME LESS AND LESS
AND WHEN SHE DID COME
SHE WAS DIFFERENT
COLDER
DISTANT
NOT BELIEVING IN ME
OR OUR FRIENDSHIP
UNTIL ONE DAY SHE JUST
STOPPED COMING
ALL I EVER WANTED WAS
ONE TRUE FRIEND
BUT I SUPPOSE THAT IT WAS
TOO MUCH TO ASK.

I'VE LOST IT ALL NOW
BUT THE ONE THAT HURTS THE MOST
IS LOSING HIM
ALEX
OH I KNOW I NEVER HAD HIM
AT LEAST NOT LIKE SHE DOES
BUT I ALWAYS THOUGHT WE HAD
A CONNECTION
SOMETHING THAT DREW US TOGETHER
SOMETHING THAT REMINDED ME
OF HAPPIER TIMES
I THOUGHT HE WAS THE ONE
THE ONE TO REDEEM ME
TO FREE ME
AND ALL IT WOULD TAKE IS
A SINGLE KISS
HE IS SO PURE AND SO GOOD
A KISS FROM HIM WOULD
PARDON MY LIPS
OF ALL THE LIES THEY'VE TOLD
FREE MY TONGUE
OF ITS WICKED AND SARCASTIC BARB
CLEANSE MY MIND
OF THE NEED TO LOOK OUT FOR ONLY ME
RID MY LIFE
OF THE ACHING LONELINESS
CLEANSE MY SOUL OF THE
EVIL I'VE DONE IN THE NAME OF SURVIVAL
AND UNBURDEN MY HEART
OF THE WEIGHT OF BETRAYAL
A CLEAN SLATE
THE OPPORTUNITY TO START OVER
TO BE THE KITTY I ALWAYS KNEW I COULD
BE WHO I ALWAYS KNEW I SHOULD'VE BEEN
A SECOND CHANCE THAT ONLY HE COULD
GIVE ME DESPITE EVERYTHING I'VE DONE
WAS THAT ONE WISH REALLY REALLY
TOO MUCH TO ASK?

I GUESS I'LL NEVER KNOW

BY
BOB TERRELL

THE WAKING HOURS, PART I KIWI

THE FOLLOWING IS AN ATTEMPT TO CHRONICLE THE EVENTS THAT OCCUR IN DREAMLAND WHILE ALEXANDER IS AWAKE. THEY MAY BE USED IN PART OR IN WHOLE BY THE AUTHOR AS CANON, AN ALTERNATE STORY FOR THE COMIC, OR ANY OTHER PURPOSE.

THIS STORY BEGINS AFTER STRIP #55, DATED 2006-03-15.

KIWI PAUSED FOR A MOMENT, HEARTBROKEN. HE'D COME BACK, RIGHT? SHE WASN'T JUST IMAGINING THINGS? SHE LOOKED AT THE VILLAGE WALL AND GIGGLED. NO, OF COURSE NOT. THE WALL WAS PRETTY SURE HE'D COME BACK! STILL, IT WAS JUST SO SURREAL. AFTER SO LONG... AND THEN TO POOF, JUST LIKE THAT...

HER REVERIE WAS INTERRUPTED BY HER GRANDFATHER, WHOM SHE SUDDENLY FOUND BESIDE HER. HE'D SEEN ALEXANDER DISAPPEAR, AND HE HAD A RATHER SHEEPISH LOOK ON HIS FACE.

"WELL, I... I GUESS THAT SETTLES THAT QUESTION!" HE DID AS BEST HE COULD TO SOUND LIKE HE KNEW IT WAS A HUMAN ALL ALONG. IT WASN'T VERY CONVINCING. HIS GRANDDAUGHTER MERELY LAUGHED AND KISSED HIM ON THE CHEEK.

"OH, GRANDPA." SHE PAUSED. "GRANDPA, IS IT ALL RIGHT IF I GO AND TELL THE OTHERS? THE TEDDIES, PADDINGTON, AND NASTAJIA? THEY HAVE TO KNOW. I'M SURE THEY'LL BE THRILLED TO HEAR ALEX IS BACK! ...I THINK HE IS, AT LEAST."

"YOU'RE NOT REALLY GOING TO FIX THE WALL ANYTIME SOON, ARE YOU?" HER GRANDFATHER ASKED, THOUGH IT WAS REALLY MORE OF A STATEMENT OF FACT THAN A QUESTION.

THIS TIME, IT WAS KIWI'S TURN TO LOOK SHEEPISH. "WELL..." SHE TRAILED OFF.

"IT'S ALL RIGHT, DEAR. YOU CAUSED ENOUGH MAYHEM AS A CHILD AT ASHENDEL THAT THEY NEVER BOTHERED US ABOUT. I SUPPOSE THIS IS ONLY FAIR."

"OH, THANK YOU!" KIWI SAID, AND GAVE HER GRANDPA A BIG HUG.

HE HELD HER HANDS FOR A MOMENT, LOOKING AT HER FONDLY. "BE SAFE, LITTLE ONE." HE FLEW BACK DOWN TO THE VILLAGE.

NEVER MIND THE FACT I'M NOT THAT LITTLE ANYMORE, THOUGHT KIWI. SHE STARTED OFF TOWARD THE TEDDIES' VILLAGE. SUDDENLY, SHE SENSED A RATHER LARGE PRESENCE BEHIND HER..

THE WAKING HOURS, PART 2: KIWI/NASTAJIA

THE FOLLOWING IS AN ATTEMPT TO CHRONICLE THE EVENTS THAT OCCUR IN DREAMLAND WHILE ALEXANDER IS AWAKE. THEY MAY BE USED IN PART OR IN WHOLE BY THE COMIC'S AUTHOR AS CANON, AN ALTERNATE STORY FOR THE COMIC, OR ANY OTHER PURPOSE.

THIS STORY BEGINS AFTER STRIP #93, DATED 2006-05-09.

————————

KIWI SAW THE CONFUSED LOOK ON PADDINGTON'S FACE AND FLEW UP. HE HAD MANAGED TO LOOK AWAY AT JUST THE WRONG TIME. "HE WOKE UP," SHE SAID. "I'D FORGOTTEN ABOUT THAT, TOO." SHE LOOKED DOWN AND SIGHED. "I WONDER HOW LONG HE'LL BE GONE THIS TIME." SHE LOOKED BACK AT PADDINGTON, WHO APPARENTLY HADN'T HEARD THAT PART.

"ALEX IS BACK!" HE SAID, WITH A BIG GRIN ON HIS FACE. THE EXCITEMENT WAS APPARENTLY TOO MUCH FOR HIM. HE JUMPED, AND UPON LANDING, KNOCKED OVER SEVERAL NEARBY GROUPS OF TEDDIES. "OOPS, SORRY GUYS." THE DAZED TEDDIES ON THE GROUND DIDN'T HAVE A REPLY. HE TURNED BACK TO KIWI. "HOW LONG DO YOU THINK HE'LL BE GONE?"

"WELL, HE WAS ONLY GONE 30 SECONDS LAST TIME. I GUESS WE CAN TRY TO WAIT IT OUT," SHE REPLIED. SUDDENLY, SHE WAS AWARE OF WHAT SHE'D INTERRUPTED. "OOOH, HEY, WHAT ABOUT YOUR DANCE LESSON?"

PADDINGTON TURNED TO THE CROWD. "SORRY, EVERYONE. IT LOOKS LIKE I NEED TO CUT THE DANCE LESSON SHORT TODAY." THIS DREW A FEW SIGHS AND WHINES FROM THE CROWD. "I'LL MAKE IT UP TO YOU NEXT TIME. I PROMISE!"

A FEW MINUTES PASSED WITH NO SIGN OF ALEX. KIWI, MEANWHILE, WAS GETTING BORED QUICKLY. AND NASTAJIA HAD TO KNOW! SHE LOOKED AROUND, THEN BACK AT PADDINGTON. "WELL, I GUESS THERE'S NO TELLING HOW LONG WE'LL BE WAITING HERE. LET'S GO TELL NASTAJIA!" SHE BEGAN FLYING TOWARD THE EDGE OF TOWN.

"KIWI? AREN'T YOU FORGETTING SOMETHING?" PADDINGTON ASKED. KIWI LOOKED AT HIM, PUZZLED. HE POINTED TO A PARTICULAR STORE'S SIGN DOWN BELOW.

"OH! YOU'RE RIGHT!" SHE SAID, AND FLUTTERED DOWN. SHE FOUND THE SHOPKEEP, A SWEET OLD WOMAN OF A TEDDY BEAR WEARING A STRAW HAT WITH A RED RIBBON AROUND IT. HER GREEN AND WHITE POLKA DOTTED DRESS DIDN'T MATCH AT ALL, AND KIWI WONDERED IF A HUMAN CHILD HAD PICKED OUT THE OUTFIT. SHE LANDED ON THE GLASS COUNTER NEAR THE SHOPKEEP AND LOOKED BENEATH HER. "CAN I HAVE ONE OF THOSE, PLEASE?"

"JUST ONE, DEAR?"

"I THINK ONE IS ABOUT ALL I CAN MANAGE," SAID KIWI. THE SHOPKEEP WASN'T TOO BRIGHT.

"RIGHT YOU ARE, DEAR. ANY PARTICULAR COLOR?"

WELL, AS LONG AS SHE COULD PICK... "GREEN, PLEASE!"

THE SHOPKEEP SCOOPED UP A GREEN ONE AND PUT IN ON THE SCALE. THE NEEDLE DIDN'T MOVE. SHE PICKED IT UP AGAIN AND DROPPED IT. THE SCALE STILL DIDN'T CARE. SHE LOOKED OUT THE WINDOW AT THE BIG ROCKY LEG IN FRONT OF HER WINDOW. A BOULDER OF A FACE CAME DOWN AND STARTED TALKING WITH SEVERAL TEDDIES. "YOU'RE WITH PADDINGTON, AREN'T YOU, DEAR?"

"YES, MAM."

"WELL ANY FRIEND OF PADDINGTON'S IS A GOOD FRIEND OF OURS, DEAR. THIS ONE'S ON ME," SAID THE SHOPKEEP, PLACING IT IN FRONT OF HER.

"OH, THANK YOU!" KIWI CRIED. SHE PICKED UP HER TREAT AND ZOOMED OUTSIDE.

SHE FLEW UP AND SAT ON PADDINGTON'S SHOULDER. "YOU DON'T MIND IF I SIT DOWN TO EAT THIS, DO YOU, PADDINGTON?"

"NOT AT ALL," HE REPLIED. "I EXPECTED IT WHEN I MADE THE SUGGESTION."

LET IT NEVER BE SAID THAT ROCK GIANTS ARE STUPID, THOUGHT KIWI. THEN SHE REALIZED THE BIG, GOOFY SMILE ON HIS FACE. "WHAT? YOU KNOW THIS IS THE ONLY PLACE IN DREAMLAND TO GET GOOD GUMMI BEARS!" HE JUST KEPT SMILING. "WHAT?"

"NOTHING," SAID PADDINGTON. THAT SMILE WOULD NOT LEAVE HIS FACE. "READY TO GO?" KIWI RESPONDED BY NODDING, CHEEKS FULL OF GUMMI BEAR. THE GUMMI BEAR'S EARS WERE MISSING.

PADDINGTON MADE HIS WAY OUT OF TOWN. A SMALL ENTOURAGE OF TEDDIES FOLLOWED HIM, MOSTLY CHILDREN. UPON REACHING THE EDGE OF TOWN, PADDINGTON TURNED TO THEM.

"HEY KIDS, CAN YOU DO OL' PADDINGTON A FAVOR?" HE ASKED. SIX LITTLE TEDDY BEAR HEADS NODDED. "AT SOME POINT MY FRIEND ALEXANDER'S GOING TO COME BACK."

"THE HUMAN BOY?" ASKED ONE.

"YEP, THAT'S HIM," PADDINGTON REPLIED. "WHEN HE COMES BACK, I NEED ONE OF YOU TO TELL HIM WE WENT TO SEE NASTAJIA. CAN YOU DO THAT?" THE TEDDIES NODDED AGAIN.

HE WAVED GOODBYE TO THE TEDDIES WHO HAD FOLLOWED AND HEADED SOUTH TOWARD ASHENDEL. THE TERRAIN QUICKLY CHANGED FROM THE GRASSY CLIFF OVERLOOKING THE OCEAN TO A ROCKY AREA THE TEDDIES CALLED A BOULDER GARDEN, THEN FINALLY TO FOREST. JUST UNDER A HALF HOUR FROM WHEN THEY'D LEFT THE TEDDIES' VILLAGE THEY FOUND THEMSELVES NEARING ASHENDEL, THE LARGE TREE UPON WHICH IT STOOD LOOMING UP IN THE DISTANCE, BARELY VISIBLE THROUGH THE TREES.

NASTAJIA FELT IT COMING WELL BEFORE SHE SAW IT. IT WAS LARGE, AND IT WAS HEADING THIS WAY. WITHOUT A WORD SHE SIGNALED THE FOUR GUARDS WITH HER, AND THE FIVE ELVES QUICKLY SPREAD OUT AND DEFTLY MADE THEIR WAY UP INTO THE TREE BRANCHES ABOVE THEM. THE SOURCE OF THE RUMBLING AND NOISE SOON CAME INTO VIEW. IT WAS A ROCK GIANT. WHAT WAS HE DOING HERE? THEN SHE NOTICED THE FAIRY THAT WAS WITH HIM. SUCH AN ODD PAIRING MEANT IT HAD TO BE HER OLD FRIENDS, PADDINGTON AND KIWI.

THE TWO HAD STOPPED TALKING A WHILE BACK AND FOR NOW WERE SIMPLY ENJOYING THE TRIP. THEY BECAME AWARE THEY WERE NOT ALONE WHEN A FIGURE DRESSED IN GREEN DROPPED FROM THE TREES IN FRONT OF THEM. A WAVE OF HER HAND BROUGHT 4 MORE ELVES DOWN FROM THE TREES, SURROUNDING THEM. KIWI PAID NO ATTENTION TO THEM, NOR TO THE DANGER SHE MIGHT HAVE BEEN IN HAD SHE BEEN ANYONE ELSE. SHE RECOGNIZED THE PURPLE-HAIRED ELF AND FLEW TO HER IMMEDIATELY.

"NASTAJIA!" KIWI EXCLAIMED, OVERJOYED TO SEE HER FRIEND. "HOW HAVE YOU BEEN?"

"GOOD TO SEE YOU TOO," SAID NASTAJIA. "WHAT BRINGS YOU HERE?"

KIWI PAUSED FOR A MOMENT. "ALEXANDER'S BACK," SHE SAID, HER VOICE BARELY ABOVE A WHISPER.

NASTAJIA TURNED COLD. AN ELVEN AMBUSH WASN'T A PARTICULARLY WARM WELCOME TO BEGIN WITH, EITHER. "NOT FUNNY, KIWI." SHE NEARLY SPIT THE WORDS OUT. HOW DARE SHE.

"YOU THINK I'M JOKING?" KIWI ASKED INCREDULOUSLY.

"WELL, LET'S SEE," NASTAJIA COUNTERED. "YOU BROUGHT FIREWORKS TO MY CORONATION. IN ASHENDEL," SHE BEGAN.

"FAIRY FIREWORKS. THEY DON'T BURN," KIWI SAID.

NASTAJIA CONTINUED, TALKING OVER HER FRIEND. "WHEN I TURNED 18 YOU TRIED SETTING ME UP WITH 'A NICE BOY' YOU KNOW. I DON'T HAVE TIME FOR THAT SORT OF THING, KIWI." KIWI LOOKED DEJECTED, BUT NASTAJIA WASN'T DONE YET. "AND ON MY 16TH BIRTHDAY, YOU TOLD ME YOUR VILLAGE WAS UNDER ATTACK. I SHOWED UP TO MY BIRTHDAY PARTY WITH HALF THE ROYAL GUARD BECAUSE YOU WANTED IT TO BE A SURPRISE!" SHE FUMED. THIS FAR OUT FROM ASHENDEL, NASTAJIA KNEW THERE WAS NO ONE ELSE IN EARSHOT ASIDE FROM THEIR PARTY AND THE BIRDS IN THE FOREST. BOTH WERE SILENT. AND HER GUARDS WOULD KEEP THIS QUIET, SHE KNEW. THE GUARD WHO SMIRKED WAS LUCKY SHE WAS BEHIND NASTAJIA.

"FINE!" KIWI SHOT BACK. HER FRIEND CLEARLY DIDN'T APPRECIATE THE EFFORT THAT HAD GONE INTO EACH OF THOSE. "BUT IF YOU WON'T LISTEN TO ME, LISTEN TO PADDINGTON!"

NASTAJIA LOOKED UP AT PADDINGTON. "HE'S BACK. HE WOKE UP, SO WE CAME TO FIND YOU, BUT HE'S BACK," HE SAID.

NASTAJIA CAUGHT HER BREATH AND DROPPED TO ONE KNEE, AS IF HER TIRADE HAD BEEN KEEPING HER STANDING AND SHE NO LONGER HAD THE STRENGTH TO DO SO. TRUTH BE TOLD, SHE'D GOTTEN A LITTLE AGGRESSIVE AT KIWI AND THIS WAS AS GRACEFUL A METHOD AS SHE COULD IMAGINE TO HIDE THE FACT SHE HAD NEARLY LOST HER BALANCE. SHE LOOKED TO THE GROUND, HER EYES DOWNCAST. HER BANGS FELL DOWN IN FRONT OF HER FACE, CONCEALING IT FROM HER FRIENDS. HE'S BACK? HE'S NOT DEAD? HER MIND BEGAN RACING. WHAT'S HE LIKE? HOW HAS HE CHANGED? HAS HE CHANGED AT ALL?

KIWI INTERRUPTED HER THOUGHTS. "NASTAJIA? ARE YOU ALL RIGHT?" SHE ASKED, FLOATING IN FRONT OF NASTAJIA AND JUST ABOVE HER HEAD.

NASTAJIA COLLECTED HERSELF AND STOOD UP, CALMLY AND DELIBERATELY. SHE HELD OUT HER HAND TO KIWI, WHO LANDED IN IT DELICATELY, FOLDED HER WINGS BEHIND HER, AND LOOKED UP AT NASTAJIA WITH CONCERN. IT WAS THE CLOSEST THING TO AN APOLOGY THAT NASTAJIA WAS WILLING TO DO RIGHT NOW, AND SHE WAS RELIEVED KIWI HAD ACCEPTED IT.

SHE TURNED TO THE GUARDS BEHIND HER. "HEAD TO ASHENDEL AND INFORM ARVAMAS THAT OUR EXPEDITION HAS BEEN CUT SHORT. I SHALL SEE YOU UPON MY RETURN." SHE GLANCED AT THE OTHER TWO GUARDS, WHO THEN KNEW TO STAY WITH HER. SHE DROPPED HER HAND AS KIWI FLEW BACK TO PADDINGTON AND STARTED WALKING BACK ALONG THE PATH HER FRIENDS HAD COME FROM.

THE GROUP MADE THEIR WAY NORTHWARD, NASTAJIA IN FRONT, HER GUARDS ON EITHER SIDE, WITH KIWI AND PADDING-TON BRINGING THE REAR. NO ONE SAID A WORD, AND SO THE ELVES MOVED SILENTLY THROUGH THE FOREST. THE SAME COULD NOT BE SAID FOR THE ROCK GIANT. THE TWO ELVEN GUARDS HEARD EVERY FOOTSTEP, BUT NASTAJIA WAS LOST IN THOUGHT.

WHY DID HE NEVER COME BACK? HE WOULD ARRIVE IN DREAMLAND EVERY NIGHT WHEN HE WENT TO SLEEP. IF HE WAS BACK NOW, HE WASN'T DEAD. IF HE WAS BACK NOW, THEN HE OBVIOUSLY COULD COME BACK. IF HE WAS BACK NOW, AFTER ALL THIS TIME, HE MUST HAVE FINALLY WANTED TO COME BACK. HE MUST NOT HAVE WANTED TO RETURN UNTIL NOW! HOW COULD HE DO THAT? HOW COULD HE CHOOSE TO LEAVE DREAMLAND BEHIND? LEAVE ME BEHIND? I'VE HAD EIGHT YEARS TO MOURN HIM, MISS HIM, AND BURY HIM, AND NOW HE RETURNS BECAUSE IT'S CONVENIENT FOR HIM?! OH, WHEN I SEE HIM... HER HANDS CLENCHED INTO FISTS AS THE FURY ROSE IN HER, BUT THERE WAS NO OTHER SIGN TO HER COMPANIONS IN TOW. AS USUAL, HER GUARDS NOTICED, AND DROPPED BACK TWO STEPS. HER FRIENDS, ENJOYING THE FOREST, DIDN'T.

THE FOREST SOON ENDED AND THE GROUP FOUND ITSELF IN ROCKY TERRAIN. NASTAJIA BY THIS POINT WAS NO LONGER READY TO PUNCH HIM IN THE FACE, INSTEAD FINDING HERSELF WONDERING WHAT HE'D BE LIKE. HE USED TO BE SUCH A TEASE, SO ANNOYING. HAS HE MATURED AT ALL SINCE OUR CHILDHOOD? IS HE TALL? HANDSOME? MAYBE HE'S... HE'S... AND THEN SHE CAUGHT SIGHT OF HIM. SHE RAISED HER HAND, AND THE GROUP HALTED.

HE WAS FIGHTING PIRATES. NO, SCRATCH THAT. HE WAS RUNNING AWAY FROM THEM, UNTIL THEY SURROUNDED HIM. HE SWUNG HIS SWORD. SWORD? IT WAS A WILD SWING, AND MISSED MISERABLY. IT HIT THE ROCK BEHIND HIM... AND... TORE THROUGH IT. NASTAJIA'S EYES WIDENED AS SHE WATCHED. THE ROCK CAME CRASHING DOWN, AND HE STOOD THERE FOR A MOMENT, STARING AT HIS SWORD LIKE AN IDIOT. FINALLY, THE SHIP'S CAPTAIN CAME DOWN. THE CAPTAIN RUSHED AT HIM AND TOOK A WILD SWING. ALEXANDER MANAGED TO PARRY IT, THANKFULLY. THE CAPTAIN'S FIGHTING FORM WAS TERRIBLE, AND THE INCOMING SWING HAD BEEN OBVIOUS. ALEXANDER COUNTERED WITH A WILD SWING OF HIS OWN, WHICH THE CAPTAIN DODGED EASILY. THE CAPTAIN REPLIED WITH A KICK TO ALEXANDER'S FACE. HE WAS FIGHTING PIRATES, AND LOSING. HE WAS FIGHTING PIRATES, WHOSE TYPICAL ADVERSARY IN COMBAT WAS SMALL, UNARMED HUMAN CHILDREN, AND LOSING.

WHATEVER FURY WAS LEFT INSIDE HER DISSAPATED. PATHETIC. IT WAS, UNFORTUNATELY, THE ONLY WORD SHE COULD THINK OF TO DESCRIBE HER CHILDHOOD FRIEND. SHE WAS GOING TO HAVE TO SAVE HIM. FROM PIRATES. SHE NOCKED AN ARROW IN HER BOW AND AIMED AT THE CAPTAIN. AS THE PIRATE CAPTAIN BROUGHT HIS SWORD TO ALEXANDER'S FACE, SHE LOOSED HER ARROW. IT HIT ITS MARK.

BY

LARRY ROTH

THE ASHENHEART CANTOS
BOOK ONE: HEART OF ASH

ONCE...

I WAS A CHILD SO LIGHT OF HEART
AND ALL GOOD THINGS FELL TO MY PART
OF MY PARENT'S LOVE I HAD NO LACK
ALL THEIR PROTECTION AT MY BACK
AND THOUGH THEY RULED WITH ROYAL MEASURE
I WAS STILL THEIR GREATEST TREASURE

LIKE ASHENDEL'S TREE THAT GROWS SO TALL
THAT GAVE TO ME MY NAME AND ALL,
MY WORLD WAS STEADY, SAFE, AND SURE
OF ASHENHEART, HEART OF ASH, I WAS SECURE
NEVER DOUBTING, YET TO LEARN
THE STRONGEST ASH TO ASHES MAY STILL BURN

WITH MY HEART'S BEST FRIENDS I ROAMED DREAMLAND
THROUGH AZURE SKIES SAILED HAND IN HAND
SO MANY WONDERS WE WERE SHARING
ALL THINGS WERE OPEN TO OUR DARING

THE WORLD WAS NEVER MORE SO BRIGHT
AS WHEN WE HEEDLESS SOUGHT DELIGHT
FINDING ADVENTURES, AND NEW FRIENDS
SQUABBLING - AND MAKING AMENDS

WE FOUR THOUGHT THE WORLD OUR TOY
FAIRY, ELF-GIRL, HUMAN, ROCK BOY
NEVER SUSPECTING THE GATHERING DREAD
OR NIGHTMARES LOOMING UP AHEAD

BEGINNING TO LOOK IN A DIFFERENT WAY
ON MY FRIEND FROM FAR AWAY
NOT KNOWING WHEN HE'D GO OR STAY
NOT YET KNOWING WHAT TO SAY
WONDERING WHAT NEW GAMES TWO MIGHT PLAY;
MY HEART TO ASHES TURNED ONE DAY

WE FOUR FOUGHT A FEARSOME FOE
WE TRIPPED HIM UP; WE LAID HIM LOW
BUT THOUGH THE VICTORY WAS WON
WITH US THE FATES WERE NOT YET DONE

A LAST ADVENTURE CALLED HIM AHEAD
WE COULD NOT FOLLOW WHERE HE LED
FROM DARK HE CRIED OF SWORD AND STONE
THEN HE MET ... SOMETHING ... ALL ALONE

HELPLESS I STOOD THERE IN THE SUN.
HELPLESS MY TEARS BEGAN TO RUN
HELPLESS MY WORLD WAS ALL UNDONE
HELPLESS I KNEW THAT HE WAS GONE
AND SO MY CHILDHOOD DAYS WERE DONE.

ASHEN WAS MY CHILD'S HEART
AND ASHENHEART MY NAME
ON THAT DAY I FIRST LEARNED LOSS
AND THE WORLD WAS NE'ER THE SAME

II

EVENTUALLY MY TEARS ALL DRIED.
I PUT MY CHILDISH GAMES ASIDE
I TURNED MY MIND TO SERIOUS THINGS
LEARNED THE TRADE OF QUEENS AND KINGS
STUDIED AT THE ARTS OF WAR
TO BE HELPLESS NEVERMORE

PREPARED ONE DAY TO TAKE MY PLACE
WITH MY PARENTS, TO GUARD MY RACE
AND ALL WHO HONOR PEACE AND JOY
TO DEFEND THEM ALL, MY SOLE EMPLOY
AGAINST THE DARK TO BE A SHIELD
TO SEEK, TO STRIVE, AND NEVER YIELD

BUT THOUGH THE ASHES IN MY HEART WERE BURNING
THE TIMES AND TIDE WERE YET STILL TURNING.

DAY BY DAY, HOUR BY HOUR
I LEARNED THE LIMITS OF ROYAL POWER
OF CHOICES MEASURED OUT AND WEIGHED
HOW OFT DISCRETION MUST BE DISPLAYED

LEARNING NOT TO STRIKE A FOE
WHEN I COULD NOT MEET HIS COUNTERBLOW
WHEN IT NOT ON ME WOULD FALL
BUT UPON MY PEOPLE ONE AND ALL
SWALLOWING WORDS AND CHECKING PRIDE
STRIVING TO HOLD OUTRAGE INSIDE
LEARNING FROM MY PARENTS, GUILE
LEARNING HOW TO BOW AND SMILE
THOUGH MY HEART CRIES "IT'S NOT RIGHT!"
MY HEAD KNOWS IT'S NOT TIME TO FIGHT

STILL, WITH MY PARENTS THERE BESIDE ME
WITH LOVE AND WISDOM STILL TO GUIDE ME
I GREW IN BEAUTY, TALL AND PROUD
I WAS A PRINCESS YET UNBOWED
AS MUCH FOR THEM AS FOR MYSELF
AND EVERYONE WHO IS AN ELF

THEN - MY HEART TO ASHES ONCE MORE TURNED
MY PARENTS LEFT - AND NE'ER RETURNED
WHAT THEY SOUGHT I DID NOT KNOW
OR EVEN WHY THEY HAD TO GO

ASHEN WAS MY YOUNG GIRL'S HEART
AND ASHENHEART MY NAME
SOON - TOO SOON - A KINGDOM'S WEIGHT
FELL UPON MY FRAME

ON MY NAMESAKE TREE I STAND
NO ONE BESIDE ME ON THE THRONE
NOW THE RULER OF THIS LAND
LEFT TO GUARD MY REALM - ALONE

III

SO MY LENGTHENING DAYS ARE SPENT
ON ENDLESS DUTIES AND DISILLUSIONMENT.
TOO SOON I PROVED WHAT I'D LONG KNOWN:
A RULER'S LIFE IS NOT HER OWN.

THE CROWN I WEAR I HOLD IN TRUST
THAT MY DECISIONS ARE RIGHT AND JUST.
I DARE NOT LET MY FEELINGS LEAD;
NOT FOR ME, BUT MY PEOPLES' NEED.

I AM A QUEEN AND MAY NOT WEEP
IF I MY PEOPLES' FAITH SHALL KEEP
AND AS I SIT UPON A THRONE,
BOTH POWER AND BURDEN ARE MINE ALONE.

ALL YIELD TO ME AT MY COMMAND
BUT THERE'S NOT ONE TO TAKE MY HAND.
WIDE AS THIS REALM IS O'ER WHICH I REIGN
MY HEART'S DESIRE IT DOES NOT CONTAIN

AND SO I ARMORED UP MY HEART
LEARNED TO HOLD MYSELF APART
REMEMBERING STILL WHAT I HAD LOST
TOO MUCH AWARE OF WHAT IT COST
I STAND AGAINST THE GATHERING DARK
LEST OTHERS SHOULD SOON FEEL ITS MARK

COLD FURY BURNS WITHIN ME STILL
AT ALL THE THINGS THAT'D WORK US ILL
AT ALL THE THINGS I LET GO BY
FOR POLITICS I DARE NOT DEFY

STILL I COUNT EACH DAY'S RUN
AS ANOTHER SMALL VICTORY, WON
STILL I KEEP MY HEAD HELD HIGH
AND HOLD WELL BACK EACH TIRED SIGH

STILL I KEEP MY BACK HELD STRAIGHT
AND LET NO ONE SEE THE WEIGHT
OF MY GROWING LOAD OF CARES
AND MY BURDEN OF DESPAIR

ASHEN IS MY WOMAN'S HEART
AND ASHENHEART MY NAME.
ASHEN HAD MY WORLD BECOME...

AND THEN ONCE MORE HE CAME.

IV

BUMBLING CLOWN, UNTUTORED LOUT
WITH NO IDEA OF WHAT HE'S ABOUT
HE'S NOT SAFE TO LEAVE ALONE
IT'S AS THOUGH HE'S NEVER GROWN

WORSE; WITH HIS WORDS HE BREAKS MY HEART
WITH ALL THE THINGS HE HAS FORGOT
WITH ALL THE THINGS HE MAKES ME FEEL
STILL HE DOUBTS THAT I AM REAL?

WHO IS THIS STRANGER NOW BEFORE ME?
WHERE IS THE FRIEND OF LONG AGO?
WITH ALL I'VE BECOME, HE DOES NOT KNOW ME
AND YET I CAN'T QUITE LET HIM GO.

AND NOW WHAT IS THIS SWORD HE BEARS?
AND NOW A SUIT OF ARMOR WEARS!
AND NOW IT SEEMS THERE IS A QUEST
AND NOW WE GO AT ITS BEHEST

I AM UNDONE; I TURN AND RUN
IT'S ALL TOO MUCH TOO FAST
A NEW FUTURE, STILL INSECURE
EMERGES FROM THE PAST

HE COMES TO ME WITH NO DEMANDS
HE COMES TO ME WITH OPEN HANDS
AND SORROW ON HIS FACE
HE FINDS ME WITH MY NAKED HEART
AND TRIES TO GRANT ME GRACE

I THOUGHT THAT I WAS DONE WITH TEARS
I THOUGHT I'D LEARNED TO FACE MY FEARS
FOUND SOME MEASURE OF SURCEASE
AND NOW IN THIS UNCERTAIN HOUR
HE HELPS ME FIND RELEASE

ASHEN IS MY WOMAN'S HEART
AND ASHENHEART MY NAME
WHAT WE HAD IN TIMES BEFORE
MAY NEVER COME AGAIN

BUT NOW BY WHAT STRANGE MIRACLE
IT IS I CAN NOT SAY
WE'RE TOGETHER ONCE AGAIN
AND FACING A NEW DAY.

V

AND NOW...
THE STRANGER WHO CAME BACK TO ME
THE FRIENDS I'D PUT ASIDE
WE GATHER ALL TOGETHER
ACROSS DREAMLAND WE STRIDE

AND NOW AT LAST THE MYSTERIES
BEGIN TO BE UNDONE
I KNOW NOT HOW MUCH TIME WE'VE LEFT
BUT AT LAST WE HAVE BEGUN

ANOTHER NOW HAS JOINED US
AND WHILE I HAVE MY DOUBT
WE TRAVEL ON REGARDLESS
SOMETIMES IN AND SOMETIMES OUT

IT'S HARD TO OPEN UP MY HEART
BUT TRY ONCE MORE I MUST
DESPITE THE LESSONS OF THE PAST
I'LL DARE AGAIN TO TRUST

TO HAVE FAITH THAT THINGS ARE CHANGING
AS THE BALANCE SHIFTS AGAIN
TO HOPE I'LL FIND MY FAMILY
AND NEVER LOSE MY FRIENDS

AND THOUGH THIS JOURNEY'S IMPORT
MAY BE GREATER THAN WE KNOW
I NOW CAN LOOK AROUND ME
AND FIND I'M NOT ALONE

ROCK GIANT, FAIRY, ELVEN QUEEN
EVEN CAT GIRL THIEF!
WAS EVER THERE SO STRANGE A TEAM?
IT'S ALL BEYOND BELIEF!

AND WHAT OF HIM WHO COMES TO ME
FROM THE OTHER SIDE OF SLEEP?
SOMETIMES HERE AND SOMETIMES THERE
WITH PROMISES TO KEEP?

BUT WHEN HE TAKES THAT SWORD IN HAND
WHEN BY MY SIDE HE MAKES A STAND
WHEN HE ANSWERS FEAR'S DEMAND
DEFIANTLY, WITH SUCH PLAN
AND LEAPS INTO THE FRAY,

THEN HE BECOMES MORE THAN HE SEEMS
A HERO OUT OF LONG LOST DREAMS
HIS COURAGE LIKE HIS ARMOR GLEAMS
ALL MY HOPES MAY BE REDEEMED
AND HONOR SAVE THE DAY

ALL THIS HE DOES AND SO MUCH MORE
YET IF I WOULD BE JUST
THE GREATEST THING I NEED HIM FOR
IS TO RETURN MY TRUST

HE SEES THE WOMAN WITHIN THE QUEEN
THE GIRL BENEATH THE CROWN
AND WHEN HE STANDS THERE, SO FOURSQUARE
MY DEFENSES CAN COME DOWN

I CAN AT LAST ADMIT MY FEARS
I CAN AT LAST RELEASE MY TEARS
I CAN AT LAST ROLL BACK THE YEARS
AND MY HOPE REAPPEARS

HE CALLS ME NAMES
HE MAKES ME SMILE
HE HELPS ME EASE MY CARES AWHILE

HE SHARES MY PAIN
HE MAKES ME KNOW
THAT I'M NO LONGER ALL ALONE

AT NEED HE CAME
BROUGHT BACK MY FRIENDS
AND HELPED ME FIND MYSELF AGAIN

IT'S NOT THE SAME
AS 'TWAS BEFORE
BUT I CAN BRAVE THE WORLD ONCE MORE

NIGHTMARE SEEKS TO TAKE HOPE'S STEAD
AND OUR DEFEAT, ITS AIM
I KNOW NOT WHAT STILL LIES AHEAD
BUT I NO LONGER SEEK IN VAIN

ASHEN IS MY WOMAN'S HEART
AND ASHENHEART MY NAME
BUT SOMEWHERE DEEP INSIDE ME NOW
I FEEL BRIGHT HOPE'S NEW FLAME

WHAT HAS GONE MAY BE REBORN
E'EN AFTER MIDNIGHT'S DARKEST HOUR
SUNSET'S FOLLOWED BY THE MORN
WHERE HEARTS MAY HEAL AND LOVE MAY FLOWER

FOR WHEN I LOOK INTO HIS EYES
JOY NOW TAKES ME BY SURPRISE
FROM ASHES WILL THE PHOENIX RISE
AND DREAMLAND WE'LL RECLAIM.

LIKE A FEATURE FILM...
THE DREAMLAND CHRONICLES
IS A TEAM EFFORT.

I HAVE BEEN VERY BLESSED
TO BE ABLE TO WORK
WITH THE MOST TALENTED
PEOPLE FROM ALL
OVER THE WORLD.

ARTISTS FROM TAIWAN,
GERMANY, RUSSIA, SPAIN,
PORTUGAL, CANADA,
AND MORE GAVE THEIR
TIME AND TALENT TO HELP
BRING DREAMLAND
TO LIFE.

CHARACTER DESIGNS:
KAREN KRAJENBRINK
ROBIN MITCHELL

CHARACTER MODELING:
IVAN PEREZ
CAN TUNCER
MARCELLO BORTOLINO
PETER STAROSTIN
DAVID CAMARASA
ERIK ASORSON

**CHARACTER
RIGGING AND MORPHS:**
JUAN CARLOS PRADOS HERRADA
ULRICH SEIDEMANN
JENN DOWNS
PETER STAROSTIN
KOBI ALONY
IVAN PEREZ
JOEL CARLSON
PETER WONG
TRUNG TRAN
JEREMY CHAPMAN
FRANK LENHARD

3D SOFTWARE:
AUTODESK'S
3D STUDIO MAX

ADDITIONAL SOFTWARE:
SPLUTTERFISH'S
BRAZIL RENDERING SYSTEM,
ADOBE PHOTOSHOP,
FRISCHLUFT'S LENSCARE

COMIC FONTS:
RICHARD STARKINGS
AND COMICRAFT

ENVIRONMENT DESIGNS:
STEFANO TSAI
KAREN KRAJENBRINK

ENVIRONMENT MODELLING:
STEFANO TSAI
ANTERO PEDRAS

**TECHNICAL AND
RENDERING SUPPORT:**
FRANK LENHARD
ANTERO PEDRAS

MARKETING:
BRIAN PETKASH
LYS FULDA
SPHINX GROUP

EDITING:
AMY BETZ
JUSTIN EISINGER

SPECIAL THANKS:
MY WIFE DONNA, MY PARENTS, MY COUSIN DR. RUSS CARAM,
AND OF COURSE THE REST OF MY FAMILY.

ADDITIONAL THANKS:
TED ADAMS AND THE IDW TEAM,
DANIELLE CORSETTO, KIDS LOVE COMICS,
CRYSTAL YATES, SARAH ELLERTON,
MIKE KUNKEL, KEVIN GREVIOUX,
ALEXANDRA MILCHAN, SCOTT AGOSTONI,
AND OF COURSE ALL OF MY READERS
WHO MAKE THIS ALL POSSIBLE.

GUEST COVERS

WHEN IDW ASKED ME IF WE COULD PRODUCE A MONTHLY SERIES OF COMICS AS WELL AS THESE GRAPHIC NOVELS... WE THOUGHT IT WOULD BE FUN TO GET SOME OF MY FRIENDS AND COLLEAGUES TO DO GUEST COVERS.

I HOPE YOU ENJOY SEEING THESE BRILLIANT WORKS OF ART. IT'S AMAZING SEEING DREAMLAND THROUGH THE EYES OF OTHER CREATORS.

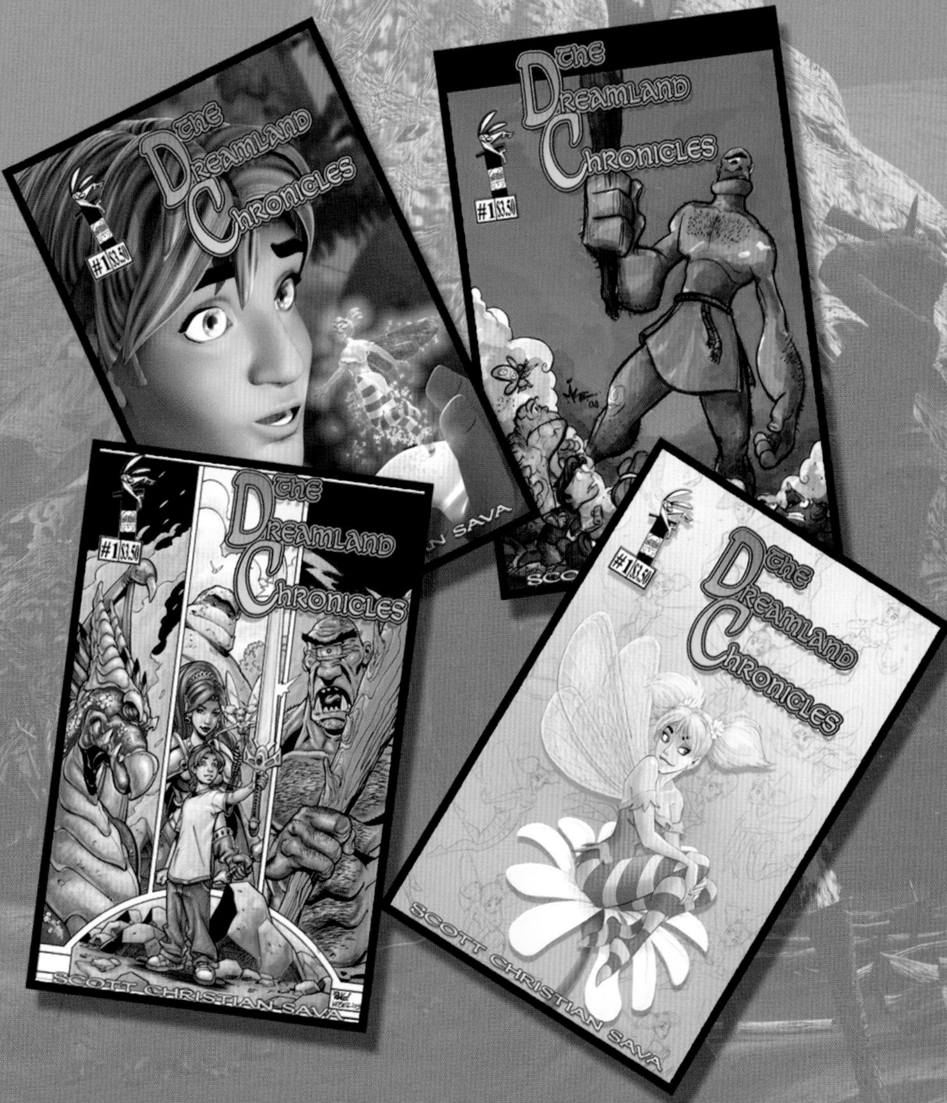
The Dreamland Chronicles
#1 $3.50
The Dreamland Chronicles
#1 $3.50
The Dreamland Chronicles
#1 $3.50
Scott Christian Sava
The Dreamland Chronicles
#1 $3.50
Scott Christian Sava

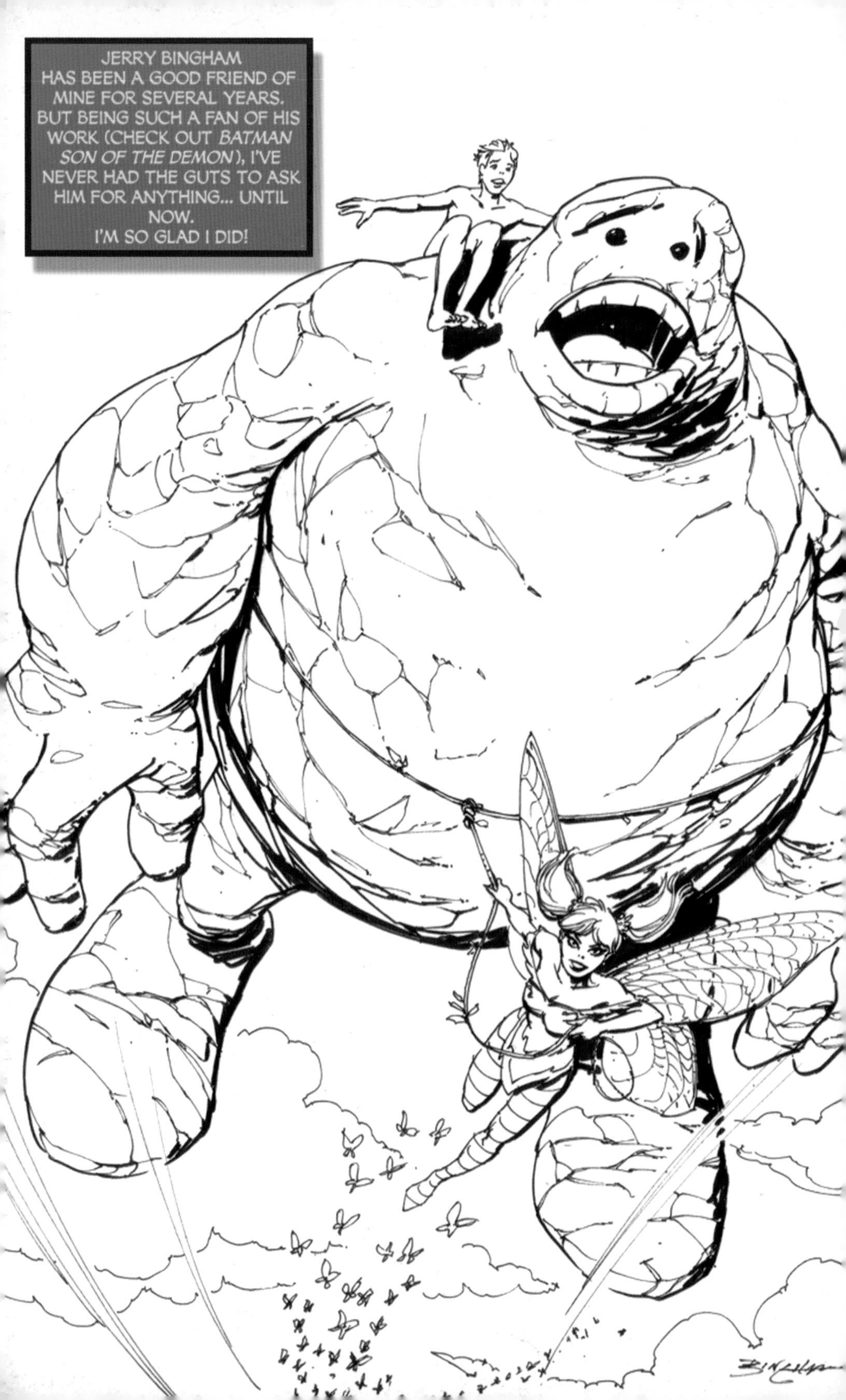
JERRY BINGHAM HAS BEEN A GOOD FRIEND OF MINE FOR SEVERAL YEARS. BUT BEING SUCH A FAN OF HIS WORK (CHECK OUT *BATMAN SON OF THE DEMON*), I'VE NEVER HAD THE GUTS TO ASK HIM FOR ANYTHING... UNTIL NOW.
I'M SO GLAD I DID!

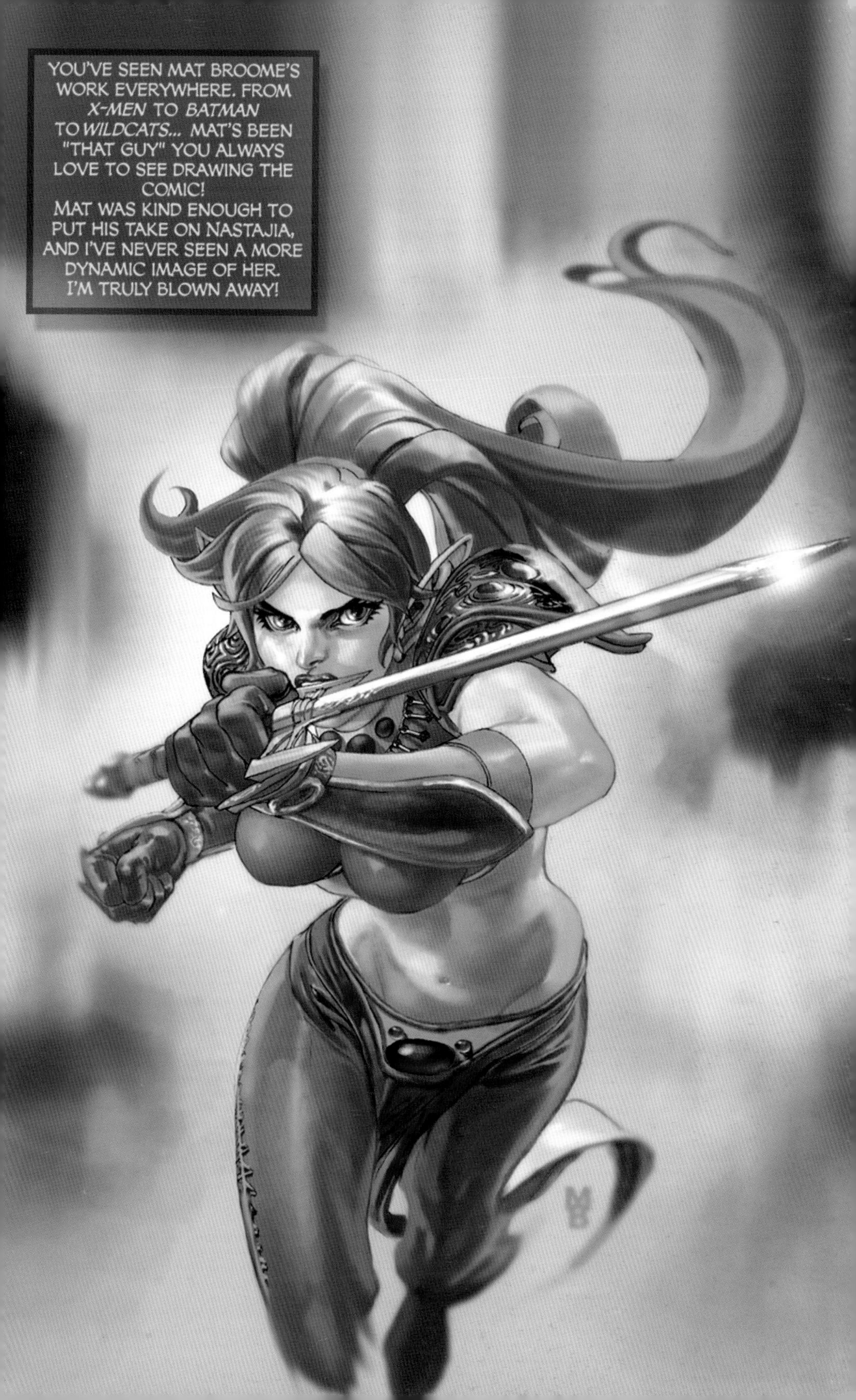
YOU'VE SEEN MAT BROOME'S WORK EVERYWHERE. FROM *X-MEN* TO *BATMAN* TO *WILDCATS...* MAT'S BEEN "THAT GUY" YOU ALWAYS LOVE TO SEE DRAWING THE COMIC!
MAT WAS KIND ENOUGH TO PUT HIS TAKE ON NASTAJIA, AND I'VE NEVER SEEN A MORE DYNAMIC IMAGE OF HER. I'M TRULY BLOWN AWAY!

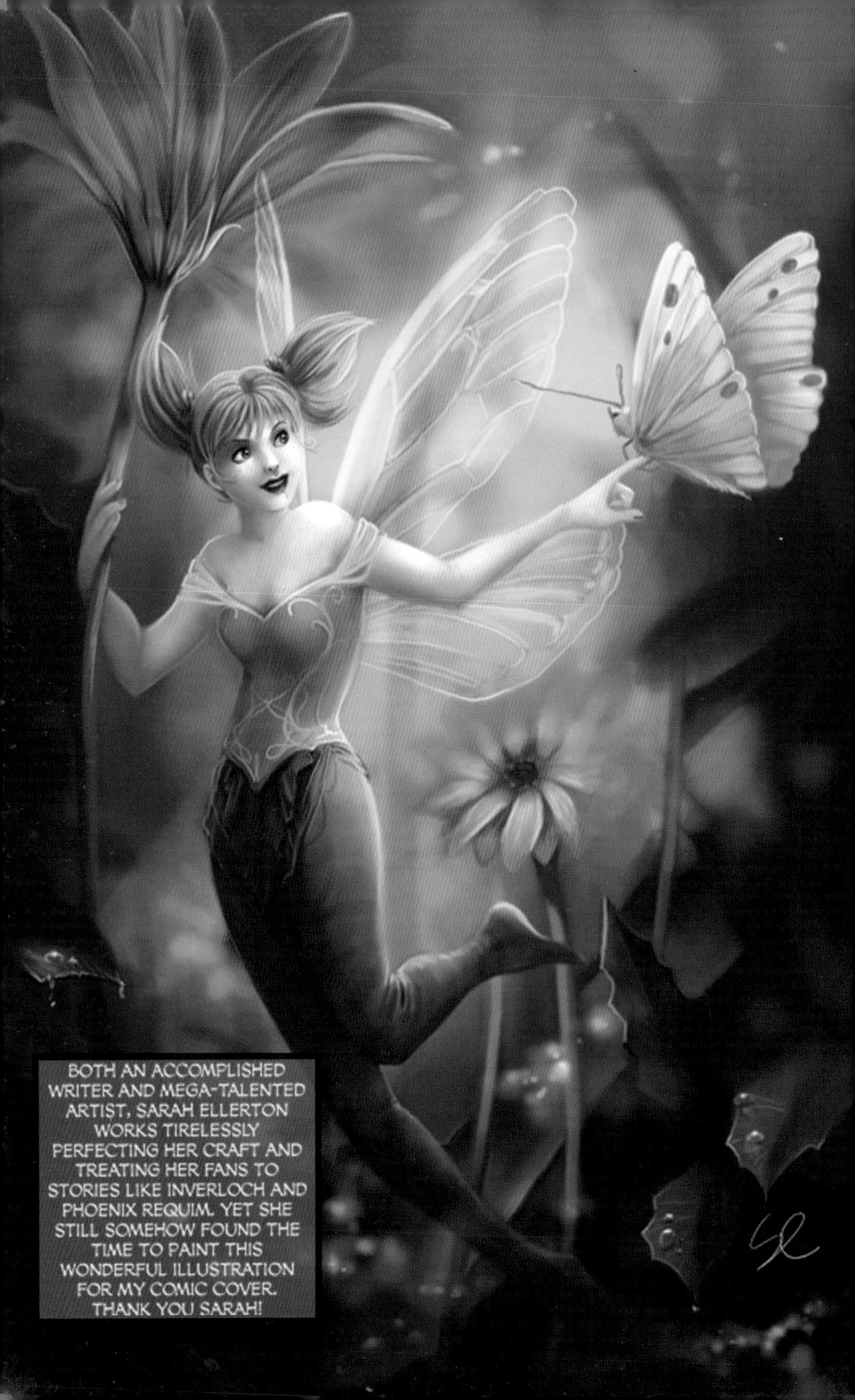

BOTH AN ACCOMPLISHED WRITER AND MEGA-TALENTED ARTIST, SARAH ELLERTON WORKS TIRELESSLY PERFECTING HER CRAFT AND TREATING HER FANS TO STORIES LIKE INVERLOCH AND PHOENIX REQUIM. YET SHE STILL SOMEHOW FOUND THE TIME TO PAINT THIS WONDERFUL ILLUSTRATION FOR MY COMIC COVER. THANK YOU SARAH!

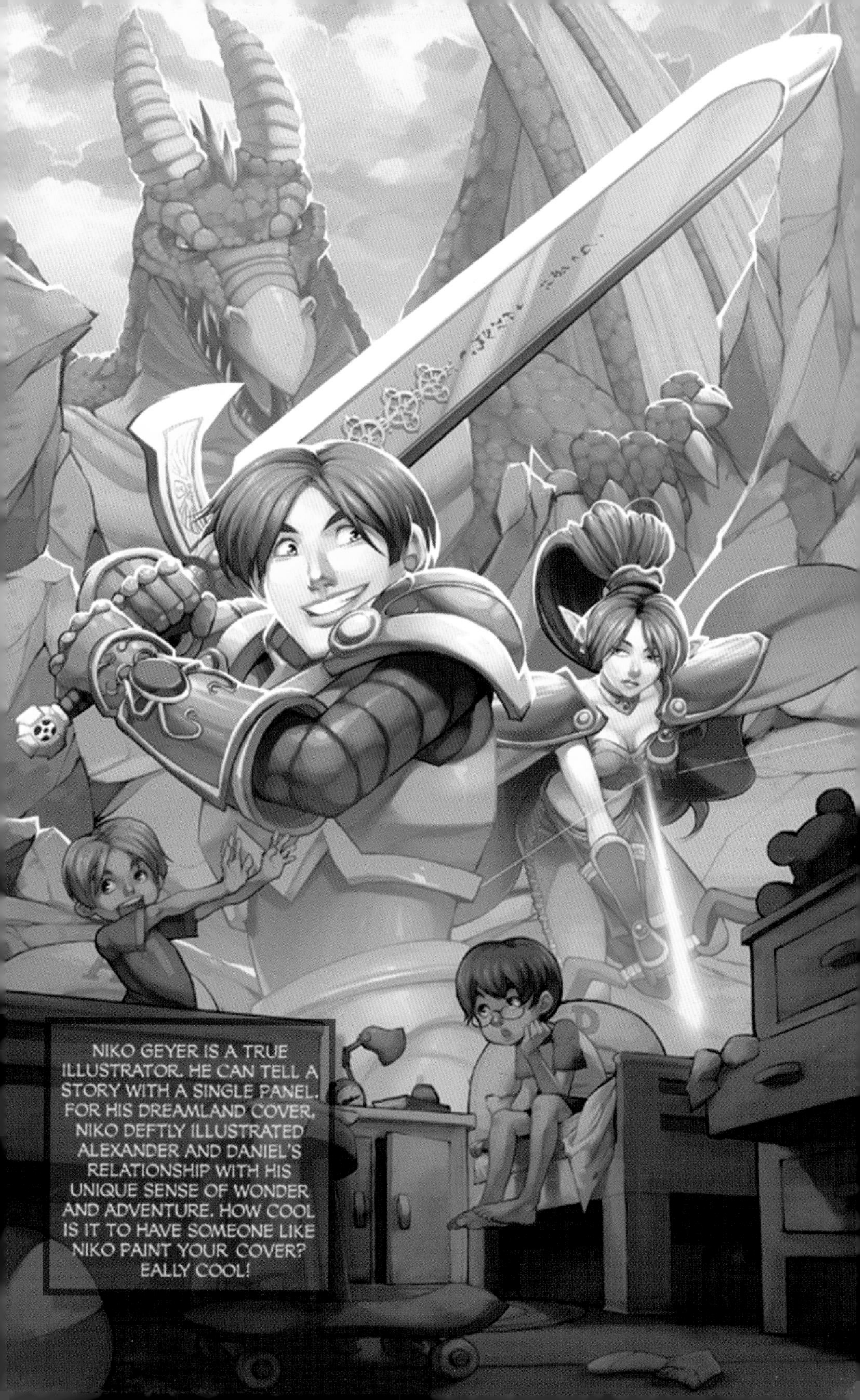
NIKO GEYER IS A TRUE ILLUSTRATOR. HE CAN TELL A STORY WITH A SINGLE PANEL. FOR HIS DREAMLAND COVER, NIKO DEFTLY ILLUSTRATED ALEXANDER AND DANIEL'S RELATIONSHIP WITH HIS UNIQUE SENSE OF WONDER AND ADVENTURE. HOW COOL IS IT TO HAVE SOMEONE LIKE NIKO PAINT YOUR COVER? EALLY COOL!

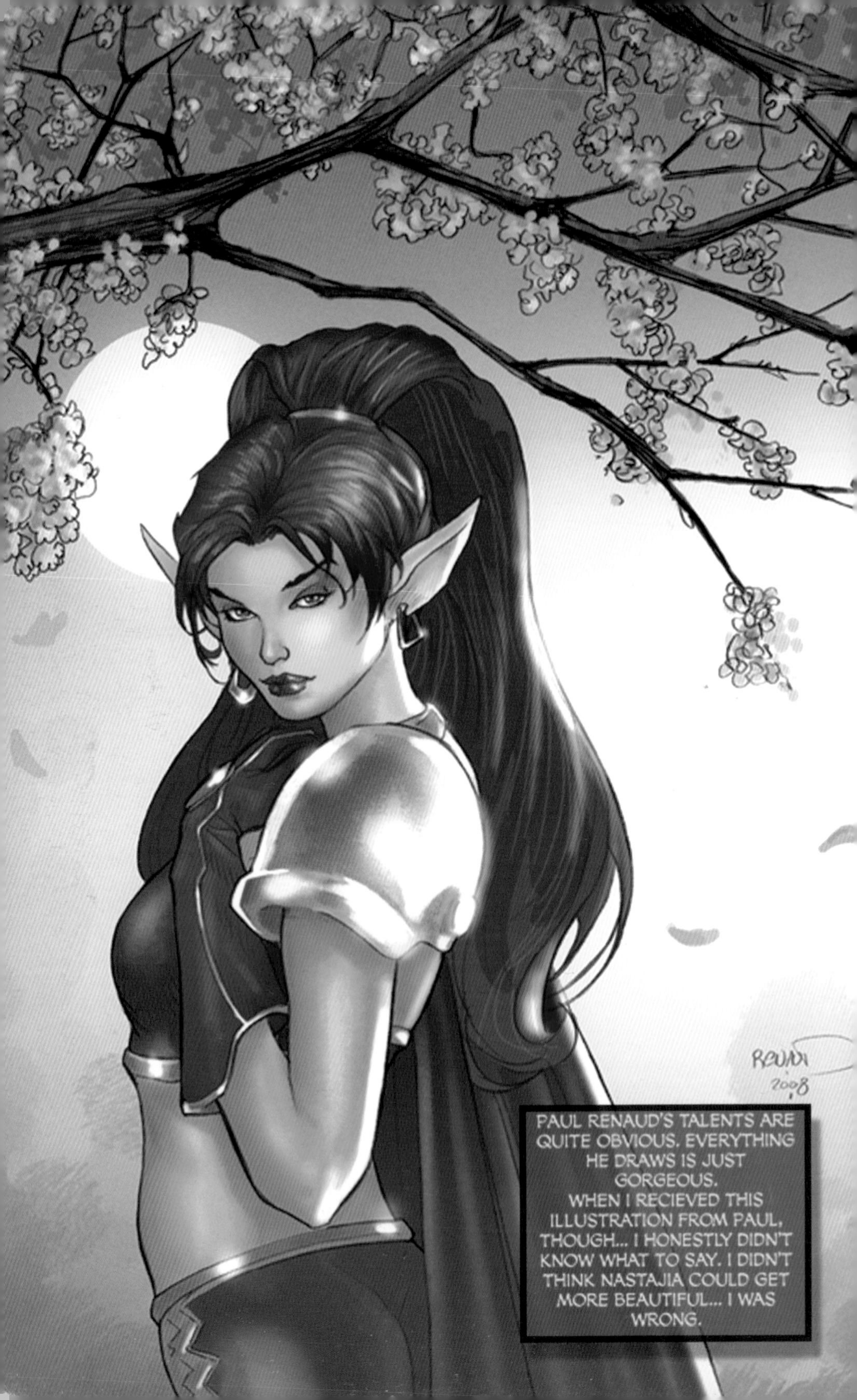
PAUL RENAUD'S TALENTS ARE QUITE OBVIOUS. EVERYTHING HE DRAWS IS JUST GORGEOUS.
WHEN I RECIEVED THIS ILLUSTRATION FROM PAUL, THOUGH... I HONESTLY DIDN'T KNOW WHAT TO SAY. I DIDN'T THINK NASTAJIA COULD GET MORE BEAUTIFUL... I WAS WRONG.

In November I was invited to be a guest of honor at the annual ***Philcon*** science fiction convention in Philadelphia. We thought it would be fun to make ***Dreamland Badges*** for everyone. It was ***so cool*** seeing everyone walk around with Dreamland badges all weekend. It felt like my very own ***Dreamland Convention.***

Hmm...that's not a bad idea...

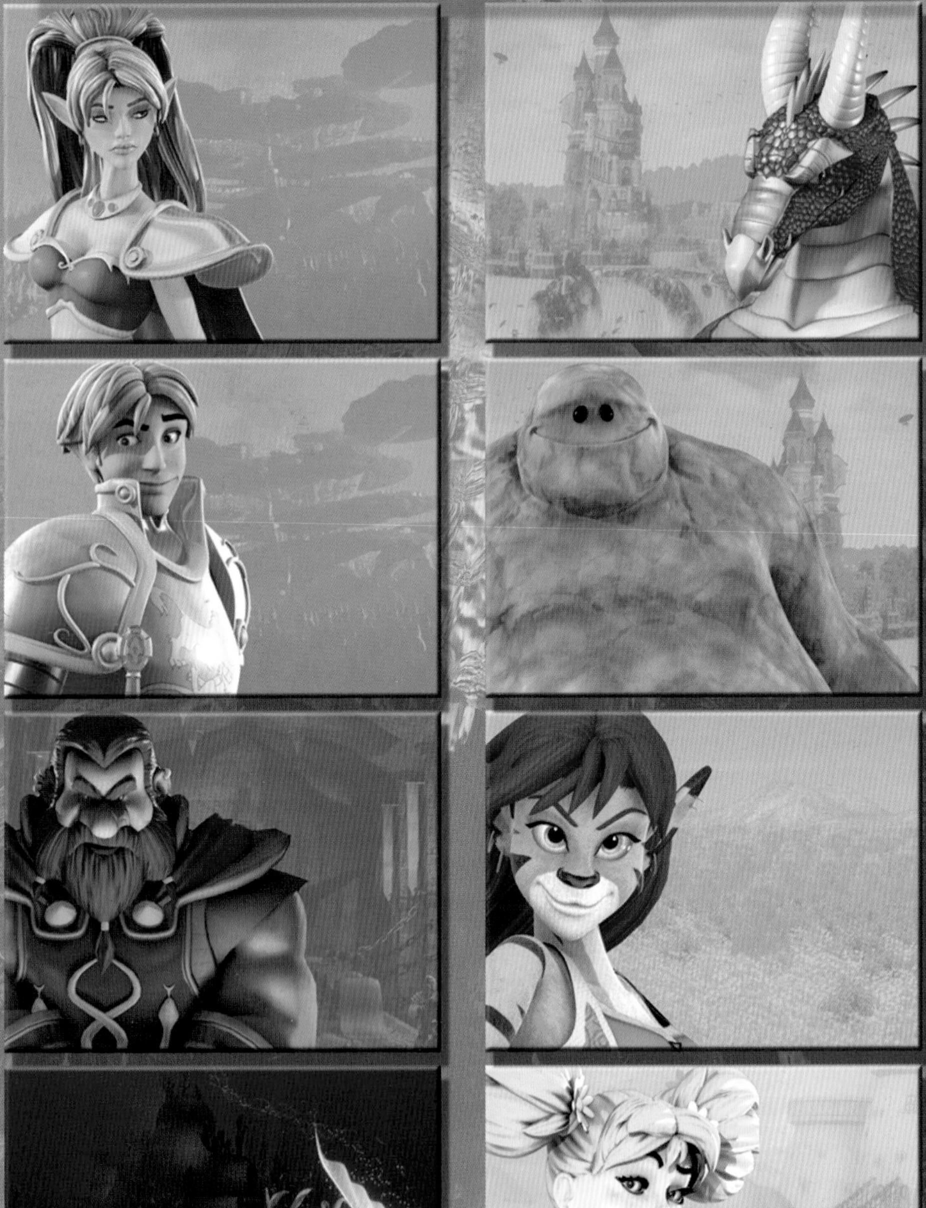

ALL ATTITUDE!
LUSH GRASS BASE!
GORGEOUS CRAFTSMANSHIP!
TOTALLY FUN!
FIVE INCHES TALL!
BEAUTIFUL PAINT JOB!

IN CASE YOU DIDN'T KNOW... WE'VE BEEN FORTUNATE ENOUGH TO MAKE SOME WONDERFUL FIGURES AND PLUSHES TO GO WITH THE BOOKS.

THESE ARE ABSOLUTELY SPECTACULAR REPRESENTATIONS OF THE CHARACTERS IN THE BOOK AND FROM A CREATOR'S POINT OF VIEW... THERE'S NOTHING COOLER THAN HAVING A TOY AND PLUSH OF YOUR CREATIONS.

CHECK THEM OUT AT YOUR LOCAL STORE OR ONLINE.

ALSO AVAILABLE IS NASTAJIA AND KIWI.

MORE TO COME SOON!

METALLIC FINISH ARMOR!
AMAZING DETAIL!
GOLD TRIM!
COBBLE STONE STAND!
PERFECT LIKENESS!
FIVE INCHES TALL!

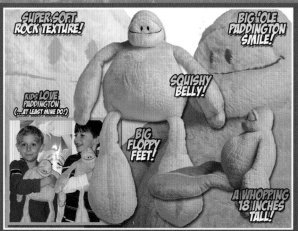

SUPER SOFT ROCK TEXTURE!
BIG 'OLE PADDINGTON SMILE!
SQUISHY BELLY!
KIDS LOVE PADDINGTON (...AT LEAST MINE DO!)
BIG FLOPPY FEET!
A WHOPPING 18 INCHES TALL!